OFFA'S DYKE

Landscape and Hegemony in Eighth-Century Britain

Keith Ray and Ian Bapty

WIND*gather*
PRESS

Windgather Press is an imprint of Oxbow Books

Published in the United Kingdom in 2016 by
OXBOW BOOKS
10 Hythe Bridge Street, Oxford OX1 2EW

and in the United States by
OXBOW BOOKS
1950 Lawrence Road, Havertown, PA 19083

© Keith Ray and Ian Bapty 2016

Paperback Edition: ISBN 978-1-905119-35-6
Digital Edition: ISBN 978-1-909686-19-9

A CIP record for this book is available from the British Library

All rights reserved. No part of this book may be reproduced or transmitted in any form or by any means, electronic or mechanical including photocopying, recording or by any information storage and retrieval system, without permission from the publisher in writing.

Printed by Printworks Global Ltd, London & Hong Kong.

For a complete list of Windgather titles, please contact:

UNITED KINGDOM	UNITED STATES OF AMERICA
Oxbow Books	Oxbow Books
Telephone (01865) 241249	Telephone (800) 791-9354
Fax (01865) 794449	Fax (610) 853-9146
Email: oxbow@oxbowbooks.com	Email: queries@casemateacademic.com
www.oxbowbooks.com	www.casemateacademic.com/oxbow

Oxbow Books is part of the Casemate Group

Front cover: Offa's Dyke negotiating the heights above Garbett Hall, north of Knighton, looking northwards from the slopes above Brynorgan. Photograph by Keith Ray. See also, Frontispiece to Part Two of this book.

This book is dedicated to the memory of

Sir Cyril Fox 1882–1967

Archaeologist of landscape

Guilden Morden 1924

(Photograph reproduced by kind permission of Charles Scott-Fox)

Contents

On Offa's Dyke (*Gladys Mary Coles*)	vi
Acknowledgements	vii
Preface	ix
Foreword: Christopher Catling (*Secretary, Royal Commission on the Ancient and Historical Monuments of Wales*)	xi
Prefatory notes	xiii
Introduction: Landscape and hegemony: Offa's Dyke in dual perspective	1

PART ONE: THE BACKGROUND REVIEWED

1 Offa's Dyke in profile: character, course and controversies	10
2 Studying Offa's Dyke: a cumulative inheritance	55
3 The Mercians: a border history	93

PART TWO: THE EVIDENCE EXPLORED

4 Placing the Dyke in the landscape	122
5 The structure of the Dyke	164
6 Building and operating the Dyke	214

PART THREE: THE CONTEXT RE-APPRAISED

7 In a frontier landscape	254
8 The material of Mercian hegemony	298
9 Offa's Dyke: power in the landscape	334
Epilogue: Reconnecting Offa's Dyke in the twenty-first century	365
Appendix: Selected Offa's Dyke profiles	377
Notes	381
List of Figures	427
Bibliography	430
Index	439

ON OFFA'S DYKE

Once a concept, now returned to concept
except where the mounded soil
hints of activity, toil,
scoopings, bendings, craft
of earthwork unknit by wind-work.

Once a long snake, sinuous over the land,
over hill heights, above cwms:
now its disintegrated skin
is ghosted in the ground,
buried in its own earth
yet visible here and there
like the life of Offa, Mercian King.
This, in itself, evidence of him,
hegemony's power, fear –
 the tangible remains.

Their truths the walls of history hold:
Hadrian's, Jerusalem's, Berlin's –
humanity walled in, walled out,
a wall for weeping on, a wall for execution:
and all our inner barriers, divisions
numerous as the species of wild growth
embedded in this dyke –
taken by the only natural army.

GLADYS MARY COLES

From 'Stoat, in Winter' (1984), reprinted in *Leafburners,
New and Selected Poems* (Duckworth, 1986, 67)

Acknowledgements

Firstly, thanks are due to our small group of scholarly 'critical friends', and to the publisher's reviewer, whose perceptive comments on the manuscript in whole or in part (and in early versions) hopefully helped make the volume somewhat less burdened by errors of fact and interpretation than might otherwise have been the case (although of course we take full responsibility for the outcome). We wish also to record our thanks to our former colleagues at Herefordshire Council, and to the archaeologists at Clwyd-Powys Archaeological Trust, Shropshire Council and Gloucestershire County Council, for their kind supportive friendship and encouragement over the years. Respectively, we thank in particular Nigel Baker, Peter Dorling, and Tim Hoverd in Herefordshire; Bill and Jenny Britnell, Chris Martin, Nigel Jones, Jeff Spencer and, latterly, Paul Belford at CPAT; Andy Wigley in Shropshire; and Jon Hoyle, Toby Catchpole and Jan Wills in Gloucestershire.

Cadw (Welsh Historic Heritage) and English Heritage supported the work of the Offa's Dyke Management Project, and the advice and assistance of their officers Bill Klemperer, Sian Rees, and Paul Stamper is acknowledged with thanks here. Jim Saunders, formerly Offa's Dyke Path Officer, was an enthusiastic supporter of that work, and during the preparation of this book we have appreciated also the help of members of the Offa's Dyke Association, and staff of the Offa's Dyke Centre, Knighton. Our thanks go also to Mike Allen of Allen Environmental Services, and to Tim Malim of SLR Consulting, for drawing our attention to their recent and forthcoming publications.

One of us (KR) has benefitted especially from the published insights of a number of recent writers who have grappled with aspects of Anglo-Saxon and later history and literature that would not necessarily have seemed at first sight to be relevant to the study of Offa's Dyke. Foremost among them are Nicholas Howe, to whom we owe the concept of a 'political sense of place' in respect to the Anglo-Saxon landscape; Joanna Story, whose work on 'Carolingian connections' has set in proper perspective the European dimension of the Mercian hegemony; and Max Liebermann, whose research on the medieval March of Wales and its origins brought us to the view that its precursor 'march' was potentially an important concomitant of the placement of Offa's Dyke in a contested frontier landscape.

We would especially like to thank our publishers, David Brown and Casemate Publishing, and our editors, Dr Julie Gardiner and Clare Litt, both of Oxbow Books, for their supportive and professional steering of the manuscript through to publication. Thanks are also due to Oxbow Books for providing the resource for the preparation of most of the maps and plans. Lizzie Holiday and Katie Allen diligently produced the digital copies concerned and Val Lamb skilfully designed the layout and typeset the volume. We thank Tim Hoverd for preparing several fine line drawings for publication and Adam Stanford provided much help with photographic fieldwork. Unless credited otherwise, all photographs were taken by Keith Ray, between 2009 and 2014. A special note of thanks is due to Charles Scott-Fox who kindly both granted permission for the dedication of the book to the memory of his father, and allowed reproduction of the dedicatory photograph of Cyril Fox at Guilden Morden, from his biography, *Cyril Fox, Archaeologist Extraordinary*, (Oxbow Books, 2002).

Christopher Catling, Secretary of the Royal Commission on the Ancient Monuments of Wales (RCAHMW) kindly consented to contribute a brief Foreword. Last but not least, Keith Ray wishes to thank Sophie Gilliat-Ray, and Anna, Robin and Dylan Ray for having lived so patiently with 'Offa' for so long in the course of preparation of the volume.

Preface

This book provides an account of Offa's Dyke from the vantage point of the middle years of the second decade of the twenty-first century. Its primary focus is upon two themes: the relation of the Dyke to the landscape (both physical and cultural) of late eighth- and early ninth-century Britain, and its role in helping to sustain the political hegemony of the kingdom of Mercia at that time. The book nonetheless also aims to provide notes towards a new characterisation of the great linear earthwork (and especially the intricacies and consistencies of its placement and build), a review of the interpretive questions that still inhibit a full understanding of its nature and purpose, and an attempt to re-situate the Dyke in wider Anglo-Saxon and Welsh history. This cannot help but involve a focus also upon the enigma that is Mercia itself, that in some respects has become yet deeper following the discovery of the 'Staffordshire Hoard' in 2009. We feel that this is justified due to the way in which the Dyke as a concept, as well as a tangible form, reflects the identity of the Mercians as frontiers-people, embodied in their very name, 'the borderers'.

Our dedication of the book to the memory of Cyril Fox needs no justification, but perhaps some explanation. Fox has been much criticised in recent years for various 'errors' and blind-spots in his characterisation and interpretation of the Dyke: such is the fate of pioneers. However, it was Fox who first fully demonstrated how Offa's Dyke cannot be understood without developing an eye for landscape and the use made of it by the Dyke builders. His archaeologist's instincts and practice led him to appreciate both the nature of linear earthworks as statements in the landscape, and the need to obtain clear dating evidence, which, before the era of radiocarbon dating, meant establishing relationships to more readily dateable features. Above all it was Fox, in dialogue with Frank Stenton, the leading Anglo-Saxon historian of the mid-twentieth century, who first (and most strikingly) laid the case for a 'political' understanding of the wider significance of Offa's Dyke in Mercian, Anglo-Saxon and British history.

Foreword

Christopher Catling

This absorbing and beautifully illustrated book rescues Offa and his Dyke from ignorance and ignominy: ignorance because, although Offa's name is familiar enough, thanks to his Dyke, few of us would be able to tell you much about the man; and ignominy because Offa has been given a bad press by historians who, taking their cue from Bishop Asser, the Welsh monk who wrote the *Life of King Alfred* around AD 895, characterised him as a tyrant, a man who was, according to Anglo-Saxon scholar Simon Keynes, 'driven by a lust for power'.

In writing this welcome corrective to past thinking about Offa and his Dyke, Keith Ray and Ian Bapty have looked at the landscape with keen and questioning eyes. A great strength of the book is that they never take any part of the Dyke for granted. Instead they constantly ask 'why was it built here and not over there?' and 'what else was there in the landscape at the time that prompted the choice of this placement rather than that?'.

Exploring such questions leads to an appreciation of the fact that this is no hastily thrown up ditch and bank, but something that involved forethought and a deep knowledge of the terrain as well as engineering skill and the power to command the resources to construct this 175-km linear earthwork. The authors' detailed knowledge of the Dyke enables them to identify patterns in the construction that have not been considered sufficiently before now – such as the segmented nature of the bank and the constant minor adjustments to the orientation. They identify another example of careful planning is the way that the Dyke approaches and crosses river-valleys, overlooking the valley-bottoms that might have been predictable lines of approach eastwards towards the Dyke.

These distinctive placement practices lead the authors to propose that the Dyke was constructed to be highly visible, especially when viewed from the west, and to enable westward surveillance. The enhanced form of the Dyke at several key locations also reinforces the idea that its course was chosen to overlook a number of highly-charged 'political places' to the west of its route. And the much-debated question of whether the Dyke really does stretch from sea to sea is addressed by some new ideas about the potential relationship between Offa's Dyke and Wat's Dyke in the northern part of the route along with evidence to show that the Gloucestershire lengths were built using the same construction techniques and placement principles as the rest of the Dyke.

While the primary focus of the book is on the archaeology and landscape of the Dyke, the Dyke's very existence raises a whole suite of questions about the ambitions of both Offa and his successor Coenwulf to extend Mercian political control throughout southern Britain. The Dyke can be seen as one among a variety of devices used by the Mercian regime in the dynamics of its relationship with the other Anglo-Saxon kingdoms of the period in which landscape features are employed to symbolise and enforce hegemony.

Comparisons with another great linear monument separating Roman Britain from the lands to the north are inevitable, along with the questions that have been asked about Hadrian's Wall: did it create peace and security or did it bring tension; was it a Berlin Wall, built to separate, or was it a more permeable structure, designed to control but not to prevent movement, trade and cultural relations. Human beings have a habit of challenging boundaries, and a fascinating aspect of this book is the authors' exploration of the impact that the Dyke might have had on the people who lived on either side. This frontier, with its mix of peoples of different cultures, may well have resulted in the creation of a distinctive 'March' culture, not unlike those of the borderlands of the Carolingian empire in continental Europe.

In saying all of this, one is acutely conscious that there are no firm dates for the Dyke, and no objective archaeological evidence to support the historical attribution of the Dyke to King Offa. The authors make the rather striking point that, by contrast with Hadrian's Wall, which has been surveyed, mapped, studied and excavated by thousands of academics, students and antiquaries for hundreds of years, Offa's Dyke has only been subjected to sustained attention three times, and only once has a full survey been published: by Sir Cyril Fox exactly 60 years ago. The result is that there are many big unknowns, including a lack of radiocarbon and thermoluminescence dates from which to draw well-founded conclusions about the Dyke's construction and phasing.

This new and comprehensive study is therefore timely, but it is far from definitive; instead, by combining the evidence from landscape archaeology with such literary and historical sources as have come down to us in the form of charters, letters, legal frameworks, early modern poetry, place-names and coinage, it points the way to the kind of comprehensive research programme that the Dyke needs and deserves.

The aim of such research would be to ask not only what purpose the Dyke served and what impact it had upon the border communities on either side when it was newly constructed, but also what it means to people today, both as an ancient monument and as a symbol that has gained in resonance in recent years with the growing sense of Welsh nationhood that has developed since devolution. This is a less tangible heritage than the physical one of the Dyke itself, but one that could, as the authors point out, underpin potential World Heritage Site status: is the universal significance of Offa's Dyke ultimately that it makes us think about such issues as nationhood, border control, migration and assimilation – questions that take us not only to the core of early medieval history but also to some of the big political questions of our day?

Prefatory notes

Abbreviations

ASC   The *Anglo-Saxon Chronicle*, an account of history in England by year date from the birth of Christ. The main 'A' version was first compiled in the late ninth century, in Wessex. Relevant entries from the various versions are to be found in EHD, below. 'ASC 792' and so on in the Notes to chapters (below) refers to the year of the entry, usually as given in EHD.

HE   Historia Ecclesiastica, an abbreviated version of the title of the *Historia ecclesiastica gentis Anglorum*, the History of the English Church and People, written *c.*731 by the 'venerable' monk Bede, of the Northumbrian double monastery of Monkwearmouth and Jarrow.

EHD   *English Historical Documents, Volume 1, c.500–1042* (1955; second edition, 1979, Eyre and Spottiswoode, London), edited by Dorothy Whitelock.

On measurements

Distances are given throughout the book in miles and then in kilometres. However, smaller measurements, whether they be heights above mean sea level (or 'Ordnance Datum' at Newlyn in Cornwall, referred to conventionally as 'OD') or metres in length or breadth, are given only metrically. Although this is manifestly inconsistent, it is thought likely to be most familiar to a contemporary readership, and is less cumbersome than producing shorter lengths and heights in both imperial and metric measurement.

On the terminology of identity

Throughout the book, we mostly refer to the 'Welsh' as the Britons, or as 'British'. Although this does to some degree risk confusion, it has the important merit of more closely conveying eighth-century attributions (although 'Wales' was also used by the Anglo-Saxons to denote the land of the west-central Britons). As we note in the concluding chapter, the existence of Offa's Dyke, as well as the stubborn resistance of the British/Welsh to further Anglo-Saxon settlement in the uplands of the 'central Marches', was largely responsible for the development of a positive consciousness of a separate, specifically Welsh, identity for most of the people who lived in what became 'Wales'. However, this was a gradual process which only became strongly articulated in the Norman era. The potential confusion regarding the term 'Britons' arises because autonomous or semi-autonomous 'British' polities and societies continued to exist elsewhere. So, for instance, in the south-west peninsula, 'Dumnonia' continued as a separate entity until at least the time of king Egberht, and in the northern Pennines the kingdom of Elmet survived at least residually into the ninth century; meanwhile in the north of 'England', the Britons of Cumbria retained their autonomy at least into the later eighth century.

On orthography

Throughout this book, we use Anglo-Saxon word formations, but not precise spellings. So, for instance, rather than rendering the proper name Æðelberht (one individual with this name being the king of the East Angles executed by order of King Offa) as 'Ethelbert', or the compromise 'Æthelberht', we have chosen to use the form 'Aethelberht'. The reader can perhaps imagine that an 'academic' explanation for this, given the nature and scope of Anglo-Saxon historical scholarship, could run to several pages of text. We have two practical reasons for doing so, however: firstly, it is we think inconsistent to use the hybrid that begins with an ash ('Æ') without using the thorn (ð) that follows it in contemporary (eighth-century) usages, for instance in land diplomas (charters); secondly, the spelling 'Ae' is more familiar to the modern eye than 'Æ', and yet is closer to the Anglo-Saxon than the simple 'E' more popular in the nineteenth century. Similarly, words such as 'ætheling' (a scion or protégé, or designated heir, of a royal family or descent-group) are rendered here as 'aetheling'. Such usage we think preserves the 'identity' of these words as used by the Anglo-Saxons without encumbering the text with archaisms (although specialists will no doubt disagree with this proposition). That said, the world of Old English, its language and literature, is a wonderful and not quite lost one, and we would encourage the reader to explore it for themselves. A fitting and fascinating introduction, including preliminary chapters on 'spelling, pronunciation and punctuation' and on 'other differences between Old English and Modern English', is Bruce Mitchell's *An Invitation to Old English and Anglo-Saxon England* (Blackwell, Oxford, 1995).

On resources

The sources that we have drawn upon are reflected in the notes and bibliographical references recorded in the text. Key resources for the study of Mercia in the context of Anglo-Saxon England remain *English Historical Documents Volume 1* (EHD, above), the *Cambridge History of Medieval England*, Vol. 1, the *Blackwell Encyclopaedia of Anglo-Saxon England*, and David Kirby's *The Earliest English Kings*. On Offa's Dyke, the only full length by length description remains Sir Cyril Fox's British Academy volume, long out of print.

A modern-day rendering of Fox's monumental record is long overdue, and when undertaken perhaps ought to comprise a project encompassing both the production of detailed documentation (including excavation) using modern methods and aids, together with the publication of an accessible popular field guide.

On maps and places

There are large numbers of often quite obscure places mentioned in the book, and it may be difficult for the reader to locate them. We have attempted to provide some mapped detail in the figures included in the volume, but many readers will seek finer resolution. Quite apart from the wondrous resources of famous search-engines on the world-wide web, including digital maps and satellite images, the Ordnance Survey 'Explorer Maps' at the scale of 1:2500 provide access in the hand to swathes of the borderlands through which the Dyke and frontier pass. From south to north the references are OL 14, 189, 201, 216, 240, 256, 265 and 266.

Although it was beyond the scope of this volume to include very detailed mapping of each section, and with the important caveat that the Offa's Dyke Path only follows just over half the course of the Dyke and only slightly more of the eighth-century frontier, Aurum Press publish an informative and colourful National Tail Guide in two inexpensive volumes, using relevant OS map extracts, written by Ernie and Kathy Kay and updated by Mark Richards. A new walking guide to the Trail, written by Mike Dunn and to be published in 2016 by Cicerone Press, takes into account some of the insights provided hereunder.

On the writing of the book

This book, as co-authored works inevitably are, is a work of collaboration. This particular volume had its origins in extended talks between the two authors when one of them (ILB) worked as Offa's Dyke Management Officer between 1999 and 2006, during which time he gained a practical working familiarity with the monument across its entire length. Meanwhile, the lead author (KR) initially contributed a perspective based upon his attempts to understand the history particularly of the eighth- to ninth-century frontier in Herefordshire, where he was employed as County Archaeologist between 1998 and 2014. By 2008, after Ian Bapty had joined the staff of Herefordshire Archaeology, and having undertaken some preliminary site visits together to consider the issues anew, we had formed the view that a fuller-length publication than at first envisaged was justified. We then approached Julie Gardiner at Oxbow Books to seek a commission to write the book. After preliminary drafting of ideas, we undertook a more ambitious series of site visits in 2009 and 2010 to inspect the Dyke closely and to debate its character at several particularly complex or topographically intriguing locations. This programme of visits encompassed many of the surviving built lengths of the Dyke, and in addition we made a study-visit to the Mercian heartlands in 2010. A turning-point came during the earlier part of that year, when it became clear to us that some significant aspects of the built form of the Dyke, and especially what we term the 'adjusted-segmented' design of individual lengths, had escaped previous notice: or their significance had been misunderstood.

The processes of researching (especially in respect to the Mercian hegemony and the development of the frontier), writing of the text, illustrations management, and drafts editing, have, throughout, been undertaken almost entirely by Keith Ray. There was, however, close consultation in the early stages concerning Chapter 2 in particular, and there was, in the years before September 2012 (when ILB left Herefordshire Council to take up his current post), extensive consultation over drafts. Several of the insights concerning the form of the Dyke and its landscape setting would not have been possible without the intimate knowledge of the monument arising from Ian Bapty's several years' work involving on-site observation and conservation action.

INTRODUCTION

Landscape and hegemony: Offa's Dyke in dual perspective

Offa's Dyke faces westwards into Wales along much of the borderland with England, and is Britain's longest linear earthwork monument. Its physical size and visual impact is in many places, even today, remarkable. Its bank and ditch trace a sustained course across hills and river-valleys, watershed and plain, southwards from Treuddyn near Mold in Flintshire to the middle reaches of the river Severn near Welshpool. After a break of just over five miles along the Severn it clearly continues southwards as far as Rushock Hill near Kington in northern Herefordshire. It then follows a seemingly intermittent course southwards again to the river Wye west of Hereford. This much of its extent spans a distance of over 90 miles (145 km). After a further apparent gap in south Herefordshire, a stretch of at least ten miles (6 km) of what has traditionally been thought to be (and which according to the present study can still be regarded as) Offa's Dyke in the lower Wye valley extends southwards from Redbrook near Monmouth to Sedbury, by the Severn Estuary near Chepstow.

The Dyke was once thought to have continued in some form or another northwards from Treuddyn to the sea at Prestatyn or thereabouts, but this is now doubted.[1] Meanwhile, between Hereford and Monmouth another discontinuous earthwork may have once existed, or the river Wye itself stood proxy for its line here. Such uncertainties about its full course, questions concerning its exact dating, and even about its attribution, and queries concerning how it was built and what it was used for, have ensured that this colossal construction remains enigmatic, with several aspects of its basic character still a matter for debate. That, of course, is part of its attraction to scholar and enthusiast alike.

This book provides an in-depth discussion of the basic questions concerning the date, attribution and purpose of Offa's Dyke, but its focus is also upon the relationship of the earthwork to the landscape which it traverses and in which it was built. Study of today's landscape and observations about the form of the Dyke within it are therefore central to this perspective, but so too is consideration of the landscape of an emergent borderland of twelve centuries and more ago. And a further, wider landscape is also central to this interpretive project: the *political* landscape of late eighth- and early ninth-century Britain, dominated as it was by the Kingdom of Mercia. Our aim is to demonstrate that the Dyke had a place, too, in the exercise, manifestation and extension of power: and that this may go some way towards explaining why the Dyke bears the name of this significant Mercian king.

The creation of such a long-distance earthwork was clearly intended to mark some sort of boundary, and it is surely the case that Offa's Dyke performed a strategic, if not exactly military, purpose. However, there can equally be little doubt that bringing the Dyke into being served as a statement of raw power. This power-play had several dimensions, not least in its demonstration of the capacity of the Mercian kingdom to conceptualise an engineering work on this scale, and to mobilise a workforce sufficient to the task of realising its construction. As such it was also a statement of both existing practical power and an intended continued political dominion. The latter was exercised not only over those disparate peoples who already found themselves embraced within the Anglo-Saxon kingdom of Mercia, to the east of the north–south line of the Dyke. So, for instance, while excluding the Welsh kingdoms to its west, when built it also potentially marked a stage in their subjugation by the Anglo-Saxons. Less obviously perhaps, this expression of dominion was arguably intended also to intimidate the leaders of the Anglo-Saxon kingdoms situated far to the south, north and east of the Dyke. The message was plain: the power that was activated to achieve this monumental enterprise could, and would, be directed upon any kingdom or people which dared challenge the Kingdom of Mercia and the writ of its formidable late eighth-century and early ninth-century kings.

Beyond even this material statement of *realpolitik*, the hegemony that the execution of such a vast construction project gave expression to was also an imperially-cast conception. As will be explored in the pages that follow, there has been much recent discussion about the scope and scale of Offa's Dyke: and there is perhaps also some burgeoning debate regarding its uniqueness as a linear frontier work. One particular doubt that has been expressed in recent writing concerns whether the statement in Asser's late ninth-century *Life* of King Alfred of Wessex that the Dyke was built 'from sea to sea' was anything more than conventional hyperbole.[2] The view expressed here is that creating some reality to this sea-to-sea convention (if such it was) was nonetheless integral to the envisioning of this extraordinary project. The reason for this is that in achieving this perception, the 'great dyke' fulfilled one among several imperial ambitions of Mercia during its apogee under Offa and his successor, Coenwulf: namely, to place Mercia, alongside continental Francia under Charlemagne, as a legitimate, even an inevitable, successor to the world of late Imperial Rome.

An important question to be addressed in an introductory way here is: why is it necessary to rehearse the uncertainties and ambiguities of the Dyke in a volume of this kind right now? After all, one of the things that we call for in and through this book is a renewed effort to gain further basic information about its form and history, using up-to-date archaeological methods involving both survey and excavation. Our answer is threefold.

Firstly, it has been asserted in recent years that the puzzle of Offa's Dyke has at last been solved. According to Margaret Worthington and the late David

A new appreciation of complexity: Offa's Dyke near Craignant

The subtleties and regularities of the placing of the Dyke in the landscape, and of its built form, have yet to be explored fully. The apparent simplicity of form, seen here looking southwards towards Selattyn Hill (right) and the Shropshire Plain beyond (horizon, left), is belied by a variety of repeated placement practices in respect to the changing topography of the borderland hills and valleys, and construction devices which have not until now been fully appreciated or explored. The Dyke here continues to mark the boundary between England and Wales.

PHOTOGRAPH: ADAM STANFORD/
AERIAL-CAM, COPYRIGHT RESERVED.

Hill (in their 2003 publication *Offa's Dyke History and Guide*, and articles published elsewhere) there is no longer any doubt that the Dyke was built to counter a specific threat to Mercia from the Kingdom of Powys, nor that it only ever existed in the length of 80 miles (130 km) where today it survives as a (mostly) continuous and conspicuous earthwork from Treuddyn in the north, southwards to Rushock Hill near Kington. This view is unfortunately becoming orthodox despite being founded upon a problematical evidence-base, on questionable rejection of the Gloucestershire lengths of the Dyke, and on a particular interpretation of a single, now illegible, inscription on a stone pillar in the Dee valley near Llangollen.[3] It also derives from seeing the Dyke as the primary entity to be explained historically, rather than the frontier of which it nonetheless formed the most obvious element. These perspectives are ones that we challenge throughout this volume.

Secondly, our field observations in recent years have led us to conclude that there are significant aspects of the construction of Dyke and its placement in the landscape that have so far escaped notice, but that may be fundamental to an understanding of its intended purpose or purposes. This volume notes several such observations, and highlights the need to follow them up with further intensive study.

And thirdly, it is now exactly 60 years since the publication in 1955 of Cyril Fox's *Offa's Dyke: A Field Survey of the Western Frontier Works of Mercia in the Seventh and Eighth Centuries AD*, which is still the most comprehensive study that has yet been made of the Dyke. It is moreover 90 years since the survey on which that volume was based was first commissioned by Mortimer Wheeler (in 1925). If a further phase of field study of the Dyke is to take place in the coming years, as we believe it should, it is important to take stock of existing ideas and data, and to create new agenda for detailed archaeological investigation. Our aim in this volume is therefore to provide a reasonably comprehensive 'baseline' statement of current knowledge and understanding, to reprise old issues in novel ways, and to contribute fresh perspectives that will challenge both previous assumptions and unwarranted conclusions. We hope that the publication of this book at this time will help stimulate further enquiry that will move beyond critical reappraisal to the acquisition of a coherent body of new data.

In this book, we therefore raise, and try to tackle, all of the questions that have properly exercised scholarly research and debate around Offa's Dyke in the past. It is vital nonetheless to observe that it is no straightforward matter to address the interpretive questions so far posed concerning the history and purpose of the Dyke. This is in part because of the inherent difficulties of coming to grips, archaeologically and historically, with what in some sense or another can undoubtedly be seen as a 'boundary work'. Moreover, the complexities of its form, the immediate political circumstances of its construction, and the consequences of its creation have also served to create multiple significances for the monument, for which no once-for-all solution is likely to be possible.

In any attempt to advance an understanding and appreciation of Offa's Dyke, there are accordingly few firm starting-points. For instance, to begin with a simple archaeological description of the earthwork, we can surely say that it is typical of a class of linear earthwork monuments dating to between the fifth and ninth centuries AD – or can we? On the one hand, the absence of firm dating evidence for the Dyke, specifically from multiple scientifically-dated samples from several (and varied) locations along its course, at present hinders such confidence. On the other hand, several of the observations we have made during our recent studies indicate instead that in several respects Offa's Dyke is quite different from other contemporary or near-contemporary linear bank-and-ditch monuments in terms of the degree to which it was engineered and 'performed' in the landscape to achieve particular effects. So it may not only be scale of the Dyke, or its naming, or its date, which differentiates it from other such works, but also the intricacy of its construction.

Clearly, then, it is our view that it is illusory to imagine that there is currently a settled consensus, based upon unequivocal archaeological research conclusions, regarding the dating and interpretation of Offa's Dyke. Nor, however, is it tenable to maintain that there is in fact no 'Offa's Dyke problem' at all, and that a particular focus on this Dyke at all somehow 'misses the point' that it is just another example of a long-distance boundary work of which many examples existed in Anglo-Saxon England. On the contrary, arguably what set apart the Mercia of Offa and Coenwulf's time from other Anglo-Saxon political hegemonies was the scale of its ambition politically. What therefore distinguishes Offa's Dyke from other linear boundary works, in addition to its built form and huge geographical span, is the extent to which the massive highly-focused construction project that created the Dyke gave material expression to that ambition. This perspective requires us to consider more closely than might at first sight seem relevant, both the history of Mercia in terms of its frontiers and neighbours, and the workings of the Mercian hegemony both in political and in material terms.

To encompass fully the matters raised here, the book is organised into three sections, each of which comprises three chapters. Part One sets out the background, reviewing in the first chapter the parameters both of the character and course of the earthwork and of the controversies concerning (for instance) the purpose for its creation. As such, that chapter identifies some of the key areas of debate that need to be addressed at the outset, such as its date, while also providing an initial detailed characterisation of the earthwork. A second chapter then traces the development of 'Offa's Dyke Studies' from medieval references, through the writings of antiquaries from the seventeenth to the nineteenth century, and the twentieth-century investigations of historians and archaeologists, to the present day. The work of Sir Cyril Fox in the years from 1926 is clearly pivotal in this context, and it is reviewed closely here. Yet it is noted also that many of the problems, issues and interpretive ideas concerning the Dyke that Fox identified (and some that he did not rehearse) were in fact first raised in the nineteenth century. Part One concludes with a chapter that reprises current understanding of the origins and development of the Kingdom of Mercia in reference to its frontiers. It provides an outline account of Mercia and its kingship in respect to its changing fortunes, and in particular it focuses upon its borders and its relations with its neighbours in the seventh, eighth and early ninth centuries. In doing so, the aim is to situate, as succinctly as possible, both Offa and the Dyke in the context of the rise to pre-eminence of the Mercian kingdom within the Anglo-Saxon world.

In Part Two, the intricacies of the character of Offa's Dyke, and what can be inferred about the way that it was designed to operate, are placed at centre-stage in three chapters that focus first upon how the Dyke traversed the landscape, then upon the specific character of its build, and finally upon the field indications concerning how that build was accomplished and what (few) clues exist about how it might have been used. The fourth chapter of the book therefore analyses the placing of Offa's Dyke within the landscape, characterising in detail, for example, the way that it approaches the various locations it traverses in repetitive but particular ways: such that it can be seen to have utilised a distinct series of locational and design practices. Details of its construction as understood from the sum of previous investigations, and to a degree also from our own recent field observations, are the subject-matter of the fifth chapter. These, and further such observations in subsequent chapters, demonstrate that there are enough similarities in its build in different locations to be positive that it is of unitary construction from Flintshire in the north to Gloucestershire in the south.

The closing chapter of this second Part of the book identifies clues concerning the organisation of construction of the Dyke and explores the nature of evidence that can be adduced for the existence of 'infrastructure' that may have accompanied the creation of the monument. This discussion extends from the nature of the obligations of the (lay and ecclesiastical) Mercian elite to provide resources for military service and works, through consideration of the physical form of laying-out works and possible gateways, to the question of the existence of a 'landscape of control' and surveillance within which the Dyke was the key element.

The nature of the frontier itself and the place of the Dyke within it, and within the strategies for developing and maintaining the Mercian hegemony, are the subject of the three chapters in Part Three of the book. The seventh chapter probes the character of the Anglo-British borderland as a landscape that became especially significant to the Mercian state towards the end of the eighth century. The physical landscape that Offa's Dyke traversed when newly-built remains little understood, but there are clues to its 'political' geography in the form of the Dyke itself: in particular through an observable correlation between zones of highly complex build and its passage across parts of the landscape that may have been especially sensitive in respect to British centres to the west. Within the frontier zone, some areas that have remained anomalous in discussion of the Dyke as a continuous earthwork are featured centrally: and the chapter therefore includes a focus upon areas to the north and south of Hereford. The political context is once again paramount, and Offa's probable presence on the frontier in just this area is noted as having been a key factor affecting decisions about the route and form of the Dyke overall.

In the penultimate chapter the aim is to profile more fully the nature of the Mercian hegemony in the late eighth and early ninth century, and how it was sustained. If Offa's Dyke was an instrument of hegemony, it existed alongside several others. Some of these have been extensively debated hitherto, others less so. The spotlight here is strongly (but by no means exclusively) upon the material realm, and in particular upon coinage, sculpture, architecture and elite martial items. The concluding chapter then examines the role of the Dyke

'It has become identified with a national walking trail': near Montgomery

At Dudston Fields between Chirbury and Montgomery, Offa's Dyke earthwork, the Offa's Dyke Path National Trail, and the national boundary between Wales and England coincide. Seen here from the north-east, the prospect is into Wales from Shropshire. The Path has enhanced the renown of the Dyke, while at the same time bringing increasing erosion, and public confusion concerning the difference between the Dyke and the Path where the latter deviates from the course of the former: as in parts of Clwyd, in Breconshire and in northern Monmouthshire.

in sustaining and deepening the Mercian hegemony, however short-lived this political domination transpired to have been. In doing so, the 'hegemonic role' of the Dyke is explored inasmuch as it exemplified a politics of exclusion and aggrandisement, of imperial allusion, and of Mercian dominance over the English. The focus then shifts to the question of how Offa's Dyke may have facilitated the development of an early march-land along the border between the Mercians and Britons, drawing upon insights gained from comparison with contemporary developments on the continent, and in particular in the Carolingian domains. The building of Offa's Dyke represented both a point in time, and a stage in the development of the frontier, and the chapter concludes with a tentative reconstruction of the historical dynamics of the frontier in the reigns of Offa and Coenwulf.

A brief Epilogue asks finally, how we can comprehend the historical and culturally enduring place of Offa's Dyke in the twenty-first century, not least in reference to the legacy of both Offa and Mercia. For a millennium the Dyke was synonymous with the border between Wales and England, and became a symbol of the separated character of Welsh identity within Britain. From the late twentieth century it has become identified with a national walking trail, and is in some respects in danger of being valued, if at all, only in recreational terms. In ending the volume, the terms of a potential 're-connection' of the Dyke at, and beyond, the local level are discussed, and the place of archaeology and historic landscape studies at the fulchrum of such re-discovery is emphasised.

PART ONE
THE BACKGROUND REVIEWED

At Crow's Nest: loking north towards the Vale of Montgomery and the Berwyn Mountains

CHAPTER ONE

Offa's Dyke in profile: character, course and controversies

> King Offa, in order to have a partition for all time between the Kings of England and Wales, built a long dyke stretching from the south past Bristol, along the edge of the Welsh Mountains....This dyke is still to be seen in many places.
>
> (William Caxton, *The Description of Britain*, c.1480)[1]

The building of Offa's Dyke is rightly regarded as being among the greatest physical achievements of the inhabitants of the British Isles during the period between the end of Roman Britain and the Norman Conquest. The most obvious characteristics of its great length and its crossing of hilly 'border' country have been understood in detail for at least 200 years.[2] The Dyke was, moreover, the subject of one of the first extended studies in what has come to be termed 'landscape archaeology'. Sir Cyril Fox made a detailed study of the earthwork, along with Wat's Dyke which runs parallel to it in the northern part of its course, in a major survey project undertaken in the period 1926 to 1934. This was published in a substantial monograph in 1955, bringing together his earlier work and providing a strong evidential basis for subsequent discussion. Fox's interpretation of the Dyke as, in effect, the product of negotiated treaty relations between Mercia and the Welsh kingdoms neighbouring it to the west, held sway for a generation. Yet although there has subsequently continued to be broad agreement concerning the identity of the Dyke as a 'frontier work' associated with the zenith of the Anglo-Saxon kingdom of Mercia, and with the eighth-century kingship of Offa in particular, there have remained questions concerning its exact date and purpose, doubts expressed about its extent, and discussion also concerning the organisation of its construction.[3]

There are a number of questions that can be posed concerning the basic characteristics of Offa's Dyke, such as 'what is the nature of the linear earthwork?', and 'what condition is it in?', and the answers to these are set out briefly here. Further questions have been asked ever since the Dyke became an object for serious historical study, at least since the nineteenth century. Prominent among these are 'when was it built?', and 'can it definitely be attributed to King Offa?' A number of features of the Dyke have been questioned, and paradoxes identified, chief among which are 'what is the significance of the apparent gaps in its

1 Offa's Dyke in profile: character, course and controversies

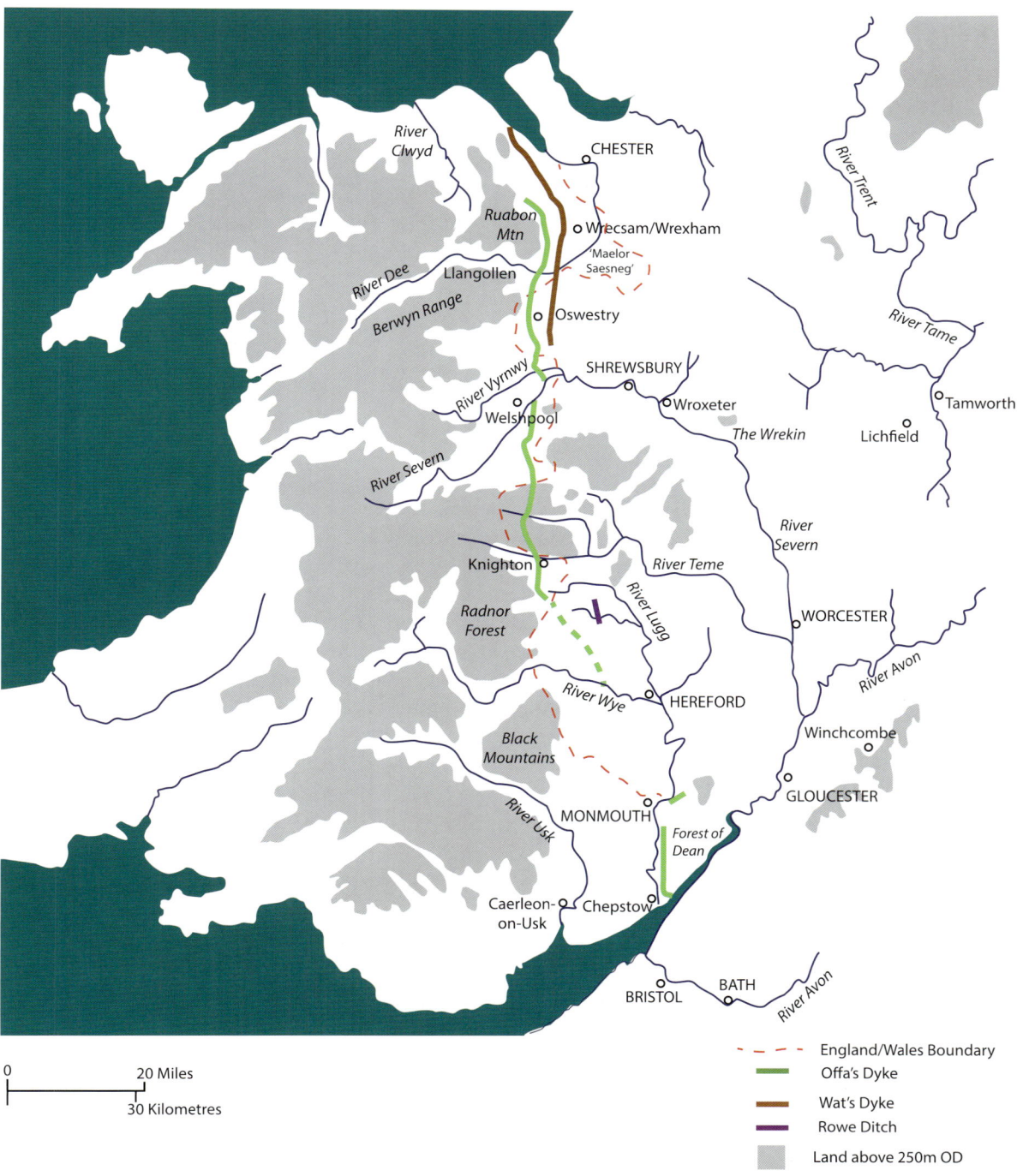

FIGURE 1.1 Offa's Dyke and Wat's Dyke in west-central Britain
Note especially the contrast between the location of Offa's Dyke in the upland margins and Wat's Dyke in the plain, and the differences between the line of Offa's Dyke and the modern Wales/England border.

course, and are they real or illusory?', and 'what is its relation to Wat's Dyke and other linear earthworks in the Marches of Wales?' These and related questions are explored here, not at this stage in the book necessarily to provide detailed answers but rather to indicate the extent and limitations of current knowledge. Finally, as a prelude to detailed analysis of its location in the landscape later in the volume, a full description of its course is provided here, northwards and then southwards from the middle Severn valley near Welshpool in the present-day Welsh administrative region of Powys.

An introductory characterisation

Visible today as a sometimes prominent feature in the landscape, Offa's Dyke is a very long distance linear earthwork that crosses often deeply dissected terrain just beyond (that is, to the west of) the western margin of the lowlands of 'west-central' southern Britain, and of the English Midlands. The Dyke follows a carefully placed north–south route, holding closely to this primary orientation throughout much of its known course. The basic structure comprises an earthen, or earth and stone, bank with a ditch dug (mostly) on its western side, such that the earthwork faces westwards (Figure 1.2). A substantial counter-scarp bank is present on the outer lip of the ditch along enough well-preserved stretches to indicate that this was a commonly-occurring original construction feature.[4] On the eastern side of the bank there are pits, or a west-facing scarp, or occasionally a linear quarry, or (more frequently than has been widely acknowledged) what appears to be a continuous ditch, from which contributory material to build the bank was derived. In some locations more than one of these features co-exists.

FIGURE 1.2
Offa's Dyke at Mainstone, Shropshire, looking north

This length of Dyke, viewed northwards as it descends to the crossing of the upper Unk valley just to the south of the Kerry Ridgeway (and close to Crowsnest, shown in Figure 1.2), illustrates the basic features of the Dyke, with a continuous west-facing profile extending down into the base of the ditch on the western side of the earthwork; and with a prominent bank to the east. The way in which the Dyke approaches the valley here is discussed in Chapter 4.

The Dyke so constituted survives remarkably, if variably, well despite many centuries of natural erosion and human disturbance to its form and course. As will be described in subsequent chapters, the form of the Dyke exhibits variety but not inconsistency: there are design characteristics in both its positioning in the landscape and its built features that recur throughout its known course. Moreover, this recurrence of key locational and build characteristics of the Dyke is far from random. It represents, rather, a consistency also in how these features were deployed: both in response to the similarities in the topographical circumstances that were encountered, and in order to achieve particular effects.

The mid-way point along the 115 miles (185 km) span of the putative western frontier of Mercia from the North Wales coast to the Severn Estuary is at the valley of the river Clun, and this is the mid-way point today of the Offa's Dyke Path. However, no definite trace of the upstanding earthwork Dyke has been recorded northwards of Treuddyn near Mold in Flintshire. Its last, impressive, length lies between Treuddyn and Llanfynydd, and it extends across 29 miles (c.47 km) or so southwards of this to the middle reaches of the river Severn to the north-east of Welshpool.[5] Across this distance it is mostly continuous, although there are gaps where it has never been traced (as for example short stretches on the north banks of both the Dee and Ceiriog), and where it once existed but has either been quarried away or levelled due to historically-recent activity, as at several points in the Trefonen area south-west of Oswestry. The river Severn stands in place of the Dyke for 5 miles (8 km) southwards from a point near Rhos, to the north-east of Welshpool. Then the earthwork appears again on the margins of the floodplain of the Severn upstream at Buttington (and immediately to the east of Welshpool). It continues southwards from this location as a mostly substantial earthwork for another 28 miles (c.45 km) to Knighton at the crossing of the Teme valley, via the Vale of Montgomery and the Clun uplands.

From Knighton the Dyke continues as a linear earthwork largely without gaps for around a further 8 miles (c.12.5 km) as far south as Rushock Hill in north Herefordshire.[6] Cyril Fox, in common with several among the earlier commentators, regarded a series of short lengths of linear earthwork in northern Herefordshire as having formed elements in a frontier line projecting the course of Offa's Dyke southwards from Rushock Hill to the north bank of the river Wye near Bridge Sollers.[7] Beyond Bridge Sollers, eastwards and then southwards mostly on the left bank of the Wye, further intermittent lengths of dyke or bank have been claimed at one time or another as part of Offa's Dyke: although there has been little support for the idea that these ever formed part of the long-distance work.[8]

Across the 25 or so miles (c.40 km) involved, past Hereford, Fownhope, Ross-on-Wye, and Monmouth, only one of these claimed lengths has ever, it seems, been closely assessed. This particular short stretch, west of Lower Lydbrook in English Bicknor parish, has been positively identified in recent years as forming a coherent and characteristic length of Offa's Dyke.[9] Finally,

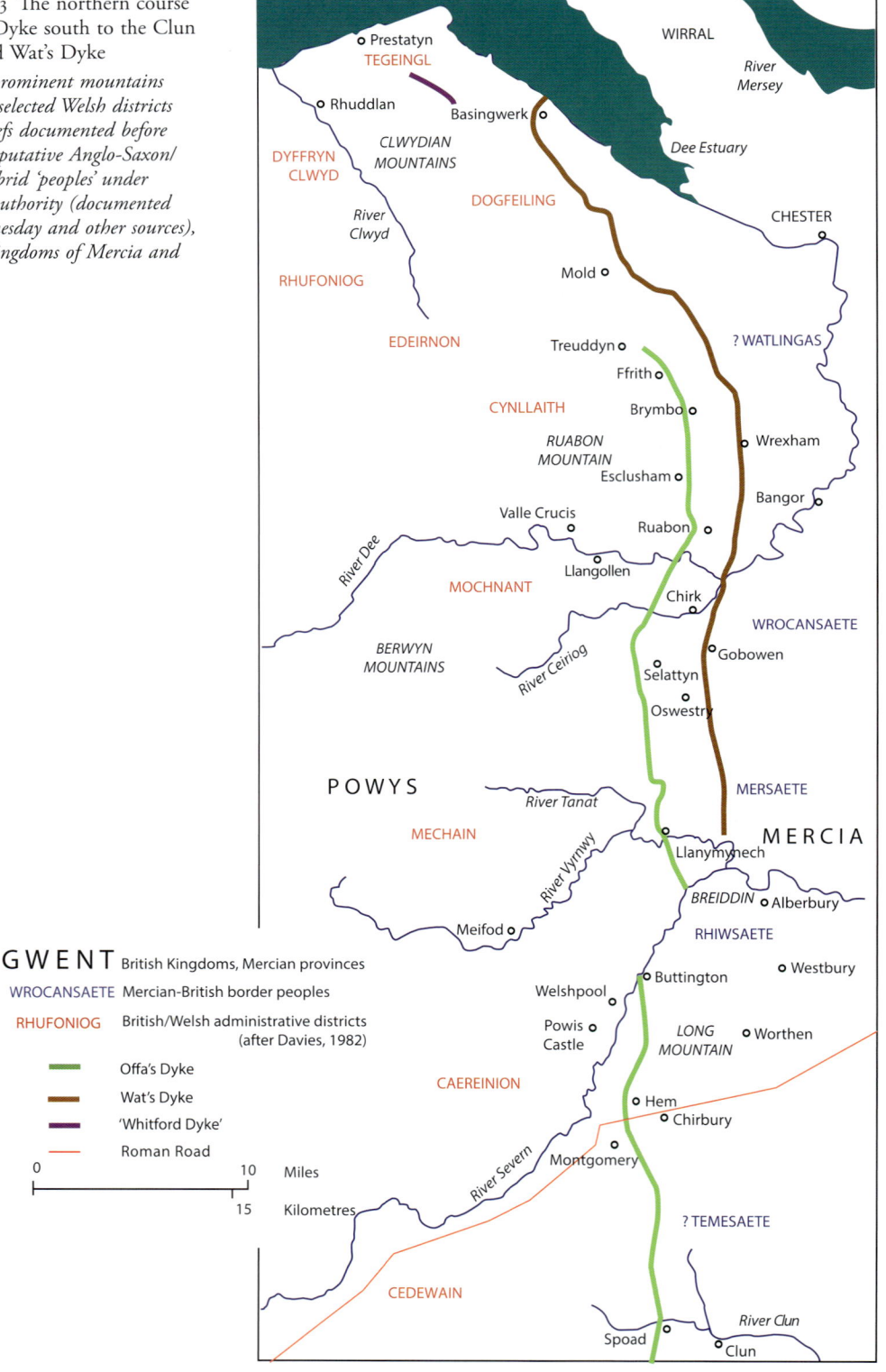

FIGURE 1.3 The northern course of Offa's Dyke south to the Clun valley, and Wat's Dyke

Showing prominent mountains and hills, selected Welsh districts and cantrefs documented before AD 1200, putative Anglo-Saxon/British hybrid 'peoples' under Mercian authority (documented from Domesday and other sources), and the kingdoms of Mercia and Powys.

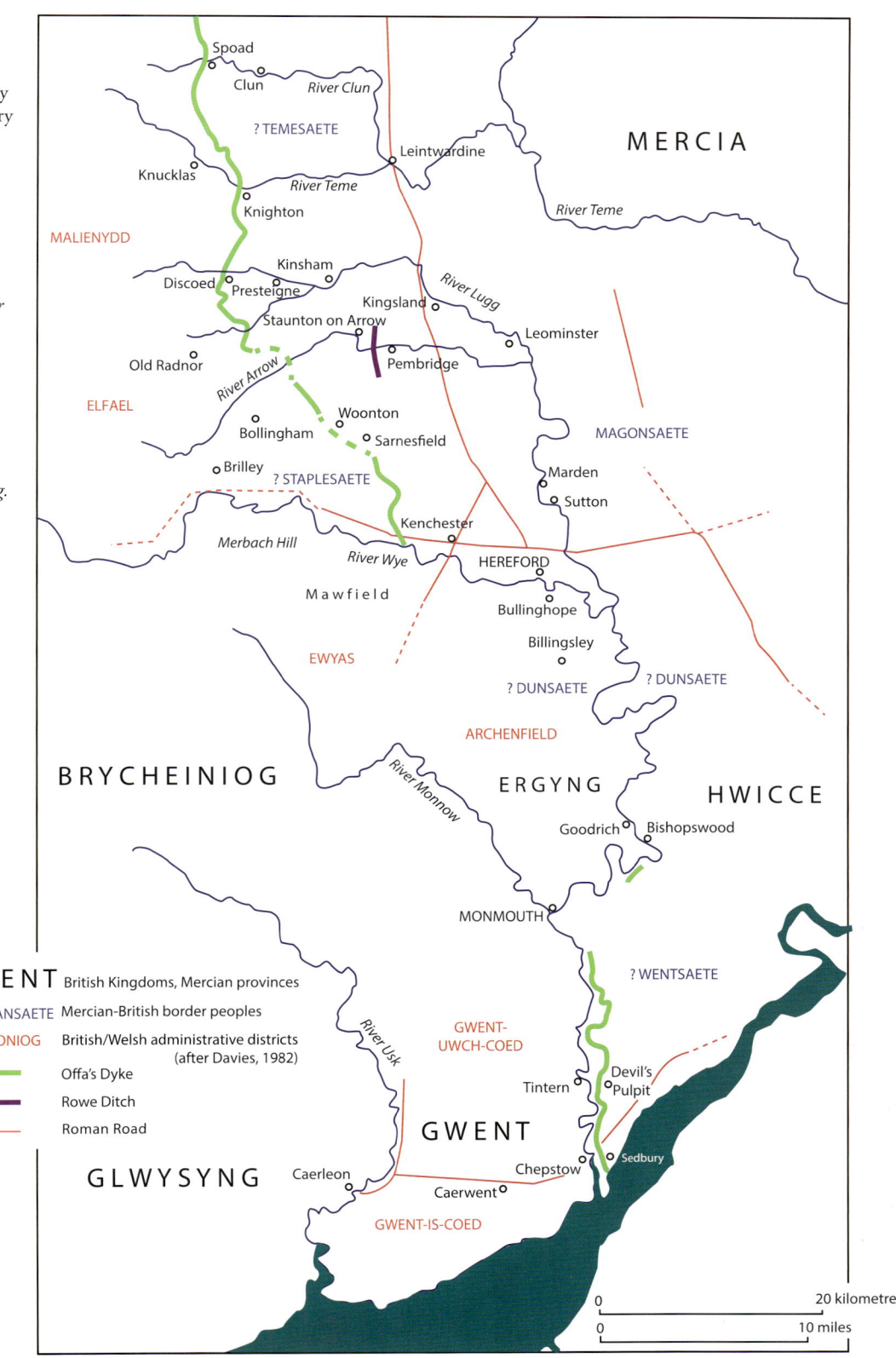

FIGURE 1.4 The southern course of Offa's Dyke, south from the Clun valley to the Severn Estuary

Showing prominent mountains and hills, selected Welsh districts and cantrefs documented before AD 1200, putative Anglo-Saxon/British hybrid 'peoples' under Mercian authority (documented from Domesday and other sources), and the kingdoms of Mercia, the Hwicce, Brycheiniog, Ergyng, Gwent and Glwysyng.

from near Lower Redbrook in Gloucestershire, some 2 miles (3.2 km) to the south-east of Monmouth, and again on the left bank of the Wye, the earthwork resumes as a continuous or near-continuous upstanding earthwork, again with an admixture of contrasting scales of build. This stretch extends southwards, again on a north–south course, for around 10 miles (16 km), with localised gaps north and south of Tutshill (within Tidenham parish on the left bank of the Wye opposite Chepstow), some of which were caused by quarrying and others possibly by modern development.[10] Close to the confluence of the Wye with the Severn the earthwork turns suddenly south-eastwards to cross the Beachley peninsula, where it terminates dramatically on the cliffs above the Severn Estuary (Figure 1.5).

The overall length of the Dyke that is clearly upstanding and closely traceable today therefore extends across some 90 miles (c.145 km).[11] Given that there are repeated characteristics that are shared between all parts of what has been known historically as Offa's Dyke, it remains reasonable to regard the entirety of this 'overall length' as having been embraced within the same scheme. The locational regularities include particular stances taken up as the Dyke traverses slopes or makes its way around the (mostly western sides of) localised summits of hills; and a series of distinctive ways in which the earthwork approaches and crosses river-valleys.[12] The characteristic build features that are visible in the field include the counter-scarp bank noted already, but more especially front-facing enhancements of the bank including some form of stone facing and the exposure of natural rock-faces; and the construction of lengths in series of segments arranged in distinctive ways.[13] Several of these repeated locational and build features are particular to Offa's Dyke, differing from those of other known linear earthen dykes, including the presumed near-contemporary and partly-parallel Wat's Dyke.

Although the largely continuous upstanding earthwork that extends southwards between Treuddyn and the river Severn near Welshpool spans around 29 miles (c.47 km), its survival varies throughout that distance. It is most clearly damaged or absent where mines, quarries, housing and industrial developments have either masked or removed it altogether, or roads have been built along its bank or ditch. The areas most strongly affected by such historically recent activity are near Rhosllanerchrugog north of Ruabon and Wynnstay Colliery south of it, and at Brymbo north-east of Wrexham. In addition, Llynclys Quarry south-west of Oswestry has cumulatively removed a substantial length, and, on a much smaller scale, the construction of a lake in a landscape park in the eighteenth century at Chirk Castle has resulted in the unusual circumstance of the submergence of 200 m of its course, with the bank surviving underwater but still visible (especially from the air) here.[14]

The 35 miles (c.56 km) of Dyke from Buttington southwards to Rushock Hill in north-west Herefordshire, although surviving better than the closely-equivalent length north of the middle Severn valley, has nonetheless been subject to localised levelling and degradation for the most part for agricultural

1   Offa's Dyke in profile: character, course and controversies

FIGURE 1.5 At Sedbury, Gloucestershire, by the Severn estuary

The view south-eastwards here, looking along the inner side of the bank of the Dyke with the ditch to the south (right), is towards the point (the skyline ridge here) at which the Dyke meets the Severn Estuary, and reaches its southern terminus, on Sedbury Cliffs. The massive proportions of the earthwork are characteristic of, rather than in contrast to, many of the other Dyke lengths in Gloucestershire. Most of the build features found along all these Gloucestershire lengths are, moreover, identical to such features deployed elsewhere along the course of the Dyke north of the Wye west of Hereford, north and south of the middle Severn valley, and north of the river Dee.

operations.[15] Considerable lengths of the Dyke are, however, continuously well-preserved in the uplands south of the Vale of Montgomery, from the Kerry Ridgeway southwards across south Shropshire and the Clun Forest, and across east Radnorshire and into Herefordshire (Figure 1.6).

In west Gloucestershire south of Lower Redbrook, the Dyke survives remarkably well except in the immediate environs of St Briavels Common (where it has been degraded due to the creation of a patchwork of small fields and closes for small-holder farming) and south of East Vaga on Tidenham Chase. From the latter location southwards, natural erosion and quarrying have cut back the limestone cliffs east of the river Wye, removing traces of the Dyke in the process. Further south towards Tutshill and Sedbury, quarrying has occurred alongside creeping suburbanisation in what have, from the mid-nineteenth century onwards, become effectively the eastern suburbs of Chepstow, the centre of which town is located across the Wye to the west.

Northwards from the river Vyrnwy close to its confluence with the Severn, the 38 mile (61 km) span of Wat's Dyke from near Maesbury (south of Oswestry) northwards to the shores of the Dee estuary at Basingwerk first mirrors the northern end of the 'continuous' Offa's Dyke, between less than 1 mile and just over 3 miles (c.1.6–4.8 km) eastwards of the latter, and then extends beyond it northwards. The date and the purpose of Wat's Dyke also remain in question, and the existence of the two dykes in such close proximity to one another demands some explanation.[16]

The earthwork sometimes referred to as the 'Whitford Dyke', and other

FIGURE 1.6 On the Clun uplands, south of Llanfair Hill

The open grasslands at high elevation (around 430 m OD at this point) and late enclosure here have meant better preservation of the earthwork, and a relatively unrestricted view of the Dyke as it snakes northwards towards the Clun valley traverse. Figures 4.9, 5.35 and 5.36 show the Dyke just to the north of this point from the air, while particular build features close to the dip in the middle distance are illustrated in Figures 5.30 and 5.34.

putative linear earthworks in the area between Holywell and Prestatyn in Flintshire, were seen by Cyril Fox as representing part of the northwards extension of Offa's Dyke through central and northern Flintshire.[17] However, cumulative field studies by the 'Offa's Dyke Project' and recent investigations by Clwyd-Powys Archaeological Trust staff indicate that none of the previously-identified lengths of earthwork bear scrutiny in these terms. At present there is therefore little to commend the view that Offa's Dyke did once extend across the 20 or so miles (32 km) from Treuddyn to Prestatyn. This is due partly to the associations of the 'Whitford Dyke', which appear to be prehistoric, and because no trace of a linear work survives across most of the area concerned.[18] This does not mean, however, that this area can be forgotten about in terms of understanding the context for, and purpose of, Offa's Dyke. The same is true of the possibly always intermittent character of the Dyke in north Herefordshire and the seemingly complete absence of the linear earthwork south from Bridge Sollers and Hereford, beyond Ross-on-Wye to Bishopswood on the boundary between Herefordshire and Gloucestershire, and between English Bicknor and Redbrook south-east of Monmouth. What these 'gap' areas represented in the wider political and geographic scheme we regard, on the contrary, as germane to an understanding of the nature of the Mercian-British frontier in the decades concerned, and thereafter.

Date and attribution: profiling two key questions

Probably the most basic question that can be asked about Offa's Dyke concerns its date of construction. What archaeological evidence is there that it is specifically an eighth-century monument? Surprisingly, we cannot yet provide a conclusive answer to this question. This is especially puzzling at first glance, given the number of excavations carried out by the 30-year University of Manchester 'Offa's Dyke Project' based at the Porth-y-Waen Field Centre, Oswestry, and the number of other documented archaeological interventions and observations, totalling 84, that had occurred by 2003.[19] The discussion of chronology in the principal publication arising from this project refers to dating evidence from earlier excavations, but not from the 57 or so project interventions, none of which apparently produced any dates.[20]

That Offa's Dyke was built after the Roman period was suggested by Fox from his excavations undertaken as early as 1927 at Ffrith village.[21] Subsequent investigations at the same site, specifically two development-led investigations in 1990 and 1995, have confirmed the general character of the assemblage from an undoubted Romano-British settlement here, and have suggested that occupation continued beyond the *c.*AD 200 limit indicated by Fox.[22] The problem is that, although it is clear that the Dyke post-dates the Roman period, we have no evidence from this (or as yet from any other excavations or interventions), regarding exactly how long after the end of the Roman Empire in the west (in the early years of the fifth century AD) the Dyke was built.

It seems as reasonable now as it was in 1955, therefore, to conclude that this massive linear earthwork is post-Roman in date, but that the *archaeological* evidence available at present does not permit greater precision for any given length.[23] To begin to specify an 'event horizon' for the building of the Dyke in one area, let alone across such considerable distances, chronometric dates would need to be obtained from a series of clearly defined construction contexts.[24] It soon becomes apparent from reading the principal published account of the results of the late twentieth-century 'Offa's Dyke Project' that many of the excavations undertaken were limited in their objectives (such as to tracing the existence of the ditch at particular points), while the nature of the interventions appears to have limited the scope for the production of definitive results.[25]

Another reason for the current lack of dating evidence for Offa's Dyke is due to the limited extent to which it passes through areas – even in such locations as Ruabon and the outskirts of Wrexham – under significant recent development pressure. This contrasts to some degree with the situation of Wat's Dyke, which, lying in more level terrain and closer to major communication routes and to urban areas, has suffered more development-based intrusion. So, for example, two of the recent development-linked excavations of Wat's Dyke have produced evidence that potentially dates its construction. One of these excavations, at Mile Oak, Oswestry, produced a date from a hearth thought to be either actually contemporary with, or in use immediately before, construction of the bank of the dyke.[26] Although this indicated a likely date for the hearth in the fifth or early sixth century, and although the impression gained by the excavator was that the hearth had not been fired long before the Wat's Dyke bank was built over it, there is nothing to prove with certainty that there was not a considerable time-lapse before the actual construction works took place.[27]

More recently, an area-extensive excavation of a levelled section of Wat's Dyke at Gobowen north of Oswestry has produced a number of new insights into the construction of the monument that have significant implications for our appreciation of observations about the construction of Offa's Dyke.[28] This excavation was important because it revealed the foundations of the bank of that linear work over a considerable distance, and because the dates obtained were retrieved from a succession of deposits in the ditch, and one from under the forward lip of the bank, using a newly-developed dating method, Optically Stimulated Luminescence (OSL), that measures how much time has elapsed since a given surface has been exposed to sunlight (Figure 1.7).[29] The series of dates have been interpreted by the excavators as centring upon the early ninth century, although a date later in that century would also be possible.[30]

The contradiction between these dates for Wat's Dyke might be readily explicable if it was a multi-phase construction. However, equally, the arguments put forward by the excavators of the Gobowen site for seeing the ninth-century dates as providing a unified construction horizon for the whole dyke could be regarded as sufficiently persuasive. In contrast, the present lack of unequivocal dating for any part of Offa's Dyke leaves discussion of the date of its construction still dependant, for the meantime at least, upon its historical attribution to Offa.[31] But how reliable is this attribution? Consideration of this question necessarily brings us to an evaluation of the only near-contemporary documentary reference to the Dyke, dating to the last decade of the ninth century:

> Fuit in Mercia moderno tempore quidam strenuus atque universis circa se regibus et regionibus finitimis formidolosus rex, nomine Offa; qui vallum magnum inter Britanniam atque Merciam de mari usque ad mare facere imperavit.
>
> *There was in Mercia in recent times an energetic king called Offa, terrifying to all the neighbouring kings and provinces around him, who ordered a great ditch to be made between Britain and Mercia from sea to sea.*[32]

This statement is embedded within a section of Bishop Asser's *Life* of King Alfred of Wessex (*c*.895) that seems to have been written to explain why the West Saxons had for some time preferred not to bestow the title 'Queen' on the king's consort. The importance that later commentary has attached to this ascription could therefore be questioned, in part because it appears only as a

1 Offa's Dyke in profile: character, course and controversies

brief prelude to Asser's re-telling of the West Saxon ruling family's moralistic story about Offa's daughter, Eadburh. The latter married Beorhtric, king of the West Saxons, whom she was said to have dominated and (albeit incidentally) poisoned. Her high-handed manner caused great offence in the West Saxon court, where she was said to have behaved 'like a tyrant after the manner of her father'.[33] Whether an aside or not, however, the statement appears to be a straightforward summary of widely-held, if inevitably West Saxon-focused, late ninth-century beliefs regarding King Offa a century after his death. It suggests that Offa was famous, or infamous, not only for his tyranny and aggressive dominance over Mercia's neighbours, but also for having built a great dyke that expressed or extended that dominance.[34]

A sceptical view could nonetheless be taken that, since we have no *independent* dating of Offa's Dyke, least of all at present from archaeology, we are not in a position to regard the work as specifically attributable to Offa's reign.[35] Could the 'Offa' of the traditional ascription indeed have been legendary, or generic? So, for instance, the general practice among the Anglo-Saxons was to ascribe the large-scale and (one would think) obvious works of men that were nonetheless incomprehensible in their purpose to subsequent generations, to creations of their gods. The earthwork known as Wansdyke in Wiltshire, similar works including the Wansdyke of north Somerset, and the various 'Grim's Ditch' works in Oxfordshire and elsewhere, are examples of the naming of dykes in this generic way. Could the Offa concerned be the semi-legendary 'Offa of

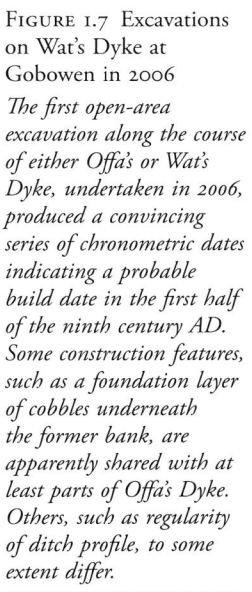

FIGURE 1.7 Excavations on Wat's Dyke at Gobowen in 2006

The first open-area excavation along the course of either Offa's or Wat's Dyke, undertaken in 2006, produced a convincing series of chronometric dates indicating a probable build date in the first half of the ninth century AD. Some construction features, such as a foundation layer of cobbles underneath the former bank, are apparently shared with at least parts of Offa's Dyke. Others, such as regularity of ditch profile, to some extent differ.

REPRODUCED COURTESY T. MALIM/ GIFFORDS COPYRIGHT RESERVED

Angeln', for instance?[36] To most authorities this has seemed unlikely, given that Offa was the most renowned of the Mercian kings, and that the Dyke clearly bears some geographical relation to the westerly limits of Mercia. The naming could in theory, however, be a later ascription of the massive construction to a prominent earlier ruler.[37]

What would we make, therefore, of Offa's Dyke in the absence of the Asser reference? Firstly, archaeologically, we might simply describe the Dyke as a long-distance boundary work extending from near Wrexham southwards as far as the vicinity of Kington in Herefordshire. It clearly faces west towards the Welsh and was therefore presumably of English construction; and this only makes sense in a pre-Norman context.[38] Secondly, we could note the oddity that this long dyke partly runs parallel with another linear dyke (Wat's Dyke) that also extends over a considerable distance and also faces westwards, but is situated to the east of the longer earthwork, on more level terrain. We might also deduce, therefore, that one of these dykes is likely to have replaced, or perhaps augmented, the other. Thirdly, we might note that a length of dyke that exists on the eastern side of the river Wye south of Monmouth shares many of the attributes of the longer of the two dykes, but is not physically contiguous with the more northerly dyke. We might also question whether short lengths of dyke (oriented roughly north–south along a parts of a broadly plausible continuous line) linked the length on Rushock Hill, with which they were frequently inter-visible, to the river Wye west of Hereford. Finally, we might attempt to place each of these dykes in some historical context by citing all the instances of border warfare between the Welsh and the English traceable in the annalistic and other literary sources of both peoples.[39]

From the historical understanding that the albeit limited documentary sources for Mercia at its zenith provide, we might nonetheless deduce, even without the Asser reference, that the Dyke that traditionally has borne his name was either commissioned by Offa himself, or was dedicated as a memorial to him. So despite the oblique context of the Asser statement, to some extent 'buried' within Asser's *Life*, it seems most reasonable, upon reflection, to take it at face value. As such, it was a remarkably concise – even abrupt – assessment of the man, his reign, and the nature of his achievement, precisely as the historically somewhat antagonistic inheritors of his world might be expected to deliver. Given the lack of other reference to the Dyke, rather than simply asserting an in-validity to the Asser statement, it might be more pertinent to note what a remarkable survival that statement is, at all.

It has been pointed out by several commentators that the naming of the Dyke in the historical sources all derive from the twelfth century or later. These vary from literary sources through to highly localised medieval land charters, and it would seem strange if they were all to have been inventions of that period.[40] What they instead illustrate is both that more records and commentaries were being produced from the twelfth century onwards, and that the likelihood of their survival into modern times was therefore greater than the chances of further Anglo-Saxon references so surviving. The lack of reference to the Dyke in annalistic events recorded for the area concerned in the late ninth century and subsequently does however suggest that it had soon lost relevance politically and perhaps to some extent also strategically.[41]

Offa's Dyke enigmas and the relationship to Wat's Dyke

There are aspects of the character of Offa's Dyke that have at various times in the past been regarded as puzzling, or even contradictory. For example, concerning the extent of the Dyke, Asser's ninth-century statement that it extended from sea to sea has been seen as difficult to reconcile with its apparent discontinuity or its 'incomplete' linkage to the coast at either end. For Fox, Asser's use of the Latin word *usque* was proof of the precision of the statement: the Dyke literally reached 'the whole way' from sea to sea.[42] Recently, however, it has been suggested that the phrase was simply 'a convenient tag', and a device that was available for Asser to use, since a number of early sources that would have been familiar to him, from the British monk Gildas to the Northumbrian cleric Bede, used similar phrases in a generic way to describe the Roman frontier works.[43] So, the argument runs, a dyke that only vaguely achieved this distance could nonetheless be regarded as having done so, especially if it linked rivers – the Dee and the Wye – that in effect did link it to the sea at either end. However, Offa's Dyke *did* extend northwards beyond its crossing of the Dee, whether or not it linked up to the Dee estuary and the Irish Sea; and it followed the river Wye to its estuary. Moreover, Asser was not the only one who had to hand a copy of Bede. We know from letters of the Northumbrian cleric Alcuin that Offa possessed a copy of the *Historia Ecclesiastica* which was at least read to him: in which case it may well have been Offa himself who advertised the Dyke in this way, and Asser simply repeated his boast.[44]

Another frequently asked question has concerned what the 'gaps' in Offa's Dyke signify. For example, the 'maximal' view of Offa's Dyke espoused by Fox requires explanations as to why the Dyke cannot be traced clearly as a continuous construction fully 'from sea to sea'. One possible view concerning this issue is that, for instance, the Dyke did once extend continuously beyond its surviving course, but has been removed where it cannot now be traced at ground surface. Another possibility is that definition of the frontier or boundary did not necessitate the construction of a continuous earthwork throughout its extent. Yet another is that what Fox termed variously 'dense forest' or 'damp oak-woods' stood where the Dyke is apparently absent.[45]

Among the enigmas that have been observed concerning Offa's Dyke is the one that most closely correlates with the question of why it appears to terminate northwards at Treuddyn. That is, why is there a parallel major linear dyke placed sometimes less than 2 miles (3.2 km) to the west over much of the northern course of Offa's Dyke southwards to the Vyrnwy? In recent years, archaeological study of Wat's Dyke has, for various reasons, progressed further than that of

Offa's Dyke. For instance, in addition to the dating and structural information retrieved from recent excavations, its course is now more fully charted, including the demonstration that gaps noted by Fox are more apparent than real.[46]

The southern end of Wat's Dyke is situated on the banks of the river Morda close to its confluence with the river Vyrnwy, south of Maesbury, to the south of Oswestry. Wat's Dyke extends northwards to include the massive Iron Age hillfort of *Yr Hen Ddinas* ('the old fort': known locally as 'Old Oswestry') in its course, whereupon it turns north-east. Here it is some 3 miles (4.8 km) to the east of Offa's Dyke which, at this point, follows part of the upper Morda valley before rising up across Baker's Hill (Figure 1.15). Wat's Dyke continues northwards across the level country of the Severn-Dee watershed to the east bank of the Morlas Brook near its confluence with the Ceiriog. Having swung north-west after crossing the Dee, it then turns north-east again to cross the Clywedog north of Erddig. This marks the halfway point of its 38-mile (61 km) length, and here it again lies 3 miles (4.8 km) to the east of Offa's Dyke which at this point continues its course north of Ruabon, towards Brymbo. A mile before it reaches the river Alyn north of Wrexham, Wat's Dyke then takes a line to the north-west on a course that it follows for nearly 20 miles (32 km) to Holywell, where it turns abruptly east for less than a mile (1.6 km) to the Dee estuary at Basingwerk.

Wat's Dyke superficially shares in common with Offa's Dyke both some similarities in construction, and also some of the same locational practices. At the largest scale, this includes the general north–south trend of much of Wat's Dyke, at least as it crosses the landscape from north of Wrexham south to Maesbury. More locally, practices such as following a course around prominent west-facing slopes, and (to some extent) the crossing of slopes on a long diagonal, are shared between the Dykes.[47] Moreover, the foundation deposit of both dykes has been found in some locations to comprise a compact spread of stones.

There are, however, also important differences. One, noted by Fox, is that there are consistent contrasts in scale, with Offa's Dyke being substantially larger, at least where the two dykes run parallel with one another.[48] More importantly, their geographical location with respect to topography is very different. Wat's Dyke avoids the uplands entirely, crossing mostly level plain and watersheds to link up a series of north–south lengths of the courses of individual rivers. Another contrast is the relation to existing features in the landscape. While Offa's Dyke for the most part entirely ignores pre-existing defended enclosures, for instance, Wat's Dyke is so designed as to link and incorporate structures such as hillforts within its scheme of defence: 'it was designed as a series of straight lines between prominent survey points whilst Offa's Dyke, in contrast, ran through sparsely populated countryside and was designed to carefully follow topographical features and contours'.[49] Wat's Dyke was built so that it 'links a number of pre-existing forts from the Mercian estate centre at Maesbury, through Old Oswestry and Alyn Fort for example, to the (former) Welsh royal residence at Bagillt and the (Mercian) fortification at Besingwerk on the Dee estuary'.[50] Differences in construction include the manifestly segmented character of the built of Offa's Dyke, discussed in detail in Chapter 5, below, whereas Wat's Dyke was 'smoothed out' across long distances, producing long straight uniform lengths.[51] The Wat's Dyke ditch is more consistently V-shaped, although the suggestion that the bank was more solidly-built throughout, with 'a carefully laid cobblestone core topped by a clay and gravel rampart' is more questionable.[52]

Misapprehension about the origins of Offa's Dyke and its relation to Wat's Dyke in particular is not new. Much of the writing from the twelfth century through to the nineteenth century demonstrated ignorance of the northern discontinuity of Offa's Dyke and of the true nature of its geographical relationship to the dyke parallel to its east; and nearly all of the mapping from the sixteenth century to the eighteenth century compounded this lack of comprehension. The character of the two dykes began to be disentangled in the eighteenth century, but it was only in the nineteenth century that the separable course of each dyke was consistently acknowledged.[53] Fox's study went further in distinguishing both the locational and the build differences, but embedded in the literature a presumed but potentially fallacious dating of Wat's Dyke to the early to mid-eighth century.[54] To some extent, and until the detailed chronology of construction is established at a number of different locations, there is a danger that each new individual investigation and its accompanying dates will 'sway' interpretation hither and thither.

Offa's Dyke and other early medieval linear works

The construction of linear dykes in Britain has a lineage in some areas that extends back to the Middle Bronze Age. They become common in southern Britain in the later Iron Age, with extensive systems having been created close to significant political centres as at Colchester, St Albans, Silchester and Chichester. Although comprising extended straight lengths of bank and ditch, these later prehistoric dykes nonetheless have as their primary stance one of enclosure, or at least delimitation, of a contained area. Dykes that crossed extensive tracts of land and were designed to mark off whole territories first appear in the Roman period and are a feature of the northern Imperial frontier.

In the years immediately before and after what transpired to be the final withdrawal of the Roman legions from Britain around 410 AD, other such linear dykes were built, that served a similar purpose of marking off whole territories, but whose 'blocking' purpose was perhaps equally important. The best known of these is probably Bokerley Dyke on Cranborne Chase on the border between Wiltshire and Dorset.[55] This dyke was clearly designed to cross and to flank the Roman road between Silchester and Dorchester via Salisbury ('Old Sarum'), regulating movement from east to west along that road. East Wansdyke in Wiltshire could be a sub-Roman parallel with Bokerley Dyke and it does indeed share some build characteristics with it (Figure 1.8). Nonetheless, its location along the crest of a south-facing scarp overlooking the Vale of Pewsey (while at the same time facing northwards away from that Vale) is very different, and, following a broadly east–west course, it transects no Roman roads.[56]

Campaigns of investigation of the linear dykes that are such a prominent feature of the east Cambridgeshire landscape has securely placed these dykes into the context of Anglo-Saxon migration (or perhaps confederacy with the former Romano-British population of these areas), and the form of these dykes is suggestive that the inheritance of dyke-building practice may have been direct.[57] The form of the four best-known Cambridgeshire dykes (from west to east, the Bran (or Heydon) Ditch, the Brent Ditch, the Fleam Dyke and the Devil's Dyke) varies considerably, not only in dimensions but also in the complexity of their build.[58] The dykes are located in parallel with one another and are each set on a north-west to south-east orientation. They are separated by around five miles (8 km) from one another, linking hilly clay country to the south and fenland to the north across what were open or at least scrub-covered chalk landscapes both south and east of Cambridge. The Fleam Dyke has produced the earliest dates, centring upon the fifth century AD.[59] It crosses broken terrain and appears to have been built in a series of stages, in places featuring complex re-cutting of its ditch. What appears to be the latest in the series, the Devil's Dyke, runs north-west from Newmarket crossing gently sloping ground. It is the largest, extending some 8 miles (12 km) and is the straightest of the dykes. Also the simplest in build, it appears to have originated

FIGURE 1.8 East Wansdyke at Baltic Farm, Bishop's Canning, Wiltshire

East and West Wansdyke, in north Wiltshire and north Somerset, had their origins in prehistory, but were re-commissioned in the Roman period. They were each likely to have been re-used by the kingdom of the West Saxons, either independently, or, along with the Marlborough-Bath Roman road (A4), as a continuous frontier. This view is westwards along the dyke towards Roundway Down, where it turns north-westwards towards the Marlborough-Bath Roman Road.

1 Offa's Dyke in profile: character, course and controversies

FIGURE 1.9 The Devil's Dyke in Cambridgeshire, near Newmarket (Suffolk)

Viewed south-eastwards at this point close to the A11 crossing, with the ditch running along the south-west facing side of the earthen bank. Devil's Dyke is the straightest and most prominent of the series of Cambridgeshire dykes which in their present form date from the fifth and sixth centuries AD, and are thought possibly to have been built by Anglo-Saxon settlers as a defence against British communities of the Chilterns.

in a single construction event (Figure 1.9). The Cambridgeshire dykes have in common with Bokerley Dyke the transecting of major communication routes, in this case the Icknield Way and the Roman road known as Ashwell Street. A feature common to all of the Cambridgeshire dykes is that their ditches were flat-bottomed, and this stands in contrast to all those discussed further here, which had mainly V-shaped or U-shaped profiles.[60]

West Wansdyke is an interesting case, not only because it differs in important respects from East Wansdyke, but also because of its similarities and differences compared to dykes of the Welsh Marches. The substantive parallels between East and West Wansdyke are that they both follow a broadly east–west course across the landscape and both face northwards. However, East Wansdyke for much of its course faces level ground northwards with a steep drop down a scarp slope to its rear, while West Wansdyke crosses between hills and for much of its course faces downhill with a wide northwards prospect (although in some places it faces uphill with no such prospect). In contrast to East Wansdyke, the course of West Wansdyke links pre-existing defensive enclosures, as does Wat's Dyke. Recent investigations along West Wansdyke show that its origins are diverse, sometimes featuring complex re-cutting of its ditch. In some locations West Wansdyke began as a prehistoric (Iron Age) linear work, while elsewhere it appears to have been built entirely within the Anglo-Saxon period.[61]

Cyril Fox sought systematic comparison not only between Offa's Dyke and

Wat's Dyke, but also with the shorter dykes of the central Welsh Marches. Among these, the closest similarity with the East Anglian dykes is probably between the Cambridgeshire Devil's Dyke and the Herefordshire Rowe Ditch in the Arrow valley near Pembridge. This latter comprises a bank with a continuous west-facing ditch and it crosses a broad level area of the valley on a course nearly 4 miles (6.4 km) long (Figure 1.10). Throughout this length, it has only one significant change in orientation, at the river Arrow itself. Moreover, just as the Devil's Dyke does, it completely ignores the inherited trend of the landscape, and cuts directly across earlier features.[62] Rowe Ditch was already an ancient feature of the landscape when it was recorded in a tenth-century Anglo-Saxon charter for an estate at Staunton-on-Arrow, and it would appear to fit best as a prominent physical manifestation of a late sixth- or early seventh-century Anglo-Saxon annexation of the Leominster district.[63]

Other dykes of the central Marches include the Wantyn Dyke of the Montgomery district, and the series of cross-dykes of the Kerry Ridgeway and other prominent hill ridges further south. Fox regarded these dykes as earlier Anglo-Saxon and Mercian attempts to block west to east movement into newly-acquired territory. Investigation of the range of works noted by Fox has in recent years produced evidence that illustrates how diverse they were. Some have proved to be of prehistoric origin, while others can be located in the mid- to late first millennium AD. These are not necessarily of English origin, however, and a recent co-ordinated study concluded that many of them were created to mark the boundaries of adjoining Welsh districts or *cantrefs*.[64] The dates of these dykes do place many of them in the same broad period as Offa's Dyke, but they are also both earlier and later in date.[65] Still other dykes in the Marches not far from Offa's Dyke have as yet received little attention at all, and could be of almost any date. An example is the cross-valley dyke linking Birtley Knoll and The Mount, Deerfold, at Lingen in north Herefordshire. This extends along a ridge that is the watershed locally, between the Teme valley to the north and the Lugg valley to the south, and so lies in the geographical sphere of both Presteigne and Knighton.[66]

What even as brief a comparative review of these other dykes as provided here indicates is that with the possible exception of aspects of the build of Wat's Dyke there is little evidence that they exhibit close parallels with Offa's Dyke:

FIGURE 1.10 The North Herefordshire Rowe Ditch

Rowe Ditch bisects the Arrow Valley on two very straight end-to-end alignments, subtly changing course only once, close to the crossing-point of the river that here meanders across a broad level valley. The simplicity of alignment and the continuous build characteristics, with no individual bank or ditch segments readily visible, differ markedly from the placing and construction of Offa's Dyke.

COURTESY OF HEREFORDSHIRE ARCHAEOLOGY AND THE WOOLHOPE NATURALISTS FIELD CLUB (HEREFORD).

except that they are linear earthen bank and ditch works, and that some of them are of likely seventh- or eighth-century date. This is a view reinforced rather than contradicted by close study of design and build.[67] The recent excavations at Gobowen on Wat's Dyke need to be complemented by sufficiently large scale new fieldwork on Offa's Dyke, but already these Gobowen results can be interpreted as indicating that yet further substantial contrasts in design characterise these two monuments.

Offa's Dyke closely traced, north from the Severn beneath The Breiddin

In the principal published accounts, Offa's Dyke has been described in detail either from north to south or from south to north.[68] The detailed characterisation provided here proceeds instead northwards and then southwards from a notional mid-point at the river Severn near Welshpool. This avoids simply making an assumption that the Dyke begins at any specific point in either the northern or the southern extremity of its course. The emphasis in this description is therefore upon describing the movement of the Dyke through a varied topography and in reference to the geography and topography of rivers and mountains. A particular concern is to trace in outline the situation of the Dyke within the landscape and what choices needed to be made to achieve the preferred course.

FIGURE 1.11 Offa's Dyke north of Carreg-y-big, viewed from the south-east

The subtlety of the placing of the Dyke in the landscape is a recurrent theme throughout this book, here well-illustrated in a carefully-controlled adjustment up (or down) the slope north of a possible gateway south of Carreg-y-big Farm, west of Oswestry. This length of the earthwork is prominent at upper-centre of the aerial photograph (Figure 1.15).

IMAGE: ADAM STANFORD/AERIAL-CAM

30 *Offa's Dyke: Landscape and Hegemony in Eighth-Century Britain*

Key-map to Figures 1.12, 1.14, 1.15, 1.18, 1.20, 1.22, 1.24, 1.26, 1.28 and 1.30

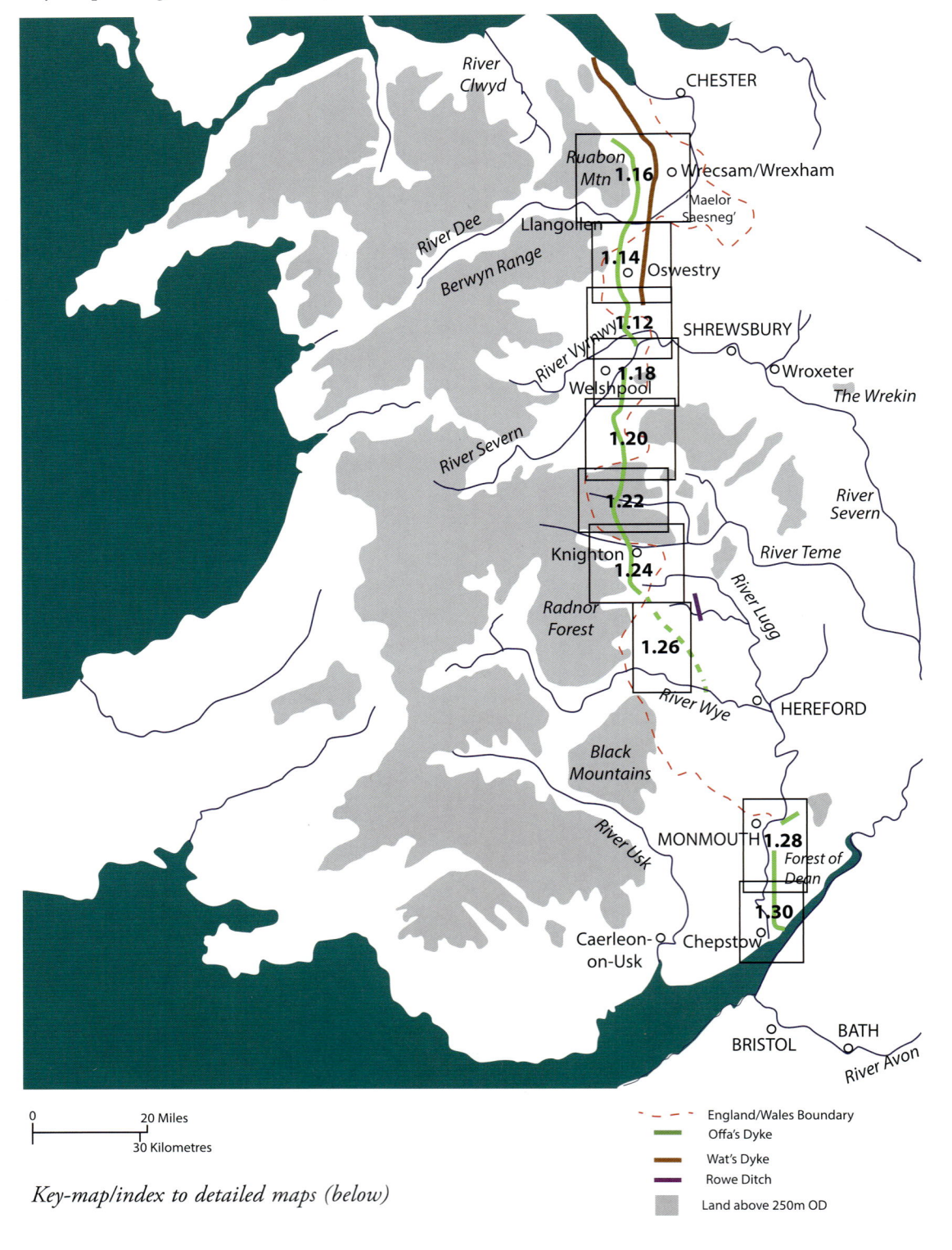

Key-map/index to detailed maps (below)

- - - England/Wales Boundary
— Offa's Dyke
— Wat's Dyke
— Rowe Ditch
▨ Land above 250m OD

1 Offa's Dyke in profile: character, course and controversies 31

The present account of the northern part of the course of the Dyke therefore begins from the river Severn on its north bank opposite the dramatically steep-sided high hill known as The Breiddin and then continues northwards to the apparent end of the Dyke just south of Treuddyn. In contrast, the southern part then extends from the Severn at Buttington near Welshpool down to the sea by the Wye/Severn estuary, with the major apparent interruption along the Wye in Herefordshire.

From the middle Severn valley northwards to the Dee

The first point at which the Dyke appears on the left (north) bank of the river Severn in its upper middle reaches is just upstream from Llandrinio, south of a place called Derwas. This location is some 5 miles (8.0 km) to the north-east

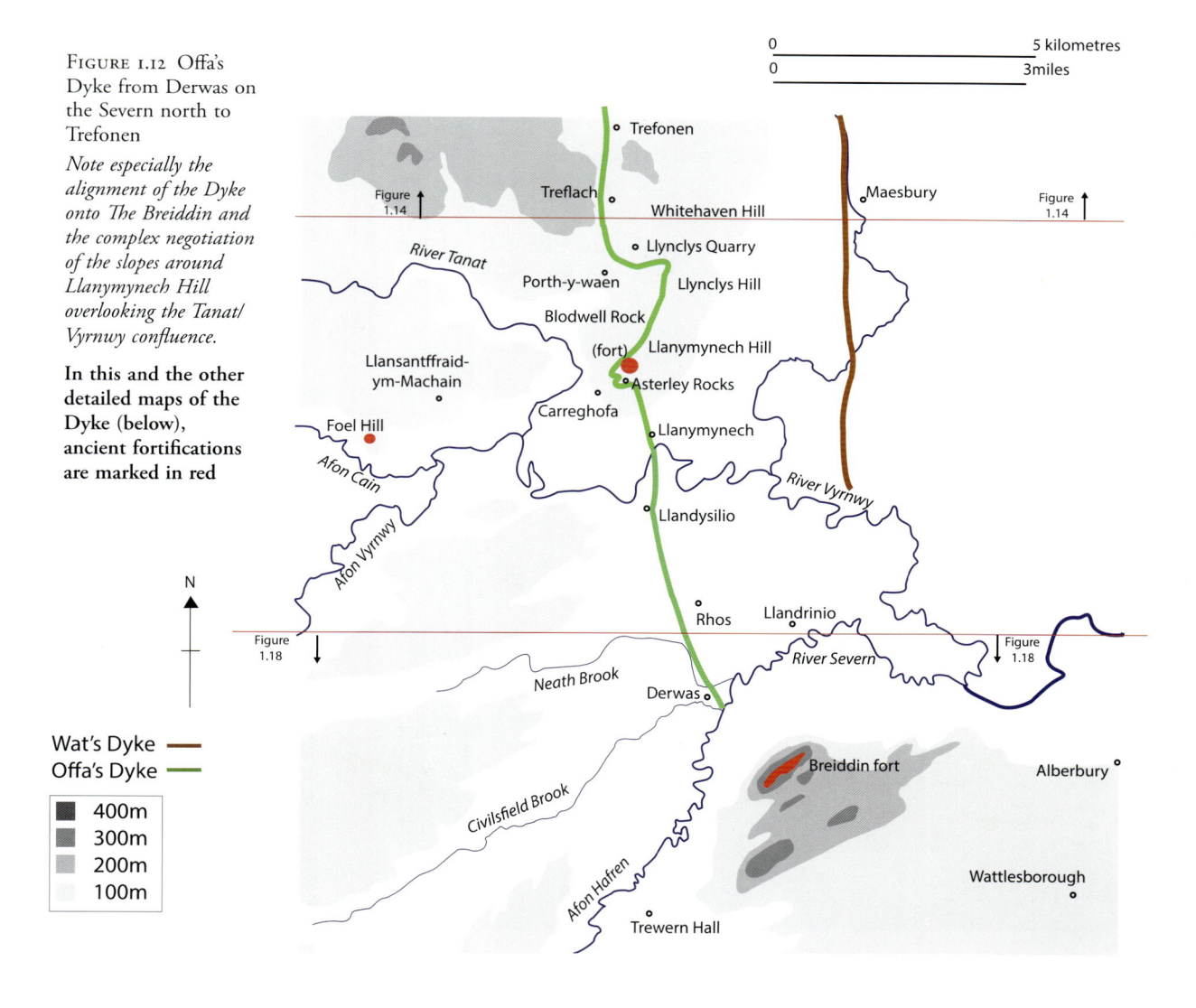

FIGURE 1.12 Offa's Dyke from Derwas on the Severn north to Trefonen

Note especially the alignment of the Dyke onto The Breiddin and the complex negotiation of the slopes around Llanymynech Hill overlooking the Tanat/Vyrnwy confluence.

In this and the other detailed maps of the Dyke (below), ancient fortifications are marked in red

of Welshpool. There are clear indications of the presence of the Dyke on the floodplain very close to where a stream known now as the Neath Brook joins the Severn on its northern (left) bank (Figure 4.10). This location is below the north-facing near-vertical slopes of The Breidden that arise directly out of the western edge of the central Shropshire plain, on the opposite (south) bank of the river Severn.[69] The Dyke strikes north-west by north across the level ground between the Severn and the Vyrnwy locally, taking a direct course for a mile and a half (2.4 km), aligned towards the church at Llandysilio. However, just to the north-west of Rhos it deviates more towards due north for the same distance of a mile and a half to a point just to the east of Llandysilio church. Assuming that it continued to follow the line of the road approaching the bridge by Llanymynech, the Dyke again shifts its orientation, this time due north, running exactly the same mile and a half distance on a straight course to the right bank of the Vyrnwy.[70]

It may be helpful to pause here briefly to consider what was achieved by the selection of this course. Had the Dyke been built further to the west in this area, it would have had to traverse more broken terrain, and to have crossed both the rivers Vyrnwy and Tanat. It managed such a double traversing of rivers close together elsewhere, however, with seeming impunity. So why does it not do so here? Equally, only 3 miles (4.8 km) to the east, it could have crossed the Severn just below its confluence with the Vyrnwy. Why was it instead so aligned that it had to cross both of these significant rivers? Given the overall north by north-west alignment from Derwas, the answer appears to concern not only a need to regain a direct north–south alignment, but also an intention to mount the western flank of Llanymynech Hill. To achieve this while crossing the

FIGURE 1.13 Llanymynech Hill and Whitehaven Hill viewed from Bryn Mawr

Bryn Mawr is a prominent hilltop crowned by a hillfort, just to the south of the confluence of the Tanat and Vyrnwy rivers. Llanymynech Hill is to the right of this view, with Whitehaven Hill being the prominent hill on the centre horizon (albeit much reduced in profile by Llyncys Quarry). The parish of Carreghofa occupies the ground beneath Llanymynech Hill and Asterley Rocks, down towards the valley at lower-centre.

Vyrnwy at the perpendicular it needed to follow the course it does northwards from the left bank of the Severn. A course around the west-facing flank of Llanymynech Hill produced an elevation that permits oversight of the Tanat-Vrynwy confluence, and commands views up both valleys as well as over the relatively narrow 'pass' that the combined rivers have carved through the gap in the hills between Llanymynech and Llandysilio. The significance of this is a matter that will be returned to later in the book, since it probably had as much to do with political as with purely physical geography.[71]

On the north bank of the Vyrnwy, Fox adduced local accounts and early observations such as those of Thomas Pennant in Volume 3 of his *Tours in Wales* (1810) to trace the line of the Dyke for half a mile (0.8 km) through Llanymynech village.[72] From there it can still be traced, albeit in a fragmentary state, climbing the south-facing scarp of Llanymynech Hill to the natural cliff at Asterley Rocks a quarter of a mile (0.4 km) away north-westwards. It then follows a curving course for just over half a mile around the western perimeter of the hillfort that takes in most of Llanymynech Hill. The Dyke subsequently maintains a northwards course with a westwards prospect from the rim of the sheer cliff-face of Blodwel Rock for a further half-mile, before dipping into the valley separating Llynclys Hill from Whitehaven Hill. It follows a mile-long curving route around Whitehaven Hill with a south-facing and then south-west and west-facing prospect.[73] For the next 2 miles (3.2 km) a series of short straight alignments trace a nonetheless somewhat sinuous course (since the nineteenth century interrupted by development) through Treflach and Trefonen, before a mostly well-preserved length drops northwards to the Morda valley, and another scarp-edge section runs for another 2 miles around Craig Forda.

Fox had much to say about the use of terrain here, where the river Morda funnels south-eastwards in a steep cleft, but turns due south for 2 miles hard against the west-facing flank of Craig Forda.[74] Coming from the south, the Dyke crosses the Morda valley with a short-and-sharp descent and rise. It regains the heights of Craig Forda by an oblique rise across the mid-slope, heading for the crest of the scarp facing westwards. This crest is then followed northwards for a mile and a half (2.4 km), but the key factor to observe here is the way that the natural vantage point over the north–south cleft of the Afon Morda was used precisely to fix and maintain the chosen strict north–south line of the Dyke. From there it pursues a route northwards across a narrow steep-sided re-entrant valley, whence it climbs around the west-facing flank of Baker's Hill (Figure 1.15). A series of straight sections carries it for 2 miles (3.2 km) further northwards across undulating country to the ridge running westwards from Selattyn Hill.

Despite major deviations around the limestone hills east of Llanyblodwel in the Tanat valley, the general course across the 10 miles (16 km) north by north-west as the crow flies from the Severn at Derwas to Craig Forda is therefore remarkably consistent, moving westwards less than 2 miles (3.2 km) over that distance. In tracing this course, a 'stance' was created for the Dyke in

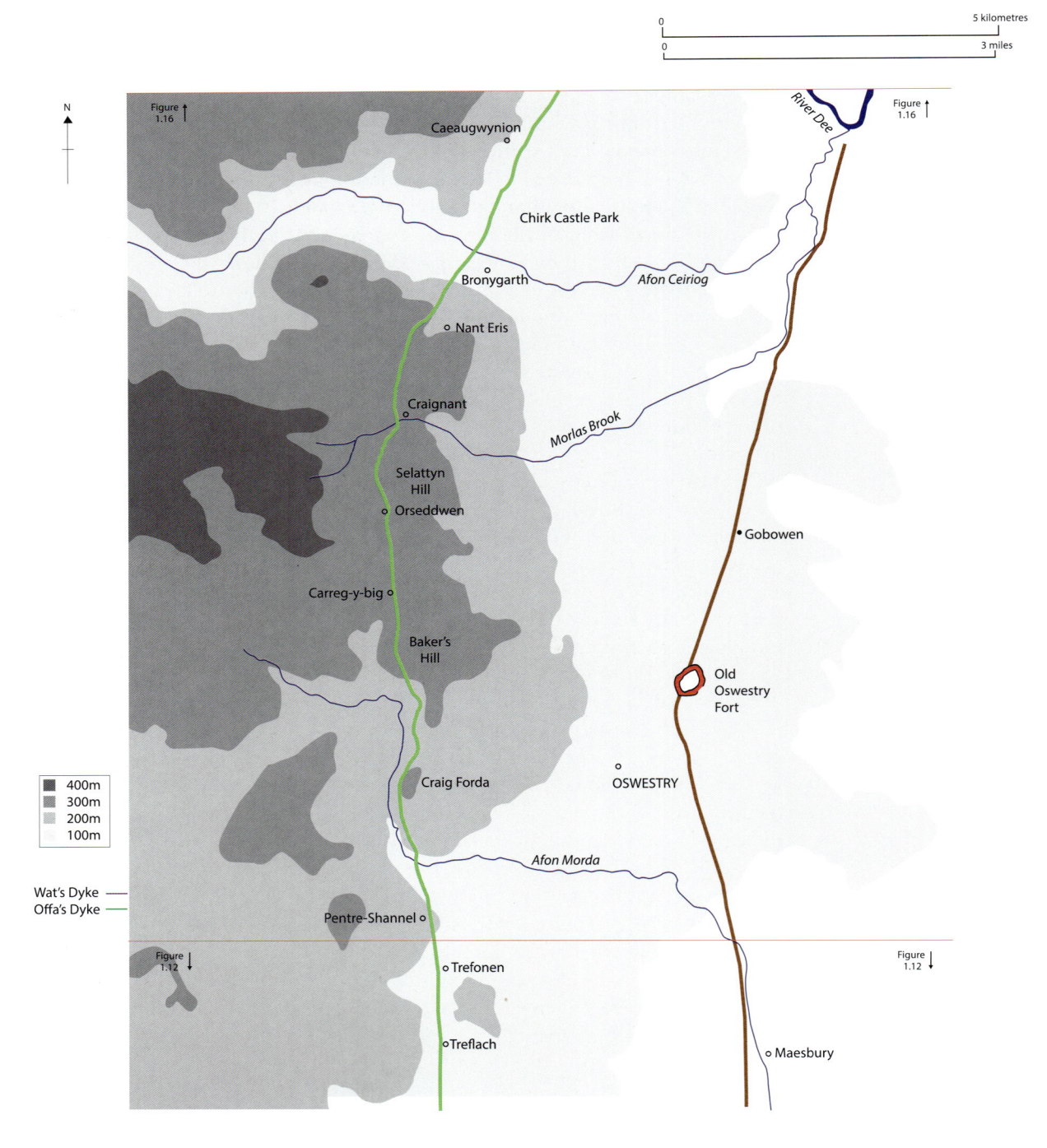

FIGURE 1.14 Offa's Dyke from Treflach and Trefonen north to Chirk Park and Caeaugwynion

Of particular note here are: the proximity of Offa's Dyke to the line of Wat's Dyke where the latter incorporates Old Oswestry hillfort; the perpendicular crossing of the Ceiriog valley; and the use made of the west-facing slopes of Craig Forda, Baker's Hill and Selattyn Hill.

FIGURE 1.15 Aerial view northwards from above Baker's Hill

In the foreground, the Dyke makes a sweeping traverse of Baker's Hill before continuing northwards to Carreg-y-big and onwards to Selattyn Hill. The way in which the Dyke makes use of prominent west-facing hilltops is especially evident here, as well as the degree to which it holds to a strict north–south course. The heavily-dissected terrain of what became north-west Shropshire between Afon Morda and Afon Ceiriog is also evident, as is the location of the hills around Llangollen in the distance.

REPRODUCED COURTESY OF A. WIGLEY: COPYRIGHT, SHROPSHIRE COUNCIL.

the landscape that prioritised oversight of the Tanat-Vyrnwy confluence region while minimising the need for digression from a line that would also require a minimum of descent and ascent of valleys and clefts. In other words, the routing was both build-efficient and tactically astute: and such perspicacity of placement is a constant characteristic of the Dyke wherever it is encountered. From Craig Forda to Selattyn Hill the 3 miles (4.8 km) of Dyke shifts to a directly north and south alignment, in only one location deviating more than 200 metres off a consistent line. The Dyke completes an impressive sweep around the western flank of Selattyn Hill, before descending northwards to negotiate the cleft of the Morlas Brook at Craignant. Just over a mile and a half (2.4 km) further north it swings north-eastwards in a major shift of alignment, sustained in a crossing of the Ceiriog valley at the perpendicular, for 4 miles (6.4 km) to the river Dee crossing, after which the same general alignment continues to some distance beyond the Dee to Ruabon.[75] The descent northwards to the Ceiriog is undertaken in a series of short straight sections, shifting ground rapidly on the steeper sections.

After crossing the Ceiriog the ascent mirrors the short straight lengths of the descent, but over a shorter distance of only a quarter of a mile (0.4 km), just to the west of Chirk Castle. From this point the only concern appears to have been to reach a pre-selected optimal point at which to meet the Dee immediately east of Cefn Bychan. It achieved this across nearly 3 miles (4.8 km) in a series of long sweeping straight sections, several of which look uphill to the west while nonetheless making the most of any opportunities for the maintenance of a tactical advantage, as at Caeaugwynion. Having negotiated the level ground above the river Dee near Plas Offa on the road between Chirk and Llangollen, the Dyke makes a direct descent at the perpendicular to the river bank.

North of the Dee

The 'displacement' of the Dyke in its crossing of the Dee is much less than that either side of the Severn, with only half a mile (0.8 km) of winding river course downstream to where it climbs on an indeterminate route through Hopyard Wood and on to Tatham to the northwest of Ruabon. This part of the route again mirrors the descent to the Dee in tracing long relatively straight sections which each define a different alignment. North of Ruabon a relatively strict north–south course is followed across 8 miles (12.9 km), crossing the river Clywedog and reaching the right bank of the river Cegidog to the south-west of Caergwrle. From Pentre Bychan south of the Clywedog to Brymbo south of the Cedigog, the north–south trend is closely adhered to apart from a significant adjustment just to the north of the Clywedog. Again it runs in long relatively straight sections, frequently facing westwards uphill while maximising tactical advantage wherever feasible, as near Coedpoeth. This means that at some points the Dyke traverses the crests of eastwards-trending spurs to achieve a view west towards Ruabon Mountain as well as offering a rearward view onto the Cheshire

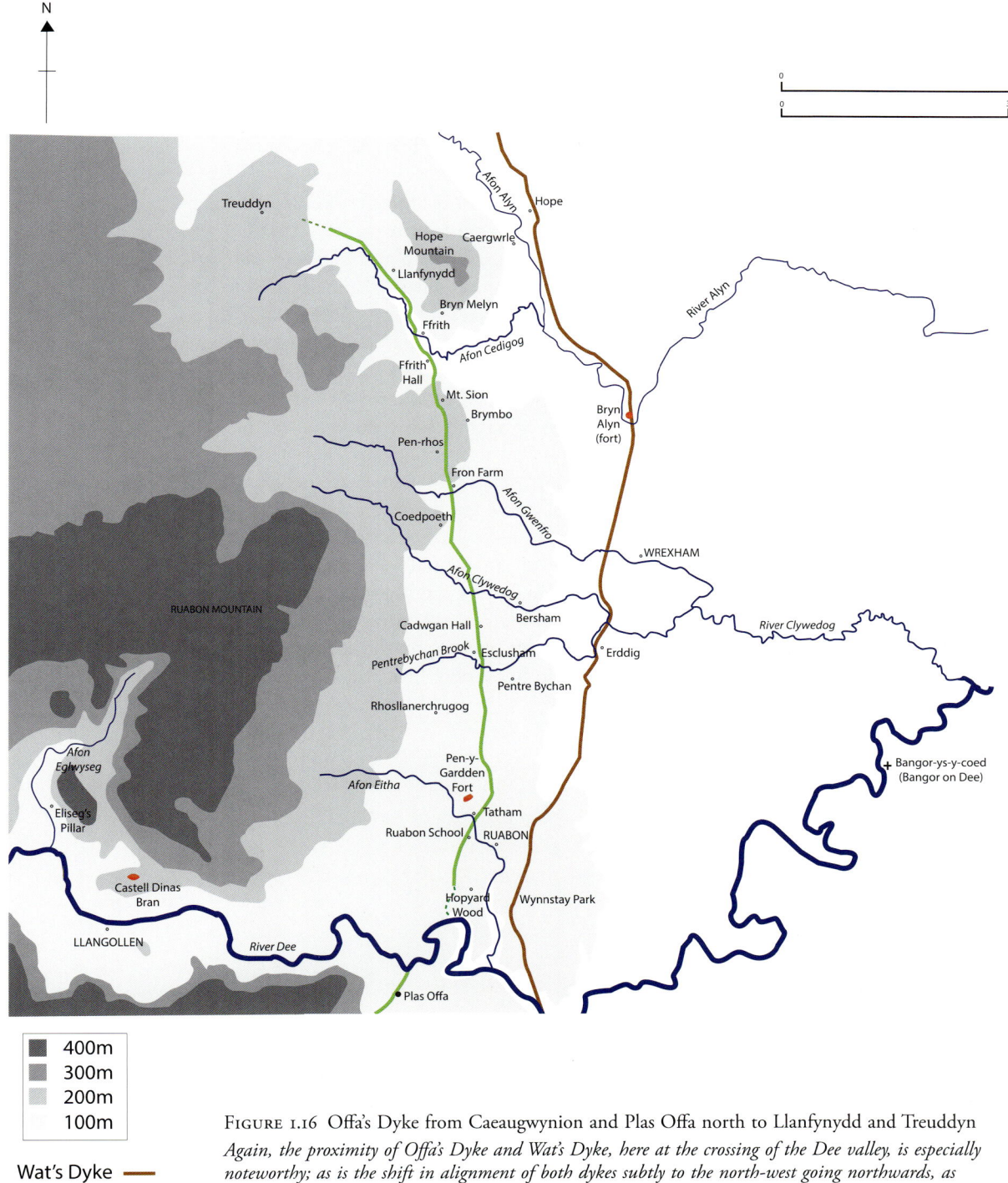

1 Offa's Dyke in profile: character, course and controversies 37

FIGURE 1.16 Offa's Dyke from Caeaugwynion and Plas Offa north to Llanfynydd and Treuddyn
Again, the proximity of Offa's Dyke and Wat's Dyke, here at the crossing of the Dee valley, is especially noteworthy; as is the shift in alignment of both dykes subtly to the north-west going northwards, as they each meet a river valley: respectively the Cedigog and the Alyn.

Plain. Meanwhile, elsewhere, this eastwards view affords the only prospect from the Dyke, apart from over the ground immediately in front of it to the west. At Brymbo the Dyke gains significantly higher ground and provides a view to the south along the line of the entire course northwards from Ruabon as well as a prospect of Ruabon Mountain south-westwards and the Cheshire Plain to the east. Just to the north the western view is foreclosed, but reciprocally the view north-eastwards expands.

From a vantage point just north of Brymbo, at Mount Sion overlooking the Cegidog valley from the south, a view extends northwards (if constrained by the equally high Bryn Melin immediately northwards) past Ffrith and Llannfynydd (Figure 1.17). From Mount Sion, by Pen-y-coed above Ffrith Hall, the Dyke drops to the Cedigog, and at Ffrith Hall it then makes the first of three shifts of alignment northwestwards. This initially places it in an uncharacteristic valley-floor position, firstly for half a mile (0.8 km) through Ffrith village and then, half a mile to the north, through Llanfynydd for another mile and a half (2.4 km). This alignment takes it up the crest of a spur in the direction of the hilltop at Treuddyn.

The shift in direction from Ffrith Hall northwards meant that the Dyke abandoned the topographic consistency that had so far characterised its course north from the middle Severn valley. Had it been consistent, it would have crossed the Cegidog south-west of Cymau Hall and would have followed the crest of the west-facing scarp to the west of Bryn Melyn, before tracing a course onto the western flank of Hope Mountain. This would have maintained a

FIGURE 1.17 The northern extremity of Offa's Dyke from near Brymbo

The view here is northwards from Mt. Sion along the upper course of the Afon Cedigog, past Ffrith village and towards Llanfynydd. Offa's Dyke descends the hill steeply at left foreground, and follows a course along the east bank of the Afon Cedigog, through the notch-like valley oriented north-west to south-east here. It continues onto the low ridge at Llanfynydd, tracing a course north-westwards towards Treuddyn (left middle distance). Bryn Melyn at the southern end of Hope Mountain rises at right-centre of this view.

northwards course and a westwards prospect as it headed towards the locations of the historically more recent towns of Mold and Flint. Indeed, only 4 miles (6.4 km) north of this point, such a course would have joined the line of Wat's Dyke as the latter follows a course north-westwards before swinging sharply north (west of Northop/Llan-eurgain) towards Flint.

A reason that could readily be adduced for such a sudden shift of alignment is the pre-existing presence of Wat's Dyke to its east, but the situation may not be as clear-cut as such a geographical observation implies. From Offa's Dyke at Pen-y-coed immediately next to Mount Sion, Wat's Dyke is situated less than two miles (3.2 km) to the east. Here, Wat's Dyke is seen in a clear view eastwards from Offa's Dyke (from the hill crest above the Cedigog) following the east bank of the river Alyn to the south of Caergwrle in a similar way, if less dramatically, as Offa's Dyke overlooks the river Morda south of Selattyn Hill. It is here on a course likewise almost due north and south, except that the landscape at Caergwrle is very much lower in elevation.

However, just to the north of Hope, instead of continuing its northwards course and making for the Dee estuary at Queensferry, Wat's Dyke continues to follow the Alyn valley by turning north-westwards in the direction of Mold. By turning north-west at Ffrith, Offa's Dyke exactly mirrors the shift in the 'stance' of Wat's Dyke to a south-westerly aspect, while keeping within 3 miles (4.8 km) to its west. At Treuddyn, Offa's Dyke disappears for no apparent reason. What we are to make of this sudden absence, or indeed the sudden change in character, is uncertain: as is the question of whether the change can be ascribed to accident or design.[76] Despite much local searching, no continuation of the line northwards from Treuddyn has ever produced anything convincingly attributable to the former presence of a massive dyke such as approaches Treuddyn from the south. The south-west to north-east aligned ridge upon which the latter settlement stands affords wide views northwards towards the Alyn valley and Halkyn Mountain, and north-eastwards the Dee estuary, with somewhat more restricted views to the west to Nercwys Mountain, beyond which lies the Clwydian Range. However, it is far from clear what objective the Dyke might have continued towards, even if it had continued as a slighter work such as is evident through much of the landscape south of Selley near Knighton, far to the south.

Offa's Dyke, and the frontier, south from the Severn at Buttington

It can only be assumed that, since both on the left bank and the right bank of the river Severn the Dyke makes straight for the river, the Severn itself must have been intended to form the north–south route along the 5 miles (8.0 km) that separate the two points where the Dyke meets the riverbank.[77] It has rarely been mentioned in print, but should be pointed out clearly here, that the valley of the river Severn reaches at Buttington its narrowest point in the whole 27 miles (c.43 km) of that river's length between Abermule (10 miles (16.0 km) to the south-west) and Shrawardine (17 miles (*c.*27 km) along the river northeastwards and then eastwards). Between Buttington and Derwas the river is, or has been historically, fordable in one or two places, but the valley is broad and full of former back-channels and marshy areas, that in the eighth century may well have been impassable in all but the very driest conditions.

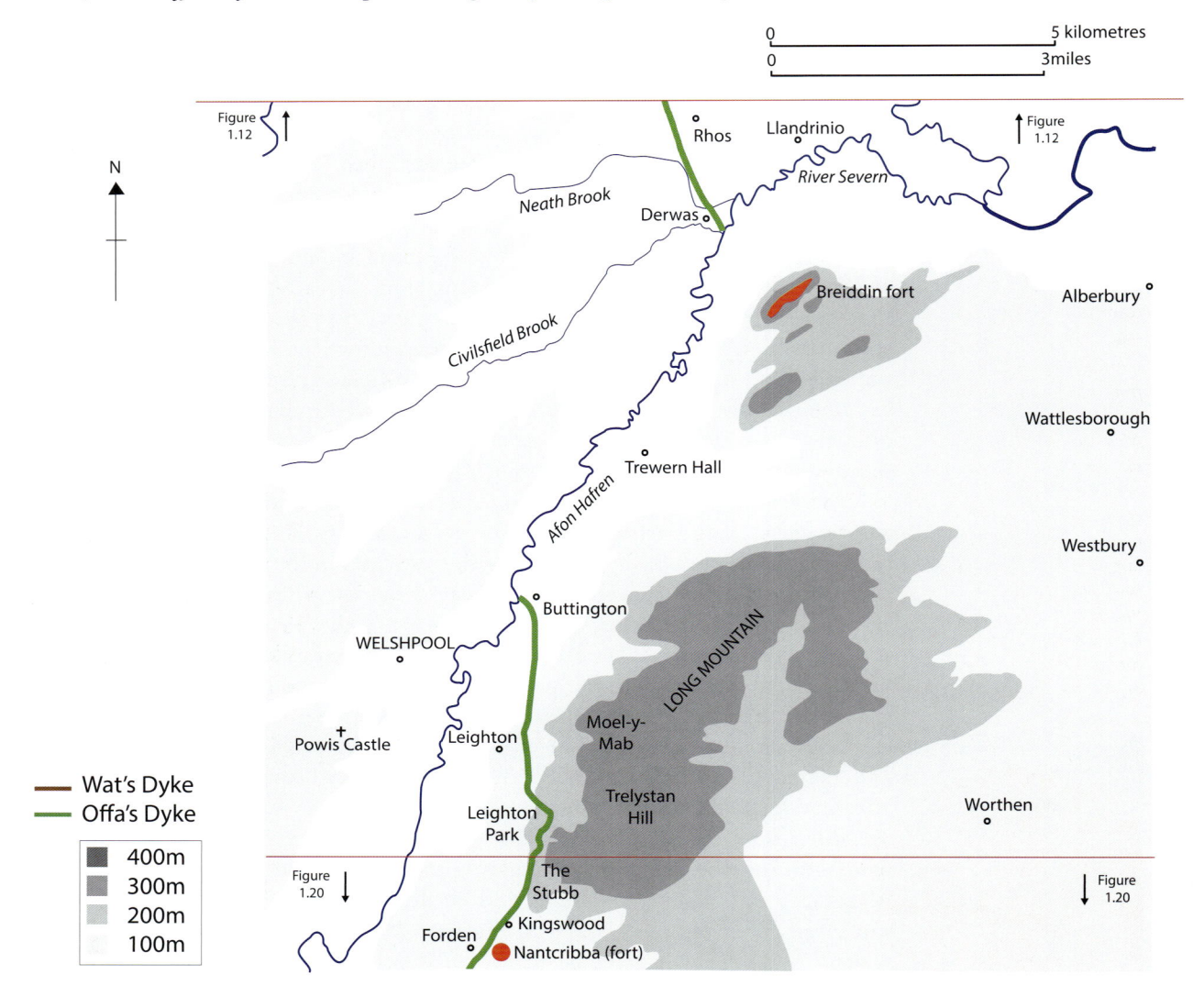

From Buttington southwards to the Kerry Ridgeway

Regardless (for the moment) of the significance of the gap at the Severn, Offa's Dyke nonetheless clearly begins its southward course from Buttington, just over a mile and a half (2.4 km) east of Welshpool. The Dyke first crosses the floodplain south-west of Buttington church, and then takes up a position

FIGURE 1.18 Offa's Dyke from Derwas along the Severn and south to Forden
The length of the 'gap' in the Dyke along the Severn valley is particularly evident here, as is the use of the river as an integral feature of the course of the linear earthwork. Also notable is the way in which the course of the dyke south of Buttington 'tracks' the course of the river while using the western flank of the Long Mountain for elevation.

1 Offa's Dyke in profile: character, course and controversies

overlooking the Severn and running due south along the low north-western slopes of Long Mountain on the opposite side of the river to present-day Welshpool. As it proceeds southwards from Hope, rather than maintaining a position directly above the Severn floodplain by following the contours of the hill around to Leighton, it continues the north–south line and rises abruptly onto the flank of Moel-y-Mab. It has to follow the contours southwards around a deep re-entrant valley east of Leighton Park, before it emerges onto the steep slopes of Trelystan Hill. Its sinuous course around and down the western flank of The Stubb hilltop promontory affords a high-level prospect both across the Severn valley westwards and also along a course that it takes, now trending south-westwards, through Kingswood and on to Forden (Figure 1.19).

The very straight mile and a half (2.4 km) long section through Kingswood is said to mark the former course of a Roman road that linked Wroxeter with the upper Severn valley.[78] In a series of adjustments of alignment between three relatively short straight sections, the Dyke then modifies its route through the next half mile (0.8 km) or so to turn southwards at the crest of the hill overlooking Hem. Here it turns almost due south towards Rownall, a mile and a half away across the valley of the Camlad stream (Figure 7.8). An interesting aspect of the placing of the Dyke within the landscape in this whole course over nearly 7 miles (11.3 km) south from Buttington to Rownal is that once it has achieved (at Leighton) a distance of around a mile (1.6 km) east of the river Severn it maintains that distance from the river almost continuously with only

FIGURE 1.19 At The Stubb, looking west towards Kingswood

The view south-westwards towards Forden here is from the last prominent spur of the Long Mountain, with extensive views westwards over the Severn valley. The bank of the Dyke is on the left here, although the ditch is largely infilled. At Forden itself excavation showed that very locally both the bank and the ditch were covered with a later soil deposit to some depth.

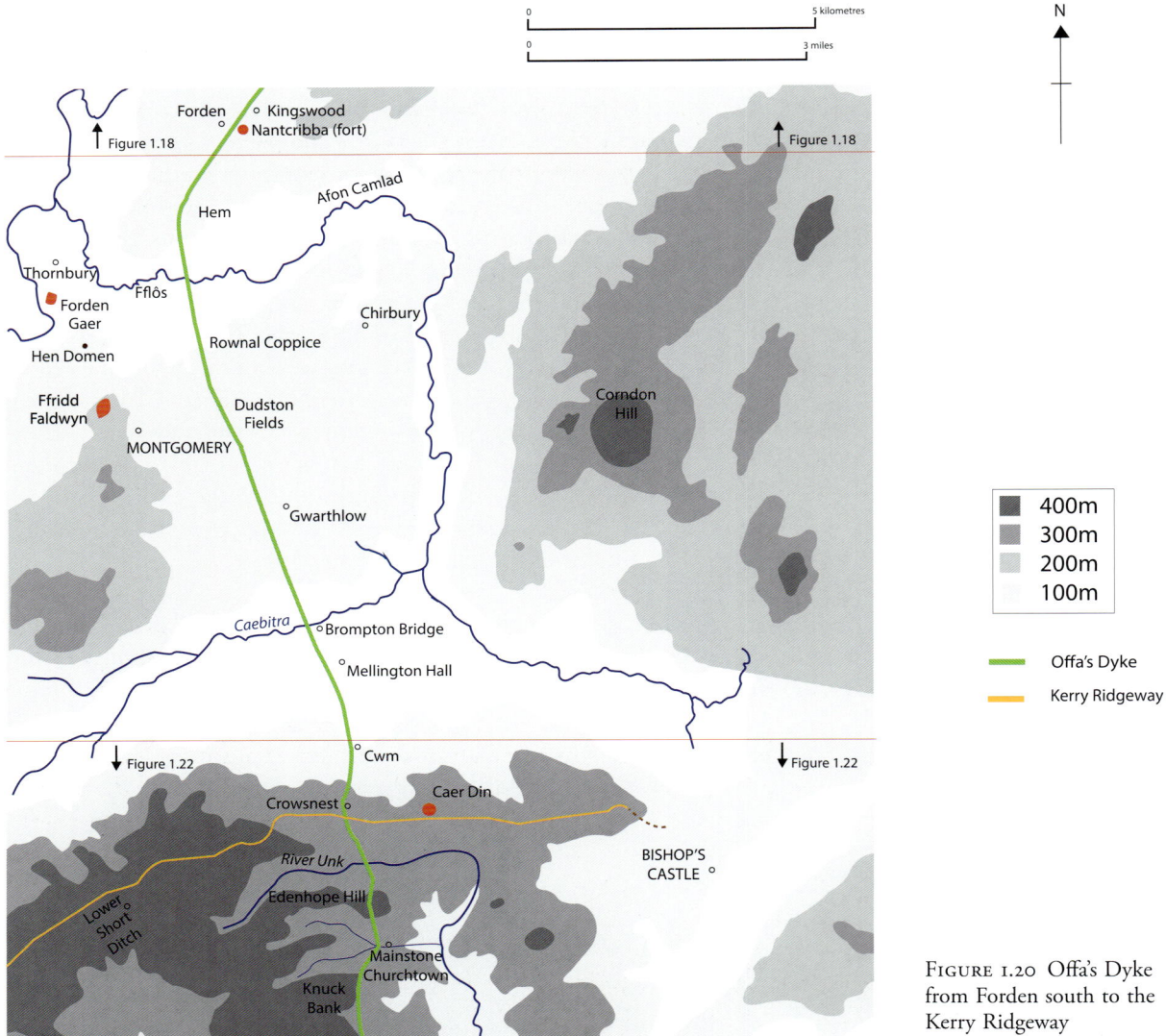

FIGURE 1.20 Offa's Dyke from Forden south to the Kerry Ridgeway

Note the dramatic shift in orientation achieved at Hem, and the way in which the Dyke carefully bisects the Vale of Montgomery while facing directly towards the east-facing slopes of the hills that lie westwards of this bisecting line. The way in which the Dyke loops up onto and across the Kerry Ridgeway is also very evident.

one point at which it strays as far as just under 2 miles (3.2 km) from it.

The crossing of the Camlad is carefully made perpendicular to its course, and at this point the Severn is just a mile to the west across the 'Fflos', or flood-flowing levels, that spread to the south-east of The Gaer (Thornbury) by the surviving earthwork of the Roman fort (Forden Gaer). From Rownal Coppice the Dyke strikes a firm course south-eastwards across the plain of Montgomery. It maintains a generally straight alignment here (with nonetheless much micro-scale deviation) for 5 miles (8 km) to a point just west of Mellington Hall that is

FIGURE 1.21 At Dudston Fields, Chirbury, looking south

As it crossed the level plain to the east of the prominent hills above present-day Montgomery, the Dyke took up a prominent position and its bank and ditch assumed major proportions, as seen here looking southwards from near the present-day Chirbury to Montgomery road. A debate concerning whether ridge and furrow traces of open field cultivation visible from the air on either side of the Dyke here pre-dated its construction gave rise to the most detailed measured earthwork survey yet undertaken anywhere along its course (see Chapter 5).

tucked in against the north flank of the high hills south of the Caebitra brook. In those 5 miles, the course of the Dyke varies from the principal alignment no more than 100 metres at any point.

One possibility for the choice of this particular alignment is that towards the southern end of the stretch of Dyke concerned, it again achieves a fully perpendicular crossing of the Caebitra. South from Mellington Hall, the course adjusts towards a north–south route for half a mile as it traverses the lower slopes of the north-facing flank of the high hills to the south, to a point at Cwm where it crosses a small stream that descends northwards to the Camlad. In the half mile (0.8 km) from Cwm to the Kerry Ridgeway the Dyke ascends 200 m in elevation, in part up a north-east facing hill-spur. It does so in order to achieve a particular saddle on the ridge that the Kerry Ridgeway track passes along, from east to west.[79]

From the Kerry Ridgeway south to the Wye

Fox termed the stretch of Offa's Dyke between the Caebitra brook and Kington 'the mountain zone', and the view northwards from the Kerry Ridgeway at Crowsnest (Part 1 Frontispiece) certainly justifies this epithet.[80] The reason why the Dyke was so placed as to aim for and to cross this particular saddle on the Kerry Ridgeway is soon evident upon reaching the summit and moving southwards. The critical feature of this location is its relationship southwards to Edenhope, the valley running eastwards here to become the Unk valley flowing south to the Clun. This is because, as elsewhere, it makes the best possible use of oversight onto approaches from the west. Here, as the Dyke descends southwards from the crest of the Kerry Ridgeway, it picks up the lip of the west-facing flank of a hill overlooking two valleys that combine just before the Dyke crosses the stream forming the infant Unk. Having traversed the narrow valley at the foot of a spur separating the two valleys from which the Unk draws its first waters the Dyke then rises vertically up the eastern flank of a deep cleft in Edenhope Hill. After this it passes over the eastern summit of that hill and drops almost immediately down into Cwm Ffrydd just below its confluence with Stevens Dingle at Mainstone Churchtown, just over a mile (1.6 km) south of Crowsnest.

The Dyke regains the opposite flank of Knuck Bank diagonally, trending slightly westwards to ensure that oversight is maintained into the upper part of Cwm Ffrydd. From the ridge of Knuck Bank for the half mile (0.8 km)

FIGURE 1.22 Offa's Dyke from the Kerry Ridgeway south towards Cwmsanahan Hill

It is particularly interesting to note the way in which the course of the Dyke deliberately picks a way along the eastern extremity of the uplands at Knuck Bank and Edenhope Hill; and also how carefully Llanfair Hill was chosen as the point at which to pivot the course south-eastwards.

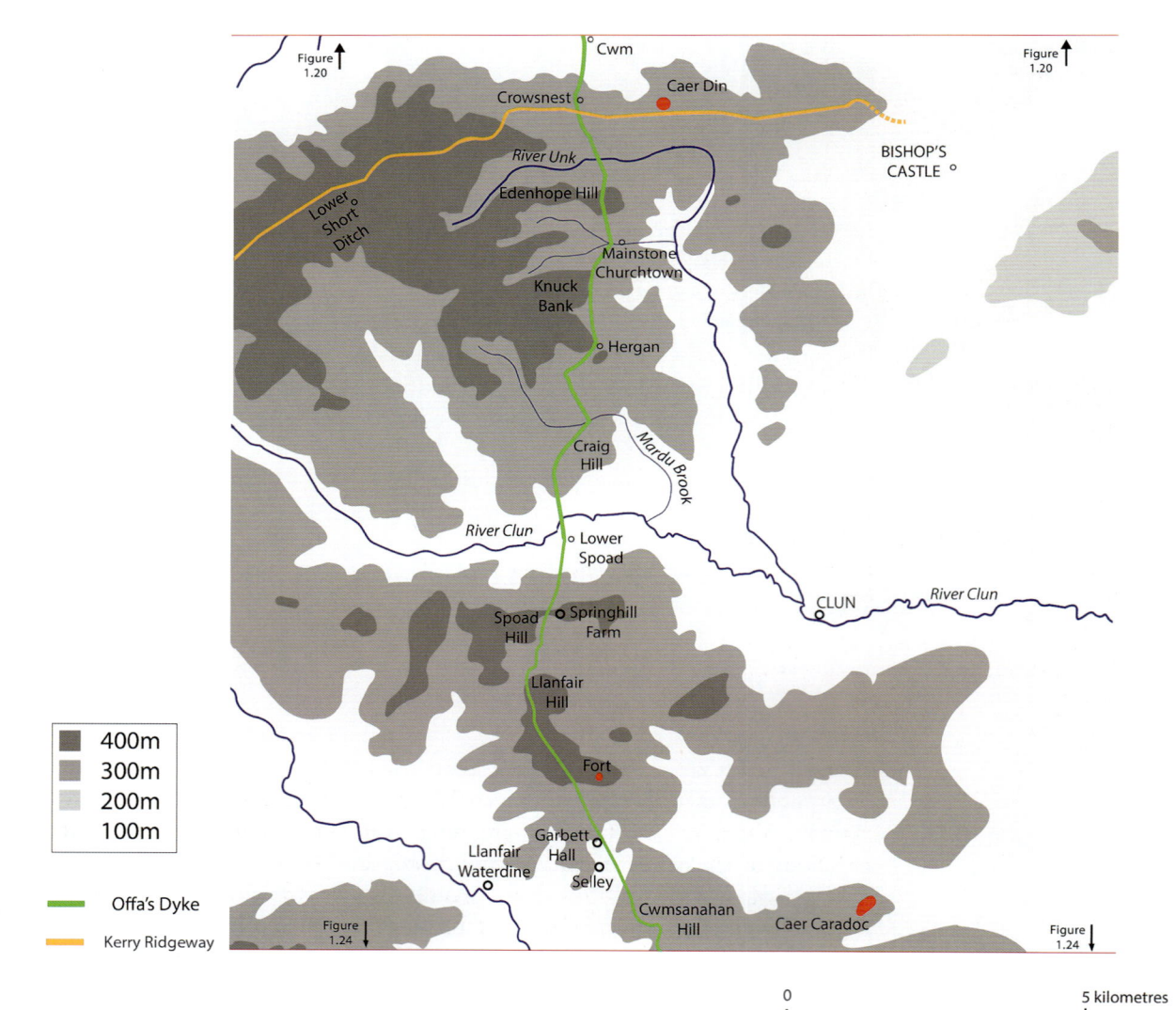

1 *Offa's Dyke in profile: character, course and controversies*

FIGURE 1.23 At the crossing of the Clun valley, north of Spoad
The way in which the Dyke was sited to negotiate the crossing of the Clun valley is very evident in this view looking south towards Spoad Hill. The line of the Dyke curves gently from the north-west down to the valley-floor, which it crosses in a straight line. It then curves slightly south-westwards up the slope above Lower Spoad. This ensured that the perpendicular crossing of the flood-plain was flanked on either side by a forwards-curving line that enabled the approach down the valley from the west to be monitored. This is discussed in Chapter 4, while the repeated adjustment in Dyke build placement on the north-facing slope at Spoad is specified in Chapter 5. IMAGE: ADAM STANFORD/AERIAL-CAM.

southwards to Hergan, the earthwork traverses two westwards-descending hill spurs and two steep-sided combes. At Hergan it crosses a watershed, and then traces a course around two west-trending steep spurs before descending into the floor of the valley of the Mardu Brook. It follows a short course along the side of the valley before rising up the western flank of Graig Hill and descending rapidly to the valley of the river Clun, which river is again crossed at the perpendicular towards Lower Spoad (Figure 1.23). Half a mile (0.8 km) of continuous steep ascent up another north-facing slope then brings it to the

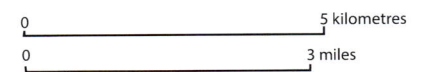

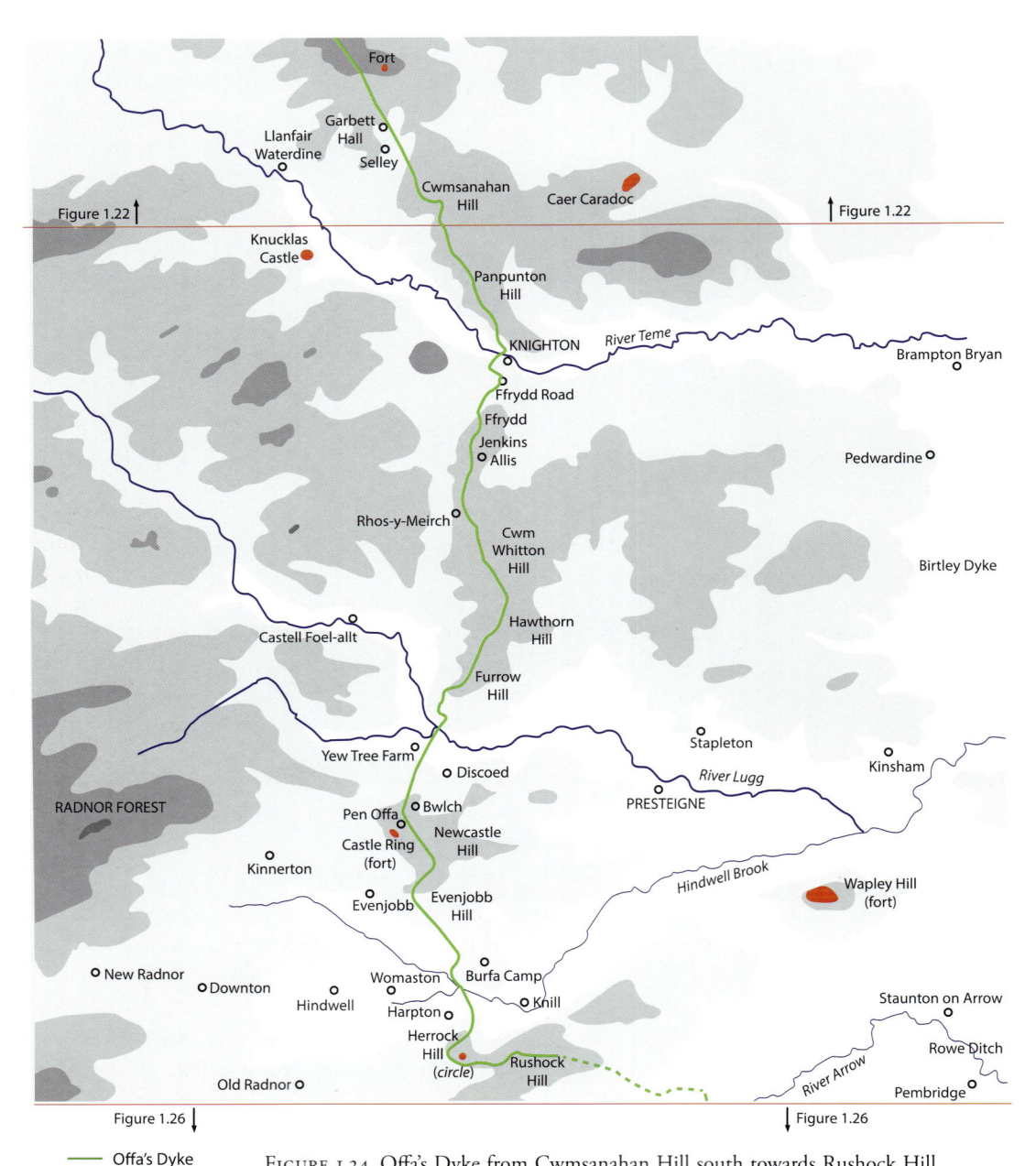

46 *Offa's Dyke: Landscape and Hegemony in Eighth-Century Britain*

FIGURE 1.24 Offa's Dyke from Cwmsanahan Hill south towards Rushock Hill

The care with which the choice of the crossing point over the river Teme was made should be evident in this map. The 'switchback' character of the course of the Dyke across the uplands is nowhere more evident than in the complex route chosen southwards of Knighton, where an 'optimal' relationship to the Walton Basin (the New Radnor – Harpton area on this map) in particular appears to have been important to the dyke-builders.

1 Offa's Dyke in profile: character, course and controversies

FIGURE 1.25 At Jenkins Allis south of Knighton, looking north

The much-levelled Dyke, with its ditch infilled, crosses the field in the foreground diagonally from left to right. Either side of Knighton, more massive lengths of Dyke across floodplains or on some level hill-tops (as here), are interspersed with much lengths of much slighter build (see Chapter 5). This is more evident along all sectors of the course of the Dyke from this area southwards, although it does occur northwards also. Fox interpreted these contrasts as arising from differences in vegetation-cover in these areas at the time of construction. Alternatively, how the Dyke appeared from the west may have been the determining factor. The Teme valley is just visible in the left background; the location of an abrupt change in Dyke dimensions is at the far end of the main run of linear earthwork shown here.

ridge at Spoad Hill, again rising 200 metres in elevation, from 200m OD at the river to 400m OD on the ridge. Southwards it then takes the most direct route onto the western side of the summit of Llanfair Hill where it begins to follow a long (4-mile/6.4 km) south-south-east alignment down towards the Teme at Knighton. This length provides a near-continuous view south-westwards overlooking the Teme valley as it follows its south-eastwards course towards Knighton.

This particular crossing-point, at what is now the town of Knighton, was advantageous for the narrowness of the Teme valley at this point; and it is certainly also an imposing location. However, it happens also to coincide exactly with the point where the distance between the broadly parallel courses of the rivers Teme and Lugg is shortest. Having crossed the Teme onto the hill across which the centre of Knighton now stands, a further half mile (0.8 km) onwards the Dyke picks up a course onto the west-facing flank of the hill known as Ffrith, up to a high vantage point at Jenkins Allis (Figure 1.25). From here it follows a course that takes it around the western sides of at least five west-facing hill-crests for 3 miles (4.8 km) past Cwm Whitton Hill and Hawthorn Hill, descending the spur of Furrow Hill to a crossing of the Lugg just to the west of Discoed.

From this point the Dyke follows an almost mile-long (1.6 km) course that takes it straight up the north-facing hill towards Bwlch and brings it over a ridge of Newcastle Hill to the east of Pen Offa. From here it makes a distinct turn to the south-east and then south-west along the north-western flank of Evenjobb Hill. Turning south-east again, it makes a protracted descent of the slope on an extended diagonal course, tracing a mile-long course overlooking the Walton Basin to the south-west. It skirts the base of the hill at Burfa and crosses the Hindwell Brook before, half a mile (0.8 km) further on, climbing nearly vertically up the side of a spur of a hill directly opposite. Here it turns abruptly south up the narrow spine of the spur itself and then winds upwards

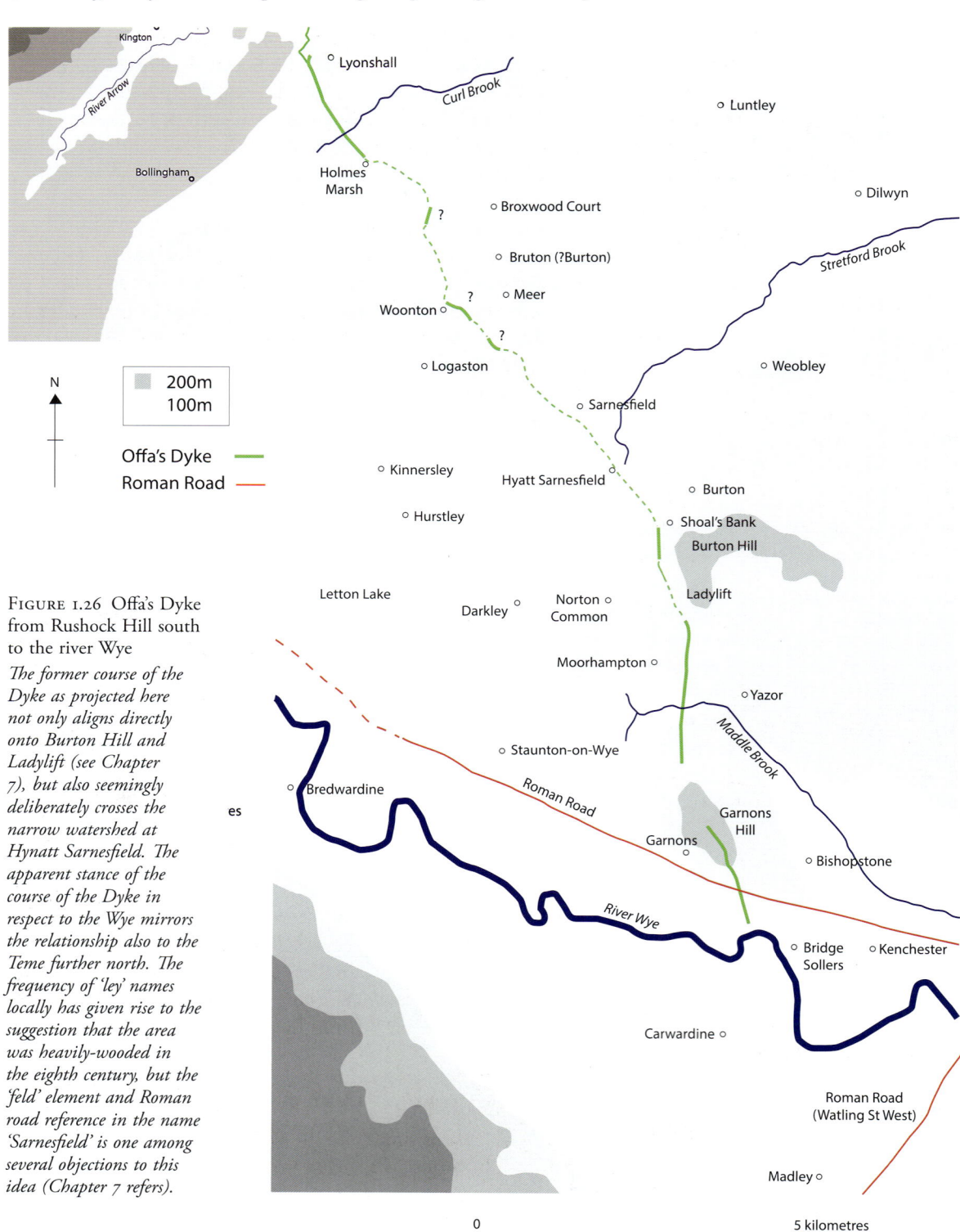

48 *Offa's Dyke: Landscape and Hegemony in Eighth-Century Britain*

FIGURE 1.26 Offa's Dyke from Rushock Hill south to the river Wye

The former course of the Dyke as projected here not only aligns directly onto Burton Hill and Ladylift (see Chapter 7), but also seemingly deliberately crosses the narrow watershed at Hynatt Sarnesfield. The apparent stance of the course of the Dyke in respect to the Wye mirrors the relationship also to the Teme further north. The frequency of 'ley' names locally has given rise to the suggestion that the area was heavily-wooded in the eighth century, but the 'feld' element and Roman road reference in the name 'Sarnesfield' is one among several objections to this idea (Chapter 7 refers).

1 *Offa's Dyke in profile: character, course and controversies*

FIGURE 1.27 At the Curl Brook valley, Lyonshall, Herefordshire, looking south

Ladylift and (background, left) Burton Hill dominate the prospect south from a field adjacent to the Leominster-Kington road (A44). Offa's Dyke lies within the hedgerow to the right of the view, and the rise in the foreground forms part of the bank of the Dyke running east–west after an abrupt turn eastwards towards Lyonshall Park Wood. The Dyke climbs the west-facing flank of Ladylift (Figure 2.8), before turning south towards Moorhampton and the river Wye.

around the precipitous west-facing slope of Herrock Hill. The Dyke traces a prominent half-mile course below the summit of Herrock Hill but rather than crossing a deep valley and ascending around Bradnor Hill immediately to the south as it might be expected to do, it heads due east and crosses a saddle that links Herrock Hill and Rushock Hill. From the top of the latter hill it unusually provides a view both northwards and south.

A length of bank and ditch, long considered to comprise a continuation of the Dyke southwards beyond Rushock Hill, exists just over half a mile (0.8 km) to the east, crossing the Arrow valley just to the west of Titley Mill. The gap that exists between the upstanding length on Rushock Hill and this Arrow valley length could be (and has been) explained by suggesting that the latter is really an unrelated cross-valley dyke. If so, it is difficult to understand why there should have been an apparent concern to achieve a north–south orientation for this length of Dyke such that it crosses the river valley obliquely.[81] The intervening landscape existed almost entirely within the 'landscape envelope' of Eywood and its surrounding parkland, which was subject to large-scale landscaping in the eighteenth century.[82]

A likely course through Lyonshall Park (also subject to designed landscaping) is traceable, but any earthwork that existed here has apparently had a post-medieval track super-imposed upon it. The Dyke makes a prominent right-angled turn where it assumes major proportions again at The Ovals just to the west of Lyonshall church (Figure 1.27). Here it picks up a line east of south sighted onto the slopes below (and to the south of) Ladylift Clump at Yazor nearly 5 miles (8.0 km) to the south-east.[83] Only the first mile and a half (2.4 km) or so, across the valley of the Curl Brook west of Lyonshall, is readily traceable as a substantial earthwork, although it reaches massive proportions as it approaches the valley-bottom from the north. The difficulty of tracing it beyond the hilltop at Holmes Marsh could be because it never existed southwards, or because, across the two and a half miles (4.0 km) from at least Crump Oak southwards to The Batch south of Woonton, its line has, since the eighteenth century at least, been followed closely by the route of the present A480 Kington to Hereford road.[84]

For a mile and a half (2.4 km) south-east through Sarnesfield parish there is no visible trace of the Dyke at all, where, if ever present, it appears likely to have made a transit close to, if not actually upon, the watershed between the Lugg and the Wye catchments at Hyatt Sarnesfield. A prominent continuous west-facing lynchet to the south of (and not actually at) Shoal's Bank rises up the flank of Burton Hill diagonally. This earthwork, if it represents the form of the Dyke locally, serves to pick up the southwards line again, but there is no indication that its half mile (0.8 km) long course across the west-facing slopes below Ladylift Clump achieved that summit. Instead, as at The Stubb, Kingswood, in Montgomeryshire (where it gains the shoulder of a hill with a prominent outlook westwards over the Severn valley), the Dyke appears to have climbed to a spur to the south of the summit, with a prominent view westwards over the Wye valley.

From this spur a north–south course was achieved across the valley of the Maddle Brook for a mile and a half (2.4 km) to Garnons Hill. Here again a south-eastwards trending line is picked up for two miles (3.2 km), firstly across the naturally north-west to south-east oriented ridge of Garnons Hill, and then down to the Wye just to the east of Bridge Sollers, where it reaches the river in a short length that still in places reaches substantial proportions.[85]

From the Wye southwards to the Severn

As it approaches the Wye, therefore, the course of Offa's Dyke utilizes whatever high ground is available, while its alignment is south-eastwards rather than southwards. This must surely offer some clues as to what (if anything) happened next. It is plausible, for instance, that there was a Mercian intention to annexe an area of the kingdom of Ergyng across the 15 miles (24.1 km) of territory between Canon Bridge on the right bank of the Wye north of Madley and Goodrich on the right bank below Ross-on-Wye.[86] However, only a half-mile (0.8 km) length of bank hugging the contours of the slopes above the steep drop to the river Wye within English Bicknor parish has, as has been noted already, so far been identified as part of the Dyke above the Wye upstream from Monmouth, although

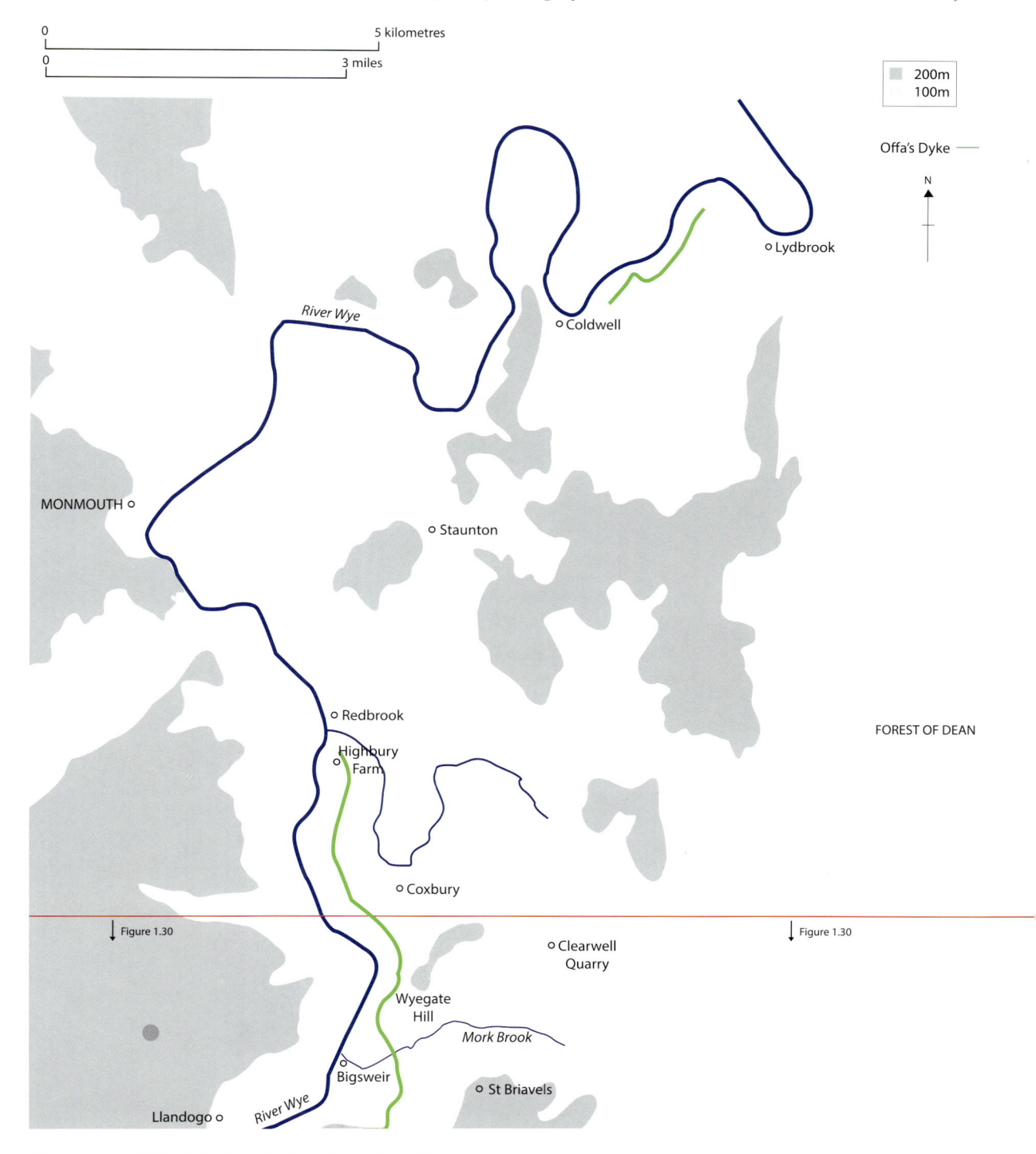

1 Offa's Dyke in profile: character, course and controversies

FIGURE 1.28 Offa's Dyke from Lydbrook south to Bigsweir
While the gap between Redbrook and English Bicknor has previously been the locus of comment here, the location of Staunton in reference to the higher ground south-east of Monmouth is perhaps more significant in establishing either a former (or intended) course of the Dyke, or the orientation of the frontier locally.

FIGURE 1.29   At Madgett Hill, looking north

Offa's Dyke makes an oblique, outwards-curving descent/ascent across the north-facing slope of Madgett Hill (from left foreground to centre-right in this view), looking up-river across the Wye valley (at left). The Dyke was once of substantial proportions here, but has been eroded by subsequent farming. The rucksack is placed on the top of the bank, and to the right of it can be made out a semi-circular construction scoop or quarry. The hill opposite is St Briavels Common, which the Dyke traverses, again in a gentle curve, from bottom right to top left. It has been 'submerged' by the farming of the commoners' crofts and paddocks in recent centuries, with consequent diminishing in size and loss of continuity which has adversely affected appreciation of its former proportions.

hints of further lengths northwards have been noted in the Bishopswood area.

The Dyke re-emerges as a continuous work some 5 miles (8.0 km) to the south-west, at Highbury above Lower Redbrook.[87] From there it follows a 9-mile (14.5 km) course along west-facing spurs, around or across re-entrant valleys and along the tops of hills with continuous west-facing and sometimes south-facing prospects, to descend to Sedbury immediately overlooking the Severn estuary. The amount of landscape and land-use alteration that has taken place along some parts of this stretch of the earthwork, and the wooded character of this landscape today, have tended to be detrimental to a mature appreciation of the nature and scale of the Dyke here.[88] For much of the distance, however, the bank (if not always the ditch) has retained proportions every bit as massive as those of other stretches north and south of the Severn described above. Moreover, there are particular features and devices along this stretch that so very closely mirror locational and build-forms and features that can be observed at many locations elsewhere along the course of the Dyke that the notion that this was not part of the overall Offa's Dyke scheme can and should be rejected outright.[89]

Just to the south of Highbury Farm, the Dyke follows the crest of a ridge for half a mile (0.8 km). This ridge closely parallels the course of the river Wye here, flowing 300 ft (91.4 m) below in its narrow floodplain. At Coxbury, the Dyke descends to mid-slope before rising to the west-facing crest of a spur of Wyegate Hill a mile (1.6 km) further on. It descends the spur to cross the re-entrant valley of the Mork Brook, before ascending the north-facing slope at Coldharbour just to the west of St Briavels, rising up to 700 ft (213.5 m) in elevation above the river in just a quarter of a mile (0.4 km) in the process.

The Dyke then crosses the upper south-facing slopes of St Briavels Common, taking a mile-long (1.6 km) course before traversing another steep re-entrant valley to gain the crest of the scarp of Madgett Hill (Figure 1.29). For over a mile from this point the Dyke closely follows the western lip of the plateau at Tidenham Chase that directly overlooks the Wye almost continuously. Although there are gaps caused among other things by quarrying and residential development, it maintains the same stance following the scarp.[90] The scarp itself in many places breaks up into cliffs for another mile and a half (2.4 km) to Tutshill opposite Chepstow, and beyond. Directly opposite where Chepstow's historic Port Wall meets the Wye, the Dyke turns decisively south-east from the left bank of the river to traverse a mile (1.6km) across the Beachley peninsula to the right bank of the Severn at Sedbury Cliffs (Figure 1.5).

While the location and form of the Dyke at various points along the stretch from Highbury to Tutshill are both prominent and highly 'performative', it is only a prelude to the flourish with which the Dyke ends in this stark cut from west to east across the grain of the Beachley peninsula, just to the south of Sedbury. Here it occupies the most advantageous and visible ground, and, free from the limitations imposed upon it by the limestone escarpment, it resumes the form (including counterscarp bank and eastern quarry-ditch) so characteristic of the more dramatic parts of the south Shropshire and Radnorshire stretches.

Past study of Offa's Dyke has focused not only on its course, changing character and anomalies, but has also devoted much effort to defining a plausible political context for its creation. In the following chapter we therefore not only review what these studies have concluded about the form and placement of the Dyke, but also what contrasting views have emerged concerning its purpose.

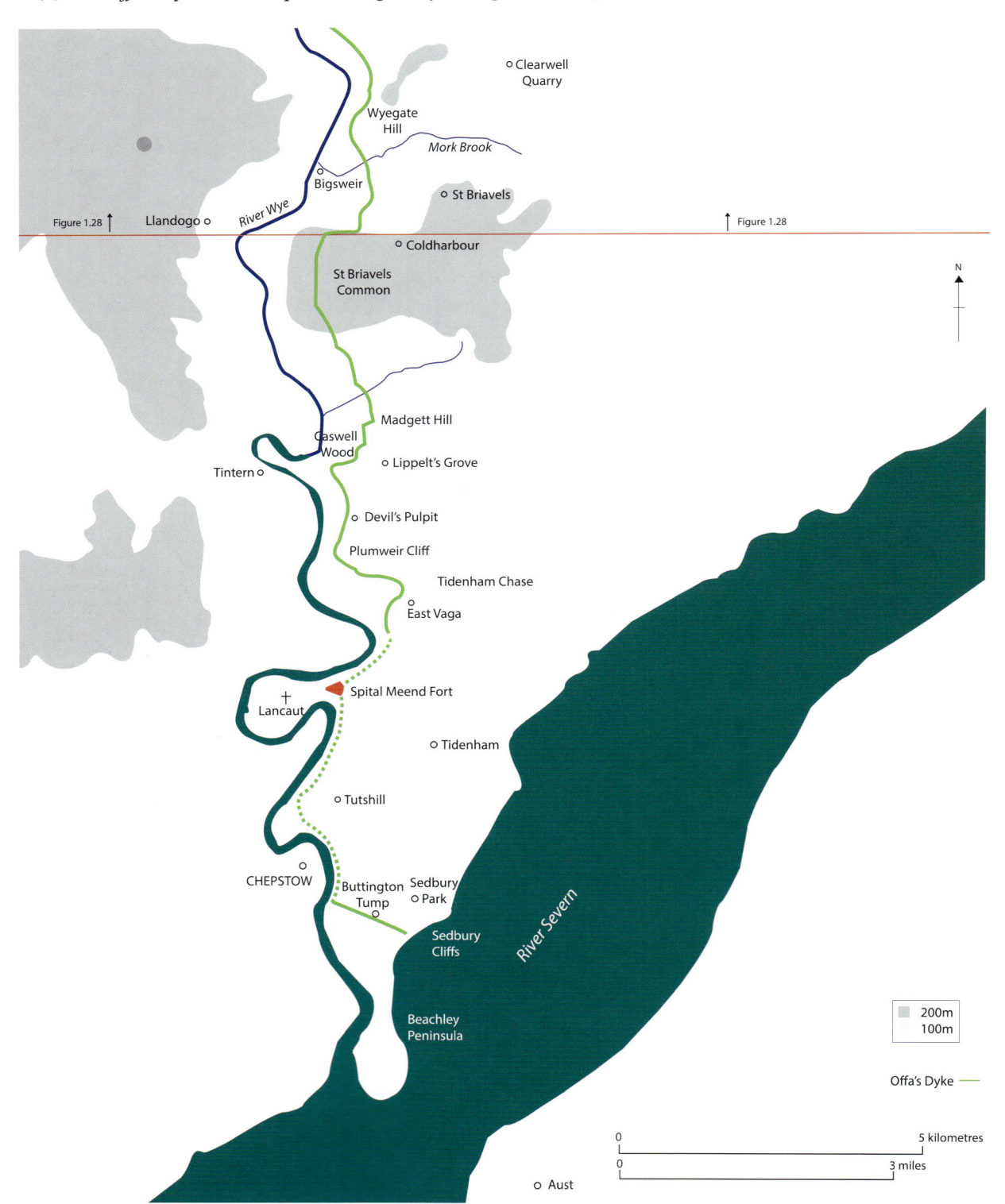

FIGURE 1.30 Offa's Dyke from Wyegate Hill to Sedbury Cliffs

CHAPTER TWO

Studying Offa's Dyke: a cumulative inheritance

> Within two myles, there is a famous thing;
> Cal'de Offaes Dyke, that reacheth farre in length:
> All kind of ware, the Danes might thether bring,
> It was free ground and cal'de the Britaines strength.
> Wat's Dyke, likewise, about the same was set,
> Betweene which two, both Danes and Britaines met
> And trafficke still, but passing bounds by sleight
> The one did take, the other prisner streight.
>
> Thomas Churchyard, *The Worthines of Wales*, 1587[1]

The sixteenth-century Welsh poet Thomas Churchyard may have inaccurately glossed the English (or specifically the Mercians) as Danes here, but his interpretation of the relation between Wat's Dyke and Offa's Dyke in this passage of his extended poem is intriguing. While the most likely explanation is that it was an inspired guess, there is just a slight possibility that it retained something of genuine folk-memory.[2] Although Churchyard's verse promoted a particular vision of the use of the dykes, he was not seemingly engaged in more protracted debates surrounding the built form or the purpose of Offa's Dyke, nor its relation to Wat's Dyke. Such debates were nonetheless not long in developing, such that by the nineteenth century a wide range of the issues that will be focused upon in this and subsequent chapters had been aired.

In tracing the history of interest in, study of and interpretations concerning Offa's Dyke there are several themes and questions that recur and that are posed and pursued again here. These include: 'when did historical interest specifically in the purpose of building Offa's Dyke begin?', and 'what questions did antiquarian study of the Dyke focus upon?' In reference to more recent studies of the Dyke, questions have centred upon what such study has discovered about the intricacies of the route chosen and the way in which the earthwork was built. These and several other questions about previous study of the Dyke have provided what is termed here a 'cumulative inheritance' for twenty-first century research into the great linear work. The history of inquiry goes back a long way, even into medieval times, so that is where the story needs to begin.

An awakening interest registered in medieval commentary

There is no mention of Offa's Dyke in the *Anglo-Saxon Chronicle*, despite its record of events that took place in the near vicinity, such as the protracted battle between the forces of Wessex, Mercia and the Welsh on the one hand and the Danish on the other at Buttington in 894.[3] The late ninth-century comment in Asser's *Life* of King Alfred of Wessex is, therefore, the only clear known reference to the Dyke until the twelfth century. The one apparent exception is a mention in a section of the so-called *Historia Regum*, a series of annals for the years 732–802 compiled in York, edited by Byrhtferth, a monk of Ramsey Abbey near Peterborough around 1000, and brought together by Symeon of Durham around 1129. This is judged to have been derived directly from Asser's *Life* of Alfred, since it more or less repeats *verbatim*.[4]

Two of the medieval references to Offa's Dyke provide insights not only into how, at least in the twelfth century and later, the great earthwork was understood to have come about, but also into its extent. In his *Life* of King Oswald, compiled *c.*1165, Reginald of Durham linked the battle at *Maserfelth* in 641 (in which Oswald was killed) to Oswestry, which he located also in reference to Offa's Dyke.[5] Reginald explicitly described the Dyke as having been built by Offa as a 'barrier' to defend his western border against the Welsh, and repeated the idea that, 'From sea to sea, therefore, he girdled in almost his entire kingdom against Wales, and set up the dyke as a boundary for both lands.'[6] The anonymous *Brut y Tywysogyon* or 'Chronicle of the Princes', compiled probably at Strata Florida Abbey in Cardiganshire from the late thirteenth century, explains the Dyke from a medieval Welsh perspective: 'Offa had a dyke made as a defence between him and the Welsh, so that it might be easier for him to resist the attack of his enemies. And that is called Offa's Dyke ('Clawdd Offa') from that day to this'.[7] Remarkably, *Brut* places the creation of the Dyke precisely under the year 798, which has been understood to represent a misplacing of the entry, given that Offa's death is correctly entered under 796. The same entry adds the observation that the Dyke extended 'from one sea to the other, that is, from the south near Bristol to the North above Flint between the monastery of Basingwerk and Coleshill.'[8]

John of Salisbury in his *Polycraticus* of *c.*1159 was apparently the originator of the story (in Folio VI.6) that in 1063, in King Edward the Confessor's time, Earl Harold (Godwin) established a law, following his victories over the forces of the kingdom of Gwynedd, that any Welshman found with a weapon on the English side of Offa's Dyke would have his right hand cut off. Gerald of Wales (*Giraldus Cambrensis*, 1146–1223) had direct links with the cathedral chapter at Hereford, and was responsible for some of the earliest references to the presence of Offa in Hereford.[9] He mentioned the Dyke in his *Description of Wales* produced towards the end of the twelfth century, in the context of the 'English kings before the Normans came ... (who) made such a determined effort to subdue the Welsh that they destroyed them almost to a man'.[10]

Ranulf Higden was the first writer, in his *Polychronichon* written soon after 1299, to mention the existence of both Offa's Dyke and Wat's Dyke.[11] William Caxton in effect pulled all these earlier sources together in his *Description of Britain* of *c*.1480. For Caxton, 'Wales or Wallia, also called Cambria' comprised the third division of Britain, the bounds of which he outlined in his Chapter 5. He noted that the boundary between England and Wales was, at that time, marked by the river Dee at Chester in the north and the 'Vaga' (Wye) at Chepstow in the south. 'In addition', he wrote:

> King Offa, in order to have a partition for all time between the Kings of England and Wales, built a long dyke stretching from the south past Bristol, northwards along the edge the Welsh mountains, following the rivers Severn and Dee almost to their sources and continuing to the mouth of the river Dee beyond Chester, close to Flint castle, reaching the sea between Colehill and the monastery of Basingwerk. This dyke is still to be seen in many places. In the time of King Edward, Welshmen were forbidden, on pain of severe punishment, to cross the dyke armed … Nowadays, however, on both this side and the far side of the dyke, and especially in Cheshire, Shropshire and Herefordshire, English people and Welsh people are intermingled in many places.[12]

The confusion between the two dykes is not surprising given their proximity, and nor is Caxton the only early example of such entanglement: as evident from the *Brut* entry mentioned above, it was present also in some of the Welsh sources. It is important to acknowledge, therefore, that these medieval references do not establish any definite 'independent' facts about the Dyke. They record what was believed about it at the time, and they may simply have been 'common sense' understandings: as speculative then as many of our ideas needs must be now. We should not too readily dismiss them entirely in these terms, however. They potentially provide insights from unreferenced documents or traditions that became inaccessible to later writers, and it is too easy simply to see them as the source of misconceptions that emerged later. For example, as in the quotation with which this chapter opened, confusion about the extent and inter-relation of the two dykes may relate to a view of their genesis that may rest ultimately in a folk-memory of a once-real relationship.[13]

Early antiquarian observations

The medieval writers in effect alluded to, rather than described, Offa's Dyke. However, by the mid-sixteenth century at least one account had appeared that was based upon some first-hand observation. This was published in the *Itinerary in Wales* by John Leland, a work which recounted his travels between 1539 and 1541. He noted that "Offa's Dike apperith manifestly by the space of a ii. miles almost in the middle way betwixt Bisshops Castell and Montgomery" and he also commented that it existed elsewhere in Chirbury Hundred. Leland provided detail that indicates that he did more than simply observe Offa's Dyke in passing. For instance, his account included reference to the appearance of the Dyke as a *limes* or boundary bank close by the mound at Nantcribba near Forden, north of Montgomery. He also related that informants in Montgomery had told him "that Offa's Dike apperith sumwhat about Radenor, and again within a iii. mile of Oswestre", both of which statements are true.[14] Churchyard's poetic account first published in 1587 that was selected to introduce the present chapter is important because it is the earliest known source that manages to distinguish clearly between the two dykes, although the extent to which it is based upon direct personal observation is less certain.

John Aubrey (1626–97) was a polymath: an observer and recorder of the vestiges of the past in the Elizabethan and Jacobean antiquarian manner.[15] His observations were of variable reliability, but his correspondence concerning the antiquities of Britain was extensive. There is a lengthy account of Offa's Dyke in his *Monumenta Britannica*, a work that had been fully assembled, although not in publishable form, by around 1690.[16] Aubrey noted that the Dyke was called 'Clawdd Offa', that it was made by 'Offa, king of the Mercians' and that it was built 'to separate the Britons from the Saxons'.[17] He related the tradition that whoever was found to be on the 'wrong' side of the Dyke would have their right hand cut off, and informed the reader that the earthwork is still visible 'here and there on the ridge of the hills'.[18] He cited two locations in Herefordshire as examples of this latter situation.[19]

Aubrey also made the earliest known 'archaeological' observation and evidential deduction about the Dyke, stating that: 'The Graff is on ye Welsh side; viz Westwards, and ye Rampire towards the English side: wch evidences that it was made by the Saxons'. He added that 'This Dyke is neer as big as Wensditch in Wiltshire'.[20] Aubrey finally included a paragraph based upon 'information' from his correspondent Henry Milbourn, Recorder of Monmouth, concerning the extent of the Dyke:

> Offa's-Ditch beginneth at Basingwerk in North-Wales in the County of Flynt: thence it runs to Montgomery-park; thence to Clun; then to Lanterden in Herefordshire (where it is called Rue-ditch) then to Ryd-ar-heleg (heleg is a willow) neer Clifford in Herefordshire, then to Bachy-hill aforesaid (where I have seen it) then to the river Wy.[21]

Clearly by the seventeenth century the north Herefordshire Rowe Ditch was mistakenly believed to be part of the Offa's Dyke scheme. Meanwhile the name 'Bachy-hill' sounds as if it may be an earlier naming of what today is known as Merbach Hill just to the south-west of Bredwardine. Either Milbourn or Aubrey, or both, were apparently confused as to which side of the river Wye Merbach Hill stood.[22]

This was also the age when the first detailed mapping of the landscape was being undertaken. Maps of the estates of major rural landowners were being created, and these maps occasionally made reference to the presence and course of Offa's Dyke where this was either more striking as a landscape feature, or was of importance to the definition of particular holdings. An example is William

FIGURE 2.1 Sir Richard Corbett's 'Mannor of Leighton' from Powis Castle

This view eastwards from the upper terrace at Powis Castle is focused upon the hillsides of the western flank of the Long Mountain. William Fowler's (1663) map of the 'Mannor of Leighton in Montgomeryshire' featured just this area, as if seen from the same direction (the West). The course of what is labelled 'Offa's Dike' on that map is better-traced to the north, at the 'Buttington' end of the estate (to the left of this view), where it impinged more closely on the farmed landscape, than above Leighton Park, and in the vicinity of the 'Viaduct Ravine'.

Fowler's (1663) map of the 'Mannor of Leighton' in Montgomeryshire, drawn for Sir Richard Corbett. On this map, 'Offa's Dike' is clearly labelled at the northern end of the estate lands as it rises southwards from Buttington (Figure 2.1), and its course is traceable for most of its route south to Forden.[23]

Edward Lhuyd (1659–1709), the Welsh philologist, naturalist and antiquary, was a contemporary of Aubrey. He succeeded Robert Plot as Keeper of the Ashmolean Museum in Oxford, and updated Camden's entries on several of the Welsh counties. He planned to write an *Archaeologia Britannica*, but only completed the first volume, on links between the 'Celtic' languages of the British Isles, by the time of his death. Lhuyd's correspondence was extensive, and his *Parochalia* (1696) included references to Offa's Dyke in Flintshire and in Oswestry parish.[24] Lhuyd was particularly keen to obtain transcriptions of inscriptions upon stones, and he recorded the lettering inscribed on the 'Pillar of Eliseg' at Llangollen, that has featured so prominently in recent interpretations of the relation of the kingdom of Powys to the building of Offa's Dyke.[25]

Later eighteenth- and nineteenth-century observations and discussions

By the eighteenth century, a received understanding of Offa's Dyke was a basic touchstone for educated people with an interest in the ancient origins of England and Wales, or indeed in the history and topography of the Welsh Marches in particular. The Offa's Dyke entry in Philip Luckombe's *England's Gazetteer; Or An accurate Description Of All The Cities, Towns, And Villages in the Kingdom* (1790) combined information from the scant historical sources with a sketchy description of the course of the Dyke which was still tangibly derived from the sixteenth- and seventeenth-century antiquarian sources discussed above.[26] Its inaccuracies concerning the northerly courses of both dykes was closely reflected in eighteenth-century maps such as William Williams' map of Flintshire and Denbighshire, of 1754, which wrongly shows Wat's Dyke reaching the Dee estuary at Flint and Offa's Dyke terminating further north-west along the estuary at Basingwerk near Holywell.

Luckombe's account was typical of contemporary 'informed opinion' concerning the Dyke, but the information it contained was already adrift of the latest published material. In 1784, Thomas Pennant, a local landowner who lived near Mold, had used information on sites of archaeological interest supplied to him by the antiquarian John Evans of Llwyn-y-Groes to amplify the observations gathered during his 1773 tour of Wales. This allowed him, for the first time, to describe accurately the course of both Offa's and Wat's Dykes in the northern Marches and to distinguish clearly between them:

> (Wat's Dyke) is so often confounded with OFFA'S ditch, which attends (it) at unequal distances, from five hundred yards to three miles, till (Offa's Dyke) is totally lost ... It is remarkable that *Wat's* dike should have been overlooked, or confounded with that of *Offa*, by all writers, except by *Thomas Churchyard* the poet, who assigns the object of the work: that the space intervening between the two was free ground, where the *Britons* and the *Saxons* might meet with safety for all commercial purposes.[27]

Following a remarkably detailed description of the course of Wat's Dyke (which Cyril Fox reproduced in full in his account of his survey of that dyke), Pennant described the course of Offa's Dyke from the Vale of Montgomery northwards to Treuddyn in commensurate detail. What is especially striking about Pennant's description is how 'modern' it sounds in its identification of aspects of the course of the Dyke. So, for instance, he noted how there is no sign of the Dyke north of Buttington Bridge along the Severn, and deduced that the river was meant to serve as the boundary here. He mentions that it suddenly ends, without any apparent reason, at Treuddyn: and he speculates that Offa may have perceived the Clwydian Mountains as somehow symbolically continuing the frontier north to the sea.

This spirit of new enquiry and observational accuracy was to be very much a feature of a renewed interest in Offa's Dyke over the next century. Although the names and observations of the nineteenth-century Offa's Dyke researchers are now largely forgotten and are neglected even within the academic literature (and the assorted gentlemen, landowners, clerics and Oxford Dons concerned do seem today more like characters from an Anthony Trollope novel than serious archaeological and historical scholars), it was their enquiries which first put the study of Offa's Dyke on a firm evidence-based footing. This extensive body of work was partly made possible by important new research tools such as Ordnance Survey maps accurately recording the course of the Dyke.[28] However, it also reflected the self-confidence and scientific endeavour of the age, and the support of the local antiquarian and natural history societies which were enthusiastically founded in many places along the Welsh borders from the mid-nineteenth century onwards.

FIGURE 2.2 Offa's Dyke at Pen-rhos, south of Brymbo, looking south
The whole landscape of the area south towards Pentre Bychan and Ruabon is in view from this elevated point just to the south of the former Brymbo Colliery, and at this point also the land rises towards the right, to Esclusham Mountain north of Ruabon Mountain. The field boundary to the left stands on the bank of the Dyke, and no ditch is visible. Fox recorded that 'indications of the ditch' could be seen here in 1927, just to the west of Brymbo Hall. However, this location is also only a short distance south of the site of the first recorded excavation on the Dyke in the early 1890s by M'Kenny Hughes, where he claimed to have found no West-facing ditch.

Practically all the nineteenth-century Offa's Dyke researchers, ranging from the gentleman-cleric T. D. Fosbroke in the 1830s to the mainstream antiquarians Boyd Dawkins and Augustus Lane Fox in the 1870s, followed Pennant in their understanding of the importance of first hand observation and the careful analysis of field evidence.[29] As the pioneering antiquarian Richard Colt Hoare had put it at the beginning of the century, the new ambition for research was to 'speak from facts not theory'.[30] Close analysis of primary detail therefore began thenceforward to characterise informed approaches to the basic Offa's Dyke problems such as extent, date, uniformity and purpose that are still actively debated, and feature so prominently in this book. Indeed, out of this cluster of new ideas and speculations came interpretations which substantially prefigure most of the Offa's Dyke 'explanations' that are current today.

A basic issue to be addressed was inevitably the date of the Dyke. The historical sources, and particularly the Asser reference, seemed to give a satisfactory answer to the question, and for most observers there was no reason to query the Anglo-Saxon, Mercian (and specifically the Offan) associations. However, Archdeacon Williams raised the possibility of a pre-Roman context for its construction, noting some of the variations along the earthwork.[31] Meanwhile, H. L. Jones pointed out that the matter could be clarified by looking at the relationship of the Dyke to other datable historic features, and that Roman roads were an obvious case in point. He identified five places where this might most satisfactorily be achievable: near Caergwrle, at the foot of Llanymynech Hill, near Forden, near Kenchester, and near Chepstow.[32] Although Jones did not carry out further research on this issue, the principle was an important one, and he understood that a practical demonstration would 'depend much upon positive excavation if ever a point of actual intersection can be determined'.[33]

At the end of the century, the question of the date of the Dyke was re-opened by M'Kenny Hughes, who became the first person to undertake direct excavation of the earthwork. This intervention was a section cut across the bank and ditch at Brymbo, which was said to have revealed that no western ditch existed there. Echoing Archdeacon Williams' earlier comments, M'Kenny Hughes used his excavation evidence both to query how uniform the Dyke really was, and to propose that the earthwork referred to as 'Offa's Dyke' might really consist of several separate structures built and used at different times.[34]

Another key question, then as now, was where the monument actually ran. Particularly as the Ordnance Survey maps were published, it became apparent that this was no straightforward matter, and that there were significant gaps in the 'sea to sea' course whereas a literal reading of Asser suggested this should not be the case.[35] For the central and northern Marches, Pennant's description of the course of the Dyke, and in particular the distinction between Offa's and Wat's Dykes, was confirmed and restated in more detail by these nineteenth-century researchers who now had access to accurate maps as well as the ability to make their own field observations.[36] However, the issue of the extent of the Dyke beyond the central Marches area was more problematical, and various among the Victorian observers sought to resolve this uncertainty.

In the south, Pennant had simply observed that 'Offa's Ditch extended from the River Wye along the counties of Hereford and Radnor into that of Montgomery …'[37] In the early 1830s the Reverend T. D. Fosbroke, who lived near Ross-on-Wye and whose son was curate at St Briavels in Gloucestershire, set about establishing in the field the evidence for definite remains of the Dyke in the Lower Wye Valley. As reported in the pages of the *Gentleman's Magazine*, Fosbroke carried out several field trips and identified significant surviving sections in the area of Tidenham Chase and St Briavels Common.[38] Interestingly, and directly pre-figuring the more recent arguments of David Hill and Margaret Worthington (see below), he added a follow-up letter to the same magazine two years later in which he amended his earlier conclusions, reporting that further research had convinced him that the southern portion of the Dyke must actually run further to the west (but whose course was yet to be identified). He concluded that the Wye Valley earthworks were really entrenchments of Roman date, therefore, and did not form part of Offa's Dyke at all.[39]

The matter was not allowed to rest there, however. Fosbroke's revised conclusion was vigorously and systematically rejected by George Ormerod, the owner of Sedbury Park which included the alleged far southern end of Offa's Dyke. As well as using his own deeds of ownership and Anglo-Saxon charter evidence to demonstrate the antiquity of the Sedbury length of the Dyke (which various early nineteenth-century commentators had suggested was a seventeenth-century Civil War entrenchment), Ormerod also mapped and analysed in detail the remains of Offa's Dyke southwards from Madgetts Wood in Gloucestershire.[40] Ormerod pointed out the largely continuous nature of the Lower Wye sections of the Dyke, their uniformity of design, the lack of connection with known Roman roads and other infrastructure in the vicinity, and the long-standing tradition naming the earthworks hereabouts as Offa's Dyke. Importantly, Ormerod also stressed the close similarity between the Gloucestershire earthworks and the character of the accepted Offa's Dyke earthworks in the northern Marches:

> In 1845 I examined the accessible points of the dyke between Mold, in Flintshire, and Bridge Sollers, in Herefordshire, and satisfied myself as to the accordance of the Tidenham mounds, where perfect, with those of the more northerly range, in form and character, and particularly in the adaptation of the dyke to the sides of hills, and its avoidance of projecting flats and headlands by the banks of rivers. This may be exemplified by comparing the dyke opposite Welshpool, after its first crossing the Severn near Buttinton, in Montgomeryshire, with the arrangement on Tiddenham Chase, and also its terminating portion, when again meeting the Severn in its passage over the southern Buttinton within Sedbury.[41]

Not only does Ormerod's attention to detail and first hand observation typify the contribution of the nineteenth-century Offa's Dyke observers, but his well-reasoned conclusion was that the large linear bank and ditch topping the eastern edge of the Lower Wye Valley was part of Offa's Dyke after all. He further remarked that, given the known historical sources, these earthworks made no real sense in anything other than an Anglo-Saxon context.

Linking the Dyke in Gloucestershire with the sections further north was nonetheless still widely acknowledged to be a problem. The respected Welsh antiquarian and Monmouthshire resident Sir Samuel Rush Meyrick used place-name evidence to chart a notional course linking St Briavels with Bridge Sollers on the Wye via Symonds Yat and Hentland.[42] However, later observers were quick to point out the absence of known remains along this course.[43] Most commentators followed C. H. Hartshorne and H. L. Jones in suggesting that the river Wye had hereabouts been utilised instead as the boundary.[44] Hartshorne further suggested that a route through northern Herefordshire from Bridge Sollers on the Wye could have incorporated surviving sections of earthwork at Mansell Gamage and Holmes Marsh, as well as following 'the line of the Turnpike road through Sarnesfield', before eventually connecting with the section on Rushock Hill.[45] Jones was more circumspect, preferring to conclude that 'nothing but close and accurate search, carried out by residents in this highly cultivated district, can throw light upon this uncertain portion of its course.'[46] It is perhaps typical of Offa's Dyke studies that, 150 years later, such 'close and accurate search' is yet to be completed here.

The northern course of Offa's Dyke was also debated by nineteenth-century scholars. If anything, this northerly question seemed more difficult to resolve, even though all serious commentators were quick to follow Pennant in rejecting the earlier confusions with the northern end of Wat's Dyke. According to Pennant's description, the Dyke terminated in the north at '*Cae-dwn*, a farm near *Treyddin* chapel, in the parish of *Mold* (pointing towards the *Clwydian* hills); beyond which there can no further traces be discovered'.[47] The 16 mile (25.75 km) gap between Treuddyn and the north Wales coast was accepted by Hartshorne, but following established local tradition, the Ordnance Survey recorded earthworks in the vicinity of Newmarket in Whitford parish (close to Prestatyn) as Offa's Dyke.[48] This identification was affirmed in the Offa's Dyke entry in the 'List of the Pre-historic Remains of Wales' published in 1854 by the Cambrian Archaeological Association.[49] Jones struggled to explain the lack of intervening remnants between Newmarket and Treuddyn: he felt that even intensive cultivation could not have completely removed such a structure, and suggested that, as with northern Herefordshire, the real issue was perhaps that 'sufficient search had not been made' locally.[50]

Perhaps acting on Jones' suggestion, just such a search was made in 1857 by the academic Edwin Guest, who, like Jones, was a member of the Cambrian Archaeological Association. Guest began his three day investigation at the recently opened railway station at Mold, and as well as visiting Wat's Dyke, 'which, bye the bye, the whole country assured me was the Clawdd Offa', he set about tracking Offa's Dyke northwards from Treuddyn.[51] His first problem was that no local informants could identify Pennant's 'Cae-Dwn farm', and it was only well to the north (and near to the coast) in the vicinity of Newmarket that he was able to find tangible remains said to be the Dyke. Local people confirmed the traditional naming of Offa's Dyke in this vicinity, which attribution could be traced in living memory back at least to the eighteenth century.[52] Guest was also told that portions of the Dyke had recently been destroyed hereabouts as a consequence of agricultural enclosure and improvement. One local man described the locally 'known' course of the Dyke from Treuddyn in detail via a route over Halkyn Mountain and with a terminus on the coast at a place called Uffern east of Prestatyn (which Guest argued was derived from the Welsh *terfyn* meaning boundary). Although frustrated in his efforts to find any indications of a continuous feature along this alignment beyond the Whitford and Newmarket sections, Guest was nevertheless happy to conclude that he had identified the northern terminus of Offa's Dyke.

Notwithstanding the complications arising from close field observations

FIGURE 2.3 Aerial view of Offa's Dyke at Ffrydd, south of Knighton

This view of the Dyke from the north-east is just to the south of the length of the Dyke that Earle observed being removed in 1856. In the foreground the Dyke rises out of the Teme valley and onto a shoulder of land where it changes direction subtly, but more importantly increases in scale. This is shown in plan in Figure 2.5 (at Point L on Fox's Fig. 60), and the contrasting dimensions of the bank are illustrated in Appendix 1. The substantial Jenkins Allis length is shown from the south-west in Figure 1.25.

PHOTOGRAPH COURTESY AND COPYRIGHT OF CLWYD-POWYS ARCHAEOLOGICAL TRUST.

of Offa's Dyke, these nineteenth-century commentators did generally accept the 'sea to sea' view of the monument. It was nevertheless acknowledged that the interpretation of the purpose of the Dyke was another complex issue, particularly since the historical sources gave very little explicit information in this respect.[53] John Earle, another professional academic, noted the paradox that, despite the supposed origin of the earthwork as a structure 'which once divided nations', it now 'so far from being the limit of the Principality … hardly even divides counties, or properties or parishes' and that this 'startling' fact was itself an interpretative problem.[54]

The answer, for nineteenth-century scholars, was both to look in detail at the actual form of the monument, and to re-address the historical sources. The Reverend Hartshorne was typical, producing precise measured sections of the Dyke, and analysing that evidence against a series of similar sections for other broadly comparable earthworks in other parts of southern Britain including Wat's Dyke, Wansdyke, Grims Ditch and Devil's Dyke:

> It is only by comparing analogous facts that we can hope to obtain any satisfactory information concerning their origin and intention. From pursuing this method in the present difficulty, we are enabled to draw a few conclusions that help us, though in a trifling degree, to dispel some of the darkness with which the subject before us is encumbered.[55]

Those 'few conclusions' of Hartshorne were, firstly, that Offa's and Wat's Dykes (with their ditches on the west) could be distinguished from other earthworks where the ditch faced south or east and, therefore, to suggest that the former dykes alone were built directly against the British. Secondly, he concluded that not only were Offa's and Wat's Dykes both built by Offa as a defence against the British, but that Offa's Dyke was the later of the two, and represented a subsequent elaboration of Offa's and Mercia's western defensive system.

This defensive model had a number of adherents. Boyd Dawkins and Lane Fox examined the central Marches section of Offa's Dyke between the Blue Bell (near Mellington south of Montgomery) and Llanymynech Hill in 1870 and commented on what they saw as the military design of the placement in situations such as the Long Mountain.[56] The Reverend Elias Owen suggested that the course of the monument on Llanymynech Hill even included a bastion- or tower-like raised platform which he recorded in a plan.[57]

The most subtle expression of the defensive argument was that offered by Professor Earle, following his visit to part of Offa's Dyke north of Knighton in 1856 (the partial destruction of a length of which by recent agricultural 'improvement' he disapprovingly recorded; Figure 2.3). He suggested that, while Offa's Dyke represented an agreed frontier line, the peace it kept would still have relied on active military patrols, perhaps by mobile cavalry units from both sides. In the case of the Mercians, he argued that later Anglo-Saxon documentary references to the 'Walhfaereld', notably in a charter issued by Burgred of Mercia in 855 concerning land at Blockley in Worcestershire, could be translated as 'the military company on the Welsh service', so demonstrating (to his own satisfaction at least) that precisely such a border defence corps had existed within the broad period to which Offa's Dyke belonged.[58]

The supposed military function was not, however, universally accepted. Others stressed the treaty or boundary-marker aspect of Offa's Dyke, and did not see that function as requiring any active military component.[59] M'Kenny Hughes, while querying the overall attribution of the Dyke to Offa, nevertheless thought it possible that the Mercian king of that name had combined sections of disparate earthworks to form a single unit. The purpose of that monument was not so much defence as demarcation, and particularly to inhibit cross border movement and prevent acts of border raiding and cattle rustling.[60]

Early twentieth-century developments

By the end of the nineteenth century, all the Offa's Dyke debates that were to be such a prominent feature of twentieth-century analysis had, as is evident from the foregoing, already been rehearsed in outline, and the problems with going beyond those debates identified. However, some techniques such as archaeological excavation had scarcely been used on Offa's Dyke and detailed survey (beyond the work of the Ordnance Survey) remained to be undertaken. Perhaps partly because of the intervention of the First World War, it was not until 1922 that the newly formed 'Oswestry Prehistoric Society' sought to redress the balance by undertaking excavation of the well-preserved length of Offa's Dyke on Baker's Hill near Oswestry. The group was formed in large measure on the initiative of Northcote Thomas, who, after his retirement from Colonial Office service in Nigeria as a government anthropologist, had returned to live close to where he grew up, at Trefonen. Thomas had recruited Lord Harlech as President of the new Society, which was established on Thomas' initiative 'with the excellent purpose of exploring and surveying Offa's Dyke'.[61] The Oswestry group dug out as much as a 30 m length of the ditch at a point south of a gap in the Dyke on Baker's Hill. However, the enterprise was poorly supported by the members of the group, perhaps because of the remoteness of the site (Figure 2.4). Finding only a single worked flint object and a piece of post-medieval pot for all their efforts, the group switched their efforts to an examination of the ramparts of Old Oswestry hillfort.

By the later 1920s, there was a widely recognised need for a professionally coordinated field-based study of the whole of Offa's Dyke (and, indeed, of Wat's Dyke) which would make full use of the newly emergent academic discipline of archaeology, and attempt finally to go beyond the uncertainties left by the nineteenth-century studies. At the suggestion of Sir Mortimer Wheeler, and perhaps in response also to the debacle of the abortive investigations at Baker's Hill, the task fell to Cyril Fox immediately upon his appointment to the Keepership of Archaeology at the National Museum of Wales in Cardiff.[62]

The view shared by Fox and Wheeler was that to make progress towards an

FIGURE 2.4 The site of the Oswestry Field Club's excavations at Carreg-y-big

It was on this hillside that a 30 m length of the western ditch of the Dyke was dug out by members of the 'Oswestry Prehistoric Society' in 1922, with little recorded gain in information. Fox recorded that this stretch of the Dyke, from near the farm up to the crest of Baker's Hill, featured a marked eastern quarry-ditch, that in some places was continuous for some distance (1955, 60).

REPRODUCED COURTESY OF A. WIGLEY: COPYRIGHT, SHROPSHIRE COUNCIL.

informed understanding of the Dyke it would be necessary to make a detailed, field by field, empirically-based observation and recording of its form, including, where possible, judiciously located archaeological excavation. It was also seen as important, for the first time, to study closely and compare Wat's Dyke and the short-dykes of the central Marches with Offa's Dyke to try to understand the overall development of what Fox was to term 'the Mercian frontier'.

The orderliness of Fox's approach to documentation of his findings in the field and subsequently, and the comprehensiveness of his reporting, has never since been matched. The magnitude of the task he undertook and fulfilled, and the breadth of his conclusions, were so considerable that they entirely shaped appreciation of the purpose and significance of the Dyke for a generation, down to the 1970s and beyond.

Sir Cyril Fox and the 'Offa's Dyke Field Survey'

> My previous work on the Dykes of Cambridgeshire was known to the Director of the National Museum of Wales, Dr. (now Sir Mortimer) Wheeler … and I was greeted by him on taking up my post as Keeper of Archaeology there in January 1925 with the news that the Council of the Museum had approved of sufficient annual leave of absence for the fieldwork involved in the research.[63]

In this manner, Sir Cyril Fox specified the genesis of his Offa's Dyke field survey. He identified as the most important part of the survey 'the detailed description of the character of the work' (that is, the Dyke) and the provision of a record of 'every yard' of its extant observable form on a six inch to one mile Ordnance Survey base map.[64] Fox's experience in Cambridgeshire working especially on the Devils Dyke and the Fleam Dyke meant that he had a clear understanding of dykes as earthworks. He appreciated their effectiveness in blocking movement along pre-established route-ways, and this predisposed him to seeing the dykes of the Welsh Marches in the same way. In the manner of the time, he had also interpreted the Cambridgeshire dykes as having been built across open ground, while in contrast terminating at each end in dense woodland.

Fox carried out six seasons of fieldwork on Offa's Dyke, and a seventh on Wat's Dyke, between 1926 and 1934; and he published a series of interim reports on each successive season of work in the journal of the Cambrian Archaeological Association, *Archaeologia Cambrensis*.[65] Events in Fox's life, and the intervention of the Second World War, meant that any planned general report did not materialise, as might have been expected, during the 1930s.[66] Instead, a series of short articles was issued, and an extended essay of synthesis, 'The Western Frontier of Mercia in the Dark Ages', was prepared for the British Academy in 1940 in response to the invitation to present that year's Sir John Rhys Memorial Lecture.[67]

When it was finally published, Fox's monograph *Offa's Dyke: A Field Survey of the Western Frontier Works of Mercia in the Seventh and Eighth Centuries AD* represented a compilation of his interim accounts across six chapters, each dated between 1926 and 1931 (with some minor editorial changes made in 1953), a chapter on Wat's Dyke dated 1934, and an edited version of the British Academy lecture of 1940. Even so, it was a monumental achievement. Sir Frank Stenton concluded his Foreword to the volume by proclaiming that: 'Through the years of labour which Sir Cyril Fox has spent upon the present survey … the frontier-line which Offa drew from the estuary of the Dee at Prestatyn to

2 Studying Offa's Dyke: a cumulative inheritance

the Severn Sea at Sedbury Cliffs… (and) the outstanding memorial of its type and period in north-western Europe now at last comes fairly into view.'[68]

Fox's attempt to understand the Dyke involved making detailed assessments of its topographical location and the formulation of an approach to the analysis of design that, by the time of the third season in 1928, was leading him to classify the different kinds of linear alignment that he had observed along its course. By the fourth season, it is possible to sense a 'eureka moment': he was beginning to detect a distinct pattern in this variability in the different forms of alignment and builds of bank as he recorded them south of the Severn in Montgomeryshire. From this he felt able to deduce what he saw as the likely condition of the entire landscape (wooded, pasture or cleared for cultivation) that it crossed, as he supposed it had been in the eighth century.[69]

A great strength of Fox's decision to reproduce the interim statements in his overarching monograph is that it retains their freshness of presentation. The narrative takes the reader along with him, providing enough of the evidence in a first-hand account for judgements to be made about the plausibility of what is being described and explained. His method involved the close annotation of the series of Ordnance Survey 6-inch to the mile (1:10,000) maps that he reproduced at a reduced scale. These annotations for instance numbered for each report (and volume chapter) those individual fields in the landscape in which occurred the specific features commented upon in the text. They also marked the presence of different kinds of alignment of the earthwork, and the position from which photographs reproduced in the text were taken, and the exact locations of the drawn profiles of the earthwork that were such an important feature of his documentation of its form (Figure 2.5).

It was inevitable that Fox's reporting of the northern sections was more detailed than for the more southerly, partly due to time pressures, but also because the 'pattern' of the build of the Dyke had become more familiar to him as he worked southwards.[70] However, it was also inevitable that what he termed the 'highland zone' of the Dyke in south Shropshire and Radnorshire attracted most attention: due largely to its better survival. Fox clearly saw this as

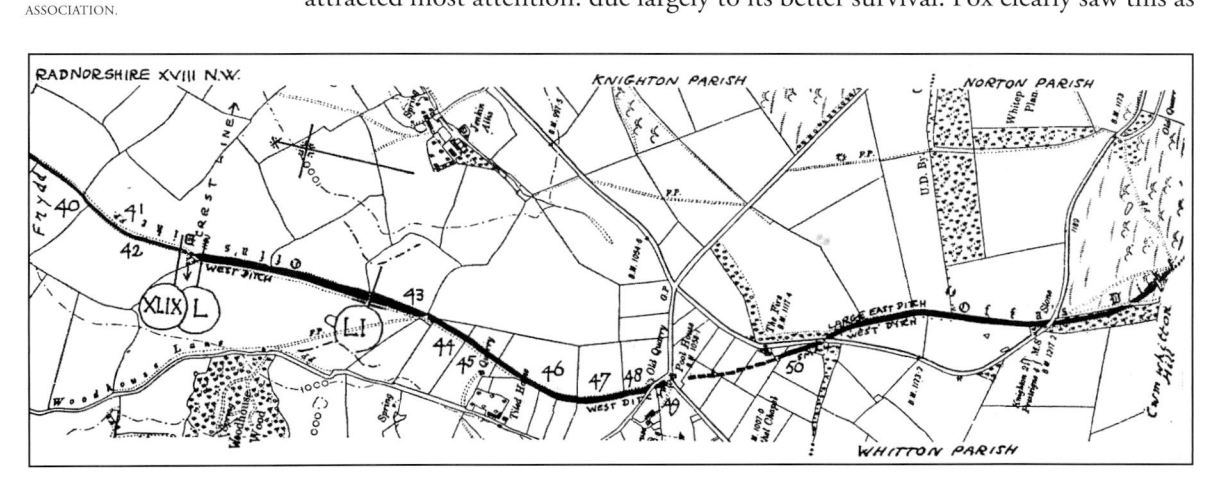

FIGURE 2.5 Fox's annotated map extract of for Offa's Dyke south of Knighton

This is one of the series of 47 such map extracts (reproduced from the yearly reports) published in Fox, 1955 (Figure 60). The scale of reproduction was four inches to the mile, reduced from the 6" Ordnance Survey series. This extract shows the length of Dyke that ascends southwards from the direction of Ffrydd, south of Knighton (away to the left, beyond this extract). Figure 1.25, above, is a view northwards from Field 44 in this extract. The Dyke crossing this and Field 45 has since Fox's survey been mostly levelled, and is now marked by the slight rise evident in the foreground of Figure 1.25. It is just visible at top left in Figure 2.3.

REPRODUCED COURTESY OF THE CAMBRIAN ARCHAEOLOGICAL ASSOCIATION.

the 'classic' part of the Dyke, as have most subsequent researchers, fieldworkers and commentators. Because of these disparities in his treatment of different parts of Offa's Dyke, his chapter on Wat's Dyke provides a better integrated account of a whole monument.[71]

Only the kind of close observation made during a careful analytical ground survey such as that undertaken by Fox could have led to the intricacy of characterisation that he achieved. An example is the summary of key differences in the method of obtaining material for the bank in the account of the course of the Dyke in east Denbighshire and north-west Shropshire.[72] He reiterated in 1955: "in the portion N. of the Dee surveyed in this chapter, the material composing the bank seems to have been derived wholly from the western ditch; S. of the Dee the material may be gathered in part from spoil holes on the E. side of the bank (e.g at Selattyn and Baker's hills, Profiles xxvi and xxvii, Figs. 33 and 32). A definite E. ditch occurs, however, in short lengths of the Dyke at Treflach (e.g. Profile xxxi, Fig. 34)."[73]

Before outlining Fox's account of what he saw as the most northerly parts of the course of the Dyke, it is worth mentioning something about his fieldwork that has perhaps not previously been highlighted sufficiently. This concerns the season of the year when most of the fieldwork took place, which was during the summers of the years spanned by the survey. While it is clear from the photographs that accompany Fox's reports and chapters that he did occasionally re-visit key locations during the winter or spring, the times of the year that are most effective for field survey were not the main seasons when he took to the field.[74] As a consequence, he may have missed much important detail obscured (among other vegetation) by fully-grown bracken, blackberry scrub and nettles. In parts of the course of the Dyke in Gloucestershire the overgrowth of vegetation made his task insuperable.[75]

Fox opened his detailed account by recording the lengths of earthwork in north Flintshire that he thought could be demonstrated were parts of Offa's Dyke.[76] The excavations at and in the vicinity of Brynbella Mound (Whitford parish), and of 'Ysceifiog Circle', were reported. These earthworks appear to be, even from these initial accounts, prehistoric in character. A description of the undoubted length of Dyke that descends a spur (and is massive enough to have a road along its crest) south of Treuddyn then opened the account of its course in south Flintshire and into Denbighshire.[77] In the account, Fox illustrated his observations in reference to a table of measurements and the first seven profile drawings of the undoubted Dyke. He concluded with a description of the results of his excavations south of the Post Office in Ffrith village, and at Ffrith Hall, just to the south and still within the valley of the Cedigog (Figure 2.6).

Fox's view of Offa's Dyke is set out cumulatively in the 1955 volume in the series of discussions and commentaries which in each chapter followed those sections of text that provided the key descriptive accounts. The first extensive reflection on the overall character of the Dyke is to be found in a commentary section towards the end of the east Denbighshire and north-west Shropshire chapter which described the 'three great stretches' of the Dyke between Plas Power Park, Bersham (east of Wrexham) and the river Vyrnwy.[78] This commentary section comprised sub-sections that discussed, in turn, the course of the Dyke, its character, farmsteads or settlements close by, the layout across the area concerned, the unity of design, the technique of construction, possible political influences on its alignment, and what Fox termed 'The Will, and the Task'.[79] A number of key conclusions concerning the Dyke are made therein. The 'will', which combined a keen 'eye for country' with undeviating purpose and an intimate knowledge of the districts through which the linear earthwork ran, was deemed to be that of King Offa himself.

Fox regarded differences in construction method north and south of the Dee as possibly indicating that different lengths may have been dug by different work-gangs. However, that a major change in direction to take in Selattyn Hill occurred not at the Dee but in the Ruabon area was, he asserted, evidence of the workings of a single authority. Fox explained the need for that change by the powerful presence of the Kingdom of Powys locally, which meant that the course the Dyke took was the result of an accommodation between the British leadership and that of the Mercians. The Iron Age hill-top enclosure of Pen-y-gardenn overlooks the Dyke close to the point at Ruabon where the change occurs, and according to Fox the 'tactical inferiority' of the position that the linear earthwork follows indicates that the fort must have been in the hands of the people of Powys. The existence of the 'Pillar of Eliseg', a memorial stone erected by a ninth-century King of Powys in the extreme north-west of the Vale of Llangollen, was cited in support not only of the fact, but also the date, of the deemed resurgence of that kingdom.[80]

FIGURE 2.6 The site of Fox's 1927 excavation by Ffrith post office, Denbighshire.
The east front of the chapel at Ffrith is immediately recognisable from Fox's (1955) Plate IXb. Fox's excavation here discovered what he thought was a 'marker post' beneath the bank, although this feature could have been associated with the Romano-British settlement, material from which was both sealed beneath, and re-deposited in, the bank. In 1927, the bank of the Dyke was a very substantial feature on this eastern side of the main village street, but has since then been mostly cleared away. In recent years, more of the Romano-British settlement here has been recorded, lying mostly to the east of the street, during various episodes of development work.

Discussion of earthworks and other features on or close to the Dyke, such as the 'out-work' at Mellington Park, the Kerry Ridgeway 'gap' and the Lower Short Ditch (to the west of the Dyke and dug across the same ridgeway route) are key features of Fox's account of the course through eastern Montgomeryshire, which also included a note on his excavation near Forden.[81] The commentary accompanying this account is where Fox's thoughts about the nature of alignments and what can be deduced from them were set out fully. Fox explained how the Dyke from Llanymynech north of the Vyrnwy to the Kerry Ridgeway south of the Vale of Montgomery could be interpreted in such a way as to enable reconstruction of the eighth-century landscape that immediately preceded the construction project.[82] In brief, straight alignments were stated to occur where arable land or open grazing or scrubland had existed in the eighth century; more sinuous routings were considered to reflect the presence of eighth-century woodland.

The course and characteristics of the Dyke in the 'mountain zone' were described in the chapter that dealt with 'South Shropshire and East Radnorshire'.[83] The section here that summarised the profile of the Dyke contrasted lengths of 'normal' type construction with 'the 'hedge-bank' dyke with eastern ditch or spoil trench' which was 'met with for the first time in the survey' in this zone.[84] Fox cited examples of the latter both north and south of Knighton. Arguably, this difference in built form going southwards from Llanfair Hill is more sudden in its appearance than Fox indicated, and first occurs near Selley Hall.[85] Two potential gaps or gateways were noted at length by Fox in the chapter, and the discussion of earthworks reverted here to a consideration largely of the significance of the location of presumed later prehistoric forts (Castle Ring and Burfa Camp, both in Radnorshire) and a series of smaller promontory forts or simple enclosures (in the south Shropshire hills). Fox was particularly struck by the variation in build in this zone and considered briefly whether this was due to a multi-phase construction. He dismissed this idea due to the unity of placement of the Dyke in a layout that was 'governed by (locational) considerations affecting the whole traverse of over 21 miles.'[86]

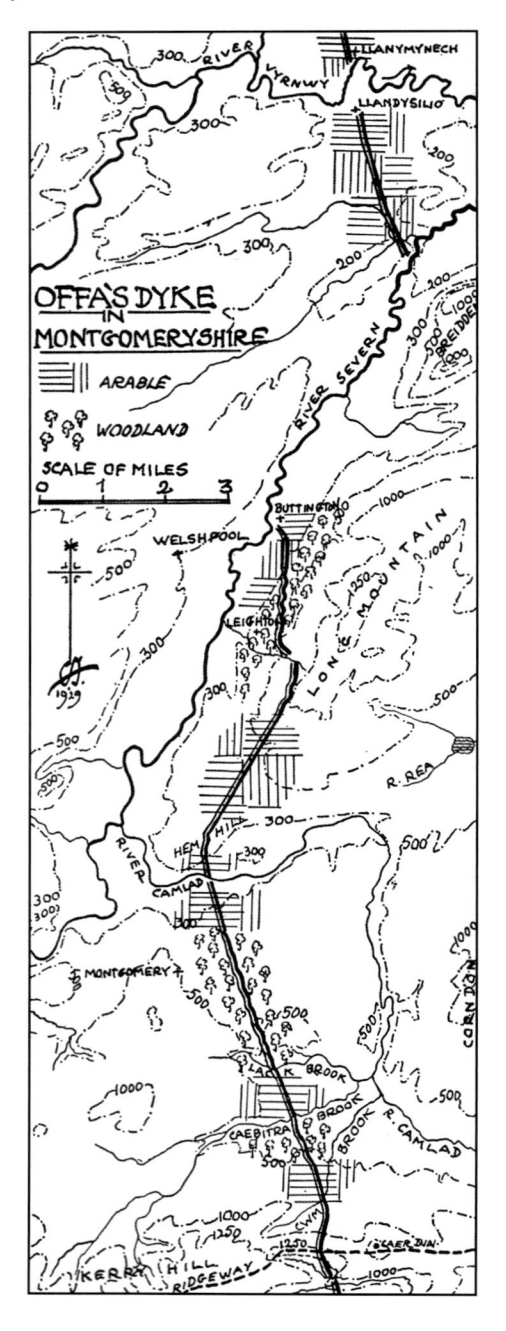

In further discussion Fox posed the question 'How then are we to reconcile the unity of the Dyke (in terms of how it is placed in the landscape) with its diversity of structure, more extreme (here) than in any sector we have hitherto

FIGURE 2.7 Offa's Dyke in Montgomeryshire (Fox, 1955, Figure 52) *Based upon his views on the comparative straightness of alignments, Fox 'reconstructed' eighth-century visibility conditions to suggest contrasting open-ness of the landscape and existing land-uses. The straightness of some stretches, as directly south of 'Hem Hill' are a reflection of modern boundary fences, however, while the deviations further south in the Vale of Montgomery are more minor than suggested here.* REPRODUCED COURTESY OF THE CAMBRIAN ARCHAEOLOGICAL ASSOCIATION.

studied?' To answer this, Fox defined 'the three constructional types (*weak, normal, reinforced*)' and related them to the 'physiography' of this sector. In the northern half, Fox noted that the Dyke was 'usually of *normal* type with occasional *reinforced* portions'[87] In the southern half, most lengths were in contrast 'of *weak* type, with occasional *normal* portions.' For Fox, this was explicable through reference to the 'short dykes' of the 'mountain zone'. These are present, and are often particularly strong, either on ridge-tops where passage on an east–west alignment was likely, or across valleys. As such, Fox saw them as localised efforts to prevent raiding from the west into newly-colonised areas of Mercian settlement. Offa's Dyke was, according to Fox, either of 'normal' or 'reinforced' form in just such locations, because these areas 'formed the chief route of raiding highlanders', while the areas with long straight alignments in valleys marked open (arable or pasture) farmland where 'the Mercian frontiersman was in the eighth century firmly planted'.[88]

Fox's proposition that the short dykes represented an early advance by the Mercians into British territory was complemented by his conclusion that the line of the Dyke to the east of these dykes represented a retreat from such a forward position. This view requires that if the Dyke was not at the 'leading edge' of English settlement, its construction must have involved ceding territory to the west. In adopting this view Fox assumed also that the Dyke and the frontier were one and the same entity, and this precluded considering the alternative possibility that the earthwork had been placed instead in the midst of a managed 'frontier zone', with land to the west as well as to the east of its line settled by English frontiers-people. Fox amplified his interim conclusion that the Dyke represented a negotiated line in a final section of this chapter, in which he went on to suggest that the building practices observable on dykes such as the 'Double Deyches' at Kerry could be seen also at the Hergan section of Offa's Dyke. He concluded that in this 'mountain zone' one could witness the genesis of the whole Offa's Dyke building project, and he raised the question of how the Dyke operated while not being 'manned'.[89]

The final Offa's Dyke chapter in Fox's *Survey* monograph traced the intermittent sections of surviving Dyke through north Herefordshire to the river Wye, and described the two 'Row Ditches' in Hereford and the 'dyke' at Perrystone Court north of Ross-on-Wye, before tracing the Dyke from English Bicknor in Gloucestershire through to Sedbury cliff on the Severn estuary.[90] 20 pages of the commentary section within this chapter were devoted to explaining the gaps and absences of the Dyke in Herefordshire, and its varied character in Gloucestershire. For instance, Fox noted how the intermittent stretches of the Dyke in north Herefordshire between Rushock Hill and the Wye at Garnons correspond almost exactly to the geographical limits of the Old Red Sandstone. In his view, before the medieval period this terrain was cloaked in dense woodland. He supported this assertion with place-name evidence relating both to individual farms and to settlements here that contain a '-leah' element, signifying (as was widely thought at the time) that they originated as woodland clearings.[91]

The alternation between the 'weak', or 'boundary bank', form of Dyke construction and the 'normal' lengths on the hills to the east of (and above) the lower Wye valley Fox again explained in reference to contrasts in vegetation cover, the former corresponding to the occurrence of eighth-century woodland, the latter to arable land or open country. He also adduced a further three reasons why the Dyke was built in the lower Wye valley in a context where it could be supposed that the river might have served as a boundary just as well. The first was 'the proximity of a belt of habitable land in Welsh occupation' in the fertile area around the former (Romano-British) Silurian capital at Caerwent just to the west of Chepstow.[92] The second was the opportunity afforded by spectacular views in all directions from the Dyke in the Madgett Hill area southwards, for surveillance of the whole Wye/Severn confluence area. The third was the existence of a large royal manor, Tidenham, that, as was clear from a charter of AD 956 that ceded it to the monks of Bath Abbey, 'in its organisation, and in the services due from its tenants, … was distinctively English'.[93]

Fox seized upon an obscure element of the Tidenham charter of 956 AD that referred to a holding 'below the dyke', presumed to be on the Beachley

FIGURE 2.8 From Sarnesfield Cross south towards Burton Hill, Herefordshire

The line of the bank that represents the Dyke here today is outlined by snow against the hillside south of the road from Weobley to Yazor, west of Hereford. The earthwork here climbs the lower west-facing flank of Burton Hill towards the spur running down from Ladylift. It was in this part of the landscape that the Dyke was such a prominent feature 'on the hills', according to Aubrey's seventeenth-century informants.

peninsula. This area was leased to 'Welsh shipmen' who, he deduced, not only controlled the ferry crossing across the Severn to Aust in Gloucestershire, but also the timber trade up the Wye.[94] He concluded that 'the frontier was drawn and the Dyke built upon the plateau edge above the Wye mainly because, the trade along the lower reaches of the river being in the hands of the Welsh, it was inconvenient to make the river the political boundary…..coastal shipping, right down to medieval times, required access up to the head of the tidal waters of a river, and Offa's Dyke on the lower Wye had to extend high enough (that is, far enough northwards) to cover with a reasonable margin the tidal traffic'.[95]

Fox's account of the survey of Wat's Dyke began with a reprise of Thomas Churchyard's 1587 poem and Thomas Pennant's late eighteenth-century account, each of which, as already noted, distinguish clearly between Offa's and Wat's Dykes.[96] After describing its course in identical fashion to the various chapters on Offa's Dyke, Fox made the important observation that, while possessing throughout 'a considerable bank and well-made western ditch' Wat's Dyke lacked a number of the built form features that so characterised Offa's Dyke.[97] An equally important observation was that Wat's Dyke as a bank and ditch earthwork is consistently 'moderate' in profile size, especially in contrast to Offa's Dyke. The latter he described as 'being on average at least half as large again as Wat's Dyke'.[98] While observing the existence of a number of Iron Age forts either on the course of the Wat's Dyke or near it, Fox noted that, again as with Offa's Dyke, there is nothing to suggest that any active use was made of them.

There is no evidence that Fox substantially revised his interpretation of the nature and purpose of Offa's Dyke between his completion of the field-based survey in 1931, his writing of the British Academy address in 1940, and his publication of the monograph in 1955. The 1940 address was reproduced in full in the 1955 volume, and in a series of sections it set out Fox's definitive conclusions concerning both Offa's and Wat's Dykes. He began with a re-assertion that Offa's Dyke extended from sea to sea, 'completely delimiting the Anglo-Saxon state of Mercia and the Welsh principalities'.[99] The frontier so defined spanned 149 miles (240 km), although 'the length of constructed earthwork is 81 miles'. Fox then emphasised the fundamental importance of an understanding of alignments in the course of the Dyke, to its character and purpose. He went on to re-iterate the view both that Offa's Dyke marked an agreed frontier, and that its unitary character underlines the veracity of its attribution to Offa.[100] Variations in the form of the earthwork in the areas south of the Vale of Montgomery nonetheless arose from giving priority to the ridge-way sections while 'the intervening spaces were filled in later and less effectively'.

Fox saw further variation throughout the course of the Dyke as deriving from inconsistency in the control of the implementation of the work locally, while 'the traverse, in meticulous detail, was in competent hands' which he envisaged having the stamp of direct royal authority.[101] He then reprised his 'discovery' that the distribution of eighth-century fields and woodland could be deduced from the variable form of the Dyke in different locations. In the next section of the essay, he summarised the implications of his study of Wat's Dyke and the other central Marches dykes: the former was sufficiently similar in form and conception to be close in date to Offa's Dyke, while the shorter dykes represented preliminary attempts to secure the western frontier.[102] The proximity of the central part of the Dyke north and south of the Severn to the Mercian heartland around Tamworth inevitably meant, in Fox's view, both that priority was given to building these sectors, and that better-marshalled resources were devoted to it.[103] Significantly, Fox attributed the uniqueness of the Dyke, as the only example of the class of monument, linear dyke, 'to which the name of the builder has consistently been attached' as representing the heroic vision widely appreciated by the Anglo-Saxon aristocracy, of 'a life's work consciously designed for posterity'.[104] He noted moreover that the close correlation of the line of Offa's Dyke with the modern 'boundary line of Cymru' was fundamentally attributable to the physiographic reality of an upland zone bordering upon a lowland one.[105]

There are several shortcomings in Fox's work, and some of these are highlighted below in reference to the views of his recent critics. Some of these criticisms, such as an over-reliance on the concept of the presence of dense woodlands to explain gaps in its course, are today (and in light of a more sophisticated understanding of vegetation and land-use history) seen to be justified.[106] The deductions Fox made about the eighth-century landscape along those parts of the course of the Dyke immediately south of the middle Severn valley probably over-determined how he interpreted other stretches further south, and in particular how he explained the less than obvious course south of Rushock Hill in north Herefordshire, and the nature of the Gloucestershire lengths.

Nonetheless, a number of the criticisms themselves, such as the charge that Fox somehow 'invented' the attribution of the Gloucestershire sections of the Dyke to Offa, are both inaccurate and unwarranted.[107] Although it has already been remarked how the season during which most observations were made was the least favourable from the standpoint of clarity of visibility, Fox nonetheless produced a record that adequately characterised most of the large-scale, and many of the localised, features of the Dyke, and produced both commentary upon and mapping of aspects of its structural variability. Moreover, the approach that Fox took to selective excavation was fully in accord with the standards of his day, and the logic of their location seems eminently sensible today. Unfortunately for him, some of the key locations that he chose for such exploration, such as at Forden in Montgomeryshire, or Garnons near Kenchester in Herefordshire, did not produce the unequivocal results he had hoped for; but it was not the strategy itself that was flawed.[108] His insistence upon the complexity of the formation and the sophistication of the location of the Dyke is, moreover, in our view entirely appropriate. What Fox showed was that the build and routing of the Dyke merit close field-based observation and analysis, and its interpretation requires an understanding of the nature both of landscape and of politics in the world of eighth- and early ninth-century Mercia. Both these needs are as real today as they were in his time.

Frank Noble and 'Offa's Dyke Reviewed'

Frank Noble was a history teacher who, having obtained a post at Knighton Secondary School early in his career in 1951, developed a close and long-standing interest in all matters relating to Offa's Dyke. He walked and re-walked the earthwork, in particular throughout the known and projected course of the Dyke south of the Severn from Welshpool, and studied the available documentary evidence for especially the medieval history of the communities through which it passed.[109] Through observation over a number of years he identified many specific and localised problems with Fox's description and questioned his overall thesis concerning its purpose. He made an especially intensive search for the Dyke in Gloucestershire because this was the part that he felt that Fox had dealt with least satisfactorily.[110]

Another concern that Noble had was that Fox had not engaged closely enough with the question of what light the study of local historical documents could throw upon the circumstances of the building of the Dyke in the eighth century. Noble therefore used later charter evidence and other documentary sources to throw light upon the form and route of the Dyke, especially in an attempt to resolve the difficulties that he thought Fox had, to some extent, himself created in his discussions of the lower Wye sections. To support his more sophisticated reading of the cultural landscape of south Herefordshire and northern Monmouthshire, Noble introduced a renewed focus upon what he regarded as a key document in any understanding of relations between the Welsh and the English in the Wye valley: the 'Ordinance concerning the Dunsaete'.[111] This undated text has been thought likely to belong to the reign of the West Saxon king of the English, Athelstan, in the tenth century, although this has recently been questioned.[112] Noble argued that its description of a situation in which there was a people divided by a river and by their Welsh or English ethnicity fits a boundary situation obtaining in south Herefordshire either side of the Wye and originating in the eighth century under Offa.

In drawing together his field and documentary researches, Noble launched into a detailed critical review of Fox's treatment and description of the monument across Gloucestershire, Herefordshire and Powys, and he set out his conclusions in a dissertation for Birmingham University.[113] This was completed in 1977 and part of it was published posthumously in 1983 under Margaret Gelling's editorship.[114] Noble reiterated an interpretation of the Dyke as a complete linear monument forming part of a coherent frontier stretching northwards from the shores of the Severn at Beachley. However he argued, in contra-distinction to Fox's view of the Dyke as marking an 'agreed frontier', that it had instead been located entirely in the Mercian interest, and may have included stand-alone palisaded sections similar to the (by then) archaeologically-attested Saxon defences of Hereford.[115] For Noble, therefore, Offa's Dyke was not 'negotiated', nor was it designed to incorporate natural obstacles such as dense forest. Rather it was a physically continuous frontier following a line 'which could be patrolled or ridden' intended to be a militarily enforceable barrier to movement eastwards from the uplands.[116] Moreover, the 'control line' that Noble envisaged the Dyke to have formed was, for him, 'set back inside Mercian territory', deliberately comprising a barrier slightly rearward of the real frontier of settlement within a border zone.[117]

Noble's detailed arguments, as published in the 1983 monograph, are set out in the two chapters of his dissertation that Gelling considered were the most closely and effectively argued. They comprised, respectively, accounts of 'the southern border' and 'the central border'. The first of these chapters opened with a section on the course of the Dyke in the Lower Wye Valley north to Brockweir. From the outset, Noble was highly critical of Fox's evaluation of the physical evidence here. For example, he noted how the north–south 'Elm Villa

FIGURE 2.9 At Sedbury Park, Gloucestershire: view towards Chepstow

This prospect along the inside of the bank is from the hillside north of the Dyke within the former Sedbury Park. This point is visible at left in Figure 1.5, but here the view is north-west and in the opposite direction. The roofs of houses in the southern suburbs of Chepstow are visible in the background here, and Buttington Tump stood on the crest of the rise at centre-right, now obscured by trees.

bank' earthwork on the Gloucestershire side of the river opposite Chepstow (that Fox had dismissed as a medieval field lynchet) was actually part of Offa's Dyke and had served to block the inherited line of the Roman road running west from Gloucester to Caerwent. According to Noble, this had diverted traffic to a new crossing where the medieval town of Chepstow developed.[118] He inferred, possibly quite correctly, that the 'Chepstow' or 'market meeting-place' was actually a creation of the Anglo-Saxons as a locus for trade with the Welsh merchants of Gwent and Morgannwg.[119]

A further part of Noble's account then dealt with the course of the Dyke from Brockweir to Redbrook, at the limit of the continuously recognisable earthwork. As noted above, particularly in the vicinity of Highbury Farm, Fox had found the vegetation so dense that it proved impossible for him to follow its course locally.[120] Between 1930 and the time when, in 1963, Noble and an accompanying group of people traced this part of the course of the Dyke, the scrub had grown into trees, and it proved much easier to trace the earthwork.[121] Noble noted the inconsistency of Fox's reading of the Dyke here in dismissing as a modern boundary feature a stony bank that represents a sudden transition from a major to a minor scale, when he had no such problem at a location such as Jenkins Allis south of Knighton where just such a transition was equally sudden.[122] Noble's section on the frontier through the Wye valley northwards featured arguments which required an appreciation of the documentary evidence for the medieval Deanery of Archenfield that had been beyond Fox's scope. It moreover benefitted from the preliminary results of ground-breaking research on the Llandaff charters only just becoming available to scholarship in the mid-1970s.[123]

The final section of Noble's chapter on the 'southern border' traced the intermittent course north from the Wye in north Herefordshire west of Bridge Sollers to Rushock Hill. Here, Noble questioned the geographical and environmental arguments that Fox had used to adduce dense eighth-century forest to explain the apparent absence of the Dyke locally, and particularly in the 5 miles (8 km) south from Holmes Marsh. Rather than relying upon arguments from soils and geology, or place-names, as Fox had done, Noble pointed to the 'remarkable tangle of parish and 'Hundred' boundaries in the Sarnesfield area' which he compared to the situation in the 'denns' of the Kentish Weald and other areas known to have comprised ancient woodlands. Given the prominent rises in the topography, and the inter-visibility of hill crests with both Ladylift Clump to the south and Rushock Hill to the north, Noble felt that either 'a ride through the woods, or a palisade line across open ground could easily have been aligned between them.'[124]

Noble organised his account of the 'central border' into five sections, the first of which dealt with that part of the course of the Dyke that extends north from Rushock Hill to Selley.[125] This is the length of the Dyke that most routinely alternates between 'weak' and more substantially-built lengths of the Dyke, including some locations – as on Hawthorn Hill between Presteigne and Knighton, and on Panpunton Hill north of Knighton – where there is a prominent and continuous ditch on the eastern side of the Dyke without, in several stretches it would appear, a western ditch at all. Throughout this account, Noble seemingly agrees broadly with Fox's assessment that the presence of a 'weak' length of bank and ditch equates to an area that was heavily wooded at the time of construction of the Dyke, while disagreeing with several of Fox's detailed arguments about the nature of the landscape concerned.

This is particularly the case in respect to Fox's deductions about the eighth-century extent of arable. For instance, at Yew Tree Farm, Discoed (Figure 2.10), Noble saw the massive scale of the dyke as it descends to the river Teme as indicative of it being 'the major control on an important route into Mercia' rather than having anything to do with Fox's postulated (but to Noble implausible) Anglo-Saxon clearance or cultivation of the steep north-facing slopes here.[126] Noble also used this section of the second chapter to discuss the question of gateways, identifying at least three such gateways – in agreement with and in amplification of Fox – in the area between Pen Offa near Discoed and Ffrydd Hill above Knighton.[127]

In a second section, on the 'short dykes' (and again mirroring Fox's approach in singling these out for discussion), Noble proposed the idea that many if not all of them may have served to delimit the bounds of the early Anglo-Saxon kingdom of the 'Westerna' or Magonsaete. Among other observations, he suggested that the Long Mynd dykes were most likely to have been of prehistoric date, which they have since been proved to be through excavation and chronometric dating.[128]

The remaining sections of the chapter were devoted to the 'Clun Forest Upland', the Vale of Montgomery, and the frontier 'Along the Severn Valley'. In the first of these he again showed how Fox's orthodoxy of straight alignments signifying open landscape had misled him into supposing the unlikely scenario of extensive arable farming in thin soils at heights of between 350 m and 400 m OD. In the second section, Noble questioned Fox's claim that the Dyke north of Brompton Hall followed a 'sinuous trace', before noting the circumstances whereby the (post-1536) redefinition of parish boundaries produced the unusual circumstance in the Vale of Montgomery that they largely followed the line of the Dyke. He saw the disposition of Welsh parishes to the west and English ones to the east here as a deliberate historical projection back to the assumed circumstances of the eighth-century construction of the Dyke.

The focus of the final section of the chapter was upon what could be deduced from the course of the Dyke using documentary material, especially in relation to the section to the east of Leighton. Meanwhile he used Welsh documentary references and the notes of the Ordnance Surveyors making the revision of 1906–8 (since destroyed in wartime air-raids) to suggest that there existed a continuation of Offa's Dyke on the right bank of the Severn beyond Buttington, tracing a route near Trewern and Criggion.[129]

Noble also introduced some ideas about the correlation of situation and scale

FIGURE 2.10 Offa's Dyke at Yew Tree Farm, Discoed, crossing the Lugg valley

The Dyke, seen here from the south-east, descends the north-facing slope in the foreground in a series of straight lengths, which continue directly across the floodplain of the river Lugg. On the opposite side of the valley, however, the concern appears to have been to achieve oversight of the valley from the north-west by tracing a sinuous course around the edge of the west-facing scarp. Noble contradicted Fox's view that these differences derived from pre-existence differences in eighth-century land-use, citing this location as an example of a place where Fox's ideas failed to convince.

of the Dyke that deserve closer attention. This is most clear in his discussion of the section of Offa's Dyke occupying the heights above the Wye opposite Tintern. Here, Noble remarked that the prominence of the bluff either side of the Devil's Pulpit was such that Fox had observed how striking the Dyke would be as seen from Tintern as a skyline feature when newly dug (see Figure 2.11). He explained that the massive proportions of the Dyke here were likely to have been deliberately designed to overshadow what he thought was still likely to have been a stronghold of the kings of Gwent.[130]

The 'review' of Offa's Dyke that Noble conducted was a useful corrective to some of the over-simplifications that Fox had made, and it also demonstrated two further ways in which a fuller account of the circumstances of the borderlands before and after Offa might be achieved. The first was that detailed reference can be made to the available local documentation for particular parts of the passage of the Dyke through a landscape rich in traditions and associations from Welsh literature and information from medieval documents.

The second was that the observations made concerning features of the Dyke in individual localities should be undertaken without the prior definition of 'overarching' principles that over-determine how the particular is viewed. However, Noble himself is open to criticisms otherwise levelled at Fox. For example, the numbers of entrances he envisaged would have rendered the Dyke inoperable as a barrier, at least in some locations such as the Vale of Montgomery. He adduced no evidence in support of his idea of a 'cleared ride'

FIGURE 2.11 The Devil's Pulpit length seen from Tintern (Fox, 1955, Plate XXXVI)

This is an example of a photograph taken in winter, beyond one of Fox's summer survey seasons. Tintern would have been readily accessible from Cardiff by motor-car, and Fox clearly wanted to illustrate how the Dyke followed the crest of the precipitous slope overlooking scarp above the river Wye here. It was Noble, however, who emphasised how the Dyke was built in a particularly impressive way along this stretch, specifically to dominate the ground on the Tintern (west) side of the valley.

REPRODUCED COURTESY OF THE CAMBRIAN ARCHAEOLOGICAL ASSOCIATION.

providing an alternative to the existence of an earthwork in Herefordshire north (or south) of the Wye. Nor did he do any more than presume that the 'Ordinance concerning the Dunsaete' referred to provisions already in place up to two centuries earlier than Athelstan's time.

A corollary of Noble's work was that, having supervised his dissertation and edited its partial publication, Margaret Gelling was moved to devote a chapter of her general survey book on *The West Midlands in the Early Middle Ages* to a consideration of the context and impact of 'The Building of the Dyke'.[131] Besides rehearsing the familiar arguments concerning who was responsible for the Dyke and what it represented, Gelling's particular contributions here were to discuss the relevance and date of parish boundaries, and of English place-names west of the Dyke. This served to emphasise the importance of Archenfield/Ergyng in understanding the south Herefordshire zone of the frontier, and to provide further amplification of the concept of the existence of a frontier patrol by reference to the distribution of *Burhtun*, *Burhweard* and other inferentially early place-names.[132]

A modern 'Offa's Dyke Project'

Frank Noble was not the only person for whom the questions remaining after Fox's survey proved an irresistible draw to further field-based study. Following on from his work on the late ninth- or early tenth-century Burghal Hidage

2 Studying Offa's Dyke: a cumulative inheritance

document which listed the fortified places or 'burhs' of Wessex, the historian-archaeologist David Hill pondered what light it might throw on how the building of Offa's Dyke had been organised. He also wanted to see whether further fieldwork could improve understanding of the structure and date of the Dyke, in reference also to Wat's Dyke. The project he devised and initiated was later assisted by Margaret Worthington and other associates, and it was eventually carried out across three decades from 1971. From the outset the project comprised a series of test excavations on Offa's Dyke and Wat's Dyke but by the mid-1990s it had encompassed not only many such interventions but also detailed survey of several lengths of Offa's Dyke, particularly in the sections north and south of the Severn in the Welshpool area.

In the early years Hill published a number of statements that set out a prospectus for his studies, and gave some indication of the preliminary results of the fieldwork.[133] The longest of these statements merits discussion here, because it illustrates the thinking behind the work, and his early conclusions concerning both dykes.[134] He noted how few excavations had taken place on either dyke since the end of Fox's field studies in 1934, and following a small-scale excavation conducted with the help of part-time students at a threatened part of Wat's Dyke, at the Exchange Station, Wrexham, he concluded that 'Sir Cyril Fox in his British Academy publication had lulled students into the feeling that the system of Dykes was explained, examined, and that nothing further needed doing. It is now our conviction that this is untrue, that the Dyke system is not understood, and that *some* of the theories advanced by Fox in the twenties and thirties are wrong and deal with only aspects of the problem.'[135]

By the end of 1976, 23 sites had been examined in one way or another on Offa's Dyke between Pinner's Hole, Knighton, in the south and Coedpoeth west of Wrexham in the north, and on Wat's Dyke between Old Oswestry in the south and Soughton near Mold in the north.[136] Hill suggested that the earlier among these excavations 'had demonstrated marking out banks under both Wat's and Offa's Dykes', and expressed the view that 'When it is realised that Offa's Dyke is said to be 149 miles long, of which some 81 miles were built, and that Wat's Dyke is 38 miles long, of which 23 miles were built, then the size, in fact the enormity of the problem may be grasped.'[137]

The initial focus on fieldwork results in the 1977 paper was on two investigations of 'gateways' that Fox had postulated to have existed at Dalford, near Whittington, on Wat's Dyke, and at Orseddwen, Selattyn, on Offa's Dyke (Figure 2.12). The work at the latter, involving a 6.3 × 2 m trench, is indicative of the small scale of interventions made by the project, in a context where the earthwork, at least at Orseddwen, is likely to have been over 30 m in east–west extent. While the results appeared informative in the discovery of a ditch less than 2.0 m wide and 0.5 m deep, if a larger ditch had been present beyond the trench, it would have been missed.[138] The bulk of the paper, some six pages, was then devoted to reporting upon the ten excavations carried out on Wat's Dyke. The project investigations had shown that the gaps along the course of

Wat's Dyke that Fox had noted and had regarded as explicable either in terms of the presence of ravines, or as a result of the presence of 'dense forest' in the eighth century, simply did not exist. In these areas, the ditch was continuous, but the bank had been levelled.[139]

Although draft reports were prepared, for instance in 1980, that summarised the results of the first few years of the project, only highly summary 'bulletins' of the results were published thereafter.[140] By the year 2000, after another 20 years of short seasons of survey and excavation undertaken as a University of Manchester external studies field school, the first in a series of articles setting out a new view of the Dyke, its built form, purpose and extent was published.[141] The view of Offa's Dyke that Hill outlined in this and other publications depended for much of its force on the claim that the University of Manchester's Offa's Dyke Project had demonstrated that Wat's Dyke was an entirely continuous earthwork throughout its course from Maesbury north to Basingwerk.[142] The techniques used to establish this continuity in Wat's Dyke did not similarly establish the existence of the ditch of the Dyke in the 'gaps' in Offa's Dyke, and it was therefore concluded that Offa's Dyke could not be regarded as having existed in areas where there are presently gaps.[143]

Only the 'continuous Dyke', that is, the earthwork comprising all the sections of Offa's Dyke to the north of Herrock Hill, was henceforward to be

FIGURE 2.12 View north towards Orseddwen, north-west of Oswestry

This is the same stretch of Dyke that is seen, also from the south, from the air in Figure 1.15, with the west flank of Selattyn Hill rising to the east at right of the photograph. This was the site of one of an excavation for the 'Offa's Dyke Project', in which the ditch that was located and defined appeared to be very shallow. The way in which the Dyke crosses the stream in front of the farmhouse here exhibits exactly the same practice of extending forwards on either side of the valley facing westwards, as it does in much larger valleys.

PHOTOGRAPH: ADAM STANFORD/AERIAL-CAM, COPYRIGHT RESERVED.

FIGURE 2.13 Offa's Dyke at Garnons, near Kenchester, to the west of Hereford

This view, looking south-west towards the river Wye and beyond to the Black Mountains, shows the line of Offa's Dyke crossing diagonally down-slope (by the hedge-row) from right to left. The Dyke in this part of the landscape was known to Aubrey's informants in the seventeenth century. It was also noted by nineteenth-century observers such as Hartshorne. The camera is positioned on the lane that follows the line of the Roman road west of Kenchester, close to the point where Fox's excavation in the autumn of 1927 failed to locate the point of intersection of that road by the Dyke.

regarded as the genuine, or 'Basic' Dyke.[144] In contrast, southwards, all the sections of dyke in Herefordshire north of the Wye and in Gloucestershire east of that river, were to be regarded as short lengths of unconnected earthwork, or cross-valley dykes of the same kind that the north Herefordshire Rowe Ditch undoubtedly is. Having eliminated these other works, the location of the continuous, 'Basic Dyke' was readily explicable to Hill and his research partner Margaret Worthington by noting that it corresponds closely to the presumed eastern boundary of the Kingdom of Powys, a polity that extended 'at its widest limits from the neighbourhood of Mold to the river Wye near Glasbury and Hay throughout the period AD 600–850'.[145]

A significant problem with this application of an 'Occam's razor' approach to defining the extent of the Dyke is that it involves ignoring a suite of questions that it in turn raises. So, for instance, just why the 'continuous' earthwork should stop so far short of the river Wye if Powys indeed extended southwards to it, is a question left un-posed, let alone unanswered.[146] A 'maximal' Powys was an entity that Nash-Williams defined in passing in 1950, and its extent was acknowledged to have waxed and waned considerably in that time.[147] Moreover, while the 'notional' mapping was of 'Wales in the late ninth century', this was based (as is evident when the reference not provided by Hill is traced) only upon the modern boundary between Wales and England.[148] 'Once the Dyke is seen to represent only the frontier between Powys and Mercia', Hill asserted, 'the remaining non-continuous other lengths of Dyke, and the longer gaps, are readily explicable: they concern the frontier between Mercia and 'Gwynedd' in the north, while 'The lands to the south were Ercing and Gwent'.[149]

Hill had already prepared the reader for the dismissal of the Gloucestershire part of the Dyke earlier in the article, in reference to the survey then recently carried out by Gloucestershire County Council archaeologists.[150] He stressed the intermittent and fragmentary nature of the Dyke as he claimed it had been recorded by the Gloucestershire team and concluded that 'There is no early (pre-1780) evidence for this isolated and anomalous earthwork being called 'Offa's Dyke''.[151] On the contrary, however, a length of this earthwork, close to the valley of the Mork Brook to the west of St Briavels, was specifically named 'Offedich' in a document of 1321.[152] Moreover, it is evident from reading the full report on the then-recent survey that the Gloucestershire linear earthwork that is so carefully placed along the scarp-edge overlooking the Wye in Gloucestershire possesses multiple locational and build features that mirror closely the form and placement of the Dyke elsewhere.[153]

Hill did acknowledge that 'truncating' Offa's Dyke in this way put his view 'at odds with the only near-contemporary source', Asser's *Life* of Alfred. However, he noted that the remark about Offa 'appears in a section of a semi-mythical nature' so need not be taken seriously, and could be compared with 'other early medieval descriptions of dykes which ran 'from sea to sea' when in reality they cover dry land only, depending for their length on the rivers at either end that connect them to the sea'.[154] He thought that in this way the statement could be disregarded because it had been used purely as a rhetorical device. Again, however, on the contrary: if Offa's Dyke merely connected such major rivers, why did it continue north of the Dee at all? Nonetheless, having cleared the ground in this way, Hill was able to establish with apparent certainty a context for the creation of Offa's Dyke in a particular episode of warfare as 'recorded' in the well-known but no longer legible inscription on the 'Pillar of Eliseg' near Llangollen (Figure 2.16). This is because in Edward Lluyd's transcription, and through much subsequent translation, this inscription appears to refer to warfare between King Elise's Powys and the kingdom of Mercia around the mid-eighth century. While this may have been the case, and while a Powysian attempt to reclaim land in the lowlands of Shropshire and Cheshire may have been one reason behind the decision to build Offa's Dyke, it does not necessarily explain the *extent* of Offa's Dyke either northwards or southwards from the river Dee.[155]

This article was published in 2000, at around the same time as Margaret Worthington's entry on Offa's Dyke in the *Blackwell Encyclopaedia of Anglo-Saxon England* in 1999. In that entry the hypothesis appears baldly as established fact. 'Offa's Dyke was built by Mercia against Powys', and 'extensive archaeological research since 1971 has shown that only the continuous sixty-four mile length is to be considered a part of the original design'.[156] It had, according to Worthington, also been established that there were no gateways through the earthwork, and that 'the Dyke was built as a continuous barrier acting as a deterrent to incursions by the Welsh'. Fox's work is again identified as in need of serious revision, and is relegated practically to having usefulness only as a point in time record of erosion: it 'remains a valuable record of the monument in 1931, as many lengths have subsequently been damaged or destroyed'.[157] Together, these articles paved the way for the book, *Offa's Dyke History and Guide*, produced jointly and published in 2003.

Offa's Dyke: History and Guide is avowedly a popular work, and this extends positively to a series of sections explaining, sometimes with the aid of cartoons, how the daily life of eighth-century England is relevant to the building of a dyke that we have no firm documentation for. Somewhat less positively, it may explain, but does not justify, a lack of attention to detail (for instance in referencing opinions adduced or observations made) and, at least in the first edition, the absence of a bibliography. Brief chapters introduced 'the background to Offa's reign', including a noting of the geography of Offa's attendance at church councils, and of his 'European' connections; and 'early studies' of the Dyke. This latter section highlighted, quite rightly, the 'sound common sense' of Professor John Earle in his mid-nineteenth-century musings on the possibilities of the existence of a border patrol linked to the operation of the Dyke.[158] However it went on to suggest that it was the work of the Ordnance Survey topographical surveyors that 'led to several unrelated portions to both north and south being marked on the maps as 'Offa's Dyke', and these were generally accepted by fieldworkers, including Cyril Fox (as fact)'.[159]

The core of the book then comprised an outline of 'the evidence', and the detail of much of this is discussed below.[160] However, this account did not amount to a full reporting of the work of the 'Offa's Dyke Project' overall, or even of that work minus the Wat's Dyke field studies. Rather, it was a description, in three parts, of the course of the 'Basic Dyke' from Rushock Hill to Treuddyn. This description was interspersed with brief, often single-paragraph, descriptions of the results of excavations along the way. There followed a series of discussion sections (on 'marking out features', 'gateways', 'river crossings', and 'fortifications'), some of which contained further reference to individual excavations.[161]

The conclusions, to which the fourth chapter was devoted, in effect begin with the final discussion section of the preceding chapter, entitled 'the monument', in which succinct generalisations are made 'after careful consideration of the 82 excavations we know to have taken place'.[162] So, for instance, the ditch is, 'with few exceptions' 2 m deep and 7 m wide, while a 'consistent relationship' exists between the crest of the bank and the centre of the ditch'.[163] It is stated unequivocally that evidence for marking out banks and posts has been found, suggesting the method used to lay out the course, and it reiterated the view that 'there appear to be no gateways through the original monument'.[164] The statements that 'This is a carefully laid out and constructed monument' in which 'any sinuosity in the line … (is due to its being) a carefully engineered defensive line that dominates the land to the west', and that 'This is a well thought out and planned structure that was not a panic response to a short-lived emergency' accord well with our own understanding of the monument, and indicates that the authors had appreciated the skill of the builders in producing these effects.¹⁶⁵

The revised interpretation of the historical context, very much as set out in 2000, provided the substance of the ten-page 'conclusions' of the book. In this view, 'It may be therefore that we should accept (Asser's statement about Offa's Dyke stretching from sea to sea) as no more than a literary device, a convenient expression, the use of which was already familiar in connection with other great fortifications.'¹⁶⁶ The 'Basic Dyke' tag had by this time been dropped, presumably because by 2003 this part of the Dyke was to be promoted as the entirety of the 'real' Offa's Dyke.¹⁶⁷ A further chapter set out the 'how and why' of the building of the Dyke, assisted by cartoons that helpfully included depictions of workers and 'ealdormen' re-drawn from later Anglo-Saxon manuscripts.¹⁶⁸ A final chapter then described 'other earthworks', several of which we regard as having, on the contrary, formed integral parts of Offa's Dyke and the frontier. The chapter recounted the fieldwork that led the authors to conclude that these earthworks were either different in time, or in purpose, to 'Offa's Dyke'. The substantial discussion of the lengths of linear earthwork between Rushock Hill and Garnons by the river Wye in Herefordshire require further consideration and will need to be taken as a starting point (together with our discussions of this region in Chapter 7, below) for further, more detailed, study of this area.¹⁶⁹

Again in *Offa's Dyke: History and Guide*, the Dyke lengths in Gloucestershire 'on the cliffs above the Wye Valley' were said to have 'little similarity to the form or siting of Offa's Dyke in the undisputed central area of the Welsh Marches'.¹⁷⁰

FIGURE 2.14 At Knighton: the site of 'Offa's Dyke Project' excavations in 1973

The form of the Dyke here may have been altered somewhat by its re-use as part of the defences of the medieval town of Knighton. Nonetheless, the abrupt right-angled turn eastwards as the bank and ditch of the Dyke meet the edge of the scarp above the river Teme (centre) is characteristic of the practice of making angled turns in prominent places, noted elsewhere along the course of the linear earthwork.

As is demonstrated later in the present book, this view is unsustainable upon closer scrutiny. However, matters were made worse by the statement that 'It was the acceptance of these lengths as Offa's Dyke by Cyril Fox that placed them on the Ordnance Survey maps' when previously they had been described as 'ancient entrenchments'.[171] This latter statement contradicted Hill's previous attribution of the advent of the naming of the Dyke north and south of the 'undisputed' part to those same Ordnance surveyors.[172] Yet neither the Ordnance Survey surveyors (who on some editions of their maps chose to be cautious and not to follow local tradition in naming the lengths concerned 'Offa's Dyke') nor Fox 'invented' the connection with Offa: this was, as noted above, a matter of provably medieval and later documentary record, or long-standing local traditions as recorded in the field.

Notwithstanding this contradictory evidence, Hill and Worthington sought to reinforce the point by describing the Devil's Pulpit earthwork and the long stretches of bank to north and south of it as 'some isolated stretches of apparent earthwork on the crest of the river cliffs, associated with quarrying', and suggested that the St Briavels Common lengths comprised a 'disparate group of features'.[173] This account bears little relation to the realities of the often monumental-scale linear earthwork that follows a near-continuous line for over four and a half miles (8.0 km) between St Briavels and Tidenham, and that is missing southwards from this mostly where quarrying has removed it.[174] Not only did Fox not 'invent' the Gloucestershire length of the Dyke, or record it incorrectly; but, as detailed above, most of the arguments that have been rehearsed as if newly developed in the various 'Offa's Dyke Project' statements of findings in recent years had in fact been discussed at some length in the first era of concerted debate in the nineteenth century.

That Hill and Worthington thought long and hard about the Dyke, and

FIGURE 2.15 The 'Pillar of Eliseg' to the north-west of Llangollen

The now-illegible inscription on this pillar, located close to the confluence of the river Eglwyseg with the Dee north-west of Llangollen, indicates that it was set up by Concenn, King of Powys sometime in the ninth century, to commemorate the martial exploits of his grandfather, Elise, against the Mercians. Although the lack of mention of warfare in this part of the frontier in the later eighth and early ninth centuries indicates that the Dyke may have successfully contained such aggression by then, the likely motivations for building the Dyke were more diverse and its effects more widely felt.

invested a huge amount of effort in tracing and documenting its course, especially in Shropshire and Montgomeryshire, cannot be doubted. However, their excavation strategy and scale of operations at individual sites has made it difficult for their efforts to bear fruit, and the published detail of the evidence is slight or altogether missing. The number of interventions sounds impressive, but with no dates obtained, many of the operations undertaken in unfavourable circumstances, and no published analysis of soils, sediments or palaeo-environmental evidence, the weight of interpretation placed upon the results is clearly too great to sustain the conclusions drawn. In particular, one can be critical about assertions that aspects such as the existence of marking-out features and the absence of gateways have now been adequately demonstrated: they have not.[175]

Equally problematical is the way that in recent years these authors have built an edifice of interpretation around the role of the Kingdom of Powys that cannot be upheld from the available evidence. The dismissal of the Gloucestershire lengths without having adduced evidence or arguments sufficient to carry the argument is equally problematical. In the abstract of his *Antiquaries Journal* article in 2000, Hill claimed that 'the interpretation presented here is based on the known earthwork and does not involve the need to explain away any perceived gaps'.[176] This is odd, given that at the centre of what he termed 'the continuous dyke' there appears to be a gap of fully 5 miles (8.0 km) along the river Severn, the reason for which is not entirely evident, unless it is simply assumed that a river could and did 'replace' its course here: and that it was the line of the frontier, rather than the presence of the Dyke alone, that was crucial to the enterprise of defining the western limits of Mercia.[177]

These are critical conclusions to have drawn regarding the Hill-Worthington programme, especially given the important role that the 'Offa's Dyke Project' has played in keeping interest in the great earthwork alive. However, they are necessary ones given how, albeit with caveats, their interpretive model now has a hold on the literature and has become a new orthodoxy.[178] Arguably, if Fox had a pre-occupation regarding the Dyke it was not, as Hill and Worthington claimed, with 'explaining away' the gaps, but rather with environmental factors determining its wider placement in the landscape, and with the details of a line determined by negotiation. Meanwhile, it could be argued instead that it was Hill and Worthington who pre-occupied themselves with establishing the presence or absence of the Dyke itself, and possible associated features, in particular locations.

Despite their close attention to detail and their over-arching interpretations, neither the 'Offa's Dyke Survey' of the 1920s to 1930s, nor the 'Offa's Dyke Project' of the closing decades of the twentieth century, undertook sufficient comparative analysis of the earthwork itself over its entire course. This is ironic, since both studies involved looking closely at Wat's Dyke, and made comparisons with the other linear dykes of the Welsh Marches. As we proceed through the second decade of the twenty-first century, another 'fresh look' at the Dyke is merited. This necessarily involves further detailed observation of its locational and build characteristics at individual locations. It must also involve, however, something that was lacking, for different reasons, from each of the major twentieth-century studies: that is, systematic comparison of the form of the Dyke at different locations along its length.[179]

A new era of study and commentary

Before going on to review briefly some more recent contributions to these debates, brief mention should be made of the contribution of another of the 'Offa's Dyke Project' associates. Marge Feryock, an extra-mural student based in the Presteigne area, contributed a chapter on Offa's Dyke to a book providing an overview of Mercian history from secondary sources, published in 2001.[180] Although the conclusions followed the Hill-Worthington orthodoxy, the field evidence adduced for Gloucestershire affirmed and augmented, rather than contradicted, some of the conclusions reached by Fox about this sector. Some of Feryock's reflections about the possible economic significance of this part of the Dyke have also successfully predicted the results of more recent research.[181]

In recent years, a more intensive series of archaeological field projects has been undertaken, especially in response to construction works affecting Wat's Dyke. New investigative and management work has also been undertaken by regional archaeological services such as the Gloucestershire survey already referred to, and Clwyd-Powys Archaeological Trust projects. The former involved the most detailed fully-reported length by length survey of any part of the Dyke undertaken since Fox, while the Clwyd-Powys Trust initiatives have included a comprehensive 'short-dykes' project in east-central Wales.[182] Under the auspices of Cadw: Welsh Heritage and English Heritage working in concert with other agencies such as the former Countryside Commission for Wales, Clwyd-Powys Archaeological Trust established the 'Offa's Dyke Archaeological Management Project'. This involved the conduct of a programme of conservation action co-ordinated by one of the authors of the present volume (IB) in the period 1999–2006.[183] It is from the latter initiative, in which both authors were involved, that a new phase of study, represented in part by this book, has developed.

Recent years have moreover seen Offa's Dyke and Wat's Dyke made the subject of further commentary and new syntheses, including in contributions on the world-wide web.[184] Paolo Squatriti has for example produced a fascinating meditation on the environmental impact of the Dyke's construction and how it stands as a kind of mediation between nature and culture.[185] He has also produced a substantial, closely documented, comparative study on the 'ditch digging' activities of the great kings of the early medieval world.[186] The latter in particular raises important questions concerning one among several reasons why Offa's Dyke may have been built.[187]

Further new historiographical studies have very recently been published, such as a major review by Ann Williams which has brought out further riches

FIGURE 2.16 The location of excavations at Plas Offa, Chirk, 2013

Excavations here late in 2013 were undertaken by staff of Clwyd-Powys Archaeological Trust in response to the worst recent case of damage to the monument, when unauthorised bulldozing of a 50 m stretch of the earthwork took place.

PHOTOGRAPH: ADAM STANFORD/ AERIAL-CAM, COPYRIGHT RESERVED.

in a meagre documentary record and a valuable summary of past studies. Its emphasis was nonetheless on how little has been firmly established about the Dyke, and it concluded, somewhat gloomily, that the Dyke 'is passing beyond the reach of history'.[188] Damian Tyler has also produced a concise survey of the readily-available historical and archaeological evidence, and of recent commentary.[189] This reiterates a number of the critical comments made above, and presents an 'ideological' interpretation of the purpose of Offa's Dyke that has much in common with a key aspect of the perspective set out in the present book.[190]

In some respects the most important new integrative writing, however, has been commentary arising from the field project already mentioned in Chapter 1 that involved excavation not of part of Offa's Dyke, but rather of a levelled, but not entirely destroyed, length of the bank and ditch of Wat's Dyke at Gobowen, north of Oswestry.[191] This meticulous investigation by Tim Malim and colleagues demonstrated what a 'longitudinal' excavated view of a dyke can reveal concerning the substructures of the bank and the form of the ditch, and what new dating methods can contribute to an understanding of its development. The perhaps surprising results of the dating programme for the site have led to further new (if necessarily limited) review of the archaeological evidence for both dykes, together again with some critical comparison with other early medieval dykes such at the Cambridgeshire dykes and Wansdyke.[192]

CHAPTER THREE

The Mercians: a border history

> Mercia or Mearc, an old English word that signified a *Limite*, for all the other Kingdomes bordered and confined upon it. This was the largest Kingdome by farre of all the rest.....augmented by Penda, who extended the marches thereof every way....But having come to the full period, within the revolution of 250 yeeres, fell at last into the dominion of the West-Saxons, after that the Danes had spoiled, weakened and wasted it many yeeres in all manner of barbarous hostility.
>
> William Camden, *Britannia*, 1588[1]

Neither the reign of King Offa, which spanned the second half of the eighth century, nor Offa's Dyke, which spanned the western margins of his kingdom, emerged without precedent: of kingship, or borders. Nonetheless, it is difficult to avoid the impression that the kingdom of Mercia came into prominence as if from nowhere in the midst of earlier Anglo-Saxon history.[2] The *Mierce* or 'border people' challenged the powerful Northumbrians in the seventh century, at some junctures in alliance with the leaders of the kingdoms, or confederacies, of Powys and Gwynedd. Their subsequent campaigns against these latter kingdoms permanently separated the Britons of the north from those of the west (in what became, respectively, north-western England and Wales). By the middle of the eighth century, moreover, not only had the Mercians in effect annexed their eastern neighbours in Lindsey and subordinated those in East Anglia, but they were also dominating (to a greater or lesser degree) all the English south of the river Humber.[3]

Despite the acknowledged fact that Offa's reign stands at the apex of this increase in Mercian power and domination, he remains a remarkably opaque figure historically, with no definite record, for example, even of where he was buried. While memory of Offa is enshrined instead within the monumental linear earthwork bearing his name, we have only the one direct written attribution of the building of the Dyke to this particular king, and even that, as was explained in Chapter 1, was produced as much as a century after its construction. Meanwhile, the creation of a more overtly 'managed' western frontier of Mercia might be attributed in some ways to both Offa and to his successor Coenwulf. In discussing Offa's Dyke and the frontier between the Britons and Mercia, however, it is not only the kings but their people who need to be taken into account. In particular, it is worth exploring what is perhaps a relatively neglected question of Mercian identity. That question is how was the 'border' character of the Mercians defined in reference to its neighbours in all directions in the course of the history of the kingdom from the mid-seventh to the early ninth century?[4]

The zenith of Mercia politically is generally accepted to have encompassed the leadership of Aethelbald (716–757), Offa (757–796), and Coenwulf (796–821), and it is during the span of the reigns of these three kings that the power of the kingdom could be said to have been fully 'hegemonic'.[5] This period has often therefore been referred to as the era of 'Mercian supremacy', although it has for some time been evident that the nature and scope of Mercian dominance is in need of critical re-appraisal.[6] Recent scholarship has also revised the view that what Mercia experienced thereafter was 'collapse'. It is possible that succession in the Mercian kingship in the ninth century may have been shared for the most part between two powerful elite lineages: those potentially represented by Coenwulf, Ceolwulf (821–823) and Ceolwulf II (874–879) on the one hand, and Beornwulf (823–826), Berhtwulf (840–852) and Burgred (852–874) on the other.[7] However, even if such a dynastic contest existed, the robustness of Mercian institutions was remarkable given the onslaught of the Danes and the rise of the dynasty of King Alfred of the West Saxons.[8]

While Mercian ambitions for overlordship south of the Thames gradually diminished during the ninth century, the evidence for extensive campaigning by Mercian forces in Wales and in East Anglia may indicate that political domination was still on the agenda for some at least of the last Mercian kings.[9] Moreover, although any hopes for a restored autonomy for Mercia was in effect terminated in AD 918 with the death of Aethelflaed, 'the Lady of the Mercians', the role of its ealdormen and people during the tenth-century re-conquest of the English territories north of Watling Street and subsequently through to the Norman Conquest indicates that much of the power and organisation of the former kingdom remained intact.[10] The foundations of such resilience had been laid, however, during the era of the dynamic, aggressive, and strategically focused Mercian kings of the eighth and early ninth centuries.[11]

In examining the 'border history' of the Mercians, there are a series of questions that can be pursued. These include, 'how does the history of Mercia reflect the specifically 'border' identity of the Mercians?' and 'what was it about the geographical location of the Mercians that led them to be identified as 'borderers'?' Also, 'whose lands did they border, and how did these borders change through time?' The present chapter opens an exploration of these and related questions, and this continues in one way or another as a recurring theme of the book as a whole, with particular reference to the 'British' west. This exploration begins with the question of where the border of the 'first Mercia' was located.

The formation of Mercia: an originating and an expanding 'border'

Nearly all the royal genealogies of the Anglo-Saxon peoples started with Woden, and this was certainly the case for the kings of the Mercians. The god Woden was the principal Anglo-Saxon deity associated (together with the god Tiw) with war and the bringing of victory, and was also linked with poetry, prophecy, magic, healing and death.[12] Whether understood as myth or reality, the ascription of a god as a kingship-founder was entirely meaningful for the Mercians. The founding series of ancestral leaders of the 'Angles' has been claimed to have originated in an area on the continent situated geographically between the Saxons to the east, the Danes northwards and the Franks southwards.[13] Questions of the exact origins and early formation of the Mercian Anglians within Britain are, however, extremely difficult to answer now. This is due to the near-absence of surviving documentation produced by the Mercians themselves that set out their myths and that can provide accounts of their origins and early history.[14]

The sources for the early history of Mercia instead derive almost entirely from their neighbours and rivals. There is for example no known Mercian chronicler, ecclesiastical or lay.[15] Some sources ostensibly represent Mercian interests, such as the 159 surviving Latin charters or diplomas issued in the name of Mercian rulers. Others have been widely accepted as Mercian productions, including a key document known as the 'Tribal Hidage'. Yet on closer inspection such items are texts that seem likely to have been prepared by individuals and interests located outside the heartlands of Mercia. For instance, the charters almost exclusively concern estates that lay in kingdoms under Mercian rule but beyond 'inner' Mercia, and were apparently prepared by non-Mercian clergy.[16] Moreover, the 'Tribal Hidage' listing is headed by figures for the Mercians themselves. One interpretation of this list sequence is that the document was a tribute tally designed to identify taxable entities for the purpose of raising payments from the Mercians as a defeated people, and was likely to have been prepared for a power that at one time held dominion over Mercia.[17]

As to the inference from their collective name, that the first Mercians occupied a 'border' location, Frank Stenton's review of the evidence in the 1940s led him to suppose that the border concerned was marked by what he termed 'the belt of high land connecting the hills of Cannock Chase with the forest of Arden'. This was because the existence of a people to the east of this watershed known from a charter of 849 as the *Tomsaete* (the people who live on the river Tame) can be posited as one of the early tribal groupings that formed the core of the kingdom, while the forests west of that watershed (Morfe, Kinver) were known by British names.[18] From this, it could be deduced that the reason why the Mercians were regarded as 'borderers' is that they settled along the 'leading edge' of the territory that by the late sixth century was being wrested by the Anglo-Saxons of the midlands from the Britons of the west (Figure 3.1).

Like many aspects of Mercian history, however, the origins of neither the

FIGURE 3.1 Mercia and major Anglo-Saxon kingdoms in southern Britain

This map shows the bounds of Mercia at its zenith, towards the end of the eighth century. Kent could alternatively have been depicted as a kingdom. The key features, as far as the heartland of Mercia around Lichfield is concerned, are the course of the Humber and the line of Watling Street. Each had implications for the origins of the kingdom and the direction of its principal trading connections.

FIGURE 3.2 Wall, in Staffordshire: Romano-British buildings

Wall (Letocetum) was an important walled staging-post in later Roman Britain, located on a hillslope close to the intersection of the boundaries of three major provinces. It may have been an early Mercian royal centre. This view is south-westwards over the foundations of the imperial guest-house (mansio) and its associated baths, terraced into the hillside overlooking Watling Street (the line of which, the present A5 road, crosses this view from left to right just out of sight behind the houses at the foot of the hill).

people nor the kingdom are likely to have been quite as simple as this. For instance, in AD 732 the Northumbrian monk-scholar Bede described the existence of two distinct kingdoms, of the Northern and the Southern Mercians, with a boundary separating them along the river Trent.[19] This correlates well with the archaeological evidence, such as it is, which indicates early settlement of the area southwards from the Humber along the Trent valley itself.[20] It would also explain why the lands of the *Tomsaete*, bordering upon the middle Trent valley, were regarded as the 'heartlands' of the kingdom, containing as they did key centres of the Mercian kingdom at its apogee. These centres were, respectively, Lichfield (the location of the bishopric and, briefly in the late eighth century, the archbishopric of the Mercians), Tamworth (the royal centre and in some senses 'capital' under Aethelbald, Offa and Coenwulf), and Repton (a royal monastery that was the burial place of Aethelbald and some of the ninth-century Mercian kings).

Bede located the northern border of the Mercians more precisely in his statement that the battle which saw the early East Anglian king Raedwald triumph over the Northumbrian king Aethelfrith in 616 was fought on the east bank of the river Idle, 'on the edge of the lands of the Mercian people'.[21] This gives rise, therefore, to another possibility. This is that it was Northumbrian recognition of the substantial Mercian presence on their southern border that provided the origin of the naming, not by themselves but, in their earlier history at least, by their more dominant northern Anglian neighbours.[22] In this sense, the 'originating border' may have been the best-known political boundary of early Anglo-Saxon England, along the river Humber. Identity was defined by living either north of this river (in the lands of the 'Northumbrians') or southwards from this river (among the 'Southumbrians'): in these terms the definition of the boundary was decidedly a Northumbrian one.

Alternatively, 'the border' that the name of the Mercians referred to might have been a yet more ancient one. A recent study of political arrangements in Britain in the later Roman period has, for instance, suggested that the limits of three of the four provinces of *Britannia* that were created following the Empire-wide administrative reforms ordered by Diocletian in 286 AD met at, or around, Wall in Staffordshire.[23] This latter Romano-British settlement, located adjacent to Watling Street, is very close to both Lichfield and Tamworth. Hints of continuity derive from the Roman name for Wall, *Letocetum*, which shares a place-name element (featuring a 'grey wood') with Lichfield.[24] Wall was moreover located close to the intersection of this major south-east to north-west road with a north–south road linking Gloucester with Lincoln, so was situated next to a key road intersection within Roman Britain. It apparently had late Roman defences that enclosed an area with substantial buildings including a government rest-house with bath-house, near which was found evidence of Christian activity, and very close to which the later church was built (Figure 3.2).[25]

It has, moreover, recently been pointed out that the distribution plots of distinctive types of fifth-century Germanic brooches may indicate that the authorities governing two of the four late Roman provinces of Britannia (*Britannia Secunda*, based upon Lincoln, and *Maxima Caesariensis*, based upon London) settled, as military federates within the provincial territories that they respectively continued to administer in the late fourth and into the early fifth centuries, people from across the seas with traditions of dress and accoutrement that noticeably contrasted with one another.[26] Among the far-reaching implications of this observation concerning the centrality of Wall is that the 'border' concerned was not simply a 'folk' frontier as previously conceived. Rather, this was a geographical threshold, with the boundary as a meeting-place, which may have reflected a fundamental aspect of the organisation of Britain as understood from both the incoming English *and* the indigenous British perspective. As such, the boundary would not only have had deeply rooted origins, but also a substantial continuing inherited meaning, for many of the inhabitants of southern Britain (whether English or 'Welsh') through subsequent centuries (Figure 3.3).[27]

Two subtly different, but on present evidence equally plausible, models for the hybrid occupation of this 'Mercian heartlands' area during the fifth and sixth centuries can be proposed from these evidential threads. One model would envisage a fusion of a resident Romano-British (and possibly partly Christianised) population with 'mercenary' forces brought in from overseas, and perhaps drawn in from the direction of Norfolk or Lincolnshire. The other model would suggest a mixing of 'Anglo-Saxon' settlers moving southwards from the Trent with a British population already present on Watling Street. Rather than being alternatives, however, these models could be regarded sequentially, and as complementary to one another. In this way the first model represents an early process that drew upon what were possibly among the earliest migratory groups in East Anglia, the other a slightly later development drawing in the groups whose primary direction of settlement had been into what became Northumbria. In this case the 'Anglian' character of the Mercians, and their continuing links with these two other Anglo-Saxon kingdoms, would be readily explicable. If this overall thesis of dual settlement direction is upheld, what is also evident is that the Mercian heartlands around Lichfield and Tamworth are located precisely where these two 'streams' of settlement coalesced. From this perspective, there can be no mystery surrounding how the 'borderers' came to be located where the earliest 'Mercia' came into existence. What became the Mercian heartlands was an originating border where several paths, whether of roads, of boundaries, or of migrants, met. As such, it is entirely plausible that Wall, with its late Roman walls still visible then, was in fact the focus of an early Mercian royal site, located in just that 'grey wood' area that both later British historical tradition and the later name of Lichfield referenced.[28]

The entry that opens the listing in the 'Tribal Hidage' (whatever that document represents), identifies this territory as comprising the lands of 'the first Mercia'. The stated scale of this land, extending to 30,000 hides, strongly contradicts Bede's total of 12,000 hides for the Mercians north and south of the Trent. This contradiction must arise from one of two alternatives. On the one hand, Bede's method of reckoning hidages might have substantially differed from that used for the 'Tribal Hidage'. On the other hand, the suggestion that 'Southern Mercia' was only 5,000 hides in extent could reflect Northumbrian propaganda of the period just after AD 656 which manipulated the figures to suggest that the larger part of Mercian territory had fallen under Northumbrian control (see below).[29]

This rehearsal of possible alternatives for the naming of the Mercians and the extent of their primary settlement area serves to illustrate that there is no 'one truth' concerning matters of identity and history, especially when the sources that might have existed among the peoples concerned are lost to us.[30] Be that as it may, beyond the heartlands, a wider 'inner Mercia' (perhaps accurately reflected in the 'Tribal Hidage' figure) can be distinguished from territories which appear to have been incorporated in the wave of expansion in the seventh century culminating in the reigns of Wulfhere (658–75) and Aethelred (675–704).

Such an expanded 'core area' may therefore have encompassed the *Pecansaete*, thought to be the dwellers of the Peak District, the Britons of the southern part of the former British kingdom of Elmet, and the *Pencersaete* of (later) western Staffordshire and eastern Shropshire.[31] It seems likely to have included also Leicester and Northampton, the territory of the 'Middle Anglians' (itself bordering the lands of the 'Middle Saxons') which extended from the northern Chilterns to the Fens, taking in the lands eastwards to the margins of the Wash, including the environs of Peterborough. All of these peoples may have been to a degree ethnically 'hybrid': not only as between British and 'Anglo-Saxon', but also in terms of the heterogeneous composition of incoming groups. The wider

FIGURE 3.3 The boundaries of late Roman provinces and distributions of early Anglo-Saxon brooch-types (map)

The location of Wall and Lichfield (and nearby Tamworth) close to or at the meeting-point of three later Roman provinces is evident here, as is the coincidence of contrasting brooch-types and likely provincial boundaries (Source: White, 2007, Figure 74).

- - - - Approximate late Roman provincial boundaries

■ Main distribution areas of Cruciform and small-long brooches

■ Main distribution of equal-arm, cast saucer and composite sauce brooches

—— (Later) line of Offa's Dyke

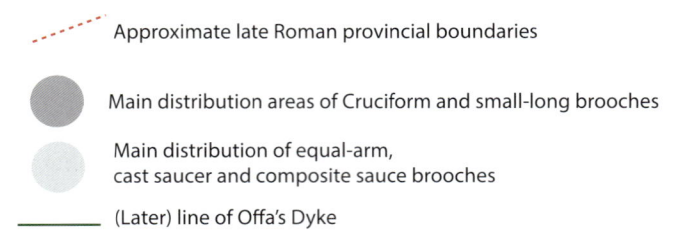

territories enveloped by the end of the seventh century included those of the *Hwicce* of what became Gloucestershire, of the 'Gewisse' of the upper Thames region, and of Lindsey to the south of the Humber estuary, although both the *Hwicce* and the people of Lindsey retained their kingships through to the later eighth century.[32] The status of the *Wrocansaete* of later Shropshire, and of the indeterminate folk of both lowland Cheshire and of lands north of the Wye in

Herefordshire and Shropshire is less certain, since they may have been formed from a later mix of Anglo-Saxon settlers and indigenous peoples. However, their absorption into Mercia must have been an established fact at the latest by the end of the seventh century.[33]

In this light, the further territorial expansion of the Mercian kingdom in the eighth century represented a logical extension of the pushing outwards of its borders from an historic core territory. Paradoxically, therefore, it was the location of the Mercians in the geographic centre of the country that enabled them continually to expand their sphere of control outwards over their neighbours in this way. So, for example, an already fluid western borderland witnessed further penetration and military expeditions into British lands throughout the eighth century. Military interventions and close involvement in the internal politics of the West Saxons during the reigns of Aethelbald and Offa resulted in consolidation of the Mercian hold on the Thames valley, and the seizure of territory on the Wiltshire/Somerset Avon. Moreover, an expansionary move into the western heartlands of Wessex in south Somerset was followed by close involvement in the internal politics of the West Saxons, no doubt at least in part arising from a wish to facilitate Mercian access to the south coast and its cross-Channel trading activity.

The extension of Mercian control south-eastwards in the eighth century was likewise focused first upon gaining sovereignty over the 'Middle Saxons' and access to and use of the port at London. Beyond this, it continued into the lands of the East Saxons, and into Kent, Surrey and Sussex. This was not a seamless or simple process, however, as will be noted in the discussion of Wulfhere's reign below. And finally, dominance over the East Anglians would have secured access to Ipswich and the eastern seaboard, and influence over all the lands north of the Thames estuary.[34] By this process, what had started out at the beginning of the seventh century as the edge-land of 'the borderers' had become, by the beginning of the ninth century in some very real ways, 'the core' – both geographically and politically – of Anglo-Saxon England.

Penda and the mid-seventh-century Northumbrian frontier

While the earliest Mercian kings remain shadowy, the accession of Penda between 626 and 634 – and particularly the extension of his power after 642 – seemingly changed everything: 'here was a Mercian leader whose military exploits far transcended those of his obscure predecessors.'[35] For the first time the Mercian kingdom appears as a significant polity and a senior partner in coalitions featuring at different times, Northumbrian (at least, Deiran), East Anglian, Saxon and British kings and forces. Because early seventh-century Mercia was still a kingdom with a pagan ruler, it is inevitable that we see Penda now almost entirely through the prejudicial lens of the Northumbrian church via Bede's writing and later commentary.[36]

Place-name study has been invoked to suggest that the home territories of several among Penda's kin-group are traceable through the names of settlements such as Pinbury (Gloucestershire), Peddimore (Warwickshire) and Pinvin (Worcestershire) and that this implies that his power-base derived from lands in, or bordering, those of the *Hwicce* focused in Gloucestershire.[37] However, his origins remain obscure, and the place of his kin within the ruling lineages of the Mercians is uncertain. What is in less doubt, even if the precise dating sometime around 628 is still a matter for debate, is that Penda led a force, possibly even before his accession, to defeat two princes of the *Gewisse* at Cirencester, as a result of which this area was annexed to Mercia.

Following Bede's account, Penda's kingship has conventionally been traced through a succession of military alliances that affected the balance of power between Northumbria and its southerly neighbours, British and Anglian. The first of these alliances was with Cadwallon, king of Gwynedd. In 633 Cadwallon led an army into the borderland between Northumbria and Mercia to attack Edwin, the Northumbrian king. This expedition was joined by Penda and it met with success at a battle in the region of Hatfield Chase close to where the river Trent joins the Humber. Edwin was killed, and it has been suggested that it was Penda's 'pagans' who then destroyed both Edwin's royal vill at *Campodonum* and the new church there.[38] The following year Edwin's cousin, Osric, who had maintained himself as king in Deira (the southern kingship of the Northumbrians) was also defeated and killed.[39] Encouraged by these successes, but no longer with Penda, Cadwallon pressed on into the vast territory of Bernicia and was defeated by the new Northumbrian king Oswald in a battle near Hexham and not far from Hadrian's Wall in 634.

Oswald proved more than a match both for the Britons of North Wales and for the Mercians under Penda, and he subsequently dominated all the kingdoms south of the Humber. It was in this period that Oswald may have installed Eowa, Penda's brother, as king of the northern Mercians. Eowa is likely to have been baptised under Oswald's sponsorship (as was the West Saxon king Cynegils, in 635). This is significant because the eighth-century kings of Mercia traced their descent – quite likely for political purposes in reference to Northumbria and to Christianity – through Eowa and not Penda.

Perhaps trying to define this domination territorially, Oswald led his army southwards in 641. Possibly he also wanted to drive a wedge between the Britons of North Wales and the Mercians, the two major peoples who may have remained in alliance to oppose him in the south.[40] If so, it was a miscalculation, because when the two opposing forces met in battle at a place that Bede called *Maserfelth*, usually identified as Oswestry, he was defeated and killed, along with Eowa.[41] Bede regarded Penda as the overall commander of the victorious army, and he gained most from the resulting disunity within Northumbria. In the aftermath, Oswiu, Oswald's brother, became king of Bernicia, while Oswine, Osric's son, acceded to Deira.[42]

In the years following the victory at *Maserfelth*, Penda's efforts appear to have been focused upon pressing home his advantage northwards, while at the same time undoing Northumbrian influence in the south and east. It is likely to have been during this time, for instance, that his sister married King Cenwalh of Wessex.[43] Moreover, he fought and defeated the East Anglian kings Ecgric and Sigeberht, and led an expedition deep into Northumbria that culminated in the destruction of the royal centres at Bamburgh and Yeavering.[44] These mid-seventh-century Mercian political manoeuvres prefigure closely the patterns of alliance and intrigue that so characterise relations between Mercia and the other Anglo-Saxon kingdoms right through the eighth and on into the ninth century.

In 651, Oswiu invaded Deira, bringing about Oswine's exile and death. Penda was so far established as an influential presence in Northumbrian politics by this time (a daughter was married to Oswiu's eldest son, Oswiu's younger son was a hostage at Penda's court), that when the Deirans put Aethelwald, a son of Oswald, on the throne, the latter promptly placed himself and his kingdom under Penda's protection. Whether or not this had the effect of rendering Deira a vassal kingdom of Mercia, the situation was inherently unstable. Before making a further intervention in Northumbria, however, Penda attacked East Anglia in 654 and killed their king, Anna.[45]

Penda then appears to have installed his son Peada as king of the 'Middle Angles' before, in 656, leading an army to seek to destroy Oswiu. Bede described this host as being headed by 30 *duces regii*, or royal military commanders, including a British contingent led by Cadafael of Gwynedd and an East Anglian force under their king Aethelhere, as well as the Deirans under Aethelwald's command. The battle that was eventually joined at a stream called the *Winwaed*, thought to be in the vicinity of Leeds, almost resulted in the destruction of Oswiu's army. Nevertheless, it was ultimately a Northumbrian victory in which both Penda and Aethelhere were killed. In the aftermath of this defeat Mercia briefly became a vassal state of Northumbria, and this could have been the point when the *Tribal Hidage* was compiled to exact tribute.

That Penda's reign was pivotal in the rise of Mercia to political prominence is beyond question. Recent re-appraisal of the nature of Mercian power under Penda has referred to it in terms of 'hegemony', although this can be a mercurial term.[46] Be that as it may, Penda undoubtedly occupied a crucial transitional place in the history of Anglo-Saxon kingship, since he was the last king who exercised overlordship while remaining pagan.[47] Moreover, he epitomised traits of kingship that both looked back to the heroic age of warbands held together by gift-giving and loosely organised polities bonded by kinship, and forward to the age of inter-kingdom relations managed through diplomacy, hostage exchange, and ever more strategic use of marriage-based alliances.

This transition continued well into the era in which Offa's Dyke was built. However, the question of the inter-relations of the Mercians and the Britons to the west under Penda deserves more attention. It has been noted, especially, that 'throughout a lifetime of strenuous warfare, Penda never fought against the Welsh', and that he saw the alliance with Gwynedd as vital to the strategic interests of Mercia in the face of Northumbrian attempts to extend their overlordship south of the Humber.[48] Penda's role in the victory against Oswald at *Maselferth* may have had as its correlate the settlement of substantial numbers of Mercians in the plain of the middle Severn between the Breiddin in the west and the Wrekin in the east (Figure 3.4), whether or not, as slightly later Welsh literature asserted, this involved the 'ethnic cleansing' of the area by Penda and his lieutenants.[49]

The exact territorial limits of Mercia under Penda are unknown. In the north, various south-facing earthworks, for instance the Roman Ridge Dykes near Sheffield and the 5 mile long (8.0 km) Nico Ditch south of Manchester, though undated, have been ascribed to Northumbrian efforts to contain Mercian expansion.[50] Meanwhile, Penda's defeat of the *Gewisse* could have provided the context for the construction by the West Saxons – or, if its origins were earlier, then at least the re-commissioning – of the 'East Wansdyke' earthwork in Wiltshire, and perhaps also the transformation of other prehistoric boundary works into the 'West Wansdyke' in Somerset.[51]

In the mid-seventh century a putative son of Penda, Merewalh, was ruler of the arguably mixed British-English people in that part of western Mercia that later approximated the Diocese of Hereford, covering north Herefordshire and south Shropshire.[52] The limited archaeological evidence, for instance the recent discovery of an Anglo-Saxon settlement at Bullinghope south of Hereford, points to a mid-seventh-century settlement of the area, but gives few clues as to the identity of the incoming English.[53] The westwards expansion involved in the establishment of the kingdom ruled by Merewalh, and he or one of his descendants could have created the Herefordshire Rowe Ditch across the Arrow valley west of Leominster.[54]

FIGURE 3.4 The hills south-west of Oswestry, viewed from near Watling Street

Where Watling Street crosses the undulating landscape at the western margins of the north Shropshire/south Cheshire plain, the hills to the west become very evident. It was across these hills that Offa's Dyke was placed, its course well within sight of (and from) the lands that the Mercians had wrested from the British. This view is towards the hills from Llynclys (left) to Baker's Hill (right), as seen from Sandford (just to the south of the A5 road, 3 miles south-east of Oswestry) on a day in mid-November.

PHOTOGRAPHIC PANORAMA/ MONTAGE: ADAM STANFORD/ KATIE ALLEN, COPYRIGHT RESERVED.

From Wulfhere to Aethelbald: 'early Christian' Mercia and its neighbours

After the defeat of Mercia and its allies at the *Winwaed*, Penda's son Peada in effect became Oswiu's client ruler over all the Mercians south of the Trent. Despite this subordination to the Northumbrians, the continuity of Peada's rule here might further explain why in later centuries the primary heartlands of Mercia were deemed to be located primarily in just that land of the *Tomsaete* focused around Tamworth and Lichfield.[55] Peada had married Oswiu's daughter Alhflæd two years before Penda's death and had accepted baptism apparently with the latter's acquiescence.[56] He may already have been active in the conversion of the 'Middle Angles', and after his accession promoted the church in the lands that remained under direct Mercian control or influence. It could have been Peada, for example, who asked Wilfrid, bishop of York, to establish Lichfield, under the former bishop of York, Chad, as the principal ecclesiastical centre of the Mercian heartlands.[57] This compromise situation, with Peada ruling over the southern Mercians and therefore only one (though probably larger) half of an originally perhaps two-part kingdom, was brought to an abrupt end by his murder in 657, an act thought to have been inspired by Oswiu. The destabilising intention of this move once again misfired, and a retaliatory revolt appears to have been orchestrated by Mercian nobles against the Northumbrian overlords late in 658. This brought a younger son of Penda, Wulfhere, to the throne.

Wulfhere soon appears to have been active not only in re-establishing Mercian dominance in east-central England but also in extending Mercian influence southwards, including to some areas south of the Thames. This is illustrated by the foundation charter for Chertsey Abbey, dated *c*.672, which was issued by Frithuwold, *subregulus* in Surrey. It is difficult in this context to conceive of Mercian overlordship existing in Surrey under Wulfhere without the same power having existed over the area of Middlesex.[58] Wulfhere apparently formed alliances with dissident branches of both the South and the West Saxon kingdoms, and conducted military campaigns as far as the south coast of England.[59] Moreover, he revived his father's Northumbrian ambitions, and led another confederated army northwards across the Humber. Nonetheless, Wulfhere was defeated in 674 by Oswiu's son Ecgfrith and died in the following year. The kingdom of Lindsey based upon Lincoln was promptly annexed by Ecgfrith, but Aethelred, Wulfhere's brother (and also Ecgfrith's son-in-law), then defeated Ecgfrith in another battle on the Trent in 679, regaining Lindsey in the process.[60] Thereafter, Northumbrian attention was preoccupied with its northern border. Arguably, one impact of the later seventh-century Mercian kings upon the course of Anglo-Saxon history was therefore to call a permanent halt to Northumbrian attempts to dominate their neighbours south of the Humber.

Aethelred reigned from 675 to 704. He has been cast as a pious king who had more concern with the affairs of the church than with secular matters.[61] He was certainly active in the re-organisation of the diocesan framework of the English church under the archbishop of Canterbury, Theodore, and was benefactor to several churches and monasteries. However, in the late seventh just as much as in the eighth century, such actions were overtly political. Monasteries, for instance, were treated exactly as if they were the property of the founding royal and elite lineages. It is therefore not entirely appropriate to regard Aethelred as having contributed little to the development of the Mercian kingdom. Both Wulfhere and Aethelred, for instance, seem to have sponsored Lichfield as the ecclesiastical focal point for the Mercian heartlands. In his earlier years, Aethelred was also militarily active. As well as his attack on Northumbria, he invaded Kent (in 676), devastating Rochester in the process. Moreover, his granting of land in Wiltshire at least indicates the extension of his influence (if not direct control) over parts of Wessex. He may also have absorbed the *Hwicce* of the Cotswold-Severn area, and the *Wrocansaete* of the Welsh border more fully into 'Greater Mercia' at this time, and he probably also campaigned in Wales.[62]

In 697 shadowy events surrounded the murder by unnamed Mercian nobles of Aethelred's queen, the Northumbrian Osthryth. This may have been a revenge killing for the role of her sister, Ealhflaed, in the murder of her husband, Peada, 40 years earlier. If this was the case, it suggests that Aethelred's hold on power over the Mercian nobility was weakening by this time. This could have been what led to his abdication in 704 to become abbot of Bardney in Lincolnshire, where Osthryth had been buried. Coenred, a son of Wulfhere, succeeded his uncle, only to abdicate in tandem with King Offa of the East Saxons in 709, and to join him on a journey to become a monk in Rome. Coelred, his successor, was a son of Aethelred (but according to the medieval Chronicle of Evesham Abbey, not of Osthryth). The verdict of both Bede and St Boniface was apparently that Coelred was an irreligious, if not actually sacrilegious, wastrel who died insane and unlamented in 716. That this was a highly partial and ecclesiastical view is hinted at by the fact that in the same year he is recorded as having fought a battle in the Vale of Pewsey against the powerful (if aged) Ine, King of Wessex. This was very likely a Mercian victory and it seems that in this period the foundations were being laid for a major push southwards into lands formerly under the sway of the West Saxons.

King Aethelbald of Mercia and his southern border

Sometime around 735–740 a monk, Felix, wrote a *Life* of St Guthlac, which throws some light on the rise of the king, Aethelbald, who succeeded Coelred. Felix composed the *Life* at the Christian community of Crowland (near Peterborough) where its subject had once lived. Crowland is located on the margins of the East Anglian fens, and was then a site occupied by religious solitaries but was not yet a formal monastery. The *Life* was apparently produced, at least in part, as a paean of praise for the then East Anglian king, Aelfwald (*c.*713–749). In this work, Felix alludes to the fugitive years up to 716 during which Aethelbald, a grandson of Eowa (Penda's brother), sought to wrest the Mercian kingship from Coelred. It appears that Guthlac was a kinsman of Aethelbald, and mediated the friendship with Aelfwald. That Guthlac was well-placed to act in this way derived from his training at the Mercian double monastery at Repton, which was close to the river Trent in the centre of Mercia, and was a place with which Aethelbald had very close associations (emphasised by his eventual burial there). The apparent accord between East Anglia and Mercia must have served Aethelbald well, since he not only went on to bring stability to 'Greater Mercia', but extended the latter to include the lands of the Middle Saxons, including London. With this enlarged Greater Mercia in place, Aethelbald then ambitiously launched a series of campaigns against the English and Welsh kingdoms to the north, south and west of Mercia.

In the period 716–733, it seems likely that Aethelbald's attention was focused upon bringing London and the south-east of England within the direct ambit of Mercian power, with the exercise of over-kingship, if not direct rule, over the South Saxons and Kent. However, according to the *Anglo-Saxon Chronicle*, Aethelbald's more aggressive assertion of Mercian power over the neighbouring kingdoms began with an attack on Wessex in 733 that resulted in his capture of Somerton. This place, located in south Somerset, was at that time a key centre of the western part of the West Saxon kingdom beyond Selwood.[63] Northumbrian sources indicate that Aethelbald subsequently led a major expedition into Northumbria in 740, while in 743 Cuthred of Wessex appears as a subordinate king on campaign with the Mercian king in Wales. In 752, towards the end of his reign, Aethelbald was again in conflict with Wessex, fighting the by now in-subordinate Cuthred.

Perhaps most remarkable in light of subsequent history was the extent to which Aethelbald appears to have weakened the power of Wessex, especially along its northern flank and in former heartlands such as the middle Thames valley, in the years between 730 and 750. In this period, for instance, what later became Berkshire was so closely integrated into Mercia that Aethelbald was seen as the protector of the monastery at Abingdon and gave the abbey at Cookham to the archbishop of Canterbury.⁶⁴ While Aethelbald's domination of England for nearly 30 years was noteworthy, so too, it seems, was the degree to which his 'military household' (to use Stenton's phrase) involved licentiousness, including towards women in holy orders. Such behaviour attracted the opprobrium of a whole group of English ecclesiastics on the Continent, and these complaints were clearly expressed in a letter sent to him by St Boniface in 746. While these improprieties of behaviour may have shocked English churchmen overseas, the latter were equally exercised by the wider oppression perceived in the demands that Aethelbald made upon monasteries in Mercia and in neighbouring subordinated territories. One of the practices singled out for criticism was the new requirement for monks to labour on (or at least to provide labour for) Mercian royal building projects. A grant made in 749 by Aethelbald at the synod of Gumley near Leicester reveals that the expected labour service included the repair of bridges and the maintenance of fortresses, although monks were specifically granted immunity from a range of other duties.⁶⁵

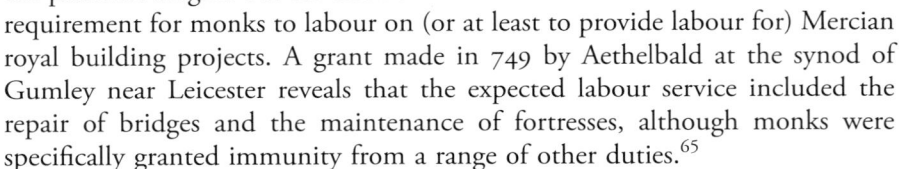

Whether or not the bridge-work and fortress-work of Aethelbald's reign extended to the construction of linear earthworks is uncertain. As noted above, Fox was the most articulate, if not the first, advocate of the idea that it was Aethelbald who could be credited with the construction of Wat's Dyke.⁶⁶ Fox also suggested that the late seventh or early eighth century could have been the time when the 'short dykes' of the Kerry Ridgeway and adjacent localities on the present border between Shropshire and Powys might have been constructed by the Mercians as part of their settlement push westwards into the uplands and valleys of mid-Wales. However, the small scale of these works means that even if they had this genesis (which now seems doubtful) they are unlikely to be attributable to direct intervention by Aethelbald or his senior officials.⁶⁷

The Boniface letter also provides some insight into aspects of Aethelbald's governance of Mercia. In the preface to the manifold criticisms of the king – also including also the seizure of monastic revenues, and actual violence against clerics – he was nevertheless praised for his generous giving of alms, his prohibition of theft, perjury and rape, his defence of widows and the poor, and the keeping of peace within his kingdom.⁶⁸ However, these positive aspects of Aethelbald's rule did not prevent renewed challenges to his authority towards the end of his reign, and these evidently extended beyond just the threat of a more aggressive stance from Cuthred's Wessex (manifest from 752 until Cuthred's death in 756).

FIGURE 3.5 Cropthorne, Worcestershire: early eighth-century cross-head
The importance of estates like Cropthorne was not only that they were within royal ownership or patronage, but that they marked the consolidation of Mercian power in the west in the early eighth century. Rosemary Cramp attributed the distinctive style of carving of commemorative crosses like this, probably located at a monastery on the river Avon here, to exactly this period.

3 The Mercians: a border history 109

East Anglia, for instance, had apparently become a client of Mercia after Aelfwald's death in 749, but under its successor king, Beonna, it began to re-assert its independence. The evidence for this is the appearance of coins that style Beonna as king of the East Angles in the period from at least 754. Such challenges, and the perceived weakening of his authority that accompanied them, may have precipitated the murder of Aethelbald in 757 by his own bodyguard at Seckington near Tamworth (Figure 3.6). The circumstances of the king's presence at this location are unrecorded, but it potentially throws some light on the location of kingly residences in the close environs of Tamworth. Beornred, who emerged as Aethelbald's successor, may very well have been behind a deliberate plot to assassinate the king. If so, this was not a popular move within Mercia and within a year he had been deposed by another claimed descendant of Eowa, Offa.[69]

Offa, King of the Mercians: an outline narrative

Offa therefore first appears in recorded history during the upheaval of 757 to 758, after the murder of Aethelbald. One reading of the evident power struggle among the Mercian nobility is that Beornred usurped Aethelbald's throne by, or at least as a result of, a gross act of treachery on the part of the latter's personal retinue. The fact that Offa eventually overthrew Beornred at the cost of many lives indicates that Aethelbald's successor (or murderer) was not without support among the Mercian ruling families. It is not perhaps surprising, therefore, that much of the early period of Offa's reign appears to have involved consolidation within Mercia and containment beyond its borders. Welsh sources record a battle fought in the vicinity of Hereford in 760, and this instability in the west may well have made a lasting impression on the newly enthroned king.

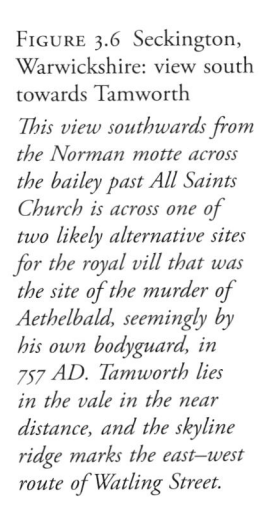

FIGURE 3.6 Seckington, Warwickshire: view south towards Tamworth

This view southwards from the Norman motte across the bailey past All Saints Church is across one of two likely alternative sites for the royal vill that was the site of the murder of Aethelbald, seemingly by his own bodyguard, in 757 AD. Tamworth lies in the vale in the near distance, and the skyline ridge marks the east–west route of Watling Street.

Had Offa's reign been recorded in the surviving writings of a Mercian churchman there would at least be a narrative such as there is for Alfred of Wessex which, however partial, would provide a basic historical framework. Perhaps his life and deeds were once so recorded, although there is no mention of such a work in either contemporary or later surviving Anglo-Saxon literature. As it is, therefore, the situation remains broadly as stated by Stenton:

> "The re-establishment of Mercian supremacy by Offa is the central fact in English history in the second half of the eighth century. But the stages by which it was brought about cannot now be reconstructed. No Mercian chronicle has survived from this period, and charters alone give any definite impression of Offa's place among English kings."[70]

The dynamics of Offa's kingship

From what can be reconstructed, the character of Offa's reign changed as its nearly 40-year span wore on. The long period of consolidation from the start of his reign in 757/8 through to around 780 may have featured some significant internal re-organisation of the Mercian kingdom, and the full integration of some subject kingdoms and attempt at absorption of others, within it. The decade from 780 to 790 saw Offa focusing his attention upon expanding the horizons both of the kingship and the kingdom, creating something of the framework and apparatus of a state along the same lines as were being developed by his contemporary, Charlemagne, on the mainland of Europe. This appears to have been a period of rapid aggrandisement and the development of an ambition not previously articulated by any Anglo-Saxon kings, except perhaps the Northumbrians at their apex in the seventh century under Oswald, to exercise control over all the English and to rival the imperial model being promulgated by the Franks. Finally, there was a relatively brief period, between 790 and Offa's death in 796, that saw not only a determination on the part of a now ageing king to tolerate no rivals, but also, by whatever means necessary, to guarantee the succession of his son, Ecgfrith.

Apart from the Hereford episode, it was not until 771, when Offa attacked and subdued the *Haestingas* of East Sussex, that an overtly martial character to his reign was felt beyond Mercia.[71] This military move has been seen as directed towards either or both of the kingdoms of Kent and of the South Saxons, and in 776 he attacked (or was resisted in) western Kent, fighting a battle at Otford on the river Darent. The Welsh annals indicate the conduct of a campaign in Wales in 778. Offa fought king Cynewulf of Wessex near Bensington (Benson) south-east of Oxford near Dorchester-on-Thames in 779 'and captured the town'.[72] A further campaign was apparently mounted against the Britons (in Wales) in, or around, 784, and another at the very end of his reign, in 796.

A new politics

What is perhaps interesting in this recounting of Offa's attested military activity is the economy with which he used the might of his kingdom. It appears that he never conducted overt warfare against either Northumbria or East Anglia, and directed only sporadic violence (rather than full-scale warfare) towards Kent and Wessex. Indeed the impression from the above rather brief catalogue of military activity is that Offa regarded warfare as a carefully constrained instrument within a political strategy that was pursued largely by other means. These means included traditional strategies such as advantageous marriage alliances as well as church patronage and the use of its clerics as intermediaries.[73]

In addition, however, Offa 'forged a new type of polity by systematically degrading the status of neighbouring kingdoms and attempting, with varying degrees of success, to make them Mercian provinces under his own rule.'[74] To this end, he made effective use of novel political methods such as the appropriation of the rights of sub-kings and the elites to confer and convey land entitlements and such as arms-length interference in the dynastic squabbles of neighbouring kingships through the opportunistic promotion of rival factions. Changes in the styling of the signatories to Offa's charters show that this appropriation was achieved through progressive erosion of their political standing. In the case of the *Hwicce* in Gloucestershire, of the South Saxons, of Kent, and even of East Anglia, office-holders designated earlier in Offa's reign as sub-kings were progressively 'demoted' to the status of regional ealdorman.

Meanwhile, Offa secured alliances with the two most powerful of the English kingdoms through marrying two of his daughters to the kings of Northumbria and Wessex respectively. In each of these kingdoms this was also a strategy of promoting a pro-Mercian faction and helping them to oust the rival group that had sought more stridently for the polity to remain independent of Mercian influence. So in 787 Offa's second daughter, Eadburh, married Beorhtric, king of the West Saxons, soon after the latter's accession to the throne in 786.

It cannot have been accidental that this alliance followed immediately upon Beorhtric's success in sending his rival, Ecgberht, into exile. In 792, Offa married another daughter, Aelfflaed, to Aethelred I, immediately upon his re-accession to the Northumbrian kingship. This in turn also resulted in the exile of the latter's rival, Eardwulf. It may be that a similar plan was being hatched in respect of Aethelberht of East Anglia, since some sources suggest that the context of his execution by Offa in 794 may have included marriage negotiations involving the latter's youngest daughter, Aelfthryth.[75] These, like those in 790 involving a suggested marriage between Charlemagne's eldest son Charles, and Aelfflaed, may have gone awry.[76]

In these later decades of Offa's reign, his concern to secure the eventual accession of his son Ecgfrith as king in his place not only involved eliminating opposition within and beyond Mercia, but also the active emulation of Carolingian practice by having Ecgfrith anointed as his successor in his own lifetime. While the anointing could also be seen as an attempt to secure his hard-won achievements in the assertion of Mercian dominance politically, it was clearly also an attempt to establish a dynasty. In the short term, moreover, it may have served only to exacerbate problems that he already had with securing dominance over Kent and Canterbury.[77]

It was at least in part a reflection of his difficulties with Jaenberht, the Archbishop of Canterbury, and the Kentish elite, that Offa attempted to re-make the ecclesiastical landscape of Britain through the creation of a new archiepiscopate (something that had not been done since Augustine's mission to Kent in 597 almost exactly 200 years previously).[78] The significance of the location of this new archbishopric at Lichfield at the very centre of Mercian power could not have been lost upon anyone, and it is not surprising that Jaenberht resisted the move with all the powers at his disposal.

The zenith of power

It seems likely that as well as routinely attending Church Councils in his reign, Offa to some degree orchestrated and presided over the visit of the papal envoys and the holding of Councils to discuss matters of mutual interest between the rulers of Britain and the papacy in 786–787.[79] This series of events was conducted in reference to both Northumbrian and Mercian interests and was facilitated through Carolingian diplomacy, but the fact that the first and the last Councils of the papal mission were both held in Mercia is indicative of the reality of Offa's domination of contemporary secular and ecclesiastical politics.[80] Nor is it surprising that politics feature prominently in several other aspects of Offa's operations, such as his stimulation of trade and of the internal workings of the economy of the monetised areas of his realm, and the development and exchange of monastic holdings.

The political as well as the economic role of coinage in Offa's reign has also received much attention. So, for example, the date and auspices of minting of coin has been seen to have significant bearing upon how fully relations of dominance and resistance among the kingships of the neighbours of the Mercians can be inferred. In the early years of Offa's reign, for example, Beonna of East Anglia issued coinage in apparent rejection of Mercian supremacy, but by the mid-770s Offa was having coins minted in his own name there.[81] Later, the background to the capture and beheading of the East Anglian king Aethelberht in 794 included the defiance of Mercian authority represented by the minting of coins in Aethelberht's name. Meanwhile, Offa authorised the issue of coins that bore not only his name, but also, on the obverse, his bust, frequently accompanied by the name of the moneyer who minted the coin. The style of these busts is such that they approximate portraits of Offa in the Roman imperial manner, and as such they projected the authority of his person (Figure 3.7). The production of a heavier and larger silver issue than had previously occurred on any scale, the minting of a limited gold issue, and the innovation of the issue of a limited

FIGURE 3.7 Coin of Offa, moneyer Ebba (British Museum)

The early years of Offa's reign marked a significant change in the character of Mercian coinage, and probably represented a more overt attempt to stimulate trade and the income it could generate for the royal household and administration. Most moneyers were based in the south and east, well outside the Mercian heartlands, and coin distributions (and by inference contemporary usage) are also heavily focused upon these 'trading' regions. Drawing by Tim Hoverd.

number of coins featuring the bust of his queen, Cynethryth, self-consciously underlined the political message of the coinage.[82]

While the focus of discussion here of Offa's dealings with his neighbours and the Church has been upon politics, the status of his cultural patronage, expressed to a considerable degree in the ecclesiastical sphere, has to some degree been neglected. While there was nothing approaching the scope or scale of the 'Carolingian renaissance', that there were significant cultural developments in Mercia and under Mercian influence, especially in Offa's later years, is now beyond dispute.[83] This concerned not only the work of scriptoria but also the workshops of sculptors and metalworkers established to embellish the churches, palaces and persons of the ruling elite.

The summit of Offa's political fortunes can probably be regarded as marked by the linked events in 787 involving the investiture of Eanberht as archbishop of the new diocese of Lichfield and, in turn, this archbishop's anointing of Ecgfrith as Offa's heir, which presumably took place in the newly 'elevated' cathedral. The alliance with Beorhtric and the West Saxons signalled by the marriage with Eadburh must have seemed to have completed the successes of 787 for Offa and Cynethryth, and the sealing of an *annus mirabilis* in the affairs of the Mercian court. If so, the triumph was short-lived. A later Carolingian source suggested that the idea was mooted by Charles 'the Younger', Charlemagne's son, in 789, that he should marry Aelfflaed, Offa's eldest daughter. Offa allegedly demanded that in return, his son, Ecgfrith, should marry Charlemagne's daughter Bertha. The answer that Charlemagne was said to have given to this proposal that would have enhanced further the

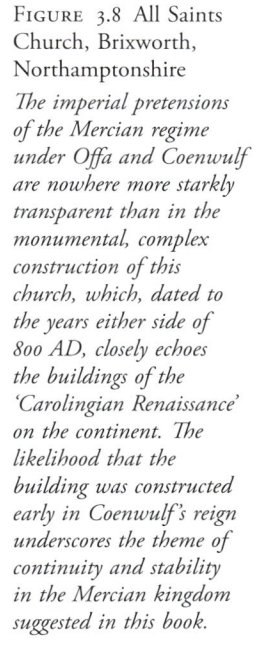

FIGURE 3.8 All Saints Church, Brixworth, Northamptonshire

The imperial pretensions of the Mercian regime under Offa and Coenwulf are nowhere more starkly transparent than in the monumental, complex construction of this church, which, dated to the years either side of 800 AD, closely echoes the buildings of the 'Carolingian Renaissance' on the continent. The likelihood that the building was constructed early in Coenwulf's reign underscores the theme of continuity and stability in the Mercian kingdom suggested in this book.

standing of Offa in the wider world was swift and negative: such that the original suggestion from the Carolingian court appears to have been withdrawn and diplomatic and economic reprisals were enacted.[84]

Lack of sound judgement was probably also at the root of Offa's probably hasty decision to execute Aethelberht of East Anglia in 794, despite the adoption of clear ecclesiastically-inspired strictures by the Mercian court concerning the unlawfulness of such an act of regicide. The act appears to have been condemned universally, and was in later hagiography ascribed to the pernicious influence of Queen Cynethryth. The political aftermath of this debacle probably explains something of the events of 796 and why they represented such a catastrophe for the Mercian regime. Early in that year, as a direct consequence of the volatility of late eighth-century Northumbrian dynastic politics, and possibly as a result of the loss of inhibitions following the execution of the East Anglian king, but also no doubt in reaction to the cruel punishments meted out by Aethelred to his rivals, the latter too was murdered 'by his own people'. Perhaps as a result of the impact of this political disaster, Offa himself died in June 796.

Coenwulf: the management of an inheritance

We shall have more to say about the character of Offa's rule in later chapters. In particular this will involve looking more closely at the various ways in which the Mercian hegemony was sustained during his reign. However, the standing of the Mercian regime and the politics of its western border were arguably just as important to Coenwulf as they had been to Offa, and this is vital to an understanding of the early use of Offa's Dyke and the building, or re-commissioning, or extension, of Wat's Dyke.

Reconstructing the succession

The process by which Coenwulf became Offa's successor is uncertain, but it is widely presumed to have arisen in much the same way that Offa himself emerged as king in 757/8, as the outcome of a power struggle among the Mercian elite.[85] Yet this was surely not the anticipated outcome given that Ecgfrith was crowned king in succession to his father, and that his few months' reign showed him to be not lacking in energy, if the several charters that he issued are any kind of guide. Historians have been strongly influenced by a much-quoted letter of Alcuin to a senior Mercian ealdorman in 797 in which he stated of Ecgfrith 'that most noble young man has not died for his own sins; but that vengeance for the blood shed by the father has reached the son.'[86] It would be easy to infer from this that Ecgfrith had been assassinated, but other possibilities exist. One that we think deserves some close consideration is that a decline in Ecgfrith's health was managed by the regime, and that Coenwulf was identified as a possible successor, during the critical months concerned.[87]

It may be pertinent to this idea of a managed transition that a charter of Ecgfrith issued in the summer of 796 was witnessed not only by Offa's widow,

Cynethryth, but also by Coenwulf.[88] Although this need only indicate that the endorsement was not drawn up until after Ecgfrith had died, among others of the earliest charters of Coenwulf's reign Cynethryth still witnessed as queen: her presence, registered in this way, suggests continuity. The ealdorman Brorda, the most frequent lay attestor to Offa's charters, was described in one of his charters as his 'patricius', a status unique among the many such documents issued in Offa's name. Brorda appears in the Ecgfrith charter in question, but then does not appear in the earliest of Coenwulf's charters. It was this same Brorda who is widely thought to have been the recipient of a letter from Alcuin that urged counsel to be given to Coenwulf to emulate Offa's sober conduct. If Brorda did then mediate a full accommodation of Coenwulf into the Mercian hegemonic 'project' it might explain why he re-appeared as a leading signatory in charters issued by Coenwulf from 797 onwards.

The establishment of Coenwulf as 'legitimate' successor to Offa, despite Alcuin's apparent hostility to him at least initially, possibly explains also why, despite the trauma of the events between 794 and 796 and the advantage its enemies sought to gain during a period of transition within the Mercian regime, Coenwulf was so evidently able to hold the polity together into the ninth century and to build upon Offa's achievements. It was certainly a struggle to do so, at least to begin with, since as early as the month of his accession, Coenwulf was faced with a potential descent into chaos. Eadberht Praen, a prominent member of one of the kingly lineages of Kent, had returned from exile in Francia and had assumed the Kentish kingship, with the consequence that the Mercian archbishop there, Aethelheard, fled from Canterbury and took refuge in London. It appears that soon afterwards, there was also a revolt in East Anglia that is registered by the minting of coins under a ruler named as Eadwald.

A strategy of assertion

The sequence of events that followed is potentially very revealing of Coenwulf's decisive character, and how far he was truly heir to Offa's power. First, rather than engaging in a rash military intervention in Kent, he asserted his authority on his western border as soon as 797 by routing the forces of Caradog ap Meirion, king of Gwynedd, who had attacked the Mercians at Rhuddlan at the northern end of the Vale of Clwyd during 796.[89] He followed this up immediately in 798 with an expedition across the region of Rhos, between the Vale of Clwyd and the Conwy, where, in a battle that extinguished the threat for the next 20 years, he killed Caradog.

In 797 or 798, while flexing Mercian military muscle in the north-west, Coenwulf sought a diplomatic solution to the situation in Kent. In a letter to Pope Leo III jointly attested by Archbishop Aethelheard, he proposed that in return for the suppression of the Lichfield archbishopric, the see of Canterbury should be transferred to London.[90] Following a negative response from Leo, Coenwulf acted swiftly, and invaded Kent late in 798. He 'ravaged the people of

Kent as far as the (Romney) Marsh, and they (presumably, the Mercian army) seized Praen their king and brought him in fetters into Mercia'.[91] Coenwulf then installed his brother Cuthred as king of Kent. While there is no contemporary record of events in East Anglia, the resumption of the minting of Mercian coinage there by 800, now featuring Coenwulf, appears to mark a similarly stark re-assertion of authority.

In 801, Eardwulf, who had become king of Northumbria in 796, invaded Mercia. Coenwulf had been sheltering Northumbrian exiles, and this may have been the pretext for the move. The Mercian king's response is uncertain, but given the support that Eardwulf had already received at Charlemagne's court during Offa's last years, Coenwulf was apparently sensible enough not to provide an excuse for direct Frankish intervention in English conflicts by ordering a full-scale retaliatory attack northwards. Although it may have been that Alcuin was brought in to mediate, further Mercian intrigue was apparently behind the expulsion of Eardwulf from Northumbria in 806.

Another setback occurred in 802 when, as was noted in Chapter 1, above, Offa's daughter Eadburh was said to have 'accidentally poisoned' her husband Beorhtric, king of the West Saxons. Whatever the truth of the matter, Beorhtric's demise created the opening for Ecgberht to return from exile to take up the Wessex kingship. 'And that same day Ealdorman Aethelmund rode from the province of the Hwiccians across the border at Kempsford.'[92] That this expedition was led by the *dux* of the *Hwicce*, and not by Coenwulf himself, indicates both that the latter may have been fully occupied on his border with Northumbria, and that Aethelmund was acting on his behalf and from his own heartlands. The Mercian forces were engaged in battle by 'Ealdorman Weohstan with the people of Wiltshire', who won the ensuing battle. Weohstan presumably deputised for Ecgberht in this engagement given that the latter was concurrently undergoing the act of succession. Both ealdormen were killed

FIGURE 3.9 Tamworth, Staffordshire: the Tame bridge and the castle

Tamworth emerged as a key centre not only for residence but also for the administration of Mercia by the mid eighth-century, although only in the ninth century did it become a regular location of Church Councils, and for the issuing of Charters, presided over by the Mercian kings. The Norman castle was probably built upon, or close to, the site of the royal residence.

3 The Mercians: a border history

in the 'great battle', which must have been fiercely contested.[93] There matters between Mercia and Wessex seemingly rested for the remainder of Coenwulf's reign, during which time he was preoccupied with Kent and with campaigns in north Wales. Ecgberht's martial efforts were meanwhile directed against the British peoples of the south-west peninsula.

Coenwulf had agreed the suppression of the Mercian archdiocese by 803, and Archbishop Aethelheard called a Council of the churches in Kent to re-state their privileges as underscored by the pope. Upon Aethelheard's death in 805, Wulfred became Archbishop of Canterbury. He asserted more vigorously the rights of the Church at Canterbury and minted coins in his own name without reference to the Mercian king. Coenwulf's brother Cuthred died in 807, and Coenwulf from then on took direct control of Mercian interests in Kent. Although relations may have improved between 809 and 815, Wulfred's visit to Rome in 814 was followed upon his return by his calling a Council of the whole Church in the archdiocese at Chelsea in 816. Among other things, this overturned the rights granted by the papacy to Offa and to Coenwulf to appoint their own nominees to vacant posts as leaders of monasteries. Since Coenwulf's daughter Cwoenthryth had only recently been appointed in just this way as abbess of the monastery at Minster-in-Thanet, the thrust of Wulfred's move was all too plain. Coenwulf responded in 817 by obtaining from the new pope, Paschal I, confirmation of the original privileges, but Wulfred continued to contest the case, so much so that at a Council in London 821, Coenwulf threatened to expel the turbulent cleric.

Shifting the territorial focus

Other aspects of Coenwulf's reign have been understood through his charters just as with Offa, but these perhaps shed less light than did Offa's concerning relations with his neighbours. Two things stand out. First, the Worcester-based charters in particular reveal the closeness of Coenwulf's links with the kingdom of the *Hwicce*, and although the Mercian king still presided over meetings at Tamworth, there is perhaps some justification for perceiving a shift in the centre of gravity of Mercian politics westwards, with the emergence of Winchcombe as an important Mercian royal centre (Figure 3.10).[94] Secondly, the terms used to describe Coenwulf in his charters echo strongly the overbearing way in which both Aethelbald and Offa had styled

FIGURE 3.10
Winchcombe, Gloucestershire

According to H. P. R. Finberg, Winchcombe not only became the location of a royal double monastery, but was also the centre where the 'state archives' were located from the reign of Coenwulf onwards. It complemented a number of centres where Mercian royal power had probably become focused from late in Offa's reign, including London (Aldwych), Bedford, Leicester, Cirencester and Bath.

themselves. Indeed, one charter in particular referred to him as 'Emperor', and this hyperbole extended also to the forms and references of at least some of his coinage.[95]

That there was some substance to Coenwulf's imperial airs does find support from what little we understand about his campaigns against the British of the west later in his reign. After Caradog's death, Cynan ap Rhodri had become king and seemingly established tolerable relations with the Mercians. However, in 817 or 818, when Caradog's son Hywel succeeded to Gwynedd after Cynan's death, Coenwulf invaded the kingdom, attacking the Britons on the margins of the Snowdon massif, and perhaps fighting in a battle between rival Welsh forces at Llan-faes on Anglesey. During that campaign it appears that the region of Rhufoniog south of Rhos was invaded by the Mercians, and in 818 or 819 a yet more extensive campaign saw Coenwulf with a Mercian army attacking Dyfed in south-west Wales.

This record of Mercian aggression against the Britons appears to have been orchestrated through north-eastern Wales, and was a prelude to a further major Mercian military campaign probably at the outset of Beornwulf's reign. This culminated, in the summer of 823, in the destruction of the eastern stronghold of Gwynedd at Degannwy on the Conwy estuary, and the conquest of the kingdom of Powys southwards from Rhufoniog. The series of operations concerned clearly has considerable implications for how we view the development and operation of Offa's Dyke. Since Coenwulf himself is recorded as having died at Basingwerk on the Dee estuary in the early summer of 821, it suggests that Beornwulf was simply carrying out an operation planned two years earlier. The position of the fortification at Basingwerk at the northern terminus of Wat's Dyke is potentially significant for what it may indicate about how the two parallel dykes at the northern end of the frontier could have operated.[96]

The western frontier in Mercian border history

The statement by William Camden with which this chapter opened demonstrates that as early as the sixteenth century Mercian history was understood in terms of a narrative of expansion, decline and fall. What is perhaps more interesting, however, is that Camden perceived the reason for the name of the kingdom not in terms of a particular frontier westwards with the British, so much as its location between 'all the kingdoms' that both bordered it and pressed in upon its territory. Such pressure could have resulted in the eclipsing and absorption of the 'tribal' groups that, early on, coalesced to form a kingdom on, and to the south of, the river Trent: but it did not. Rather, it appears to have served as a spur for this vigorous people to expand their territory and their influence outwards, while retaining a sense of localised constituent identity for the originating groups.

Under Penda, a key focus for outwards expansion arose in part from resistance to Northumbrian dominance. His incursions north of the Humber, his intrigues in Deira, and the campaigns of his later seventh-century successors in effect ended forever Northumbrian ambitions for supremacy southwards. But arguably his lasting legacy was the way in which the western borderlands became settled by Mercians, perhaps, as Finberg suggested, largely by peaceable absorption of indigenous British political groupings and communities.[97] Be that as it may, the eighth-century kings of Mercia appear to have viewed these territories less as protectorates and more as a platform from which to orchestrate further moves westwards at the expense of their British neighbours.

The character of the Mercian kingdom changed markedly under Offa, with a more sophisticated politics underscoring a more supremacist ambition. This was sustained by Coenwulf, but the new cohesion and confidence of the regime under both monarchs was also reflected in a change in stance towards the western borderlands. It is here that Offa's Dyke finds its historical relevance, but not only as a marker of the limits of Mercia, and certainly not only as some kind of defence against raids by the Britons. Camden's use of the word 'limite' to gloss the word 'mearc' underlying the name Mercia may also be relevant to what Offa's Dyke was meant to achieve. It intriguingly references the Latin word *limes*, denoting a frontier. While Camden clearly saw this as signifying the boundaries of those mostly Anglo-Saxon kingdoms that surrounded Mercia, it has clear resonances also for the particularity with which the western borderlands of Mercia were being newly defined in the eighth century, at least in part through the creation of the Dyke and a recognisable 'frontier zone'.

PART TWO
THE EVIDENCE EXPLORED

The view north from Cwmsanahan Hill towards Garbett Hall and Llanfair Hill
Offa's Dyke, facing to the left towards Wales, curves northwards up (or down) the hill above Garbett Hall in the background here, in western Shropshire. It survives as a low, denuded bank in the foreground, with a presumed infilled ditch. After crossing the valley it ascends the slope in one of its most dramatically-sited and largest-scale lengths.

CHAPTER FOUR

Placing the Dyke in the landscape

> When we look at OFFA'S DYKE, even at the present day, we shall be surprised at the boldness of its conception. It is carried over the summit of lofty mountains, across morasses, and through places where every natural obstruction is presented. These difficulties are, however, successively overcome ... with as much ease as though the engineer had felt himself superior to every natural impediment which he had to contend with.
>
> Charles Hartshorne, *Salopia Antiqua*, 1841.[1]

In his book on the antiquities of Shropshire, Reverend Hartshorne introduced the idea that the building of Wat's Dyke could have served as a precedent for a west-facing Mercian frontier work, which Offa's Dyke more completely fulfilled.[2] He was also among the first of the nineteenth-century observers to make the point that in order to discover more about the organisation behind its construction a greater familiarity with the physical form of the Dyke was needed; and that this was to be achieved, at least in part, through systematic observation and measurement at different localities.[3] Perhaps equally important as these ideas, however, was Hartshorne's conviction (which the above passage makes plain) that the work represented an organisational confidence, and evinced a 'boldness of conception', that enabled even the most challenging terrain to be traversed with apparent ease. In this way his insights can be seen to have anticipated the approach adopted (and some of the conclusions reached) by Cyril Fox almost a century later.

Fox observed at an early stage in his field study how the Dyke was carefully sited and deliberately constructed, and he also summarised, mostly in brief commentary sections within the reports on his successive seasons of fieldwork, how he thought such intricate location of the linear earthwork had been achieved.[4] He did not, however, systematically apply an analysis of form and location developed in one season in reference to the particular stretch of the Dyke covered, subsequently to all sections.[5] So, for instance, his comparative analysis of alignments along the earthwork in Montgomeryshire was not applied to the rest of the Dyke, although he apparently felt that the classification he used there was applicable elsewhere along its course.[6] Neither of the two extended accounts of the Dyke that have appeared subsequently have made good this deficiency, despite each having been based upon long-term and close study of the monument.[7]

Consequently, there a number of questions that may occur even to a casual observer concerning the placing of the Dyke in the landscape, and that have been asked in the past, but that have not yet been addressed fully from an archaeological or landscape perspective. Among the more general of such questions are, 'What determined where the overall north–south course of the Dyke was situated in respect to its exact geographical position eastwards or westwards?', and, 'Why did the Dyke consistently follow the courses that it did in relation to major topographical features that recur along its route?'

Other questions about the landscape placement of Offa's Dyke appear not to have been asked explicitly before at all. They include several that are of a more intricate nature, such as 'How was the position of the overall line of the Dyke across any broad stretch of country 'translated' into its exact topographical positioning along that line?' and 'In what ways was the Dyke made observable from different points along its course, and from a variety of locations especially to the west of it?' The aim of the present chapter is therefore to look again at the way in which the Dyke was placed in the landscape at a variety of scales from the broadest to the more local, and across its entire length, to see whether there are consistent patterns: and, where possible, to begin to explain them. The appraisal summarised in this chapter should not be mistaken for an exhaustive study, however. Rather, it is a statement of potential. The aim is to establish that such an approach can be fruitful, and to illustrate the nature of the insights that can be gained.

Some primary dimensions of the placing of Offa's Dyke

Fox envisaged the location of the western frontier of Mercia as primarily a reflection of the long-term influence upon human activity of a geographical transition between highlands and lowlands that is evident across much of Britain. Such a broad environmental explanation involved climate as well as physiography, and he first expounded this idea as a general proposition in his *Personality of Britain* essay in 1932.[8] For Fox, the choice of location for the course of Offa's Dyke, crossing dissected terrain actually within the uplands, represented the creation of a Mercian foothold just beyond the natural boundary between what he termed the 'Highland Zone' and the 'Lowland Zone' of Britain.[9] It is certainly the case that across at least that part of the landscape north of the Severn near Welshpool, the land to the east of the Dyke is largely 'lowland' and that to the west very generally 'upland'. Moreover, Fox strongly emphasised the contrast in the positioning of Offa's Dyke on the one hand and Wat's Dyke on the other in respect to uplands and lowlands. While the latter made careful use of the local topography, including the course of rivers, it was for much of its course nevertheless firmly placed within the Cheshire and north Shropshire plain. In contrast, Offa's Dyke only descended to that plain once, when it crossed the interfluve between the rivers Severn and Vyrnwy.

Although it provides a generalised view as to why the Dyke may have been placed in this 'threshold' zone between the uplands and lowlands, this idea does not adequately explain why Offa's Dyke took in so much of the uplands south of the middle Severn valley. Fox explained this fact, rather, in terms of an initial thrust of Mercian settlement that the 'mountain zone' part of the course of the Dyke, from the Vale of Montgomery to north Herefordshire, was created to consolidate. He regarded this explanation as the key to an understanding of the sequence of completion of the Dyke project: this most central part of the frontier was, for Fox, significant due to its proximity to the most important but vulnerable core area of Mercia, and he therefore regarded it as the first part of the scheme to have been built.[10]

Despite this overtly political inference, Fox had no doubt that geography was the primary determinant of the Dyke's location: 'I venture to attribute the correspondence (between the modern boundary between Wales and England and the line of Offa's Dyke) to natural causes, to which politics have proved unconsciously subservient'.[11] In other words, the enacted placing of Offa's Dyke was inevitable given the transition between uplands and lowlands that its course reflected. For Fox, political and human settlement considerations had been important, but they had not been the determining factors.

As was noted in Chapter 2, for some among the more recent interpreters of the rationale for the Dyke, the question of why Offa's Dyke was placed where it was can be answered primarily again, in terms of politics: its course corresponding to what was in the later eighth century the eastern boundary of the Kingdom of Powys.[12] The inherent circularity of such an argument regarding Powys has already been pointed out, but given on the one hand the westwards thrust of Anglo-Saxon settlement (and the fundamentally Mercian affiliations of such settlement), and the continuous or near-continuous nature of much of Offa's Dyke on the other, it is impossible to argue that the linear earthwork had no boundary purpose in relation to the numerous British communities and kingdoms westwards of its line. It is relatively uncontroversial, therefore, to suggest that although it did not necessarily mark the then westwards limit of English settlement, at least one motivation for building the Dyke was nonetheless to consolidate the major extent of such settlement or control.[13]

Past emphasis upon the division between upland and lowland Britain on the one hand, and assumed political boundaries on the other, has nonetheless contributed to a neglect of some distinctly different observations about the position of the Dyke. At the broadest scale, for example, irrespective of the existence of a transitional zone between uplands and lowlands in what has become the Welsh borderlands, there is a geographical logic to the placing of Offa's Dyke that refers instead to the seas surrounding west-central Britain. This is reflected in the fact that the Dyke was created on a course that in its overall north–south orientation extended towards the Dee estuary to the north and the Severn estuary to the south. These two estuaries frame the north-eastern and south-eastern limits, respectively, of the westwards projection of the mainland of Britain that Wales occupies. So even if the northern course of the Dyke was

4 *Placing the Dyke in the landscape*

FIGURE 4.1 Orientation and seas: Offa's Dyke southern limit at Sedbury Cliffs.

There is a need to explore alternative geographic perspectives in seeking to understand the location of the Dyke at the widest scale. One such perspective concerns the surrounding seas and dominant orientation. The view here, south-westwards from the terminus of the Dyke at Sedbury, takes in the first Severn Bridge and the Gloucestershire littoral beyond it.

never carried to the shores of the Dee estuary, its overall trend northwards from the middle reaches of the Severn east of Welshpool was clearly set towards that estuary somewhere in the vicinity of Flint. In the context of a power with the ambition of wresting control of north-central Britain from Northumbria and southern Britain from Wessex, while annexing British territory in west-central Britain on at least a client-kingdoms basis, the securing of a line that linked these two major estuaries could be seen as a key tactical move.

Another alternative observation concerns the dominance of a strict north and south orientation in the placement of the Dyke, within a limited margin of deviation for much of its course. So, although there are stretches where its line runs from north-west to south-east, and from north-east to south-west, its route predominantly and recurrently follows a strict north–south alignment that is highly constrained in its lateral shift. Throughout the whole of its course between Treuddyn in the north and Discoed near Presteigne in the south, for example, the Dyke runs through a relatively narrow corridor of landscape, such that it never deviates more than 4 minutes west and 3 minutes east of a line 3 degrees 5 minutes west of the Greenwich Meridian. Moreover, for well over half of this course the deviation is less than a minute east or west of this primary longitudinal position. After a shift to a north-west to south-east orientation from a point overlooking the Walton Basin just south of Discoed to the Wye west of Hereford, its orientation reverts to a strict north–south line along the lower Wye valley to once more deviate no more than a minute east or west from 2 degrees 40 minutes west to reach the Severn estuary at Sedbury.[14]

Arguably, any demarcation of a frontier line between areas to the east and to the west of that line is likely to have had a consistent north–south trend, and it is remarkable in this light that extensive north-east to south-west trending or north-west to south-east trending stretches of the Dyke were created at all. And yet it is the consistency of line over such a great distance that impresses: while economy of effort was no doubt a consideration, the discipline with which the line is maintained indicates in its own right the nature of the dominant authority involved, which Fox saw as emanating from Offa himself.[15]

Routing and large-scale 'stances' in respect to topography and landscape

Whatever the reasons for the broadest geographic location of Offa's Dyke, it was situated in a series of deliberate large-scale stances in relation to the major areas of upland, and the principal rivers, of what has become the borderland between England and Wales. These stances include or exclude to the east or west of the line of the Dyke discrete areas of lowland and upland, while their placement also makes positive use of the existence of three major rivers that any such routing will encounter. Several major areas of upland were therefore excluded from the line followed by the Dyke. This is especially the case north of the middle Severn valley: Ruabon Mountain (including Eglwyseg Mountain) stands prominently to the west, as does the major area of upland that forms the eastern flank of the Berwyns mountain range. South of the Severn, the Long Mountain was traversed and largely included within the line, while the hills that Montgomery is sited upon the eastern margin of, were excluded. The Clun Forest uplands, to the north of the river Clun, were in contrast bisected, thereby including within the line of the Dyke significant areas of upland such as Corndon Hill and, further east, the Long Mynd. Both the Radnor Forest massif and the Black Mountains were left well to the west of the line, while Harley Mountain east of Knighton, and similar uplands south of the Clun valley, were included within it.

Meanwhile, both the Dee and the middle Severn rivers were used in place of the Dyke at points where their courses could help the transit of its planned course through the landscape.[16] In contrast, the Wye was quite probably used not so much in place of the line, but as an alternative element of the frontier southwards until that river enters its gorge-like entwinements south of Ross-on-Wye and south of Monmouth, when there is once again the opportunity for the Dyke to follow a course consistently along prominent crests or crags at a level far above the river itself, but frequently overlooking it. The Severn estuary was then used in a very different way, as the point of dramatic terminus southwards.

So, given that the dominant north–south orientation of the Dyke north of Discoed traverses more than 70 miles of broken terrain, the consistency in its routing is remarkable. But within this overall north–south corridor, there were nonetheless some noticeable adjustments in orientation. It helps the definition of these adjustments to identify first, the five stretches that are oriented most strictly north–south. One extends between Brymbo and Ruabon north of the river Dee, and another from Craignant north of Selattyn Hill southwards to the middle reaches of the Severn. A third extends from the Severn southwards via the Vale of Montgomery and Clun Forest to the uplands at Llanfair Hill, and a fourth (the shortest such stretch) from Knighton to a point just south of the river Lugg near Discoed. Finally, a fifth stretch extends south from near Monmouth to the Wye estuary. However, these were linked together, and extended, by the river Severn itself east of Welshpool, and by four stretches of Dyke on subtly contrasting orientations (Figure 4.2).

The first of the stretches of Offa's Dyke orientated in a contrasting way to the strict north–south line comprises the south-eastwards trending length north of Brymbo towards Treuddyn. The second is the south-westwards trending course across the Dee and Ceiriog valleys that links the first and second of the more strictly north–south routings. The third is the short north-west to south-east oriented stretch from Llanfair Hill to Knighton, and the fourth the long south-eastwards course extending from a point just south of the river Lugg at Discoed in effect all the way to the river Wye.

The systematic routing involved in such a pattern of orientation suggests that a particular zone had been demarcated in advance for the total 'traverse' from north of the Dee southwards to the Severn estuary. This zone is definable despite the extent of displacement eastwards, south of the middle Lugg valley near Discoed. This very considerable adjustment that the course of the Dyke makes in a south-easterly direction from the Discoed area appears likely to have been designed at least in part to enable an approach to the Severn estuary that flanked the lower reaches of the river Wye on its eastern side. The reasons for the displacement, however, were probably both practical and political.[17]

The relation to the uplands to the west of the line is not simply a matter of their exclusion, however. The carefully-planned lengthy 'stances' appear, rather, to be placed in such a way as to deliberately 'face' these uplands. So, the most northerly stretch of the Dyke that is on a north-west to south-east orientation, extending south-eastwards from Treuddyn, holds a position facing south-westwards that at its northern end provides a view towards the northern flank of the Ruabon Mountain massif. Southwards, having traversed the Cedigog, and having regained high ground around Brymbo, the Dyke then becomes oriented almost directly north–south (Figure 2.2). Here the route it traces southwards again faces the same Ruabon Mountain massif, but this time looking directly westwards towards it. The stretch extending south-westwards that crosses both Dee and Ceiriog valleys also faces north-eastwards towards the same high ground of Ruabon Mountain and further high hills to the west. Across the length once more on a strict north–south course southwards towards the Tanat-Vyrnwy confluence, the Dyke faces westwards to the hills that rise gradually towards the Berwyn Mountains.

South of the middle Severn near Welshpool, Offa's Dyke follows once again a southwards course looking west over the Severn valley towards the hills beyond. Then it traces a course adjusted slightly south-eastwards to face the hills to the west of Montgomery, and at a consistent distance eastwards from them. On a due southwards trajectory again, the Dyke follows a course weaving its way through the deeply dissected hills of the Clun Forest uplands before rising to its highest point at Llanfair Hill, all the while facing hills of equivalent height westwards.

The south-easterly course from Llanfair Hill down to the crossing of the Teme at Knighton takes up a stance facing south-westwards. This not only overlooks the Teme valley but also faces towards the hills around the Radnor Forest massif. The subsequent stretch from Knighton southwards is again oriented due north and south, with a view directly westwards to the Radnor Forest uplands. Having made its extraordinary loop to overlook the Walton Basin and link onto Rushock Hill, the Dyke faces in part south-westwards towards another major upland massif: this time the east-facing scarp of the Black Mountains.

From Rushock Hill, the course trending south-east is resumed (if the Dyke did once exist continuously here), towards the lower slopes of Burton Hill/Ladylift in north Herefordshire. The short length of Dyke forming the eastern 'arm' of the angled turn on Rushock Hill is oriented towards the south-west facing eminence at Burton Hill/Ladylift, and this orientation is regained down in the north Herefordshire plain where, after crossing the Arrow valley, the alignment towards the same hill is picked up at Lyonshall (Figure 1.27). The consistency of the sighting here suggests that even if the Dyke was not completed across the north Herefordshire landscape, it was planned to be continuous across this area. Along most of this stretch towards the north bank of the Wye, it would have faced south-westwards towards the east-facing scarp of the Black Mountains.[18]

Finally, whatever happened in the intervening distance, the again directly north–south orientation that was followed in a course traced for 10 miles (16 km) above the east bank of the Wye south of Monmouth included prospects

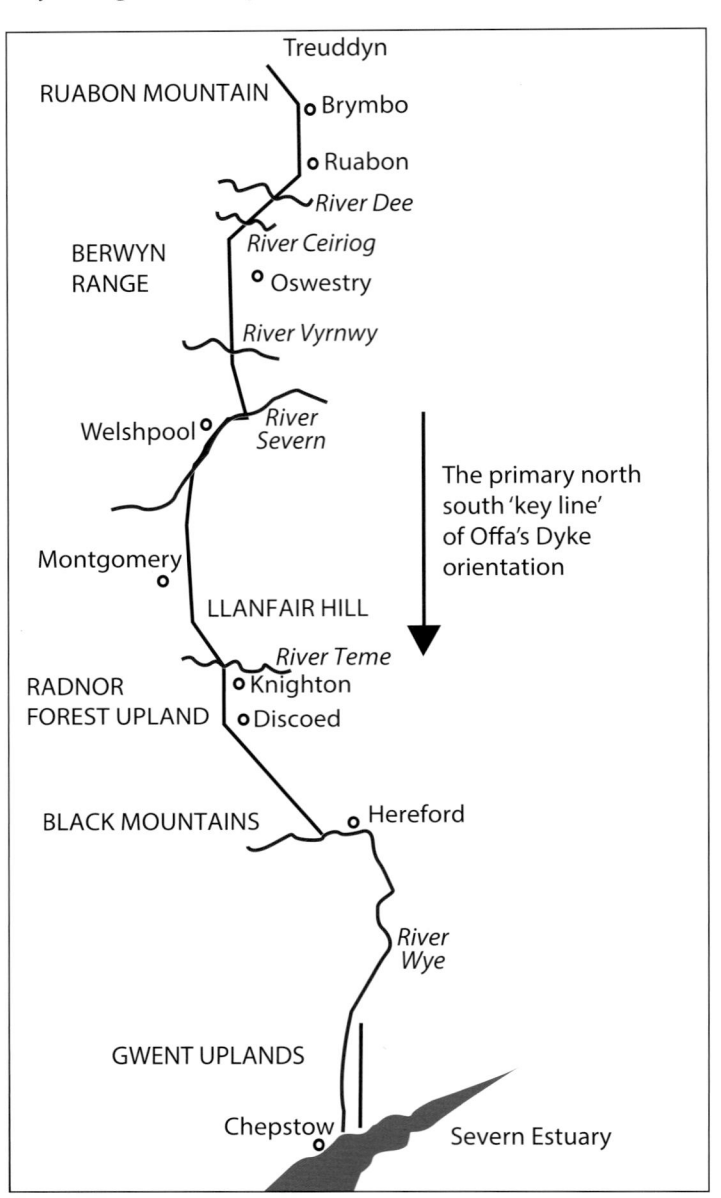

FIGURE 4.2 Major 'stances' of the Dyke, facing the uplands (schematic map)

This schematic map aims to highlight the way in which the gross location of the Dyke respects prominent landscape features westwards.

FIGURE 4.3 South-west facing orientation: the Teme valley from Panpunton Hill

The ideas of demarcation of a territory is evident here, but may be less important than the visual dominance of the Dyke over a protracted distance, and its surveillance capacity, here over a distance of two miles, directly overlooking the valley.

westwards towards the Gwent uplands north-west of Chepstow. In respect to these stances, therefore, there is once again a remarkable consistency in the placement of the Dyke, to face, both visually and symbolically, the uplands often of significantly higher elevation to the west.

Use of the major rivers

Offa's Dyke was brought directly to the banks of the major rivers it encountered (Figure 4.4). Yet neither at the Dee nor at the middle reaches of the Severn was it deemed desirable to traverse the river concerned on opposing banks at a single point, even though it would have been quite feasible to have done so. Rather, the choice was made to off-set the Dyke on either side of the river in

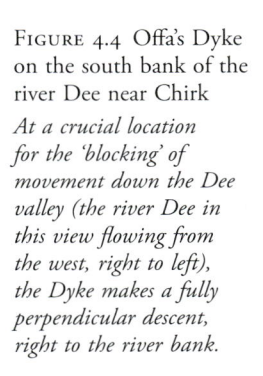

FIGURE 4.4 Offa's Dyke on the south bank of the river Dee near Chirk

At a crucial location for the 'blocking' of movement down the Dee valley (the river Dee in this view flowing from the west, right to left), the Dyke makes a fully perpendicular descent, right to the river bank.

question. In doing so, it was made clear that the river was in each case to be seen as integral to the definition of the route of the Dyke.

The crossing of the river Dee to the east of modern-day Llangollen is contained within one of the main 'stances' that runs counter to the strict north–south course of the Dyke. This major alignment nonetheless maintains a strict line from a point to the west of Ruabon to another at Craignant to the north of Selattyn Hill despite the presence of such a major river. To do so, it meets the bank in one location, and leaves it a short distance upstream (or downstream, depending upon the direction one is facing), but the choice of location was determined not only by the overall trend of the Dyke, but also by what the river does at this point. The Dee follows an 'S-shaped' course, with the Dyke meeting it at the bottom (western) end of the 'S', and leaving it at the upper (eastern) end, such that while the actual crossing is displaced, the route is not. As such, the river itself in a sense *became* part of the Dyke, and this reveals an important aspect of its placement: that it in effect incorporated key natural features both to maintain consistency of line, and (in respect especially to the hills it traversed) to provide advantageous oversight westwards.

In the middle Severn valley north of Welshpool, the natural course of the river follows a south-west to north-east orientation, although its floodplain broadens markedly from a point north of Tirymynach on the west bank and Trewern on the east. Here, a broad area of level ground between the rivers Severn and Vyrnwy separated the lowlands of their confluence, and areas eastwards towards Shrewsbury, on the one hand, from the upper Severn valley and the Vyrnwy-Tanat hills on the other. This was therefore a crucial area for both the settlement and the protection of the Mercian frontier zone. Had the intention been to minimise the length of the river used as a proxy for the Dyke here, the earthwork could have been built to follow a single alignment south

FIGURE 4.5 Offa's Dyke approaching the middle Severn valley from the north

The Dyke at this point (near Rhos, south of Four Crosses), was purposefully aligned southwards, straight towards the western summit of The Breiddin massif. It approaches (or leaves) the river-bank here in a successive series of three alignments.

from the crossing of the Vyrnwy. Instead its course was adjusted locally, slightly eastwards through two subtle changes of alignment to approach the river-bank more directly.[19]

It could be argued that the reason for this adjustment was practical: the aim was to minimise the extent to which the earthwork had to cross the softer ground of the flood-plain. This could have been achieved more effectively, however, by bringing the Dyke yet further around to the east, to approach the river more or less at the perpendicular. The course chosen was instead aligned onto the western end of the upper slopes of The Breiddin (Figure 4.5).[20] This act achieved two things simultaneously. Firstly, it broadly maintained the strict north–south orientation set out from the crossing of the Vyrnwy; and secondly, it did so while most effectively and efficiently closing the topographical gap that can be seen to exist between the twin mountainous 'bulwarks' of The Breiddin to the south and Llanymynech Hill to the north.[21]

Deliberate alignments in the placement of the Dyke

The alignment of the Dyke onto prominent topographical features, as with the western end of the upper slopes of The Breiddin just mentioned, is not surprising. However, the sophistication of sighting practices is often remarkable. A particularly striking instance is to be found in just this middle Severn valley area that was inevitably such a crucial point in the frontier. Here, as the course of the Dyke approached Buttington from the south it was carefully oriented very slightly east of due north on a line that, if projected, would pass just to the east of the present site of the church. Just over half a mile (1.0 km) south of Buttington it quite subtly shifted orientation westwards to a point on the edge of the floodplain. From there it appears to have turned more sharply westwards again, towards Buttington Bridge, and this reinforces the sense that the manifest intention was to meet the left bank of the Severn at this point.

Buttington is located at the narrowest part of the floodplain both north and south of Welshpool, so was clearly of strategic importance for a crossing of the river: hence the presence of the bridge here from at least the medieval period. The Dyke need not have descended to the Severn floodplain at all if not heading for this point, but could have continued northwards past Garbett's Hall overlooking Buttington from the east, continuing to Cefn, and then along the lower western slopes of The Breiddin past Trewern to Criggion. Here it would have been located directly opposite Derwas, where the Dyke approaching the north bank of the Severn terminates.

Yet if the intention was to meet the south bank of the Severn where Buttington Bridge now stands, why did the Dyke not trace a more direct line towards this point but instead followed a course for most of the distance north from Pentre that was aligned past Buttington church? One possible answer is that this alignment is in fact sighted not onto anywhere as close as Buttington, but, rather, beyond it towards Llanymynech Hill fully nine miles (14.5 km)

FIGURE 4.6 The west-facing slopes of the Long Mountain, from Buttington Bridge
The Dyke is traceable from the hill-slopes in the background, down to a point just beyond the clump of trees in the left centre foreground. It rises up onto the shoulder of the hill in descending profile in the background, before continuing along towards Forden, maintaining a consistent distance from the river Severn (see Figure 1.19 for the view westwards from near Forden, and Figure 2.1 for the view from Powis Castle towards The Long Mountain).

to the north. As noted in Chapter 1, this was a key location, both for its prospect westwards over the valleys of the Tanat and Vyrnwy and as a vantage point southwards up the Severn valley and onto the west-facing flank of Long Mountain. Perhaps it was the centrality of a particular point on Llanymynech Hill that led to its memorialisation, not as 'Asterley Rocks' (as today), but instead as 'Carreghofa'.[22]

Not only did alignments of Offa's Dyke vary in their length, but in some terrain they could be 'nested', with both localised and long-distance alignments co-existing. This practice is evident in the crossing of broad level areas of the landscape such as the Vale of Montgomery. Here, an encompassing single alignment maintained closely over a distance of more than six miles between Hem and Mellington (*c.*9.5 km) included as many as 10 very straight lengths varying in length from 140 m to 1000 m. These were repeatedly separated from one another by connecting lengths that varied more obviously in orientation over short distances, continually and subtly adjusting to the variations in terrain present, but that still maintained closely the dominant alignment.[23]

Some alignments comprised precisely straight lengths entirely, as in the stretch of Dyke overlooking the Severn valley between The Stubb (south of Leighton Park) and a point south of Forden, in which an overall length of two miles (3.2 km) is made up of three precisely straight alignments placed end to end, with orientations only minimally distinct from one another. Different stretches of Dyke that also followed single overall alignments meanwhile had few or no lengthy straight runs of Dyke, and were adjusted continually to take account of terrain subtleties. A case in point is the length of Dyke south of Buttington with an alignment possibly sighted towards Llanymynech Hill, just discussed. This length extends from a point north of Pentre just to the east of Leighton (across the Severn from Welshpool) northwards to a point just north-west of Hope Villa south of Buttington (or, of course, vice-versa). This length of just over a mile (1.8 km) comprises nine straight lengths laid end-to-end, on contrasting orientations but deviating only minimally from a single alignment.[24] These lengths vary from 60 m to 400 m, and alternate between long straight lengths, and much shorter lengths that subtly adjust its passage across the landscape. The significance of these subtle adjustments and varied-length straight lengths is of more than passing interest for the light that it throws upon the way in which the Dyke was built, and to what ends such subtlety of build was directed.[25]

In light of the above it is not surprising to find that it was through reflection upon the observations he had made during his survey of the Dyke in Montgomeryshire that Fox attempted to make sense of its alignment practices by identifying four different types of alignment and specifying their incidence.[26] His first type was a direct alignment across an area between two identifiable points, where both ends of the straight length were clearly inter-visible. The second type was a variant of the first, where the alignment concerned deviated over the course of direct line at a specific location (or between two further points of a shorter length), not visible from either end.[27] A third type was again a direct alignment between two points, but the 'trace' between these points was regarded as sinuous rather than straight. As Fox described this, 'Parts of the earthwork which between two mutually visible points are sinuous, but which at no point markedly diverge from the straight line'.[28] His fourth kind of alignment was present in 'parts of the earthwork which, within the broad limits of general direction, are sensitive to the relief of the country-side'.[29]

FIGURE 4.7 Along Offa's Dyke at Mainstone, looking southwards

The orientations along the Dyke have both near-distance and longer-distance objectives, as here, looking in the opposite direction from the one reproduced as Figure 1.2, facing the Kerry Ridgeway. In the near distance is the ravine-like valley at Mainstone Churchtown, while even from this distance (around 13 miles, or 20 km away to the south-south-west) the Radnor Forest massif is a glowering skyline presence.

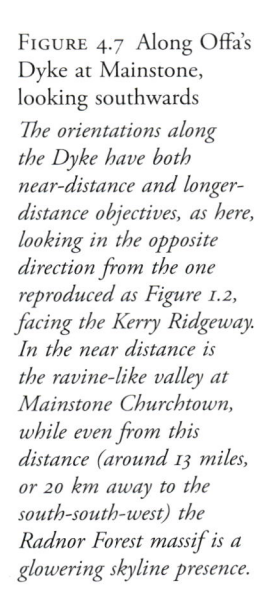

It is clear both from this classification and from its analytical application to 14,610 yards (8.3 miles; 13.36 km) of Dyke in Montgomeryshire, that this contour-following type cannot be described as an 'alignment' at all: rather, it simply follows the general trend of the course of the Dyke. The degree to which the third type can be regarded as a deliberate alignment is also questionable, since a line between any two points is liable to be sinuous if it is not straight.

Fox's first type of alignment, with or without a slight or subtle deviation, recurs in characteristic ways throughout the course of the Dyke, just as does the tracing of a line around the contour of a west-facing slope. In Montgomeryshire, most of the straight alignments occur where the Dyke crosses level or only slightly undulating terrain.[30] Fox identified 14 stretches of the earthwork that featured straight alignments in that county, and expressed a view that the explanation for their occurrence was the existence of 'country not of marked elevation, flat or with moderate variations in level, and free from dense woodland'.[31] This view was of course central to one of the main theses that Fox was concerned to develop: that the detail of the changing form and placement of Offa's Dyke across the landscape could itself be interpreted as having been a consequence of whether the pre-existing eighth-century land-use and vegetation of the area concerned was arable, pasture or open moorland, or dense woodland.[32] Where the straightest type of alignment was present (such as across some but not all level areas, or across the flood-plains of some rivers), it could according to Fox be inferred that sighting-in such an alignment had been easy because the land was under arable.

However, although topography was clearly an influence, and vegetation may have inhibited or facilitated the ease with which alignments could be created, did the presence of open or cultivated land in one area and woodland in another actually *determine* the placement of the straight alignments? Noble certainly used the example of the Dyke on the north-facing slope at Discoed to argue that this was not the case. There, the topographic position down a slope was not obviously conducive to the creation of a straight alignment. Nor were the thin-soiled north-facing slopes optimal for arable farming.

The north-north-west to south-south-east course of the Dyke across the Vale of Montgomery evidently secured the upland and lowland areas to its east and served both to occupy a stance facing the group of hills to the west of Montgomery itself and to block west–east movement along the valleys of the Camlad and Caebitra. It achieved this traverse in 3 major orientations but with 8 straight alignments between Pound House, Hem, and Cwm, where the dramatic half-mile ascent to Crow's Nest begins. The straight alignments nonetheless encompass subtle adjustments of line, representing only minor deviations from a continuous line from north to south. Fox recorded 4 straight alignments, three subtly varying alignments, and two short sections where he thought that there was no direct alignment. He made sense of this 'mix' in terms of the influence of former forest. However, this gives the false impression that there was no overall alignment trend to the whole of this 6-mile (*c.*9.5 km) transit. Although disrupted to some degree by local topography at Rownal and at Lower Garthlow, the consistency of the line is remarkable: it can be characterised therefore instead as a running series of end-to-end alignments. Moreover the location of the 'adjustment' lengths is far from random, and their situation, providing significant outlook points along the course of the Dyke across the plain, argues strongly against the existence of any woodland at all in the vicinity of the Dyke here in the eighth century.[33]

Meanwhile, Fox's overall analysis of the straight alignments in Montgomeryshire showed that these varied enormously in length, from 140 to 1,830 yards (*c.*150 m to 1.6 km). If straight alignments could vary so much in length, how could their presence or absence have been dictated entirely by topography or by eighth-century land-use? The answer is that neither explanation need be invoked, if we instead see the Dyke as a *wholly-designed* structure. That is, that the decision to create a straight alignment had more to do with what the Dyke was supposed to achieve in terms of visual effect or local oversight than with the answering of the simple practical question 'how do I lay out a Dyke as directly as possible in a landscape of varied topography and vegetation cover?' Rather, the Dyke was both locally and extensively planned and engineered to produce particular effects in particular places, that when put together amounted to a clear strategy for control, containment and in effect re-definition of a landscape in defiance of the inherited pattern, whether environmentally-shaped or socially and culturally constructed.

The placement of the Dyke in respect to rivers and streams, and their valleys

The route of Offa's Dyke as described in Chapter 1, and in reference to major topographical features such as mountains and rivers above, can be viewed as having encountered and traversed a series of challenging obstacles. These included the rivers and river-valleys, streams and side-valleys, and various deep ravines, that so characterise the dissected landscapes of the eastern uplands of what is now the England/Wales borderland. Fox's predecessors, Fox himself, and those who have written subsequently have, like Hartshorne, pondered the skill involved in negotiating this difficult terrain; and Fox in particular noted the intricacies of this achievement. However, the carefully-managed ways in which Offa's Dyke approached rivers, river-valleys and chasms, large and small, also reveals something of the strategic planning and the practical and tactical thinking behind its landscape placement.

The crossing of flood-plains

In contrast to its approaches to the major rivers, the Dyke crosses most of the valley-bottoms of the smaller rivers along its course at the perpendicular, with lengths of bank and ditch approaching the stream-course of each river across

FIGURE 4.8 Crossing the flood-plain of the river Lugg near Discoed

This view southwards from the northern edge of the valley is in the opposite direction to the one shown in Figure 2.10, above. The prominent scale of the earthwork descending the north-facing slope of the hill by Yew Tree Farm is evident in the distance, as is the effect of placing the Dyke at the perpendicular to cross the floodplain at left-centre. This served to divert the Cascob Brook from its former course, to meet the Lugg at a right-angle along the line of the ditch of the Dyke (confluence visible at left foreground).

PHOTOGRAPH: ADAM STANFORD/AERIAL-CAM, COPYRIGHT RESERVED.

its floodplain from points directly opposite one another (and often regardless of how the floodplain itself has been approached). From north to south, perpendicular crossings of rivers and streams were achieved in this way in the flood-plains of the Gwenfro, Clywedog, Pentrebychan, Eitha, Ceiriog, Morlas, Morda, Camlad, Caebitra, Unk, Clun, Teme, Lugg, Hindwell, Curl, Maddle, Mork and Brockweir valleys. Such crossings of the rivers themselves at right-angles to their courses may have been determined by a pragmatic concern to minimise the extent to which the Dyke builders had to cross soft ground and water flowing mostly from west to east along these channels.

In contrast to this wholly pragmatic placement across the floodplain itself, in several cases considerable care was taken to control how the Dyke was located in the landscape as it approached the slopes down the valley-sides concerned. This is seen very clearly at the northern end of the Vale of Montgomery, where the Dyke, having been tracing a north-east to south-west course, reached a prominent point on the ridge above the river Camlad. Here, it was turned sharply southwards at Hem down a steep slope to effect a perpendicular crossing of the floodplain of the river (Figure 7.8). This manoeuvre also facilitated an alignment southwards onto a rise immediately west of the later Rownal Covert, where the Dyke runs south-eastwards to effect another perpendicular crossing of the Caebitra Brook 3 miles (4.8 km) away.[34]

In contrast, the crossing of the Hindwell Brook valley in Radnorshire involves no descent from the western side, with the Dyke seemingly deliberately avoiding the impressive Iron Age bulwarks of Burfa Camp and running instead in a loop at the foot of the hill on which they stand. However, it then takes a direct west–east course across the floodplain where it crosses at the perpendicular to their flow not only the Hindwell but also Ridding's Brook, to the foot of Herrock Hill, where it ascends the side of a north-facing spur.[35]

4 Placing the Dyke in the landscape

Meanwhile, most of the other perpendicular valley traverses involve a 'symmetrical' ascent and descent of the Dyke across valleys with a broader or narrower V-shaped profile. The crossings of the Gwenfro valley south of Brymbo (in Denbighshire), the Curl Brook valley west of Lyonshall, and the Maddle valley at Yazor (both in north Herefordshire), and the Mork and Brockweir valleys (in Gloucestershire), all conform to this pattern: although the most northerly and the most southerly among these valleys are more ravine-like in profile.

Carefully-planned approaches to valleys

So the course of Offa's Dyke as it approached the valleys concerned was by no means always determined by the particular requirement for a perpendicular crossing of the river itself; or indeed as at Hem near Montgomery (Figure 7.8) by the need to achieve both a major shift in course and a key vantage-point. In several places the Dyke was carefully and deliberately positioned such that it overlooked the valley from either north or south as it moved towards the point at which it then crossed the floodplain. The Dyke was in most such cases positioned to follow a north-west to south-east course as it approached the valley concerned from the north, before changing its course suddenly at or close to the river itself to traverse the valley-bottom at the perpendicular. Such a course provided an outlook over the river valley in question from a north-easterly direction.

It is difficult to see such an angled approach to the valleys in question as having been arrived at co-incidentally, and the presumption must surely be that

FIGURE 4.9 Approaching the crossing of the Teme, overlooking the valley

This aerial view in winter picks out the course of the Dyke on its extended course running south-eastwards to (or northwestwards from) Tref-y-clawdd (Knighton), in near-constant oversight of the Teme valley from the north. In the near-distance here, the location of the Dyke crossing the southern flanks of Llanfair Hill clearly anticipates or follows from the placement of the Dyke on Cwnsanahan Hill (just discernible at top left here).

REPRODUCED COURTESY OF A. WIGLEY: COPYRIGHT, SHROPSHIRE COUNCIL.

close surveillance of the approaches from the west towards each river-crossing itself was intended. Such oversight could be provided at a variety of scales. So, for example, the Dyke was so located as to follow such a course on the fully two-mile (3.2 km) stretch from Cwmsanahan Hill down to the crossing of the Teme at Knighton. Throughout this length there are broad views south-westwards over a 3 to 4 mile (4.8 km to 6.3 km) stretch of the Teme valley from high ground to the north of it, and from a number of points along this part of the Dyke there are vistas right down between the hill-slopes onto the river itself and the surrounding valley-bottom (Figure 4.9).

At a similarly grand scale, the Dyke approaches the river Wye obliquely from the north-west along the natural orientation of the ridge of Garnons Hill to the west of Hereford near Bridge Sollers, then makes a slight adjustment southwards before continuing the south-eastwards alignment to meet the north bank of the river. All the while the Dyke maintains south-westwards facing prospects across the river, with the Black Mountains ridge directly in frame on the horizon beyond it, rather than facing directly up the valley (Figure 2.13). This achieves both oversight of the river and its valley from the north-east, while occupying a stance facing the distant upland massif. In this location, the Dyke also directly overlooks an area that may have been closely contested in the early years of Offa's reign.[36]

In several other places such oversight of a significant river-valley from the north-east on the approach to the river-crossing is achieved through a length of the Dyke whose location is equally dramatic. At Llanymynech Hill, for example, the course the Dyke took around the outer crest of the precipitous hillside directly overlooked the lower Tanat valley and the Tanat/Vyrnwy confluence.[37]

Near Discoed, the Dyke approached the Lugg valley west of Presteigne by curving around the western edge of the descending flank of Furrow Hill to reach a point where it suddenly swept around to traverse the valley-bottom at the perpendicular (Figures 2.10 and 4.8).[38] In these cases the Dyke followed the crest of a steep slope overlooking the river concerned for some distance prior to descending the valley-side to cross the river itself. This enhances the sense the observer today has, that the Dyke was deliberately placed to monitor movement in the valley below, as well as to provide a looming presence eastwards when seen from the bottom or the western flanks of the valley.[39]

This pattern, featuring an oblique approach from the north-west followed by the perpendicular crossing of the river itself, was repeated at the crossing of several of the more minor streams the Dyke traversed, for instance south of the Kerry Ridgeway at the crossing of the head-streams of the river Unk in Edenhope and in Cwm Ffrydd, and at Mainstone Churchtown. Only at the river Clywedog north of Ruabon, where the Dyke also approaches from the north-west, but instead crosses down the east-facing flank of a ridge descending to the point where the direct north–south traverse of the valley-bottom, can it be seen that oversight of the cleft through which the river descends was not a concern of the Dyke-builders.[40]

4 *Placing the Dyke in the landscape* 139

FIGURE 4.10 Offa's Dyke north of the Afon Morda valley, looking south

At centre foreground is Carreg-y-big, with the curve over Baker's Hill beyond clearly facilitating views over the steep-sided Afon Morda valley at right. The Dyke crosses the side-valley by Oswestry racecourse to take a route along the crest of Craig Morda (wooded, in the middle distance). Long Mountain, across the Severn, is hazily visible at left horizon.

REPRODUCED COURTESY OF A. WIGLEY: COPYRIGHT, SHROPSHIRE COUNCIL.

At the crossing of the Morlas stream north of Selattyn Hill, the Dyke was placed to achieve an oblique oversight of the valley before a traverse of the river itself at the perpendicular, but in this case a north-west facing prospect was achieved as it approached the stream from the south. At Discoed west of Presteigne in Radnorshire oversight of the valley of the Lugg from the east as the Dyke approached from the north was matched on the south side of the river crossing by a prospect westwards over a tributary valley. Here, the Dyke was carefully placed at the point where a flank of the hill facing north turned south-westwards. Such subtle use of folds in hill-slopes to achieve westwards-facing prospects above river-valleys can be seen to have been implemented in several other locations where the flood-plain crossing itself appears to have been entirely at the perpendicular.

'Mirrored' oversight of valleys looking upstream from Offa's Dyke

There appears to have been a deliberate attempt at some valley-crossings to create a concave curving line facing westwards down the slopes both north *and* south of the valley, with only the valley-bottom traverse itself undertaken at the perpendicular. This is dramatically the case at the crossing of the Clun valley at Spoad near Newcastle, where the curve is particularly evident when viewed from north or south (Figures 1.23 and 9.12), and is also evident at the crossing of the Ceiriog at Chirk (Figure 4.11).

In each of these two places, the descent the Dyke made from the south was precipitous and was woven around the west-facing leading edge of a near-vertically disposed spur or shoulder of land. In each case also, the ascent to the north took advantage of the presence of a south-flowing stream to achieve an outlook angled westwards up the valley, despite being much less steep than its north-facing counterpart on the opposite side of the same valley. Exactly how the slopes in each case vary as they descend into the valley differs somewhat in each case, but it is very hard to avoid the conclusion that these two widely geographically separated traverses were conceived and executed by the same group of 'Dyke designers'.

The valleys stopped up

In traversing these smaller rivers and streams, the building of the Dyke across their floodplains and literally onto their banks effectively interrupted their flow. In some valleys, such as those of the Teme and the Lugg, its impact was similar to the construction of a low dam across the valleys, and some care must have been taken to construct channels that prevented the Dyke from simply being washed away when the river was in flood. This 'stopping up' of rivers, however, was not just a matter of water. In effect, the blocking was of the valley as a whole: serving also to control the movement of people and stock along these valleys that had taken place from time immemorial. This cannot have been other than deliberate, and the choice of where to block or check movement along the valleys concerned is revealing. So, for example, north of the Dee the Clywedog valley was blocked just before it enters its gentler lower course at Bersham. Similarly, west of Oswestry, the Morda valley was blocked at precisely the point where it emerges from a steep-sided gorge into a broad, almost level, area (Figure 4.15).

In the Dee valley itself, the oblique crossing line of the Dyke closely girdles the higher ground successively at Gardden and at Cefn north of the river, and at Fron southwards from it. As it does so, it also prevents transit along the south side of the valley and effectively stops up movement either up or down it. The very same 'stance' serves to block movement along the Ceiriog abruptly at Bronygarth to the west of Chirk, well into the higher ground. Meanwhile, the Dyke blocked the Vyrnwy valley at exactly that point where it issues onto the central Shropshire plain. This is also just below its confluence with the Tanat, therefore effectively curtailing movement between uplands and lowlands along either river-valley.

The blocking effect of placing of the Dyke across river-valleys in distinctive

4   *Placing the Dyke in the landscape*   141

FIGURE 4.11 Offa's Dyke negotiating the crossing of the Ceiriog valley at Chirk

The Dyke is visible in the foreground at right, at the beginning of a series of carefully-located adjustments of orientation on this north-facing slope. It is evident again across the valley, turned slightly outwards in a similar series of adjustments, rising from/descending to the river-crossing, traversing the south-facing slope below Chirk Castle.
PHOTOGRAPH: ADAM STANFORD/ AERIAL-CAM, COPYRIGHT RESERVED.

FIGURE 4.12 Blocking routeways and valleys: the Dyke north from Crowsnest
This view is from a point adjacent to the Kerry Ridgeway east–west ridge-top track, a likely prehistoric and later routeway (cf. Figure 4.13). In the Vale of Montgomery in the middle distance, the Dyke crossed both the Caebitra and Camlad streams, and blocked off access along them. Following the Dyke alignment onto the ridge beyond the large (Lymore Park) wood, the key location at Hem is just discernible, where the Dyke turns north-east, overlooking the river Severn.

ways is also evident south of the Severn, but in markedly different ways. Across the Vale of Montgomery, for example, the primary concern (and possibly the reason for the choice of route) may have been to obstruct eastwards movement along the Camlad and Caebitra valleys. The streams concerned flow in opposite directions to one another, the first and more northerly flowing westwards and the second eastwards. Crossing the Camlad close to its confluence to the Severn, however, served to inhibit movement eastwards up its (at this point) largely level, if meandering, course. Meanwhile, crossing the Caebitra at Brompton served to block eastwards egress from the narrow valley onto the broader lands of the Vale (Figure 4.12).

Further south again, the crossing of the Unk headwaters served in only a limited way to inhibit west–east movement since in this area the ridges were probably more important than the valleys. However, the crossing of the Clun so far up its course prevented any movement down its valley towards the Teme catchment lowlands south of the Long Mynd, while the crossing of the river Teme itself at Knighton clearly blocked access to the same area. This also created a long controllable corridor to the east of the Dyke through to the Clun-Teme confluence lowlands east of Brampton Bryan, and the same was true of the point at which the Lugg was crossed at Discoed. Here the Dyke was brought around the uplands south of Presteigne to block movement from the Walton Basin lowlands towards the lower Lugg valley.[41] From the Wye southwards, the drainage pattern is very different, and it seems possible that, if the Dyke was built at all in this landscape, it followed the left bank of the river.

So the effect of such 'stopping up' of the river-valleys was to contain the areas of the upper catchment in such a way as to frustrate as well as to control movement. In this way, the Dyke did not just exclude access from the west to the lower-lying richer farming lands to the east, but interfered with *any* movement along the major valley routes outwards towards the lowlands from the British lands to the west. By the simple expedient of careful location of the Dyke the Mercians effectively truncated the 'eastern' world of their potentially hostile western neighbours. That said, it should not be forgotten that the Dyke was not necessarily designed as an impermeable barrier to movement, but perhaps rather as a controlling or regulating one.[42]

The placement of the Dyke in respect to natural eminences

Although its orientation was not fixed invariably along a north–south compass setting, a dominant trend for the course of Offa's Dyke does not deviate strongly to take in particularly prominent locations. Indeed, its course often ignores vantage points that are quite close to its 'minimal' route, as if to eliminate detours as far as practicable. Economy of effort is one obvious explanation for this invariance, and no doubt the human resources available at any one time would have required that any deflection from a straight course was minimal. However, the situation is more complicated than this, and involves paradox.

So, for example, if the intention was to dominate areas to the west, it is surely odd that at various points even a minor shift to the west to encompass obvious vantage points was missed.

This apparent failure to capitalise fully upon what might be perceived as 'strategic advantage' in setting the course of Offa's Dyke was one of the factors that led Fox to see it as a defensive boundary work marking a 'negotiated frontier' through which its course was determined by a process of mediation between Welsh and Mercian interests.[43] Yet in very many places, it is also the case that the Dyke did occupy a position only just upon the western side of a hilltop when it could easily have been built over the crest of such eminences, where it would have achieved a prospect both eastwards and westwards. If the location of the Offa's Dyke had really been a matter of negotiation, then surely the position of the earthwork would not so frequently have given anyone to the east of its line such an advantage of oversight westwards?

As with the perpendicular crossing of rivers, it could be argued that the course that the Dyke followed as it was carried over and around hills was a matter of expedience. So, for example, 'wherever it did not cause too much additional work, the earthwork was taken to a point above the source of small streams'.[44] Although this was sometimes the case, it was not invariably so. There are placements of the linear earthwork in relation especially to hill tops and flanks that are sufficiently consistent throughout the whole course of the Dyke to prompt the question as to whether, as with the care often taken to approach valleys to achieve oversight, the Dyke was in fact placed deliberately in such locations to produce particular surveillance effects.

These placement practices in respect to eminences appear to have served to achieve three things simultaneously. Firstly, they maximised the visibility of the Dyke around west-facing hilltops or across west-facing slopes. Secondly, they minimised the disadvantage of crossing areas where the hill-slopes to the west rose higher than the position occupied by the line of the Dyke itself. Thirdly, they maximised the visibility of the Dyke as it crossed level areas, when seen from higher ground.

Making an extended curve over a west-facing summit

Although Fox did not isolate a series of placement practices in the way that they are characterised here, he did recognise their existence. So, for instance he noted that:

> The course of the Dyke over the Kerry ridge is especially interesting (since) the deflection to the westwards, manifestly made to avoid eastward-facing slopes, has several parallels further N. and is another valuable piece of evidence in favour of the unity of the structure.[45]

The odd thing about the course of the Dyke as described by Fox here is that while its traverse of the Kerry Ridgeway does indeed curve westwards in a broad shallow arc when seen on a map, on the ground its ascent towards that ridge from the Vale of Montgomery south of Cwm *does* follow an uphill-facing (eastwards-looking) stance ascending the spur of the hill just below Crowsnest (Figure 4.13). So it is questionable whether the deflection was made simply to avoid an east-facing slope here. The reason was, rather, to cross the Ridgeway at a key vantage-point, and then, to the south of the ridge, to hold the southwest-facing crest of the slope overlooking the narrow but steeply down-cutting upper Edenhope valley to the south of that ridge (see also Figure 1.2).

Fox was in no doubt as to the ultimate purpose of such placement: 'the trace was as usual designed to give, wherever possible, a wide view to the W.'[46] If so, what did Fox have in mind when he spoke of a 'deflection to the westwards' with 'several parallels further N.'? One close analogy with the Kerry Ridgeway traverse is the place where the Dyke crosses over the col to the west of the main summit of Selattyn Hill. Here, the extended curving crossing of the western-facing flank of the hill combined the locational advantage of the gaining of higher ground with the minimising of the deflection of the otherwise straight course of the Dyke locally (Figures 2.12, 9.9).

The 'several parallels further north' are instead, therefore, also examples of this more common locational practice, that involved minimal deviation, but that took maximum advantage of the opportunity for wide westwards prospects by making a long curving transit of gentle west-facing slopes running just below a summit. The practice has its most northerly occurrence in the shallow curve traced around the hilltop at Brymbo Hill, north of the Cedigog valley. It is evident again trending around the western side of the hilltop just to the south of Pentre Bychan north of Ruabon. The next occurrence southwards is the one at Selattyn Hill just mentioned, and scarcely a mile further south the transit of Baker's Hill west of Oswestry racecourse was effected in exactly the same way, although its course ran closer to the summit here and the westwards deflection was more subtle.

South of the middle Severn valley, besides the Kerry Ridgeway example, the practice is manifest in the course of the Dyke traced around the west-facing flank of Llanfair Hill. North of Knighton the Dyke made a series of such curves around the flank of the summit of the ridge just to the north-west of Panpunton Hill. Meanwhile, to the south again a whole series of such curves were created close upon one another in Radnorshire, at Ffridd, at Rhos-y-meirch, at Cwm Whitton Hill, and at Hawthorn Hill, before the descent southwards to the

FIGURE 4.13 Offa's Dyke traversing the Kerry Ridgeway: from the north

This aerial photograph indicates clearly the 'outward' curve over the ridge and down into the Unk valley beyond. Figure 4.12 is the ground-level view north from the field just to the west of the Dyke in front of the ridgeway route (at right-centre).

PHOTOGRAPH BY CHRIS MUSSON, COURTESY OF CLWYD-POWYS ARCHAEOLOGICAL TRUST, WITH PERMISSION.

4   *Placing the Dyke in the landscape*   145

FIGURE 4.14 A gently-curving course around a west-facing hill-top: Llanfair Hill

Springhill Farm lies on the ridge above Spoad and the Clun valley beyond. Figures 5.35 and 5.36 feature this length from the air, while Figure 6.1, below is a view looking in the opposite direction, south from Springhill.

PHOTOGRAPH: ADAM STANFORD/AERIAL-CAM, COPYRIGHT RESERVED.

valley of the Lugg. In Gloucestershire, an exactly similar example of the practice having been being implemented exists at The Fields (west of Windward House) on St Briavels Common, where, having emerged from its descent into the deep valley of the Mork Brook, the Dyke followed a gently curving course southwards around the south-west facing upper slopes of the hill.

Along the contours of west-facing slopes

Another recurrent placement practice is the location of the Dyke such that it follows a route carefully sited along the contours of steep west-facing slopes, placed either at the crest or some way down the slope in question. North of the middle Severn, there are several stretches of the earthwork south and south-west of Oswestry where this practice is very evident. The first is the course of the Dyke around the crest of the slopes on the western side Llanymynech Hill running northwards along Blodwel Rock. A similar, though probably not quite as precipitous, route was followed along the south-facing slopes of Llynclys Hill. A third example is the course followed at a closely maintained level along Craig Forda above the river Morda west of Oswestry, Here, for nearly a mile, the Dyke was cut as a continuous notch in the upper slopes of a west-facing hillside with what is often an almost sheer drop to the river.

South of the middle Severn this practice is yet more common. For example, it occurs at several points south of Pentre on the western slopes of the Long Mountain. Immediately south of the Kerry Ridgeway, the practice is evident along the west-facing crest

FIGURE 4.15 Craig Morda from the south, from just west of the Dyke

The view here is into the steep valley of the Afon Morda, seen from a point just west of Pentre-shannel farm. Offa's Dyke follows a route just below the conifers and above the steep scarp overlooking the river.

PHOTOGRAPH: ADAM STANFORD/AERIAL-CAM, COPYRIGHT RESERVED.

above Nut Wood (overlooking Upper Edenhope; see Figure 1.2), and around the slopes to the east of Upper Mount, dominating the ravine through which a tributary of the Mardu flows. It is also found at several points along the stretch of Dyke linking the west-facing hill-crests from Cwmsanahan Hill to Panpunton Hill north of Knighton. South of the Teme valley there are several examples of such a practice along shorter stretches of the Dyke, such as where the Dyke traced a course that descended southwards around the western edge of Furrow Hill overlooking the Lugg valley near Discoed.

Other locations where this practice is evident are along the northern flank of Evenjobb Hill, around the lower slopes of Burfa Bank overlooking the Walton Basin, and around the western and southern sides of Herrock Hill. It is evident also on the hill crest overlooking the river Arrow at Lyonshall, and around the southern slopes of Burton Hill/Ladylift near Yazor in Herefordshire. South of Lower Redbrook in Gloucestershire the course of the Dyke along the crest of the west-facing slopes of Highbury Plains and down to Coxbury above the river Wye is a good example of the practice, and a position at mid-slope was then taken up southwards again towards Wyegate.

Probably the most sustained length of Offa's Dyke that is characterised by this practice is, however, that further south again which runs above the Wye in Gloucestershire from Madgett Hill in the former Woolaston parish to Worgan's Wood in the north-west of Tidenham parish, and then on to East Vaga and down to Woodcroft north of Tutshill (all still in Tidenham). For much of this stretch, the Dyke followed a line close to the top of the west-facing crest directly looking down upon the river Wye up to 600 feet (180 m) below. Particularly striking in this regard is the course the Dyke traced around the top of the westwards-extending spur of land at Lippetts Grove southwards past the Devil's Pulpit and on to Plumweir Cliff, opposite Tintern. The line of the Dyke was sustained southwards towards the Wye-Severn confluence through to and beyond Woodcroft, but, as noted previously, its exact course here has been disrupted by quarrying and by residential development through much of its former extent.

Repeated placement practices elsewhere in the landscape

There are further clearly identifiable and repeated locational practices that can be observed at various points along the course of the Dyke, but some of which occur less frequently than those described above. One such practice was the careful threading of the Dyke through a valley. In such instances a course was carefully chosen along the base of the west-facing slopes, as above the Afon Cedigog at Ffrith in Flintshire. A similar, if shorter, course was traced through the valley at Treflach Wood south-west of Oswestry. In the valley of the Mardu Brook north of the crossing of the river Clun, the Dyke was similarly carefully placed close to the base of west-facing slopes. Other practices were more dramatic in their incidence and effect, and are potentially more revealing of the logic of placement followed by the Dyke builders. They are therefore the subject of more detailed commentary here.

Perpendicular ascents/descents of a steep slope

This placement practice most commonly occurs close to rivers, and the examples on the north-facing slopes above the river-crossings of the Cedigog, the Ceiriog, the Teme and the Lugg have already been noted in this regard. Another place where this occurs close to a river is opposite Burfa by the crossing of the Hindwell Brook south of Presteigne. Here the valley-bottom and its two streams were traversed by the Dyke built on a massive scale, which then diminished dramatically as it ascended sharply the side of a north-facing hill-spur almost vertically before abruptly turning south to trace a course along the spine of the spur. Another example is at Lippetts Grove in Gloucestershire where, having traversed a stream dropping steeply westwards to the Wye, the Dyke ascended a very steep north-facing slope.

Such dramatic descents and ascents tend only to be implemented over relatively short distances. This is hardly surprising, given the effort involved in such operations, and the inherent instability that could result. The striking nature of such ascents was one of the qualities that Fox, in particular, was appreciative of: and especially in regard to the planning involved. An example that he cited in this regard is the abrupt '70-yard' ascent up a 1 in 2 slope onto higher ground from a point just north of Pentre in Leighton parish east of Welshpool, at the southern end of the run of straight alignments that was discussed earlier in this chapter, above.[47]

The latter characteristic, that such 'vertical' ascents of steep slopes are almost always enacted when the slope in question faces north, is of particular interest. It has significant implications concerning how the Dyke was designed to be seen in general, as well as how it was to be seen from particular places along its course (see below). It is also of considerable relevance to the question of vantage-points and surveillance.[48]

Descents down (or ascents up) the spine of a tapering ridge

This practice involved the enlistment of a prominent topographical feature to project the earthwork itself prominently within the landscape, by placing it precisely following the crest of a spur of steeper or gentler gradient. One of the best examples of this practice is at the very northern-most extremity of the Dyke, just to the south-east of Treuddyn, at Llanyfynydd (Figure 9.13). Here, a particularly massive length of Dyke was placed along the north-west trending spine of a spur of the hill ascending from the Cedigog valley towards the prominent broad upland ridge upon which Treuddyn is located.[49]

Although it did not ascend the whole length of the spur, another example of this practice is to be found on the border between Radnorshire

FIGURE 4.16 The Hindwell Brook and the valley below Burfa Camp

The view east from the west bank of the river that drains the Walton Basin takes in the largely ploughed-out but formerly massive bank and ditch of Offa's Dyke where it crosses the floodplain at the perpendicular (above the fence at right-centre). The earthwork is then picked out in the early morning sunlight as a much slighter feature climbing vertically onto the north-facing shoulder of Herrock Hill at upper right-centre.

and Herefordshire, where, as noted above, the Dyke made use of the spur descending from Herrock Hill facing north towards Knill (Figure 4.16). Further to the south, the practice is in evidence in two locations where field or parish boundaries have replaced the former line of the Dyke. The first is on the north-facing slope of Garnons Hill east of Mansell Gamage and just north of the river Wye west of Hereford. Here, having crossed a valley between hills, the course of the Dyke swung south-eastwards to follow the trend of Garnons Hill up a spur ascending to the summit. The next prominent occurrence southwards again is up a north-facing spur south of Redbrook, ascending towards Highbury.

Traverses of east-facing slopes

At various points along the course of the Dyke, the crossing of gentle east-facing slopes was made very carefully so that although there was an 'uphill' prospect westwards, the terms and ground upon which the slope was met maximised the visibility over the ground westwards from the Dyke itself. This placement practice occurred most frequently where the Dyke made a traverse of a spur leading eastwards from a prominent massif. The most northerly example of the practice of careful positioning to minimise the slope disadvantage is at Tyn-y-Coed facing westwards up the spur that descends from Minera on the north-eastern lower slopes of Ruabon Mountain. Here the ground to the west rises up nearly 100 m in height in only a quarter of a mile (0.35 km), but the Dyke was 'slotted' onto and along a shallower interruption to the slope just above the point, half a kilometre to the east, where the slope becomes much shallower. Such positioning indicates the great concern not to deviate from a

FIGURE 4.17 Offa's Dyke at Caeaugwynion, south of the river Dee

As at Middle Knuck near Mainstone and at Coedpoeth west of Wrexham, the Dyke here occupies on overtly disadvantageous position facing uphill as it traverses an east-facing slope. This length is close to the location of one of Fox's sections across the earthwork.

regular north–south course, even if it meant a loss of visibility of the Dyke when seen from a distance westwards.

Further south, at the stretch of Dyke at Caeaugwynion south of the river Dee, and facing the Fron spur before the top of the slow descent towards the Dee, there are two or three lengths of earthwork that also face upslope to the north-west (Figure 4.17). In this area the Dyke was carefully placed on the eastern edge of a north-east facing shoulder of land to minimise the impact of a westwards prospect facing uphill. The Dyke was also carefully placed in this way between Pentre-shannel and Trefonen south-west of Oswestry, where it traversed the lower slopes of the eastern summit of Mynydd Myfyr; as it ascended the spurs north of Cwm at the southern end of the Vale of Montgomery; and where it crossed the broad spur of land descending eastwards from the north-eastern flank of Ruabon mountain.

In the upland course of the Dyke immediately south from the Kerry Ridgeway, the practice occurs again at Middle Knuck near Mainstone. Here the Dyke traverses three significant west–east spurs and their intervening combes before reaching Hergan (Figure 6.10). On the upland stretch of Dyke south of the Clun valley, the practice is evident again along a length of the earthwork on the north-facing slope at Spoad Hill (Figure 9.7), as it is also in short stretches of the Dyke in the vicinity of Brockweir in Gloucestershire, south of Monmouth.[50]

Extended diagonal traverses of hill-slopes

There are very many cases where the Dyke has been placed such that there is a gradual straight-line but diagonal ascent (or descent) of the westwards- or southwards-facing flank of a hill over longer or shorter distances. The most prominent instances of this practice are arguably the route southwards from Buttington up onto and along the western flanks of the Long Mountain overlooking the Severn opposite Welshpool, and the somewhat shorter but in some ways more vivid diagonal strike of the Pen Offa to Burfa descent/ascent overlooking the Walton Basin in Radnorshire.

FIGURE 4.18 The long diagonal traverse of the southern slopes of Evenjobb Hill

The substantial bank and ditch in this stretch of the Dyke makes a bold slice across the lopes of the hill to pass at the foot of the hill on which Burfa Camp stands. This manoevre has the effect of emphasising the dominance of the dyke over the Walton Basin landscape beneath it, and of boldly facing the early political centre at Old Radnor (see Figures 7.5, 7.11 and 9.6, below).

The impact of the Long Mountain traverse is best appreciated from the terrace at Powis Castle (Figure 2.1). Although the Dyke is no longer prominently visible here due to the wooded character of the landscape around Leighton, the west-facing flank of the mountain which it ascended form north to south is continuously visible from the west across the broad valley of the river Severn. In contrast, the mile-long stretch of Dyke between Evenjobb Hill and Burfa has a more intimate relation to the Walton Basin lands immediately in front of it than does the Leighton section over the Severn. One apparent purpose of the diagonal strike in practical terms in this instance was to keep the Dyke pushed forwards above the Basin and to provide a continuously descending rather than undulating line.[51]

Two other straight diagonal traverses exist just to the south, where the Dyke rises from the Weobley road at Norton Canon in north Herefordshire before following a sinuous course around the slopes beneath Ladylift Clump at Yazor (Figure 7.14), and where the Dyke subsequently drops to the Wye at Garnons with a short but dramatic half-mile descent to the river in three straight alignments (Figure 2.13). The drama of such adjustments of descent or ascent across steep slopes is also well-illustrated by the length of Dyke that runs across the north-west facing slopes of Selattyn Hill (Figure 4.19), and by the length directly above the Wye at Coxbury/Church Grove, south of Redbrook, Gloucestershire

Several other shorter straight diagonal hill-slope traverses might be thought to have more to do with the practical business of climbing a steep hillside, as at Brynorgan north of Cwmsanahan, to the north of Knighton, and at Great Ffrith Wood south of that town. However, while the 'drama' of the Brynorgan

4 Placing the Dyke in the landscape   151

FIGURE 4.19 The long diagonal traverse of the north-western flank of Selattyn Hill

This placement of a prominent length of the Dyke here again emphasises the boldness with which the earthwork has been executed, standing out against the slopes rising behind it. The prospect south-eastwards from Plas-crogen towards this Dyke length is just to the right of the view featured in Figure 9.3.

PHOTOGRAPH: ADAM STANFORD/ AERIAL-CAM, COPYRIGHT RESERVED.

ascent/descent is really only evident when seen from the Garbett Hall section of the Dyke itself, the vividness of the strike – albeit made by a smaller-scale section of the Dyke as an earthwork – must have been very evident when seen from the floor of the Teme valley upstream of Knighton. At Hergan north of the Clun valley, however, the device of the gradual diagonal ascent of a hillslope is used to good effect, if only for a short distance, in a setting where the area from which it can be viewed is not extensive.[52]

The Dyke viewed in the landscape from the west

It is inevitable that the perspective on the Dyke that is developed today is strongly influenced by present-day familiarity with mapped representations, or aerial or satellite views of the landscape as if from a great height, such that, at the flick of a button, the entire course of Offa's Dyke can be viewed in a number of ways, both across whole tracts of the landscape and also in close detail. New ways of seeing the Dyke can also be created using a variety of visual modelling devices, including view-shed analysis and LiDAR-derived digital terrain models.[53] As such, it is now possible to see how the Dyke is placed in the landscape in ways that were not accessible to the 'planner(s)' of the great earthwork. Nonetheless, it is important to continue to experience and to interpret the Dyke from the more limited physical perspectives accessible to eighth-century people.[54]

The limitations of such a ground-based perspective can too easily be overstated. For example, signal fires lit on still, clear days could be seen for many miles. Moreover, elevated vantage points enable sighting over long distances, and the maximal scope of visibility can be considerable. So, for example, from the 330 m high vantage point of Croft Ambrey in north Herefordshire it is possible on exceptionally clear days to make out to the north-west the outline of the Aran Mountains at the western end of Llyn Tegid (Lake Bala) in north Wales and simultaneously in the opposite direction to the south-east, the Cotswold scarp, for instance at Cleeve Hill south of Cheltenham in Gloucestershire. The distance between the Arans and Cleeve Hill is around 110 miles (177 km).

It has already been noted here how frequently the particular traverse that the Dyke followed across a hilltop or around and along the contours of a west-facing slope appears to have been designed to provide a prospect over land to the west of the Dyke. However, as viewed *from* the west, this meant that the Dyke appeared repeatedly as a skyline feature, or, especially where the course was consistently at mid-slope or below the crest (as for instance at Craig Forda west of Oswestry, or along the Gloucestershire stretches above the Wye), as a line picked out against a hillside.

Along the river-valleys

It would not only have been the 'rawness' of the physical scar of the newly-created linear earthwork upon the landscape that would have struck the observer of Offa's Dyke in the last decade of the eighth century, but also the way in which it was visible in the landscape as a traversing line. The build of the Dyke was designed to impress, especially when seen from the west, and was repeatedly manipulated to privilege certain views from that direction. Moreover, these often correlate precisely with likely approaches along ridgeways and, especially, along valleys extending downwards towards the east.

This can best be demonstrated in reference to a particular location, and with the benefit of illustrations. At Discoed west of Presteigne in the Lugg valley there are two approaches to the Dyke from the west that coalesce at just that point where the line of the earthwork crosses that river. One approach follows the line of the Cascob Brook as it flows eastwards along a narrow flat-bottomed and steep-sided valley south of Llan-Fawr. Meanwhile, the other approach is from the north-west, along the more U-shaped profile Lugg valley from the direction of Pilleth, the site of a much later battle between the Welsh and the English.

The Yew Tree Farm to Bwlch length of the Dyke occupying the north-facing slope down to the river Lugg here faces almost due west, on the flank of the hill at just that point where it turns from a fully northwards prospect to a north-westwards one. North from Yew Tree Farm across the bottom of the valley, the alignment shifts very slightly north-eastwards again. However, while the dimensions of the bank and ditch in the valley bottom were once considerable in their own right, it was always the length occupying the rising ground southwards from the valley-floor that was visually the most prominent.

When approaching the Dyke from the west here, from the direction of the Cascob Brook valley, the course of Offa's Dyke becomes visible firstly on the south-facing slope below Hawthorn Hill as it traces a long winding descent hugging the edge of the west-facing scarp, overlooking the river-valley (Figure 2.10). At the point where the tributary stream flows down onto the narrow Lugg floodplain, the stretch of the Dyke crossing the valley-floor would also have become visible for the first time. However, it would have been that part of the Dyke occupying the north-facing slope at Yew Tree Farm that was most striking given its scale and the fact that at that point the observer would have

4 Placing the Dyke in the landscape

been facing it at the perpendicular and would have looked directly up towards it (Figure 4.8).

However, this was a view that would only have been revealed at close-quarters, and as such it stands in contrast to the view of the earthwork when moving southwards from the north-west along the Lugg valley itself. From this direction, the Dyke would have been first visible as a skyline feature on Hawthorn Hill from as far away as just east of Pilleth. As the person approaching the Dyke's crossing of the valley got closer to it, the length of the Dyke situated on the north side of the valley at this point was entirely obscured by the convexity of the slope, unless seen from the western side of the valley from which the lower lengths might have been visible. Meanwhile, that stretch of the Dyke traversing the north-facing slope of the hill above Yew Tree Farm and up to Bwlch, and overlooking the valley from the south, would have been visible prominently, if obliquely, the further down the valley the observer travelled. The fact that the approach along valleys both from due west and from the north-west focused upon this length contributes strongly to an explanation of why it was so elaborated.

The situation of some other valley approaches towards the Dyke closely echo the Discoed situation, as at Edenhope on a smaller scale where one stream

FIGURE 4.20 Offa's Dyke crossing the Clun valley, viewed from the north-west

Despite being fully aware of the drama of a traverse such as this when viewed from the west, Fox used such images (1955, Plate XXVIII) only 'locationally', to specify the route taken, rather than to illustrate the visual impact. Fron Camp (right) directly overlooks the river Clun and Newcastle, from the north (Figure 4.23).

REPRODUCED COURTESY OF THE CAMBRIAN ARCHAEOLOGICAL ASSOCIATION

approached the Dyke from the north-west, while another encountered it head-on from due west. Here, the length of Dyke occupying the south-facing slope curved around the edge of a west-facing scarp, just as on the Lugg making it visible from a distance, while the length placed upon the north-facing slope was readily-visible only at closer quarters. In other locations the approach was subtly different, but exemplified some of the same principles. The situation at Spoad on the Clun crossing is interesting here not only because of the intricacies of the built form, but also because of the visual impact that the approach of the Dyke from the north has as the Dyke in the valley-floor is approached from the west (Figures 4.20 and 9.12). The earthwork appears to envelop the onlooker, the closer they get to the Dyke. The effect is of engagement within the 'arms' of an aggressively co-ordinated fortification – whether or not the work itself had sufficient strength at closer quarters.

Across from the hills and along the vales

Another way to envisage how the Dyke was and is experienced when viewed from the west along a relatively narrow valley such as that of the upper Lugg is in terms of several alternative perspectives: the 'skyline' or the 'slope-transit' views when looking up towards the earthwork as it crosses the hill-slopes, and the 'valley-bottom' view where the Dyke would have appeared as a barrier across level ground, framed by the rising ground on either side of the floodplain. At Discoed, both kinds of view would have been apparent for different stretches of the earthwork as the observer moved towards the point where the Dyke traversed the Lugg valley.

However, in considering views towards the Dyke from the west that are at all elevated, not only are sight-lines towards it directed slightly upwards to it, or along a more or less level plane, but there are also views that can be directed downwards onto it. The Dyke could appear as a skyline feature in any such elevated situations, in the same way that it often did in respect of views from the valleys. However, as with the valley-bottom views, the Dyke could be viewed as it stood out boldly against the hillside above and below the course that the earthwork took across the slopes. As previously noted here, the Dyke is especially visible standing out in this way highlighted against the hillsides as viewed from the west wherever it makes a diagonal traverse of a hillside. Arguably, for example, the entirety of the southern section of the Dyke from Highbury to Sedbury in Gloucestershire was designed so that, while it was always seen from some distance across the Wye valley 'gorge' from the west, it was always experienced either as a skyline feature or as a mid-slope feature.

Oblique views of the Dyke are common from the west, and are especially striking in those situations where it can be seen crossing a variety of terrain, and again particularly also where the land in front of it and the land behind and above it are simultaneously in view. Views downward onto and across the Dyke are not uncommon, especially north of the middle Severn valley, but they are most striking where the earthwork crosses substantial level areas, and when viewed from much higher ground. This is for instance the case where the Dyke makes its traverse across the west-central part of the Vale of Montgomery (Part Three Frontispiece and Figure 9.1).

The view from an elevated point such as the bluff upon which the ruins of Montgomery Castle now stand produces the same effect as seeing the Dyke from the landscape westwards from it where it crosses a slope diagonally. That is to say, both the ground in front of it and the land behind its course are visible simultaneously; such that when it was dug it would have stood out strikingly as a stripe across the landscape. On the plain itself, however, when viewed from the west it is the ground behind the Dyke that most vividly 'frames' its course visually. The subtleties of the placement of the Dyke in such situations are difficult to explain simply. The situation at Gwarthlow, on the shallow northern edge of the valley through which the Caebitra stream flows from west to east, provides an instructive example (Figure 4.21).

The only deviations on a straight course here between Rownal Covert to the north of the Chirbury-Montgomery road and Brompton Bridge to the south (a distance of 3 miles/5 km) are a very minor one at Dudston Fields and a longer one to take in, at its maximum extent, not the ridge southwards from, but the dip directly below, the Lower Gwarthlow knoll. Why should this be? One possibility is that the rise and fall of the Dyke on either side of and beneath this knoll was deliberately choreographed such that the eminence at Lower Gwarthlow both had a view over the Dyke at this point and was very prominent behind the Dyke when seen from the west (Figure 4.21). The knoll site was thereby 'framed', when seen from the west, by the Dyke rising through the landscape to north and south.[55] As such, this particular course maximised both the visual impact of the Dyke and features behind it when viewed from the west, while at the same making the most of the surveillance potential of the work when looking outwards from it towards the west. Seen in this light, the ridge to the south of Gwarthlow was just as important a location as the Dyke itself: the transit of the Dyke across this ridge maximised the scope to overlook both the Lack Brook and the Caebitra valleys southwards while at the same time providing a vantage point in several directions southwards, westwards and eastwards simultaneously.

Where the views eastwards towards the Dyke were from a farmstead or other settlement, they could be regarded as 'static' in that they remained the same from this (relatively) fixed point. However, it needs to be borne in mind that prospects inevitably changed with *movement through* the landscape, and that at the time of its construction, just as now, some prospects would have been obscured by vegetation-cover, and especially by the presence of trees. In other words, views towards the Dyke will always have been shifting as the observer moved around the landscape.

In these terms, as the Dyke descended into a valley and ascended the opposite side it could be observed from the west across some parts of that course

FIGURE 4.21 (composite) The Dyke at Gwarthlow, viewed from the west

The prospect here is from a point near Geryeryn Farm, just to the east of the Brompton Bridge to Montgomery road (B4385) a mile south of Montgomery town. The Dyke appears at left on the crest of a rise behind which the low hills above the right bank of the Camlad south-east of Chirbury are just visible. The Dyke then descends into a slight hollow immediately west of Lower Gwarthlow farm, which stands on a localised knoll in the landscape (centre). It then rises again to a slight ridge above the Lack Brook (which flows eastwards to join the Caebitra just above its confluence with the Camlad at Church Stoke). Just to the right of the Lower Gwarthlow knoll, the summit of Roundton, south of Corndon Hill, is visible as a prominent peak on the sky-line (right).

silhouetted against the horizon, or standing out against the hillside, or it could be seen obliquely, rising up (or descending) a hillside with the hillslopes both behind and in front of it viewable simultaneously (Figure 4.22). Equally, while from a distance of a mile or more a particular length of the Dyke could be seen standing out against a hillside, closer in towards the earthwork the same length could appear as a skyline feature.

The careful siting of the Dyke in the landscape served to privilege the more striking among such contrasting views, with the Dyke often running along ridges that interrupted the descent of a slope. Such subtlety of placement is, for example, readily apparent in the visually striking (and therefore clearly strategically-important) location of the Dyke on its long diagonal ascent/descent of the hillside between Newcastle Hill/Pen Offa and the Hindwell Brook below Burfa Camp, overlooking the Radnor Basin (Figure 4.18, above).

FIGURE 4.22 The Dyke silhouetted on the skyline: Baker's Hill from the west

The curving course of the Dyke round the west-facing part of the summit of Baker's Hill is very clear from the air, as evident in Figures 1.15 and 4.10. As noted above, this had the effect of making its course more visible from the west and of offering better surveillance vantage from the Dyke, westwards (including over the valley of Afon Morda). That the westwards dominance of the earthwork was deemed important is apparent even from a point, as here, only a kilometre away, at Rhydycroesau. The placing of the earthwork forwards on the summit had the effect of making it a continuous skyline feature when looking upwards from below.

PHOTOGRAPH: ADAM STANFORD/AERIAL-CAM, COPYRIGHT RESERVED.

Prospects *from* and *along* the Dyke

There is no evidence that at any point walkways were built into the structure of Offa's Dyke along its crest in the same manner as provided, for instance, along parts at least of Hadrian's Wall. In these terms it is difficult to discuss views outwards from the Dyke either eastwards or westwards, except as obtainable even today simply by standing on the bank, or just behind it. It is clear, however, that at many points along the bank of the earthwork as it traverses strong contrasts in elevation, views along the Dyke are frequent occurrences.

The land viewed from the Dyke, westwards and eastwards

It has been observed that 'the chosen line always attempts to take a position where there is a clear view to the west, even when this means moving slightly away from the direct line but always with the overall plan in mind'.[56] Whether this generalisation really holds true depends upon what is regarded as a 'clear view'. There are, for instance, cases where the view westwards up a slope, as at Coedpoeth west of Wrexham, at Caeaugwynion near Chirk, or at Knuck near Hergan north of the Clun valley, was very restricted, and at the latter two cases it would have been possible to deviate 'from the direct line' to avoid this. Equally, there are valley-bottom routes as at Ffrith in Flintshire, at Treflach Wood, north Shropshire, and along the Marddu Brook valley close to the Clun valley crossing, where there is in effect no extensive westwards prospect other than towards hills to the west overlooking the Dyke.

It is nonetheless the case that for at least nine-tenths of its course the Dyke sought out and achieved sometimes very wide views westwards. In the discussion of the placement practices deployed by the Dyke builders above, it is very evident not only that the approaches to the crossing-points of rivers were deliberately planned so that the valleys upstream of the intended floodplain crossing were overlooked for sometimes considerable distances, but that many other kinds of 'overlooking' were encompassed. As noted in the case of the Newcastle Hill to Burfa stretch, the view outwards could be across a broad level area, in that case the Walton basin which formed the eastern heartland of later Radnorshire. Elsewhere, as at Craig Forda above the defile of the river Morda, at Llanymynech Hill overlooking the confluence of the rivers Tanat and Vyrnwy, along the Long Mountain, and above the lower Wye in Gloucestershire, what was overlooked westwards was the course of the river itself.

Techniques such as view-shed analysis could (and in future arguably should) be used to illustrate and illuminate such patterns of overlooking.[57] However, it is evident from visual field study simply walking the landscape along and to the west of the Dyke that while strong visibility of the earthwork as seen from the west, and the creation of an imposing line across the landscape, were key concerns of the Dyke designers and builders, at least equally important was maximisation of the surveillance-potential westwards along most of its course. In these terms it was not just a vague overlooking, but rather the places and areas that were carefully overlooked, that are important to an understanding of why the Dyke was built along the line it took. The key questions here are, what was it that surveillance was directed towards, and why. While river-valley approaches from the west as well as track-ways and traditional route-ways were of obvious potential importance, it was some particular places other than these that the Dyke appeared to reference by its prominent location. The potential significance of this is highlighted further by an apparently deliberate elaboration of the build the earthwork in several such locations. The significance of this observation will be touched upon also in Chapter 5, but will be explored in successively greater detail in Chapters 6 and 7, below.

One corollary of the placing of the Dyke in the landscape such that there is rising ground to the east of it, is that these upper slopes of hillsides or summits of hills provided further scope for surveillance. So it is that views over the Dyke from west to east might in some locations have been as important a consideration in the location of the Dyke as the specific route taken itself.

It is perhaps natural to focus upon views westwards from the Dyke, since this is the direction in which the Dyke faces, with the ditch on the west and the bank (mostly) on the east. While this was undoubtedly the most important direction of sight from the point of view (literally) of those who created the earthwork and whose lands lay mostly to the east of its line, views eastwards and their significance should not be neglected. It is worth considering what some, at least, of these views encompassed. From Llanymynech Hill northwards, at several places there was a view eastwards over the plain that runs northwards from Shrewsbury to Chester. This provided a direct reference-point to lands settled by the Mercians in the century and more prior to the late eighth century. The significance of this is explored further in Chapters 7 and 9, below.

Meanwhile, the exact points chosen in some cases for the approaches and descent/ascent to the rivers crossed broadly at the perpendicular often afforded

FIGURE 4.23 Eastwards towards Clun from the southern limit of Graig Hill

The bank of the Dyke in the foreground traces a zig-zag course across the south-facing slope down to the river Clun opposite Spoad Farm (see Figure 9.12). The position of the earthwork here provides a wide prospect down the Clun valley.

FIGURE 4.24 Looking westwards up the Clun valley over Newcastle village

The drama of the siting of the Dyke at the Clun crosses can readily be appreciated not only in the prospects directly across the valley north and south (Figures 1.23 and 9.12, but also obliquely south-eastwards down the valley (Figure 4.23), and, as here, north-westwards up it. The siting of the crossing itself, just to the east of this pronounced bend in the river between two prominent hills, meant, unusually, that the Dyke could not be seen from a distance when approached along the valley. However, the traverse the Dyke makes across the Clun valley is very visible when seen from any of the surrounding hills (see Figure 4.20).

views down along significant stretches of the valleys concerned, eastwards from the Dyke. One example is the extensive view down the valley towards Clun from the point at which the Dyke makes its final descent southwards to the flood-plain of the river Clun opposite Spoad (Figure 4.23). Again, the possible 'surveillance' reasons for choosing such vantage-points are self-evident, especially when the view westwards from approximately the same point on the slope above the Clun flood-plain (Figure 4.24) is taken into account.

Views along the Dyke, northwards and southwards

When seen from key vantage points such as Crowsnest by the Kerry Ridgeway or the possible look-out facility at Bwlch by Discoed, it is evident that surveillance of the route *along the line of the Dyke itself* was also an important consideration in its design.[58] This is the case whether the vantage-point was on the earthwork itself, just behind it to the east, or just in front of it to the west. Besides the obvious surveillance importance of being able to see the land either side of the Dyke from the earthwork itself, it is difficult to avoid the impression that the intention was in almost all cases to maximise the visual impact of the Dyke as it was viewed from north or south negotiating its way across the landscape, and particularly as it traversed defiles and river-valleys. Just why this would be important is a question that therefore springs to mind.

Views northwards and southwards along the course of the Dyke encompass dramatic abrupt perpendicular rises that the earthwork accomplished up valley-sides, along with extended oblique crossings of steep slopes, and long curving traverses around the flanks of hills with sharp drops in elevation westwards. While this provided a kind of 'theatre of landscape' for the observer in these places, it was unlikely to have been a performance produced chiefly to satisfy an aesthetic of dyke-building (though pride in the achievement could have been a factor in producing the precision of the work). Instead, it provided a reassurance of the strength and connectivity of the earthwork sustained over wide tracts of country. As a consequence, the creation of the Dyke endowed those viewing its course from the work itself, or from points just eastwards from it, with a sense of security that the earthwork was not a structure that could easily be out-flanked. These observations would have enhanced appreciation of the scale of the power and of the achievement of the Mercians in creating the barrier.

It is noticeable that it is where careful treatments of the descent/ascent towards river-valley crossings are located on south-facing slopes north of the crossing itself that they appear most 'performative'. At these latitudes, these are precisely the slopes that are seen to best effect as the sunlight falls upon

FIGURE 4.25 View north along the Dyke, south of Gwarthlow

Looking long the course of the Dyke almost anywhere in the Vale of Montgomery, the appearance is of a level plain. That this is deceptive even here, is evident when it is realised that the view here is along the length feature in Figure 4.21. Between the ploughed field in the foreground and the one just visible at right centre by the woods in the background, there is the considerable dip below Lower Gwarthlow farm.

them from the south for most of the year. The reasons for such preference also perhaps relate to the configuration of the hillsides themselves: at several points, the 'spread' of the Dyke laterally across the slope serves to accentuate its size and strength even where the build is less massive.

The Dyke viewed from the east

Locations with views westwards from close proximity to the eastern side of Offa's Dyke in many cases improved the surveillance characteristics of the landscape viewed westwards, whether or not the dyke could be seen from these locations. Comprehensive analysis of westwards prospects of this kind could be conducted but are arguably unnecessary to demonstrate this point here. However, another aspect of the westwards prospect towards the Dyke from the east might explain another frequent feature of its placement. One reason why the Dyke is sometimes placed such that it faces uphill to the west, besides a perceived need to maintain a closely-held line north and south, is so that it stood proud either as a skyline feature or as picked out again ground rising to its west. This is in a sense the inverse of the situation where it was possible for those standing west of the Dyke to see the land from which the earthwork excluded them. The psychology looking westwards was the impact of being able to see very clearly the line of the Dyke as a protective device providing security from marauders from the west.

So it is, that both from the lowlands to the west of Wrexham the view of the Dyke in the environs of Coedpoeth, and from the lands around northeast of Chirk the view of the Dyke in the environs of Caeaugwynion would have included lengths of the earthwork framed by the uplands directly above its course. Further south, the same was true at various points in the vicinity of Oswestry, as at Baker's Hill when viewed from the racecourse or at Pentreshannel when viewed from lands to the west of the Morda. South of the Kerry Ridgeway, the same was true of lengths north of the Clun valley in the vicinity of Middle Knuck north of Hergan, and south of the Clun at Spoad Hill. At some prominent locations such as at Cwmsanahan Hill north of Knighton, the Dyke was just as prominent when viewed from the hills to the east as it was as viewed from the uplands to the west. This was also true of much of the course of the Dyke in the northern part of Tidenham parish in Gloucestershire.

Offa's Dyke: wholly-designed and implemented placement in the landscape

The way in which the overall route of the Dyke negotiated mountain masses, river-valleys and major rivers was neither random, nor entirely dependent upon the 'dictates' of topography. Rather, the techniques of overall routing in each case concerned a deliberate traversing, or facing, or circumnavigation, of major features of the landscape in such a way as to exercise control over the way in which each would be experienced henceforward. Fox admired the subtlety of line chosen for the Dyke, but at an early stage in his fieldwork and reporting, and based upon some of his earliest observations, he made two key inferences about its placement that unduly influenced the conclusions he drew from his field study. The first was that, although major route choices determined its overall course, the detail of placement was decided as work progressed. The second was that the route followed, being the outcome of negotiation, represented a compromise between Mercian and British requirements.

In the foregoing, it has been shown how the Dyke was located at the broadest scale within the landscape, and then how alignments were used to subtly adjust its course in a number of ways. It has been possible to identify a series of locational practices whereby the Dyke was repeatedly placed in particular ways in reference to the continually encountered topographical features along its course, whether rivers, valleys, ravines, hilltops, slopes or level areas. This approach to characterisation has necessarily isolated analytically the different kinds of observable placements, but it is important to appreciate how these various practices were brought together to effect the placement of the Dyke across any particular stretch of landscape. Indeed, with the suite of practices described above in mind, it is possible to see how they are deployed in different combinations sequentially as any one stretch of the Dyke is followed. The various sequences and combinations were created in reference both to the changing topography itself and to the opportunities for surveillance and visual dominance that could be afforded by continually shifting the stance the earthwork was made to take.

Another way of envisaging the overall planning of the work is to observe how the major shifts in orientation and the more localised groups of stances not only excluded or included major features of the natural environment, but also large areas of the landscape that may have had historic significance for the Mercians. In this way, for example, it may have been that the Ruabon Mountain massif was faced on its eastern side by the three most northerly 'stances' precisely because it had a particular significance in reference to an important political focus for the kingdom of Powys. It was indeed in the upper part of the Vale of Llangollen to the west of this massif that the fortress at Castell Dinas Bran stood on its great eminence, and it was here also that the Eglwyseg river ran past the spot where the engraved 'Pillar of Eliseg' stone cross had been erected.

South of the Dee, the Dyke traverses the Ceiriog at Bronygarth and traces a course past Craignant and around the western side of Selattyn Hill before proceeding southwards to the Morda and beyond this to a point overlooking the Tanat valley, then turning somewhat eastwards of south on either side of the Vyrnwy. This effectively created an arc whose trajectory curved around Oswestry on the rim of higher ground to the west and then across lower slopes to its south-west (see Figures 1.14 and 4.2). Could this have reflected Penda's seventh-century campaigns in this area, including the battle at *Maserfelth* (if it occurred here), as well as the location of Maesbury lower down the Morda valley chosen as the southern 'anchor-point' for Wat's Dyke?[59] Similar configurations existed where the Dyke extended westwards to take in much of the Vale of Montgomery while facing higher ground to the west; and also where it traced a broad loop around and to the west and south-west of Presteigne on the river Lugg. In these cases also, it may have been political rather than topographical considerations that determined the essentials of the placement of the Dyke.

Meanwhile, at a more local level, the placing of each alignment resulted from a decision that a straight length of Dyke would work best in a particular place in terms of the effect (more formidable barrier, more visually impressive form, more effective linkage of key areas) that its presence would achieve. In other words, the straight alignments were highly deliberate (and deliberated upon) and were therefore fundamental and not incidental to the plan for and design of the Dyke throughout its course. In this way they were also a 'linking' device that integrated design and build at the scale of the whole landscape. That design and build were inter-related at a more intimate scale will become evident when the specific contributions of the built form of the earthwork to these questions of alignment, localised design, structure and surveillance are taken up in the next chapter.

CHAPTER FIVE

The structure of the Dyke

> Those who have had opportunities of examining the regular method in which OFFA'S DYKE is constructed, and of tracing its course in the secluded and remote districts through which it is carried, must regard it as a very extraordinary effort of human labor and skill.
>
> Charles Hartshorne, *Salopia Antiqua*, 1841[1]

Over eighty years on from first publication of Cyril Fox's archaeological descriptions of Offa's Dyke, there exists surprisingly little in print that illuminates the detail of its construction through close description at different locations. To some extent this is due to the lack of adequately large-scale excavation of the earthworks of the Dyke despite more than eighty recorded interventions.[2] There has also, however, been little discussion of exactly how any defined length of the Dyke may have been built, nor of how closely the practices of digging and building relate to those of landscape placement that were discussed at some length in the previous chapter.

This is a subject that needs to be approached with caution, for several reasons. There is, for example, the danger of making inferences from observations at one location that may not hold for others. Meanwhile, the causes of observable variation may differ from place to place, such that in one place differences may primarily have been a response to variations in geology, and in others in topography. Elsewhere again, a deliberate design effect may have been sought. Moreover, it needs to be borne continually in mind that around 1200 years have elapsed since the earthwork was built. The natural processes of initial settlement and the subsequent decay or collapse of any timber bank components will have had a significant impact. And the subsequent effects of erosion from water ingress, slippage, and watercourses, from animal burrowing, and from human activity (and especially enclosure and farming and the breaches and infillings that this has involved) will also have been considerable.

Bearing in mind these caveats, and despite the scrutiny to which Fox and others have subjected the Dyke, there are nonetheless new observations concerning its construction that it is possible to make, with care, from the surface form of the earthwork. Equally, although so few of the archaeological excavations across or into the Dyke bank and ditch have been published in detail, it is possible ascertain some aspects of the build characteristics that are shared more widely along the span of the linear earthwork. These include the depth and character of ditch profiles as dug, the existence and form of bank 'foundations', and the nature of stabilisation features or facings that may have been added. What it is not yet possible to do, however, is to compare systematically the method of building up the bank *as observed at multiple locations* to determine whether this differs in any repeated or regular way from length to length and from place to place along its course.

In pursuing enquiries about the build of Offa's Dyke, there are questions that can therefore be posed that necessitate close scrutiny of the readily visible traces and interrogation of the limited available archaeological survey and excavation record. This is in part to gain some understanding of the sequence and processes of construction, but mainly to gauge the potential significance of the completed built form. Such questions include 'what is the incidence and what the significance of different styles of build throughout the length of the Dyke?', 'are there any lengths of Dyke that exemplify especially complex patterns of build?' and 'if so, where are they to be found, what form do they take, and what can be inferred concerning their purpose?' In framing and responding to such questions, the chapter focuses first on the details of how the bank and ditch and other build features were created, and then upon how the definable lengths of Dyke were laid out in relation to one another. It is in this latter sphere, especially concerning the patterns of subtle adjustment of the position of build lengths, that the most potentially significant among the observations and deductions made in this book concerning its build occur. The 'regular method' of its construction highlighted by Reverend Hartshorne in 1841 is therefore very much at centre-stage in the following pages.

The formation of the Dyke as an earthwork: contrasting construction modes

That Offa's Dyke was not built in a uniform manner everywhere along its course is evident to the most casual observer: there are variations not only in the size of the bank but also in the depth of the ditch, for example. It is evident also that, although differential erosion is a factor in such contrasts, it cannot explain either the nature or the incidence of such variability in build; nor can geology, causing greater or lesser difficulty in ditch-digging, be enlisted as the fundamental reason for observable variations; although both factors were undoubtedly an influence on present form in many locations.

In his summary of the build characteristics of the Dyke in north-west Shropshire, Fox expressed the view that 'differences in method of construction … (and) … the differences in scale which were constantly met with in comparable portions' were '(within the limits laid down by higher authority) dependent on the resources of the locality and the energy of, and command of technique possessed by, the gangers in charge of the actual work of digging'.[3] Nonetheless, Fox was soon to realise that some differences, at least, were more regularly encountered. So, in respect to lengths across, and southwards from, the 'mountain zone' in western Shropshire and Radnorshire, he highlighted a contrast in construction type between what he termed the 'normal' Dyke and a slighter build, the 'boundary bank' form.[4] Moreover, he observed that the distribution of the lengths of these contrasting forms was not random, but rather was amenable to analysis that might provide clues as to its rationale. He recorded, visually, this contrast between these two forms as they sometimes existed side by side (or, rather, end to end) only once by his usual method of drawn profiles across the bank and ditch. This was to illustrate a dramatic change between kinds of build where the two forms abut one another in adjoining lengths on the crest of a hill to the south of Ffrydd, Knighton (Figures 2.3; 2.5; 7.2).[5] He correlated the two contrasting forms with differences in the kind of alignment of lengths of the Dyke, and the location of these latter in different parts of the landscape. So, he noted, the 'normal' (that is, larger) size of the earthwork was to be found where straight alignments of the Dyke predominated, as in areas of open country, especially in river-valleys, but also along some plateau-like hill-tops.[6] Meanwhile the 'weak' or 'boundary bank' form was present where a more sinuous course was taken, often around the crests of hills.

It would be possible to follow Fox in recognising the reality of such a primary contrast, such that the more northerly course of the Dyke could be seen to have been built in a uniformly strong 'normal' manner while the more southerly course was built in that way also, but in lengths interspersed with the weaker 'boundary bank' form. This in turn might lead to the suggestion that the Dyke was built at a different time or at least in a different way, north and south from Selley near Knighton, the most northerly point where the weaker construction form regularly occurs. Such an idea would be mistaken, however.[7] This is not so much because the 'boundary bank' form can be found further north, although in at least one location it clearly can be (see below). Rather, it is because such a view ignores the fact that the contrasts in construction are somewhat more complex than this, and a fuller appreciation of these contrasts leads to an altogether more subtle understanding of build variability and its logic.

This is not to deny the contrast in scale of build that Fox highlighted, but rather to note that there are two further forms (and scales) of construction that, like the 'normal' bank form, are found intermittently throughout the whole course of the Dyke. These two further types were recognised by Fox, but he did not highlight their ubiquity. The first of these additional forms of build he termed the 'major scale', although he nowhere specified all the places where this occurred. Indeed, he only noted its existence in passing, as in his 'Wye Valley' chapter, where he stated: 'In the lowlands of N. Herefordshire the Dyke is of normal Offan type with W. ditch, and in most places on the major scale, such as one sees at important points farther north'.[8] The phrase 'important points' is significant here, since it indicates Fox's awareness that there were key places whose importance was denoted at least in part by the scale of construction deployed by the Dyke-builders. The further, fourth, build form can best be termed the 'scarp' form. Fox noted the existence of this form, but related its incidence only to contrasts in the character of the ditch. This 'scarp' form refers to lengths where the Dyke was built on a steep, mostly west-facing, slope in such a way as to exaggerate the scale of the bank or to suggest the existence of a ditch where in reality there was only ever a notch or berm.

Fox's 'normal' scale of the Dyke is also more variable than he implied, differing considerably from one area to another. Moreover, lengths built in the 'normal' way, the slighter manner and the 'scarp' form may each also feature, in at least parts of their course, the presence of an eastern ditch. There is sometimes also the anomaly of the apparent absence of a western ditch in a number of places where the eastwards one is present. In practice, it was the effect sought and the most efficient means of achieving it, that seems to have mattered most to the Dyke designers and builders, rather than slavish adherence to a construction template.[9] This does not mean that the contrasting forms and dispositions observable do not have significance, however: only that there is more subtlety to their deployment and conjunction than Fox apparently recognised.

Given that variability in scale and execution is observable throughout course of the Dyke, it is perhaps better to describe the four different forms and scales of build, rather, as 'modes' of construction, to which the Dyke as built conforms to greater or lesser degree in any one place. In order to clarify these 'modal' contrasts in construction form, and, to some extent, where they occur, they are described separately here, along with examples of locations where they are readily discernible. To create this classification, it is first necessary to remove potential confusion arising, especially, from the term 'normal'. Our preferred terminology therefore firstly contrasts a *substantial* (instead of 'normal') mode, with the more massively *monumental* (in preference to 'major') mode. In turn these two modes differ from the *slighter* (replacing the awkward and potentially misleading 'weaker', 'hedge-bank' or 'boundary bank' terminology) mode and, finally, the *scarp* mode, which is less a matter of scale and results instead from the deployment of a particular construction practice.

The substantial construction mode

This mode of build comprises a prominent western ditch only rarely less than 2 m deep, and a broad bank or rampart standing at least 2 m above the surrounding ground.[10] Lengths built in *substantial* mode are found along most of the course of the Dyke north of the middle Severn, and they are especially evident where it crosses level ground, or where it traverses land sloping gently upwards to west or east of its line. Examples are the lengths at Esclusham west of Wrexham, on the hill above Bronygarth south of the river Ceiriog (Figure 5.2), at Pentre-shannel/Trefonen west of Oswestry, and at Rhos south of the crossing of the Vyrnwy (Figure 4.5).

South of the middle Severn this regular, *substantial*, mode is evident along the course of the Dyke at Leighton and at Forden near Welshpool (Figure 1.19), and along much of the stretch from the Vale of Montgomery southwards across

FIGURE 5.1 Offa's Dyke above Garbett Hall, continuing to Cwmsanahan Hill

As the earthwork descends southwards here from the heights around Llanfair Hill, its route directly overlooking the Teme valley north of Knighton becomes clearly established. As with many lengths in the 'Mountain Zone' the good preservation of the earthwork enables the identification of original features such as the counterscarp bank in front of the ditch and the constituent segments carefully arranged down the slope.

FIGURE 5.2 Along the prominent ridge overlooking the Ceiriog valley above Bronygarth

As it approaches the Ceiriog valley crossing from the south, the dimensions of the Dyke reach the upper end of the scale of build that is in this chapter termed the substantial mode of construction, with a very considerable ditch and proportionately large bank.

uplands to the Clun valley. It is evident from Newcastle Hill (Pen Offa) to Burfa in the Walton Basin in Radnorshire. In Herefordshire the *substantial* build mode is apparent at the Arrow crossing at Titley Mill, along the crossing of the Curl Brook valley west of Lyonshall (Figure 7.13), at Yazor (Moorhampton), and at Garnons (close to the Brecon to Hereford road) above the Wye west of Hereford. In Gloucestershire, it is present at Collins Grove in English Bicknor parish, near

Highbury south of Lower Redbrook, and in long lengths of the stretch from Madgetts to East Vaga above the river Wye opposite Tintern (Figure 9.2).

The monumental *construction mode*

Some stretches of Dyke that are broadly of the *substantial* mode of construction with a deep western ditch are nonetheless truly monumental in scale. Examples of this *monumental* mode to the north of the middle Severn are the passage of the Dyke down a prominent spur south of Treuddyn and north of Llanfynydd (Figure 9.13), the length around the prominent hilltop at Brymbo, the stretch to be found crossing level ground north of the Dee at Ruabon School (Figure 7.10), and that extending around the west-facing summit of Selattyn Hill, south of the Ceiriog (Figure 2.12). In places along these lengths, the bank may still survive up to 3.5 m high, and the slope between the base of the ditch and the top of the bank can be as long as 8 m.

South of the middle Severn valley, other such monumental-scale lengths were built, for example, at Dudston Fields near Chirbury in the Vale of Montgomery (Figure 1.21), around the west-facing summits at, and south of, Llanfair Hill south of the Clun valley (Figures 1.6; 5.8), and at Knill in northwest Herefordshire, where the Dyke crosses the valley of the Hindwell Brook south of Presteigne.[11] A particularly fine, if short, stretch is that at the southern end of the length of Dyke at Sedbury Park that terminates dramatically on the crest of the cliffs overlooking the Severn estuary (Figures 1.5; 2.9).

The slighter *construction mode*

The *slighter* mode, in which the bank is manifestly of smaller proportions yet nonetheless is still a significant element of the earthwork, comprises a bank sometimes little over a metre in height, fronted by a ditch of similar proportions. This commonly occurs where the Dyke takes a meandering course around west-facing scarps or slopes, and where the proportions might easily be regarded as greater than they in fact were, when viewed from lower ground to the west. This mode of construction is evident north of the middle Severn valley throughout the course that the Dyke takes around the western perimeter of the hillfort on Llanymynech Hill north of the Vyrnwy; and it is of interest in this context that its course around the promontory fort at Spital Meend above Lancaut on the Wye in Gloucestershire may also be marked by a bank of

FIGURE 5.3 The 'slighter' mode of construction: at Rhos-y-meirch

In some locations, what Fox characterised as a 'hedge-bank' scale to the build of the Dyke may have resulted instead from erosion.

these proportions. It might also be suggested that at several locations south of the Teme, including across much of north Herefordshire (where the Dyke may well have existed but if so has been all but erased), it may have been of this form.

Fox saw this mode, interspersed with what he referred to as 'normal' (termed here, *substantial*) construction mode lengths, as characteristic of large parts of the course of the Dyke through Radnorshire, on Herrock Hill and Rushock Hill in north Herefordshire.[12] He also regarded most of the Dyke in Gloucestershire as having been built in this mode. However, the recent field (Dyke presence and condition) study of the lengths in Gloucestershire has shown that the *substantial* mode of build can alternate with the *scarp* mode within short distances, and they can occur together – as also can the *slighter* mode co-occur with the scarp mode there.[13] The Gloucestershire archaeologists developed a sophisticated classification scheme for combinations of build mode, and such an analysis could be applied elsewhere along the course of the Dyke.[14] Another area where such modes both alternate and co-occur, for example, is at Hergan and southwards to the crossing of the river Clun near Newcastle-on-Clun (and see below).

Fox related the geographical incidence of the demonstrably lower bank to another 'anomalous' feature of the Dyke south of Selley. This is the occasional presence of an eastern ditch.[15] His sketch plan of the 'junction' on the crest of the hill north of Jenkins Allis, mentioned above, showed how to the north in the Knighton direction the much lower bank has an eastern ditch – which he specifically described as an 'east (spoil) ditch'. Here he also recorded no ditch present forwards to the west, while in contrast the 'normal scale' (our *substantial* mode) Dyke southwards past Jenkins Allis was marked to show a west ditch.[16]

FIGURE 5.4 The 'scarp' mode of construction: at Hergan
In some locations, what Fox characterised as a 'hedge-bank' scale to the build of the Dyke may have resulted instead from erosion. Photograph by Ian Bapty.

The scarp *construction mode*

The *scarp* mode involves the active modification of natural landforms to emphasise the Dyke as a prominent linear landscape feature, while minimising the construction demands involved. In a number of locations, an practically 'token' bank is therefore sited along the crest of a scarp, while the natural slope of the scarp itself has apparently been artificially steepened.[17] This is dramatically demonstrated along Craig Forda above the Morda west of Oswestry. It is also evident at Lynclys north of Llanymynech. The scarp mode is evident also through parts of the course of the Dyke above Leighton east of Welshpool, and is markedly present along parts of the course of the Dyke at and immediately to the south of Cwmsanahan Hill north of Knighton. The appearance of this form at this location is remarkable for the scale of the work: at one location it extends from the crest, where there is a half-metre high bank, down across a carefully scarped 9 or 10 m drop to a clear base of slope marked also by what appears to be a slight berm, notch or ditch (Figure 6.12).

Southwards again, the *scarp* mode occurs also just to the south at Panpunton Hill close to Knighton, and it features prominently around the west-facing slopes of Herrock Hill above the Walton Basin. It was enacted through much of the Gloucestershire course, whether at English Bicknor, Lippetts Grove, or the Devil's Pulpit. The drama of some of these locations is striking, and the views over the Dyke into the landscape westwards are often down precipitous slopes.

Interleaved and hybrid construction

Just as has already been noted above for Gloucestershire, the *scarp* mode length at Cwmsanahan Hill is interwoven with short stretches of *substantial* mode build, whilst being 'bracketed' at either end (after negotiating several sharp changes in direction) by *slighter* build mode lengths. The Dyke oscillates between construction modes within a relatively short distance elsewhere, for example in the area north of Llanymynech, where, as the Dyke approaches from the north from the Treflach direction, it is in *substantial* mode. It then switches to *scarp* mode at Lynclys, before adopting the *slighter* mode along Blodwel Rock to Llanymynech Hill. It then returns to the *substantial* mode to enter Llanymynech itself and to cross the Vyrnwy to continue down to the Severn.

The length southwards from Newcastle Hill/Pen Offa, overlooking the Radnor Basin west of Presteigne, is interesting in this respect because this interleaving also reflects differences in the scale and form of the Dyke while for the most part it is in *substantial* mode. So from Pen Offa there is a length that is of *slighter* construction mode, which remains of slight build but adopts a *scarp* mode along the northern flank of Evenjobb Hill. As it then made the long diagonally-placed run down to the base of the hill below Burfa Camp it resumed the *substantial* mode of construction. At the crossing of the flat valley bottom of the Hindwell Brook, however, the Dyke for a short length became of (formerly) *monumental* proportions, before suddenly adopting, as it rose onto Herrock Hill, the *slighter* mode. Nor does this account exhaust the subtlety of 'interleaving' of construction here, either. At Herrock Hill, the *scarp* mode takes the form of a notch or berm rather than featuring a ditch as such, and the Dyke then resumed the *substantial* mode to continue on to Rushock Hill.

Meanwhile, at Esclusham west of Wrexham, the *substantial* mode bank is sited upon a bluff, the west-facing slope of which was deliberately steepened to enhance the visible scale of the bank. Excavation showed that the bank had been

FIGURE 5.5 A 'hybrid' length of Offa's Dyke at Lippetts Grove, Gloucestershire

This view eastwards along the north-facing course of the earthwork indicates the massive scale of construction of the Dyke throughout the two miles facing (mostly) west towards Tintern, and of which the Devil's Pulpit forms the centre-piece. The scarp (right) is an enhancement of the natural slope, as at Hergan. (A bank surmounts the scarp at right, top, but is not visible here. The bank has a large quarry ditch to its south, upslope out of sight here). The path is around 1.5 metres wide at this point, occupying the outer half of a former approximately 3 m wide ditch, while the counter-scarp bank, visible here to the left of the path, becomes more substantial eastwards from this point.

rendered 'substantial' here, precisely through the manipulation of a natural rise: the hybrid nature of the monument combined both *scarp* mode and *substantial* mode build practices.[18]

Localised diversity despite the major construction trends

Although the above characterisation accurately portrays the modal forms of Dyke construction, variability as well as hybridity is a frequently-noticeable aspect of the build design of the Dyke. The purpose of features such as the 'Mellington Park outwork', a massive north–south mound extending westwards from the counter-scarp bank of the Dyke next to a ravine close to the crossing of the Caebitra stream, is uncertain.[19] More extensive features such as the double-bank (or parallel bank) south of the right-angled turn at Hergan are found in very short stretches elsewhere, as at Brynorgan near Selley north of Knighton. At Hergan, these two banks formed one above the other along the west-facing scarp could represent an attempt to magnify the Dyke as seen from the west along the approach to the right-angled turn at 'Hergan corner'. If so, they could reinforce the sense that a gateway once existed here.[20]

Some implications

Close study therefore reveals that the Dyke builders continually and intricately adapted the built form of the earthwork from length to length, drawing repeatedly and systematically upon a palette of different placement, design and construction practices. The deployment of these in any one locality or across any one linear span of the earthwork produced a unity of concept and execution

FIGURE 5.6 Contrasting Dyke forms and build modes in Gloucestershire (Spital Meend to St Briavels Common length) after Hoyle and Vallender, 1997, Figure 4B

Type 1 (and Type 1 hybrids) correspond to 'substantial', 'monumental' and 'scarp' modes of construction (with the latter mode predominating). The 'Type 2' forms appear, from surface inspection, to have originally been 'substantial' but to have been reduced by subsequent agricultural activity on gentle slopes or by erosion on steeper slopes (see also chapter 5, note 14).

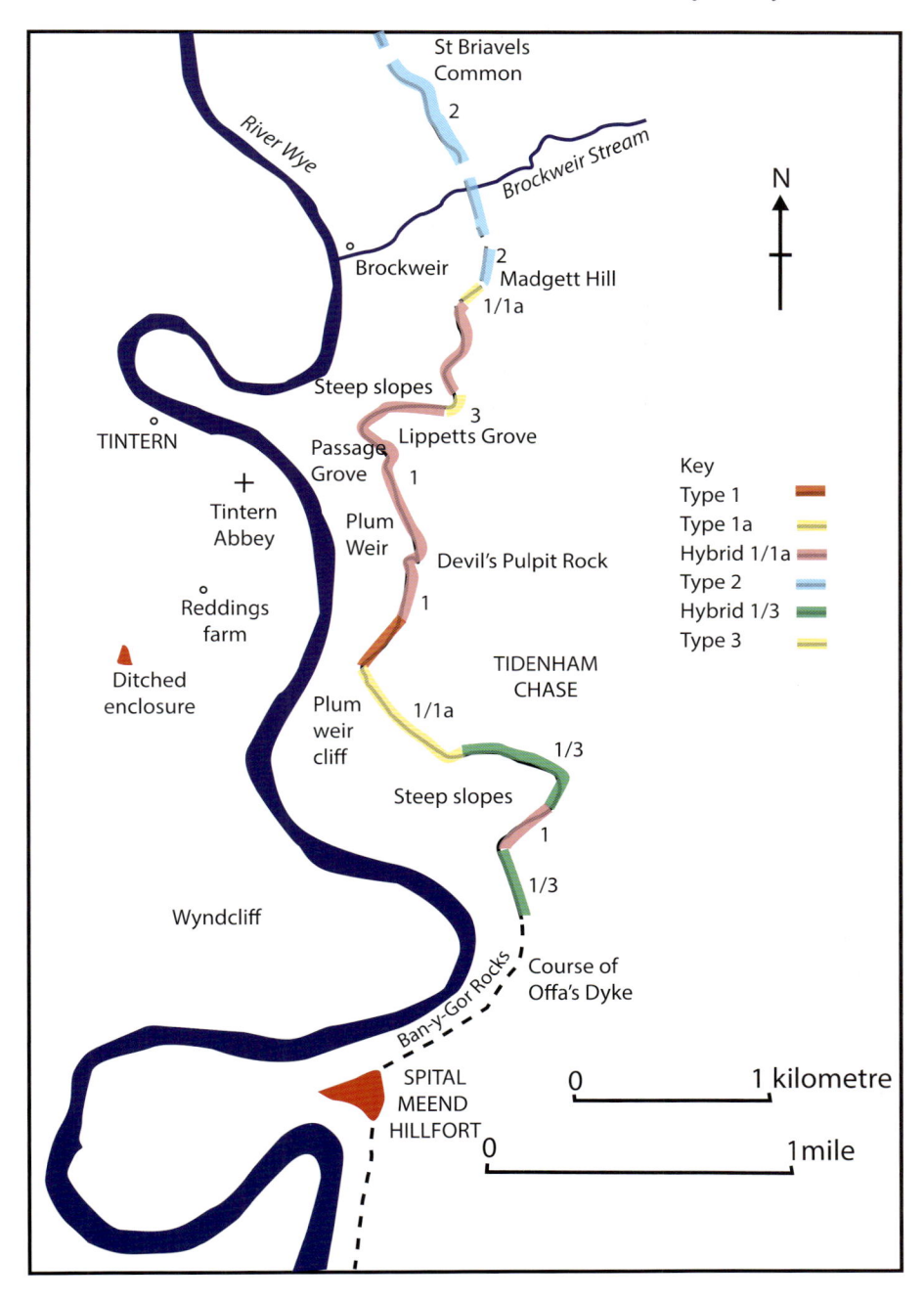

such that it is possible to distinguish an 'Offa's Dyke construction formula' wherever it occurs. This suite of practices is manifestly different from that which characterises Wat's Dyke, even though there are some build similarities that indicate their shared origin as works of what Fox termed 'the Mercian school of dyke-building'.

Moreover, recognition of these more complicated arrangements of different build modes indicates the possibility that the absence of the Dyke in some places may be more apparent than real. Such absence could, for instance, be ascribed to the loss or 'submergence' within later landscape transformations, of a slighter, or a scarped, form. So while it is likely to be the case that the 'Whitford Dyke' in the far north in Flintshire is prehistoric in origin, and that it was utilized as a boundary in medieval times, it cannot be entirely discounted that it may have been incorporated into the late eighth-century scheme.[21] That the existence of a linear earthen bank with a ditch front and back, and a relatively small scale to the earthwork overall, *automatically* disqualifies a length of linear earthwork of this character as having anything to do with Offa's Dyke is surely no longer sustainable in light of these observations.

The dominance of the *slighter* mode of construction along some stretches of Dyke in its course south of Selley means that we cannot simply hold to Fox's dictum about manifest continuity being necessary to the charting of a possible course to the Dyke in areas where it is apparently absent. On the contrary, any length of linear earthwork that may have been part of the Offa's Dyke scheme needs to be evaluated first in reference to the number of characteristic locational and (in particular) build features that can be regarded as characteristic of the design/build repertoire discussed in these two chapters. It is primarily for this reason that all the lengths of earthwork described by Fox as part of the scheme in Gloucestershire need still to be regarded as part of Offa's Dyke.

As to reasons for the variability of form, the evidence from Gloucestershire that will be discussed below might be taken to suggest that in some parts of the course of the Dyke, the underlying geology could be a key determinant. However, it would seem that, just as the placing of the Dyke in the landscape reflects the deployment of a consistent series of placement practices, so too does the choice of built form represent its own 'repertoire' of alternatives, for instance when encountering the different opportunities (as well as challenges) provided by contrasts in rock and soil, and by localised topography. These opportunities concerned how stable the structure could be made to be, how imposing it could be made to appear, and what surveillance advantages it could gain.

The form of the ditch and bank: profiles and sections

What we understand about the detail of the build of Offa's Dyke at multiple locations is at present highly dependent upon observations about its form across its breadth rather than along its lengths. In other words, apart from verbal descriptions and Fox's annotated plans, the manner of recording the surface form of the earthwork most often deployed has been to measure and draw the profile at different points. Most of the eighty or so excavations have meanwhile been limited in scope such that few sections have been cut across the whole ditch, or the whole bank. Hardly any have been dug across both bank and ditch in one place. In contrast, several of the excavations undertaken in recent years

5 *The structure of the Dyke*

have simply involved the recording of a machine-cut made for purposes other than archaeological study.[22]

The build of the Dyke as apparent from surface traces

Besides his detailed written observations and a series of photographs, Cyril Fox published 50 profile drawings for the Dyke south of Treuddyn.[23] These form an important archive recording the profile of the earthwork throughout its course and especially at well-preserved points. As well as publishing the drawn profiles, Fox also quantified the recorded dimensions (at least for the course of the Dyke as far south as the Kerry Ridgeway) in a series of 'Table of Measurement' figures.[24] From Treuddyn southwards he provided comparative measurements in these tables from 32 profiles. This work is one of many reasons why Fox's contribution is indispensible in archaeological terms, beyond simply providing 'an inventory of the state of the Dykes in the 1920s and 1930s'.[25]

Comparisons based upon close examination of Fox's profile drawings are instructive, although they are considerably more useful (because more numerous) for the earlier, northern, parts of the Dyke recorded in the 1926–32 survey than for more southerly ones. They show for instance that the location of the ditch and its associated bank in respect to east–west variation in topography varies considerably. Among the 49 profiles for which analysis of such variability is possible, 13 were recorded in areas where from one side of the Dyke to the other it is located on level ground, or on mostly level ground that slopes up slightly to the west. In 5 further cases the ditch is located on the western facing side of a slightly domed summit of ground. In another 10 profile locations the Dyke was positioned on a moderate to steep slope to the west, and in a further 8 cases the ditch was located on a very steep drop to the west or on a brow with a steep drop beyond it. In three unusual cases (all at Treflach) the ditch and bank were located at the foot of a west-facing slope. In fully 10 locations, the ditch and bank together were located in a situation where the Dyke faces uphill to the west (that is, sited on an east-facing slope), and in three of these cases this slope is steep.[26]

Any observations on the proportions and profile characteristics of the ditch based upon surface observation are obviously prone to error, since the way that the ditch has partially infilled through time may give a misleading impression of its original (or its at present buried) profile.[27] An example where excavation by Fox revealed the complete masking of the ditch represents an extreme, but instructive, case. This was the site he examined to the south-west of Court House, Forden, in 1929. Fields to the north-west of the Dyke here were entirely level, but the bank of the Dyke had clearly been 'submerged' by silt in this direction, to a depth of over a metre.[28] Nonetheless, there are 44 profiles that are informative about the ditch characteristics, and these can helpfully be grouped according to their general form. In this way, 15 of the ditch profiles can be classed as conforming to a deep V-shape, while 19 can be said to possess a shallow V-shaped profile. Of those on very steep slopes 4 have notch-like or berm-like level areas in front of them that might, or might not, have ditches. Very shallow depressions that may approximate shallow flat bases were recorded in 6 places, but only one such profile certainly featured a flat-bottomed ditch. The 15 deep V-shaped ditch profiles recorded correlate in 5 cases with land sloping slightly or markedly to the east, and in 5 other cases with land sloping to the west. On only 2 of the 10 occasions when there is a level area or gentle slope to the east is there also a deep V-shaped ditch profile: and both of these are in the Llanfair Hill area.

Fox's profiles show that the form of the bank, as with the ditch, reflects its topographical position, although a shallower profile may, for instance, reflect the impact of erosion down steeper slopes. The breadth of the bank he recorded in profile correlates closely with the difference in scale between his 'normal' (our *substantial* mode) and his 'major' (our *monumental* mode) forms of construction. So where the more massive build occurs there is often a breadth of 12 m or more at base. Meanwhile, for the *substantial* mode of build, this breadth averages between 8 and 10 metres. Understandably, Fox tended to choose locations where the Dyke was better-preserved for measuring profiles, so

FIGURE 5.7 Contrasting profiles of Offa's Dyke on Long Mountain, after Fox (1955, 109)

REPRODUCED COURTESY OF THE CAMBRIAN ARCHAEOLOGICAL ASSOCIATION. COPYRIGHT RESERVED.

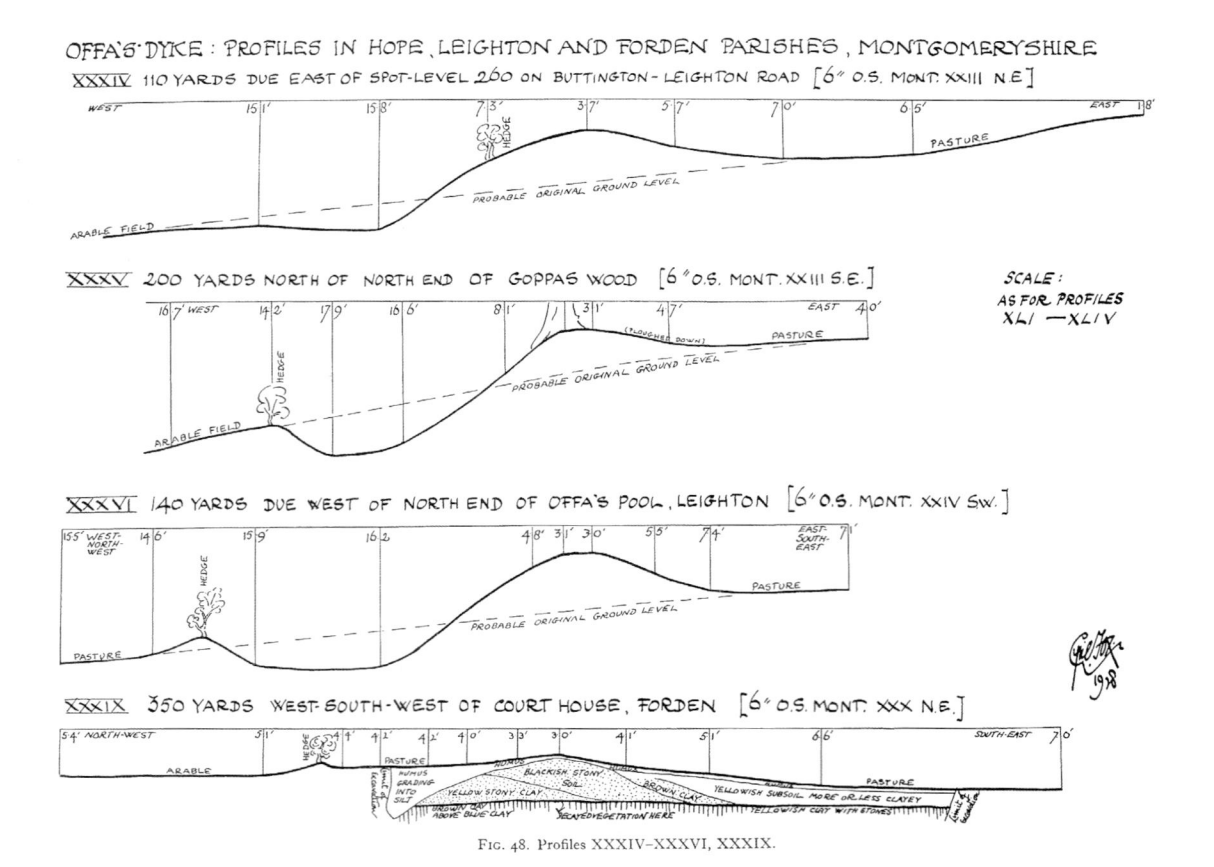

FIG. 48. Profiles XXXIV–XXXVI, XXXIX.

it is not surprising to find that in 37 out of the 50 profiles that he measured, it is possible to estimate the original form of the bank.[29] At 21 of these locations, the bank had a symmetrical profile and in 16 the slope on the broadly 'western' side was markedly steeper than the west-facing slope situated to the 'east' of the Dyke. In 6 of these 16 cases, moreover, the western slope bore indications of deliberate steepening of the slope profile, and in light of the observations above concerning the *scarp* mode of construction, such locations require further detailed study.[30]

One area relatively deficient in profiles in Fox's study was the Dyke where it overlooks the Wye south of Monmouth.[31] This deficit was made good in the mid-1990s by the recording of 48 profiles along the course of the Dyke from Sedbury northwards to English Bicknor (Figure 5.6). In some places (as across much of St Briavels Common) the earthwork was almost completely levelled (4 instances), and in others quarrying or modern tracks had obscured the profile (14 cases). The remaining 30 profiles revealed three main contrasting types of situation currently existing and observable. In the first category, there is a bank with a west-facing scarp in front of it that takes the form either of a berm or a notch (9 instances). In the second there is a ditch which in many cases is a slight feature at surface but at each location concerned there are indications of a more substantial below-ground form (16 cases). In the third, the ditch is still a massive feature, as at Sedbury (4 profiles).[32] Of these latter, only the Sedbury ditches can be described in terms of their full profile, and these are all of the deep V-shape type.

The profile of the bank as recorded in the 1995 survey of the Dyke in Gloucestershire confirmed that near its southern terminus, the Dyke was indeed built at a truly *monumental* scale, with the profile close to Sedbury showing that the height of the eroded bank was at least 5 m above the part-infilled ditch, while the scarp from bank-top to ditch-bottom extended over 10 m. The counter-scarp bank is also very evident in this stretch. Fully 30 of the 1995 profiles showed that the Dyke was placed on a steep slope (including at English Bicknor and Bishopswood), often in the *scarp* mode of construction, but with a bank built at the *substantial* scale in key locations.

An important observation in the 1995 survey was that aspects of these contrasting surface traces and profiled forms could in several places be matched closely to the underlying geology, which was mapped against the survey results; while in other cases the situation was more complex. So on the limestone, as opposite Tintern, the ditch is most likely to be shallow (or its place occupied by a notch or a berm), on the Old Red Sandstone (for instance south of Redbrook), the ditch is most likely to be entirely in-filled from erosion products derived from the softer rock, and on the Keuper Marl (at Sedbury) it had massive proportions except where it has been in-filled by modern ploughing (as to the east of Buttington Tump).[33]

Apart from comments made in passing by previous field researchers, there is no indication that there has developed an awareness of any sophistication in the

FIGURE 5.8 The *monumental* build mode well-preserved: above Garbett Hall

At the southern limit of Llanfair Hill (see also Figure 5.1), the Dyke earthwork approximates something of its original scale. The counterscarp bank is just discernible, but the massive ditch here is barely visible, when seen from the west. What still impresses, however, is the great mass of the near-vertical west face of the bank, reinforced with stone (see Figure 5.16, below, where part of the facing is seen exposed).

build of the bank from surface inspection, other than observations concerning how it may have been faced. These comments have mostly been derived from observations of the eroded west-facing elevations. While the new observations we have made remain localised (and therefore somewhat anecdotal) rather than comprehensive (arising from systematic project-based recording), they can now be made for several more locations than previously noted.

At a number of places, for example, the bank appears to have been built deliberately in bays: that is, in 'box-like' divisions, using slab-like stones as lateral

FIGURE 5.9 Bank length with possible slab-defined bays at Discoed on the Lugg

The individual segments of bank on the north-facing steep slope here, close to Yew Tree Farm, feature carefully-tapered overlapping terminals that facilitate subtle changes in the alignment of successive segments. Each segment appears to have been divided also into 'bays' that may have been designed to help contain the spread of quarried material both laterally and down the slope.

5 *The structure of the Dyke* 179

and presumably also as length-ways structural dividers. At Yew Tree Farm, Discoed (near Presteigne), edge-set stones passing laterally across the bank build can be observed today, set from east to west within the thickness of the bank. In one bank segment (see Figure 5.9) a number of distinct divisions or bays, each 5–6 metres long, can be postulated from the occurrence of three 'sets' of edge-set stones that appear to pass laterally through the bank. Edge-set stones can also be seen set at right-angles to the longitudinal line of the bank close to the crest of the ridge on Edenhope Hill (Figure 5.10). That this build practice co-exists in locations where stones quarried from the lower part of the ditch were carefully laid in 'layers' (that is, not coursed, but piled horizontally) suggests that the whole enterprise of 'box-building' may have been carefully devised and executed for a particular purpose.[34]

FIGURE 5.10 The bank of the Dyke on Edenhope Hill: further laterally-set stones

As at Yew Tree Farm, but less likely to concern stabilisation on a slope, there may have been a deliberate embayment here within individual bank segments.

The character of the ditch as understood from archaeological excavations

Fox's focus upon profiles reflects the limitations both of time upon an already ambitious project, and the methods of his day. It is not therefore surprising that his few excavations involved the cutting of narrow slots through ditch and

FIGURE 5.11 The excavated ditch at Ffrydd Road, Knighton: in section

PHOTOGRAPH COURTESY OF CLWYD-POWYS ARCHAEOLOGICAL TRUST (COPYRIGHT RESERVED).

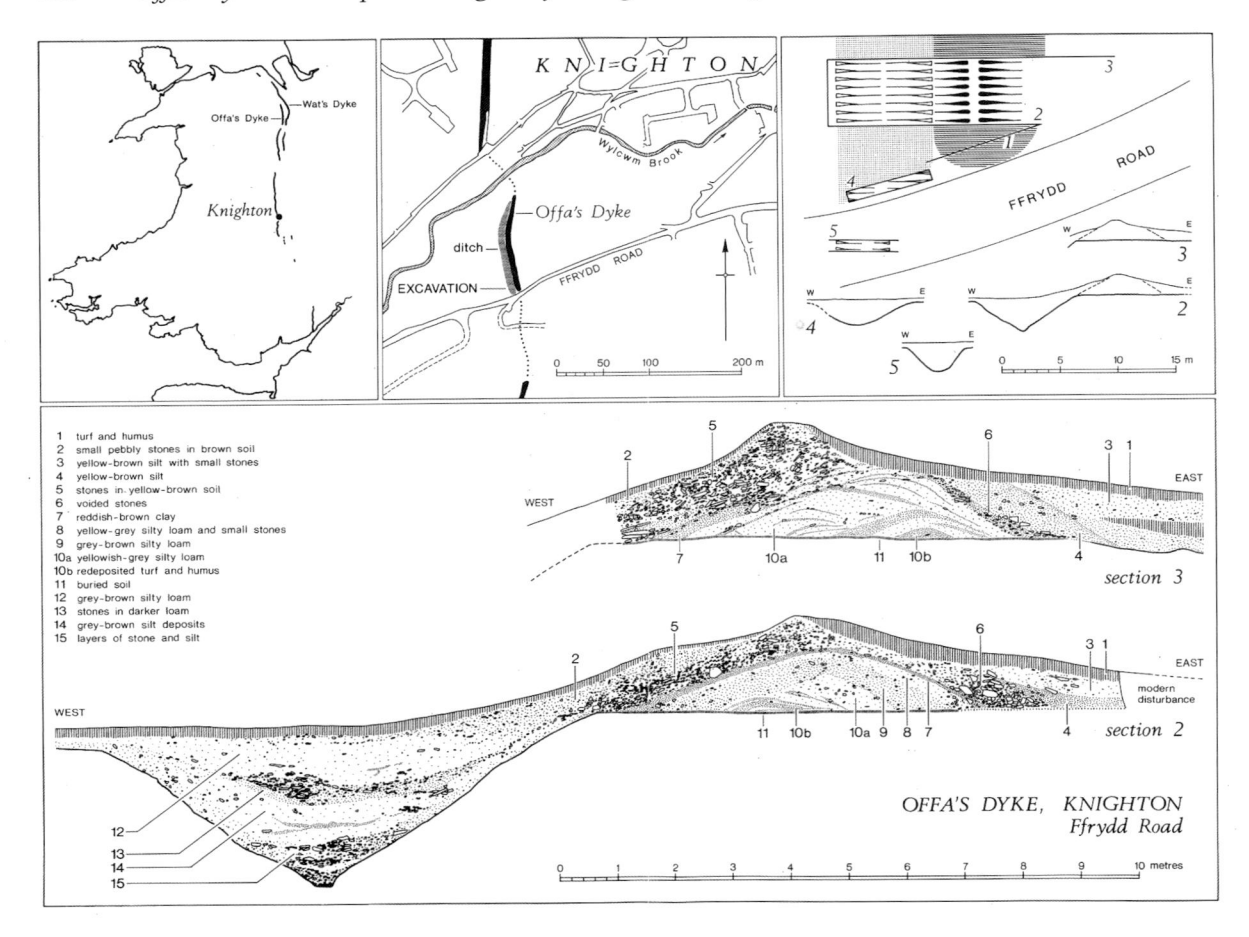

bank. What is perhaps more surprising is that to this day what we understand of the build of Offa's Dyke is entirely limited to equivalent simple lateral cuts through parts of the bank or ditch, or, rarely, through both.[35]

Very few of the excavated ditch sections along the Dyke have shown it to have been dug to a consistent width or depth, despite the published suggestion that 'excavations have shown that the ditch, with few exceptions, is 2 m deep and 7m wide'.[36] The one fully excavated ditch section published by Cyril Fox, at Caeaugwynion near Chirk Castle Park, was near enough to these dimensions, at 2.3 m deep and 5.5 m wide.[37] However, at Mainstone, Shropshire, the ditch recorded in the more northerly of two machine-cut drainage pipe trenches was found to be 3 m deep and 9 m wide. At Redwood Lodge, Buttington, it was recorded as 3 m deep and 6 m wide. At the other extreme, at Orseddwen, south of Selattyn Hill, the ditch was thought to be only a metre deep and less than 3 metres wide, despite the massive proportions of the bank here.[38]

The only other full ditch sections so far published are those from excavations at Ffrydd Road, Knighton, and at Bronwylfa Road, Esclusham near Wrexham.

FIGURE 5.12 The bank and ditch in the well-recorded Ffrydd Road investigation

DRAWINGS COURTESY OF CLWYD-POWYS ARCHAEOLOGICAL TRUST (COPYRIGHT RESERVED).

5   *The structure of the Dyke*   181

At the former, during road-widening works in 1976, an area of bank and ditch to the north of the road was machine dug and then hand-excavated to a width of around six metres, and a complete profile of both bank and ditch was drawn.[39] Two further narrow cuts were made specifically across and into the ditch, the first immediately next to the road on the north side and the second along the centre line of the road itself, and the sections were recorded as profiles. On the downhill (north) side of the road, the ditch had been dug 8.5 to 9 m wide and up to 3 m deep in both sampled locations. In the centre of the road, however, only four metres to the south of the section directly adjacent to the road, although the ditch had been dug to a comparable depth, it was only 4 m wide.[40] The northerly ditch segment was a broad open V-shape with a slot at its base. The inner slope featured two gradients, the upper one of which was shallower and continued without interruption onto the outward-facing slope of the bank. In contrast, the narrower southerly ditch had only a simple U-shaped profile.

At Bronwylfa Road, near Esclusham Farm, a machine-dug trench for a gas pipeline was recorded in section, and this showed the ditch to be 5 metres wide and 2 metres deep.[41] A field drainage ditch had been inserted into the eastern side of the Dyke ditch, but probably did not account for the apparent eccentricity of a notch cut into the west-facing slope forwards from and below the level at which the bank had been created. As already mentioned, this location is of considerable interest to the extent that it shows a combination of the *substantial* with the *scarp* mode of construction. The ditch had deliberately been dug at the base of a natural west-facing declivity so that anyone approaching from the west was confronted by a much greater scarp than could have been achieved simply with a built bank: the vertical contrast in height from the base of the ditch here is some 5 m, while the sloping front of the work extends as a continuous line over 6 m. Moreover, the exposure of a rock-face might well have given the impression of a (possibly coursed) built wall-facing when seen from the west.

The full ditch profile of Offa's Dyke appears to have been observed and recorded at a further 10 locations, although even indicative dimensions have

FIGURE 5.13 A 20 metre long section through Offa's Dyke at Esclusham

This is the most extensive section through Offa's Dyke yet published from records made during the cutting of a pipeline trench through the Dyke in 1990.

DRAWING COURTESY OF CLWYD-POWYS ARCHAEOLOGICAL TRUST (COPYRIGHT RESERVED).

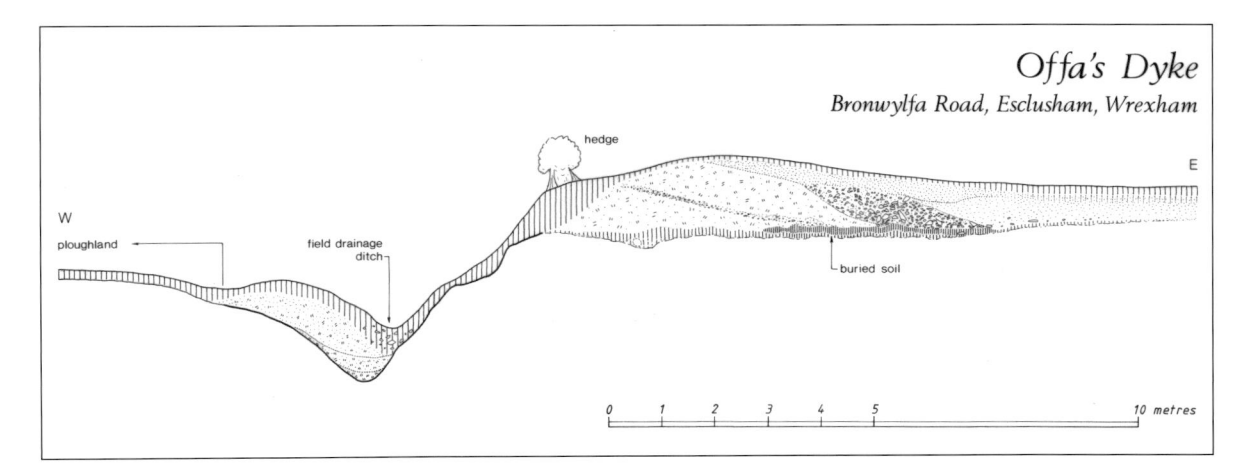

Offa's Dyke
Bronwylfa Road, Esclusham, Wrexham

been published for only 6 of these. Along the stretch linking the Vyrnwy and Severn, at the Nea, Llandrinio, the proportions given were '5m wide and more than 1.5m deep', while a mile away to the north at Four Crosses, Llandysilio, it was 'over 1m deep and 4.5m wide'.[42] Near the Old School House by Llynclys Hill, 'the excavation revealed a considerable ditch'.[43] An oblique section across the Dyke at Home Farm, Chirk Castle, did not provide an accurate measurement of the width of the ditch, but demonstrated that it was over 2 m deep here.[44] At Ffrith Farm near Llanfynydd, a ditch presumed to belong to Offa's Dyke measured more than 8 m in width but was only 1 m deep.[45] Meanwhile, at the Schoolfield, Llanfynydd, the width was found to be more than 4 m while the ditch depth as given was 1.5 m.[46] The published section at Buttington Tump, Sedbury (Tidenham, Gloucestershire) indicates a ditch that is again just over 4 m wide and 1.5 m deep.[47]

There have been several other excavations in which the lip of the ditch or the upper levels has been traced, but in no cases was it attempted, or indeed possible, to test the depth.[48] Nonetheless, even this limited sample indicates that the ditch depth could vary between as little as 1 m and in excess of 3 m. Meanwhile the width could be as little as 3 m, was often 5 m, and could be as much as 9 m. The shallow ditch depths can be found not only on the heights of the uplands, but also in the lowest parts of river-valleys. Deep ditch depths might be more common in lowland settings, but can also be found on the hills.

There is similar broad variety in excavated ditch profiles. It has been suggested that 'the ditch was usually cut in one of three formats, a V-shape or a U-shape … (and places where) the natural slope was steepened by cutting it back just below the crest and a shallow ditch dug a few metres below the steepened slope'.[49] Fox's thumbnail sketch of the Caeaugwynion ditch section clearly shows this, however, to have been flat-bottomed, with a base 1.8 m wide. Moreover, among the published sections only the narrower one at Ffrydd Road, Knighton, has a U-shaped profile; while, for instance, the Mainstone section described as U-shaped is more properly to be regarded as V-shaped. What does vary considerably is the angle of cut, possibly with the deeper lengths of ditch having a steeper profile. In some places the limited scope for silting due to the rocky character of the adjacent bank has resulted in the excavated profile differing little from that visible at surface, as in the case of the U-shaped ditch recorded at Lippetts Grove in Gloucestershire.[50]

The most common as-dug ditch-profile appears therefore, based upon this limited sample, to be a V-shape. That variations of profile do exist is undoubted, however, and contrasts in silting profile in adjacent lengths of the ditch indicate that such variability may have been deliberate and systematic, rather than random, or resulting from different multi-phase creation of the monument, or contrasting geology. The Ffrydd Road, Knighton, excavations showed this variation graphically in a context where several sections were examined close together.

Among the few published full sections, only those from Redwood Lodge,

Buttington, and at Ffrydd Road, Knighton, exhibit any apparent fill complexity. At Redwood Lodge, although the cut as drawn does not closely fit the fill lines shown, there appears to be a re-cut following a four-context 'primary fill' sequence. In contrast, at Ffrydd Road, Knighton, the published sections appear to show a succession of silting episodes followed by a collapse, and then a subsequent re-cut.[51]

The practice of steepening a natural slope by cutting it back, and the inserting of the ditch below this, as at the foot of the slope at Bronwylfa Road, Esclusham, was also recorded, if not noted as such, at Porth-y-Waen, Shropshire. Here, the artificial steepening of the slope occurred at least twice, while the bank itself (if it had ever existed as a notable feature here at all) may have occupied an upper levelled area, or ledge, to the east.[52] Meanwhile, a similar creation of terraces or ledges appears to have occurred in the face of the rock at Buttington Tump in Gloucestershire, except that the third, upper, terrace in this location facing the Severn Estuary was capped by a bank 2.5 m high.[53] This suggests that the *scarp* mode of construction could be brought into play wherever the opportunity presented itself to thereby exaggerate the scale of the barrier facing west, and in many places this involved building a hybrid form.

The recent work on Wat's Dyke at Gobowen, especially when placed in reference to other excavated sections of ditch of that dyke elsewhere, has led to the conclusion being drawn that there is some consistency in the form of that ditch along its course. It has moreover been suggested that the depth to which the Wat's Dyke ditch was cut (often over 3 m in depth) is greater than the depth of the ditch of Offa's Dyke.[54] Given the evidence adduced here for Offa's Dyke ditch sections extending to a depth of 3 m or more, there are nonetheless few grounds for suggesting that the ditch was *consistently* shallower than that of Wat's Dyke.

The idea that the ditch of Wat's Dyke was deeper than that of Offa's Dyke certainly runs counter to the suggestion that Cyril Fox made, backed up by measurements from very many drawn profiles, that the reverse was the case.[55] It may well be that the depth of the Wat's Dyke ditch lengths was more consistent throughout its course than was the case with Offa's Dyke, or that the Wat's Dyke

FIGURE 5.14 The stony 'foundation deposit' beneath Wat's Dyke at Gobowen

The view north across the excavations at Gobowen in 2006 shows the basal layers of the bank, with, to the west (left) the V-shaped ditch. The Optically Stimulated Luminescence dating sample points within the ditch sections are clearly visible.

PHOTOGRAPH COURTESY OF TIM MALIM.

ditch lengths have become more in-filled, but this does not necessarily mean that Offa's Dyke was therefore a more composite or piecemeal work. Rather, the Offa's Dyke ditch appears to have featured contrasting patterns of depth and profile that recurred at different places throughout its course. While this is perhaps not so surprising given the stark contrasts in topography and geology that it encountered, it reinforces also the sense that a suite of build practices was brought into effect that complemented the suite of placement practices also deployed throughout its course.

Excavated evidence for the structure of the bank

At Ffrith village and at Ffrith Hall, near Llanfynydd in Flintshire, Fox cut two contrasting sections across the bank, but not across the ditch.[56] His account of this work focused almost exclusively on what the first of these excavations demonstrated regarding the post-Roman date of the Dyke. The only observation he made about the way in which the Dyke had been built was to speculate that a post-hole-like void sealed beneath the bank might have held a post used as a marker to establish its course.[57] Fox's published Ffrith village section drawing indicates a concentration of stones at the rear of the presumed core of the bank, and a mounding up of soil from the east to the west against this core, cutting into the Romano-British deposits that are located mainly on the eastern side of the Dyke here. The Ffrith Hall section in contrast produced no finds and the schematic rendering of the stratigraphy in the drawing implies a more homogenous structure that possibly included turf and subsoil piled, or even perhaps placed, from both east and west. At least one continuous 'interval'

FIGURE 5.15 Section through the bank exposed in the side of a track at Bronygarth

The photograph is of part of the bank on the north-facing slope just uphill of the length featured in Figure 4.11, and downhill from the length in Figure 5.2, above. The earth and stone matrix, with some larger boulders towards the rear (left) of the bank are a recurrent feature of the build method.

PHOTOGRAPH: ADAM STANFORD/ AERIAL-CAM, COPYRIGHT RESERVED.

layer between construction phases is also hinted at in the drawn section that Fox published.[58]

Only two other sections excavated through the Dyke were reproduced in Fox's 1955 volume. One of these was simply a sketch rendered as part of a larger profile at Caeaugwynion north of Chirk Castle Park. While Fox published a full, if thumbnail, profile of the ditch here, only small-scale cuttings were made into the front and back of the bank, from which he deduced that it 'was composed of gravelly and sandy clay'.[59] The other section, cut to the south-west of Court House, Forden, north of Montgomery, was similarly schematic.[60] This section was re-cut in 1976 to try to trace a deposit of 'decayed vegetation' located on Fox's drawing on the old ground surface beneath the rear of the primary deposit of 'yellow stony clay' at the centre of the 11 m wide bank. This primary deposit was presumed both by Fox and by the 1976 excavators to have been derived from the ditch, on whose eastern lip it would therefore have been deposited.

There were a further three sites at which observations had been made before 1955 that are pertinent to an understanding of the build of the bank. One of these Fox had observed himself in the disused quarry at Treflach Wood, which had cut through the Dyke, leaving a bank section visible. Fox annotated a photograph to show the bank again 'composed of gravel and clayey sand in diagonal layers.' The primary dump of material he thought had evidently been placed on the edge of the ditch, 'and it was brought to full size by adding material to the reverse slope and the crest.'[61] Another observation site was on the cliff scarp overlooking the south bank of the Dee near Plas Offa, where Fox observed that the bank comprised 'river pebbles in a sandy matrix'.[62] The third site was where an access roadway had been cut through the Dyke in 1922 at Ruabon Grammar School, whose then Headmaster had observed the resulting section. Here, the core material was 'sandy stony soil', but it had been kept from spreading to the rear of the bank and into the ditch by 'numerous large waterworn boulders placed at the base of the bank at either side (but chiefly on the E.)'.[63]

The fullest published examination of the bank is again that at Ffrydd Road, Knighton.[64] Here, not only were the two main sections across the larger bank on the downhill (north) side of the road meticulously recorded, but their utility was enhanced by their close proximity to one another. An expected pattern of successive dumping to form the bank was observed here, comprising 'progressively coarser material, from freshly stripped turf to large quantities of shale slabs and boulders'. However, the location of the finer primary dump material, including turves, differed such that 'in (the more northerly) Section 3 the turf and soils peaked towards the rear of the bank, and the major part of the stony material had been piled onto the front of this initial mound.'[65] The careful cleaning of the surface of spits dug into the 6 m wide length of bank between the sections dug across it here enabled the excavators to observe that 'the dumps of material overlapped each other in haphazard fashion, and meandered freely with no apparent signs of constraint.'[66] There was no evidence

FIGURE 5.16 Possible roughly-coursed stone facework on the bank at Llanfair Hill

In a number of locations along the Dyke, traces of facings in rubble, or surviving as roughly-set bands of stone, can be noticed. Sometimes (as at the length of Dyke north of Carreg-y-big near Oswestry (Figure 1.11)) these can be dismissed as having formed part of later field-walls, but here, and at various points between Madgett Hill and Lippett's Grove in Gloucestershire, the stone concerned is set well down in the profile.

for any timberwork in the main body of the bank, nor of any revetment to either front or rear. The excavator expressed the view that the character of the shale stones at the front of the bank was such as to indicate that there had been a deliberate attempt to create a 10 m long slope from the top of the bank to the base of the ditch, faced with loose stones, possibly to deter attempts to scale the bank.[67]

Several other excavations have produced limited observations on the form of the bank, although few have been published fully enough to enable the drawing of firm conclusions. One of these excavations followed up another of Fox's excavations, at Sunnybank, Ffrith.[68] Here an old land surface was found, sealing Romano-British levels. Immediately above this, the surviving 0.8 m of bank was composed of layers of silt-clay with stone, which could indicate the former presence of turves. At Coedpoeth near the river Clywedog the recorded partial bank section survived to over 2 m high, and was said mostly to have been formed of turves.[69] The section cut across the Dyke a mile south from this, at Bronwylfa Road, near Esclusham Farm, showed that the bank comprised a series of dumps and survived to 8 m wide and 1.5 m in height. A buried soil was noted here, as at several other locations, but perhaps more remarkable was an apparently large dump of stone at the rear of the bank. Unless this represented a much later episode of dumping, it is likely to have derived from a quarry somewhere to the rear of the Dyke. Its composition was seemingly in marked contrast to the mixed character of the material towards the front of the bank.[70] To the rear of the dumps of material making up the bulk of the bank at Buttington Tump, Sedbury, was similarly added a significant sealing deposit of bulky material.[71]

Both of the excavations at Nutwood, Edenhope, encountered and examined the bank. In one of these sections 'a reasonably large surface of the lower part

5 The structure of the Dyke

FIGURE 5.17 Surviving bank facework at Madgett Hill, Gloucestershire

This view along the front of the bank looking southwards up a steep slope traversed by the Dyke here provides a clear indication of the amount of stonework originally deployed to create a 'wall-like' façade. The stonework evident at various locations along the length of Dyke facing Tintern across the Wye gorge hereabouts has sometimes been claimed to be 'modern', forming post-medieval field-walls. Such re-use clearly has occurred, but the crucial evidence visible in this photograph is that the ancient yew tree actually retains such stonework against the bank, and has clearly grown up over it.

of the bank (was) examined and some evidence for the use of turfs in the build of the bank was observed'.[72] In the more southerly of two sections cut across the Dyke in the bottom of the Unk valley nearby at Mainstone, the bank was interpreted as comprising simply dumps of material derived from the ditch and was composed of layers of gravel and clay, some of which contained also stone.[73] Between the Vyrnwy and Severn, the base of the bank was traced in two excavations at Four Crosses, Llandysilio. In one, two distinct deposits were recorded, the lowest comprising sandy clay with a few stones, with the subsequent dump comprising clay with stones that reflected closely the underlying natural deposits of glacial drift.[74] In the other, the bank survived to almost 1 m in height.[75]

Across the river Severn at Redwood Lodge, Buttington, 'a distinct layer of stone was to be seen at the base of the bank'.[76] This phenomenon was also observed at Woodside, Selattyn, where half of the width of the bank was revealed and was shown to survive to a metre in height. The layer forming the basal deposit here was composed of large stones, and this was covered with a layer of 'hard-packed clay with some stone', itself overlain by a layer of 'looser clayey material'.[77] In the south in the Vale of Montgomery at Brompton Hall, it was suggested that the front of the metre-high remains of the bank had been faced with turves set at a steep angle to form a sloping front to the earthwork.[78] A similar pattern was revealed at one of the sites examined at Johnstown north of Ruabon, where part of the western face of the bank was thought to have been constructed with turves.[79] Meanwhile, the oblique section through the earthwork at Home Farm, Chirk Castle, revealed an old land surface overlain by the main dump of clayey bank material.[80]

The recent work on Wat's Dyke at Gobowen has provided some clues as to the lateral complexity in the form of the bank of that dyke. These findings appear to echo at least some of the more anecdotal observations from sections cut across Offa's Dyke. So, for example, there was a half-metre high linear spread of 'upcast earth generated while de-turfing the line of the ditch and bank area'. This was recorded as extending for 10 m northwards from the southern limit of the excavation. It tapered towards its northern end, and was located on the inner lip of the ditch.[81] This earth bank was interpreted as a 'marker bank' that had been partially overlain immediately to its east by a stony bank deposit itself surviving to just over half a metre in depth. This stony deposit extended within the excavated area for over 25 m along the line of the bank before a point was reached where it had been removed by later ploughing. There were localised indications that this had in turn been overlain by a turf rampart deposit.

It therefore appears likely that both Offa's Dyke and Wat's Dyke often, but not necessarily always, had a foundation of spread stones, in at least some cases laid up against, or across, a preliminary narrow linear pile of up-cast topsoil. The bulk of the bank of Offa's Dyke then comprised dumps of earth, at some points stabilised by stone and turf spreads. Larger stones might be placed at least at the back of the bank, presumably to further inhibit uncontrolled spreading of dumped material. Turf was sometimes used as a facing material, as was loose stone or piled stone.

Quarry pits, quarry ditches and scarps

It is beyond question that the western ditch, although primarily a strengthening of the obstacle presented by the Dyke, was in part also designed simply as a quarry for material with which to build the bank. However, whether in Gloucestershire, Radnorshire, or Shropshire, another recurring feature of the construction of Offa's Dyke is the presence of quarries located to the east of the Dyke, and very frequently directly upslope from the rear of the bank. The presence of such quarries, and their clear disposition as shown on aerial photographs, has previously been noted. However, there is no indication that, with the exception of the 1995 survey in Gloucestershire, such features have been accurately mapped, let alone investigated.[82]

Fox in particular noted the existence of quarries mostly in passing, and it is evident from his reports that his recording of their presence was more frequent in the accounts of the form and location of the earthwork in Shropshire and Montgomeryshire than at points further south.[83] While Fox no doubt regarded these pits and quarries as part of the overall scheme, he appears only to have noted them where their presence was very obvious.[84] Close observation throughout the course of the Dyke suggests, however, that such features can be traced wherever the ground conditions favour their potential recognition. They cannot, for instance, easily be recognised where the Dyke crosses a floodplain, as on the north side of the Severn north of Welshpool, or, on a much shorter length, where the Dyke crosses the valley of the Hindwell Brook in Herefordshire. They are most obvious, inevitably, in areas where the underlying rock is hard.

It is also the case that in any one stretch of the Dyke where conditions are suitable, inspection of the area immediately to the east of the Dyke results in an appreciation of the various means used to extract material to be used to augment the bank of the Dyke. So, for instance, along the length of Dyke from Yew Tree Farm, Discoed, near the Lugg valley crossing, and southwards from there up to Bwlch near the top of Newcastle Hill, the quarries vary from simple terraces to apparently shallow scoops, to deeper delve-like hollows and

FIGURE 5.18 Former quarry for Offa's Dyke stone on Madgett Hill, Gloucestershire

This quarry-face is located immediately behind the Dyke at exactly the same location as Figure 5.17, and the view here is looking just to the left of that image. The quarry (with a block more recently prized out) is one of a whole series of quarries located immediately behind the Dyke all the way southwards from here to (and a little way beyond) The Devil's Pulpit rock. Their antiquity is indicated by medieval and later references to a 'stone wall' (in practice, the exposed west-facing quarry-faces) along the hilltop here.

very clearly-defined pits. Along the prominent length of Dyke from Plumweir Cliff north to the Devil's Pulpit in Gloucestershire, they are particularly well-preserved and comprise a linear band of linking quarries that often still exhibit exposed west-facing rocky outcrops on their steeper eastern sides. Although most evident along this length, such features are found throughout the course of the Dyke in Gloucestershire.[85]

Quarry pits

Consistencies in the form of the quarries are most evident where the Dyke descends steep slopes. So, for example, on the lengths of the Dyke that are the most obviously performative, such as on the north-facing slopes at the crossings of the Lugg, Clun and Ceiriog rivers, not only are the bank sections carefully disposed (see below), but the location of quarry pits, scoops, terraces and cuts in the bedrock has apparently also been chosen with considerable forethought, and the rock and spoil extraction appears to have been carefully undertaken to avoid slippage.

The ubiquity of such features can be judged with reference to the profiles that Fox recorded primarily in the northern parts of the course of the Dyke. For example, 7 of the 9 profiles drawn between Baker's Hill and Porth-y-Waen, west of Oswestry, showed indications of quarry-scoops or linear hollows to the rear of the Dyke. The one excavation that has produced some evidence at least for shallow scoops at the rear of the bank was the section cut and then observed during road widening at Ffrydd Road, Knighton.[86] The quarries at the rear of the bank in Gloucestershire 'are usually a series of shallow inter-

FIGURE 5.19 The bank and part-infilled rearward former quarries at Madgett Hill

The massive scale and developed form of the bank of Offa's Dyke along this north-facing length (looking east) here is evident when it is realised that to the right the huge hollow is the site of quarries for the bank, and the bank itself crowns the steep scarp to the left, and its back is to well to the right of this image.

5 The structure of the Dyke

connected hollows, running parallel to the bank within a *c.*10–20 m wide zone. The quarries are generally *c.*0.5–1.5 m deep, although empirical measurement of depth is confused as these are often cut into the downslope of the natural hillside.'[87] While they were clearly dug simply to obtain bank material and 'have no specific function as part of the finished monument' they are potentially revealing about how the Dyke was built.[88]

The potential for more complete archaeological examination of such quarry-pits is considerable, and not only for the 'design and build' implications in terms of their form and placement. Estimation of their projected cubic productive capacity from both survey and excavation evidence may tell us more also about the original build height and form of the accompanying bank. More detailed surface survey recording is therefore desirable, but arguably in some locations this should be augmented by excavation to determine the original limits of the quarrying, and thereby to establish both the scale of extraction and (for instance) the nature of quarry-face working.[89]

The eastward ditch

Fox explicitly described the rearward ditch north of Jenkins Allis near Knighton as 'a broad shallow E. ditch (spoil trench)'.[90] Although in some places the linear quarries to the rear of the bank are conjoined, they are not necessarily of uniform width, nor are they fully continuous. However, in several locations, and particularly noticeably both north and south of Knighton, the eastern ditch is both regularly cut and was established as a continuous feature (Figure 5.20).

Such regularity in some locations but not others could be taken to suggest that

FIGURE 5.20 The eastern quarry-ditch on Panpunton Hill, north of Knighton

There is no question that the Dyke faces south-west here, overlooking the Teme valley. There is apparently no ditch at the front of the earthwork, and the rear ditch is in effect simply a quarry. The segments of bank are nonetheless ordered such that there is continual adjustment as the Dyke traverses the hillside. It is clearly the impact of the earthwork in the landscape, rather than its defensive capacity, that was the main concern in this area: as also at Hawthorn Hill, only a short distance south of Knighton, overlooking the Lugg valley.

this was the work of distinctive groups of Dyke-builders, and such a possibility should not be dismissed without further examination of the co-occurrence of other distinctive construction practices. However, other possibilities need to be considered. So, although the eastern ditch undoubtedly provided material for the building of the bank, where it occurs it is unlikely that this was its only purpose. To appreciate the impact of cutting a linear trench at the rear of the bank, it is necessary to observe the bank from a distance as it crosses the landscape (Figure 5.21). In such locations, the effect of a continuous ditch is twofold. Firstly, it makes the bank stand out more prominently as either a skyline or mid-slope feature regardless of the fact that there is sometimes no western side ditch at all, as at Hawthorn Hill. Secondly, the digging of an eastern ditch created a 'notch' to the rear of the bank when seen in profile, and this itself served to accentuate the appearance of mass or height in the dimensions of the bank.

The presence and role of scarps

Fox's concern to ensure that the bank and ditch were adequately represented through drawn profiles has inevitably had the effect that scarps which were deliberately created to sharpen the slope down to the rear of the bank, although frequently encountered, were not always recorded as being present. If the eastwards ditch was often created to enable a particular effect to be achieved, this is also true of the scarps that are a frequent feature of the same kinds of location. So, for example, at Yew Tree Farm, Discoed again, rearward scarping occurs not only at the point where the slope becomes markedly steeper going uphill, but also where the bank becomes slighter and the ditch disappears. The scarping here is not entirely parallel with the rear of the bank, but is instead slightly angled on a south-west to north-east tangent. The effect is to make the bank stand proud of the hillside, when it might otherwise have been in effect lost to view when seen from the west. An exactly similar phenomenon is noticeable at Bronygarth above the Ceiriog, where there was also careful positioning of individual lengths and segments of bank and ditch on the steep north-facing slope overlooking the valley.

The linear form of the ditch and bank from field study

Discussion of the form of linear quarries and an occasional eastern ditch serves to highlight the relative lack of focus upon the lateral form of the Dyke along its constituent lengths in the past. Fox published drawn profiles either to provide a 'representative' record of better-preserved areas, especially in illustration of the shape of the bank and ditch, or to demonstrate particular relationships in the situation of the Dyke in respect to the ground to east or west. He did not deliberately or systematically characterise lengths of ditch and bank in a continuous linear way except through use of Ordnance Survey base maps at the scale of 1:10,560.

FIGURE 5.21 Subtle scale and form adjustments: above Garbett Hall

The rationale for the construction of lengths of Dyke which exhibit continuous modification over relatively short distances, as at this location north of Knighton, is occasionally difficult to comprehend. Yet they are potentially highly informative of build processes and design practice. While the disposition and form of individual lengths of bank, ditch and counterscarp bank here are far from neat (and could therefore be dismissed, as Fox sometimes did, as examples of poor workmanship or control), they appear to reflect a concern to produce particular configurations, perhaps here to enhance the drama of the traverse of a steep slope (see also, Part Two frontispiece), or, as at Carreg-y-big, possibly to enhance the setting of a 'gateway' (see Figure 6.8).
REPRODUCED COURTESY OF A. WIGLEY: COPYRIGHT, SHROPSHIRE COUNCIL.

5   *The structure of the Dyke*   193

Meanwhile, although it has not been published except to illustrate the method, the survey work that Hill and Worthington and their associates undertook in recent years does seem to have attempted a linear characterisation, apparently mostly around the Vale of Montgomery and in the Ruabon area.[91] The published illustrative half-kilometre length in the Montgomery Plain provided a schematic rather than a full record of the lateral nature of the earthwork.[92] Moreover, it seems likely that because the surveyors regarded the bank as very rarely surviving to something approaching its original height due solely to erosion, the significance of longitudinal variability to an understanding the original built form appears to have been missed.[93]

The detailed survey of the Dyke in Gloucestershire in 1995 did in contrast systematically map, for the first time even if only schematically, the character of both bank and ditch along a substantial length of the Dyke.[94] The primary importance of this survey is that it has demonstrated comprehensively that, although adapted to local circumstances, in Gloucestershire the construction modes characteristic of Offa's Dyke north and south of the middle Severn valley are all present.[95] Moreover, the construction modes 'interleave' in exactly the same complex ways in several locations as they do elsewhere (See Figure 5.6).[96]

'Straight alignments' and the detailed form of the Dyke

Although Cyril Fox did provide a continuous account of the lateral form of the Dyke in reference to the 1:10,560 base-mapping, his published extracts obscure the mapped detail because the form and presence of the Dyke is shown in dark ink overlay upon the base mapping. This means that it is his interpretation, rather than the mapped evidence, that has become the published record –

although the Ordnance Survey base mapping itself remains of course readily available for consultation. Comparison between Fox's representation and that mapping can, therefore, be instructive.

This is especially so where Fox noted that particular straight alignments can be contrasted with lengths of the Dyke that trace an ostensibly more meandering course. So, for example, Fox explained the difference between a long straight alignment located immediately south of the Camlad in the Vale of Montgomery with the apparently more irregular alignment to its south, directly east of Montgomery town, as a difference in land-use and vegetation-cover (and therefore visibility) at the time of Dyke construction.[97] He did note that midway along this length there was a noticeable deviation 'in the hollow at Rownal', but suggested that this was explicable because the Dyke in this particular location was invisible from the sighting-points at Hem to the north and Rownal Coppice to the south. However, it may be significant that Fox had used an arguably 'tidied-up' 1912 Second Edition of the 1:10,560 scale Ordnance Survey map as his base: no doubt for the sound reason that this version best reflected the landscape as he was recording it. Reference to the First Edition map of 1888 at this scale nonetheless reveals that the entire middle third of the length from the Camlad to Rownal Coppice comprises 'variance' from the overall alignment, and this must surely bring into question the 'straightness' of this length. The alignment from Hem to Rownal Coppice was no doubt direct. The course of the Dyke between these points comprised, however, a continual process of subtle adjustment to the lie of the land and to enhance the appearance and surveillance capacity of the earthwork.

As noted in Chapter 4, the alignments were used to set the course of the Dyke not only pragmatically, but also strategically. Was the continual adjustment of the line between sighting-points in contrast simply a pragmatic response to local circumstances, however? While it is possible to gain a strong sense that this was not the case, the question remains as to whether a deliberate choice to make adjustments beyond what was necessary to cope with local topography can be demonstrated to have existed. There are three scales at which the question can be addressed: those pertaining to subtle alignment shifts over lengths of 100 m or more; those relating to adjustments in individual, shorter, segments of the bank and (often) also of the ditch; and those relevant to the relationship between individual segments. As it happens, the necessary analysis of how these contrasts can be identified is only so far possible in a location close by Rownal Coppice.

Dudston Fields, Chirbury: structured variation in alignment and build

There is only one location anywhere so far where the intricacies of Dyke lengths have been recorded in a detailed measured archaeological survey plan. This is a 570 m length surveyed in April 1986 by Paul Everson and colleagues from the then Royal Commission on the Historic Monuments of England

FIGURE 5.22 Analytical field survey of Offa's Dyke at Dudston Fields

SURVEY PLAN REPRODUCED COURTESY OF ENGLISH HERITAGE; COPYRIGHT RESERVED.

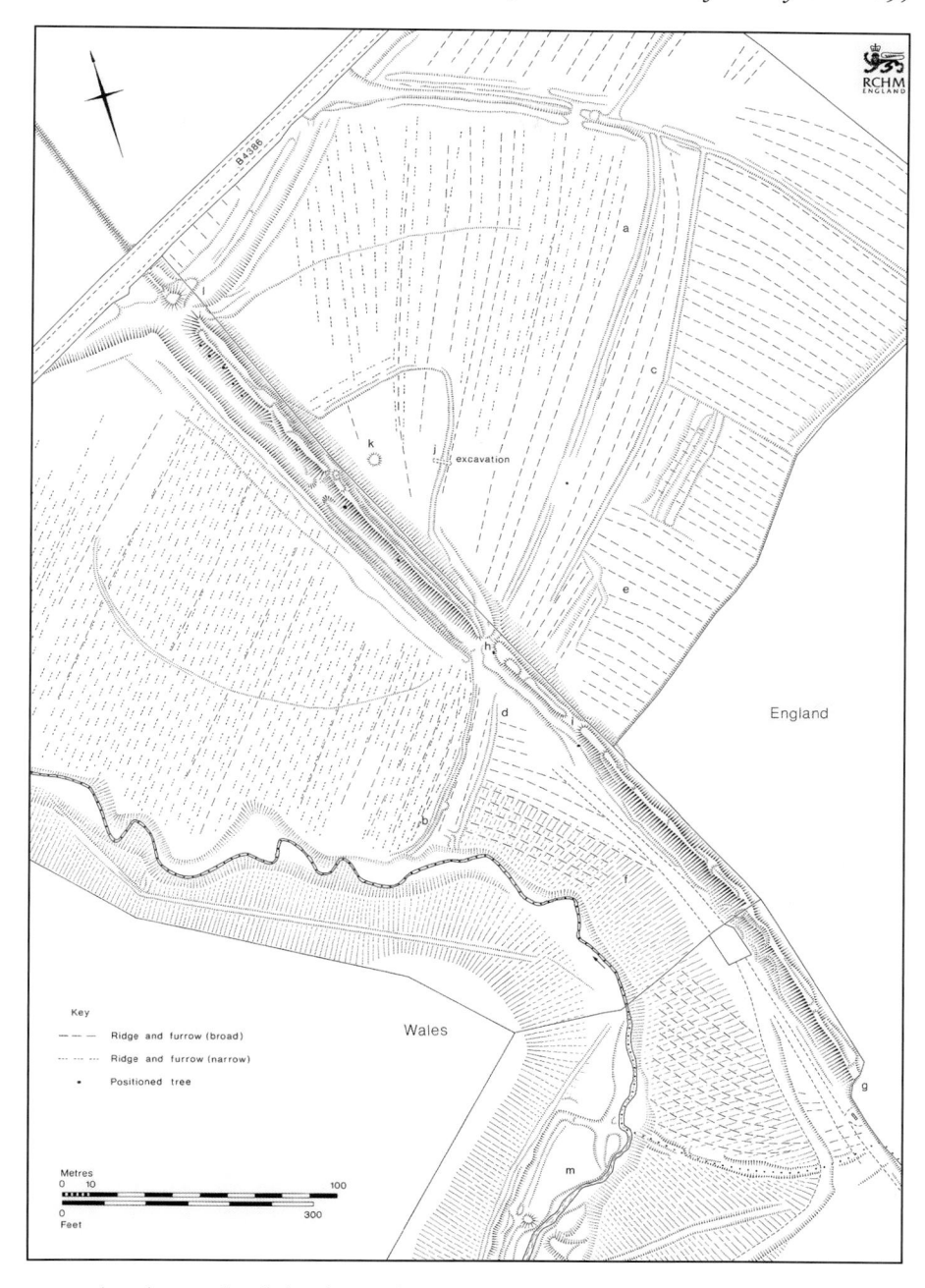

immediately south of the (B4386) Montgomery to Chirbury road at Dudston Fields (Figure 5.22 – RCHME plan). The primary aim of the survey was to examine a postulated relationship between the Dyke and the furlongs of an open field system on either side of it, but the detailed record of the Dyke earthworks that the survey produced enables a level of sophistication of analysis not yet possible anywhere else.[98]

The first thing to note from the plan of the Dudston Fields length, published in 1991, but that was not commented upon in the article that it illustrates, is that although the Dyke follows one major alignment, oriented broadly north-west to south-east, it is possible to discern the presence of three distinct alignments here (Figure 5.23). Such localised adjustment to the orientation of the Dyke may be a feature only of this length, and could reflect simply a need to avoid a west-facing scarp down to the stream that has long marked the boundary between England and Wales locally. However, the degree of adjustment is such that sight-lines perpendicular to each of the 'adjusted' orientations that contradict the overall alignment (followed by the 'central' aligned length) converge on a particularly prominent hilltop location overlooking the plain from the west here.

The second thing to note is that within these alignments it is possible to define individual bank and ditch segments that may also exhibit subtle adjustments of orientation (Figure 5.24). It is noteworthy firstly, that the minimally-definable segments of bank and ditch appear consistently to vary in length between 20 m and 80 m. Moreover, while there are interruptions to the flow of the bank that could be attributed to post-construction breaches and erosion, there are subtleties and consistencies in the positioning of the terminals of the bank segments that could well have arisen from deliberate design in the initial construction. There is, for example, some consistency in the manner of overlap between the tapering bank-ends joining the various earthwork segments here. So the overlap between first

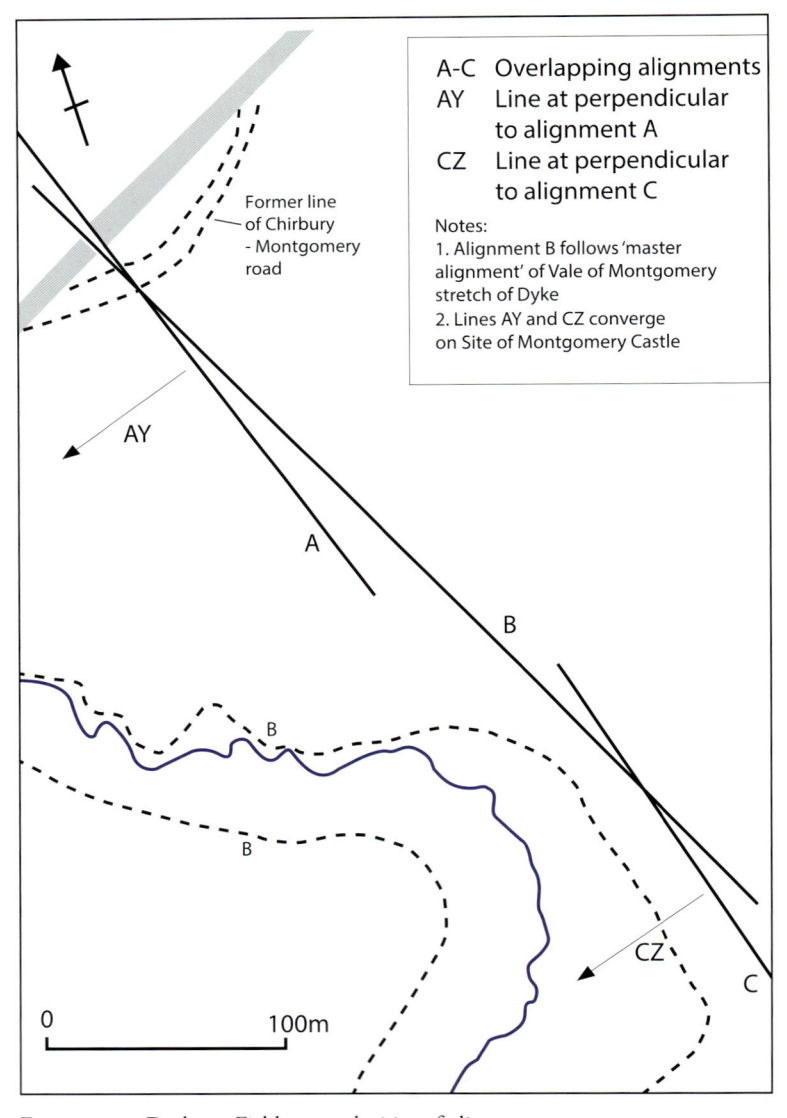

FIGURE 5.23 Dudston Fields: complexities of alignment
Three alignments of bank and ditch lengths are defined in this figure, representing adjustment to immediate topographical constraints while maintaining a key alignment; but also reflecting a concern, apparently, to achieve a particular configuration directly facing Montgomery.

and the second bank segments south of the breach caused by the earlier route of the Chirbury-Montgomery road is located such that the more southerly segment trends eastward at the point of contact and tapering (Point C on (Figure 5.24). A closely similar overlap is present also at the next junction between bank segments southwards, and in neither case can the angled 'groove' across the earthwork be ascribed simply to the presence of former boundaries.

The next southerly segment extends for 80 m, and at its southern end there is an angled breach in the Dyke where it is crossed by a disused track-way that rises up one side of the bank and descends down the other (shown as 'D' in Figure 5.24). This track follows an early headland boundary between two former open fields to the west of the Dyke, and cuts across the furlong ridges of another former open field to the east of the Dyke. Although it is difficult to be certain, the angle of transit may reflect the presence of another tapering bank-end overlap here, wherein the northern end of the next southerly segment again turns to the east while the southern end of the more northerly of these two segments turns to the west. The more southerly of these two segments then extends for 40 metres before a significant dip in the bank corresponds to yet another overlap with a very short (20 m) segment set at a markedly different angle to the south of south-east ('E'). This very short segment is then overlapped by an 80 m long segment on an alignment that is only subtly different from that of the similarly long bank length northwards, already

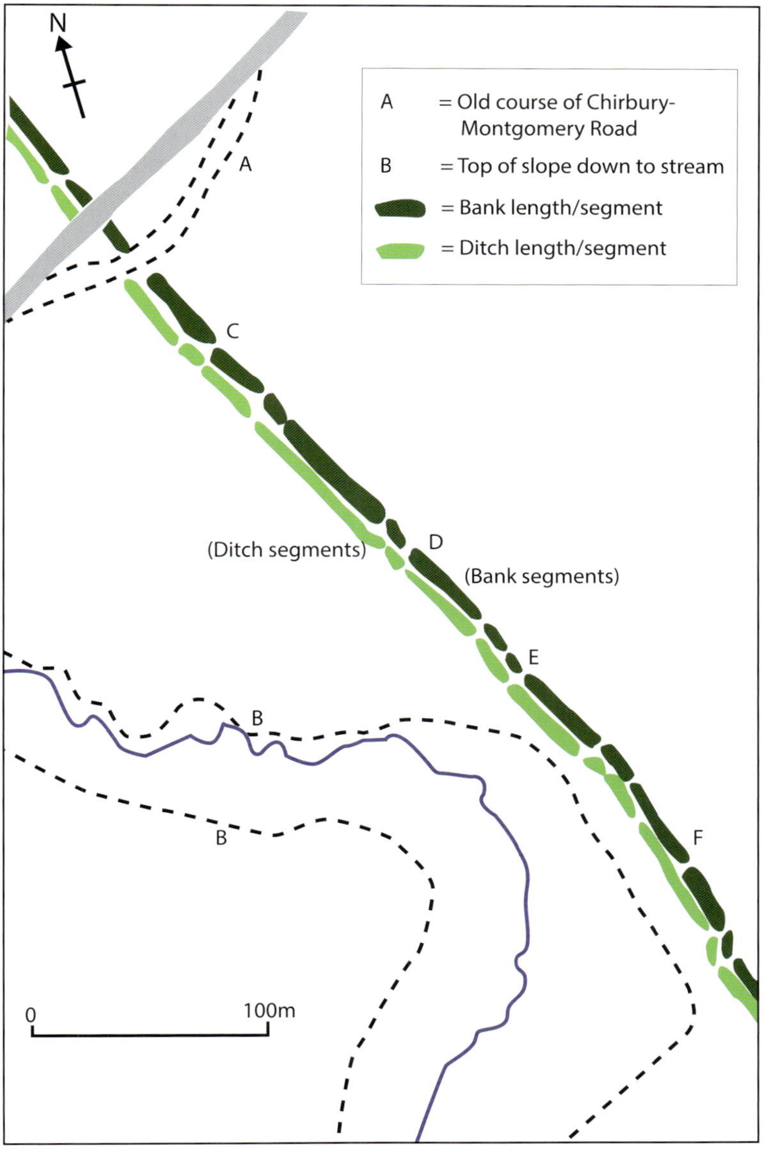

FIGURE 5.24 Dudston Fields bank/ditch lengths and segments
This is an 'abstracted' plan of bank forms, since on the ground the earthwork is uninterrupted. Rather, the figure highlights the upper parts of each segment and the lower parts of each ditch, to accentuate the subtle and adjusted differences in orientation and inter-relation.

mentioned. At the southern end of the longer segment, there is a further bank length of 80 m ('F') on an alignment that mirrors that of the very short segment northwards. The Dyke then again reverts to an orientation closely comparable with that of the two longest segments northwards, but it survives in substantially worse condition southwards and its orientation line is 20 m to the west.

The complexity captured in this way reveals two aspects of Dyke build at Dudston Fields. Firstly, it is surely not accidental that the segment lengths are for the most part multiples of 20 metres. At least three of the segments possess subtle indications that they comprise 'sub-segments' of 2m or 4m length. This suggests that for this stretch of Dyke at least, there may have been a 14-foot 'standard length' for the construction of the bank. Secondly, although the changes in orientation and positioning of the earthwork reflect an adjustment to a particular topographical feature, they also involve the positioning of the bank lengths and individual segments in such a way as to maximise the visual impact of the Dyke as it traverses that part of the plain directly opposite a prominent hilltop vantage-point. Moreover, the same topographical feature provides the point of perpendicular focus for the two alignment lengths that contradict the overall alignment trend here. It surely cannot be co-incidental that the point of focus for both kinds of build adjustment at Dudston Fields was subsequently the location chosen on which to build Montgomery Castle.

FIGURE 5.25 At Dudston Fields: the adjusted bank segments
This view directly along the line of the bank southwards indicates clearly the pattern of adjustment of ditch segments evident in plan.

Co-ordinated build design in a prominent setting: Yew Tree Farm, Discoed

In many cases the junction between two adjacent lengths or segments such as recorded at Dudston Fields is marked simply by a dip in the crest of the bank and a rise to the following crest. This is more obvious where the orientation of one length of the bank can be seen to be distinctive when compared with the lengths to either side. However, in several other particularly prominent locations, not only are discrete lengths and their constituent segments readily identifiable, but it would appear that the junctions between them have been carefully positioned, and this is even more readily apparent than at Dudston Fields. In these cases also, the junction point where a subtle or marked change in alignment is evident is often also where the end of one length or segment tapers in complementary relation to that of the next, so that the two tapering bank-ends overlap and 'dovetail' with one another. This again can superficially give the impression that there is an oblique cut or former 'path' across the monument, and it appears likely that in the past it has been assumed that such segment junctions owe their origin to such paths, or to other forms of erosion or modification.[99] This is presumably the reason why this frequently traceable characteristic of the bank segments has not previously been noted. What is also noticeable is that the segments concerned often have a distinctly, rather than subtly, different alignment. It is this, as well as the tapering configuration of the bank-ends, that suggests that this is a feature of design in the build of the bank as originally constructed, rather than a simple consequence of a modular form of construction.

The length of Offa's Dyke at Yew Tree Farm, Discoed, as was described in Chapter 4, extends from the south side of the Lugg valley southwards through to the crest of the slope at Bwlch west of Presteigne, rising 150 m in height from the floodplain in the course of half a mile (0.8 km). This stretch of Dyke Fox regarded as exhibiting a 'normal' scale of construction, reducing to 'boundary bank' form as it ascended the hill-slope.[100] He provided a detailed description of the earthwork here, for example noting that southwards from the Lugg valley floodplain, there are three different alignments, one of which crosses the southern part of the floodplain, the next of which crosses the Cascob to Discoed lane onto higher ground, and the other of which, more certainly conforming to his direct alignment type, climbs higher up the gradually steepening north-facing slope. Fox noted that, where the hill-slope steepens yet more markedly, the earthwork then changes its character to the 'boundary bank' form. It then curves up onto a shoulder of land that leads to the tellingly named Bwlch (Welsh: 'pass').[101] Fox considered that the earthwork changed again to an intermediate scale again here, where it approached the point where a ridge-way road crosses the line of the Dyke.[102]

What Fox took to be his first (possible) straight alignment across the floor of the Lugg valley and up onto higher ground to the south is here marked A1 (Figure 5.26). Length A2 is then the stretch of Dyke that corresponds to the alignment that crosses the Cascob-Discoed road which runs along the south side of the Lugg valley. Immediately south from the field gate here there is a clear trace neither of the bank nor the ditch for the first 40 metres, although there is a raised level area to the east of where the ditch has been infilled. Past another recent field gate to the east and its causewayed track to the west, the Dyke immediately takes on a massive form with the bank standing more than 4 metres above a westerly ditch that from the outset has a substantial counterscarp bank on its outer lip.[103] This length (A2) terminates uphill where the Dyke changes alignment subtly southwards as it meets the first small 'brow' of land, and on the ground it achieves this change through a very short linking segment of bank, while the successive lengths of ditch apparently maintain the same profile and depth around the turn. No trace of overlapping terminals can be deduced here, however.

From this turn the principal straight alignment recognised by Fox extends southwards (and upwards) across three fields, and he saw the southern end of this alignment as being coterminous with the end of the west ditch here. However, within the stretch conforming to his perceived single straight alignment it is possible to define instead five straight lengths, comprising three longer ones (A3, A5, A7) following a more strictly north–south line corresponding most closely to Fox's single alignment, separated by two slightly smaller ones on a subtly different orientation (A4, A6). These latter lengths are oriented such that they face very slightly north of west compared with their adjoining lengths. Moreover, the junctions between the upper lengths (A5–A6, and A6–A7) especially, feature very obvious tapering and overlapping bank ends.

The 'final' straight length of bank (A7), takes in a much sharper rise in the profile of the hill. The ditch does indeed run out at the point indicated on the annotated plan here by the end of the dotted line representing the ditch. However, although there is as Fox noted a dramatic change in the scale of the bank also at this point, the alignment of the 'boundary bank' (our *slighter* mode) continuation remains fixed for another 30 m up the hill. A further straight length then adjusts the line westwards and in doing so reflects the alignment of the course of the small stream running down the slope and parallel with the Dyke to its west. After another 40 m, the bank with at this point almost no discernible western ditch traces a much more sinuous course, but it is by no means as casually built as Fox implied. Rather, there is a carefully levelled 'berm' in front of the bank, while the quarries at its rear feature not only ditch-like lengths, but also pits, scoops, and terracing.

It is also in this stretch of the Dyke that there are clues in eroded areas of bank surface as to the details of building methods. The hints of an elaborate

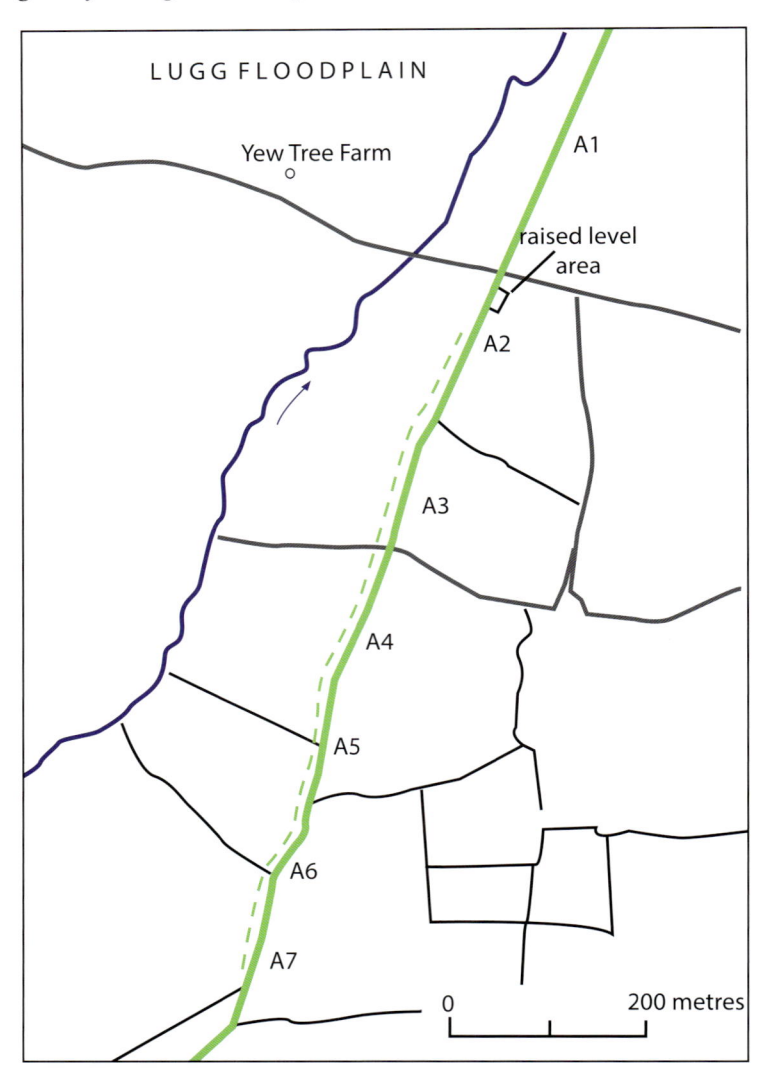

FIGURE 5.26 The stance of adjacent Dyke lengths at Discoed (plan)

build of the bank in compartments that was noted above were found in length A7. Moreover, along the front of the same and adjacent bank lengths (A6, A7) it is possible to observe the piling up of quarried flat stones from the ditch at the front of the bank that continue up the 'layered' (natural) form of the exposed west-facing inner side of the ditch in such a way as to give the impression of a wall fronting the earthen bank. The likely reality of course is that the bank was indeed mostly of simple dump construction: when freshly built, however, that is not necessarily how it would have appeared. Here also, the lengths of bank whose ends were dove-tailed such that they faced subtly towards the north-west would have provided the effect of approaching an overlapping series of walls rising beyond the earthen counterscarp bank.

Spoad and Bronygarth: further complex, 'performative' build locations

At Spoad near Newcastle-upon-Clun and at Bronygarth near Chirk there are short stretches of Offa's Dyke that occupy north-facing slopes extending down to significant valley-crossings (the Clun and the Ceiriog, respectively), just as at Discoed above the Lugg. These stretches comprise individual lengths of bank and ditch that were in several cases distinctively and deliberately oriented to face towards an approach along a valley from the west. For this reason, and the selection of the position for climbing the slope that was mentioned in Chapter 4, and the contrast in elevation between valley-bottom and the neighbouring heights (200 m or more in each case) the Dyke lengths in these locations can be described as 'performative'.

At Spoad, the orientation of the earthwork changes on the southern side of the Clun valley floodplain, and ostensibly it follows a single straight alignment

FIGURE 5.27 The continuously-adjusted bank lengths on the hill above Lower Spoad

PHOTOGRAPH: ADAM STANFORD/ AERIAL-CAM, COPYRIGHT RESERVED.

FIGURE 5.28 Detail of the adjustment of bank lengths above Lower Spoad

PHOTOGRAPH: ADAM STANFORD/ AERIAL-CAM, COPYRIGHT RESERVED.

up a spur of Spoad Hill for 800 metres. However, when this length is examined closely it can be seen to comprise, rather, a series of shorter lengths, three of which maintain the principal alignment, and two of which are short segments that adjust the stance to create lengths set at an angle to that alignment, and that are oriented such that they overlook the valley floor from a south-easterly direction. The next length up from this is also 'angled' and extends for at least 80 m, running just below Scotland Cottage. Another straight length extends for around 160 m, while a yet further angled one curves at its southern end to rise onto the saddle of the Spoad Hill east–west ridge at Springhill Farm.

Overall, this north-facing Spoad length makes a dramatic traverse of the slope, rising 200 m in height from valley floor to ridge-top across three-quarters of a mile, placed on the western flank of a spur with a stream just to the west (Figure 5.27). One result of this arrangement of lengths is that the prospect afforded from them is directed deliberately and advantageously down onto the valley-floor approach to the Dyke from the west, at different heights and therefore with contrasting fields of view. This is also mirrored on the south-facing slopes lying northwards across the river, where the stance of lengths of the Dyke is adjusted to provide equally dramatic oversight of the Clun flood-plain below (Figure 9.12). Conversely, looking up from the valley-floor the lengths are perceived as more substantial than they really are, and are viewed sequentially, with the higher lengths evident further away, and the dominance of the lower ones becoming both more apparent and less avoidable, the nearer the viewer gets to the Dyke itself in the valley-bottom (as seen in detail in Figure 5.28). At no point is it obvious to the viewer from the west that the local course and form of the Dyke has been manipulated in this way: it simply seems to be massive, and was no doubt more so when freshly dug.

The span across the north-facing slope above the Ceiriog at Bronygarth is slightly tangential to the river-valley rather than perpendicular as at Spoad, and the steep descent has a height differential of 250 m. There are again straight alignments, with that from the river to a narrow level terrace above it at Pen-y-bryn being followed by an angled length overlooking the broadening of that level area westwards, and another straight length being followed by a strongly angled section that looks right down onto the river to the west (and again possessing an enhanced prominence when viewed from the valley floor). The Dyke then proceeds in a series of adjusted lengths southwards, to eventually achieve the brow of the hill: although none of the lengths are angled in the same way as the principal two at the lower elevation are. The massive scale of the earthwork was still important at this height, although it was less visible from the river valley which is here narrower than where the Dyke crosses the Clun away to the south.

'Adjusted-segmented construction' along the Dyke

While the effect of creating a string of segments that could either be built as single links or grouped together in approximate multiples is to produce a chain, the term 'adjusted-segmented construction' is used here to capture the deliberate, planned, nature of this significant build practice deployed in the creation of Offa's Dyke. In addition to its occurrence at Dudston Fields, Discoed, Spoad and Bronygarth, the practice is evident throughout the four-mile (7 km) course of the Dyke from a point to the south of Spoad Hill to Garbett Hill, on Llanfair Hill north of the river Teme crossing.[104] Within this latter stretch the Dyke maintains an elevation of over 1300' for nearly two miles. Fox noted that there was a very limited prospect westwards here from along the western flank of the hill.[105] He observed that a course on the 'western scarp' of Llanfair Hill (a quarter of a mile west above the Crochen Brook) would have afforded a wider view, but that the scarp edge is very dissected along that route, and the line of the Dyke would have had to be very sinuous to effect a traverse successfully there.

It is perhaps therefore to compensate for the degree to which there is level, or in some cases higher, land to the west that the Dyke is as prominent as it is along this stretch. So, for instance, the bank may have reached its most massive proportions here (although the remoteness of the location has also ensured optimal preservation) and it possessed here also a substantial counterscarp bank. This formed a small bank beyond the outer lip of the ditch that added to the effectiveness of the Dyke as a barrier to movement.

The series of lengths southwards from the south-west flank of Llanfair Hill itself illustrates well all the features of the 'adjusted-segmented' build identified above. This is seen clearly at the crossing of a small stream on the saddle of the ridge just to the south of the south-west flank of higher ground already mentioned. Here, the deployment of the 'adjusted-segmented construction', and its local configuration, resulted in a series of segments positioned parallel with one another, but continually off-set, segment by segment (Figure 5.30). It is interesting that it is just at this point that the Dyke faces rising ground immediately to the west of the chosen line of the earthwork. The segments serially 'adjust' the position of the Dyke here, to bring the earthwork close to the head of the stream where the crossing is made, while exaggerating its bulk in this topographically disadvantageous position.

Half a mile (1 km) south of this massive section along Llanfair Hill, the Dyke becomes sited very directly onto Cwmsanahan Hill, an alignment it maintains for over two miles (3 km). At a series of locations where there is a wider prospect to the south-west, and particularly towards the Teme valley 200 m lower in altitude, the adjusted-segmented form was deployed, presumably to 'bulk out' the Dyke's appearance when seen from the west. What was achieved here and elsewhere was a thoroughly designed manipulation of the Dyke featuring the adjusted-segmented practice. Perhaps the reason for this (quite possibly functionally needless) elaboration may have served, like the pattern-welding of the most prestigious among Anglo-Saxon swords, to express a particular

FIGURE 5.29
Longitudinal bank and counterscarp bank profiles at Baker's Hill
The raking evening sunlight here enables the segmentation of both bank profiles to be clearly distinguished from one another in an area where there is no indication of the former crossing of the Dyke by now-lost field boundaries. The fact that the segment terminals correspond so closely indicates the way in which the Dyke segments were built as distinct entities.
REPRODUCED COURTESY OF A. WIGLEY: COPYRIGHT, SHROPSHIRE COUNCIL.

5   *The structure of the Dyke*   205

aesthetic: in this case, for the joy of a continuous *facetted* form in the performance of a built work. Such a practice ensured that, when such a length was viewed from a distance, the earthwork would have stood out in the landscape disproportionately to its actual size.

Nor are other river-valley traverses featuring these complex build forms and sequences adjacent to deeply incised rivers restricted to such north-facing hillsides. For example, Fox included in the relevant survey report of 1927 a photograph looking down the slope southwards from Fron Farm towards the crossing of the river Gwenfro. This image clearly shows three short segments descending the south-facing slope. It is also therefore noteworthy that Fox must have been aware that these segments existed and could be recognised in today's landscape (Figure 5.31). However, since he makes no mention of these segments either in the caption to the photograph or in the accompanying text, he clearly did not appreciate their significance to an understanding both of the unity and the sophistication of the build of the Dyke here, or indeed elsewhere.

FIGURE 5.30 Clearly co-adjusted bank lengths at Llanfair Hill, looking north

The continuous adjustment of bank/ditch lengths is widely evident along Offa's Dyke (see also, for example, this volume, Figures 1.6, 1.15, 2.4, 4.9, 5.1, 5.20, 5.21, 5.22, 5.25, 5.28 and 5.29, above)

FIGURE 5.31 Fox's photograph of distinct bank segments at Fron Farm

These clearly-defined features were not noted, even in passing, during the 1927 survey.

REPRODUCED COURTESY OF THE CAMBRIAN ARCHAEOLOGICAL ASSOCIATION.

FIGURE 5.32 Adjusted-segmented' lengths on the western flank of Rushock Hill

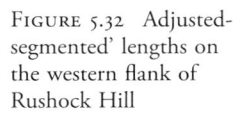

The adjusted-segmented build practice is not to be found everywhere, but it nonetheless can be observed throughout the course of the Dyke. Another example is at Rushock Hill, where it is observable in a stretch of the Dyke rising eastwards from the col linking Rushock to Herrock Hill (Figure 5.32). The practice featured almost wherever complex build arrangements were put in place at the especially prominent vantage points that the Dyke encompassed.

At the Devil's Pulpit in Gloucestershire, as at Cwmsanahan Hill north of the Teme at Knighton and at Llanymynech Hill north of the Vyrnwy, for instance, the Dyke traces a course along the outer lip of a steep west-facing scarp in such a manner that it appears as an imposing sky-line feature when seen from the west. Like these other cases the Gloucestershire length north and south of the Devil's Pulpit also features the distinctive angled turns that are discussed briefly in Chapter 6. However, the length of Dyke here additionally features the adjusted-segmented form of build (Figure 5.33). The reason for the elaboration of build in this length appears likely to concern the proximity of Tintern in the Wye valley immediately below the site and to the west. No more eloquent evidence could be found to corroborate the idea that the Gloucestershire course of the earthwork was constructed as an integral part of Offa's Dyke than the co-occurrence of these very distinctive design and build features here.[106]

FIGURE 5.33 'Adjusted-segmented' bank lengths at the Devil's Pulpit

Further build complexities: a Llanfair Hill example
Another feature along the prominent Llanfair Hill stretch of the Dyke southwards towards Selley deserves special mention. This is not an example of adjusted-segmented construction, but it demonstrates in an equivalent way the extent to which deliberate and careful design appears to have been brought to bear on the construction finish of the monument.

This feature is located half a mile south of the bank segments discussed above, at a point not far north of the diagonal traverse down to the Selley valley past Garbett Hall. Here a length of bank crosses what may be a natural declivity in the ground. This is a perfectly normal thing for it to do, but what is noticeable is that as it does so, the top of the bank maintains a continuous line while its base levels upwards from the declivity. This involved dumping many more tons of soil than was necessary, had the top of the bank been allowed to 'follow' the base in and out of the declivity (Figure 5.34).

Clearly, the resulting construction indicates that the Dyke builders wished to maintain the top of the bank at a high level. Why they should want to build the bank up in this way here is unclear, but the effect is remarkable. When viewed from a short distance rearward of the Dyke to the east, it is evident that the north–south profile *along* the bank top closely mirrors the horizon profile of the hilltop a mile or so beyond the Dyke to the west. It would appear that this is a non-functional but purposeful work, designed to create a particular – and particularly striking – effect. This is one of the best preserved lengths of the bank at a point where its setting can be fully appreciated. It seems likely that this is not an isolated occurrence, however, but simply one that it has been possible to record here because of the open landscape and lack of vegetation cover, minimal erosion of the bank, and absence of other encumbrances in the present day.[107] Arguably, this demonstrates that Offa's Dyke was deemed to be a special construction, not only by those who commanded or commissioned it to be created, but also by those responsible for the most intricate details of its execution.

The creation of a Dyke façade by the integration of build practices

One way in which the straight alignments worked was as a means of adjustment of a continuous work as it traversed particular areas definable in both topographical and no doubt also in cultural and political terms. This included visual effects when viewed either along its course or (mostly) from the west, south-west or north-west. The whole of the course of the Dyke could be analysed in terms of the 'stringing together' of aligned stretches sequentially, and the composition of individual stretches can also be 'dissected' to reveal their component elements in shorter lengths, and yet smaller segments, of bank and of ditch. As such, the whole course of the Dyke can be seen as a complex 'kit' of straight-length builds that produced a kind of chain-link draping of the Dyke across the landscape that it crossed. While this may have been a practical build-related occurrence, it is not so pervasively evident in other dykes of the middle centuries of the first millennium AD, even where they cross dissected terrain. Moreover, such a build pattern produced a facetted but also continuous appearance to the Dyke when seen from across the landscape, and the deliberate effects of this merit some discussion.

FIGURE 5.34 Precision design: a 'compensating' build at Llanfair Hill

The prospect here is westwards from the rear of the Dyke. Both to create a continuous 'wall', and to maintain a precise profile, the bulk of the bank of the Dyke has been carefully augmented at this point. Either there was a pre-existing highly localised dip in the ground on the chosen alignment, or an area on the line of the Dyke was quarried before the exact course had been fixed. It may also be noteworthy how closely the line of longitudinal profile of the bank mirrors the hillslope just beyond the Dyke to the west.

FIGURE 5.35 Dyke length adjustments around the crest of Llanfair Hill (1)

At a distance from the earthwork, the continuous adjustment of earthwork lengths, and their organisation in segments of subtly varying orientation becomes very evident (see also Figure 5.36, under contrasting conditions, and the view over Herrock Hill and Rushock Hill, viewed from the air in Figure 6.9, and from the ground in Figure 5.32, above).

REPRODUCED COURTESY OF A. WIGLEY: COPYRIGHT, SHROPSHIRE COUNCIL.

To recapitulate, the placement of the tapering and overlapping segments rendered them adaptable to any orientation effect that the builders sought to achieve, by making those segments more like the links in a chain rather than the strands of a rope. However, what is also clear is that the subtleties of adjusted alignment that were achieved by these means enabled the monument to be presented visually in striking ways, particularly when viewed from the west. The principal aim seems to have been to create a kind of 'façade' that exaggerated the engineered form of the Dyke to maximum dominant visual effect when seen from particular positions to the west. The features concerned – and in particular the overlapping terminals and subtly altered bank segment alignments of 'adjusted-segmented construction' – have been observed in areas as widely separated as the Ceiriog valley in Flintshire and the Wye cliffs near St Briavels in Gloucestershire over 80 miles to the south.

As the above should have made clear, the 'worked' nature of the planning and placement of the individual segments, building up to and down from alignments of stretches of the Dyke, served to create a monument that continually deliberately 'presented' its form in the landscape, with a particular eye to how it was to be experienced both from the west and along its course. It is not surprising, therefore, to find that the correlation of form with visual effect extended to the surface treatment of the face of the bank, and beyond this to a feature that we have not considered at all so far, the counterscarp bank.

The counterscarp bank

Slight banks located along the outer lip of the Dyke at Cadwgan Hall, Esclusham, at Chirk Park, and on the northern flank of Selattyn Hill were held by Fox not to be 'part of the Dyke as originally designed', presumably because in at least two of these cases they were crowned by a hedge-bank.[108] However, not only are Fox's arguments for not regarding at least the latter two of these as 'genuine' counterscarp banks unconvincing given their location on the very lip of the ditch, but at least one other of the profiles in the same series, at Pentre-Shannel Farm, above the river Morda north of Trefonen, indicates again the presence of precisely the same feature.[109] On Edenhope Hill, Fox recorded 'a small but definite bank on the counterscarp', while on the north-facing scarp of Knuck Bank 'a rounded bank, some 15–18 ft. broad and 2 ft. high, appears on the counterscarp of the Dyke; it is present.... for some 270 yards'.[110]

In the next section southwards from Middle Knuck, at Hergan, Fox noted the continuous nature of the counterscarp bank from Hergan 'corner' for a mile almost to the valley north of Bridge Farm and its considerable proportions.[111] He also recorded the counterscarp bank on the northern flank of Llanfair Hill, but curiously failed to note its (admittedly more patchy) survival further south. He then entirely omitted reference to the counterscarp bank surviving patchily also at Jenkins Allis south of Knighton, despite the fact that he drew them in plan to illustrate a possible entrance gap there.[112] Not far south from here a length of the counterscarp bank survives far more completely, if somewhat spread by vehicular movements, at Yew Tree Farm, Discoed. More curiously still, Fox made no mention of the very substantial counterscarp bank at the very southern limit of the Gloucestershire part of the Dyke, as it approaches Sedbury Cliffs from the west at The Coombe.[113]

Very occasionally, it seems, there have been observations on the nature of the counter-scarp bank from excavations. One example is the section at Orseddwen, about which no details have been published.[114] Another is at Lippets Grove, Tidenham in Gloucestershire, where the counterscarp bank, like the bank itself, appears to have been built using stone quarried from the quarry-ditches to the rear of the bank, which was placed directly upon the underlying clay deposit.[115] Counterscarp banks are extremely vulnerable to loss from agricultural operations, and the correlation of survival and loss respectively in pasture and arable in stretches such as that north of Hergan in the Clun forest uplands is a good indicator that the bank was a more common build element than might otherwise have been appreciated.

The purpose of the counterscarp bank has been a related area of deliberation for those who have made a close study of the built form of the Dyke. Fox's view was that the counterscarp bank was an 'enhanced' form of the Dyke only pertinent to the 'mountain zone' where the Dyke was designed to oppose

FIGURE 5.36 Dyke length adjustments around the crest of Llanfair Hill (2)

At a different angle and under different conditions, the adjustments of bank and ditch here are even more pronounced than in Figure 5.35.

REPRODUCED COURTESY OF AND COPYRIGHT OF CLWYD-POWYS ARCHAEOLOGICAL TRUST.

FIGURE 5.37 The counterscarp bank at Llanfair Hill, looking north

transgression from the west along the prominent ridgeway routes.[116] It did not seem to occur to him that the extended presence of the counterscarp bank in areas such as Hergan could be a result simply of the unusually good preservation of earthworks here. At Carreg-y-big, Selattyn, it was suggested that the postulated counterscarp bank was built to give an impression of greater depth to the ditch where the bedrock was particularly hard and the bank correspondingly slight, but this does not explain why the counterscarp bank is so prominent where the bank is massive, as at Llanfair Hill.[117]

Two conclusions need now to be drawn from this reconsideration of the presence and scale of the counterscarp bank. Firstly, it is a widespread, rather than a rare, feature of Offa's Dyke. Secondly, it often a relatively large, and by no means ephemeral, feature wherever it survives in anything approaching what might be considered its original form. At both Llanfair Hill and at Hergan, for example (Figures 5.37 and 5.4, respectively), it is sufficiently large as to give the impression of a doubling of defensive depth. Given that the counterscarp bank survives in such a vestigial condition in so many places, it is difficult to be sure whether it was a general feature of the build of the Dyke, or if it was only built where some particular effect was intended. It certainly features in several of the most highly 'worked' locations that we have described in this chapter. While, therefore, it cannot be said with certainty that the same effect was sought in each of the different locations where it is still present, the fact that it did produce the effect of enhancing the 'façade' is evident even today.

Berms and glacis

Although the existence of berms has been identified at various points, there is little definite evidence that they were a deliberate feature of Dyke construction. In contrast, although it has been suggested that turves were used in some locations to create a forward retaining structure, there is a strong indication that the use of both turves and stone clitter was often deliberately focused at the front of the bank to create a continuous slope from the base of the ditch to the top of at least the west-facing side of the bank. This is difficult to prove, given the effects of erosion on the front of the bank: and the limited amount of excavation of upstanding lengths of the bank of the Dyke has meant that this has rarely been observed closely.

Bank facings and 'walls'

In contrast, visual inspection of eroded sections of the bank at various locations, for example at Edenhope Hill, at Llanfair Hill, at Discoed, and north of the Devil's Pulpit, leads us to suggest that there were deliberate 'facings' of the bank comprising if not exactly a dry-stone wall at least the deliberate laying down of large stones horizontally to appear to be wall-like (see Figures 5.16 and 5.17, above). The fact that these have remained in place for so long indicates that as-built these were not necessarily unstable facings. Of particular interest is the 'stepped' nature of some of these pilings. Instead of creating a wall vertically from the inner side of the ditch, with the spoil piled directly behind it, the Dyke builders in these situations created a series of low horizontally-laid linear stone piles, each successively higher one set back slightly from the one below.

FIGURE 5.38 The Offa's Dyke 'wall': crossing the southern flank of Graig Hill

This finds a direct parallel in the way in which rock-faces forming the inner side of the ditch, but rising significantly higher than the corresponding outer ditch face, were 'stepped' at a number of locations to exaggerate the steepness of the front of the ditch/bank. This observation gives rise to two possibilities. The first is that the aim was not only to steepen the face confronting anyone approaching the work from beyond the ditch, but that it was also to reproduce the appearance of a built wall in living rock. The second is that the slighter 'ledges' of this kind cut into shallower slopes, as for instance at Buttington Tump, were created specifically in order to support horizontal pilings of rock.

The practice of creating the impression of a walled 'front' to the bank of Offa's Dyke can therefore be traced at Yew Tree Farm, Discoed, at Llanfair Hill, at Porth-y-Waen, at Bronwylfa Road, Esclusham, at Cwmsanahan, and possibly also at Buttington Tump. This last is particularly significant given that the Gloucestershire survey already discussed also recorded 'deliberately laid stonework, intermittently exposed on the outer face of the bank' at no fewer than eight locations between Wergan's Wood in the south and English Bicknor in the north, all at places where the *substantial* mode of construction was present.[118] The archaeologists concerned interpreted these traces as possibly 'the remains of a dry stone revetment acting as a near vertical, and highly visible, facing on the outer side of the monument'.[119] While this no doubt reflects the remarkably good state of preservation of much of the surviving Gloucestershire course, it does lead to the suspicion that systematic observation and recording elsewhere may result in a fuller appreciation of the incidence and purpose of this practice.

It could reasonably be argued that all these effects were aesthetically pleasing, perhaps more than being 'practical'. It has been suggested by military historians for example that wherever a counter-scarp bank was built, the purpose was to expose on-comers to fire from the rampart behind the ditch as they approached the lip. While no-one has yet seriously proposed that Offa's Dyke was designed to be a wall fortified and patrolled in the same way as, for instance, Hadrian's Wall, this observation, and the highly-worked and 'performative' nature of many of the more prominent locations, does echo the elaborations present on that northern British construction. This in turn raises a question about the degree of emulation of the famous predecessor structure involved in the building of Offa's Dyke, and another query concerning the purpose of both.[120]

CHAPTER SIX

Building and operating the Dyke

> The King himself, or a small group of thegns closely associated and belonging to the Mercian school of field engineering, planned the work. The course having been laid down and the dimensions and character in general terms defined, the local economic and social organization of this small Germanic state was utilized. Each land-owning thegn on or near the border was made responsible for a certain length of the Dyke, proportionate to the extent of his estate or resources.
>
> Cyril Fox, *Offa's Dyke*, 1955[1]

With characteristic economy, Fox set out in this passage his vision of how construction of Offa's Dyke was organised. He saw King Offa himself as the 'presiding genius' who conceived the project, but he also clearly appreciated that such a complex task could not be undertaken without the involvement of a core group of his close political associates. These were no doubt drawn from among the elite of 'duces' and other leaders whose names recur in the witnessing of his charters.[2] Fox's mention of a 'school' of engineering is especially significant here, given the intricacies of design and build of the Dyke are such as to implicate the involvement of a specialised cadre of officers within what in the twenty-first century might be denoted the 'project team.' Whether the labour for the work was drawn exclusively from estates held 'on or near the border' is less certain. The fact that in one of Offa's Kentish charters duties of service were explicitly restricted to actions within Kent indicates that this situation was deemed exceptional. It strongly suggests that elsewhere within the Mercian domains the location of service was at the king's discretion. The inclusion in the workforce of people drawn from the Mercian heartlands in the Trent and Tame valleys and from other key territories seems likely, given their strategic (if not exactly immediate) proximity, and the relative rapidity with which transit between at least from the middle Severn region and the heartlands could be achieved.

The final proposition by Fox, above, that the extent of responsibility of the land-owning local leaders for particular sections of the Dyke would have been proportionate to the size of their estate or the scale of their available resources, was probably written with the provisions of the late ninth-century West Saxon 'Burghal Hidage' document in mind. This referred to the secondment of a certain number of people for each hide of land for the building of specified lengths of the perimeter of fortified places in Wessex.[3] Eighth-century Mercia was very likely to have been hidated, and therefore organised according to standardised land-holding units. At the same time, the clauses of many of the charters in that century referred to the duty of fortress-building. It is reasonable to suppose therefore that similar arrangements relating the scale of land-holding to duties of 'public service' may have been put in place for building Offa's Dyke. However, it was the scale of the work required that distinguished the enterprise of long-distance building of dykes from the localised construction of defended forts. Moreover, the uniformity of design and build of Offa's Dyke already noted suggests a greater degree of control over the finished form of the earthwork than might have resulted from responsibility resting only with the leaders assigned to the completion of different sections.[4]

Historians and archaeologists have long posed questions about the way in which the Dyke was built, and examples of some of these include, 'what was the exact method of ground preparation for dyke-building?', 'have we really understood the potential significance of gateways through the Dyke to its purpose and operation?' and, 'are there any other features of the Dyke itself that can provide clues as to its use, that have not before been discussed in this light?' In this chapter these and other questions are addressed, but the discussion opens with a focus upon the effect that the dyke building operation may have had at a very local scale, and upon what evidence exists for the first steps in the physical process of construction.

The impact of Dyke creation and the work of building

If there is one certainty about the construction of Offa's Dyke, it is that it was dug entirely by hand. This must have involved thousands of pairs of hands, working under what were no doubt often extremely difficult conditions. Any first hand experience of the Dyke in the border landscapes that it traverses results in an immediate appreciation of the obstacles to be overcome, and the effort involved, in digging and piling soil and rock to create the massive linear work.[5] Study of the intricacies of construction of the earthwork serves to deepen such appreciation, but also results in questions about how the work was organised on the ground, and exactly who was responsible for co-ordinating the work and carrying it out. If the impact on the observer 1200 years after the event is so great, we may speculate how much greater it may have been for people who had seen nothing on this scale before and whose lives were so suddenly affected by the presence of this new structure in the landscape.

The human dimension: 'shock and awe' in the late eighth-century landscape?

One spring day around the year 787, Welshmen riding the cattle-rustling trails into Anglo-Saxon England came back with astonishing stories. Thousands of Anglo-Saxon levies had moved into the border country with horses and carts carrying rations, tents, rope, nails and weapons. (Rather than waging war) they had come to use tools – spades, axes, adzes and hammers. For they had been ordered to create a huge bank and ditch....Like modern motorway constructors they were to cut a swathe through the green countryside.[6]

Michael Wood took his cue here for the year in question from the deductions made by Fox and Stenton regarding the most 'opportune' moment in Offa's reign when hostilities on the western frontier of Mercia were at a low enough ebb to permit the construction of the great earthwork.[7] This envisioning of the work of construction no doubt captures something of the lived reality, and the impact on both the builders and the 'recipient' communities, British and Anglo-Saxon alike, of seeing such a great work take shape is likely to have been considerable. That there were English communities on both sides of the Dyke in several areas seems probable from place-name evidence, and there must have been some way in which the placing of the earthwork in the landscape was, if not negotiated, at least the subject of local briefing.[8]

The fact that the Dyke bears little direct relation to land divisions that can be understood from medieval or later documentation, including parish boundaries, need not be of great significance. The organisation of boundaries at the level of individual fields that pre-existed the building of the Dyke will probably only have been a feature of certain areas especially favourable for early farming settlement (whether British or English), such as the Vale of Montgomery and north Herefordshire. In the case of the latter area, the Dyke could have determined the subsequent orientation of fields, but it is suspected instead from archaeological research elsewhere in the lower Arrow catchment that these boundaries reflected a pre-existing orientation of enclosures locally, into which the Dyke was simply slotted.[9] Likewise, the existence of place-names indicative of the prior existence of woodland, such as '-leah' names denoting clearings, need not, contrary to Fox's assertion, signify that these places were heavily wooded in the eighth century – particularly if what these names reflect instead is the clearance of 'reverted' countryside a century or more earlier, or the existence of wood-pasture.[10]

Nonetheless, the arrival of the large Mercian workforce in the areas concerned must have had a strong impact on the local populace. This was particularly so where, and if, the workers were gathered together before their allocation to different work-groups. Camps for housing the workforce have been postulated, but as yet we have no means of knowing either where these existed or what form they might have taken.[11] It can be inferred from study of a single episode that occurred in 679 that there was an expectation that the army would comprise not only the fighting soldiery of the war-band, but also camp-followers who would accompany the baggage train.[12] If the 'dyke-building project' was envisaged as a campaign, we would need to ask what role the 'soldiers' and what role the 'supporters' respectively took in the progress of the work.

FIGURE 6.1 Landscape impact: Offa's Dyke traversing dramatic topographies

Even in landscapes transformed by nineteenth-century and earlier enclosure, as here at Llanfair Hill between the Clun Valley and Knighton, it is possible to imagine the impact of the sudden advent of Offa's Dyke in the late eighth century. Such a massive and largely continuous linear earthwork imposed over such a distance irrespective of the topographic obstacles must have been awe-inspiring to locally-resident contemporaries.

PHOTOGRAPH: ADAM STANFORD/AERIAL-CAM, COPYRIGHT RESERVED.

'Marking out' features

The discussion of the build of the Dyke in the chapter preceding this one concentrated upon the composition of the bank and its constructed form rather than the processes of construction as such. Previous Dyke investigators have noted the existence of posts sealed beneath the bank, and the repeated presence of a small bank at the base of the mounding sequence, as being indicative of the presence of 'marking out' features.[13] Just how extensive such features might have been (if indeed they existed) is difficult to determine, because there have only so far been excavations of sections across the Dyke at widely-spaced intervals. Another problem that such features present is to decide whether there is enough evidence from the details of their stratigraphic position and associations to confirm that they were indeed contemporary with the initial building of the Dyke, as opposed to being features that belonged to some previous activity at the location in question. Such a concern naturally arises at a site such as that at Ffrith village west of Wrexham where there is clear evidence for earlier occupation. Was the post-hole feature concerned (in this case more properly apparently a post-void) simply a feature that was integral with the Romano-British settlement, and that happened to become buried beneath the bank? Fox appeared to think not, but his published descriptions and illustrations do not permit definite resolution of this point.[14]

It has been suggested that the 'marking out' bank in particular recurs frequently enough to establish a pattern, and that 'these features would seem to indicate that a system of marking the course the earthwork was to follow was undertaken prior to its being built'.[15] However, the publication of this material at present remains somewhat anecdotal: for example, only three sections showing alleged continuous marking out banks or ditches sealed beneath the bank (at Coedpoeth, near Wrexham; at Bryn Hafod, Forden; and at Carreg-y-big, Selattyn) have been published.[16] These show no consistency of form, and without accompanying plans, their 'linearity' cannot be assessed. The 'marking out' process has been envisaged as occurring 'no more than a year' before the construction of the Dyke.[17] It seems more likely, however, that the 'marking out' represented by these small banks was both more casual, and was enacted closer to the full construction event, than such an estimate suggests. The only part of a well-preserved bank to have been excavated so far such that its manner of construction could be observed in plan, the 6 m wide strip examined at Ffrydd Road, Knighton, provides the best evidence on this point so far. Here, each of the drawn sections at either end of the excavated strip showed what might have been regarded (if seen only in a narrow trench) as a 'marker bank' at the base of the sequence. And yet, 'the initial dump of turves…(was) centred some 3.5 m from the lip of the ditch in Section 2, but was traced snaking across the trench to disappear into Section 3 some 6 m from that point. Even though this may represent a marking out bank, its meandering character was quite at variance with the straight course of the dyke'.[18] The question can probably only be resolved by considerably more excavation, undertaken within at least relatively well-preserved lengths of Dyke. While the setting up of lines of posts might represent a logical way of marking the planned route (though not necessarily a practice that occurred), the creation of a 'micro-earthwork' as a dug feature would nonetheless have required a lot of effort given that it would soon be superseded.[19]

Primary builds

Despite the range of different materials from which the bank of Offa's Dyke was built there is a reasonable amount of evidence that in many places the intended front and rear of the bank were framed by the creation of low linear retaining structures composed of turf, or stone, or both. There is also an indication from sites in considerably different topographical locations that a foundation of stones may deliberately have been laid before the bulk of the mounded or dump make-up of the bank was added. Material for the dump construction of the bank core-work was apparently obtained either from quarry pits, or scoops, or terracing, or linear ditches behind the bank, and from the ditch, notch or terrace cut to its front, or from both (or all) of these sources and directions. Sometimes a stony or subsoil layer, and sometimes topsoil or turves, formed the basal deposit. Where 'soft' material formed the base, the upper dumps often included stone and turf layers or lenses of material to help stabilise the body of the bank. It would appear that sometimes both this and the softer deposits were 'capped off' with stiff clay and sometimes with clay mixed with stone (especially where the underlying rock was shale-like sandstone or schist, as is so often the case in the Welsh/English borderlands).

We have noted that there are hints at least that, perhaps especially when the Dyke traversed steep slopes, there may have been some form of cellular build structure, with stones set in lines at the perpendicular to the course of the bank, apparently to stabilise the dump build. As already described in Chapter 5, in some places the bank was fronted with loosely layered stone that may once have approximated a 'dry-stone wall' but which in some places may have slumped somewhat to form a battered (sloping) revetment. At least one of the excavated bank sections appears to represent a decayed facing of this kind. There are hints from some excavations that an alternative form of facing might have involved laying turves at an angle to form a slope.

The overall process

It is when all the elements of construction are assessed together that the processes of construction can best be understood. The sum of this operation brought together the sighting-in and possibly also the marking of planned lengths, and the quarrying, scarping, shifting and the mounding of rock, soils and turf for the earthwork. At several points along the course of the Dyke, and in the uplands over considerable continuous tracts of landscape, much of the process of construction can still to a degree be 'read' from surface indications, even if the latter are often subtle. So, for example, whether between Lippetts Grove and Tidenham Chase above the Wye opposite Tintern, on Llanfair Hill north of Knighton, or across Selattyn Hill west of Oswestry, and at very many places in between these locations, the quarry pits, ditches and scarps to the east of the bank, as well as the ditch and scarps in front to the west, can still be traced. In future, they will need to be systematically recorded.[20]

In some of the sections dug through the Dyke an indication can be gained of how material was thrown to form the bulk of the bank. The tip-lines spreading eastwards from the crest of the bank demonstrate how in many locations most of that soil was cast onto and over that crest from the west. The spread and dumps of soil on the east-facing slope nonetheless also appear to include deposits whose tip-lines face west, or that at least do not derive from the west. This indicates the likelihood that not all the constituent deposits were derived from the ditch in these places (and clearly where the ditches and quarries to the east of the bank predominate, the bulk of the material for that bank is likely to have been derived from the east). In several places, the segmentation implies that the work-teams were required to build 20 m long segments, or multiples thereof. In some places the correlation and alignment of these segments was not so crucial, while in others they were more carefully-placed. In some places little care seems to have been taken to mask the junctions between the Dyke segments, while in others some effort was apparently made to ensure that the completed earthwork presented a seamless face.

What kind of barrier was the Dyke?

From statements recorded in the boundary clauses of tenth-century Anglo-Saxon land diplomas, or charters, it is clear that at least by that time, the term

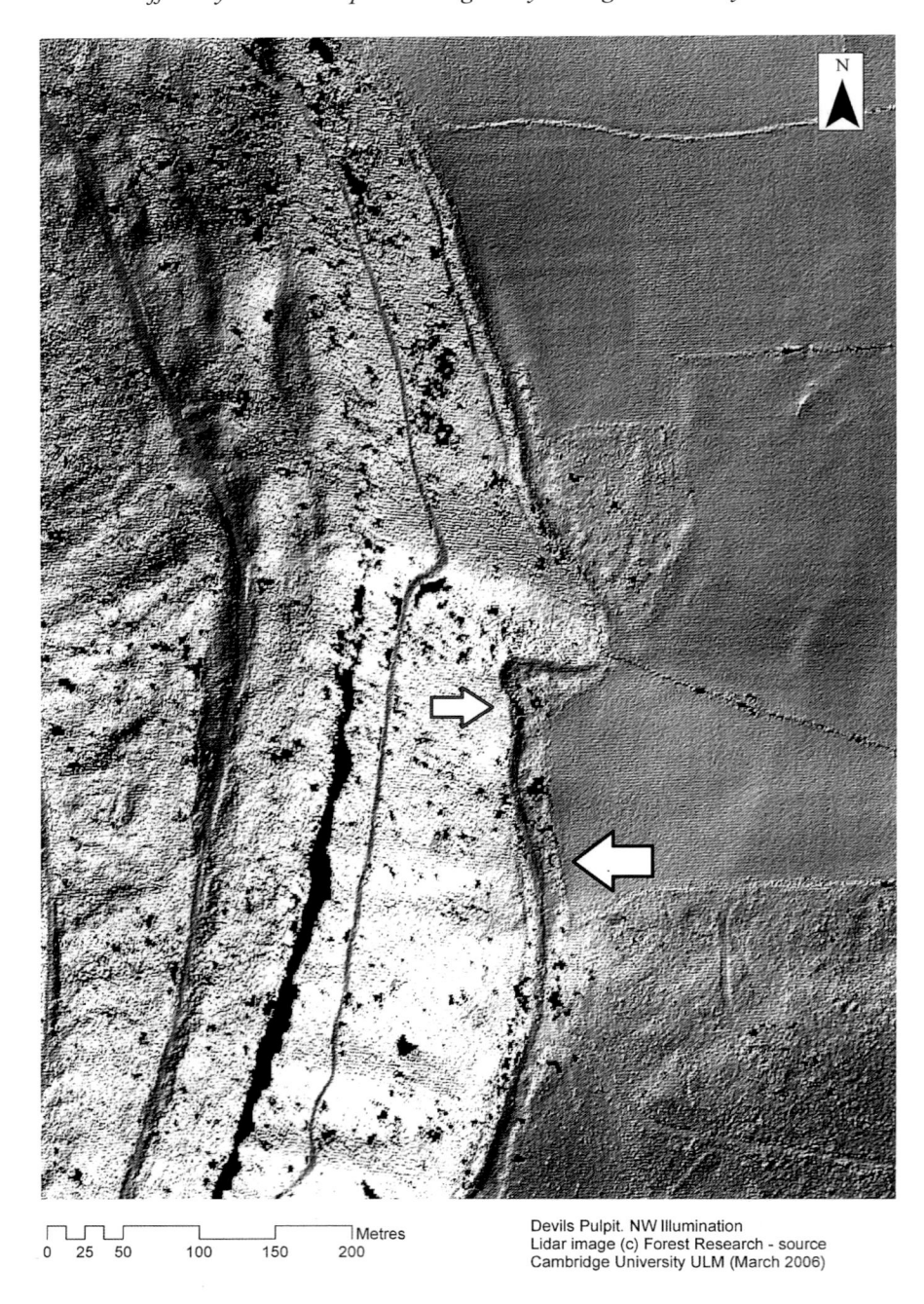

FIGURE 6.2 By the Devil's Pulpit, Gloucestershire: LiDAR plot

This greyscale plot derived from LiDAR data (see chapter 4, note 53) illustrates several of the points made in Chapters 5 and 6. The location of the Dyke on the forward edge of the west-facing scarp is very evident, as are modern track-ways running north–south lower down the scarp. The larger arrow indicates an area where ditches that served as quarries exist to both front (left, west) and rear (right, east) of the bank. The smaller arrow indicates the 'Devil's Pulpit' area itself, where the angled turn features carefully-adjusted earthwork segments (see also Figure 5.33).

REPRODUCED COURTESY OF FOREST ENTERPRISE. CROWN COPYRIGHT RESERVED.

that we now represent as 'dyke' had the same ambiguity of meaning concerning the form of boundaries that we see in the wider landscape of enclosure today:

> *Ondlong ridiges on **d**one dic*, 'along the ridge to the dyke' (956 AD)[21]; *Of **d**am broc on **d**a ealdan dic*, 'from the brook to the old ditch' (969 AD)[22]; *On anne micelne dic*, 'to a great dyke' (979 AD).[23]

The term could refer then, to a bank associated with a ditch, to the dry ditch itself, to a wet ditch, or to a channel cut to convey water from one place to another. It was not necessarily the form of a ditched linear earthwork, as much as its landscape context and purpose, which defined the way in which it was perceived by those who built it. In some places, a dyke may have originated as a drain, but have become a boundary. In others its primary purpose may have been to signify a land division. The 'great dykes', however, are a case apart, due both to their scale as structures and across distances, but also in the specific manner in which their bank and their ditch were inter-dependent.

In the simplest terms, the ditch of a linear earthwork of the 'great dyke' kind is a quarry for material to raise a rampart. The ditch on the western side of Offa's Dyke was, for most of its course, the source of material for the construction of the bank: and this is evident not only from the composition of the bank deposits in many places, but as we have just noted, also from the pattern of the tip-lines of material. Soil was dumped eastwards from the ditch in such places, with a steep 'leading' face and tapering deposit to the rear of the bank. The ditch was inevitably dug through a variety of different rock types, but the eventual form of the ditch was probably dictated as much as by the design requirements in terms of how the various segments were placed across the area concerned as by the practical requirements of excavating and dumping at any one location.

The ditch of a linear earthwork was inextricably linked with the bank not only because the latter could not exist without the ditch having been created as a quarry, but also because of its defining and defensive role. Quarries to the rear of the bank could have supplied ample material for the building of a bank, so, rather, the ditch was arguably the primary line both of definition of the earthwork, and of creating the 'blocking' of transit towards it. This much had not only been understood, but had been extensively written about, by Roman military commanders and theorists. As such it was without doubt part of the inheritance of post-Roman armies and their officers across Europe.

As a military work, therefore, the ditch of Offa's Dyke had added significances beyond its use as a quarry, and both its form and its stance (in terms of exact location) indicated its anticipated role in any particular location. It is clear from the above that although dyke-building was not an unusual activity for the Anglo-Saxon peasant, the building of as massive a long-distance and coherent work as this (as, presumably, also work for the defences of fortresses) was a qualitatively different enterprise. Such a major public work involved a greater degree of design elaboration than had probably hitherto been necessary. It must also have required a more sophisticated level of command and control for the successful co-ordination both of the work-force and materials, and for the execution of the build process itself, and this is a question that we shall soon address.

Human resources and the Dyke building project

Although Fox's interpolations about the organisation of the work quoted at the beginning of this chapter are entirely plausible, the question of which among Offa's subjects was responsible for providing labour or other resources for the building of the Dyke is essentially unanswerable, since no documentation directly bearing on the matter exists. We can, however, deduce something of the terms of required provision of such resources from charter and other documentary evidence concerning the demands made by the Mercian rulers of the subjects who held land within their domains. Discussion of the significance of such demands has been intense in Anglo-Saxon studies, and we can do no more than summarise some key points here.

'Bridge-work and fortress-work': providing labour for the Dyke project

Fox, following Stenton, noted the relevance to the construction of the Dyke of the existence of the 'three burdens' placed upon the holders of book-land: bridge-building, fortress-building and service in the army recruited for particular purposes.[24] In Mercia and in others of the Anglo-Saxon kingdoms, the mid- to late eighth century witnessed an acceleration of the gradual changes that had occurred over a protracted period concerning the terms of lordly service. The balance was gradually shifting between, first, the customary service demanded by kings that their *comes* (their leading magnates or 'companions-in-arms') should participate in their lord's personal war-band; second, the burdens of martial duties as expressed through specific land-holding agreements recorded in charters; and third, the commutation of service by monetary payments.[25] The process involved a transition from a situation in which the existence of customary rights predominated, to one in which there was a greater emphasis on 'book-land', the recording of tenure explicitly in terms of services due to the overlord.[26] This reflected a concern on the part of those administering each kingdom to formalise arrangements for the provision of services. Central among such services was the means by which landholders provided support for the creation and maintenance of armed forces and major infrastructure works, and the specific innovations of the eighth century appear to have related additionally to the building and maintenance of bridges and fortresses.[27]

The principal means by which we know of the existence of such arrangements in Mercia is through charters that identified among other provisions the granting of exemption to the duty to provide some services, but that also specified explicitly that the grantee should not be exempted the provision of those services that involved contributing to public works. At least from the closing years of Offa's reign, this could explicitly include service in military operations.[28] In many cases the clauses concerned referred to immunities granted to religious communities, or to their founders, and this gave rise in the ninth century to concern that the granting of many such exemptions could lead to a situation in which it was difficult to raise armies.[29]

FIGURE 6.3 The process of establishing Offa's Dyke length by length
On the ground at locations where the Dyke is better-preserved, as here at Dudston Fields in the Vale of Montgomery, the intricacies of Dyke construction are very evident. Three of the 20 m or so 'adjusted-segmented' lengths of bank are visible here, their upper profile silhouetted against a field of oilseed rape. Despite considerable infill over the centuries the deep V-profile of the ditch is also prominent, even in this lowland setting. The view is looking north, just south of the Chirbury-Montgomery Road.

The earliest fully corroborated mention of obligations to provide military services that might involve building earthworks is to be found in a charter issued by King Aethelbald at the Synod of Gumley in Leicestershire in 749.[30] This charter specifically mentioned the need to provide services for the construction of bridges and fortifications, although it granted exemption for the churches within the kingdom.[31] However, the public services mentioned indicated a range of public works, and not only provision of the labour to build bridges and fortresses. We know from one of Boniface's letters, moreover, that among the specific complaints of the clergy at this time was the direct conscription of clerics to perform manual labour.[32] Such works, together with service in the army, were mentioned in a number of charters issued by Offa and by Coelwulf, Coenwulf's brother and successor. Indeed, the aims of the specification of such duties were made manifest in a charter issued in respect of the 'churches of Kent' in 792, which in effect predicts what later became the primarily defensive purpose of the provisions. The Kentish churches were to be exempted services, 'except for fighting against sea-borne pagans with invading fleets....or the construction of bridges and fortified works'.[33] This clearly registers the presence of Scandinavian raiders who had already made an aggressive appearance on the West Saxon coast in Dorset and who had ransacked the abbey at Lindisfarne.[34]

That similar provisions could have been made in respect to the western frontier with the British seems logical, and can, perhaps, be inferred from the evidence of at least some charters. Fox noted, for example, that the use of a term implying the digging specifically of ditches in several Worcester charters, including one of 836, may indicate the survival of a particular local tradition of specifying that work on fortifications would normally take the form of digging linear ditches rather than, or as well as, enclosures of the fortress or 'burh' type. He appears to have believed that this tradition could have derived directly from the experience of working on Offa's and Wat's Dykes: 'half a century of pick-and-shovel work on the frontier had left its mark on legal phraseology in the Mercian state'.[35]

Local levies or a central force

As evident from the quotation that opened this chapter, Fox assumed that local leaders would have been responsible for assembling the work-force to build the Dyke. This was based largely on his settled view that the form of the Dyke itself, with its changing character reflecting the presence or absence of cultivation, could be taken to indicate that sufficient numbers of hands existed to provide local levies from among the population that had been tilling the neighbouring fields. While, as noted above, the archaeological evidence for the clearance of cultivated land is at present somewhat equivocal, that there were likely to have been English settlers in the vicinity of the Dyke is indicated from place-names. Nonetheless, it seems unlikely that sufficient capacity existed locally to achieve the work of Dyke creation over such a great distance within a span of, say, five years, which might be the maximum length of time that such a campaign of construction could reasonably be sustained.

This leaves a number of other alternatives. Offa's Dyke could, for instance, have been constructed using a general levy such as would be called upon in a campaign conducted by the army.[36] The mobilisation of such a force could be contemplated, but what we know of the actions of the Mercian army where they were under the documented leadership of individual ealdormen is that those *duces* led 'their' people, such as the Hwicce, in particular campaigns.[37] It seems reasonable to suppose, therefore, that any wider mobilisation that took place was, at least in part, of particular sub-kingdoms or 'earldoms' that (in Wessex at least) were becoming the nuclei of what were soon to develop as counties.

Be that as it may, in the context of later eighth-century Mercia, despite the difficulties in exact attribution of peoples to areas, it seems likely that the groups concerned would have included the Hwicce, the Wrocansaete, and the Magonsaete. To these we could add the local groups of 'Mercian' Anglo-Saxons that it can be adduced had settled, or had been settled, on particular parts of the frontier, and the likelihood of a more general component of the *fyrd* or 'army of the folk' drawn as a 'lighter' levy, from elsewhere across Mercia. The potential existence of particularly close links between 'the original Mercia' and the Wrocansaete could have meant that there was a more direct supply of contingents from 'central' Mercia to the parts of the Dyke easily more reached from Watling Street. This may indeed go some way to accounting for the change in build pattern that is evident from Llanfair Hill southwards. These points will be returned to, but in the meantime, the question of how any or all of these groups were co-ordinated on the ground raises the further question of how oversight was achieved, and by whom.

6 Building and operating the Dyke

Organising the work: the question of oversight

Fox thought that it must have been Offa himself who decided upon the nature and execution of the work, and who chose the exact line. This is inherently implausible, however, except in the broadest terms, given the manifold other matters of state that no doubt preoccupied the Mercian king. Whether or not this was so, the construction workforce for the 'Dyke project' would have needed to have been under close supervision and direction, particularly in those locations where highly 'choreographed' effects were sought.

Close study of the siting and design of Offa's Dyke in the landscape provides for us today, as it did for Fox almost a century ago, an enduring respect for the perspicacity and ingenuity of those responsible for placing and building the Dyke. The project required a considerable sensitivity to the changing forms of the landscape, as recounted in the preceding chapters, as well as advanced military engineering expertise. Yet what most strikes the observer who has become immersed in the 'design repertoire' of the Dyke-builders is the degree of subtlety of thought involved in the entire design-and-build process. These practical and militarily-adept people made full use of the opportunities that the inherited landscape afforded, to achieve the maximum tactical advantage and impact with the minimal amount of unnecessary 'travel' across the landscape. It was seemingly as much about what not to do, as what to do, that mattered in achieving the traverse – both broadly across the landscape and more locally.

Such carefully-applied decision-making about routing and placing in turn required a familiarity with the transitional upland and lowland landscapes in question that cannot have been achieved at a glance. Rather, it must have involved a ranging over the landscape well in advance of the commencement of works, and reconnaissance both forwards/westwards and rearwards/eastwards of the route eventually followed. It then involved careful implementation of a 'build repertoire' that ensured that at the micro-scale, similar placement and design solutions were applied at similar kinds of location along the route. This necessary reconnaissance is surely indicative in its own right of the existence of a cadre of 'professional officers' with a dedicated role to observe, to plan, and to operate within the framework of an agreed 'Dyke project'.

This is again where the massive scale of the undertaking impresses the discerning observer. It is one thing to construct a Dyke that crosses, as with the Cambridgeshire dykes, a widely inter-visible landscape at the perpendicular to an obvious direction of transit. It is equally straightforward to construct dykes that cut across a ridge-way or that traverse a single steep-sided (or indeed a broad) valley. It is a considerably greater task, and achievement, to construct a Dyke across a landscape that encompasses not only a great distance, but also some topographical variety, as in the cases of East Wansdyke and of Wat's Dyke. The earthwork across the 'neck' of lowland Scotland built during the emperorship of Antoninus Pius in the second century AD, and the 'Wall' of the Emperor Hadrian across the historic counties of Cumberland and Northumberland, were fully engineered works with a supporting infrastructure of roads, forts and watch-towers carried out by one of the most organised military forces in history.

However, the 'frontier' whose spinal course is marked in large part by Offa's Dyke was as long as both of these Roman imperial works placed end to end, and it crossed a more diverse landscape than either of them. It moreover kept to a line with a precision unmatched by an army command in these islands for a thousand years afterwards until General Wade built his military works in the eighteenth century. As we have seen, it did so not by the application of a 'rule of thumb', but rather by subtle and sustained application of design principles that ensured continuity of visibility, and the sustaining of practical utility across long distances, that was far in advance of its time. This was not the only construction of surpassing elegance and effectiveness created at the apex of Mercian achievement towards the end of the eighth century, but it was certainly the one conceived on the grandest scale and executed with the most considerable precision given that scale.[38]

The organisational operation of the Dyke: a 'frontier patrol'?

The question of how the Dyke was supposed to operate once 'completed' has also, inevitably, been the subject of considerable past discussion and debate. Each of the students of the Dyke has had their own ideas about how the Dyke could have been used.[39] This has sometimes involved a full envisioning of the process in action, as with a recent account that followed up on Noble's suggestion of a 'patrol line'. This projection envisaged that 'a patrol of perhaps ten men moving at four miles an hour would pass any given point at 90-minute intervals' and this would mean that 300 men working in shifts could have provided 24-hour cover of the central 64 miles, with less men required if the patrol was on horseback.[40]

A contrasting approach to the question of supervision of the frontier when the Dyke was in place was first promoted in the nineteenth century, and involved attempting to trace the existence of officials who were responsible for watching over the frontier. The earliest mention of someone who might have been in overall charge of the Dyke and its frontier may be in the *Anglo-Saxon Chronicle* for the year 896, in an entry that recorded the death of Wulfric, described as the 'king's marshall' and as the 'Welsh companion' or 'Welsh reeve'.[41] That the office was likely to have been a Mercian innovation is suggested by the reference to 'those men whom we call in English wahlfaereld' who were included among a list of soldiery or officials including mounted men that the recipients of the grant were excused from feeding and lodging in a charter of 855 in Burghred's reign.[42]

It is possible, therefore, that the predecessor to King Alfred's 'Welsh reeve' was an official whose role was created in the late eighth century to co-ordinate the construction, and beyond this, the operation of the Dyke, with a retinue

FIGURE 6.4 A 'frontier patrol' in the landscape?
The impression of an open landscape under surveillance from an imposed frontier work is best achieved today when walking along the Dyke on the sweeping uplands of the area Fox termed 'the mountain zone'. This impression is formed nowhere more so than here, on Llanfair Hill. This view is northwards, just to the south of Springhill Farm.

whose activities ranged over a much wider area. The task of surveillance is also something that can be interpolated from the actions of the reeve of the West Saxon king Beorhtric who rode down to the Dorset coast in 787 to intercept 'three ships of the Northmen': an intervention that cost him his life. This reeve specifically had the duty of meeting traders or other 'arrivals', and conveying them into the king's presence.[43]

Margaret Gelling produced an avowedly 'highly conjectural' account of administrative arrangements in western Mercia with particular reference to Offa's Dyke.[44] The names of some individual settlements could, in Gelling's view, be indicative of arrangements put in place to defend the frontiers and districts of Mercia even before the building of the Dyke. This thesis was developed to account for the distribution, in particular, of the name (or compound element) *Burton* throughout England.[45] What Gelling thought especially relevant to the Dyke's use was the concentration of such names in the border counties. Another borderland concentration of names related to oaks she saw as potentially related to the demands of fortress-work.[46] The problems associated with the elasticity of the term 'dyke' apply equally, however, to the term 'burh', since it is likely that many kinds of enclosure fell within the scope of this term.[47] It is clear that minster precincts, major manorial sites and the 'vills' of the aristocracy could all be surrounded by defences, but equally, the term 'burh' could also in the eighth century refer to abandoned prehistoric sites and former Roman enclosures – even before it began to be applied to towns. It is becoming clear that minsters, monasteries and royal 'vills' were the nuclei for proto-urban settlements, in contrast to the sites of fairs, markets and productive sites that included 'wics', but not exclusively so.[48]

There is also an element in some place-names, *burhweard*, which Gelling thought might be significant to the discussion of how the frontier was organised, given their concentration in the border counties.[49] She suggested that although the *burhweard* element in these names has in the past been read as a personal name, and although there is no record of an official with the title in other Anglo-Saxon sources, its meaning 'fort-guardian' was meaningful administratively. Gelling argued that its presence at Buscot in Oxfordshire indicates that the term was used to designate officials 'who had charge of a group of defence posts and were given estates from which to operate'. Certainly, the frontier distribution in this regard is suggestive of a localised purpose.

Dyke infrastructure: gateways and access

While the operation of the Dyke may have relied on a mobile force of armed officers, there may have been structures in place that facilitated the task of observation and control of movement beyond and along the Dyke. Such a possibility requires some attempt to identify possible control and access points, and look-out posts.

Gateways: an intractable problem?

The difficulties of determining the prior existence and detailed form of any original 'gateway' features are inevitably considerable. There are, for instance, many breaks that are the result of a cut through the Dyke to create tracks and access points, especially in the farmed post-Medieval landscape. The creation of at least some of these tracks could have involved the widening or complete obliteration, of any original passage-ways. Moreover, although there are ridgeway routes that are clearly of considerable topographical prominence and likely antiquity, many other potential track-ways are more difficult to be sure about. Fox correlated certain breaks in the Dyke with early ridge-ways and valley-routes. He identified several possible 'gateways' for which some earthwork evidence could be adduced. In two cases, at the Kerry Ridgeway and at Bwlch near Discoed, he went further and suggested that there had been a deliberate manipulation of the former line of the ridgeway track concerned, to take it through a Mercian 'control point' along the Dyke.[50] In contrast, Noble maintained that there were many and regular gaps or gateways through Offa's Dyke, and that these were of greater or of lesser formality.[51]

In several places where gaps exist the ditch does clearly continue across the area concerned, and the presence of an original crossing-point is unlikely to be signalled simply by the presence of an interruption to the bank of the Dyke. A case in point is on the south-west facing slope of Selattyn Hill north of Orseddwen Farm where Fox identified an 'original' gap that he thought represented a crossing-point (Figure 2.12). His published photograph of this gap, with a modern field wall built along the crest of the bank and dipping across the point where he suggested that the 'gap' existed, shows clearly that such an interpretation was unwarranted.[52] It should come as no surprise, therefore, that more recently excavation has demonstrated that the ditch was present here, if

FIGURE 6.5 Supposed 'gateway' at Jenkins Allis south of Knighton

Both Fox (1955, 157–8, describing the location as 'Frydd Hill') and Noble (1983, 44) interpreted the unusual configuration here as a 'passage-way' through the Dyke, albeit a narrow one. This was entirely dismissed by Hill and Worthington (2003, 91) due to the continuation of the ditch across the area concerned (clearly visible in the foreground here). There was clearly some manipulation of the form of the Dyke here, to turn the bank inwards at just the point where, in the manner of Iron Age fortifications, the counter-scarp banks turn outwards to flank what appears to be a deliberately expanded ditch.

only as a slight feature in the hard rock that outcrops very close to the surface locally.[53]

A number of excavations have been carried out at the location of entrances suggested by Fox, and more intensively along the stretch of Dyke crossing the Vale of Montgomery, that could reasonably have encompassed farmlands on both sides of the Dyke.[54] From the results of this work it has been claimed that the question of the alleged gateways has been substantially resolved: they were 'either non-existent or extremely scarce'.[55] The stated premise for this work was that 'any excavation that discovers the evidence for the ditch shows that a gateway had not been part of the original design at that point.'[56] This reflects a further premise that it is unlikely that bridges could have been built across the ditch near gateways (despite the explicit contemporary references to bridge-work that exist). It has recently been pointed out that it was not conclusively demonstrated that the ditches concerned were of late eighth- or early ninth-century date; and nor are such premises warranted given that it was easily possible for the Mercians to have built bridges to operate at such locations.[57]

To suggest that disproving that gaps existed by looking primarily at locations identified either specifically by Fox or generically by Noble implies that both of these Dyke students adequately set out the criteria by which entrances could be predicted. There are yet more fundamental possible objections to the idea that no gates existed through Offa's Dyke. One such objection is the documented presence, at least by the tenth century, of just such gateways through dykes, as recorded in 958 for the Rowe Ditch across the Arrow Valley east of Leominster.[58] While it could be suggested that this reflected a changed situation locally, given that it is so much further on in time from the eighth century, it was not at that time a frontier that was markedly more peaceful.

Meanwhile, close examination of one of Fox's postulated entrances, at Bwlch near Discoed, suggests that Fox was right about an entrance or crossing point

FIGURE 6.6 Dyke configuration at a likely gateway at Bwlch, Discoed

The nearest of the segments of bank in the foreground has been truncated by the present-day Kinnerton-Presteigne lane. The 'hollow-way' leading from the west towards the gap where two contrasting alignments, or trends, of bank meet is very clear in this photograph. So too is the natural ridge just beyond this which overlooks the gap/gate from the south; and which may have been enhanced as a surveillance platform. Evenjobb Hill forms the horizon, and Pen Offa Farm is just visible to the right.

PHOTOGRAPH: ADAM STANFORD/AERIAL-CAM, COPYRIGHT RESERVED.

having existed just to the south of the modern ridge-top lane running from west to east from Kinnerton to Presteigne. This is not only because, as Fox put it, this lane follows 'the only possible upland traffic line from Radnor Forest to the Presteigne area'.[59] It is also because the configuration of the Dyke is indicative of something unusual occurring here.

The run of the earthwork as it approaches from the south at Bwlch has a straight alignment from the crest of the ridge at Pen Offa down to a point just to the south of the present road. At this point the Dyke, here clearly in segmented construction, makes a slight turn eastwards just before a clear gap is evident (Figure 6.6).[60] Reciprocally, the bank and ditch that approaches this point from the north clearly curves markedly inwards (eastwards) as it traverses a gentle south-facing slope towards the road to approach the northern limit of the straight alignment (Figure 6.7).[61]

Immediately to the west of the 'gap' there is a pattern of banks and linear hollows that appeared to Fox to represent a 'deep trackway (that) leads to the opening from the NW, but cannot readily be traced on flat ground on the E. side of the Dyke.'[62] This track remains as an earthwork exactly as Fox first described it 85 years ago, although the bank that runs parallel with the Dyke where the latter approaches from the north is more continuous and substantial than indicated by Fox. As he did note, however, this configuration clearly serves to divert southwards the route-way that otherwise follows a course along the ridge from the west, and crosses the Dyke at the very point where the latter most radically changes its alignment.

Fox found support for the idea that this was a deliberate crossing-point from another striking observation. This was that for some distance both to the north

6 Building and operating the Dyke

FIGURE 6.7 The Dyke north of the Kinnerton-Presteigne ridge-way

The approach of the Dyke towards the gap in the Dyke shown in Figure 6.6 (and immediately behind the camera in this shot) is very evident here. The curving 'slight' mode of build around the bluff at top right rapidly changes to a more substantial, straight, build on a length of earthwork that is bisected by the lane at left (foreground in Figure 6.6) but that terminates at the gap. This length clearly overlooks the lane/ridgeway as the latter approaches from the west.

PHOTOGRAPH: ADAM STANFORD/
AERIAL-CAM, COPYRIGHT RESERVED.

and south of this gap the Dyke is of his minor 'boundary bank' (our *slighter*) mode of construction, but that it increases in size as it approaches the entrance gap itself from both directions, with the 'gateway' placed centrally within this enlarged length. To this we would add that the course of the Dyke is itself adjusted in a significant and not trivial way as it approaches the gap from each direction. So, its curve south-eastwards from the hillcrest overlooking the Lugg ensures that it faces south-west and overlooks the trackway exactly along the zone in which that track is deflected southwards. Reciprocally, from the south the subtle adjustment north-eastwards just before the gap is reached re-directs the earthwork to overlook the approach to the 'gateway' from the west more directly.

A trench dug in this location by an associate of Hill and Worthington was placed 'to confirm that the gap in the bank and ditch was the result of it being crossed by post-medieval drainage.'[63] The relevant highly summary publication of this excavation did not locate it on the ground, but it is presumed to have been dug across the gap evident today (or slightly forwards from it, to the west). As such, the half-metre deep gully recorded on the published section-drawing does not necessarily approximate the ditch associated with the Dyke.[64]

The course that the Dyke takes in its approach to the point where there is a gap in the earthwork corresponding to a change of alignment just to the south of the lane from Kinnerton to Presteigne, and the configuration of banks at the gap itself, therefore do indicate that the case for a former gateway here remains a compelling one. However, there is another factor in play here that has not yet received the attention it perhaps deserves. This relates to the place-name of the cottage, 'Bwlch', only a matter of 100 m north-east of the gap. In Welsh, 'bwlch' means 'gap, pass, or notch'.[65] This naming corresponds closely to the English 'yat' (OE 'geat': gate or pass).[66] The gap or pass could simply refer to the natural notch in the ridge through which the route-way passes. However, its occurrence at exactly this point appears more likely to reflect the fact that there was here a coincidence of a natural notch and the construction of a gate through the earthwork that the Dyke-builders themselves sought to create.

Dyke configuration, gateways and route-ways

One way that the (as yet unresolved) question of the presence or absence of gateways could be approached, therefore, would be to make a close examination of the disposition of the Dyke in relation to topography and place-names (for instance), and in reference also to any areas of heightened complexity of earthwork dispositions and built form. Such a procedure might produce an *a priori* case for the former existence of a gateway at Dudston Fields, Chirbury, even without the apparent former configuration of the roadway here.[67] This latter observation is important because it potentially frees us from reliance upon the assumption of the importance of specific route-ways (as at the Kerry Ridgeway crossing), or upon the consideration of otherwise unexplained gaps such as apparently caused by the later cutting of hollow-ways (as at Hope Farm, Leighton), or of works that may simply have been associated with the Dyke's crossing of streams (as with Fox's 'outwork' at Mellington Park).[68] On this basis, the oddity (noted by Fox) of the configuration of the Dyke as it approaches the stream at Orseddwen Farm is potentially more explicable by proposing that if there was a crossing-point hereabouts at all, it was on the southern side of this dell, rather than at the dip in the bank immediately to the north on the flank of Selattyn Hill.

Given that there are a number of such locations where the configuration of the Dyke indicates a point where the Dyke transects a plausible east–west route, the idea that there were indeed deliberately-constructed 'gateways' or access points through the Dyke appears to be a reasonable working hypothesis. The argument that there cannot have been bridges across the Dyke is a spurious one, not only because of the historical documentation for bridge-work, but also because of the likelihood that timber bridges associated with gateways were a feature of Mercian defensive works attested in the archaeological record, as at Tamworth.[69] In some cases there may have been causeways left when the Dyke was built, in other cases bridges could have been added: but it is the configuration of the earthworks of the Dyke itself at key points like Bwlch, Discoed, that offer the best clues to their presence (Figure 6.8).

These gateways would have provided points of access and egress to permit trading and to facilitate the passage of Mercian forces on campaign, as well as to act as control points to monitor and if necessary to block the transit of British raiders moving eastwards. The view has been advanced recently also that 'it would have been essential to maintain these main highways as communications

FIGURE 6.8 Candidate gateways: the case of Carreg-y-big, Oswestry

Four lanes converge here, on the (likely medieval) farm straddling an otherwise straight length of Dyke. Aerial photograph (a) shows the adjustment made in the course of the Dyke to accommodate the side-valley in which the farm lies. It is at a point 200 m to the south, however, that the configuration of the Dyke indicates the possibility of a gateway: since as (b) and (c) show, there is a careful choreography of bank segments and alignments here. Although not yet fully explicable, it seems more likely that this was to accommodate a purpose, rather than simply a mis-alignment of lengths of Dyke here.

REPRODUCED COURTESY OF A. WIGLEY: COPYRIGHT SHROPSHIRE COUNCIL.

(links) between neighbouring kingdoms.'[70] Moreover, the existence of mined and manufactured resources on either side of the frontier needs to be borne in mind. So, for instance, copper and lead were mined in north Wales, while on the English side salt was produced in Cheshire and at Droitwich in Worcestershire. Iron was smelted and forged on the margins of the Forest of Dean, and this no doubt had important implications for the placement and operation of the frontier in the lower Wye valley. By 'deflecting the movement of goods and people' to specific entry-points, the Mercian king could ensure the collection of tolls while permitting entry into Mercia only to those engaged in legitimate trade. As such, Offa's Dyke had an economic, regulatory and revenue-raising role for the emergent bureaucracy: 'in today's terms the crossing points of the Dykes can be seen to have formed immigration, excise and border controls to ensure the safety and continued prosperity of the Mercian state.'[71]

Surveillance and impact: the significance of the angled turns

A key feature that we have noted about the overall placement of Offa's Dyke in the landscape is that it provided oversight over locations to the west. This is more subtle than has previously been realised, with frequent location of the earthwork such that an observer standing well behind the Dyke had a clear view over its bank and down into valleys or across landscapes beyond it to the west. The deliberate sophistication of surveillance in this manner, however infrequently monitored, explains why for instance, as was noted in Chapter 4, the Dyke so often approaches river and stream valleys from the north-west. Moreover, there are other features along the Dyke that might have served to enhance its operation as a means of surveillance. This is perhaps best illustrated by the sharp changes in alignment, some of which Fox termed 'right-angled corners', but which we have more inclusively denoted here, 'angled turns'.

At least 15 locations where the Dyke features a pronounced abrupt turn are readily definable. These are places where the earthwork changes direction at a right-angle, or at least very sharply. This is surely a greater incidence than would occur if such features arose as the result of a mistake or a failure to adequately bring two work-gangs to the same place, which are among the explanations that have previously been adduced for them. Such turns exist, then, at East Vaga, at Worgan's Wood, at the Devil's Pulpit, at Lippetts Grove, at Madgett Hill and at The Langett in Gloucestershire (the county total is six examples), at Lyonshall and at Rushock Hill in Herefordshire (two), at Pinner's Hole, Knighton, in Radnorshire (one), at Cwmsanahan Hill and at Hergan (north and south), and at Llanymynech Hill in Shropshire (four), at Roundabout Plantation (Leighton) in Montgomeryshire (one), and at Craignant (Weston Rhyn) in Denbighshire (one). Other such turns may have been lost or obscured by later reworking of the earthwork.[72] A likely example of the latter is the angled turn at Pinner's Hole above the south bank of the Teme in Knighton. This is attached to a section of Dyke that may have been re-used for town defences in the medieval period.[73] Nor is this a full representation of the presence of angled turns, since some less acute-angled turns appear to be very abrupt when seen from a distance, and some abrupt turns form part of more elaborate winding ascents of steep hillsides. A length of the Dyke spanning a bluff above the south-facing slopes north of the river Clun at Spoad, near Newcastle-on-Clun, is a case in point.

Given that the first 6 angled turns noted here occur within the space of 9 miles (15 km) along the dissected ridge top in Gloucestershire above the river

FIGURE 6.9 The 'angled turn' on Rushock Hill, from the west

This aerial photograph again illustrates more than one of the characteristic features of Offa's Dyke. The 'angled turn' in the middle distance is placed at the highest point of the hill, arguably to achieve a maximal viewpoint north and south rather than to reach a pre-determined, negotiated, location. The subtle and near-continuous adjustment of build-segments is very evident across Herrock Hill in the foreground.

COPYRIGHT WOOLHOPE NATURALISTS' FIELD CLUB/CHRIS MUSSON.

6 Building and operating the Dyke

Wye, it can be seen immediately that more appear to exist in the southern and central sectors than in the northern sector of the Dyke north of the Wye. It might also be adduced that they are more common the more broken is the terrain, but strategic considerations may also have been to the fore. Even such a basic observation as that 15 such turns exist, 6 of which are in Gloucestershire and 2 in north Herefordshire,[74] strongly contradicts the claim that the sections of Offa's Dyke to the south of Rushock Hill represent entirely unrelated earthworks to those to the north.

Not all of the forms and circumstances of such turns are identical, however. For instance, Fox noted three of what he termed 'right-angled corners' in the south Shropshire to north Herefordshire sector at Rushock Hill, Cwmsanahan and Hergan, none of which closely approximates the other.[75] There are, arguably, several more such turns in this area, however. So, for instance, although Fox clearly recorded the Lyonshall turn on the relevant map extract, he both underestimated its proportions thereon, and then neglected to mention it at all in the accompanying discussion.[76] Moreover, two rather than one such turns are present at Hergan: although one of the turns represents a full right-angle at what Fox referred to as a 'col', there is an equally sharp turn 400 m to the south-west, but located on the outside of a spur overlooking the Mardu Brook.

At Lyonshall, the turn is a full right-angle and occurs at the top of a slope before the routing of the Dyke swings north-eastwards to follow a sinuous course through Lyonshall Park Wood, and around to where it makes a curving crossing of the narrow and not very steep-sided Arrow valley. What the angled turn here represents, then, is both a marked change in alignment, and apparently also the prelude to a considerable change in character from *substantial* build mode proportions to the *slighter* mode. It is also an outward-facing turn at precisely the point where the Dyke stops being very evident as a brow-line feature when seen from the west.

In marked contrast in plan at least, the angled turn on Rushock Hill is an 'inward' turn as two lengths of Dyke meet on the crest of a ridge, where they are set at 90 degrees to each other. On a map or even from the air (Figure 6.9), this arrangement appears to make little sense. This was presumably why Fox regarded it as an example of a consequence of following the planned design 'to the letter of the law', in this case a requirement to reach the highest point of each hill while deviating as little as possible from its 'agreed line' in doing so.[77] However, there are myriad instances where the Dyke passes near to, but does not achieve, such high points. What is instead achieved by this particular manoeuvre in this particular place is a vantage point both forwards from, and to the rear of, the Dyke at a crucial location. Such an arrangement facilitated broader alignments, and brought adjacent lengths of the Dyke to positions that afforded a fine prospect to the south-west and to the south-east, respectively.[78] However, the view north from the turn itself was quite possibly what may have mattered most: the prospect north-eastwards extends more than 3 miles (4.8 km) down into the Lugg valley near Presteigne.[79]

Meanwhile, Fox explained the Hergan angled turn in terms again of the need to reach a pre-determined location on the col to the east of Cwm Farm, agreed in advance with representatives of the Kingdom of Powys.[80] The reason for the perceived awkwardness of this 90-degree turn was a lack of co-ordination between two work-gangs building 'their' lengths of Dyke in opposite directions towards one another. According to Fox, the two gangs built their sections according to different traditions of Dyke-building, with the southern-most of the two gangs completing theirs first. 'The Hergan men were building the Dyke on a westward-facing slope, and they continued on this slope to the bitter end. The connexion was the affair of the Middle Knuck gang, not theirs; but they turned their banks through a right-angle and made a neat job before downing tools.'[81]

However, as discussed in Chapter 5, the different forms of Dyke deployed in any one place were more plausibly related to careful use of the terrain to achieve maximum visual effect when seen from the west. Moreover, the complexity of the form and disposition of the earthworks at Hergan suggests that what mattered was how the Dyke approached the head of the side-valley here. The enhancement of the counter-scarp bank into a full bank on the outer lip of the ditch for some distance southwards away from the turn presented an impression of formidable strength to the earthwork in this significant location. The configuration of the angled-turn suggests that overlooking of this point from all directions had been an important design consideration, and this raises the possibility that there was another passage-point or gateway here (Figure 6.10).

Meanwhile, at Llanymynech Hill, overlooking the confluence of the Tanat and the Vyrnwy south-west of Oswestry, there may be an entirely different purpose to the sharp turn. The route chosen for the Dyke here follows the western defences of the Iron Age hillfort, and it is not always easy to distinguish the form of one from the other. However, there is a location (close to the point where the earthwork links southwards onto Asterley Rocks) where a series of segments extends out to a small level area above a near vertical drop westwards and above a narrow defile southwards. Here it turns abruptly at a right-angle where these two drops meet. This angled turn is overlooked by the crag to the south also occupied by the Dyke, so it was possible to look down over it and trace the onward course of the earthwork as it followed the lip of the west-facing scarp northwards.

The purpose of these right-angled turns, as is evident from the discussion of the Rushock Hill and Hergan earthworks presented here, has been much debated. The angled turns are, however, neither 'gang junctions' nor legal imperatives as Fox suggested, nor are they attempts to avoid watercourses and follow watersheds, as Hill and Worthington have claimed in respect to the best-known example at Hergan.[82] Rather, the turns for the most part provide sometimes complex surveillance facilities at key points along the Dyke. In some cases they also provide a striking image when seen from the west, and as such provide a further clue to the importance of the areas where they occur, in reference to the landscape and the people beyond the Dyke to the west.

This can be seen dramatically at the Devil's Pulpit and its neighbouring turns, at the more southerly of the two Hergan turns, and, on a smaller scale, in the case of the feature at Llanymynech Hill that we have just noted. In all these cases, the Dyke suddenly swings out westwards to meet the sharp crest of a westwards-facing spur, and this in effect protrudes each of these features outwards beyond the general line of the Dyke at the point concerned. This phenomenon is nowhere more dramatic than at Cwmsanahan Hill where the outwards turn provides a dramatic prospect over the confluence of the Ffrwdwen Brook and the river Teme at Knucklas.

At this point on Cwmsanahan Hill, the eminence is visible from the approaches from the south, even though they are at a slightly lower altitude, due largely to the steep scarps that drop away westwards here. Although we have described it above as featuring a single right-angled turn, the behaviour of the Dyke at Cwmsanahan Hill is, upon closer scrutiny, considerably more complex. While Fox was concerned to emphasise what he saw as a primary requirement for the Dyke to take in a specific high point on the edge of the south-west trending spur, it can perhaps be better characterised as seeking to occupy every part of the near-vertical south and west facing scarps facing directly down across the 'tremendous gorge of Cwmsanahan' onto the floor of the Teme valley here.[83] On the ground there are in fact a series of abrupt turns here, although only the most northerly turns at fully 90 degrees.

Cyril Fox recorded a rectangular enclosure at this spot, but upon closer

FIGURE 6.10 An angled turn and possible gateway at Hergan

Viewed in opposite directions here, the right-angled turn at Hergan represents more than what Fox saw as a change in construction traditions and an error of linkage of the work of two 'gangs'. Rather, it can be understood as a carefully choreographed configuration of earthworks to achieve maximum visual and tactical effect.

inspection the feature concerned resolves itself instead into a small L-shaped trench with a long side around 5 m long and a short side less than 3 m long. This is intruded into what is otherwise a simple right-angled turn in the earthwork. Beyond the shorter length of ditch here there is a short projecting length of very slight bank parallel with it, and also lying parallel with, but just westwards from, the established line of the Dyke running up the hill from the north. This short parallel bank then turns at a perfect right-angle and runs as a broader bank for some 30 m eastwards along the top of a south-facing rock outcrop (Figure 6.11).

In turn, this bank then swerves abruptly southwards and descends the slope obliquely before turning equally sharply east again where it is evident as a very slight bank running along the top of another south-facing scarp. There does seem to be a possible accompanying ditch here, but if so it is some 15 m lower in elevation, at the base of the scarp that has the bank running along its crest. The scarp may have been cut back to accentuate the height of the 'wall' at this point by exposing the underlying rock.

The elaboration of this Cwmsanahan Hill location must indeed have had much to do with surveillance and visibility. The view back along the Dyke northwards extends to the southern extremity of the Llanfair Hill stretch, above Garbett Hall (Figure 6.1). Meanwhile, looking southwards much of the remaining course above the Teme valley and, south of the valley, the traverse of the landscape made by the Dyke all the way to Hawthorn Hill above the river Lugg is visible. Reciprocally, the Dyke appears as a skyline or otherwise prominent feature as viewed either from the Teme valley or the hills on either side of it westwards.

The angled turn at Pinner's Hole, Knighton, is located where it might have been expected that the Dyke, descending onto the bluff above the river Teme, would have continued down to the right (south) bank of the river. Instead, as it reaches the northern edge of the bluff, it turns abruptly eastwards in 'boundary bank' form and gradually descends the slope before merging with the river scarp. Erosion may have removed it eastwards of this point, but the impact of the turn would again have been such as to render this angled turn visible as a prominent bulwark or bastion as seen southwards from the slopes of Panpunton Hill to the north-west of the town. While no trace of it is evident down the bank to the river Teme here, it seems likely that it once made yet another right-angled turn to cross the river itself at the perpendicular here.

Finally, there is the example of the less sharp turn in the Dyke that nonetheless appears from a distance to be abrupt, north of Spoad on the Clun. Here, the Dyke rises from the lower valley-side in a gentle west-facing convex curve up a steep slope, and then curves in the opposite direction westwards to reach the end of a rise above the valley, where there is a pronounced turn northwards. This created a dramatic multiple effect: firstly, it made the Dyke maximally visible from points in the floodplain below and immediately to the west of the earthwork by keeping it in view; secondly, in occupying a stance running along and over the rise, it also appeared larger than it in fact was; and thirdly, by extending forwards subtly from its general trend in this way, it maximised its surveillance efficacy in overlooking the approach to the Dyke from the west (Figures 1.23 and 9.1).

The incidence of these features has never been mapped systematically. It might be possible to go back through Fox's notebooks to do so, but it is unlikely that his recording programme was carried through sufficiently consistently to have achieved this. There is a sense in which you have to be actively looking for such features, having already established their potential significance, to satisfactorily record them. What the presence of angled turns does reinforce, however, is the sense that the Dyke was very much about being *seen* from the west, particularly through siting and builds that served to dramatise its presence; while at the same time, they facilitated the reciprocal process of active surveillance westwards, and especially over the valley approaches.

Roads, route-ways, and dykes

So far the discussion has focused only upon features directly associated with the Dyke. However, if the Dyke was to operate in a zone of control to any degree successfully, it is plausible to suggest that other elements might have contributed to this process. Roads and route-ways have a particular significance in this regard.

The network of communication: inheritance and maintenance

The Roman road network inherited by British and English people by the eighth century was more extensive than has been appreciated until relatively recently, with many more by-roads and paved connecting ways existing than has previously been envisaged. The extent to which even major routes were maintained, however, is more doubtful. As with dykes, the terms that the Anglo-Saxons themselves used to denote these inherited route-ways varied considerably. In Welsh, the word 'Sarn' tended to be used to denote a major route. Meanwhile, the English registered the presence of roads of this nature using the term 'straet', and occasionally particularly prominent lengths of such existing roads were denoted 'portway'.[84] More specialised terms were used, at least in the later Saxon period, to specify the use of a particular route as an 'army road' or 'herepath', while 'salt-ways' were referred to in the descriptive clauses of charters in areas radiating from such centres as Droitwich.[85]

How these terms embraced tracts of the frontier landscape can be illustrated in reference to Herefordshire. Here, in the area west of Leominster and of Hereford, the road north from Hereford towards Wigmore (the former 'Watling Street West') was labelled the Portway some 3 miles (5 km) north of the city, and within another 5 miles (8 km) passed through Stretford, while another 2 miles (3 km) northwards it passed by 'Street Court'. Meanwhile, the road leading

6 Building and operating the Dyke

FIGURE 6.11 The angled turn at Cwmsanahan Hill, overlooking the Teme valley

The view westwards here is towards the triangulation pillar that stands beyond the small north–south bank. The broader east–west bank extends towards the camera position having turned at a right-angle just to the left of the pillar.

FIGURE 6.12 Indicative plan of the configuration of Offa's Dyke at Cwmsanahan Hill

The plan illustrates something of the complexity of the Dyke and its choreography in a location where it uses the dramatic topography to maximum effect in terms of the surveillance capacity of the location. It also indicates the cumulative impact of the work as viewed from the Teme valley (and in particular from the castle hill at Knucklas).

Figure 6.11 is the view along the Dyke from the uppermost 'B'; Figure 7.9 is the view south-westwards from 'E'.

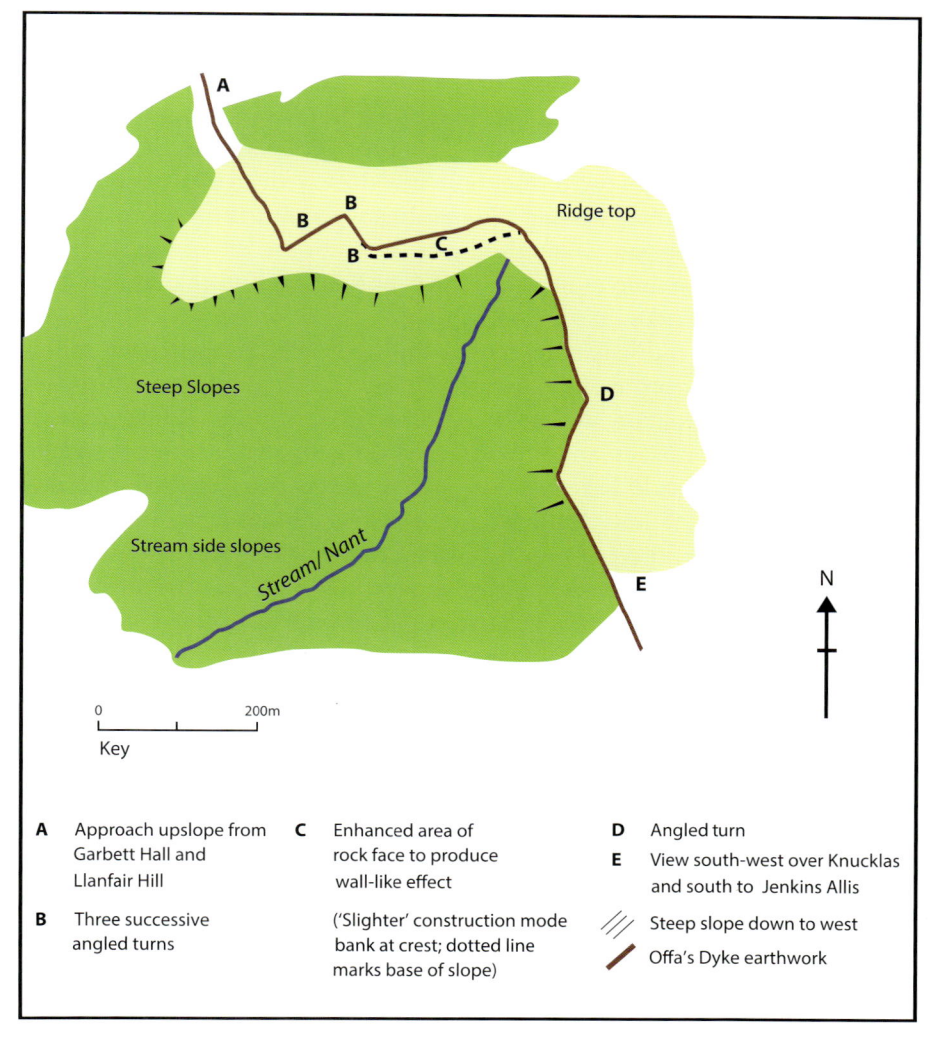

A Approach upslope from Garbett Hall and Llanfair Hill	**C** Enhanced area of rock face to produce wall-like effect	**D** Angled turn
B Three successive angled turns	('Slighter' construction mode bank at crest; dotted line marks base of slope)	**E** View south-west over Knucklas and south to Jenkins Allis
		/// Steep slope down to west
		Offa's Dyke earthwork

west from the former Roman town at Kenchester just to the north-west of Hereford was also termed 'Portway' at a location two miles beyond the point at Garnons where it was bisected obliquely by Offa's Dyke. Meanwhile, the name 'Sarnesfield' not far to the north suggests the existence of yet another road, indicated by the Welsh element 'sarn' (= road) that extended south-westwards from Leominster towards the upper Wye valley. That most of the course of each of these roads remains extensively 'paved' and in use today as significant routes around the west Herefordshire landscape is eloquent enough testimony to the post-Roman continuity of transit paths here, and is yet further evidence to adduce to counter the idea that this landscape was obscured by extensive tracts of forest in the eighth century.[86]

A charter of 958 in King Edgar's reign relating to land at Staunton-on-Arrow is important for its reference to the 'community of the Lene' and apparently to Rowe Ditch.[87] However, it also sheds some rare light for the frontier zone upon other route-ways. It referred, for example, to the 'straet' that passed through that dyke and which formed the boundary of the estate concerned for some distance. It might be safely supposed that this was itself yet another Roman road of at least by-way status, in which case part of the logic of the placement of the dyke across it can readily be understood. However, at least of equal interest is the fact that the road was gated. Not only was there a 'dyke gate', presumably to facilitate (or to inhibit) passage through this work and along the road, but there was also a 'swing-gate' and a third gate. Nor was the 'paved way' the only road or track in the vicinity, since the bounds of the Staunton charter also refer to a 'snaed way' (perhaps, 'back road').

The impression (and it is only that) given by the references to such routes is that several major and many minor paved routes and route-ways continued in use through the period in which Offa's Dyke was in use. While some of these extending north and south, and particularly through south Shropshire and Herefordshire, could have been used as communication routes to the rear of the Dyke, they are not clearly part of a deliberate infrastructure for such support. In contrast, there is much evidence, and not only in Herefordshire, for the existence of east–west routes that in effect traversed (or were intercepted by) the Dyke. This would have facilitated the movement of forces westwards in support of the blocking of opposing forces trying to move eastwards, but argues just as strongly for the 'trade' model of movement already noted.

Other linear works and dykes along the frontier

While the spatial relation of Offa's Dyke to other dykes along the frontier is readily apparent, their place in a relative sequence of construction is less certain. Fox registered the presence of several of these dykes on maps and noted their character in his text, but it was those along the Kerry Ridgeway south of the Vale of Montgomery that he regarded of especial significance to the history of the frontier. Although he understood that 'their construction may have covered

FIGURE 6.13 The Rowe Ditch traversing the Arrow valley in Herefordshire

A typical example of a cross-valley dyke, the Rowe Ditch crosses the valley of the Arrow in two long straight alignments either side of the river. This view is southwards from the likely site of one of the 'gates' mentioned as located upon the 'old dyke' in the bounds of a charter issued in 958 AD.

a considerable period of time', he saw this period as being most likely the century or so of 'local (Mercian) effort at defence and consolidation' from the age of Penda in the mid-seventh century onwards.[88]

A recent field study of the twenty or so 'short dykes' of this and adjoining areas of central Powys has found that these earthworks are more diverse than might otherwise have been supposed.[89] It was not possible, for instance, to define a consistent difference between 'barrier dykes' designed to inhibit movement along a ridge or a valley, and 'boundary dykes' that served to demarcate areas of landscape. While some of the cross-ridge dykes might have served as barriers, they could equally well have simply served to reinforce a boundary largely definable topographically or in reference to watercourses. Lacking the scale of Offa's Dyke in profile as well as length (only three are longer than a mile in extent), some of them even apparently lack a ditch. A model for their interpretation has therefore been put forward which has largely discounted the Fox idea that they were early, pre-Offan works. Rather, in many cases they approximate the *cantref* boundaries with which five linear works at the margins of the territory focused upon Mechain north of the Severn, for example, appear to coincide.[90] As for their date, there was found to be an equally wide range, albeit that they nearly all fell within the 'Anglo-Saxon' period.

This diversity is mirrored by the dykes that exist in Shropshire and Herefordshire. Those in Shropshire to the west of Offa's Dyke are largely similar to those that have been studied in similar topographical locations in Powys, while those on or near the Long Mynd have been dated to the Bronze Age.[91] In north Herefordshire, the only definite dyke other than Rowe Ditch is the Birtley Dyke, a short length of east–west bank less than half a mile in extent with a ditch along at least part of its southern flank. Of the two east–west oriented linear earthworks at Hereford denoted 'Row Ditch' and comprising a substantial bank with a ditch along their south-facing flanks, the one on the right (south) bank of the Wye that defines the southern side of the enclosure surrounding Hereford has now been firmly dated to the mid-eleventh century. The other, located in contrast on the left (north) bank of the Wye is the longer of the two, extending nearly half a mile across a southwards-trending loop of the river. This dyke is located along a terrace facing the river, but also has the effect of cutting off access northwards into the valley of the Eign Brook. It remains undated, but could plausibly also be considered to be a work associated specifically with the late Saxon defences of Hereford.[92]

South of Hereford, Fox examined another east–west and south-facing dyke that survives in remarkably good condition to the east of the Wye south of Fownhope. This dyke, at Perrystone, would have bisected any route-way tracing a line along the hilly country overlooking the river Wye from the east. This is just the area that Noble and others have insisted must have been the location of the 'Dunsaete', an apparently hybrid group that lived either side a major river that has been assumed to have been the Wye. Meanwhile, to the north in Cheshire Wat's Dyke is complemented by various linear works, all of which have been ascribed to medieval or later boundaries. Those on Ruabon Mountain recently thought to be the equivalent of the dykes of the Kerry area and southwards have now been discounted as features associated with post-medieval mining activities.[93]

In summary, then, there is little to commend a view that other linear earthworks in the frontier zone either in what might be considered to be British- or English-dominated areas to the west or to the east of Offa's Dyke served somehow to reinforce the Dyke. This is not to say that at a certain point or points in time, some of them could not have served to do so. However, there is no indication that a number of these short earthworks could have in some way have 'backed up' the Dyke, still less to have served as meaningful precursors of the great work.

Strongholds, look-out points and potential surveillance works

Strongholds

So far, there is no indication from archaeology that any fortresses of the kind mentioned in the charters of Aethelbald or his successors existed in the vicinity of the Dyke. Some of the nineteenth-century commentators, as we have seen being 'military men', supposed that a military infrastructure must have existed. It would certainly be curious if, with the repeated mention of the building of fortresses in the charters of Offa and Coenwulf noted above, none were constructed in the strongly contested landscapes of the western frontier. However, it was not until the late twentieth century that attempts were made to locate earthworks and other features that might constitute such sites.

The most obvious 'candidate' sites for strongholds are the various hillforts and other apparently later prehistoric enclosures that exist on or close to the line of the Dyke. These were assiduously listed by Fox at the end of each season of fieldwork, but none had then, or have yet, yielded any indication of likely re-use in the eighth century, or indeed in any post-Roman context. At Llanymynech Hill where Offa's Dyke is clearly constructed over the defences of the prehistoric enclosure, for instance, it is clear that the primary concern of the builders was to place the linear earthwork as close to the edge of the scarp as feasible, whatever the disposition of the fort banks and ditches.

6 Building and operating the Dyke

However, Fox did single out one enclosure for special consideration, as a later prehistoric site that may have been remodelled in the manner of the Dyke-builders. This was Caer Din, an embanked and ditched fort occupying a hilltop overlooking the Dyke in the Vale of Montgomery from a vantage point at 400 metres above sea level immediately to the north of the Kerry Ridgeway and only half a mile to the east of the Dyke where it gains the ridge at Crowsnest. This enclosure was thought by Fox to be unusual because 'in plan it tends to be polygonal with rounded angles; in other words, its defences seem in part to have been designed in straight stretches.'[94] Moreover, 'the deep trackway which passes across the enclosure, utilising the original openings, suggests that when it was occupied a good deal of the ridgeway traffic was deflected in order to pass through it.'[95] While there is no doubt that Caer Din occupies a prominent and strategic location, the arguments presented by Fox for considering it a candidate Mercian (re)fortification are somewhat thin, given that the 'straight sections', while present, do not define the enclosure sides that they form part of, and that unlike known Middle to Late Anglo-Saxon fortress works it is in no sense rectilinear.[96]

The one instance of the Dyke apparently having been built deliberately below an Iron Age hillfort is also of some considerable interest, since it does

FIGURE 6.14 Burfa Camp and the course of Offa's Dyke from Herrock Hill

The view here takes in the descent of the Dyke from Evenjobb Hill (left-centre horizon) to the foot of Burfa Hill. The earthwork sited around the steep slope of Herrock Hill in the foreground, although slight, is very prominent as seen from the valley below. An earthwork 'beacon' on the top of this hill could be part of the 'surveillance infrastructure' supporting the Dyke throughout much, or all, of its course.

perhaps increase the possibility that there was a purposeful attempt here at least to incorporate such a pre-existing feature within the defensive scheme. This is at Burfa Camp above the Hindwell Brook/Riddings Brook confluence on the parish boundary between Knill in Herefordshire and Evenjobb in Radnorshire. Burfa Camp occupies the crest of a steep-sided hill aligned due east and west, and although the earthworks of the fort are not well understood, there is at least a hint that the defences at the western end, above the slope around the base of which the Dyke runs, might have undergone some modification. The elongated plan of the fort is such that it overlooks the narrow 'exit' of these streams through a gap in the hills, and looks directly southwards down upon the projecting spur of land overlooking the river, upon which Knill church stands. It was noted above that the Dyke traverses the valley here at the perpendicular to both streams, above and to the west of their confluence. The earthwork then climbs in an unusually direct fashion in a straight alignment up a very steep incline to gain the crest of an eastwards-trending spur that descends into the valley in the direction of Knill.

A sub-rectangular moated enclosure at Court Farm (Cwrt Llechrhyd), Llanelwedd, close to the river Wye near Builth Wells has a defended perimeter of bank and ditch extending to 660 metres. Excavation of a section through its defences produced a possible construction date of the late ninth to late tenth century.[97] This prompted speculation that its regular form and substantial dimensions could be taken to indicate that it may have been built as a fortress in response to the prior existence of Mercian forts along the line of Offa's Dyke.[98] Two closely similar, but somewhat smaller, rectilinear moated enclosures have been noted also just to the west of Welshpool, at Mathrafal near Meifod at the confluence of the rivers Banwy and Vyrnwy, and at Plas-yn-Dinas just to the south of Llansantffraid-ym-Mechain near Llanymynech, which is located on a low bluff in a former loop of the Vyrnwy, and features a rectilinear enclosure of which only parts of the bank and ditch survive on its western and southern sides. The enclosure at Mathrafal has since been demonstrated to have been an entirely post-Norman creation, probably of the thirteenth century.[99]

The suggestion has also been made that three other less well preserved defended sites of somewhat more varied form but that are closely grouped on or close to Offa's Dyke just might represent Mercian forts occupying key strategic locations.[100] One of these, Nantcribba Gaer, ostensibly has little to commend it as a Mercian fortification, given its sub-circular form; although its location on a prominent ridge only 200 m east of the Dyke at Forden would make it a good look-out point.[101] A rectilinear enclosure site at Buttington is mostly known from early observations of earthworks around and to the south of the church, and is difficult to assess adequately now. The *Anglo-Saxon Chronicle* reference to an Anglo-Welsh force besieging a Danish army here in 893 indicates the existence then of a fortification, but its origins are uncertain.[102] The moated enclosure at Old Mills, Trewern, faces the important Gorther Ford on the Severn in just that stretch in which the Dyke is absent, below the steep west-facing slopes of the Breiddin, but its form is indeterminate and the results of excavations here ambiguous.[103] A fourth site, again noted as being adjacent to areas of English settlement, is New Radnor. That these sites form a coherent group of 'forts' of later first millennium date nonetheless has to be considered highly unlikely.

Where does this leave us in reference to the idea of fortifications in the frontier zone? That Mercian fortresses existed is undoubted, given the number of charter references to the requirement to build them. That there was a 'network' of these forts is far less certain.[104] It is perhaps possible to suggest an alternative, that rather than seeing a system geared to the fixed production of particular types of enclosure, the kinds of work to be constructed could have been matched to the circumstances concerned. In one context, the 'fortress' might have been a defended boundary circuit around a minster; in another it could have involved the refortification of a defensible position, as in the case perhaps of some hillforts. Only rarely, as in all probability in the case of a place like Hereford, it might have involved building a four-sided enclosure, perhaps in that place at the same time as the cathedral for the see of Hereford was first built.

The term 'fortress' may have referred to sites that have not so far been understood to constitute defended locations at all. An example might be a stockaded or palisaded area, as has been recorded archaeologically at Sutton north of Hereford. At any rate, Gelling's work has served the useful purpose of drawing attention to the relative concentration of place-names in or close to the Mercian frontier zone of the west, which may in some cases denote a fortified place. This becomes more significant in reference to the place-names that still occur along the frontier. As such, they will be discussed in detail in the chapter after this one; in the meantime, it is worth looking at some of the features in the landscape that may indicate the presence of more minor facilities.

'Look-out posts': some possibilities

The placing of the Dyke in the landscape itself provides clues as to how surveillance was a key part of the way in which the Dyke was designed to work, as was noted when discussing the prospects from it, along it, and over it from the east in Chapter 4. Offa's Dyke was frequently positioned in the landscape in such a way that it could be viewed extending across tracts of landscape, and in this respect it mirrored the way that at least the central section of Hadrian's Wall could also be observed from different points along its course.

Some particular features have been identified as locations that could have served as observation points. For example, as noted above Cyril Fox observed that at Cwmsanahan 'at the right-angle by spot-level 1343 – a remarkable alignment – the bank is broadened and then hollowed out to make a little three-side enclosure, 3 × 6 ft., like a watchman's post'.[105] The rectangular earthwork here could indeed have served such a purpose, not least because, although Fox also noted that it 'is about 25 yards from the edge of the plateau and does not command the valley', there is a prominent spine of rock running for some 30m westwards from the angled turn. From the end of this spine, upon which is set an Ordnance Survey triangulation pillar, the prospect is panoptic.[106]

Meanwhile, at Bwlch by Discoed, west of Presteigne in the Lugg valley in Radnorshire, at mid-slope from the hill crest east of Pen Offa, and just before the Dyke in its northwards course meets the likely 'gateway' by the Kinnerton to Presteigne ridge-top road, it traverses an east–west linear 'bench' or band of more resistant rock. Immediately to the east at this point, there is a broad level sub-rectangular terrace-like area around 40 metres in east–west extent by 20 metres north–south extent. It is evident that this level area to the east of the Dyke at this point contrasts with the more continual slope westwards of the Dyke.[107]

Although there is no obvious earthwork trace of any former structure on this level 'terrace', an observation post or timber tower located here would have directly overlooked the Bwlch 'gateway' immediately below it to the north. Moreover, the course of the Dyke remains in view beyond the 'gateway' and is very evident as it passes over the shoulder of land northwards down towards the Lugg valley. The elevation of this 'look-out' place is such that beyond this shoulder of land in the near distance, the Dyke can be seen climbing the south-facing side of the Lugg valley up Furrow Hill and can then be traced even today making its way across Hawthorn Hill and Hengwm Hill before crossing Cwm-Whitton Hill to begin its descent towards the Teme valley at Knighton, through Rhos-y-meirch and Ffrydd. This possible 'look-out' place at Bwlch, therefore, would have provided a facility that both overlooked and presumably in effect guarded the 'gateway' where the ancient ridge-way track was diverted to pass through the latter. Beyond that, its elevated position also afforded a more extensive prospect across the four miles of landscape to the northern horizon.

The complexity of such possible arrangements for oversight using purpose-built platforms is reinforced by observation of the earthworks just half a mile to the north near Yew Tree Farm and directly adjacent to the Cascob to Presteigne road to the west of Discoed village. The configuration of bank lengths southwards above this point as they traverse the north-facing slope, with lengths and segments deliberately angled towards the valley-bottom, raises the possibility that there was once a gateway through the Dyke in the valley here. Whether or not this was the case (and unlike at Bwlch, there is no marked deviation of the line of the bank as it approaches this road), there is a feature to the east of the Dyke that comprises again a level platform, onto which the bank of the Dyke extends after it has descended the slope and before continuing on the other (north) side of the road. This level area provides clear oversight across the floor of the Lugg valley and along the line of the Dyke as it makes its traverse of the floodplain.

Neither of the 'candidate' look-out platforms at Discoed has been examined through excavation. In contrast, another location suggested for such a

6 Building and operating the Dyke

platform, at Buttington Tump near Sedbury at the southern end of the Dyke in Gloucestershire, has been examined.[108] Here, the 'tump' is located directly adjacent to the spinal road that bisects the Beachley peninsula, and would have provided views in all directions over the confluence between the Severn and the Wye. It appears from the account of the excavation here, that the bank was deliberately widened to create a platform.

Fortified watch-towers?

The site at Nantcribba Gaer mentioned above, may, as was supposed there, have nothing to do with the Dyke. Its proximity to the rear of the earthwork does, however, raise an interesting possibility: not in isolation, but rather in reference to a number of small enclosed sites that, although undated, share this proximity. A prominent example survives as an earthwork, and is located on the south-east facing flank of the hill north of Garbett Hall and south of Llanfair Hill. Hartshorne observed this to be: 'a small pentagonal camp … on the summit of Llan-du'. The enclosure comprises five approximately equal lengths of bank and ditch, which form might be significant in light of the observations Fox made about Caer Din just to the north. Its proximity to the Dyke is very evident from the air today (Figure 6.15), and another feature of

FIGURE 6.15 The Dyke north of Garbett Hall, with a small 'fort'/watchtower

The five-sided embanked enclosure visible here at centre-left may be the site of an Iron Age or Romano-British farmstead. However, its shape is unusual and its location on a prominent hilltop just to the east of Offa's Dyke may not be coincidental.

PHOTOGRAPH COURTESY OF A. WIGLEY: COPYRIGHT SHROPSHIRE COUNCIL.

the location of this small enclosure is also interesting. This is not so much for its view of the Dyke, which is limited, as much as that it has a view eastwards, down along the Redlake valley, across to Caer Caradoc and towards the Teme valley near Bucknell, and southwards towards the Teme above Knighton.[109] If there were to have been a watch-tower here, the indication is that it was placed to communicate *back*, to locations well behind the linear earthwork to the east. Another small enclosure recorded as a crop-mark is located in a closely similar topographical position and close to the Dyke, just five miles (8.0 km) north of the 'Garbett Hall' work, across the Clun valley, on the flank of Edenhope Hill.

An extremely small ditched feature is also located just within the line of the Dyke, in this case as it circumnavigates the south side of Herrock Hill. This sub-circular ditched feature is less than 20 m in diameter, and stands on the very summit of the hill, well above the line of the Dyke that circles the hill. This might be the site of a historically-recent beacon, but it is also curious in that it also has a multangular form comprising a series of straights lengths of ditch.

Further investigation is needed to elucidate these features fully, and it would be premature to build too much upon such a slim base without any corroborating information from close archaeological investigation. However, it seems at least possible that what they represent is points of fortified surveillance. The suggestion of a 'surveillance infrastructure' for the Dyke overall, whether in the form of gateways and related oversight facilities, the location and nature of angled-turns, or of look-out places or watch-towers nevertheless does indicate that debate and investigation of these matters is far from concluded.

The use of the Dyke: a beginning rather than an end

One possibility that we have not so far mentioned is that the search for any form of infrastructure, elaborate or otherwise, would be futile if Offa's Dyke was never designed to be 'used' as such. That it did not have a protracted 'use-life' would seem to be underscored, for instance, by the apparent lack of substantive evidence for the re-cutting of individual ditch lengths. The extended treatment given above to the possible existence of features facilitating surveillance need not, however, be predicated upon the idea that the Dyke was in fact maintained and used as a patrolled work in the same way that Hadrian's Wall has widely been supposed to have been used.

Again, therefore, the question needs to be addressed as to the purpose served by the building of the Dyke, but to do so more explicitly in the context of the 'point in time' rationale of that act of creation, whatever else the great earthwork came subsequently to symbolise. One simple answer is to suggest that in common with such grandiose works built at various places across Europe and Asia at this time, the Dyke was created more for the action of doing it (to prove the ruler could) than for any longer-term aim.[110] While it can be accepted that this was at least partially true in respect of Offa's Dyke, more important perhaps was the development of a long-term strategy for Mercian political domination

FIGURE 6.16 An array of construction devices at Madgett Hill, Gloucestershire

The ascent/descent of the north-facing slopes here constitutes one of the most remarkable series of deployments of build devices (shared with other parts of the long-distance linear earthwork) anywhere on Offa's Dyke. This view westwards along part of the Dyke running along the upper mid-slope not only features this angled turn (to the right), but also some 200 m west of this point, an extraordinary 'bastioned' extrusion of the bank projecting outwards above the valley at another angled turn southwards.

in Wales that the building of the Dyke as an act of appropriation may have made possible. A strategy that witnessed a more direct pattern of intervention deep into the west was arguably already underway with Offa's campaigns into the south-west. In this light the campaigns of Coenwulf in the north and those of subsequent Mercian and West Saxon armies elsewhere represented the further unfolding of such a strategy.[111]

Although Offa's Dyke was apparently not maintained for long, it does not mean that it was redundant soon after its construction. Part of the expectation that we should find evidence of palisades, wall-walks, and so on derives from the idea that the Dyke not only marked, but in some ways *was* the frontier. Frank Noble long ago challenged the assumptions behind such a view, and suggested that we should instead seek to understand the Dyke as one feature, albeit the primary one, of the frontier as a whole. In pursuit of this suggestion, the next chapter is devoted in large measure to just such an enquiry.

PART THREE
THE CONTEXT RE-APPRAISED

Offa's Dyke from the air, view north towards Montgomery (Trefaldwyn)

The Dyke ran, according to Leland c. 1538, "by the space of a ii. miles almost in the middle way betwixt Bisshops Castell and Montgomery". Seen here from the south-east, it bisects the Vale of Montgomery, following a course between the Caebitra and Camlad streams. The 'stance' of the Dyke clearly faces the block of upland surmounted by the early fort at Ffridd Faldwyn (left centre). Upper and Lower Gwarthlow farms are visible at lower right, Dudston Fields at right-centre, and the site of the later timber castle at Hen Domen, and the Severn valley, are at upper left and centre, with the Berwyns mountain range in the distance. Photograph courtesy of Toby Driver. © Herefordshire Council.

CHAPTER SEVEN

In a frontier landscape

> If Offa's Dyke is a brilliant form of political display meant to remind all concerned of its maker's might, then we need to adjust our accounts of the Anglo-Saxon landscape to include the ways it embodied and manifested a political sense of place.
>
> Nicholas Howe, *Writing the Map of Anglo-Saxon England*, 2008 [1]

This statement appears in the introduction to a volume that advocated a new understanding of the landscape as perceived by the Anglo-Saxons through their own words, in literature. The question it draws our attention to is, how did the Dyke 'embody and manifest' a character of place that was specifically *political*, in the sense that it encapsulated relationships between peoples across a frontier? There are several answers to this question. One is, as described in the final chapter of this book, how this 'brilliant form of political display' represented the workings of hegemony at the level of inter-kingdom and international politics. Another, and more immediate, answer concerns the 'frontier landscape' itself: and this is the subject of the present chapter.

In characterising the placement of the Dyke in the landscape (in Chapter 4) we suggested that it may have existed in reference to a wider corridor of landscape rather than constituting a simple and singular line. It was also created within a landscape of settlement, both British and Anglo-Saxon, as Frank Noble showed. There may be enough clues to indicate that there were both similarities and differences as to the land-holding, defensive and other arrangements, and as to the physical 'depth' of the frontier zone, in different parts of the landscape north and south along the line of the Dyke. That there appear sometimes to have been correlations between different political dispensations and the form and even the presence of the Dyke in some key locations is also of some interest, but we must always be aware of the same kind of circularity of argument that Fox entered into here. Beyond an immediate landscape of settlement close to the Dyke, it should be asked to what extent the Mercian heartlands were connected with, and were implicated in, the existence of the Dyke. It is for instance plausible that contributions at least to the northern lengths of the earthwork were co-ordinated through this core, centrally located, region.

The course that Offa's Dyke follows locates a frontier for which the linear earthwork was no doubt the defining, but perhaps not the only, element. The frontier was more than a hundred miles in length and did not exist within an undifferentiated space throughout this distance, either topographically or indeed politically and culturally. Rather than comprising one homogenous zone occupied by the Mercian frontiers-people and by their British neighbours, this huge tract of landscape comprised more a series of contiguous zones in the north, the centre and the south. From this perspective, we think that it is difficult to argue that the political and cultural complexities of the frontier can be envisaged as a simple confrontation between the kingdoms of Powys and of Mercia, as if these were internally homogenous entities, and as if this particular political fault-line somehow defined the entire frontier. Rather, the frontier was a dynamic entity, spanning different regions with different histories and contrasting relations, both east–west and north–south.

In thinking about how the frontier was constituted, then, there are several pertinent questions that can be posed. For example, at a general level of enquiry, what was the character of English settlement of the area? How can we recognise the existence and nature of 'political places'? Another question that it is worth posing at the outset is, 'how much do we really know about the frontier zone in terms for instance of the prevalent (eighth-century) land-use'?

The eighth-century landscape and Offa's Dyke

Offa's Dyke recurrently crossed river-valleys and traversed steep slopes, and would have passed through landscapes that presented contrasts in soils and aspect. Fox was right to suggest that such physical contrasts offered varied opportunities for settlement. However, the ways in which different peoples and communities inhabited these landscapes was not merely a rational response to such opportunities either as if there had been no history of settlement already manifest in those places by the later first millennium AD; or as if there was not a cultural history of practice and expectation that, for example, the Mercian settlers brought with them. In each area, therefore, it will never be sufficient to try to define 'the environment' as though this might simply match 'an economy' which developed to maximise the productive capacity of the land. Rather, the extent of pasture, woodland, and arable, and the way in which these changed from decade to decade, and how other resources were exploited, would have varied locally in subtle ways according to inherited cultural patterns and practices and contemporary choices.

Land-use and the vegetation record

It may therefore be a vain exercise to try to portray 'the eighth-century landscape' in any unified way. However, there are already patterns that are beginning to emerge at a national scale, and from the evidence of individual locales. There is, for instance, evidence for an increase in the productive capacity of the land across Anglo-Saxon England from the eighth into the ninth centuries, whether this involved intensification of pasturing in the South-West, or wheat-growing in East Anglia and the East Midlands.² It has been suggested that such increases in the productive capacity of the land were accompanied by (or indeed may have been made possible by) a 'replanning' of the landscape at this time.³ Although the evidence remains somewhat thin, the intensification of land-use which is attested at a number of localities across England does suggest that population was growing and that settlement, too, was becoming denser and more closely organised: at least in some areas.

This has particular relevance both to the likely intensity of colonisation of those areas of the British west that had been newly absorbed into Mercia as well as into Wessex, and to the probability of yet stronger eventual British challenges to the westwards-expanding sphere of English settlement, rather than simply of political influence. The availability of newly-colonised land in both Wessex and Mercia may in part be registered also in both kingdoms, and among other things, by an increase through the eighth century in the frequency with which lands were granted by the relevant kings both to retainers and to clergy for the founding of monasteries. These were often in lands close to, but lying just behind (that is, eastwards from), the frontier zone: as witnessed by the West Saxon King Aethelheard's grant of 20 hides of land at Crediton in Devon to Forthhere, bishop of Sherborne, *c.*739, or Aethelbald's grant of land at Acton Beauchamp (nowadays in eastern Herefordshire) to his *comes*, Buca, in 718.⁴

It is at present almost impossible to reconstruct the eighth-century landscape along the frontier from the usual sources for vegetation history, because, perhaps surprisingly, so little relevant information has so far emerged from pollen analysis or other work on early environments anywhere in the surrounding landscape.⁵ It may therefore be misleading to extrapolate from the few samples currently available, to attempt to deduce a wider pattern. One sequence that has been studied in a location less than ten miles away from the Dyke is that obtained from Crose Mere, Kenwick, in Shropshire, eight miles (14 km) to the east of Oswestry near Ellesmere. Here, a sample dated within the period 250–610 AD (most likely therefore representing the situation in an early post-Roman context) produced evidence of the presence of more than 50% woody species, but also a localised decline in hazel and the growing of cereals nearby.⁶ The high percentage of oak suggests woodland regeneration, and this is mirrored at Lindow Moss in north Cheshire, where heather was being replaced by oak and hazel woodland in the same period. This suggests that the long-held impression that there was re-growth of woodland in the immediate post-Roman period may hold true, at least to some extent and in some places.⁷

What is also interesting about the Crose Mere sequence is what followed immediately after this period of apparent woodland regeneration. The samples bracketed beneath a horizon dated 790–1160 AD are marked by the presence of high levels of *Cannabaceae* pollen, probably hemp. This abundance has been taken to imply hemp-retting on the banks of the mere rather than simply hemp growing nearby, but its wider implication is that there was a more intensive

FIGURE 7.1 Offa's Dyke north of Trefonen, from the east

The natural lake at Crose Mere, south of Ellesmere, lies just over nine miles (15 km) due east from this location south-west of Oswestry, in a gently undulating lowland landscape. The dated vegetation sequence at Crose Mere suggests that there was an intensification of arable farming and possibly some specialisation in crop cultivation, probably during the eighth century AD.

PHOTOGRAPH: ADAM STANFORD/ AERIAL-CAM, COPYRIGHT RESERVED.

exploitation of the local landscape in just that period during which the Dyke was built.[8]

Interpreting the form of Offa's Dyke as a 'register' of land-use

As noted above, Cyril Fox categorised the alignments that are a feature of the placement of the linear earthwork in the landscape to show how carefully planned the earthwork was. What is of particular interest here, however, is how he used this classification to attempt a reconstruction of the whole eighth-century landscape that the earthwork traversed. He related the pattern of the different kinds of alignments he traced to topography, to geology and soils, to place-names and to variations in the form of the earthwork, and his creative use of this evidence needs therefore to be reviewed here. In brief, his thesis was that straight alignments occurred in what, in the eighth century, were parts of the landscape that were naturally lightly vegetated, or that were grazed pastures, or that had been cleared and cultivated. According to Fox, in such locations the Dyke was built mostly in 'normal' or 'major' forms (our *substantial* or *monumental* modes). Meanwhile, Fox also thought that more sinuous lengths of the Dyke had been built in woodland, and were accordingly of 'boundary bank' form (our *slighter* mode).

The way in which Fox made his inferences about early landscape from the form of the Dyke is clear from his account of the course of the Dyke at Discoed, on the north-facing slopes overlooking the Lugg valley from the south:

> Between the 800- and 900-ft. contours the earthwork is well wooded and its fine scale is maintained; the views to the W. are magnificent. The slope now is at its steepest, the Dyke diminishes in size and becomes sinuous, retaining at first its W. ditch. From the *a* of Off*a* (on the accompanying annotated Ordnance Survey map extract) onwards to the crest of the Newcastle Hill spur, where the Dyke changes direction, and thence, on the level, to the road by Bwlch, it is a mere hedge-bank, and no W. ditch is apparent, but there are spoil holes on the E. side....

There can be little doubt but that the transition from the major to the minor scale here, associated with a change from straightness to irregularity, has a physiographic origin; *the slope was open uncultivated country, the hill-top was forest* (emphasis added).[9]

Despite the categorical certainty expressed by Fox, how far the inference from Dyke form to landscape conditions can be sustained is open to question. At Discoed it is just as plausible to argue that the manifest change in topography was itself a determinant factor, or that there was a deliberate design reason to explain why the Dyke changed its character at this point. So from the valley floor to the west and north-west the earthwork is less visible as it moves from 900-ft contour upwards, and yet from further away this upper part of the course of the Dyke appears prominently as a sky-line feature. To create an impression of continuing large scale of the Dyke in this upper stretch it was therefore only necessary to scarp the hillside and build a slight bank. Frank Noble moreover pointed out the irrationality of supposing the cultivation (or at least clearance) of north-facing upland slopes while south-facing slopes in several places (including on the opposite side of the Lugg valley here) would have been left as woodland.

Just to the north, at Jenkins Allis south of Knighton, there is a situation where the change in build form from the *slighter* mode to the *substantial* mode is so abrupt as to appear strongly to support Fox's interpretation. This occurs as the Dyke approaches up a slope from the north at a modest scale and meets head-on a length of earthwork proceeding along level hilltop ground from the

FIGURE 7.2 The junction of *slighter* and *substantial* mode builds at Jenkins Allis

This point of transition in the form of the Dyke south of Knighton is of sufficient abruptness and contrast to be visible on the aerial photograph, Figure 2.3, above.

south as an altogether more impressive work. A movement from woodland (on the slopes to the north) to open country (along the top of the spur southwards) and the crossing of a tenurial and land-use boundary seems, at least superficially, to offer a feasible explanation for this sudden transition. One problem with such a view is that this abrupt change in form would also make sense in terms of the meeting of two gangs building the Dyke according to differing practice, and from opposite directions, as Fox postulated in similar circumstances elsewhere. Meanwhile, an equally viable explanation concerns the application of the 'economy of effort' principle. It is just at this point that, if regarded as moving southwards, the Dyke attains an elevation where it is clearly visible from land of equivalent height to the west. It is arguably therefore only from this point southwards that there is a need for an earthwork that impresses when seen from the west from relatively close range.

Fox's arguments concerning how the Dyke could be 'read' to reconstruct the eighth-century landscape first appeared in the chapter of his monograph that described the course of the earthwork through East Montgomeryshire. Here he claimed that a series of minor localised deviations from the main course of the alignment of the Dyke to the south-east of Montgomery town was due to the presence of a pre-existing wooded landscape through which it was difficult to make clear sightings. Yet the straight sections across the rivers at either end of these more 'meandering' Vale of Montgomery sections between them are more apparent than real. The arrow-straight course of the Dyke across both the Camlad and the Caebitra streams is arguably a product of later land-use, since the Dyke itself is no longer visible here today, submerged as it is within the silts of the alluviated valleys concerned. Its line across each valley-floor is therefore marked by straight enclosure-period hedge-lines in each case, giving a false impression of its original straightness.[10]

Having noted the way in which the straight sections of Dyke alternated with more meandering lengths, Fox felt able to apply his analysis of the form and 'physiographic' location of the Dyke as a register of the character (cultivated or open versus uncultivated or wooded) of the eighth-century landscape to its course from the Caebitra Brook near Montgomery southwards to Rushock Hill in north Herefordshire in his 'mountain zone'. This was mapped in such a way as to identify alignments of 'Type I' as marking areas that 'were probably arable fields or meadows in the eighth century' (Figure 7.3).[11]

Fox was not always consistent in the way that he 'detected' these contrasts, and he must surely have been aware of the dangers of circularity in his argument. The claim that it is the presence of straight alignments of the Dyke itself that indicates the former presence of 'cleared areas', and correspondingly that the presence of less carefully and more sinuously laid out sections indicates that it was laid out here in woodland cannot be disproved as such, because once the correlation has been set up the interpretive 'loop' is closed.

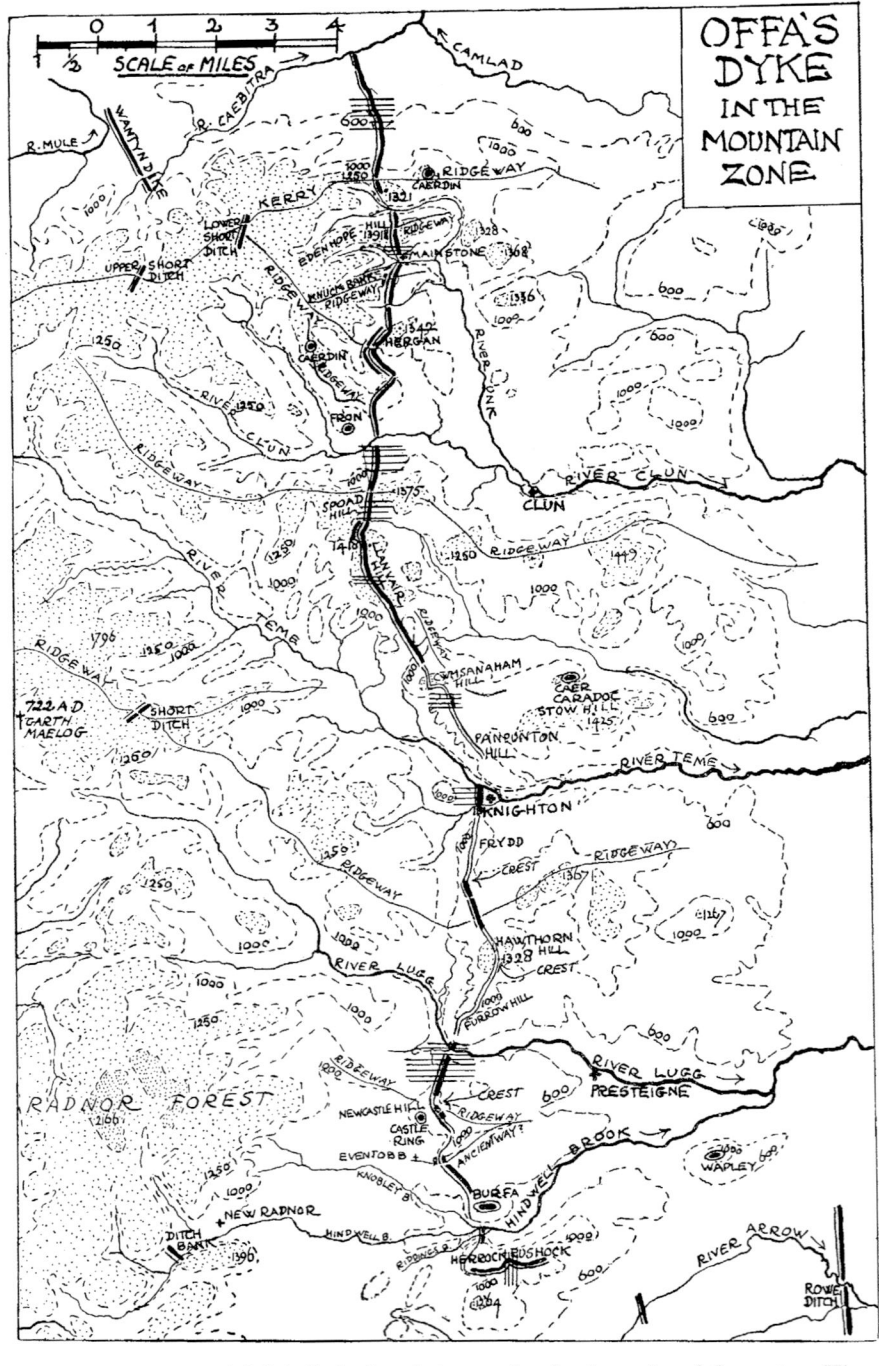

260 *Offa's Dyke: Landscape and Hegemony in Eighth-Century Britain*

FIG. 69. Structure of Offa's Dyke in relation to the physiography of the region. The more important hill forts, ridgeways, and the Short Ditches within the area are also shown.

Symbols: ‖ = Normal Dyke with W. ditch.   ‖ = Weak Dyke with E. ditch.
‖ = Reinforced Dyke with W. ditch. | = Dyke on a steep hill-side where no distinction between types is possible.   ≡ = Alignments of Type I (these areas were probably arable fields or meadows in the eighth century).

FIGURE 7.3 Fox's 'reading' of contemporary land-use from the form of the Dyke

The linkage between 'straight alignments' and open farmed land led to the doubtful conclusion that contemporary farmed landscapes of arable or pasture were prevalent on steep north-facing slopes and areas of high elevation.

REPRODUCED COURTESY OF THE CAMBRIAN ARCHAEOLOGICAL ASSOCIATION. COPYRIGHT RESERVED

The landscape under *the Dyke*

Meanwhile, Fox was also aware that there might be some potential to determine the original land-use from soils buried beneath the bank, as at his section cut at Court House, Forden.[12] Such preserved old land surfaces or buried soils have been found at a number of locations more recently where the ground sealed by the bank has been examined. However, samples taken from these deposits failed to produce useful results. An example was the machine-dug section through the bank at Home Farm, Chirk Castle, where 'The exposed section revealed a buried soil *c.*4cm thick underlying the bank, a sample of which produced no environmental or dating evidence after flotation (of retrieved samples, to separate out organic material)'.[13]

In other cases, such deposits have been dated to much earlier times, or contain material derived from earlier deposits and do not provide clear indications of the conditions prevailing in the eighth century. A case in point was the excavations in 1990 at Sunny Bank, Ffrith, near Treuddyn, where a promising 12-centimetre thick 'dark grey silt' layer was found to contain sherds of 2nd century AD Roman pottery.[14] Part of the problem in both these cases, as with most of the 'Offa's Dyke Project' excavations, was the narrowness of excavated sections through the bank. However, even at a site such as the recent (2006) excavations of a length of Wat's Dyke near Gobowen, where an extensive 'old land surface' deposit was found underneath a length of the bank, no suitable organic material to reconstruct land-use from pollen or plant remains could be retrieved.[15]

The length of Offa's Dyke at Dudston Fields, Chirbury (situated close to Montgomery) has already been discussed in this book in reference to the complexities of its build. In December 1985, aerial archaeological surveyor Chris Musson photographed this location from the air and noted the survival of earthwork traces of the selions (furlongs or ploughland strips) and headlands of a medieval open-field system that was situated on either side of the Dyke here. Given that it appeared that there might be some correlation of the orientation of the cultivation furrows from one side to the other of the Dyke the question he raised was which came first, the field system or the Dyke? The survey conducted by Royal Commission on Historic Monuments (England) field archaeological surveyors, led by Paul Everson, which we have already noted the results of (Figure 5.22), sought to establish with greater clarity the relationship between these various features.[16]

The survey was considered by those who undertook it to have demonstrated that all the slight features on either side of the Dyke here were demonstrably created *after* the great linear earthwork was in place. These features included a 'pendant enclosure' on the eastern side of the Dyke that it had been suggested might be contemporary with it. At least one track-way and another historically-recent field boundary clearly crossed the bank and ditch from west to east, and contrasts in the preservation of the bank in particular were thought to be the result of differences in land-use affecting different land parcels at different times.[17] Philip Barker, who had examined the Musson photographs and had postulated the imposition of the Dyke over an eighth-century open-field landscape here, accepted the conclusion that the selions turned before they met either ditch from the west or bank from the east. However, he questioned whether this necessarily meant that the field system overall post-dated the Dyke, suggesting instead that while the strips pre-existed its construction, they could have continued as arable thereafter, such that what is evident today is their adjustment to the newly redefined landscape.[18]

This latter interpretation was, Barker claimed, in accord with the results of his excavations at the Hen Domen motte and bailey only some three miles (5 km) to the north-west, and with subsequent aerial photography, also by Chris Musson. At Hen Domen, Barker had been able to demonstrate that the bailey bank had been built over pre-existing ridge and furrow, indicating that this field system was in place before the early twelfth-century construction of that enclosure. Musson's aerial photographs of Hen Domen showed the later ridge and furrow making a change of orientation to 'swerve' around the bailey ditch, as if the latter had caused the ridge and furrow to be reconfigured after the earthwork castle had been built. Barker's main point was that only excavation could prove the case one way or another. Whether the field system was 'pre-Offan' or not is clearly of considerable interest in reference to Fox's interpretation that the Dyke was built within what he termed 'low-level woodland' here, rather than open cultivated land.[19]

All the above may caution us not to take too simplistic a view of, for instance, the contrast between farmland and woodland in the eighth century. So while we may see the laying out of some areas of arable more formally in some particular places (Dudston Fields just possibly being one example of this), we should expect much of the landscape to include both managed woodland (as coppice and for more substantial timber) and common pasture. In this light, recent appreciation not only of Domesday arrangements but also of mid-to late Saxon period landscapes includes awareness of the likely considerable extent of wood-pasture, managed for timber, grazing and pannage within the same cycles of use.[20] It may therefore be in such a relatively open landscape that the 'wavy' route that the Dyke took, and which was highlighted by Fox, in the southern part of the Vale of Montgomery may have come into being – tracing a course not through woodland, but through a parkland landscape featuring mature oaks and grassland.[21]

The landscape behind (and at) the frontier: Anglo-Saxon settlement

Although relatively little is known about the physical landscape of the frontier in the late eighth century, any intensification of land-use eastwards of the Dyke is surely likely to have related substantially to the different histories of English settlement that characterised the different areas. There are considerable difficulties in approaching the question of the nature and timing of initial English settlement (let alone specifically in the eighth century) in any of the areas concerned, quite apart from the problems facing the archaeological study of the whole of the borderlands in respect to the 'invisibility' of settlement due to the lack of material culture, and especially pottery, from the periods concerned. Some clues as to the complexities can be gained from using three contrasting evidential routes into the eighth-century context, and these will be examined in turn here.

A landscape of territories: *a* Tribal Hidage *perspective*

There are a variety of views that it is possible to take concerning the 'Tribal Hidage' document.[22] For example, if this was a tribute list, one possible juncture for its compilation would be, as we noted in Chapter 2, during Oswiu of Northumbria's annexation of Mercia following his victory at the Winwaed in 655. However, as Simon Keynes has pointed out, there is no compelling reason to see the Tribal Hidage as a tribute list at all.[23] One context for its production alternatively as a Mercian administrative document (reckoning the extent of potential productive capacity and service provision) would be that period when the Mercian kings were beginning to specify the extent of obligations upon landholders in terms of service, and when they exercised the maximum control over the areas listed. The inclusion of West Saxons, somewhat vaguely and in 'round figures', and at the end of the list, need not imply that Wessex had been formally subjugated. On the contrary, the point of its inclusion may have been largely rhetorical: a statement of intent rather than necessarily a statement of fact. One period when a Mercian king may have regarded himself as being on the brink of exercising such a 'maximal' overlordship was late in the reign of Aethelbald, which also of course correlates closely with the first specification of military obligations in charters: but there is also no reason to suppose that it could not equally well belong later in the eighth century.[24]

There have been a number of studies that have found links through other – and inevitably usually later – documentary references to tie down the names listed in the 'Tribal Hidage' document to particular places. By these means, for instance, it has been possible to create a map of the possible locations and areas concerned, that for instance place the bulk of the 'minor' groups in the areas to the east and south-east of the 'heartlands'.[25] Our focus here, however, is upon the areas to the west of the Mercian core area. Some peoples are relatively easy to trace in this zone: for instance, the 'Hwinca' are presumably the Hwicce of present-day Gloucestershire, Worcestershire, and west Oxfordshire. Equally simply, it seems reasonable to suppose that the 'Wocansaetan' are the same people later referred to as the *Wrocansaete,* and that the name element refers to those people living in the vicinity of the Wrekin. While this locates these latter people close to the frontier, it is only their stated hidage that provides any clue to the extent of the territory concerned: which, at 7,000 hides, was extensive.

FIGURE 7.4 The middle Severn valley near Buttington, looking north

The mass of The Breiddin (at right) dominates the landscape east of Welshpool and west of Shrewsbury, seen here 100m east of Offa's Dyke at Hope. The river Severn stood proxy for the Dyke in this landscape, for nearly six miles northwards from Buttington. Prominent features such as The Breiddin, referred to in early documents as 'Rhiw', lent their names to the peoples who inhabited the frontier zone, in this case, Rhiwsaete.

At least, however, the *Wrocansaete* can be localised to the area that encompasses, and that presumably extended well beyond, the Wrekin and Wroxeter. Immediately after mention of the presumed Shropshire-focused group, there is a curious term, 'Westerna', for which it is much more difficult to establish a location. The most popular supposition has been that the area referred to is to be equated with those lands that are later referred to as occupied by the *Magonsaete*, on the basis that this is a people who are associated with the area that later became the diocese of Hereford, that is today's Herefordshire and south Shropshire.[26] Another view has been that the entities identified in the 'Tribal Hidage' are ordered clock-wise after the mention of the 'first' Mercia, the heartlands. If the rotation begins with the *Wrocansaete*, so the argument runs, then the lands of the *Westerna* cannot lie to the south: they must instead be located in what is today Cheshire.[27] While neither possibility is entirely implausible, there are problems with each. For example, leaving aside the difficulties with the sources that have been cited to identify a 'kingdom of the *Magonsaete*' ruled at some point in the seventh century by a king Merewalh, the somewhat thin documentary evidence from late Saxon charters places them firmly only in the region immediately north and east of Hereford. As for the idea that they simply 'equate' to the 'Westerna', this might be supported by a reference to the 'western Hecani' being in this area, but is not decisively so.[28] A location of the *Westerna* in Cheshire leaves the problem of why there is no mention of the *Magonsaete* in the 'Tribal Hidage'.[29] One possibility is that, theoretically being last in a clockwise rotation that started with the Wrocansaete, their entry has been 'lost in translation' through the various versions of the document that have come down to us.[30]

An ingenious solution to this problem has been offered, that, also taking the order of naming in the 'Tribal Hidage' as indicative of real geographical relationships, locates the *Westerna* not to the north of the *Wrocansaete*, but rather, in clientship, as the British of north Wales beyond the frontier.[31] Arguably, this creates more problems than it solves, however, since despite the suggestion from the same quarter that the *Wrocansaete* themselves formed a British political entity, there are in fact no grounds to believe that the 'Tribal Hidage' listing included any non-English peoples.

There is however a further possibility that has not previously, as far as we are aware, been phrased before now. This is that, rather than denoting a closely demarcated territorial group, *Westerna* was a term used to describe the western frontiers-people in general, spread along its length. In this way, what the term could rather have referred to was the peoples of forward settlement, 'those of the far west', who were resident actually along the frontier, rather than a people focused in a particular territory to the north or to the south of the *Wrocansaete*. As such the term *Westerna* may account for *all* the small groups so located, whether situated in Cheshire, what are now eastern Montgomeryshire and eastern Radnorshire, parts of Shropshire close to where Offa's Dyke crossed the middle Severn valley, or Herefordshire. This would be problematical if we could not identify any of the groups concerned, but in addition to the *Magonsaete*, there may have been several smaller peoples that are to some extent traceable right at the end of the Anglo-Saxon period. The hidages in this case would be, as several seem to be, a very general approximation of the 'taxable value' of the lands they farmed.[32]

A landscape of peoples: *clues from charters and from Domesday*

It is interesting to note the omissions rather than the inclusions of the 'Tribal Hidage'. The *Tomsaete*, for instance, are first recorded in ninth-century documents, and do not appear in the Tribal Hidage listing. Was this because, located on the river Tame in what is now (mostly) eastern Staffordshire in the midst of the heartlands, they were not administered separately? Meanwhile, the *Pencasaete* thought to have been based around Penkridge in western Staffordshire, in what might have been regarded as part of the heartland, are listed. To the west, as we have noted, there is no mention of the *Magonsaete*, again first referenced by name in the ninth century.

The problem is a complex one, since it does not only concern scale, given that other 'minor' groups such as the *Arosaete*, usually identified as a people within the kingdom of the *Hwicce*, or at least on its northern margin, are listed. It may be that those drawing up, or transcribing, the list had more detail for some areas than for others. This would explain why so many other peoples, again not listed, can nonetheless be traced by other means. The wealth of surviving Worcestershire charters, for instance, enables further groups to be identified, such as the *Weogoran*, north of Worcester.[33] For Herefordshire and Shropshire few charters survive, but it may be significant that the one or two that do survive identify equivalent entities. So it is that we learn that Yarkhill to the east of Hereford was regarded as lying within the lands of the *Magonsaete* in 811, while Staunton-on-Arrow was, in 958, on the western boundary of the same people.[34]

Among the 'unlisted' groups are several peoples whose territory close to the frontier we can locate with some confidence. For example, the Breiddin, the mountain that dominates the landscape on the eastern side of the river Severn north-east of Welshpool, appears to have been known as 'Rhiw' in the eighth century and later. The latter name reflects the term used to denote the Domesday hundred of Rhiwset, centred upon Alberbury, just to the south of the river Severn to the west of Shrewsbury.[35] This in turn appears directly to reference a people known as the *Rhiwsaete*, those 'who dwell in the vicinity of the mountain, Rhiw.' This naming of a group in reference to a prominent hill echoes the naming of the *Wrocansaete* nearby, who were undoubtedly 'the dwellers in the vicinity of the Wrekin', presumably originally those Anglo-Saxons who settled the lands bordering Watling Street as it approached the Severn at Wroxeter, or at least a people resident there comprising an amalgam of British and Anglo-Saxon groups (see Figures 1.3 and 1.4).

Another frontier people may have occupied a territory based upon Maesbury, the hundredal court for the Domesday hundred of Mersete. This name appears to refer to the *Meresaete*, 'the people living on the boundary', located between the Severn, where their southern boundary was with the *Rhiwseate* (who were as we saw located to the south of the river), and Oswestry.[36] Just why this group, rather than any of the others, should be denoted in this way, is an interesting question. Three circumstances may have contributed to it: firstly, the possibility that this was a location of early Mercian settlement in the aftermath of Penda's victory at Maserfelth; secondly, the geographic location of the area in respect to the Watling Street road and its connection through the lands of the *Wrocansaete*, back to the Mercian heartlands; and thirdly its location in the area where Wat's Dyke terminated. This set of interrelationships may be of some interest in trying to reconstruct both the terms of the hegemony overall, and in understanding a special relationship that may have existed between the heartlands and this part of the borderland due to their direct linkage via Watling Sreet.

Other such people located on the frontier with the 'Welsh' Britons are to some extent recoverable through post-Domesday references, although here the security of identification of eighth-century arrangements may be reduced. An example is the 'Tempeseter' mentioned in medieval documents for the lordship of Clun. This group name, if such it is, may refer to a geographically-defined territory, that of the *Temesaete*, a people who may have occupied the lands between the rivers Teme and Clun.[37] To their north were possibly the *Hahlsaete*, a name thought to be linked to the district named in later sources as Alcester, located in part of the large parish of Church Stoke; while to their south were the people also apparently defined through topographical reference as the *Stepelsaete*, who lived in the 'land of steep slopes' in the area of the later Domesday hundred of Staple, in Herefordshire north of the Wye.[38]

The question of the identity of these groups, both in terms of ethnicity and in reference to their political status, is a complex one. Another apparent such group, the *Dunsaete*, by the tenth or eleventh century were living either side of a significant river somewhere along the border. They are described in the late Saxon 'Ordinance concerning the Dunsaete' document as if they were a recognised grouping with a population comprising both Anglo-Saxon and British elements.[39] Ruled over in one form or another by the kings and ealdormen of the (by that time) 'English' kingdom, they appear to have had distinct traditions of paying tribute either to the Mercian or to the West Saxon kings.

Two deductions have been made about the *Dunsaete* from study of the text of the 'Ordinance', one geographical and the other political. The first assumption, which may well be correct, has been that, given that there is mention also of a group termed the *Wentsaete* (to be identified either as 'the people of Gwent' or, probably more accurately, 'the people who border the kingdom of Gwent'), the *Dunsaete* can be located fairly closely to the north of them. The area concerned was probably that centred upon Archenfield, an entity documented in the Llandaff Charters, from an eleventh-century mention in the *Anglo-Saxon Chronicle*, and in the Herefordshire Domesday. Archenfield occupied a tract of land south of Hereford and west of the Wye. The *Dunsaete* could plausibly be described as having lived either side of the Wye between Hereford and Monmouth because, on the one hand, there are indications that the British kingdom of Ergyng from which Archenfield derived its name once stretched to the east beyond Ross-on-Wye, and on the other there were reasonably well-documented Welsh communities occupying locations on the east bank of the Wye into the medieval period.[40]

The second deduction is seemingly that the *Dunsaete* was at root a British polity or political entity with a substantial English 'settler' population, only partially incorporated within Mercia. The correct inference to be drawn from the terminology of the 'Ordinance concerning the Dunsaete' is in this regard uncertain. While it continues to be assumed that the *Dunsaete* were a Welsh/British grouping, the 'Ordinance' preamble can be read as suggesting something rather different. This is that the people concerned were a hybrid community (and political/administrative entity) under Mercian/English authority, but with a population that was evenly divided between indigenous British people and an Anglo-Saxon settler group, both of whose interests were acknowledged, but who did not necessarily enjoy parity.[41]

It has been suggested that the *Wrocansaete* were a hybrid but fundamentally a British people, albeit with numerous Anglo-Saxon communities settled upon their land, and that arguably the *Magonsaete* were similarly so constituted.[42] The *Dunsaete* arrangements, with dual (or parallel) ethnicity under English authority, may instead have characterised all these border-occupying or -straddling '-saete' groups located along the frontier.[43] The broad organisation, and stability, of these dispositions may go some way towards explaining the particular association between some of the named groups and their hundredal court (the legal assembly for the Domesday Hundred concerned), which existed through to and in some cases beyond, the Norman reorganisation of the frontier in the twelfth century.

English settlements west of the Dyke: place-names and histories

The focus of Margaret Gelling's discussion of the frontier was strongly landscape-based, whether discussing the relevance of the position of parish boundaries in relation to the Dyke, or the significance of place-names denoting the existence of woodland. On the latter, she disagreed with Fox's view that the various *–leah* names denoting clearings in woodland that he suggested (especially in north Herefordshire) had reflected the predominantly wooded nature of those parts of the eighth-century landscape. She suggested rather that these names indicated the nature and location of primary Anglo-Saxon settlement: 'the whole strip of country is likely to have been settled, and the land to have been either under the plough, or systematically exploited for pasture or for timber production, within boundaries which neighbouring communities had agreed at a much earlier date.'[44] Moreover, 'If no part of the boundary is assumed to have been crossing a landscape empty of people it becomes easier to conjecture how the work could have been accomplished'.[45]

The twin departure-points of Gelling's study of place-names in the frontier region were Noble's work on the names of English groups living on the frontier derived from the documentary referencing of particular places and the place-names, and her own work on key place-names and name-elements that might yield clues as to both the earliest English settlement of the frontier region and to the working of the Dyke-related frontier system when it was put in place.[46] The case for early English settlement beyond the line of Offa's Dyke was focused upon two areas: that between Buttington on the Severn and Hopton by the Kerry Ridgeway south of Montgomery and places in the Teme, Lugg and Hindwell valleys, mostly in Radnorshire.[47]

In the 'middle Severn' region 10 settlements bearing English names exist to the west of the Dyke, and 3 places with such names are located upon it. In

FIGURE 7.5 Offa's Dyke overlooking the Walton Basin at Herrock Hill and Burfa

In the landscape west of Kington and immediately west of Radnor Forest, the Dyke gained maximum visibility either side of the Hindwell Brook valley. The concentration of English place-names in the Walton Basin has been taken to imply early settlement of an area that was nonetheless situated to the west of the Dyke.

east Radnorshire and west Herefordshire, no fewer than 19 English settlement names exist to the west of the Dyke. Several of these names first appear in Domesday, the rest in medieval documents, but it is their form, that includes in several cases elements that elsewhere are seen by some scholars to belong to the earliest stratum of English place-names, that has led to their ascription as denoting early English settlement.[48] On present evidence it is not possible to distinguish between settlements that originated before or after the eighth century, but archaeological evidence elsewhere is beginning to suggest that at least some settlements with the element –hope (a place located within an enclosed valley leading up into hills) correlate closely with settlement activity dating from the later seventh century.[49] This has yet to be demonstrated for any of the settlements west of the Dyke, however, and in order to place them confidently within the framework of the frontier, we need to look at landscapes in which other material can be regarded as relevant.[50]

The landscape west of the frontier: British kingdoms and districts

Among whatever many doubts there are about the interpretation of Offa's Dyke, one thing cannot be debated: it clearly 'faces' westwards. If, as seems most likely, it is a monument the construction of which is to be dated sometime between 600 and 850 AD, it must also be regarded as a matter not for debate that it was the kingdom of Mercia that was responsible for its creation. The question then becomes, what were the British kingdoms that the Dyke could have faced? Just as one or other of the kings of Mercia must have commissioned the Dyke, since Mercia stood eastwards of it, there were several British kingdoms, and smaller polities (including those likely to have been included within a 'maximal' Kingdom of Powys), in existence to the west, and more than one of these could have opposed specific episodes of English colonisation or particular military campaigns by Mercian or composite Anglo-Saxon armies. And yet the main reason why the Mercians built Offa's Dyke has widely been seen to have been either military enterprises or endemic cattle-raiding on the part of the Welsh.[51] A recent example is the statement that:

> On (Offa's) western border, the dyke which bears his name is regarded as a more substantial structure than was once believed, and its interpretation as a work of compromise in a time of peace has given way to a perception of it as a work of almost studied contempt for the Welsh: no point in expanding further west, but necessary to prevent them from mounting smash-and-grab raids into English territory and then escaping back across the border with their cattle and crops.[52]

However, as Wendy Davies has pointed out, the evidence for such raiding to any extent to the east of Offa's Dyke is thin, to say the least. The cattle-raiding suggestion depends largely upon the provisions of the 'Ordinance concerning the Dunsaete' (and upon later practices well-documented from medieval sources), yet this document clearly envisages *reciprocal* arrangements between the Welsh and English populations for the restoration of property.[53] There is little evidence for any resurgent British military activity, while even entries such as that in the *Annales Cambriae* for AD 760, which recorded the battle that was fought in the vicinity of Hereford, could be taken instead simply to have referred to armed conflict *at* the frontier. In contrast, there are a considerable number of references in both English and Welsh sources to westwards campaigns by the Mercians, sometimes deep into British lands.[54]

The British of the kingdom of Powys

There are a number of problems with adopting too simplistic an approach to the situation of the British kingdoms west of the frontier that in a sense mirror those that we have just been discussing to the east. Whatever the situation of Offa's Dyke in respect to Powys, its more northerly reaches may also have 'faced' princedoms at least occasionally allied to the kingdom of Gwynedd, and, towards the southern parts of its course, the kingdom of Gwent and its satellite territories. That among these kingdoms Powys was in a state of resistance to Mercian pressure in the eighth century cannot be doubted, and this would certainly have been a key factor in determining the location and form of the Dyke in any one part of the frontier in which Powys exercised influence. However, as was noted in Chapter 2, the idea that the Dyke simply marked the late eighth-century eastern boundary of Powys involves some circularity of argument, since the eastern boundary of Powys at that time is not known by any independent means. The eastern limit of Powys would, according to this argument, have been where the Dyke marks it to be, while the Dyke would be regarded as standing where it is because that was the boundary.

The complexities of the situation in north Wales in the ninth century should perhaps serve as a reminder of the difficulties of determining exactly what constituted 'Powys' then, or indeed earlier. For example, the status of the northern districts between the Conwy and the Mersey, and in the Vale of Clwyd is far from clear. There were at least four such districts, with the 'Perfeddwlad' ('middle country') comprising the cantrefs of Rhos, Tegeingl, Rhufoniog and Dyffryn Clwyd (Vale of Clywd), and with Edeirnion and Cynllaith to their south (Figure 1.3). In some sources referring to the situation in the early ninth century, the first two of these were mentioned in passing as 'kingdoms'. Meanwhile, to their east there were also distinct districts such as Dogfeiling (which occupied the southern part of the area that became Flintshire), that may also have been the focus of independent princedoms before the acceleration of Mercian involvement in the area in the eighth century.

The idea that a kingdom could be considered to have anything approaching a monolithic unity when the areas that at one time or another were under the control of its ruling dynasty extended from as far north as Deganwy on the Conwy estuary to as far south as Glasbury on the Wye is probably as anachronistic as imagining that the Mercian 'state' comprised an undifferentiated entity across the span of midland England that it occupied. Indeed, although clearly a powerful polity had emerged in mid-Wales by the late seventh century 'Powys' itself is not referred to as such in the Welsh sources until 808.[55] More likely, was that Powys comprised an affiliation or confederation of sub-kingdoms or princedoms that, at least at its northern and southern margins, fell under the sway of more powerful neighbours, or exercised some independence of action and policy.

One approach to the question of what 'Powys' comprised can therefore be to answer it in the same way that we have attempted to define English or Mercian groups living along the frontier, by attempting to define similarly-scaled entities in the 'British' landscape. In this way, districts north of the Severn that are known from medieval documentation, such as Arwystli, Gwrtheyrnion, Cynllibiwg, and Mechain, for instance, may have had a pre-Norman existence as sub-kingdoms, at some point (or at various points) brought into alliance or confederation with 'Powys'.[56] To the south of the Severn, if anything the situation is yet more complex. The districts of Ceri, Maelienydd, and Elfael, for example, had an identity in the twelfth century that seems likely to some degree at least to have been an inherited one. Extrapolation backwards into the eighth century is particularly difficult in light of the way that lordship was re-defined for both English and British areas with the advent of the Normans. While in the eighth century (or, more properly, the early tenth century), the *Anglo-Saxon Chronicle* could describe warfare pursued by Aethelbald of Mercia and Cuthred, king of the West Saxons as against the 'Walas', it was not until the Norman period that the British in 'Wales' were beginning to regard themselves as 'Welsh' when viewed in a wider perspective.

It may nonetheless have been that some attributes of the Dyke, including its exact location, were as they were in the areas 'facing' Powys because of a particularly bellicose stance of that kingdom in at least the first half of the eighth century. The early transcriptions of the inscription on the 'Pillar of Eliseg', a commemorative stone cross-shaft located to the north-west of Llangollen, indicate that it was set up by a king, Concenn, known from other sources to have reigned in Powys in the early ninth century.[57] The inscription apparently proclaimed that the stone was set up to commemorate Concenn's great-grandfather King Elise, and it does appear to have referred to the recovery, however short-lived, of 'the inheritance of Powys' from the English, making the landscape concerned 'a sword-land by fire'. This has been considered, at least since Cyril Fox drew attention to it in 1928, to provide unequivocal testimony that Elise regained extensive lands that had been annexed by the Anglo-Saxons in previous generations.[58] It has even been suggested that the cross was set up overlooking land that itself had been invaded by the English in this way.[59]

Recent reviews specifically of the form of the 'Pillar of Eliseg' transcription have elucidated, to a much greater degree than hitherto, the content and purpose of both pillar and inscription. Nancy Edwards has not only affirmed the erection of the pillar as a response to the 'increasing threat to the ruling dynasty of Powys during the second half of the eighth century and first half of the ninth century',

FIGURE 7.6 From Offa's Dyke at Pont Adam, Ruabon, towards Llangollen

The prospect westwards here, from one of the lengths of Dyke built in monumental mode (see Chapter 5), is dominated by the high hills on either side of the upper Dee valley. The Eglwyseg tributary lies beyond the lower southern slopes of Ruabon Mountain (at right here), and behind the dramatic outcrop on which Castell Dinas Bran stands (for the view along the Dyke here, see Figure 7.10).

but also noted that it marks an important stage in the public recording of the asserted lineage of that dynasty monumentally.[60] The question of the date of Elise's 'recovery' of British lands, and therefore of the context of the building of Offa's Dyke, at least along this part of the frontier, is more problematical. David Stephenson may well have moved this historical problem along substantially, in a recent important observation that Vaughan's version makes sense of part of the inscription as a 'dating clause'. This refers to the recapture of formerly British lands by Elise as having occurred '*post mortalitatem*', that is, after 'a period of pestilence that caused widespread mortality'.[61] Stephenson has suggested that this may correlate with a Northumbrian record for the year 759, in which just such dramatic mortality from 'distempers' and dysentery is described. If this epidemic was, as seems likely, widespread among the Mercians as well as their northern neighbours, it could have provided the context, at the very start of Offa's reign, for the British resurgence recorded on the inscription.

In this case, the building of the Dyke north and south of the river Dee east of Llangollen could indeed mark a subsequent regaining of the lowlands in the area, especially, between Chester and Shrewsbury by the Mercians under Offa.[62] And as such, also, the building of the Dyke could have represented a 'hardening' of the frontier in this area, and this may explain the 'curious silence'[63] of the Welsh sources concerning Offa's military activities in respect of just this part of the frontier, in contrast to his documented 'vigour' elsewhere. The 'Pillar of Eliseg' was erected several miles to the west of Offa's Dyke, moreover, in a location where it 'spoke' to a people hemmed in on all sides – by both hills and rival polities.

Glywysing, Gwent and Ergyng

At Rushock Hill in north Herefordshire, Offa's Dyke does what it does nowhere else: it travels for more than a mile on an east–west course. One way to explain this is to suggest that it ends here, and to imply that southwards of this point it was unnecessary because the writ of Powys no longer ran there. It has been suggested that the Dyke was not built across south Herefordshire because Ergyng was in some kind of federation with Mercia, and the later history of the area has been adduced to support this idea.[64] Yet the evidence could be read alternatively to point out the likelihood that at least part of Ergyng remained a dependency of Gwent for much of the later second millennium, with strong ecclesiastical ties to the see of Llandaff. However, it has not been made adequately clear in any commentary that Ergyng was itself a divided land already by the late eighth century, and it is the very likelihood that this area was in transition, that may explain the absence of the Dyke here, rather than the existence of any treaty. This is a point worth exploring more fully here.

There is, for example, no indication that Mercia and Gwent were in treaty relations with one another at this time.[65] There is therefore no reason to suggest that the Dyke was somehow not needed to 'face' Gwent. In the seventh century, the kingdom of Gwent emerged in the coastlands between the estuaries of the Wye and Usk under a king called Meurig ap Tewdrig. The sway of his dynasty can be gauged from the grants of lands (recorded in the medieval period at Llandaff) not only there but also in the Vale of Glamorgan, Gower and between the Wye and Monnow in what is now south Herefordshire.[66] The kingdom of Glywysing (later, Glamorgan) to the west of Gwent moreover sometimes exercised overlordship over it. Indeed, at the time of Offa's accession, Meurig's great-grandson Ithel was sole ruler of a very considerable dominion ranging from south-west Herefordshire throughout Gwent and Glamorgan. In the late ninth century, as Asser makes clear, although King Alfred recognised Brochfael and Ffernfael as kings in Gwent, charter evidence indicates unequivocally that Hywel ap Rhys of Glywysing was recognised as overlord throughout Gwent.[67]

The kingdom of Ergyng was in existence as an independent British polity in the sixth and seventh centuries, although kings of Ergyng are only evident up to the middle of the seventh century.[68] After this, and certainly from the beginning of the eighth century, the kingdom appears to have been administered as a sub-kingdom of Gwent. Although its extent in the period c.450–650 was uncertain, it has been suggested that since the name correlates with the Roman name 'Ariconium', a settlement just to the east of Ross-on-Wye, it once took in land to the east of the Wye.[69] By the eighth century, its eastern limits were along the Wye and its western limits along the Monnow, with Gwent to its south. However, in Aethelbald's time, the Mercians were penetrating the areas south of Hereford, and this may have involved the seizure of land at least in northern Ergyng. Recent archaeological evidence from Bullinghope south of Hereford appears to indicate Anglo-Saxon settlement of this area at least by the late seventh century.[70]

British leadership locally in Ergyng in the later eighth century may have been passing from the kings of Gwent to the bishop of Ergyng, and it is recorded in one charter that churches lost to Aethelbald were subsequently 'recovered' by Bishop Berthwyn.[71] This was perhaps by negotiation in the aftermath of the battle at Hereford in 760 when it is not impossible that the British of Ergyng, perhaps even in defiance of Gwent, actually fought alongside the Mercians against the British of Brycheiniog. More certainly, by 1086 the northern boundary of Ergyng was established between the Worm Brook and the Taradr Brook close to the Wye, with the presumably anglicised hundred of Webtree being referred to in Welsh as *Anergyng*, or 'non-Ergyng'.[72] This is important, because it could mean that the people of Webtree hundred/Anergying, whose lands were assessed in hides in 1086, and some at least of whose lands were so assessed early in the ninth century, could be the very same Dunsaete as described in the 'Ordinance'.[73]

The last grants of land in Ergyng by the kings of Gwent were those of Ffernfael ap Ithel, who died in 775, and this has been taken to indicate that it was from that point onwards, and from the later years of Offa's reign, that the Welsh of Archenfield were brought into the same relation with Mercia and then with the unified kingdom of England that is recorded in Domesday in 1086. Whatever reading we place upon the 'Ordinance concerning the Dunsaete', Domesday is unequivocal about the military duties of the men of Archenfield in respect to the requirements of the English crown as expressed through the command of the shire reeve: 'Anyone who does not go when ordered by the Sheriff to go with him into Wales, is fined....When the army advances on the enemy, these men by custom form the vanguard and on their return the rearguard. These were the customs of the Welshmen in Archenfield before 1066'.[74]

This focus upon the character of an otherwise obscure Welsh kingdom or sub-kingdom south of the Wye is of more than trivial relevance to the understanding of the frontier and Offa's Dyke precisely because it is in just this area, where we might assume that the Dyke would continue northwards from the vicinity of Monmouth or southwards across the Wye from Bridge Sollers, that there is no trace of it at all. In light of the foregoing discussion, the suggestion that Ergyng was somehow in alliance with, or in treaty relations with, Mercia is to overstate the British case. What little evidence there is appears to indicate, rather, that Ergyng was held, from the late eighth century, in formal client status with Mercia. So it was, also, that when the Vikings captured Cyfeiliog, the Bishop of Archenfield, in 914, it was the English King, Edward the Elder (brother of Aethelflaed 'Lady of the Mercians'), who paid his ransom. The role of Archenfield was to be more than to act as a buffer state, however: perhaps from Bishop Berthwyn's time in the mid-eighth century, it was to provide the protective 'shock-troops' for the advance of Mercian armies westwards up the Wye valley against the British of Brycheiniog and beyond, and then their rearguard, as recorded in the Domesday survey.

Brycheiniog

Meanwhile, there are polities further west that have a much more certain identity in the period concerned. The Llandaff charters record several kings of

Brecheiniauc (Brycheiniog) making grants in the mid-eighth century.[75] This is particularly pertinent to Offa's reign because, if the identification of 'Rienuch' or 'Rienneth' with this kingdom in the Welsh Annals for 795 is correct, Offa devastated its lands not long before his death. It is of interest in terms of our understanding of the importance of Hereford to Offa, therefore, that he may have closed his reign as he began it, fighting on the middle Wye and potentially across the watershed into the Usk valley at Brecon.

Not only were Offa's campaigns in this area hard-fought but they were also protracted, as witnessed by the references in the Annals to campaigns in 'south Wales' in 778, and in 'Wales' in the summer of 784. There are several references to ninth-century attacks westwards into Wales, for instance under Burgred. However, the only specific mention of a Mercian campaign specifically against Brycheiniog was when in 916, Aethelflaed sent an army into Wales which destroyed the royal site at Llangorse near Brecon at midsummer, and 'captured the king's wife and 33 other persons'.[76]

'Political places': some clues from the 'Dyke landscape'

So far, the 'political sense of place' along the frontier has been discussed in this chapter only in terms of peoples, and, in the case of the British, mostly their 'receipt' of the campaigning attentions of the Mercian armies, often in particular places. However, how can a sense of place be defined, that was 'political' in reference to particular localities? The course of the Dyke itself does have some implications for the state of the frontier behind it, and it was noted in Chapter 4 how some whole lengths of the Dyke are especially carefully positioned in the landscape in respect to specific places to the west of it. Fox regarded some lengths of the Dyke as marking 'important points', and in Chapter 5, above, it was observed that some such individual locations appear to have been remarkably highly 'choreographed', perhaps particularly to achieve specific effects when encountered from beyond the Dyke to the west. It happens that some further cases where such choreography is evident may also correspond to places where there was a deliberate motivation to create an impact not so much across a tract of landscape, as upon a particular place. If at such locations the Dyke was built in an especially 'performative' way, could these be regarded as 'political places' where a particularly striking location, or an impressive construction, was deemed essential?

From an archaeological perspective, the significance of recognising the possible identity of districts associated with major kingdoms such as Powys and their having some political coherence as sub-kingdoms in the eighth century is that the princely families ruling in these areas are likely to have been based at a defended centre: what in later times would be termed in Anglo-Norman Latin, the *caput* of a lordship, or in Welsh, the court, or *llys*. Not only does this create the possibility of identification of particular places as potential former centres of this kind, but it also means that these 'political places' may correlate

Overlooking Tintern: Offa's Dyke at the Devil's Pulpit

In Gloucestershire, high above the east bank of the Wye from Lippetts Grove southwards to the Devil's Pulpit and onwards towards East Vaga, the Dyke occupies every point along the crest of the crag that can be seen prominently from the narrow floor of the Wye valley from a number of different directions. This prominence is perhaps particularly notable from the bend at Tintern Parva south-eastwards along the reach of the river downstream to Plum Weir. The length from Lippetts Grove follows the contours of the hill above the steepest part of the west-facing slope before negotiating the head of a combe and embarking on a short east–west course that utilises the top of the near-vertical north-facing slopes in Caswell Wood in such a way as to provide a dramatic prospect northwards up the entire course of the Wye as far as Llandogo three miles (5 km) away. Meanwhile the turn just to the north of the Devil's Pulpit is along an outcrop of rock that provides a vantage point in all directions northwards and westwards. From Lippetts Grove southwards, the Dyke achieves massive proportions as it faces instead westwards and overlooks Tintern.

The part of the Dyke that approaches and negotiates the Devil's Pulpit rock outcrop is particularly memorable. Moreover, the build devices from here southwards to Plumweir Cliff are the most sophisticated along all the Gloucestershire stretch of the Dyke. At both the Devil's Pulpit and Plumweir Cliff, the Dyke achieves massive proportions and its impact is enhanced by 'adjusted-segmented' build lengths sited to take careful advantage of prospects northwards and southwards as well as westwards, by angled turns that as suggested in Chapter 6 approximate the form of 'turrets', and by the recently recorded laid courses of stonework that at least give the impression of a built wall facing out over a ditch which in reality in many places is no more than a notch or a berm.[77]

Noble observed that 'Tintern seems to have been a stronghold of the Kings of Gwent, and the traditional site of their victory over an attacking (West) Saxon army in 597'.[78] Whether or not this was

FIGURE 7.7 Tintern from the Pulpit Rock, Devil's Pulpit, Gloucestershire

This view is down through woodland that regenerated in the mid- to late twentieth century, and is named from the ledge of rock upon which Offa's Dyke was built. Considerable care was taken to project the Dyke close to the precipice here, where its construction necessitated cutting a forward notch into the solid rock, and substantial quarrying immediately to the east of the bank. This ensured prominence for the earthwork as seen from Tintern, and a dominating prospect over the loop of the river Wye in its gorge over 200 m below.

the case, the builders of Offa's Dyke took full advantage of the drama of this location to produce a work that towered over the river in its impressively deep and massive defile below.⁷⁹ It seems curious that such an effort was made in this location unless there was something about Tintern itself that merited a show of dominance in this way.

The Dyke at the middle Severn: particularly politically 'charged' locations?

A similarly dramatic location of the Dyke is evident in the great loop that it makes along the Llynclys slopes, on to the crag-edge at Blodwel Rock, and then around the top of the precipitous slopes on the western flank of Llanymynech Hill south-west of Oswestry.⁸⁰ Here, placed prominently along the upper flank of the high scarps overlooking the Tanat valley near its confluence with the Vyrnwy, the Dyke does not need to reach massive proportions to achieve its impact in the landscape: it simply dominated all views eastwards from Llanyblodwel on the banks of the river Tanat. Moreover, southwards around the south-west facing bulwark of Llanymynech Hill and up to Asterley Rocks, the view from the Dyke opens out to take in also the confluence itself immediately below the hill, and beyond this the winding narrow course of the Vyrnwy as it descends from the direction of Meifod. All along these stretches it closely follows the lip of a steep west-facing scarp and crag in an exactly similar way as the Lippetts Grove to Plumweir Cliff length does in Gloucestershire, and we noted in Chapter 6 how one of the angled turns here served to further dramatise its location by protruding the earthwork out from the hillfort defences along the flank of Llanymynech Hill.

The effect of the form and siting of the Dyke here was to dominate the location where any movement east from Meifod, a possible early power-base of what we might now term the 'Powys confederacy' in the middle Severn, might occur. There may be an echo of this sense of dominance in the naming of the prominent south-west facing part of Llanymynech Hill from at least medieval times as 'Carreghofa' ('Offa's Rock').⁸¹ It may even be that a royal site within the realm of Powys and linked in some way to the centre at Meifod may once have existed not far to the west of the Dyke here, and as such was the 'target' for this remarkable display of Mercian control.⁸²

Another British political centre may have overlooked the Severn valley from the west at a location south of Welshpool, since, as Noble put it, 'the stretch of massive Dyke on the highest part of its Leighton course may have had that same purpose of a display of power which seems evident opposite Tintern in the Wye valley'.⁸³ The 'primary' placement feature of this stretch of Dyke is the long diagonal transit from the riverside at Buttington southwards and upwards onto the slopes above Leighton, but a range of more localised features were also deployed here, from the diagonal transit of the hillside through to elaborate hillslope contouring. Structurally, the whole course of the Dyke from Buttington through to the slopes above Kingswood provided a continuous 'façade' culminating in the southernmost heights of the Long Mountain, and it was deliberately sited throughout this stretch to present a formidable mid-slope and then skyline feature when viewed from the west (Figure 2.1).

The elaboration of this length of Dyke extended also to details of construction. For example, south of the 'Viaduct ravine', the Dyke traverses a steep north-facing scarp and crosses the slopes on the western side of Pole Plantation in a series of short lengths on different alignments that on Fox's map extract clearly comprise a series of adjusted segments.[84] This length of Dyke certainly impressed Fox, who wrote 'There is a Roman quality about engineering work of this class which compels admiration'.[85] It is notable how the most elaborated parts of the Dyke here are not those on slopes that face westwards as much as those that have a north-westerly prospect. Such prospects today, as very possibly also in the eighth century, focus upon a large knoll crowned in pink stone. This eminence is known as *Castell Coch*, the red fort; and otherwise as Powis Castle.

Further south again, there is a dramatic shift in alignment near Forden, where, at Hem, the Dyke is brought around through nearly 90 degrees to strike a course southwards across the Vale of Montgomery. The drama of this location is remarkable, given the relatively modest elevation of the ridge-end (at 130 m OD) at which the turn is made. The view outwards here in all directions is impressive, looking as it does southwards towards the twin eminences of Ffridd Faldwyn and Montgomery Castle, south-eastwards towards the Kerry Ridgeway, eastwards towards Corndon Hill, and westwards towards the upper

FIGURE 7.8 Offa's Dyke, Montgomery and the Kerry Ridgeway, south from Hem

The prospect southwards from the carefully-sited turn in the Dyke (foreground, left) at Hem takes in the line of the Dyke (prominent tree-dominated hedgerow running due south at left-centre) and the hills above Montgomery that it faces (right-centre). The Dyke heads for, and traverses, the ridgeway that is here a prominent skyline feature.

Severn valley (Figures 7.8 and 1.9, respectively). The 'political nature' of this location is evident, however, not only in the physical location, but also in its naming. The place-name 'Hem' is represented both sides of the Dyke here, at Hem Farm half a kilometre to the west and Great Hem the same distance to the east. At Domesday this was rendered 'Heme', and this derives directly from the OE word *hemm*, a hem, margin or border. This crucial location for display and surveillance was literally at the edge of the Mercian world: the very epitome of the frontier.

The particularly complex stretch of the Dyke at Dudston Fields directly opposite Montgomery Castle was described at length in Chapter 5. It was noted there that a double change in orientation faced whole alignments directly towards the crag on which the medieval castle stands. This site, subsequently chosen as the centre of a lordship that encompassed lands in eastern Wales, Sussex, and beyond, was very plausibly a place that had once had a pre-eminent status in late British times also. The adjusted-segmented form of build is especially pronounced in exactly the same stretch of Dyke, lending it the 'facetted' appearance, and a more impressive façade, than might otherwise be the case, at just the point where the formidable nature of the work when viewed from an elevated position to the west might have warranted emphasis.

Dramatic siting, impressively large or complex build: further 'political' locations

When we come to look at similarly dramatic stretches of the Dyke to those at the Devil's Pulpit, Llanymynech Hill, or Dudston Fields, therefore, we might wonder whether they were also deliberately 'enhanced' through adjusted-segmented construction, angled-turns and other devices in order to dominate or at least to 'challenge' equivalent centres of British power. At Cwmsanahan Hill, for example, the Dyke suddenly swings out westwards to meet the sharp crest of a westwards-facing spur, here with a dramatic prospect over the Teme valley and surrounding hills. The location of the Dyke along a steep crag and the top of precipitous slopes, the deployment of angled turns, and the enhancement of scarps to create the impression of a stone 'wall' (though here relying almost entirely on banding in the living rock) produced exactly the same effect as at the other locations noted above (Figures 6.11 and 6.12).

The 'audience' for this display in this case may have been the British-Welsh aristocracy (presumably a Maleinydd-Powys princely family) who may have occupied the hill across the Teme valley to the west upon which Knucklas Castle was later built. The prospect upwards from the defended knoll here would have been fully focused upon the dramatic sweep of the Dyke, at places appearing to be a work of 10 m or more in height, around the head of Cwmsanahan.

While some potential British/Welsh political centres may have been faced by particularly dramatically sited and elaborately designed and built lengths of Offa's Dyke, others may have been confronted by lengths that were especially

FIGURE 7.9 Knucklas viewed from the Dyke south of Cwmsanahan Hill

The prospect over the Dyke here (foreground) is down onto the Teme valley from a point midway between Hawthorn Hill and Cwmsanahan Hill. The castle hill at Knucklas is the prominent wooded knoll visible just to the right of the railway viaduct.

massively built. So, for instance, in that part of the course of the Dyke that spans the Dee valley as it emerges from its more 'constrained' valley above and somewhat below present-day Llangollen there is a highly engineered and choreographed length north of the river. This runs up towards Gardden, immediately to the west of Ruabon School, and then past Tatham. The more southerly of the two particularly high and broad lengths of bank of the Dyke here is nowadays bisected by the Chester to Shrewsbury railway line, but its northern end it still survives much as it did when Fox photographed it in 1928 as it then stood amidst the works of Wynnstay Colliery. This half-mile long stretch of Dyke is linked to the more northerly one by a short straight length by Tir-y-fron farm that assists a shift in orientation north-eastwards to meet the better surviving half-mile long stretch up to Ruabon Road, Tatham, past Ruabon School. A particularly remarkable feature of this traverse is how massive the bank is in a setting where the ground both in front and to the rear of the Dyke is very level (Figure 7.10). In places the bank stands to as much as 4 m high above ground-level while the ditch is entirely filled in. If the ditch was 3 m deep here, then the combined forwards-facing slope could have been as much as 9 m in height. The effect of this as a barrier would have been accentuated had the initial build also included a counterscarp bank.

As well as serving to block the 'exit' from the upper Dee onto the lowlands, the scale and placement of the Dyke in this impressive way here was also surely political, perhaps as an act of defiance of, or calculated aggression towards, the Kingdom of Powys, one of whose centres, as discussed earlier in this chapter, was in the Dee valley west of Llangollen. Valle Crucis, the site of a later Welsh Cistercian monastery and a location near to which the inscribed stone 'Pillar of Eliseg' stands, is situated at the confluence of the Eglwyseg river with the Dee above Llangollen. This may have been the ecclesiastical centre, and nearby Castell Dinas Bran on a rocky eminence above the Dee to the north of Llangollen the secular centre, of the princely lineage of this part of Powys in the eighth century.

7 In a frontier landscape

FIGURE 7.10 Offa's Dyke at Pont Adam, Ruabon, looking north

The stretch of Dyke north from the former Wynnstay Colliery to Tatham on the western outskirts of Ruabon is the most monumental length of the Dyke anywhere, with the bank as much as 10m higher than the base of the ditch in some places. The wide prospect westwards contrasts with a more intimate engagement with the local landscape, as in reference to the hilltop and prehistoric fort at Gardden (skyline left).

If this was the case, not only was the positioning of Offa's Dyke so close to the east a bold statement, but the stance of the earthwork at Tatham, facing Eglwyseg Mountain (the alternative name for the southern end of Ruabon Mountain) might also therefore have been chosen for its symbolism.

Further light on the political significance of this location may be gauged through a study also of the geographic inter-relation of Offa's Dyke with Wat's Dyke along this stretch. In the area just to the north of the Dee crossing the two dykes are only just over a mile apart, while to the north at Pentre Bychan two and a half miles separates them, and to the south at Chirk Castle, there is a distance of four miles eastwards until Wat's Dyke is crossed at Glynmorlas. Why were the dykes brought into such close relationship here? The answer lies not only in the difficulty of containing the forces of Powys within the upper Dee valley, but also the need to under-write the appropriation of the lower Dee valley by preventing access to the symbolically important British monastic centre at Bangor only 6 miles (10 km) downstream.[86]

FIGURE 7.11 Old Radnor Hill as seen from Offa's Dyke on Evenjobb Hill

The view here is southwards, from the upper western end of the long diagonal traverse of the southern slopes of Evenjobb Hill overlooking the Walton Basin. Old Radnor Hill is at upper right centre of the view, with half of its bulk removed by quarrying. Hergest Ridge is the long prominent ridge at left horizon.

The elaborately-configured course of the Dyke along the eastern margin of the Walton Basin west of Kington was described in Chapter 4. This may have been due to the importance attached to the broad level area in the vicinity of Presteigne northwards (see below), but viewed from the hills across the Walton Basin to the south, this configuration was also very impressive. This was especially the case where the Dyke made the crossing of the 500m broad floodplain from Ditchyeld ('Dyke slope') Bridge over the Hindwell Brook immediately beneath Burfa Bank, to a point just to the east of Lower Harpton ('settlement in the valley by Herrock Hill'), traversing Riddings Brook, which marks the present-day boundary between Wales and England, in the middle of the span. This short stretch of Dyke across the Hindwell Brook valley where the stream flows down into a narrow valley from the broad Basin was nonetheless of monumental proportions, as noted in Chapter 5. To understand why it should have been built so massively here, one only needs to look southwards to the most prominent hillside, the northern slope of Old Radnor Hill, which it faces directly onto. This was the site of the early borough which gave its name to the county of Radnorshire, and which may have had a 'late British' predecessor.

And finally, the most southerly section of Offa's Dyke brings the frontier-work down to the cliffs overlooking the Severn Estuary. While there is no part of this short three-quarters of a mile (1.2 km) length that is more carefully choreographed than another, it would be true to observe that as it moves eastwards the boldness of its execution increases, and possibly also its scale.[87] The stance of this length of Dyke is interesting, since it was deliberately designed to link the north-facing loop of the Wye on which Chepstow stands, south-eastwards to the locally prominent hillcrest at Sedbury Cliff. There is higher ground to the north at Sedbury Park, but what was chosen instead was that part of the landscape locally that has a continuous prospect south-westwards down the lowest reaches of the Wye and across the Severn estuary.

It is noticeable, in the view southwards across the fields rolling gently towards the Wye-Severn confluence here, how massive is the now somewhat

FIGURE 7.12 Towards the Severn Estuary, from Offa's Dyke near Sedbury Park

This view down the Beachley peninsula here is across the massive apparent counter-scarp bank of the Dyke (crossing the field in the foreground from left to right) just to the west of Buttington Tump. The bridge in the background crosses the Wye at its confluence with the Severn on the northern approach to the first Severn Bridge south of Chepstow.

spread counterscarp bank (Figure 7.12). This is a feature that is constant along the line of the Dyke across the breadth of the peninsula, but it is not the only feature that marks this length of the earthwork as an integral part of the whole Offa's Dyke scheme. Across the remaining quarter of a mile eastwards to the cliffs looking north-eastwards across the Severn estuary, the earthwork not only increases in size, with a bank formerly of monumental proportions. It is also fronted by a deep ditch, while as a whole being set forwards prominently on the south-facing slopes here.

This represents the lowest point down the slope that the earthwork could occupy while also minimising the distance it covers. While it is a skyline feature from the peninsula itself, when seen from the south-west across the Wye south of Chepstow it is (as elsewhere) viewed as a linear feature with rising ground (at Sedbury Park) beyond it northwards. This choice of location means that it has to traverse the steep-sided valley at The Coombe before reaching Sedbury Cliffs. Rather than being seen as a problem, however, what this enabled the Dyke builders to do was to complete its course with a flourish, with the earthwork seen to great advantage from the east and from the west both along – and forward from – its line (Figure 1.5).

Why was it built so massively here, apart from the achievement of this terminal flourish? If the aim was simply to impress 'Gwent' with the power of such a flourish, the Dyke dug across the peninsula here could have been angled more towards a north-west to south-east course. Instead, the most impressive eastern half of the course from Buttington Tump very deliberately faces southwards not down the line of the peninsula but rather down the course of the estuary, today between the central suspension supports of the bridge crossing the Wye estuary before crossing the Severn (Figure 7.12).

Before the building of the bridge, such a prospect afforded a view right down towards the mouth of the Avon on the south bank of the Severn estuary ten miles (16 km) to the south. Given the interest of both Offa and his son Ecgfrith in Bath as a monastic and royal centre, such a concordance might not have been entirely accidental. Indeed, if the Avon was regarded as in effect marking the boundary between Mercia and Wessex in the late eighth century, the idea that Offa's Dyke might have been regarded as one element in the creation of a Mercian 'state frontier' that faced southwards as well as westwards becomes that much more plausible.[88] The Dyke can be seen therefore to have been built as it was here in order to 'face' the Avon estuary some to the south. Even if only symbolically, therefore, the power that the Dyke was intended to oppose here was arguably that of the West Saxons.

The Dyke and the frontier in Herefordshire

One of the several problems created by a view of Offa's Dyke as having been constructed southwards only as far as Rushock Hill on the northern border between Herefordshire and Radnorshire is that the place of Hereford in the frontier with the British of Wales is left undefined. And yet as we have already mentioned more than once, this latter location figures prominently during Offa's reign, in the early years of which as we have already noted it was apparently the site of a significant battle (in or around 760) between the Mercians and the British.[89]

Offa and the early development of Hereford

Arguably, the place of Hereford was central and not marginal to the working of the western Mercian frontier, not least because according to later hagiographical legend the one instance where Offa is himself described as having been resident close to the Dyke is near Hereford.[90] It was only in the twelfth century that a tradition concerning King Offa, King Aethelbert of East Anglia, and an alleged royal vill at Sutton just to the north of Hereford emerged, but the details are compelling. The story runs, quite plausibly but without corroborating documentary evidence from the Anglo-Saxon period, that in 793 or 794, Offa was in negotiations with Aethelberht, the young king of East Anglia, concerning a possible alliance with Mercia enacted through marriage to Offa's youngest daughter. It may be that Aethelberht had made it known that this union would be advantageous to East Anglia in reviving its role as the leading Anglian kingdom. In order for arrangements to be finalised, Offa and his queen invited the young king to their 'villa australis' ('southern vill or palace', or 'Sutton') near Hereford. Once received there, Aethelberht was then treacherously beheaded by the Mercians, to which atrocity the local people of the Hereford region responded by treating the dead East Anglian king as a martyr.[91]

Sutton is known to have been located within the royal manor of Marden at the time of Domesday, and it was with some excitement that cropmarks were seen from the air in the 1990s that appeared to approximate the multi-cellular form of a late Saxon palace, with associated buildings including an apparent aisled hall, at Freen's Court just to the south-west of Sutton on the edge of the floodplain of the Lugg. These remains, excavated in 1999 and 2002, are now unequivocally dated to the twelfth century and are interpreted instead as what may at that time have been an administrative centre of the Marden estate. However, in the floodplain of the Lugg directly below Marden church to the west, excavations in 2000 in advance of gravel quarrying intercepted the timber foundations of two separate and formally contrasting mills, each of which was dated to the eighth century. Moreover, to the east of the church, trenching in an area of earthworks revealed a substantial bank overlain by deposits associated with the medieval village of Marden.[92]

When discussing the apparent absence of the Dyke through a stretch of central Herefordshire, Noble suggested that its course may have been marked by a palisade. In 2000, in the course of investigating what appeared to be an embanked enclosure next to the church at Sutton St Michael neighbouring Marden, a slot for a timber palisade was found. This was a substantial two-

FIGURE 7.13 Offa's Dyke west of Lyonshall in north Herefordshire

Viewed here from the south, the line of the Dyke as it traverses the Curl Brook, a tributary of the river Arrow, is very evident here. The Lyonshall angled turn (turning right from the north–south line of the Dyke) is just visible in the distance (at upper centre of the image), while Holmes Marsh is just beyond the frame at bottom right.

COPYRIGHT WOOLHOPE NATURALISTS' FIELD CLUB/CHRIS MUSSON.

phase structure, the later of the two construction phases of which was dated to the eleventh century. The exact historical context for such a construction is unknown, but it appears to have formed part of a network of palisades that enclosed the landscape and divided it into discrete areas on the south-facing slopes between Sutton Walls hillfort and the river Lugg. Underneath the deserted medieval village to the west of the church was found a ring-ditch possibly around a barrow that, containing as it did a sherd of East Midlands ware of seventh-century date perhaps marks the place out as the site of elite pagan burials of the earliest Anglo-Saxon settlement of the area – possibly explaining why it later became a royal vill.

The archaeology of Hereford itself throws little definite light upon the eighth century, since neither the earliest settlement activity nor the earliest phase ramparts have as yet been accurately dated. South of the Wye, however, there is the recent archaeological evidence for Anglo-Saxon settlement at Bullinghope. More recently still, a large ditched enclosure with an east-facing entrance has been located at Rotherwas nearby, and has been dated to the seventh century. Although this cannot be proven to have been Anglo-Saxon, it would fit with a Mercian advance into this area in the decades immediately before Aethelbald's reign.[93]

The Dyke in north Herefordshire

As noted especially in Chapter 3, above, much discussion about the apparent interrupted nature of the Dyke in north Herefordshire has centred upon the alleged former existence of forest there. While it is the case that there is some place-name indication that settlements existed in 'clearings' here, it may be that such names refer to the initial process of Anglo-Saxon colonisation and that the clearance concerned was from a landscape that contained abandoned farmlands.[94] The names need reflect neither the situation before the collapse of the Romano-British rural economy, nor the situation in the eighth century. The existence of 'dense woods' in north Herefordshire can be challenged now from a number of directions. Accumulating palaeo-environmental data for instance indicates that there was no marked break in the presence of open country species in the vicinity of Hereford in the relevant period.[95] Moreover, across much of the area the Dyke crosses here it co-existed, it seems, with a co-axial pattern of enclosures that predates all other field patterns, indicating that much if not all of the area south of Kington and down to the river Wye had long been enclosed and cultivated.[96]

In north Herefordshire, it is possible to note, as others have done before us, that the only fully extant sections of the Dyke (if such they be) are those that cross the valleys of rivers or significant streams, or that otherwise 'connect' topographic prominences. In the past, there has been insufficient attention paid either to the overall potential placement of the Dyke in respect to these surviving upstanding lengths, or to the build devices used, such as the right-angled turn north of Lyonshall to which we have already referred. However, a further neglected aspect is adequate attention to early accounts of the nature of the Dyke in this area:

> Offa's Dyke (called Clawdd Offa) was made by Offa King of the Mercians (his seat was at Sutton-wall in Herifordshire), It was to separate the Britons from the Saxons....This Dyke is still visible (here and there on the ridge of the hills). It is to be seen on the top of Bachye Hill, and on Stocky-hill neer Morhampton-park in Herefordshire: in some places above a mile together.[97]

'Stocky-hill' is to be identified with the eminence now known as 'Ladylift', while Moorhampton is a hamlet located close by the dyke half a mile west of Yazor church. In this light, could the disposition of the Dyke currently perceived as a series of disconnected lengths in north Herefordshire be read instead as elements of construction of what was designed to be just as massive an undertaking as further north, but was not completed?

An alternative possibility is simply that the absence of the Dyke in north Herefordshire may be more apparent than real: the earthwork once existed in this location, but no longer does. This has been roundly discounted in recent years, but perhaps prematurely so.[98] Moreover, the simple fact that Henry Milbourn, Aubrey's informant in Monmouth, apparently first thought of Herefordshire immediately north of the Wye when he thought of lengths of the Dyke with which he was personally familiar suggests that in the seventeenth century at least, it survived in recognisably good enough condition there. From his topographical references, Milbourn clearly specified that he was referring to the north Herefordshire sections, and he noted that here (as indeed in many another area where the impact of medieval farming was particularly strong and the Dyke no longer marked the national boundary, or was close to it) the earthwork (then) survived very much better on the hills than in the valleys.[99]

North of Yazor, Fox traced the line of what he believed was Offa's Dyke northwards up into the woods on the southern flank of the eminence at Ladylift. Noble also followed it closely in this area, failing to see why Fox had

FIGURE 7.14 Continuous lynchet formed from the bank of the ?Dyke near Weobley

This continuous earthwork is the one below Burton Hill that is also shown in Figure 2.8, above, from further away. Noted by Noble, and plausibly part of the earthwork first noted in the seventeenth century by John Aubrey's informant, it continues in woodland to a point adjacent to the northern extent of the valley-traversing length at Moorhampton, that connects southwards to the Wye at Garnons.

not regarded a bank facing south-westwards and continuing north-westwards as part of the scheme (Figure 7.14). Noble recorded a continuation of this bank taking a sinuous course down towards the Norton Canon to Weobley road. Unfortunately he did not mark this course on a map, so it is not possible to be sure exactly where the feature he mentions met that road. We have traced a bank descending from the shoulder of the hill below Ladylift that survives as a west-facing lynchet. As it approaches the road, this bank curves westwards as if continuing towards Sarnesfield, but although its course is clearly truncated by that road, there is no sign of it in the fields to the north-west of the road.

The name 'Sarnesfield' itself here is of interest in demonstrating both that, contrary to Fox's assertion, the 'feld' element indicates that this was open land at the time of the English settlement, and also that it was traversed by a Roman road that continued to be recognised as such not from an English naming but from a British one. Recent ground inspection has revealed that there are short lengths of bank and ditch observable on either side of the Lyonshall to Sarnesfield road in both Almeley and in Norton Canon parishes that broadly follow its course northwards from Sarnesfield. These traces first appear (going northwards) just to the west of Little Batch Farm, and a well-preserved stretch of bank appears to survive in a spinney close to Hall Mote. This bank is evident just to the south and east of Little Woonton Farm, and just to the west it turns northwards to the east of the modern road. It is next well-preserved in Crump Oak Wood, again to the east of the road, and surviving in exactly the same form as in the spinney near Hall Mote (Figure 7.15). The possibility that the road is located actually upon the course of the Dyke for up to two miles of this three mile distance deserves further examination.

The course of the Dyke north of Holmes Marsh has at least three characteristics that it shares with lengths of Dyke elsewhere. The first is that as it crosses the valley of the Curl Brook, and especially in the valley bottom, it faces uphill in a location that appears to have no strategic sense. However, as Fox and Noble both observed, viewing northwards from the hill by Holmes Marsh, Rushock Hill is clearly in view; and when looking southwards from near the Nursery at Lyonshall, Ladylift likewise provides a clear sighting point (Figure 1.27). This is a second shared characteristic. The third is the angled turn at the northern end of the traverse of the Curl Brook valley, already discussed.

The frontier and the Dyke south of Hereford

The Domesday Stretford Hundred is interesting for the fact that it is divided into two parts, one of which is located west of Leominster, mostly west of the Roman road that passes through the village that lent its name to the Hundred. The other 'half' is located in the district of Straddle, which itself occupied an extensive area on the southern side of the Wye, extending to land either side of the ridge overlooking the Wye valley from the south, and extending into the eastern margins of the Golden Valley.[100] Lands in this area to the south of the Wye to the south of the Roman town at Kenchester form a natural part of its hinterland, and several places such as Madley, Eaton Bishop, and Kingstone that are identified as belonging to an apparent sub-district of Straddle were said in the medieval period to lie within 'Mawfield', which is the name of a farm east of Kingstone. The name is almost certainly simply an English version of the British names 'Mail Lochou', or 'Malochu' that are identified from the seventh-century Llandaff charters as being the referents for Madley ('Mais Mail Lochou', or 'the plain of Mailauc') and for Eaton Bishop ('Campo Malochu', the 'field' – or just possibly given the presence of the large presumed Iron Age enclosure at just this location – the 'fort' of Mailauc).[101]

The *Annales Cambriae* entry for 722 lists three British victories, one in Cornwall, one at Pencoed in Gwent, and another at an unknown location called 'Gart Mailauc'. The name has been traced to Caerfaelog in Llanbister and to Garth Maelog in Llanharan, in the Vale of Glamorgan, but neither of these places seems plausible given that they are 'both places deep inside Welsh territory'.[102] However, the record that we have already noted, of Aethelbald campaigning into Ergyng at just this period, places an English army in just the right place for a battle with the British. Given that the Welsh 'Garth' can mean 'enclosure', the place of the battle of 'Gart Mailauc' could plausibly be

FIGURE 7.15 Wood-bank or *slight* mode Dyke length at Crump Oak Wood, Broxwood

Photographed during woodland clearance in 2004, this bank standing more than 2 m high above a west-facing ditch appears unusually massive for a woodland boundary bank in this part of Herefordshire. The location is adjacent to the modern A480 former turnpike road south of Lyonshall, in an orientation that continues that of the Dyke shown in figure 7.13, above, just over a kilometre northwards.

PHOTOGRAPH COURTESY OF PAUL WOOD.

identified as Eaton Camp above the Wye at Eaton Bishop.[103] A British victory here might explain both the battle that Offa subsequently fought in 760 'near Hereford', and the way in which his Dyke, if such it is, descends at an angle from the north-west down to the north bank of the Wye at Bridge Sollers, only two miles upstream of Eaton Camp.

A possibility that has only rarely been entertained is that the Dyke did exist south of Hereford and followed the Wye throughout its course. In some ways this would mirror the situation south of Monmouth, but with some important differences. Here, Fox examined a number of earthworks claimed to be part of Offa's Dyke. For example, citing J. G. Wood's comments about features in the vicinity of Ross-on-Wye he wrote: 'The 'deep ditch at Duxmere, S. of Ross, is an ordinary Holloway, and the 'well-developed' bank in Furnace wood is a modern spoil heap'.[104] Noble pointed out that Fox's dismissal of ideas that there may have been frontier works, however slight, in the Wye valley between Monmouth and Hereford rested upon a series of questionable assumptions, and was made without close reference either to the landscape itself and the traces of earthworks present, or to the available documentary evidence for the early British and Anglo-Saxon history of the area concerned. There are traces of lengths of bank and ditch, some of which are continuous but slight, others of which are substantial but short, at various points on the left bank of the Wye, as at Cherry Hill above Fownhope and at Perrystone north-east of Ross-on-Wye, and these, like the banks south of Lyonshall, could have been linked together by less dramatic lengths of Dyke of the *slighter* mode of construction.[105]

Dykes and the frontier in the far north

At the northern end of the surviving continuous earthwork, a simple projection of the existing line north-westwards from Treuddyn would traverse Moel Findeg towards Cefn Mawr overlooking the upper Alyn river from the east, which river could easily have been crossed at Pont-newydd near Cilcain. A line northwards just to the east of Nannerch would have continued to the east of Ysceifiog to Bryn Glas, and it is here that the Ordnance Survey maps, following the work of the Royal Commission for the Ancient and Historical Monuments of Wales (RCAHMW) in 1910, mark the line of an earthwork identified as Offa's Dyke that was traced subsequently by Fox through the western part of Whitford parish to Trelawnyd within three miles of the coast at Prestatyn.

Such a projection does not of course in any way establish that such a course ever existed. Nor do the earthworks identified by the early RCAHMW fieldworkers necessarily correspond to linear works of the eighth or ninth century. A series of excavations that took place between the 1970s and 1990s across the Whitford earthwork and at Trelawyd failed to locate any sign of a linear feature at the latter location, and produced clear evidence for a bank flanked by ditches on either side linked to prehistoric monuments at Brynbella and at Ysceifiog.[106] We should nonetheless not make the mistake of assuming therefore that this work proves that the Dyke never did continue northwards from Treuddyn, since there are numerous possible routes that this could have taken. The problem is compounded by confusion of the northern section of Wat's Dyke with Offa's Dyke in place-names and on the ground. Such local ascription in at least one case is documented as far back as 1378.[107]

This latter is a point that we shall return to in Chapter 9. For the meantime, however, we might note that although it seems likely that there was no link between the dykes at the northern end of Offa's Dyke, and no 'original' continuation of that Dyke simply northwards for instance to the vicinity of Mold and to the sea at or near Flint, there is nonetheless one alternative possibility that needs to be considered closely rather than dismissed out of hand. This is that the naming of Wat's Dyke instead as 'Offa's Dyke' in certain locations from Hope northwards (reflected not only in the medieval example at Hope itself, but also names such as 'Clawdd Offa', a farm at Soughton north of Mold) contains the grain of a tradition that this section once actually was a detached part of Offa's Dyke that continued northwards to Basingwerk.

In such a scenario, the Alyn valley north-westwards of Hope would have provided Offa's armies with a 'campaigning route' into the 'Perfeddwlad' or 'middle country' of the cantrefs of Rhos, Tegeingl, Rhufoniog and Dyffryn Clwyd (Vale of Clywd). Such a route would have been flanked to the west by the 'extension' of Offa's Dyke in its otherwise uncharacteristic valley-setting north from Brymbo to Treuddyn. This is turn would have been unfinished (as Pennant had speculated in 1798) because the Vale of Clwyd was never fully incorporated into Mercia (as was seemingly planned, if the establishment of the bridgehead at Rhuddlan that was attacked in 796 or 797 is seen as a statement of intent).[108] If the ninth-century dates established for the 'southern' part of Wat's Dyke near Oswestry are sustained through further such results, it may be that rather than the whole of 'Wat's Dyke' having been built at one time, the southern part was added as a means of protecting the Cheshire-Shropshire Plain during the aggressive campaigns into Gwynedd by Coenwulf, or in reaction to resurgent British attacks subsequently.[109]

East and west across the frontier: Presteigne

Before discussing the 'anomalous' frontier areas of Herefordshire and northern Flintshire, we identified a number of 'political places' where the Dyke may have been elaborated to 'face' particularly important locations associated with British kingdoms, or, more symbolically, the Anglo-Saxon kingdom of Wessex across the Severn estuary. What we did not do was consider the breadth of the frontier zone that was traversed, but not necessarily entirely defined by, Offa's Dyke. At the river Dee crossing, it may be surmised from the closeness of Offa's and Wat's Dyke to each other, and the proximity of the historic British centres at Eglwyseg to the west and Bangor-on-Dee to the east, that the frontier was relatively narrow and highly contested. Elsewhere, it may have been the presence of Mercian power-centres close to the frontier that gave the latter both the depth and the complexity that it quite possibly had. While Hereford may be one example of this, that there may be other such locations is suggested by the situation of the frontier and the Dyke near Presteigne.

To the north-west of Presteigne, the Dyke descends southwards from Hawthorn Hill and the hills to the south of Knighton. Its highly elaborated form above the crossing of the Lugg was discussed in some detail in Chapters 4 and 5, above. In Chapter 6, the possible gateway surveillance features at Bwlch and at Yew Tree Farm were noted. The Dyke's long diagonal descent from Newcastle Hill and Pen Offa, again travelling southwards and here overlooking the Walton Basin in the lee of the mountain massif known as Radnor Forest, has also been described. The loop that the Dyke makes beneath Burfa Camp to cross the narrow valley of the Hindwell Brook with a bank on a massive scale, before ascending to the heights of Herrock Hill to provide a significant vantage point over the Walton Basin to the west was also discussed. In the present chapter, the fact that the monumental bank across the Hindwell Brook valley would have been particularly impressive when seen from the hilltop at Old Radnor was taken to indicate that, as possibly at Knucklas just to the north, this latter may have been a British political centre in the eighth century. In tracing this course, the Dyke effects a massive partial encirclement of the broad level part of the upper Lugg valley in the vicinity of Presteigne, cutting off access to the area from both the west (down the Lugg valley) and from the south-west (along the valley of the Hindwell Brook). Why should this be so?

The area concerned appears to have comprised a major pre-Norman estate known as 'Lugharness', containing the OE element *(ge)herness*, denoting 'obedience, jurisdiction'.[110] Attached to the river name, this specified an area forming 'the lordship of the Lugg'. The territorial definition of this early political entity can be framed in relation to the lands that lay within the medieval lordship of Stapleton, which formed part of the lands of the Mortimers at the time of the Domesday survey in 1086. This territory included the modern parish of Stapleton, plus Willey, Kinsham, Combe, Rodd, Nash and Little Brampton, Titley and the western parts of Staunton-on-Arrow, together with Stanage on the Teme just to the east of Knighton.[111] There is moreover a clear overlap here with the extent of the medieval ecclesiastical parish of Presteigne, which included the later parishes of Stapleton, Willey, Kinsham, Combe, Rodd, Nash and Little Brampton and, perhaps most significantly, Discoed.

Its name suggests that Lugharness/Stapleton was in origin an English (rather than only a Norman) lordship, so it is worth asking exactly when this entity might have originated. So, for example, its relationship to the course of Offa's Dyke across the valleys of the Teme, Lugg, Hindwell Brook and Arrow is, to say the least, striking. As ever, it is worth looking at the landscape environs to gain some clues. Stapleton is located just across the river Lugg from Presteigne, to the north. It is today a hamlet that contains the remains of a medieval castle-borough marked by the earthworks of both the castle and its dependant settlement. The castle itself occupies a bluff overlooking the Lugg valley from the north. While this might have been an advantageous site for an earlier fortification, no investigations have taken place that could throw light onto its status in the pre-Conquest period.

However, the place-names of some of the other settlements locally offer further potential insights into the early organisation and significance of this frontier area. For Kinsham, for instance, we find the namings 'Kingesmede' and 'Kingshemede' in the thirteenth century.[112] The element *humede* can be understood as a contracted version of the OE *hemmaed*, 'meadow on a boundary'.[113] The scope of 'the meadow' can be gauged from the early versions of the naming of Presteigne itself (Humet in 1086).[114] This suggests that 'the meadow' concerned was the alluvial plain at the confluence of the Hindwell Brook with the Lugg that was divided between the priests' settlement and its immediate environs at Presteigne to the west, and the King's portion at Kinsham to the east. Given that the medieval ecclesiastical parish of Presteigne included also Discoed, the 'boundary' in question can perhaps most logically be regarded as the one marked also by Offa's Dyke.

There are yet more interesting possible links with the Dyke hereabouts. The valley-floor route eastwards along the Lugg valley from the Dyke at Discoed converges with another route just to the south that in contrast can be traced along a prominent ridge from the Radnor Forest uplands, eastwards through the Dyke at Bwlch, to a place immediately to the west of Presteigne. This is now in the western suburb of the latter town, and is intriguingly called 'Warden'. The name 'warden' derives from OE 'weard-dun': 'watch hill'.[115] This could be simply a folk allusion to the medieval 'Wardens of the March'.[116] Alternatively, however (and although there are no known early name references for the location) 'warden' could be a *-wardine* name, denoting an 'enclosure'. In either case, it may be significant that the ridge-top site directly overlooking the place called Warden is the site of a castle or other early earthwork fortification.[117]

The Lugg is the largest of the tributaries of the Wye, extending from the uplands of Radnorshire down to Mordiford east of Hereford. Why should the lordship that took its name from the river be located so far upstream? One simple answer is that it was located on the border with Wales. However, its full significance only becomes apparent when an examination is made of the way in which this area was discussed at the time of the compilation of the Herefordshire Domesday. A recent study of the dynamics of the medieval borderland between Shropshire and Powys has noted the distribution of the holdings of Norman lords in 1086 in just this area.[118] It is stated that both Ralph de Mortimer, whose centre was at Wigmore, and Osbern fitz Richard, whose father's pre-1066 castle was at Richard's Castle, held vills lying 'in marcha Wallia', that is, 'in the March of Wales'. This is the only pre-1100 usage of the term, and 'marcha' is presumably here derived from the Old English *mearc*, which denotes a boundary.

The interesting point to note, however, is that these vills are concentrated in the valleys of the river Lugg and the Hindwell Brook *on either side* of Offa's Dyke. Moreover, all of the vills on the western side of the Dyke in the Lugg valley correspond to a place with a putatively English settlement name, discussed above. Although it is risky to interpolate a late eighth- or early ninth-century situation from an eleventh-century one, it does seem quite plausible to infer from this that the frontier was thought of not as a border but as a *zone*. In this case, not only would it be incorrect to think of Offa's Dyke simply as a line, but it would also be wrong to suggest, as Noble did, that the Dyke marked the *rear* of a frontier zone. Rather, Offa's Dyke can be seen as having provided in a sense the 'backbone' of such a zone, with the lands on either side instead being seen as having represented 'the frontier'.

From the particular to the pattern: a Mercian 'March'?

> If Offa did indeed transfer the Magonsaetan see from *Lidebiri* (Lydbury North or Ledbury) to the defended frontier site at Hereford, it was probably in the context of a defensive and administrative reorganisation connected with the building of his Dyke.[119]

That the building of Offa's Dyke may have been connected with a recasting of both administrative and military arrangements along the frontier in the late eighth century is surely an entirely plausible idea. And, as is indicated in John Blair's interpolation of events quoted here, it would hardly be surprising to find that this may have had implications also for diocesan organisation.[120] What exactly, however, might this 'defensive and administrative reorganisation' have involved, besides the building of the Dyke itself? There may have been an infrastructure that supported at least some aspects of the working of Offa's Dyke, in the form of controlled access points, observation posts, and routeways, if not necessarily fortifications, as was suggested in Chapter 6. Moreover, as suggested earlier in this chapter, Offa's likely presence in Herefordshire and what little is known of Gwent and Ergyng suggests that this part of the frontier was experiencing 'flux' during the late eighth century, and the lack of clear definition of a route for the Dyke here may reflect this volatility.

More widely, however, the pattern of Domesday hundreds spanning either side of the Dyke may be indicative of a more general process whereby English communities were linked together and regarded as units with more important east–west expression than north–south. North of the Wye, this can be seen in the adjacent Domesday period hundreds of Hezetree, extending from Burrington in the north-east near Ludlow to New Radnor in the south-west and 'centred' at Presteigne close to the traverse of the Dyke north to south from Discoed to Herrock Hill;[121] Elsedune to the south, with its eastern boundary at the north–south Roman road south-westwards to Huntington and Whitney-on-Wye, 'centred' around Kington; and Staple, extending from Kenchester and Wormsley to the east of the Dyke to Brobury opposite Bredwardine to the west.

While there are difficulties with identifying 'Burton' names precisely with fortifications, the proximity of some such names to the Dyke, in the context of *other* such names as with the element *burhweard*, –bury, and possibly also –worthing, rendered locally often as –wardine, does merit some exploration. Some –bury names in the area to the east of the Dyke correspond closely to places that from later sources were clearly fortified. So Chirbury to the east of Montgomery, for example, was the site of a fortified *burh* constructed in the early ninth century, while Westbury was the site of a massacre of English forces by the Welsh in 1016. In either case, the enclosures that are documented could have comprised a re-fortification of an existing, earlier, work. This may also be true of the documented Buttington fort, and this could indicate a concentration of defended locations around the middle Severn that would not be surprising. Meanwhile, the location of place-names such as Burrington and Berrington on or near the river Teme could equally represent a non-random distribution of 'burh' localities, in this context perhaps unlikely to have been religious centres. In some cases, relatively recently documented but clearly ancestral place-names may substantiate such linkages. So, for example, in north Herefordshire not only is there a 'Burton' place-name less than a quarter of a mile to the east of the course of the Dyke west of Weobley, but in the Arrow valley only four miles to the north, Burton Court and Lower Burton in Eardisland parish are situated within a stone's throw of a series of fields that in the early nineteenth century shared the name 'Bodbury'.[122]

Other places in similar relation to the Dyke in the Chirbury–Buttington area are potentially also of some interest. One example is Worthen, the name of which settlement appears to represent a direct 'descent' from the Anglo-Saxon word *worthign*, a fortified enclosure, which is located just five miles (8 km) east from the Dyke on the eastern side of the Long Mountain, equidistant between Buttington and Chirbury. In terms of potential communication-routes, its position just to the east of the Camlad and seven miles (10 km) from the crossing of the Dyke over that river is particularly interesting. While Nantcribba Gaer has (as noted in Chapter 6) been cited as a defensible place in possible direct association with the Dyke at Forden nearby, overlooking the Severn valley south of the long Mountain, what is perhaps surprising is that fortified locations indicated to the west of Forden have received no attention. Here, south of the confluence of the Camlad with the Severn, and immediately west of the dramatic re-orientation and prospect at Hem, there survive the prominent earthworks of a large Roman fort. Between the fort and the confluence is a ridge of higher land on which stands a farm named The Gaer. The ridge itself is known as Thornbury, and it is at least possible that this was the site of a 'forward' fortification that may have pre-dated or post-dated the Dyke, or could have been established to operate in tandem with it.[123]

That the Worthen name is not an isolated instance is indicated by the presence of Worthenbury on the river Dee seven miles (10 km) east of the Dyke and close to the British monastic settlement at Bangor-is-y-coed. This is, perhaps fortuitously, an identical distance behind the Dyke to Worthen in

Shropshire. The distribution of 'Burton' names in the borderlands is similarly placed close to the rear of the Dyke, from the Wirral through central Shropshire and southwards, and as already mentioned the name is particularly common in Herefordshire. By the same token, *burhweard* derived names, which Gelling has rendered 'fort guardian', are found both sides of the Dyke, with two in Cheshire (Burwardsley and Brewer's Hall), another a Domesday manor of Burwardestone straddling the Cheshire/Flintshire border, two in Shropshire (Broseley and Burwarton) and another Domesday 'Burardestune' near Eardisley in north-west Herefordshire.

The incidence of other names derived from *worthign* could be taken to reinforce this pattern. In particular, the names of places ending in -wardine may indicate those that were in some sense or another regarded as defensible settlements. Again, these latter exist on both sides of Offa's Dyke, although the majority are to the English side. More northerly examples include Shrawardine and Stanwardine to the west of Shrewsbury and north of the Severn, while to the south of the Severn Worthen may be matched by an example closer to the Dyke in 'Treverward'. This latter place is recorded as 'Trewardine' in at least one medieval source.[124]

The -wardine name element occurs most frequently in Herefordshire, however, where in the north on the margins of Shropshire, Pedwardine occurs close to the Stanage which formed part of the medieval lordship of Stapleton. Eastwards of Pedwardine across the Teme was Leintwardine.[125] Going south from there, Blackwardine near Leominster, Marden ('Maurdine' in 1086) and Lugwardine near Hereford represent an eastwards 'limit' of such names. Westwards, the name Carwardine occurs directly across the river from Bridge Sollers, perhaps significantly in exactly the area of 'Straddle' known as 'Mawfield' which we envisaged above as potentially significant in respect to warfare in the eighth century and the siting of the Dyke on the north bank of the Wye opposite.

The examples west of the Dyke in Herefordshire are even more interesting, forming a line running northwards from another point on the south bank of the Wye at Bredwardine.[126] These include 'Mateurdin', an as yet unidentified place within Brilley parish, and Chickward(ine) to the south of Kington. The latter is extremely close to the 'Burardestune', the *burhweard*-settlement of Domesday, which has been firmly identified as Bollingham House just to the north of Eardisley.[127] Meanwhile, the location of Llanfair Waterdine in the Teme valley to the west of Knighton may represent a northwards continuation of this 'forward' pattern of -worthing names, and it is of further potential interest that Trebirt in the same parish 'is an obvious Welsh rendering of Burton…about half a mile west of Offa's Dyke'.[128]

Although we have focused here upon the -wardine places in the north-central and south-central parts of the frontier, there were other names that might represent the 'continuation' of the pattern (if such it is) to both the south and the east. The first of the eastern examples is northwards also, at Northenden near Middlewich, in Cheshire ('Norwordine' in 1086). Two other such places, both in Shropshire, are also considerably to the east of the Dyke, but both are close to Roman roads that lead directly towards the Mercian heartlands. The first is Wrockwardine, immediately to the north of Watling Street beneath the Wrekin. The second is Ingardine, near Cleobury Mortimer, close to the Roman road leading east from Ludlow towards the Severn valley.[129]

It may or may not be relevant to note also the repeated presence of estates in royal hands in near proximity to the Dyke, as at Alberbury and Trewern south of the Severn, either side of The Breiddin, and Marden just mentioned. In addition to these there is Chenistetone, the king's place, as Knighton (in Welsh Tref-y-clawdd, the settlement on the Dyke) was denoted in 1086.[130] To the east of the Dyke, Chinerestone (Kynaston, Shropshire) was similarly titled in the Domesday survey. In Herefordshire, while Kingsland (*Kingeslen* in 1137–9, the 'Royal estate in Lene') to the rear of both the Dyke and Rowe Ditch just to the north-west of Leominster was traditionally the location of Merewahl's court, both Chingtune (cyning-tun, present day Kington, 'Royal estate', 1086) and Kingstone (Chingestone, 'cyninges-tun' = 'royal estate', 1086) were in areas to the west of the Dyke but putatively within the frontier zone.[131]

Finally, Kingston at Sedbury is referred to in a charter dated 956 granting Tidenham to the monks of Bath Abbey, and this is the one explicit mention of the Dyke in a localised Anglo-Saxon document. Fox drew attention to the mention within this charter, under 'Cingestune' (the 'king's settlement', which he supposed to be the Beachley peninsula), of the Welsh *scipwealan* ('shipmen') to whom part of the unenclosed land was rented.[132] The majority of the enclosed land (5 hides) was clearly in the lower part of the peninsula, since there was 1 hide 'bufan dic' (above the Dyke). While the rental arrangement is unlikely to go back to the eighth century, once again it demonstrates that land on both sides of the Dyke was regarded as an integral part of the frontier arrangements.

Although individually, some of these place-names and place references going back in many cases to the time of Edward the Confessor or earlier may not stand close scrutiny, cumulatively they help define a swathe of landscape either side of the Dyke, and along the north–south extent of the frontier from north of the Severn in Shropshire down to the Severn estuary. This strip of territory would have been of variable 'depth' from east to west, and could have been adjusted to fit at least sub-regional circumstances. It would not in any sense have been closely comparable with the later 'Marchiae Wallia', the medieval march of Wales, which was composed of individual and often competing lordships, and was secured by castles.[133]

This strip of land may or may not have encompassed 'forts', and in some cases such places would more likely have been simple palisaded enclosures around essentially domestic settlements. In light of the discussion of the Presteigne area above, however, and the question of the depth of the frontier zone, it is not only the breadth of the hundreds in north Herefordshire and south Shropshire that may be especially significant, but also their eastwards 'anchor-points'. It is for example of some interest to note that the eastern termination of Lentuerden Hundred is near Leintwardine, a former Romano-British enclosed settlement with military/administrative links at the strategic crossing-point of Watling Street West over the river Teme.[134] The eastern limit of Hezetree Hundred meanwhile carefully encompasses Burrington near Downton and the 'East-tun' (Aston) within the same territory. And Elsedune Hundred terminates at Eardisland/Burton, already discussed. This correspondence is underscored by the association of all of these settlements with the north–south Roman road, 'Watling Street West', and may hint at a quasi-military organisation of the frontier here and elsewhere, with Roman roads acting as links for the swift passage of forces along the frontier. The story of what this frontier strip (potentially comprising a series of parallel east–west territories) represented in a wider strategic context cannot be told without reference to a much wider canvas. And it is through consideration of the historical and strategic frame of Mercian political hegemony – with resonances in the Carolingian world – that its real purpose perhaps begins to emerge.

CHAPTER EIGHT

The material of Mercian hegemony

> That Offa was a popular ruler seems unlikely but he was a powerful king and everyone knew it. Charlemagne, for instance, no mean authority on such matters, recognised Offa as the sole ruler of the southern English. The general tenor of Mercian policy at the time was expressed in a charter by one of Offa's successors, when he called himself *imperator*... He calls himself Emperor of Mercia because all the English south of the Humber were deemed to be Mercian, whether willingly or not.
>
> Eric John, *Re-assessing Anglo-Saxon England*, 1996[1]

The successor concerned was Coenwulf. Eric John is characteristically rhetorical here in overstating for effect the case that Charlemagne saw Offa as 'sole' ruler in southern England. Had this been the case, the Frankish king's granting of refuge to Ecgberht of Wessex in the period from 780 or 790 until his return in 802 would have been pointless.[2] And yet there is more than a kernel of truth in the observation that Offa and Coenwulf saw themselves not as rulers of 'the English' but of 'the Mercians', reflecting a Mercia that dominated the other Anglo-Saxon kingdoms and whose kings clearly intended to subsume them, along with, in effect, the British of the west. In the late eighth and early ninth centuries, moreover, relations between kings and clergy became more central to the definition of the body politic. So tensions over patronage were registered in terms especially of disputes between the Mercian kings and successive Archbishops of Canterbury and bishops (for instance of the *Hwicce* at Worcester) over the control of monasteries and estates. These disputes highlighted the difficulties that kings had in controlling both lay and ecclesiastical interests. We see in Offa, particularly, but also in Coenwulf, an almost obsessive drive towards political dominance of elites and competitors through patronage, alliances and occasionally violence on the one hand, and through the political manipulation of the clergy for financial and tactical purposes on the other.[3] Among other possible outcomes of such concerns to dominate was an increasing impetus to control, and in some circumstances physically to delimit, the frontier.

The existence of the Mercian hegemony has been referred to at various points in this book, but to understand the place of Offa's Dyke within that hegemonic framework, and particularly as that framework developed in the closing stages of Offa's reign, its nature and its workings need to be examined more closely. If the Dyke fitted into a wider strategy (or series of related strategies) of political control it is important to understand how that strategy was expressed materially and in a variety of spheres. It is necessary also to identify the ways in which the strategy was directed upon a wider canvas: for instance, towards rivals within 'England', westwards into Wales and southwards overseas to continental Europe. What exactly, however, is meant by 'hegemony'? 'Hegemony' refers, at its simplest, to the leadership of a grouping of political entities, whether kingdoms, states, or so on. However, when searching for words to express a greater degree of control than 'first among equals', the term that is most commonly used to refer to the period concerned, 'the Mercian supremacy', is surely inadequate. Although there was a reality to the dominance of these two kings in both the practical and ideological spheres, the term 'supremacy' simply states a fact and does not describe the nature of the authority concerned. Alternatively, 'imperium' is the condition of exercising absolute power, yet while this may adequately capture the status of a ruler such as Charlemagne, it does not accurately represent the kind of pre-eminence enjoyed by the Mercian kings concerned.

The word 'hegemony' is therefore to be preferred in reference to the power of the eighth-century Mercian kingship under both Offa and Coenwulf, because even at its zenith the might of Mercia was contested within England. Although these Mercian kings sought to exercise an enhanced form of overlordship (and this was especially so in at least the last decade of Offa's reign) they at no time enjoyed such pre-eminence without strong resistance, not only from Wessex and Northumbria, but also from East Anglia and Kent. Mercian kingly power was hegemonic also, in that, as Mercia grew in dominance, it nonetheless did so in and through alliances. So while describable as at least an 'emergent state' Mercia remained the leader of an independent, if increasingly interdependent, grouping or confederacy of kingdoms.[4] The nature of the hegemonic power that Offa in particular wielded in this way corresponds closely to the meaning of hegemony used by late twentieth and early twenty-first century political scientists. This is a leadership that would tolerate no challenge to its exercise of authority within its immediate political sphere of interest, and which interfered chronically in the affairs of peoples in whose lands it perceived itself to have an overriding strategic interest.

In considering the politics of power in the wider landscape of eighth-century Britain and beyond, there are many questions that can be posed concerning the nature of the Mercian hegemony as exercised in the reigns of Offa and Coenwulf, such as 'what light do the exchanges between Offa and Charlemagne in the closing decade of the eighth century tell us about Mercian power in and beyond England?', 'what distinguishes the practice of hegemony in these years in terms of specific instruments of control or propaganda?', and 'how was the hegemony exercised in respect to the different kingdoms and areas of southern Britain?' While all of these aspects have been the subject of much debate among Anglo-Saxon historians in recent years, and we shall summarise aspects of such debate and its conclusions in this chapter, there are further dimensions that concern the character of the Mercian hegemony, that demand greater attention in the light of recent discoveries and new perspectives.

Such further general questions such as 'what can coinage tell us about politics and the personal projection of the Mercian ruling elite?', 'how did royal attempts to control economic activity within Mercia reflect their strategic interests?', and 'what does an assessment of late eighth- and early ninth-century church architecture suggest about the international pretensions of the Mercian regime?', are also posed here, and they are discussed also in reference to the possibility of particular insights arising from archaeological discoveries. The discussion extends therefore to posing and considering such questions as 'where do elaborate carvings like the 'Lichfield Angel' fit into the emerging picture?', 'where, if at all, does the 'Staffordshire Hoard' find a context in this discussion of Mercian dominance?' In turn these questions prepare the way for the opening section of the final chapter, with its key question being 'what was the role of Offa's Dyke in the context of such hegemonic strategy and activity?' In this chapter the main focus is therefore upon the *material* of the Mercian hegemony, by which term is meant two things. Firstly, it refers to the substance of political action: the nature of power and the means by which it was exercised. Secondly, it specifies the material expression of power and the physical means by which it was made manifest and effective. The chapter opens, therefore, with an exploration of the former, and goes on to focus upon the latter: of which, of course, the Dyke is the ultimate example.

Offa: the epitome of hegemonic leadership

Much has been written in recent years in re-assessment of the nature of Offa's leadership, for instance by examining closely what commentary exists upon him from writers of subsequent generations, both Anglo-Saxon and medieval, who may have based their testimony in part on documentation that no longer exists.[5] The only near-contemporary view of Offa is to be perceived from the letters of the Northumbrian cleric and correspondent Alcuin, based for much of the time at Charlemagne's court. His writings indicate something of the complexity of opinions that could be held about Offa at one and the same time. So, though apparently well-disposed towards the Mercian king, among other things for his 'modest and chaste customs', Alcuin nonetheless had misgivings concerning Offa's exercise of power and the manner of his pursuit of his ambitions, at least towards the end of his forty-year reign. The nature of such misgivings became apparent soon after the death of both Offa and his son Ecgfrith, and this has given rise to serious re-appraisal of Offa's supposed 'statesmanship'.[6]

The character of Offa's kingship

King Aethelbald's military successes and political activity had, by the mid-eighth century, clearly established Mercia as the leading power among the Anglo-Saxon kingdoms, building upon the achievements of Penda, Wulfhere and Aethelred in the preceding century. However, Offa has been singled out by those writers anxious to create a narrative of English unification between the seventh and ninth centuries as not only the greatest over-king of the eighth century but also as the first accepted ruler of all England, at least south of the Humber.[7] A question that has been raised in recent years, however, is to what degree was Offa's reputation as a wholly remarkable leader as perceived by mid-twentieth-century historians deserved, and to what extent has it been imagined?[8] The answer to this rests to a large degree upon the status we accord to the evidence upon which an assessment of his rule is based. A remarkable series of letters to Offa and to Coenwulf, and to their associates and contemporaries, from the Carolingian court and the papacy survive especially from the period c.790 to at least 805. Apart from this, of greatest importance evidentially, at least to an earlier generation of historians, is that material provided by the charters witnessed by the Mercian kings. More evidence on the nature of Offa's political dealings is also accumulating from study of Offa's coinage, largely through re-assessment of an already massive, but still growing, corpus.

Sir Frank Stenton was in no doubt that the location of grant-giving, the titles accorded to Offa and others, and the tone of address in the charters indicates an altogether different set of relations and scale of Offa's authority from what had gone before. It has nonetheless been shown fairly conclusively in recent years that the terms of address indicative of over-kingship of all the English in the charters cited by Stenton can now be dismissed as later embellishments inserted long after Offa's reign had ended.[9] The genuine surviving contemporary formulas instead all style him as 'King of the Mercians', just as the inscriptions on his coinage do.

However, it is not just the terms of reference directly to the king himself that illuminate the nature of his kingship through the charters he was the primary witness to, but also the witness-lists in their entirety. The charter formulas and detail denote a manner of rule that exercised a high degree of control and specification of statuses and relations. Moreover, careful analysis has shown that a 'core group' of close associates recur in complex and revealing ways such that it is possible to identify the presence, if not the exact constituencies, of representatives of the princely or at least the patrician lineages most closely associated with kingly authority. There appears to have both a 'core group' whose names recur frequently in Offa's charters and in certain cases also in Coenwulf's, and a wider group who appear from time to time, and who are thought to represent more regional interests. In these terms, although Offa may have purged its ranks of serious rivals to the kingship itself, there was nonetheless an identifiable Mercian 'regime' comprising an elite corps of powerful men (and some women).[10]

Offa's aptitude for political intrigue became evident soon after his accession, although the decade or so through to the early 770s is probably the least well documented part of his reign. His actions in respect to the kingdom of Kent provide an instructive indication of the character of his political manoeuvrings, nonetheless. A period of instability in Kent began in 762 when Aethelberht of Kent died and his co-ruler Eadberht appears to have been ousted by Sigered (possibly of East Saxon origin) who by 763–764 was styled 'king of half Kent' with a new co-ruler Eanmund.[11] One Heahberht, who had witnessed a grant of land in Rochester by Sigered in 762, then appears as a 'King of Kent' in the witness-list to another Rochester charter granted by Offa at Canterbury in 764, accompanied by members of the Mercian elite.

This latter presence in particular was presumably the outcome of an opportunistic intervention by Offa into a situation of political instability. If so, with the advent of yet another co-ruler, Ecgberht, who in 765 issued a grant to the bishop of Rochester witnessed also by Heahberht and confirmed by Offa at Peterborough, it may be that Kentish independence re-asserted itself. Both Heahberht and Ecgberht issued their own coinage, but little more is heard of the former after 770. Ecgberht was still witnessing charters in 779, and it may have been him who fought the Mercians at the battle at Otford in 776: an event which is widely regarded as having been, if not a defeat for Offa, at least an inconclusive engagement that resulted in a political stalemate. The level of Offa's interest in Kentish affairs did not necessarily abate, however. So following the appearance there of yet another king, Ealhmund, by 784, and from at least 785, Offa regularly witnessed grants in Kent, and in the period to 789 he even revoked grants formerly made by Ecgberht and the reeve Ealdhun because 'his minister (subordinate thegn) had presumed to give land allotted to him by his lord (Offa) into the power of another without his witness'.[12]

The relationship between Mercia under Offa and the various kings and leaders within Kent is clearly of considerable importance to the whole unfolding of Offa's reign, and especially his economic, ecclesiastical, and political strategies, in so far as these can be reconstructed from the available evidence. Two fundamental factors affecting any understanding of the degree of Mercian focus upon the south-east of England must be kept in mind when considering much of the detail of events in the sixty-year period from c.765–825. The first is the strategic and economic importance of London to the Mercian kings, and of the maintenance and further development of trading links with the continent, which will be discussed briefly below. The second is the political importance of Canterbury within Anglo-Saxon history as seen from the vantage point of a Mercian state emerging onto a world stage. In the face of these two factors, the political fate of the Kentish kings might seem to be of lesser importance, and yet awareness among the Mercians of the historical legacy of the Kingdom of Kent among the Anglo-Saxon kingdoms was crucial to the development of policy towards that place and people.

Offa and Charlemagne

The last decade of the eighth century in particular is set apart from other periods in the history of Mercia in that, although we still have no surviving documentation from the Mercian court itself, the existence of letters representing the continental side of the flow of correspondence provides some fascinating glimpses into the workings of the regime. The insights into the thoughts and actions of Offa in the last years of his reign and those of Coenwulf at the opening of his own, as well as some of the attitudes and actions of their English contemporaries, indicate something of the complexity of the politics of an emergent state that some historians appear to regard as something of a 'rough diamond', and somewhat primitive.[13] By far the largest part of this correspondence was that of Alcuin, who served Charlemagne at the Frankish court. Although as a Northumbrian, Alcuin's closest concern was with events and relationships north of the Humber, he acted widely as a mediator in Carolingian diplomacy, and this included helping to manage the relationship with King Offa.[14]

It is likely to have been in the context of the well-established intercourse evidently propagated by Alcuin, and possibly also due to the successful mediation of other clerics in the context of the 'marriage dispute' of c.789–790, that it was possible for Charlemagne to address Offa directly in a letter written early in 796 that reveals the scope and scale of their inter-relations.[15] It opens:

> Charles, by the Grace of God king of the Franks and Lombards to his dearest brother, Offa, king of the Mercians. Having perused your brotherly letters we first give thanks to Almighty God for the sincerity of the Catholic faith set down in your pages; recognising you to be not only a most strong protector of your earthly country, but also a most devout defender of the holy faith.[16]

Charlemagne went on to respond to requests by Offa concerning the protection of English merchants overseas, the return of exiles, and the supply of 'black stones'. He agreed to address these matters, but in return listed a series of his own concerns over, for instance, how some English merchants were posing as pilgrims to avoid trade tolls, that so many exiles arrived at his court in fear of their lives if they returned to England, and that English merchants were shortening the cloaks they traditionally traded to Francia to enhance their profits unfairly. He ends with a noting of the gifts he had sent to accompany the letter, to the various bishoprics within the five Mercian sees, and, for Offa himself, cloaks of silk, a belt and a 'Hunnish sword'.[17]

'In the very year of his letter to Offa, (Charlemagne's) armies obliterated the Avar empire of the Huns in central Europe, and rifled its great treasure hoard. That (he) could give Offa a cut of the proceeds, and address him as an equal, conveys some idea of the status to which Mercian kings could now aspire, as does an earlier (though abortive) proposal for a marriage alliance between Offa and Charlemagne…Charlemagne, moreover, saw England as if it were ruled by two kings only: Aethelred ruling Northumbria, and Offa everywhere to the south.'[18] This assessment is in effect a re-statement of Stenton's perspective on Offa, but it focuses too strongly upon the specifically Mercian dimension of relations between the Anglo-Saxon kingdoms and Francia. For instance, it leaves out of account the degree of involvement of Charlemagne and his ambassadors in the internal dynastic and ecclesiastical politics of Northumbria, and in the struggle for autonomy in Kent. Nor does it adequately acknowledge the status of the West Saxon kingship, whereby Cynewulf was specifically mentioned as having been in attendance at one at least of the southern Councils of the visit of the papal legates in 786, or register the extent of Carolingian interference in the struggle between the rival factions of the West Saxon ruling elite in the period after Cynewulf's death.[19]

The terms of address used by Charlemagne, and by Alcuin (on behalf of the Frankish court, and in his references to Offa in correspondence with others) have been re-evaluated in recent years to suggest that the latter's influence upon Charlemagne was not as great as suggested by earlier scholars.[20] Not only was the extent of Charlemagne's domain many times larger than Offa's, but the resources available to him and the scope of his patronage far exceeded what the Mercians could achieve. While such re-assessment of the relative status to be accorded to Offa and Charlemagne is no doubt necessary, it is important to remain mindful of the scope of engagement of the Mercian regime with the Frankish empire evident in the correspondence, and the care with which, while not regarding Offa in any real sense as an equal, Charlemagne nonetheless adjusted his policy towards the Anglo-Saxons to take account of Offa's power and influence.

The Frankish regime, working closely with the papacy, to some extent choreographed the visit of the papal legates to Britain in 787: among other things probably to moderate Offa's ambitions concerning Lichfield and Canterbury. Moreover, Charlemagne reacted almost theatrically to Offa's reciprocal proposal concerning the marriage alliance involving his daughter, Bertha. And he managed the presence of dissident exiles from among Offa's English neighbours such that while not discouraging their flight to Francia, he nevertheless packed several of them off to Rome to avoid giving the impression that he was showing anything more than compassion for their plight.[21] All this indicates a degree of Mercian impact upon Frankish policy that cannot easily be ignored. Whether the letters convey simply the conventions of the age in the expression of brotherly esteem between the two monarchs, and whether or not they exchanged anything on equal terms, there can be little doubt that Charlemagne saw Offa as a major player on part of the northern margins of the Carolingian empire.[22]

Arguably, by seeking to extend the scope of Mercian trade (see below) and by establishing some form of diplomatic mission or presence in the Carolingian court, Offa was playing a dangerous game. It opened the possibility that might not otherwise have been so obvious, for Charlemagne to enter the field of Anglo-Saxon inter-kingdom politics, and thereby to potentially extend the reach of Francia's own 'imperium'.[23] That this is precisely what was happening is clear from the extent to which close contact and relations were maintained by Charlemagne with Northumbria (and not only through Alcuin's direct

FIGURE 8.1 Tamworth: Market Street and the Town Hall from the west

The Town Hall, built in 1701, is located on the same ridge as the parish church, on the highest part of the settlement, at or near the site of the Mercian royal residence, north-east of the later castle. Tamworth only emerged as a regular site for Councils in the early ninth century, but was from an early point in time recognised as the Mercian 'capital'.

intercession) and to which exiles from Kent and Wessex and no doubt elsewhere were given safe haven. Seen in this light, much of the thrust of Offa's stance towards Francia could be interpreted as defensive rather than one of rivalry.

For example, Offa's counter-proposal that as well as the marriage of Aelfflaed to Charlemagne's eldest son, Charles, the Mercian king's own son, Ecgfrith, should marry Charlemagne's eldest daughter, Bertha, could, and has, been interpreted simply as proof of Offa's megalomania. Yet it could instead be read as resulting from a concern to guarantee that Charlemagne would not use Aelfflaed's connection to Mercia as an excuse to intervene in Mercian politics in the way that Offa himself was doing, or was about to do, in respect to both Wessex and Northumbria.[24] It is perhaps important to focus much more on Offa's immediate preoccupations in the English context, and here we can see two dimensions that are of particular significance. The first concern was to exercise control over a Mercia that encompassed East Anglia integrally by emphasising a shared Anglian identity. The second was to dominate the south-east (and specifically Kent) both for the economic power that it secured, and for the very real opportunity it provided to exercise control over the church across England and beyond. Both of these aspects are examined more closely below.

Sustaining the Mercian hegemony: Coenwulf, king and 'emperor'

The case for viewing Coenwulf as having been in some sense a scion of the late eighth-century Mercian regime was put forward in Chapter 3, above. Though essentially impossible to prove, and apparently contradicted by Alcuin's attitude to Coenwulf as a man he saw as a brusque interloper, this thesis does at least have the attraction of explaining the degree to which Ecgfrith's successor appeared to sustain key aspects of Offa's political programme. Stenton was at pains to emphasise the degree to which Coenwulf was unable to maintain the same degree of power and influence beyond Mercia that Offa did. However, such a view underestimates the brittleness of the latter's hold over events in either Wessex or Northumbria. It also ignores Coenwulf's considerable successes in the far west in Wales that, arguably, Egberht of Wessex strove to emulate in his conquest of the south-west peninsula of Britain.[25] While there is no doubting therefore 'the skill with which Coenwulf conserved Offa's *imperium*', we can nonetheless also agree with Kirby that this key feature of his reign should not obscure some divergence in policy.[26] Whether this shift in emphasis in reality reflected a less flexible and more insular regime is a matter for debate, but in light of the amount of continental diplomatic traffic of the decade after his accession, this seems doubtful.

The view generally taken by Anglo-Saxon historians towards some of the first actions of Coenwulf's reign in abandoning the Mercian archdiocese of Lichfield is that it represented *realpolitik*, an understanding that the weight of papal and Carolingian authority was against its continuation in the face of opposition from Canterbury.[27] While this is probably true, the nature of this exercise may, at least in its intent, have been more subtle politically. It is certainly remarkable how much of the thrust of Offa's strategy was sustained and developed by Coenwulf, despite the fact that he had to react to the opportunism of Offa's enemies and the leaders of the southern kingdoms, in the aftermath of Ecgfrith's death. This is well illustrated by Coenwulf's actions in Kent. Here, he maintained a concern to control events, first by biding his time and having the pope excommunicate Eadberht Praen in 798 before moving to seize him and the kingdom; and then by tightening his grip on power there by inserting a permanent Mercian royal presence by appointing his brother Cuthred as (sole) king of Kent.[28] In 799, Coenwulf had made a treaty with the West Saxons, and was working to supplant the newly-installed king of East Anglia, Eadwald.[29] Small wonder, then, that in 798x799, it was in a *Kentish* charter (albeit one issued at a Council elsewhere) that Coenwulf had himself styled 'leader and emperor of the kingdom of the Mercians'.[30]

Coenwulf emulated Offa's strategy of ecclesiastical control by installing his female kin as abbesses of key monasteries such as Minster-in-Thanet, presided over by his daughter Cwoenthryth. Such moves were resented by Canterbury and the people of Kent just as much in the early ninth century as Offa's actions had been in the later eighth, and if anything, the power of Canterbury had grown in the interim with the appointment of the reformer Wulfred as Archbishop. It is in this light interesting to note that in his correspondence with the papacy Coenwulf stressed the hatred Offa had for the people of Kent in general and Archbishop Jaenberht in particular as having been the reason behind Offa's wish to create the new see of Lichfield.[31] Instead of leaving Canterbury well alone, however, Coenwulf proposed to move the archdiocesan centre to London. The reasoning again could have been pragmatic, since the 'Mercian' Archbishop of Canterbury, Aethelheard, had in effect abandoned his seat in the face of the Kentish rebellion. However, Coenwulf's motivation for such a transfer was arguably nonetheless strategic. While he overtly argued that such a move would return to what was widely understood to have been the original intention of Pope Gregory I to have one see based in York and another in London, it cannot have been lost on his contemporaries that this move would also have brought the archdiocese more overtly within the Mercian sphere of control.

Coenwulf's relations with Charlemagne were in some ways just as complex as Offa's had been. This was nowhere more evident than in the strife between Eardwulf of Northumbria and Coenwulf in the early years of his reign, in a war between the kingdoms that had begun at least by 798 and ended only in 802 as a result of protracted mediation by the English bishops. The forcing of Eardwulf into exile in 806 was then followed by his restoration in 812 with Carolingian support. Charlemagne's intervention in Northumbrian affairs was much more direct on Eardwulf's behalf than during Offa's reign, and only deft diplomatic work by Coenwulf's ambassadors in Rome prevented the Carolingian policy from immediately upsetting the terms of his control of the key monasteries in Kent.[32]

Coenwulf and his successors continued to hold Councils in and around Tamworth in the Mercian heartlands, including at such places as Croft in Leicestershire, as well as by the Thames at Chelsea and elsewhere to the west of London. It was in one of his charters issued at such a Council at 'Clofesho' in 798 that Coenwulf was titled 'emperor'.[33] While Kent remained a significant preoccupation in respect to Canterbury and no doubt also in regard to trade, at least part of the focus of royal activity appears however to have shifted westwards during Coenwulf's reign, especially towards Winchcombe and the former kingdom, principality and, latterly, 'province', of the *Hwicce*. Had this shift to a more westerly location for the seat of Mercian power occurred in later times it may have been explicable in reference to the Danish presence and their annexation of the lands to the north and west of Watling Street. In the early ninth century, however, it is harder to fathom. It may have had to do, in a personal sphere, with Coenwulf's ancestry,[34] and with his investment in monastic foundations; but in a political sphere it seems more likely to have been bound up with his ambitions for territorial expansion westwards beyond the areas of English settlement.[35]

The political mechanisms of hegemony

There is no simple answer to the question of how the Mercian hegemony among the Anglo-Saxon kingdoms of the period 760 to 820 was sustained. As we have seen, the overall picture varied through time, and especially according to the contrasting character of Mercia's rulers. We can perhaps, however, recognise the workings of several distinct strategies of control, or 'political mechanisms' of hegemony. These represent actions and policies affecting numerous distinct political spheres, several of which had particular and distinctive material dimensions. Among these, the creation of Offa's Dyke and the active development of a western frontier was but one of the most visible.

Overlordship and authority

From the accession of Aethelbald onwards, and perhaps due to documentary losses the extent of which is unknown, historians rely disproportionately on charters to record the movements and dispositions of the Mercian kings in different parts of their realm. It has been noted that such charters refer to the kings who were the *dictators* of such documents as leaders of their peoples, significantly until Aethelbald himself issued a charter that referred instead to his dominion. "Apart from Kent no territorial charters are used in any charter with a reasonable claim to authenticity until the first half of the eighth century, when Aethelbald of Mercia uses one." This was the charter of 749 in respect of an estate at Ismere, near Kidderminster in what became Worcestershire, held by the Bishop of Worcester, in which Aethelbald is styled 'Rex Britanniae'.[36]

It is surely the case, as Damian Tyler has pointed out, that the character of Mercian kingship, in respect both to its expression and its ambition towards its neighbours, was significantly transformed during the eighth century.[37] He has noted, firstly, that the adoption of Christianity by the kings of the late seventh century had both mundane and ideological impacts on those, and particularly upon later, Mercian kings. On the practical side, royal patronage of Christian clergy provided a pool of literate individuals from which a bureaucracy could be drawn. Meanwhile on the ideological side, the Mercian kings could now draw from Biblical and Roman models of kingship, as well as the more traditional Germanic ones, to emphasise their plenipotentiary, and heavenly-sanctioned, status. This affected in particular their sense of distinction from the noble elites that surrounded them, and in the process they developed 'a more expansive vision of powerful kingship'.[38]

It could be claimed from study of the events of the period 780 to 796 that Offa did intend to move to a position of absolute power and to exercise 'imperium'. However, the process by which he alienated through grants of bookland the landholdings of the kings of dependent territories, and gradually reduced the status of such former rulers, had been a protracted one.[39] Those leaders referred to in charters near the beginning of Offa's reign as kings, such as Ealdred of the *Hwicce*, were soon termed 'subregulus' and by the end of it were denoted instead by the term *dux* (or equivalent: that is simply lieutenants, or in later terminology, *ealdormen*).[40] This process of 'demotion' of neighbours and potential rivals had as its counterpart the process of elevation of the Mercian kingship to a more exalted status. In this light, the anointing of Ecgfrith as Offa's successor was not only about securing the succession, but also served to set apart and further legitimise through divine sanction the position of the king himself. This was a process underlined for Offa by the overt deployment of a genealogy that linked him back (whether or not fictively) to Eowa, the brother of Penda, and by his portrayal as having the kingly attributes of the biblical David on his coinage.[41]

Although the evidence for Coenwulf's exercise of power is more limited, it is likely that he adopted similar strategies to those of Offa regarding how the subject kingdoms were to be kept under hegemonic control. The situation in Kent is reflected in a charter of 809 in which he was titled 'King of Mercia and of the Province of Kent'.[42] In the case of the East Saxons, who also may have rebelled after Ecgfrith's demise late in 796, the 'King Sigeric' of Essex who is recorded as having gone on pilgrimage to Rome in 798 may have been an ealdorman under Offa and Ecgfrith. His successor may have been another Sigered, who was styled in a charter of Coenwulf as 'rex', although it is not clear of which kingdom. Whatever the case, the same individual appears as 'subregulus' in 812 and as ealdorman in 814. By this measure, we can see Coenwulf treating the wider circle of until recently independent or semi-independent kingdoms, which included Lindsey, East Anglia, Essex, Kent, the *Hwicce*, and probably also the *Magonsaete*, as 'provinces' of the Mercian kingdom in very much the same way that it appears that Offa had begun to do.

Warfare and diplomacy

We have noted how, compared with the vigorous pursuit of war as an instrument of policy by his predecessor, Aethelbald, Offa was apparently sparing in his military commitment of his forces, especially in reference to his Anglian neighbours. Whenever he moved to reinforce a policy of quiet advance of political control, it was only at the point of firm resistance or challenge that he committed to a fight. This approach, coupled with a predilection for opportunism whenever instability occurred within kingdoms whose destiny he wished to influence or control, is apparent not only in his dealings with Kent, but also in Sussex.[43] An even clearer example of the exercise of the mailed fist in the velvet glove may be witnessed in Offa's relations with Cynewulf, king of the West Saxons. Soon after Offa's accession, the latter had advanced northwards into the middle Thames valley and had seized the monastery of Cookham which Aethelbald had granted to Christ Church, Canterbury. Offa was absorbed by events in Kent until at least 776 when the situation of temporary stalemate after the engagement at Otford was seemingly used by Offa as an opportunity to exert pressure on Wessex. This may have been a gradual process of re-absorption of Thames valley territories, but it culminated in what was probably a short, sharp, engagement at 'Bensington' (Benson in Oxfordshire) in 779. However, his relations with neither Wessex nor Cynewulf himself were defined by this military action, since as we have seen barely seven years later the latter sat in the same Council as Offa at the time of the visit of the papal legates.[44] That Coenwulf showed a similar appreciation of the need to balance shows of force with diplomatic activity has been well illustrated by his actions in respect to the Kentish kingship.

While the more immediate sphere for Offa's diplomacy was at the courts of the kings of Wessex and Northumbria, it was through the envoys sent to Rome and to Francia, and received from these directions, that Mercian diplomacy was most evident. Diplomacy must have played its part in Offa's moves to have Ecgfrith consecrated as his successor, whether his ultimate motives concerned securing the succession, or emphasising the divine nature of kingship, or demonstrating the equivalence of the Mercian realm to the Carolingian, or all of these.

It must have been clear to Offa well before 786 that Archbishop Jaenberht would not necessarily comply with his wishes to consecrate Ecgfrith, and that to secure the act, he would need to create a new archdiocese. This would need to be based upon a location securely and unequivocally at the centre of the Mercian kingdom, presided over by an archbishop whose loyalties were beyond question. Offa's plan to raise Lichfield as the centre of the first new archdiocese in England for over two hundred years was likely to have been formulated, therefore, and his case put to the pope, before the arrival of papal legates in Britain in 786. Indeed, it seems likely that the principles were agreed between Pope Hadrian and Offa, and quite probably Charlemagne also, in advance. As such, Offa completely outmanoeuvred Jaenberht, and although the papal legates apparently nowhere addressed the issue of Lichfield directly, and the terms of agreement on kingly powers and the privileges of the church appear quite one-sided from the pronouncements of the various Councils, it soon became evident that the plan was to entirely re-organise the southern English church to Offa's advantage.

The intricacy with which political diplomacy was managed has been indicated in the observations made above concerning Charlemagne's letter to Offa of 796, and the 'marriage dispute' that preceded it. The role of third parties in this dispute is critical to an understanding of how this diplomacy was conducted, and it was probably only possible to exercise influence on either party in respect of their vital commercial and economic interests.[45] Nor did Mercian overseas diplomatic activity necessarily diminish significantly under Coenwulf: 'it is clear that, in the first quarter of the ninth century, Mercian politics retained a high profile on the Continent in a manner similar to, but less well documented than, the period of Offa's reign. The number of Mercian missions to Rome in the years around the turn of the ninth century is remarkable. It is notable too, that contact with the Frankish court was sustained beyond the death of Charlemagne.'[46]

Diplomatic processes must have had local and material consequences, and we see glimpses of this from slightly later Mercian charters. One specific reservation of duties concerning diplomatic activity was to be found among the provisions of a charter of 848 in benefit of the monastery of Breedon-on-the-Hill in (later) Leicestershire, not far from Repton. The requirement was specifically to provide hospitality to envoys from the West Saxons or Northumbrians, as well as to ambassadors who came to visit the Mercian king from overseas.[47] Another potentially significant charter reference is the one of 855 concerning an estate at Blockley near Worcester that referred specifically to the *Wahlfaerald* ('Welsh expedition') and to 'mounted men of the English race or foreigners', either of whom may have been operating as messengers to and from the British beyond Offa's Dyke.[48]

Political manipulation, and regicide

As already suggested, Offa sought to gain influence in Wessex in the later 780s through a marriage alliance at the level of the kingship, and soon afterwards as we saw above, he had the opportunity to follow this up with a marriage into Charlemagne's family, apparently on the latter's initiative. Having failed to capitalise on the Frankish opportunity, he went on to successfully arrange another alliance with Northumbria in the early 790s. If the later sources are correct (there is no corroborating contemporary record), Offa was contemplating another union to secure direct association with the East Angles through a match between yet another daughter and their ostensibly young and energetic king, Aethelberht.[49] While the motivation of the other alliances may have been ultimately to secure pro-Mercian dynasties which could eventually lead their people into absorption into an ever-greater Mercia along the lines suggested by Eric John and others, it has been suggested that Offa may in this case have been hatching a somewhat different hegemonic plan.

FIGURE 8.2 'Offa Rex' pennies, promoting a particular view of Mercian kingship
Top, moneyer Eadhun (MEC 1126[50]*, Fitzwilliam Museum, Cambridge). Bottom, moneyer unknown (BMC 30*[51]*). The 'curly hairstyle' on the Eadhun coin is consistent with contemporary manuscript depictions of King David, and this association directly evoked the sacral qualities of kingship.*[52]*Although highly formalised, the depiction of clothing and apparent ornaments both follows Roman imperial conventions and at the same time hints at the existence of a Mercian court dress 'style'. Drawing by Tim Hoverd.*

This is based in part on a contrary reading of the 'Offa Rex Anglorum' formula used on certain of his charters, some or all of which instances might represent tenth-century interpolations, and the more certainly contemporary appearance of the abbreviation 'Of Rx A' on some of the coinage of Offa produced in London by the moneyer Alhmund. In tenth-century usage, the formula could be taken, as it largely has been, as an expression of lordship over all the Anglo-Saxons, and as 'King of the English'. However, usage in the eighth century was likely to have referred instead to a dominion over the *Anglians* that extended beyond Mercia to encompass East Anglia. 'Here the continued acceptance of a dependent relationship with the Mercians on the part of the East Angles was crucial' to Offa's building of an 'Anglian empire'.[53] In this regard, Offa's 'creation of an Anglian archdiocese could have been primarily intended as an expression of a new southern Anglian political community (whose) ecclesiastical centre was Lichfield, its principal trading emporia London and Ipswich.[54]

We know from a letter written by Alcuin to one of Offa's leading ealdorman, probably to be identified as his 'patrician', Brorda, that Offa was understood to have secured his son Ecgfrith's succession by the elimination of potential rivals.[55] While this no doubt included liquidation of some of the leading members and aethelings of the 'subsidiary' kingships and patrician families of Mercia itself, the most memorable incident was the execution of King Aethelbert in 794. However, Offa was not without blood on his hands in respect to other kingdoms also. The timings of the atrocities of Aethelred of Northumbria are particularly relevant here. In 792 Aethelred tried to execute his rival, Eardwulf, at Ripon before having the aethelings Oelf and Oelfwine killed. Then, 'on 14 September 792 the ex-king, Osred, having ill-advisedly returned from exile, was executed at *Aynburg* and buried at Tynemouth. Barely two weeks later at Michaelmas, Æthelred married Offa's daughter, Ælffled, at Catterick'.[56] It is difficult not to see these events as interconnected, though whether the widely-vilified Aethelred inspired Offa's regicidal acts, or vice-versa, will never be known.

It may have been due to this history of king-killing not long before his accession, and its repercussions for the Mercian regime, that Coenwulf appears to have been careful not to have eliminated his rivals through such direct means. There have been suggestions that he may have come to power either through (or following) a putative murder of Ecgfrith, but as was suggested in Chapter 3, what evidence there is can be read in an entirely different way. That Coenwulf was ruthless in the suppression of kings who challenged his authority is evident in the case of his seizure and 'removal in chains into Mercia' of Eadberht Praen of Kent, whether or not the later tradition that he had the latter's eyes put out or hands cut off is true. There is in contrast a more familial sense of political control under Coenwulf, for instance in the gathering of 811 in which a number of members of the immediate ruling family, including his daughter, assembled for what has been described as 'a meeting of heirs', possibly following the death of Coenwulf's son Cynehelm.[57]

Managing the church

Beyond Northumbria, English church synods or Councils of the eighth century were not convened by kings for their own purposes, as they were in the Frankish and Visigothic kingdoms. However, nor was a king like Offa in attendance 'because they happened to take place in his territory...carrying no further political implications beyond the fact that the king took advantage of such occasions to transact some business of his own.'[58] Rather, the convocation was deliberately orchestrated by the king and metropolitan(s) working in concert. So, for instance, a meeting in 789 at Chelsea was explicitly described in a charter that arose from it as 'a pontifical council (which) was held in the famous place which is called Chelsea, under the presidency of archbishops Jænberht and Hygeberht with King Offa mediating, with all his leading men'.[59]

Nor was Offa above potentially mis-representing his own (contested) plans for the church as an idea that had arisen out of the workings of their own concordat. For example, Pope Leo III wrote to Coenwulf in 798, that Leo's predecessor Pope Hadrian had 'diminished contrary to custom the authority of the bishop of Canterbury, and by his authority confirmed the division into two archiepiscopal sees...because your excellent king Offa, testified in his letter that it was the united wish and unanimous petition of you all, both on account of the vast size of your lands and the extension of your kingdom, and also for many more reasons and advantages'.[60] This latter point reveals much not only about how Offa represented his own wishes as a wider consensus (and hence the nature of his political strategy), but also how he perceived the expanding situation of his kingdom in the mid-780s. Meanwhile, although the creation of a new archbishopric at Lichfield was motivated largely by a wish to have Ecgbert anointed by a metropolitan bishop, and the act of elevation of Lichfield in this way was also hegemonic in character (since it released Offa and Mercia from an inherited dependence upon Canterbury for its connection to Rome), it may have also have occurred within a wider pattern of influence of Carolingian reforms upon the emergent Mercian state.[61]

It was however in the sphere of church appointments, either to bishoprics and the Canterbury archiepiscopate, or to leading monastic or minster establishments, that both Offa and Coenwulf involved themselves in church affairs in order to control or at least to influence them. So, for example, not only did Offa 'promote' Hygebeht to become archbishop of Lichfield, but he also engineered succession from the recalcitrant Archbishop Jaenberht of Canterbury to the presumably more compliant bishop Aethelheard from Lindsey, arranging with the pope for Hygebehrt to carry out the consecration as the senior metropolitan.

The promotion of female royal kin, and the creation of a Mercian 'court culture'

The very recognition of Offa's spouse Cynethryth formally as 'Queen of the Mercians' represented both a departure from previous Mercian practice, and a contrast with all contemporary royal houses among the English (and especially that of the West Saxons, among whom an abhorrence of the practice did not only stem from the behaviour there of Eadburh, Offa's daughter and Beorhtric's queen). The remarkable series of coins issued on Cynethryth's behalf by a single London-based moneyer can be interpreted in a number of different ways, but her representation thereon as 'Regina' was clearly a political statement, while the frequency and order of her witnessing of charters (named directly following Offa's inscription in each case) reinforces the point that she was accorded a special status as queen-consort.[62]

One of the most revealing aspects of this status is the way in which Alcuin addressed Cynethryth in his letters to her. She was 'dispensatrix domus', the 'controller' or 'administrator' of the royal household, and although this has been read simply as an emulation of the practices of the Carolingian court, it could well represent a process underway from earlier in the reign.[63] Offa's eldest daughter Aethelburh was singled out for a particular path of promotion in respect to a monastic 'career'. What is especially interesting in this context is the familiarity with which Alcuin addressed Aethelburh as 'Eugenia' ('the nobly born') in his letters. The degree of respectful intimacy he exhibited in such correspondence towards both mother and daughter echoed the way in which clerics interacted with the ladies of the Carolingian court. Alcuin clearly saw them as intercessors with the king, and as potential allies in a clerical project which sought, in respect to both the Frankish and Mercian rulers, to promote a 'court culture' in which the role of leading churchmen was pivotal.

FIGURE 8.3 Penny of 'Cynethryth Regina', promoting Mercian Queenship
Moneyer Eoba (Coins and Medals Department, The British Museum). 'The florid, well-modelled features are reminiscent of Eastern Mediterranean influences, possibly to be seen in the context of an ongoing dialogue with the Carolingian Court.'[64] Drawing by Tim Hoverd.

The practice of promotion of female members of the royal family continued under Coenwulf, but his personal behaviour (we learn from Alcuin that he 'cast aside' his first wife) meant that the chief object of similar manoeuvres was his daughter Cwoenthryth. Like Offa's daughter Aethelburh before her, the destiny of this pre-eminent Mercian princess was to achieve power through the office of presiding abbess. The power that this endowed her with, as Abbess of Minster-in-Thanet and daughter of the Mercian 'king-emperor' is evident from her capacity to resist the attempts of Wulfred, Archbishop of Canterbury, to regain control over the Kentish monasteries.[65]

FIGURE 8.4 The site of the monastery at Reculver, Kent, in the late Roman fort

Minster-in-Thanet and Reculver were, by the late eighth century, two of the wealthiest and symbolically most important monasteries in Kent. They were both under the control of the Mercian ruling family, with first Offa's Queen, Cynethryth, then Coenwulf's daughter, Cwoenthryth, presiding over their management. The twin west towers are of late twelfth-century date, but the ruined nave is of seventh-century origin. This early morning view from the east shows the remains of the third-century 'Saxon Shore fort' within which the monastery was located, and half of which has been lost to coastal erosion.

PHOTOGRAPH COURTESY OF JAMES LANCASTER/CASTLESFORTSBATTLES. CO.UK. COPYRIGHT RESERVED.

The very fact that Coenwulf sought to place Cwoenthryth in control of the same key Kentish monasteries that were 'managed' at the end of the eighth century by Offa's female kin shows the degree to which the strategy both of promoting regal female power and controlling monastic production (in all senses) by this means continued: the personnel might change but the regime was still in charge (Figure 8.4).

Moreover, that Cwoenthryth appears as a witness to at least one of Coenwulf's charters indicates again a degree of innovation he brought to the regime in respect to the privileging of female kin.[66] This was particularly a feature of the zenith of Coenwulf's rule, such that while Coenwulf's first queen did not appear to have been given formal recognition, his later consort, Aelfthryth, appears as a signatory to charters from 808, and more frequently so from 811.[67]

Creating 'capital territories': Tamworth, Winchcombe, London and their hinterlands

There were clearly many significant places in the Mercian realm under Offa and Coenwulf, that had either ancestral significance, as with a cluster of locations around Peterborough, or the monasteries at Bardney and Breedon, or those which are likely to have received royal patronage, including – in the ecclesiastical sphere – Repton and Winchcombe. Such places included such royal places as Croft in Leicestershire, Chelsea on the Thames in Middle Saxon territory, or the location 'Clofesho' whose provenance is uncertain, that were at one and the same time important venues for (albeit peripatetic) secular government and church councils.

The locations of places that recur in this way, especially as the sites of councils at which charters were issued during the reigns of Offa, Ecgfrith and Coenwulf possibly indicates the emergence of a landscape of what might be termed 'capital territories', that is, zones within which different significant individual places had complementary roles. Perhaps the most important such territory was the Mercian 'heartland' itself, centred upon the royal residential site at Tamworth but extending to the ecclesiastical centre at Lichfield and the monastic (and royal burial) complex at Repton. Other locations within

FIGURE 8.5 Winchcombe, a key place in a western Mercian 'capital territory'
Part of the defensive perimeter banks (to the left here) around the Mercian 'burh' that developed around the monastery and palace complex (probable site next to the present parish church, right). Apparently founded by Offa, this settlement became an important place during Coenwulf's reign. It has been suggested that the monastery housed the Mercian royal archives.

such a 'heartland' territory may have been important, such as the residence at Seckington overlooking Tamworth from the north (which might equally have been the vill of another of the Mercian elite), Polesworth to the east (an ecclesiastical estate, later the site of an important monastery), or Hammerwich to the south-west (a possible production or processing centre for metalwork).

Another such 'territory' can be envisaged as having emerged in the west, in the lands of the *Hwicce*, where Winchcombe (a royal centre paralleling Tamworth), Worcester (a parallel to Lichfield), Droitwich (the primary centre for salt production in Mercia), and Gloucester, Cirencester, and Bredon (monastic locales) were another such group of potentially inter-related places. The London area may have had another such cluster of key sites, although here the commercial dominance of 'Lundenwic' and the politically significant Thames-side places to the west including Chelsea, Brentford and Cookham may represent a distinction not so evident elsewhere. The economic and productive links to royal and ecclesiastical interests were no doubt paramount in the emergence of significant complexes, and the distinctive nature of such sub-regions can easily be over-emphasised. Other places linked to specific ambitions of Offa (such as Bedford, Bath or St Albans) were clearly significant in the geography of the Mercian hegemony, at least under Offa, as were places that the kings of the hegemony may have promoted in the newly 'absorbed' kingdoms, such as Dommoc (?Dunwich) in East Anglia or Rochester in Kent.

An awareness of the influence and uses of history

Moving to an even less obvious sphere, it is difficult to avoid a sense in which certainly Offa, but possibly also Coenwulf, drew upon a sense not only of Roman but also of Anglo-Saxon history in some of their activities and strategies.

It has, for instance, been suggested that another motive for Offa having proposed a union between Ecgfrith and Charlemagne's daughter Bertha was to set up resonances with the marriage of the Merovingian Pippin's daughter, also called Bertha, to Aethelberht of Kent in 560.[68]

There seems also to have been a particular royal attachment to the cult of the Northumbrian king Oswald and those of the Mercian clerics Guthlac and Chad. Offa is known to have lavished gifts upon the shrine and cult centre of St Oswald at Bardney, and Coenwulf to have gifted estates to the monastery dedicated to him at Gloucester.[69] The political dimensions of such attachments are not hard to appreciate. For example, the link to Oswald ran back through Eowa, the brother of Penda who supported the Northumbrian king at Maserfelth; the link through Guthlac to the East Anglian dynasty provided legitimation for Mercian control within that kingdom; and the focus on St Chad provided yet another Northumbrian historical link and an historical legitimation of the elevation of Lichfield to archiepiscopal status due to its having for some while been Chad's cult centre (see below).[70]

The encoding of law

King Alfred of Wessex mentioned that in compiling his law code he had drawn upon what was available to him in an inheritance from his predecessors that included both Ine of Wessex and Offa of Mercia. Modern historians have differed in their opinions as to whether this referred to a code of Offa's that had since been lost, or whether it simply referred to the provisions of the capitulary that Bishop George of Ostia issued following the visit of the papal envoys in 786.[71] This is a somewhat arcane debate, because whether or not a formal code existed, it seems certain that Alfred was reflecting a concern that he had every reason to be aware of, that Offa must surely have had to encode laws for the promotion of both kingly powers and the divine sanction of those powers.[72] In his case for accepting that the capitulary could well have constituted for contemporaries an Offan law code, Wormald noted that Offa alone among the signatories professed to subscribe 'statutes'[73], and that there was a remarkable similarity between Alcuin's encouragements concerning sound moral practice, the twenty provisions of the capitulary, and the entirely Frankish (rather than papal) elements of Charlemagne's own code the *admonitio generalis*, issued three years after the legatine capitulary.

Coinage and the political economy of the Mercian hegemony

A particularly perceptive review of the development of market centres and towns in Mercia between the seventh and later ninth centuries opened with the comment that 'it is possible to overstate the case for the sophistication of the economy of Mercia in the seventh to ninth centuries', comparing the flows of material goods in the midlands in the Roman period and the later twelfth century, and the dearth of material from the area in between.[74] It would however be more accurate to suggest that, rather, there were two contrasting economic spheres, perhaps just as today. On the one hand, commercial activity and the degree (for instance) of monetisation increased the closer anyone came to the south-eastern English ports, and on the other hand there was a Mercian 'core territory' westwards, that was less monetised and organised in a different way with, in historically-recent terms, more of a 'command economy'. There can surely be little question that this had most to do with the proximity of the Carolingian empire and its predecessor and successor states across the English Channel. It may also be a reflection of how difficult it can be to locate even major Middle Saxon settlements, and here the case of London/Lundenwic, unrecognised until the late 1980s as the location (at Aldwych) of the most important trading centre within the Mercian realm, is salutary.[75]

Coinage in the Mercian economy

The issue of heavier and more formalised coinage early in Offa's reign, and its volume later, has been taken to mark out Offa's from previous administrations.[76] The character and formulas of Offa's coinage also indicate the workings of a monetary policy that is wholly different from what had preceded it. Not only did the mints active under Offa produce coins in great numbers, but they were produced in full cognisance of continental trends. It is difficult to regard it as a coincidence that the two major reforms of Offa's reign, firstly from the smaller and lumpier *sceatta* to the thinner flan penny in the 760s, and then the heavier coinage following directly upon Carolingian reforms in 792, were contemporary with Continental innovations. The extent of royal control over minting was probably limited, certainly before the 780s, with individual moneyers such as 'Mang' apparently simultaneously striking coins for Offa at the London mint and for the independent Kentish kings at Canterbury.[77]

The practice whereby the moneyers' names appear on the coins but not the mint is in stark contrast to the more standardised and centralised production of Charlemagne's coinage, and there was much greater variety and innovation in the forms and styles of the English coins. However, it is only under Offa that the king's head appears regularly on the obverse and the royal inscription that ties the coinage directly into the authority of the kingship becomes common.[78] The changing terms of the Mercian hegemony can be mapped in reference to the 'rival' production of coins by the kings of Kent and East Anglia in particular, and this reflects the strategic importance of controlling the process of minting, and the revenues raised from it, in the mints of Canterbury and possibly also Ipswich.[79] The scale of the production of coins under Offa is registered not only in the numbers of single finds during his reign, now numbering in the many thousands, but also in the number of moneyers (at least 37 are currently known) who produced coins featuring his name.

Vills, production and trade

A major change in building and burial practices across England in the late seventh century appears to correlate with a shift in settlement and the move towards an intensification of agricultural production that was noted briefly in Chapter 7. This seems to correspond also with the initial appearance of the coastal productive and trans-shipment places that have become known as *wics* and that have been seen as so vital to the development of trade and specialisation in the Anglo-Saxon economy of the eighth century. These settlements, and in particular the places Hamwic (Southampton), Lundenwic (London), Ipswich and Eoforwic (York) have been seen as the key 'ports-of-trade' of their respective kingdoms, and therefore as centres dominated by the kings and controlled for their own purposes.[80]

The status of these sites is gradually becoming better understood. The popularity of the view that these sites were entirely controlled by kings and that they had clearly discernible 'economic hinterlands' has diminished, while the contrary view that such sites were simply key nodes on a wider network of economic and productive places that served a variety of purposes has been gaining ground. Such places are set apart by their location on rivers and at obvious points of Continental exchange, by the operation of mints, and by the range of economic activity and imported goods including pottery found there.[81] Periodic royal places of residence, or 'vills', are referred to widely in contemporary documents, sometimes as 'famous places', but their exact status as settlements, and their economic role, remain uncertain. Some, such as Tamworth and Sutton by Hereford, have produced evidence of significant estate investment in the form of water-mills dated to the eighth and ninth centuries, while Hereford, Tamworth, Winchcombe and possibly also Worcester, have traces of defences pre-dating the late ninth century.[82]

The upper tier of rural settlements identified from fieldwalking in Northamptonshire and Leicestershire, for instance, is recognised from the existence of 'Ipswich ware', and it has been suggested that these represent sites with royal or at least elite connections. The ceramic form has been found at several sites that on other grounds might be regarded as potential 'proto-urban' centres in north-east Mercia, including Northampton, Bedford and Nottingham. The first of these featured extravagant lordly structures and the second is a place that Offa and his entourage apparently had some interest in, late in his reign. The role of 'productive sites' has been much debated in this context, and the purpose and significance of finds such as metal writing 'styli' which are such a common feature of sites such as Flixborough, itself close to the boundary between Northumbria and Mercia, has attracted much comment. The key interest that the Mercian kings may have had in any of these places by the later eighth century was not that the goods assembled there could be appropriated and used for redistributive purposes, as much as that they were sources of revenue through taxation, whether under ecclesiastical or royal patronage. Whether the styli were wielded by clerics or administrators, among their purposes in contexts where quantities of goods were being exchanged was surely the recording of transactions.[83]

However, this is not to say that the hegemonic Mercian kings were not interested in controlling key aspects of trade more directly. One concern was that relating to critical resources, perhaps the most obvious being salt. This commodity was important in the Mercian economy because the principal brine-works were located within the bounds of the kingdom at Droitwich in Worcestershire and probably also at Middlewich in Cheshire. The existence of the 'saltways' recorded in West Midlands charters emphasises the commercial importance of the trade in salt, and hints at the royal maintenance of highways that has resonances also in 'bridge-work'. Mercian kings had moved to secure control over the works at Droitwich in the late seventh century, and the archaeological evidence indicates an intensification of production in the eighth.[84] The import of quern-stones of Mayen lava from Germany was possibly a royal prerogative, since this could also have provided another source of revenues. Certainly, they appear on sites such as Northampton, which may have attracted royal interest, and in association with mills almost certainly under direct royal control, as at Tamworth and Sutton near Hereford.[85]

Another kingly interest was in the role of trade in international relations, as revealed by the correspondence from Charlemagne noted earlier in this chapter. The degree of control that could be exercised by the Carolingian regime, in at least threatening to close Frankish ports in 794 to Anglo-Saxon trade, was mirrored by Offa's apparent ability to respond reciprocally by closing English ports. The resolution of the quarrel over the failed marriage negotiations that prompted these actions, and a need to maintain trading networks, was mediated through Alcuin's contacts with both courts, but not exclusively so. Gervold,

FIGURE 8.6 Gold's Clump, Watling Street, Hints, west of Tamworth

The spur of Hint's Hill on which the 'Clump' (the sharply-defined summit at right-centre in this photograph) stands is denoted 'Snake's Hill' on the Ordnance Survey maps of the area. 'Hints' is an alternative Welsh-derived name for 'Sarn', denoting a road.

Abbot of St Wandrille, may for example have had a pivotal role. A mid-ninth-century record of events affecting that monastery noted that Gervold was 'closely connected in friendship to Offa, the most mighty king of the English or Mercians', and that he had often been sent to the latter on diplomatic missions from Charlemagne, one of which had included conveying the initial suggestion of the marriage.[86] Since Gervold had been appointed as 'procurator' (toll-collector) for the trading ports on the Frankish side of the English Channel including Quentovic, he was well placed to negotiate their continued operation, which it was claimed he had achieved.[87]

The material of hegemony: some significant innovations

While there were institutional and economic dimensions to several of the political innovations of Offa's reign, these were underwritten by material products that gave physical expression to, and in turn reinforced, the Mercian hegemony. In the monastic context, the output of the scriptoria included illuminated manuscripts in which architectural forms were more closely linked to the lavishness of the lettering, and that thereby gave new meaning to the spiritual 'kingdom'. The fusion of classical and insular styles of decoration represents a world at a political and an institutional crossroads in a number of respects.

More publicly, the architecture of the age and its sculptural adornment provided both subtle and overt messages on a number of different levels. In particular, the style of the buildings and the nature and symbolism of the embellishments indicates a new internationalism in Anglo-Saxon culture, and a probable intensification of contact with the continental world. A survey of the full range of such material expression is beyond the scope of this book. Five aspects are therefore given slightly closer treatment here, in large part for illustrative purposes: they concern the iconography of coinage; architectural innovation; the location and subject-matter of sculpture in reference to a single, but key, context; the control of gold; and the holding of items of 'finery'.

Images of power: the other side of Offa's coin

The role of coinage in what we have termed the political economy of Mercia under Offa and Coenwulf was of obvious importance. However, power was not only exercised through the issuing of coins, the influence over commercial transactions, and the financing of operations that have already been noted. Coinage was clearly also a medium for conveying political messages outside the sphere of commercial activity, and this may have operated at a number of levels.[88] The possible connotations of the appearance of Offa's spouse Cynethryth on an issue of coins albeit apparently limited to a single moneyer have been highlighted already. However, while accepting that the issuing of coins with the names of moneyers upon them indicates a degree of private initiative and enterprise that was largely self-regulating, the naming of the king in such a repetitive manner on Offa's and Coenwulf's coins also indicates that the moneyers concerned were working under licence from the king, however loosely enforced. Moreover, to an essentially illiterate population, it was the appearance of the king's image rather than the presence of any particular inscription, that would have served best to affirm royal authority.[89]

The iconography of Offa's coinage has only recently enjoyed the level of analysis that it has long merited. Among the aspects that have been isolated as significant is the choices made about the representation of the images of the king on his coins in respect to coiffure, portraiture, and drapery, for example, and the manner in which Cynethryth was depicted or referenced on her much more limited issue. So the wavy hairstyle that is represented on the heads of Offa on coins such as that minted at Canterbury by Eadhun is thought to be an 'embodiment of the ideal' of kingship in the person of King David. The 'refined dignity' of many portraits, including some that portray him as 'heaven-gazing', are thought perhaps to have aimed to stress the 'otherworldliness' and sacral nature of kingship (see Figure 8.2, for example).[90]

Moreover, among coins for which there are few numismatic parallels are those that show extravagant drapery ranged in tiers and that echo, in the schematic rendering of images, the miniatures that appear in Continental manuscripts.[91] What is evident here is not only the experimentation in visual perspective, but also the sheer flamboyance of the clothing and cloaks, and perhaps also the applied jewels and devices, involved. These stand in marked contrast to the more naturalistic renderings of drapery clearly based on Roman imperial models.[92] Experimental, also, appear to be the additional symbols located in close proximity to Offa's portrait in such a manner as to suggest that they were regarded as well-known symbolic attributes of the king. In one example, of the moneyer Dud, what looks very much like a direct representation of a sword that 'doubles' as a stylised cross, could be a real object with which the king may have been associated (Figure 8.7).

On other coins, the appearance of the device of a coiled but not interlaced snake in close juxtaposition with Offa's name adds an extra dimension to the fact that 'the only animals represented on coins struck for Offa are snakes'.[93] A protective role for the snake in respect of warrior-heroes harks back to pagan practice, and it is conceivable that Offa deliberately adopted the device both to reference his heroic ancestry and to evoke the divine protection enjoyed by contemporary kingship. Symbols of power in the form of swords potentially associated personally with him, and snakes perhaps acting as personal symbols, suggest that there may have been a deliberate creation of images that were conveyed in life through worn items of dress and other accoutrements and that were represented in art and depictions not only in coins but potentially also in other media. This in turn may represent an elaboration of the iconography of power not hitherto witnessed on a 'public' scale (other than through the ceremonials attending funerals and commemoration, such as is attested at Sutton Hoo) in Britain since the Roman period.

8 The material of Mercian hegemony

FIGURE 8.7 Pennies of Offa, with contrasting drapery styles
Left, moneyer Ibba, with abstract folds (CM 1896 4–4–17b); Right, moneyer Dud (MEC 1124A, Fitzwilliam Museum, Cambridge), with naturalistic (but conventionalised Roman imperial) folds.[94] Note that both renderings of the king are idealised representations and not 'portraits', with the imperial diadem very much to the fore. Drawing by Tim Hoverd.

Meanwhile, representations of Coenwulf appear to be more conventionalised and to concentrate not on a variety of attributes but simply to reinforce an imperial presence that harked back more explicitly back to Roman styles. The fact that these were developed out of antique prototypes obtained by some of the key moneyers of his reign only serves to reinforce the idea that there was an 'official policy' of representation that the moneyers were encouraged to promote.

Hegemonic constructions: churches of Carolingian and Roman inspiration

The subsequent history of Mercia and England has resulted in the loss of most of the evidence for a 'remarkable flowering of Continental-inspired classicism' in the architecture of churches, monastic buildings and ornament in the years leading up to, and immediately after, 800.[95] There are nonetheless some remarkable survivals, and archaeology is steadily adding new evidence concerning structures that are otherwise entirely lost. Foremost among the former is the magnificent church at Brixworth, with its massive proportions, brick-built arches and rows of side chapels or 'porticus', whose presence and form has been confirmed through excavation.[96]

The character of the eighth-century semi-subterranean mausoleum that appears to have formed the first stage of building at Repton, and the similar form of the church at Wing, also echo Frankish models. Meanwhile the broadly basilican style of (at least partly) excavated churches such as that at Cirencester may have been derived not only from Francia but more directly from Italian models and from Rome itself. Given that there was an English quarter in Rome from at least the earlier eighth century and as noted above there was much direct diplomatic traffic during both Offa's and Coenwulf's reigns, this is less surprising than might easily be imagined.

Whatever the immediate source or sources of inspiration, the ultimate models for these structures derived from Imperial Rome. In this context, the re-use of Roman materials removed from former imperial sites in Britain need also occasion no surprise. This was a long-standing practice: some of the earliest churches in Kent (at Reculver and at St Augustine's, Canterbury) and in East Anglia (Bradwell-on-Sea) had been built within Roman forts using material robbed from the walls, and the churches at Hexham in Northumbria, Ripon in Yorkshire and at Peterborough were built in the seventh century from stones recovered from nearby structures.

Notwithstanding this early practice of using materials easily to hand, the large quantities of Roman tiles, wherever they were derived from, used in the arches at Brixworth must surely have been a deliberate statement. Moreover, the stone used in much of the fabric was drawn not from local quarries which would have been entirely viable, but, according to petrological study, had come from Leicester, 25 miles away.[97] This very public re-use of Roman imperial building material, together with the deployment of a basilican architectural style (if not the exact basilican form) for the building, was surely a purposeful appropriation that served as a form of overt display signalling the neo-Imperial pretensions of the regime in the period 780 to 820, to which the church at Brixworth is now generally assigned.

The elaboration of the mausoleum at Repton before the middle of the ninth century featured the insertion of vaulting supported by four substantial 'barley twist' columns 'recalling the antique columns around the apostles tomb in the old basilica of St Peter in Rome'.[98] The 'black stones' that were mentioned in Charlemagne's letter to Offa in 796 are of interest here, since it had clearly been a key concern in Offa's letter to Charlemagne to obtain some of these items. The query in return was to know the length of stones required, and it

FIGURE 8.8 Brixworth Church: evoking Roman imperial structures
Much of the focus of architectural discussion of the church of c.800 here has in the past been upon the side-chapels – or porticus – attaching to, or leading from, the nave (left and right in this view). However, as viewed here from the western end of the nave, the importance of the two monumental north–south walls separating nave and presbytery, and then presbytery and apse, is very evident, despite the later medieval insertion of a high chancel arch. Each of these walls featured tall narrow central arches and pairs of flanking openings set one above the other. As such, the walls can be understood as directly replicating the form of imperial triumphal arches in Rome itself.

has therefore been suggested that, rather than being the quern stones of Mayen lava that archaeologists had been so keen to see this as a reference to, they were instead columns of black porphyry that Charlemagne had been 'quarrying' from the imperial buildings at Ravenna in Italy for trans-shipment and re-use where they can still be seen today at the 'Palatine Chapel' of his new palace complex at Aachen.[99]

It may be speculative to link this to particular activity in Mercia, but we have a hint of a connection here not with activities at Lichfield or Tamworth, but instead at a site where a more grandiose suite of baths was available for possible conversion for royal use, on a site already replete with Roman imperial associations. It may not therefore be coincidental that both Offa and Ecgfrith are recorded as presiding over councils in Bath close to the very time that the request for 'black stones' had gone to Charlemagne. Given the traffic between the Carolingian court and the Mercian court attested in the documentary records, it would hardly be surprising that the Mercians were aware of Charlemagne's architectural innovations. Was Bath therefore intended as the Mercian regime's 'Aachen', with its equivalent 'Palatine Chapel' built lavishly using columns from Ravenna (via Francia), and its baths rebuilt for use by the inner circle of the royal court?[100]

Lichfield and imperium: an angelic testimony

The fragments of late eighth- and early ninth-century Mercian architectural sculpture with strongly biblical themes and allusions that survive at a number of later churches including Castor near Peterborough and Breedon-on-the-Hill demonstrate that Continental classicising influences and the development of a Carolingian Romanesque style extended not only to buildings but also to their embellishment.[101] The surviving pieces are clearly only a small sample of what must once have existed, and the sculptural form extended to free-standing crosses as at Sandbach in Cheshire and elsewhere.[102] Such open-air works, occurring widely in western Mercia as at Wroxeter in Shropshire, Acton Beauchamp in Herefordshire and Cropthorne on the river Avon in Worcestershire (the latter a royal estate centre close to the important royal monasteries at Fladbury and Evesham) were a very public statement of these cosmopolitan and royal connections, presumably reflecting deliberate policies of patronage.

Some of these pieces, like the Breedon 'Archangel Gabriel' relief panel, may indicate the presence of overseas master-carvers in Mercia, potentially under royal patronage.[103] However, yet more remarkable was the discovery under the nave of Lichfield Cathedral in 2003 of the carving, in Ancaster limestone, of another representation of the Archangel. In view of the fineness of its execution, its apparent date, and the likelihood that it formed part of a shrine structure associated with the cult of St Chad, its significance is extraordinary.[104] Bede had in 731 mentioned the creation of a wooden house-shaped shrine dedicated to Chad and placed within the church of St Peter in Lichfield, itself rebuilt

FIGURE 8.9 The 'Lichfield Angel' stone-carving, probably from St Chad's shrine

From the time of King Wulfhere, the shrine of St Chad had been a place of pilgrimage. This figure was part of a frieze or panel, probably depicting the Annunciation, which was most likely an integral feature of an encapsulation in stone of the original wooden shrine. The quality of the execution of the stone-carving is quite without parallel for the late eighth-century period to which it is currently ascribed, and suggests Continental craftsmanship. Such a dramatic 'upgrading' of the shrine would fit comfortably with the elevation of the see of Lichfield. Drawing by Tim Hoverd.

and rededicated in December 700.[105] The location of the pieces of the 'angel' sculpture, comprising one half of a formerly upright bas-relief end-panel, within a pit adjacent to a central chamber within the walls of the earlier cathedral (also located in the excavation concerned) unequivocally locates it at the cult focus. Meanwhile its form, clearly designed to take a coped lid, surely represents a replacement or encasement in stone of the original timber shrine.

The 'Lichfield Angel' has also revealed the polychromatic colour schemes of the painted surfaces applied to such carvings, and the quality of its carving has led to the suggestion that the carver responsible may have been brought to Lichfield from southern Europe, or even further afield, purposefully to execute the work, or to produce a series of such works. It has been dated stylistically to the later eighth century, and its presence at Lichfield in the manner outlined here has been taken to indicate a likely correlation with the raising of the see to archiepiscopal status by Offa in 787. This is therefore indicative of the lengths to which the regime was prepared to go to introduce new styles, with inspiration drawn not only from Carolingian Europe, but also from the eastern Mediterranean and the much wider cosmopolitan sphere of Byzantium.

8 The material of Mercian hegemony

Gold control: the significance of Coenwulf's London 'mancus'

A gold coin found on the banks of the river Ivel at Biggleswade in Bedfordshire in 2001 has thrown significant new light on innovations in monetary policy in the reigns of both Offa and Coenwulf. This coin is an exceptionally fine gold issue that equates to the *mancus* referred to first in England in a charter of 799 and especially in tenth- and eleventh-century Anglo-Saxon sources, particularly wills.[106] The Coenwulf coin has led to a re-assessment of the three other known examples of similar gold coins in Offa's reign. Only one of these three, an imitation dinar found in Rome, bears the 'Offa Rex' inscription, but the other two were produced by moneyers known to have been operating in the 780s. The other two coins are interesting due to the closeness with which they were modelled on Roman imperial issues.[107]

While it is likely that the production of gold coins was never significantly large in England in this period, it has been suggested authoritatively that the vanishingly small number of gold coins surviving is not a reliable guide to the number produced.[108] So, while it may be that the production of the dinar with the 'Offa Rex' inscription was indicative of a purposeful issue to meet the requirements of the pledge that Offa was alleged (in 798) to have made in 786 to send a donation of 365 mancuses annually to the see of St Peter in Rome, it is perhaps equally likely that the dinar imitation was an attempt by the Mercian regime and its moneyers to convert gold in other forms into transferable currency to break into the Italian 'market' in goods that could only be transacted using dinars or their derivatives, in gold.[109]

However, it is the particular characteristics of the Coenwulf *mancus*, dated stylistically to the period 805–810, that is of greater interest here. The first significance is that the legend 'De Vico Lvndoniae' is so far the only known reference to the *wic* of London on a contemporary coin. This inscription not only potentially emphasises the distinct location of the *wic* at 'Aldwych' a kilometre to the west of the walled area of the Roman city, but also implies official recognition of the settlement as a formally constituted place of governmental business and royal patronage, with royal officials and functions based (or at least operating) there.[110] Moreover, the care with which the coin was produced and the restrained formality of its composition suggests that it represented a special issue. One possibility that has been raised was that it was produced, in part at least, as 'an attempt to standardise the English mancus and introduce a second denomination into the monetary system, albeit one only used for certain limited purposes'.[111]

That purpose may have been to regulate and standardise production of mancuses, or to introduce a royal monopoly over it, or to limit the circulation of rival Frankish

FIGURE 8.10 Gold *mancus* of Coenwulf, found at Biggleswade in Bedfordshire

The style of both the bust of 'Coenwulf Rex M(erciorum)' and of the inscriptions places the coin firmly in the manner of the Canterbury silver issues of both Coenwulf and his brother Cuthred, King of Kent (798–807).

COPYRIGHT THE TRUSTEES OF THE BRITISH MUSEUM.

currency, or all three. The assertion of royal control could also be reflected in the omission of the name of the moneyer, it being felt that the name of the king on the coin stood as sufficient guarantee of its worth. This coin, and its contrasting characteristics with the less directly regulated gold issues of Offa's reign, can therefore be seen, along with the creation of the Rochester mint, as the extension by Coenwulf of hegemonic control of the higher value end of commercial and official transactions by finally moving to a position of direct patronage and control of moneyers.[112]

The materials of hegemonic practice: (re)placing the 'Staffordshire Hoard'?

Sometimes a single discovery may appear to have the capacity to re-write a whole period of history. Such has been thought likely with the discovery in a ploughed field between Cannock and Lichfield in 2009, initially through casual metal-detecting, of the remarkable, dazzling, group of gold, silver and bejewelled objects that has come to be known as 'the Staffordshire Hoard'.[113] This find, which ostensibly represents a gathered-together group of fragments of elite items (mostly war-gear) stripped from their original composite artefacts, was not associated with any definite archaeological features and is assumed to have been hastily buried in a box or in a bag in a pit, the original matrix of which has been ploughed away.[114]

The 3,000 or more items or fragments comprising 'the hoard' include among the so-far identified items 69 elaborate sword pommels wrought in gold and 10 in silver, 8 sword pyramids in gold and 1 in silver, and more than 207 sword hilt plates (178 gold, 29 silver).[115] However, although this appears at first sight to upset entirely our understanding of the 'splendour' of the seventh-century Mercian court (since this is the date of manufacture so far ascribed to the majority of the items), it may not represent exactly what at first sight it might seem to. This is due primarily to uncertainty as to the place of manufacture of the items, and the need to distinguish between what we term here the three different contexts which the 'hoard' implicates.

The three contexts pertinent to an understanding of the 'Hoard'

The unexpected discovery of such a group of items inevitably presents some intriguing difficulties for the archaeologist, not least because it cannot be assumed that the most numerous objects present provide a date for the assembly of the group, let alone for its deposition.[116] In particular, it is critical to an understanding of the date and significance of the 'hoard' to recognise that there are *three* key historical 'contexts' surrounding the existence of the assemblage that need to be taken into consideration. Working backwards from the latest 'event', the first of these contexts is the date and circumstances of its deposition; the second, the date and circumstances of its assembly as a group of objects;

8 *The material of Mercian hegemony* 329

and the third, the date(s) and circumstances of the manufacture and use of the included items. The determination of each of these contexts, or sets of contexts, follows a different logic and each has potentially contrasting resonances. The second and third of these contexts might not have been separated by a long interval, but they were not necessarily inter-dependent either.[117]

The circumstances of deposition may be hinted at by the condition of the items, which could for example be 'scrap' collected together for purposes of re-working. Alternatively, they could reflect a relatively rapid 'rendering down' of formerly whole items, undertaken hastily and for the purposes of transport or concealment. Yet a further alternative is that they may simply represent material that once formed part of composite objects which had, by the time of deposition and through the passage of time, become broken or even largely disintegrated. While the circumstances involved could therefore have been a deliberate act of breakage or at least dis-assembly, the nature of the selection involved (which included some martial gear but not others, there being no saddle-mounts or belt-straps for example) is such that it seems *least* likely that this was enacted in the chaos of the immediate aftermath of battle.

More probably, the 'hoard' represents an attempt to conceal material that had either been looted, or had been transported from a place of hitherto secure storage, and then placed in an intended temporary hiding place. A location so close to Lichfield and Tamworth seems an unlikely place to store loot, for example derived from the activities of the Danish 'great army' in the winter of 877 when they over-wintered at Repton. In contrast, the idea that the hoard represents a deliberately and carefully, if hastily, concealed component of a larger treasury appears highly likely, in that a location such as this, barely five miles to the south of Lichfield, constitutes a place that was within easy reach for recovery. The exact date of concealment in these terms does not particularly matter: there was no shortage of difficult times for Mercia between the mid-ninth and the mid-eleventh centuries, after all.

The circumstances of assembly are, if anything, even more difficult to unravel. The group could only have been brought together in its entirety at a time following the manufacture of the latest dateable item, but whether this was soon after the latter event, or some considerable time later, is impossible (as yet) to judge. This does not mean that the materials did not exist within distinct associated groups before the time of 'final' assembly, however. The third series of contexts – of production – is important here, because it seems very likely from studies carried out so far that while the bulk of the items are dateable to the mid- to late seventh century, the included items span a range from the late sixth century through to the late seventh or even early eighth century.[118]

One fact that is clearly evident is that a number of the pommels and other items show considerable signs of use-wear. Recent scientific research may even demonstrate that repairs were made to some of the finer items, such as the inlaid gold pommels. This indicates that the objects concerned are likely to have had an extended use-life, and that therefore their date of manufacture might

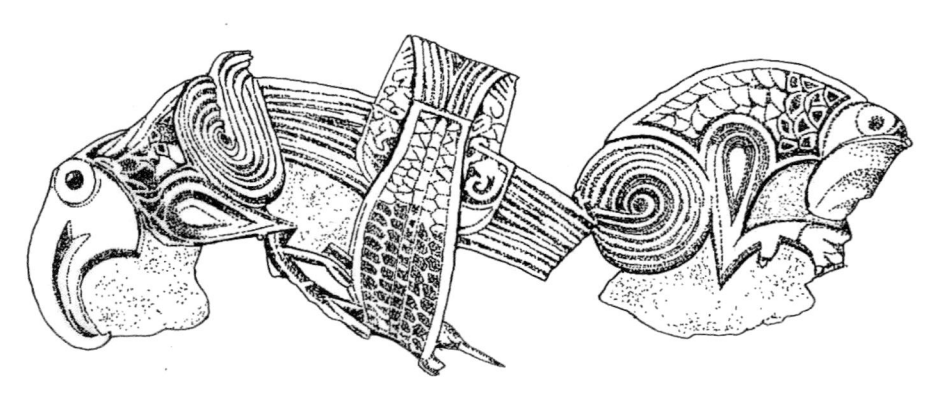

FIGURE 8.11 Gold ornamental mount from the 'Staffordshire Hoard'
This 'eagles and fish' 20-carat gold mount has been conserved and a drawn reconstruction shows it to have featured a central fish figure flanked on either side by eagles gripping its head in their beaks – presumably an allegorical reference. What the mount was fixed onto is at present unknown. Drawing by Tim Hoverd.

considerably antedate their gathering together (and their breaking up) in this particular 'Staffordshire Hoard' configuration, and their subsequent deposition. But the wear also raises the possibility that some at least may already have been heirlooms when *first* brought together in this particular grouping. Those items that are so far stylistically the most closely-dateable objects are also, quite possibly, those potentially most capable of being 'located' in reference to their place of manufacture and initial use. These are the items associated with the hilts of swords and daggers that feature elaborate cloisonné work and metalworking, as well as the very many fragments of helmets and shields. All such items are so far without close parallel anywhere in central Mercia, but on the contrary find close exemplars in both East Anglia and Kent.[119] The intensive research into both the techniques of metalworking (and other craftsmanship) and into the stylistic parallels and contrasts will hopefully throw further light on this matter.

An alternative context for the assembly and deposition of the 'Hoard'

Among the welter of commentary and speculation that has flowed following the discovery, some of the most perceptive comments have been those of Nicholas Brooks in an early letter to the team leading the study of the hoard contents.[120] Brooks noted the absence of certain key military items that might be expected to be associated with sword-pommels and other hilt 'furniture', and with helmets and shield embellishments. He suggested that this was due to the majority of the items having been drawn from the workshop of the court armourer, while the items that might otherwise have been expected to be used alongside the sword-fittings and helmets are just those that might be associated with a court leather-worker and harness-maker.[121] If the 'hoard' items were therefore the 'stock' of the court armourer, Brooks felt that an explanation for their assembly could be found in the practice of *heriot*, whereby a king gifted items of martial regalia 'on loan' to members of his subordinate elite and immediate entourage, which would be returned following the death of the person concerned. The items could then be reworked into new 'gifts' of this kind.

8 The material of Mercian hegemony

Brooks observed with interest that much discussion had already centred around the identification of the gold strip that bore an inscription, as an indication of the date of the hoard more generally. He thought that even Michelle Brown's tentative dating of the piece to the early eighth century was too late, despite Elizabeth Okasha's suggestion, on analogy with inscriptions on metalwork elsewhere, that a late eighth- or even early ninth-century context for the piece was not impossible.[122] We are not in a position to comment authoritatively on this point, but it may be worth pointing out that, despite the quotation finding parallels in a number of literary contexts in Anglo-Saxon England, there was a particular potential resonance for the Mercian regime in Felix's quotation of the passage in reference to the destiny of the future king Aethelbald as enunciated by Guthlac in the second decade of the eighth century.[123]

In re-considering the context for the assembly of the items in the hoard, a key question has to be 'when was there the motive and the opportunity to bring together in the heart of Mercia materials that would likely have represented key items of the treasury not of Mercia but rather those of each of the kingdoms of East Anglia and Kent?' The material could have been gathered from the scene of a battle near Lichfield in the seventh century, but when, at that time, were the warriors of both East Anglia and Kent in the field against, or even with, Mercia? We know of no such military confrontation on Mercian soil.[124]

The Staffordshire hoard items could alternatively have been seized from defeated leaders, as when King Anna was killed by Penda in 654. However, if the action took place on the battlefield, we would by this reasoning be compelled to assume that the 'comitates' of Anna were in the field beside him, in all their battlefield splendour, and that they were so heavily defeated that this material was stripped from them in the aftermath (and in a highly selective manner) by the victorious forces. This is not impossible, but perhaps unlikely. We have moreover no record of battles by any of the seventh-century Mercian rulers against the kings of Kent.

FIGURE 8.12 Inscribed gold strip from among the 'Staffordshire Hoard' items

The inscription is from a Latin Biblical Vulgate text (Numbers 10, 35): 'cumque elevaretur arca dicebat Moses surge Domine et dissipentur inimici tui et fugient qui oderunt te a facie tua', 'When he had lifted up the Ark, Moses said "Rise up, Lord, and may your enemies be dispersed and those who hate you flee from your face"' (a better-known version of this text appears in Psalm 67, 2). Drawn by Tim Hoverd.

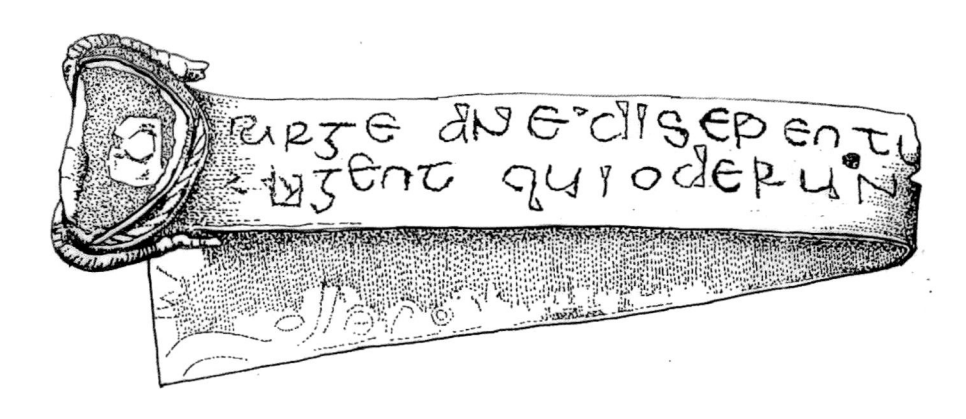

Turning however to the late eighth and early ninth centuries, there were two circumstances in which seizure of the royal treasuries (in whole or part) of both kingdoms could have been linked to a Mercian attempt not simply to defeat the respective kings, but to extinguish their line. The first was in 794 when, by whatever means and wherever it occurred, King Aethelberht of East Anglia was seized by Offa's lieutenants and summarily executed. The second was in 798, when Coenwulf so crushingly invaded Kent and seized Eadberht Praen. The focus has inevitably been on the fate of the captive king, probably mutilated and then imprisoned in Winchcombe. However, with Coenwulf's brother Cuthred installed as king and the kingdom highly subjugated, the Kentish treasury would surely have been entirely in the hands of the Mercian regime.

Taking it back to the Mercian court

Whatever the date of assembly of the 'Staffordshire Hoard' items, the suggestion that it betokens Mercian hegemony in a very material way nonetheless provides an important lens through which to perceive the manner in which such control could be exercised in practical terms. As was evident in reference to coinage, display was an important means by which the Mercian rulers projected their image.[125] The re-use, reworking or simply just the advertised ownership of such an important and in many senses priceless group of items could provide no better demonstration of hegemonic power.[126] And some items that are as yet without close parallel could represent the 'Mercian' component of the group, related to a 'revised' ownership. The fact that some items that are as yet undated had tabs for attachment, possibly to clothing, may be of some interest in this regard.[127] In the context of the years immediately before 800, the affront that the elite of Kent would have felt at such a seizure of the tangible remains of their heritage just might to some extent explain why, in addition to possible kinship, they were relatively content to recognise the authority of Ecgberht of Wessex over them by the mid-820s. Meanwhile, the anger of the East Anglians not only over Aethelberht's death but also at the loss of significant elements of their royal treasury may also partially explain the ferocity with which they engaged and defeated the Mercians under Beornwulf in 825, and killed him.

Another implication concerns the court itself. The role of queen Cynethryth in controlling the Mercian royal household was noted above. In a Frankish court context, the management and provisioning of the palace was assigned to the queen and her chamberlain. As a microcosm of the empire, the smooth running of the palace was vital to the prosperity and stability of the kingdom, and moreover, 'a Carolingian queen's attention was required especially for the 'trappings of royalty' (*ornamento regali*)'.[128] It is just conceivable that, at the Mercian court focused upon Tamworth, one or both of the relevant presiding queens of the late eighth and early ninth century had a similar responsibility, and that this extended to control over the 'bling' that may be represented not only by some of the martial gear such as present in the 'Staffordshire Hoard', but also by those items like the snakes that could have been worn, attached to the kind of clothing of the finery suggested by the gift of Avar-derived silks from Charlemagne and, just possibly also the rich drapery depicted on the coinage. The Avar-derived elaborate sword given to Offa by Charlemagne might indeed have been the sword 'owned by King Offa' mentioned in the aetheling Aethelstan's bequest: if so, it surely took its place in a treasury of such items assembled or augmented, at the same time.[129]

Offa's Dyke as a device of hegemony

What should be evident from the foregoing is both the number and the intricacy of the mechanisms developed by the two great Mercian kings (albeit with the example and inspiration of the Frankish kingdom to draw from and with the spur of competitive emulation to drive them to innovate) to exercise hegemony but also to redefine the terms of a wide range of political and social inter-relationships. The speed of the change in the last ten years of Offa's rule arguably created frictions that were its own undermining, and it is perhaps in this light that the building of Offa's Dyke should be seen. The terms of reference that Asser used to describe the Dyke as an example of vaunting ambition (a point picked up again towards the end of Chapter 9, below), and the monumental scale of its conception and placement, indicate something of its contribution to the hegemonic project. However, arguably its built intricacies, the organisational demands of its construction, and the innovative nature of its formalisation of a frontier zone, indicate just as forcefully how the Dyke was not only a symptom of, but also acted as a mechanism for, the sustaining of that project. It is with a focus upon these aspects, and the exploration of a series of other dimensions of linkage with the parallel hegemonic strategies discussed in this chapter, that we therefore open the final chapter of this book.

CHAPTER NINE

Offa's Dyke: power in the landscape

> And finally, there is the Dyke. This boundary between Wales and England is great in conception, and must have required much driving force and administrative, as well as engineering, skill to bring to completion. It looks as if this massive work were intended to be a memorial – as indeed it has been – to carry down his name to later generations.
>
> Whitelock, D. *English Historical Documents, 1, c.500–1042*, 1979[1]

The idea that Offa's Dyke was *intended* as a memorial to King Offa of Mercia is an intriguing one. What survives of correspondence between the Mercian regime, the papacy and Charlemagne's court shows that intrigue, negotiations, tactical moves and propaganda were familiar features of political strategy in the Europe of the period *c.* AD 780 to 820.[2] In this light, both the scale of the enterprise and also the notion that the Dyke stretched 'from sea to sea' could have been a means of signaling that the creation of the earthwork was a way of memorialising 'greatness' – of both Offa and Mercia. So rather than simply being conventional hyperbole Bishop Asser's comment on the Dyke may have reflected a more particular, though not necessarily definitive, understanding of what it represented.

In bringing this contemporary exploration of what is known, and what more there is to be known, about Offa's Dyke to a close, a final simple question is posed. This follows on directly from the theme of the previous chapter, and can be phrased as: 'In what ways can Offa's Dyke be seen to have reflected or furthered the hegemony of the late eighth and early ninth-century Mercian regime?' In devoting the present chapter to answering this question, it is important to draw together, and in some limited ways to extend, the threads of the preceding argument, to express a *revised*, but not a wholly *revisionist*, perception of what the Dyke was and what it stood for.

Offa's Dyke: the power of construction in the landscape

The design and build of Offa's Dyke involved a co-ordination of practices that operated at different scales. Firstly, the overall design involved a route-planning and positioning within the landscape that determined, for example, the careful direct alignment of sometimes considerable stretches of the Dyke across two miles (3 km) or more at a time, and continually the subtle transit of valleys, hill-tops and hill-slopes to achieve both oversight and maximum visibility.

Secondly, not only was the Dyke built in linear segments, but the form of these segments was deliberately manipulated in recognisable – and recognisably repeated – ways, throughout its course. The constituent lengths of Dyke were designed and built to incorporate subtle adjustments of alignment and disposition of successive runs of bank and ditch. Individual segments and groups of segments along such lengths were themselves adjusted in scale and alignment both to take practical account of the local topography and to maximise visual impact.

Thirdly, although for parts of its course Offa's Dyke may have comprised a simple dump construction earthwork, with material quarried from the ditch being piled up to form the bank, in many places the Dyke featured a more complex build-structure involving the deployment of a whole palette of earthwork treatments and constructional devices. These included ditch digging in segments with a variety of profiles and subtle control of depth; builds of the bank with foundation deposits and controlled dumping; dump- or dry-stone- revetment, or west-facing scarping of the bank; the digging of quarry pits and ditches to the immediate east of the bank; bank profiling; bank segment junction building; west-facing berm construction; counter-scarp bank alignment and construction; and west- or south-facing landscaping of scarps to produce enhancements of perceived scale. In some places the build complexity was further refined through the deployment of the distinctive practice of constructing off-set overlapping terminals.[3]

In several places, but most noticeably on some dramatic slopes overlooking river-valleys such as at Yew Tree Farm on the Lugg, at Spoad on the Clun, and at Bronygarth on the Ceiriog, the cumulative effect of such choreography was, and to some extent still is, visually dramatic. A series of subtle adjustments to the stance of the segments was made in these locations such that, as the overall trend of the Dyke traversed the slope at the perpendicular, its localised built form was nonetheless continually re-orientated to position alternate bank lengths to face fully into the valley below. Besides the practical purpose of minimising damage potentially caused by slippage on such steep slopes, this practice had a dual function in terms of visual efficacy. On the one hand, it provided deliberate oversight from each of these segments down over the valley below. On the other, it presented to the observer from the valley-floor an impression of greater size to the construction than would have been the case had the Dyke followed a straight-line course up the slope. Without the application of this adjustment the earthwork would have appeared to diminish the further up the slope it went, according to the usual rules of perspective.

Meanwhile, other distinctive construction practices, such as the making of abrupt turns in the earthwork, sometimes to create 'bastion'-like effects, have been highlighted in different locations throughout the course of the Dyke.[4] The case for recognising design and construction features claimed in recent years to have been proven *not* to have existed, such as access/egress 'gateways', and supporting works such as 'look-out' platforms has now been re-stated. For example, the evidence that Fox adduced in support of an entrance-way and gate at Bwlch near Discoed, has been found still convincing, although more careful field testing than has so far been achieved will be needed elsewhere. A need to subject the close environs of the Dyke to more comprehensive investigation has also been identified; in particular to attempt to locate other features of 'surveillance infrastructure' such as defended watch-towers or small forts.

This developed perspective on the particular placed and built character of the linear earthwork now enables us to return afresh to Cyril Fox's comments about how the 'genuine' Offa's Dyke can be identified in the field.[5] Fox defined what was 'characteristic' of the Dyke in reference primarily to 'the height or breadth of the bank, the well-defined deep or broad ditch (that) bespeak a work of military character'. For Fox, where the earthwork is of slighter build, continuity of its course over considerable distances and proximity to 'characteristic' (large-scale) lengths could be the only criteria to be used in their identification as part of the overall Dyke scheme. There needs to be a greater awareness, however, of the distinctiveness of both placement practices (how the Dyke approaches and crosses valleys, for example) and of build practices (adjusted-segmented lengths, for example) that enables attribution of a length of earthwork to the overall 'scheme', even if detached in the way that the Gloucestershire lengths in the English Bicknor and Lydbrook areas are.

The single most important conclusion to be drawn from this review of the evidence is therefore that Offa's Dyke was an intricate, fully 'engineered', construction: careful thought was put into every aspect of its creation. The deployment of this massive frontier work concerned both visibility and surveillance, achieved through the visual prominence of the earthwork, and the care with which its individual lengths and vantage points were located in the landscape. It was the strategic control of the landscape over great distances provided in this way that was important, rather than any 'garrisons' or 'patrols' that could have supported its presence.

Offa's Dyke and the western-facing aspect of the Mercian hegemony

We have argued that despite a greater awareness of the location and form of the earthwork, the focus needs to shift from a border defined simply by the Dyke to a wider frontier territory that was itself transitional: topographically, politically, culturally, and historically. This territory encompassed on the one hand a series of tracts of landscape from which the Dyke could be experienced visually: especially along its length, and from the west. On the other hand it comprised a frontier *zone* that extended northwards and southwards, but also laterally from east to west. The Dyke was created within an existing landscape of settlement, both British and Anglo-Saxon, and however sparse in some areas. Although as with so much else about eighth-century Mercia, and the British/Welsh polities, this landscape is in effect undocumented, there may be enough clues to indicate that there were both similarities and differences along the

FIGURE 9.1 Power in the landscape: Offa's Dyke crossing the Vale of Montgomery

If the Dyke (upper and lower centre, on the diagonal) seen from the south here, from near the Kerry Ridgeway can make such a vivid impression today, how much more did it do so when first created? Unlike the aerial views reproduced elsewhere in this book, this prospect was one that has been afforded from the ground for all of the 1200 years since the earthwork was built.

FIGURE 9.2 At the Devil's Pulpit, Gloucestershire: Offa's Dyke distinctiveness

Not only locational details, but also specific aspects of its design and its built form, enable parts of the Dyke in widely separated locations to be identified confidently as part of the same overall 'scheme'. These details are well-exemplified at locations such as the Devil's Pulpit, where the topographic positioning of the earthwork, its scale, its performance of an 'angled turn', its 'adjusted-segmented' build, and the form and disposition of its flanking ditches (or berm) and eastern quarries, are features shared with Dyke lengths as far distant as north Shropshire and Denbighshire.

frontier as to land-holding, defensive and other arrangements, and as to the east–west breadth of the frontier zone in any one area.

That the Dyke was built 'against' the British/Welsh is of course a truism: a truth hard to deny when it so obviously faces west and so frequently occupies a stance that dominates the prospect westwards, presenting a striking appearance when viewed from that direction. Despite traversing the landscape in some locations in a less than wholly dominating way (for instances where it faced uphill westwards), Offa's Dyke nevertheless has characteristics that suggest that it represented a 'blocking' response to a continuing opposing British presence in many places, while permitting a degree of permeability in others.[6] Such permeability, which includes the likelihood of gateways, suggests a Mercian awareness of a continuing need for contacts and commerce further west, while it nonetheless also perhaps represented a potential for further appropriation of land, or at least the extension of dominance westwards, in some areas.

The course that the Dyke followed was not simply a line of demarcation: rather, it had a *connective* purpose. There were a series of key places along the developing frontier that the Mercian ('emergent state') authorities wished to place the Dyke westwards from. The connecting up of these places was achieved by creating a particular 'stance', or series of such stances, towards the wholly British lands to the west *beyond* the frontier zone. So for example, the Oswestry area, with its historic resonances extending back to Penda, was to be embraced within the Dyke. South of the Dee the stance adopted faced north-eastwards towards a key locale for the kingdom of Powys, located west of present-day Llangollen. Southwards from the Clun uplands, where the developing Welsh power was that of the kingdom of Brycheiniog, both the Mercian territory of *Lugharness* in the area of modern-day Presteigne in the Lugg valley, and the new diocesan and military centre at Hereford, were to be included: so the course of the Dyke extending southwards to the river Wye was oriented so as to face south-westwards. Between such key areas (among which also was the Vale of Montgomery), the connective line needed to be oriented as directly north–south as it was practicable to achieve.

The politics of exclusion

Especially across extensive areas both north and south of the middle Severn valley, the building of Offa's Dyke served radically to disrupt movement from west to east. The ancient route-ways along river-valleys or ridge-ways were blocked or at least controlled, and the points where major valleys entered the plains, lowlands or lower broad valleys were rendered inaccessible except under Mercian supervision. Yet the Dyke did more than interrupt and dislocate free passage: it excluded people. The dislocation involved in creating a controlled barrier was therefore not simply physical and practical; it was fundamentally also political and psychological. The very presence of the Dyke conveyed in a brutal manner that the British were forever to be denied access to, and occupation of,

FIGURE 9.3 View southeast across the Shropshire Plain from Plas-crogen

Offa's Dyke is just discernible on the edge of the wood in the foreground and along the hedgerow with large trees to its right. To the right the Dyke descends into the deep cleft at Craignant west of Sellatyn village (just visible among the trees at right-centre). The Wrekin and Wenlock Edge occupy much of the hazily-visible horizon. In between lies the landscape of British/Welsh dispossession.

PHOTOGRAPH: ADAM STANFORD/AERIAL-CAM, COPYRIGHT RESERVED.

extensive tracts of the landscape formerly under their control, such as the fertile plain that stretches north from the Severn through Shropshire and Cheshire to the Dee estuary. The positioning of the Dyke across this broad area serves to highlight the contrast between the barren hillsides of the west and the rich plains of the east, as for example from the uplands to the west of Oswestry or from the eastern flanks of Ruabon Mountain.

This is accentuated in those locations where it is located facing uphill such that it is possible to see directly, if often somewhat hazily, over the Dyke eastwards, and out across the fertile plain below (Figure 9.3). Standing at such places even today you can find yourself reflecting closely upon the words of Gerald of Wales (1145–1223). In his *Description of Wales* Gerald summarised the sustained efforts of the English kings to 'subdue the Welsh' before the Normans came. As the first of three examples of early attempts at subjugation he identified that:

'King Offa shut the Welsh off from the English with his long dyke on the frontier'[7]

Apart from the usefulness of this reference in underlining the clearly understood and long-standing association of this particular king with this Dyke, it emphasised two things that had a strong and cumulative resonance for the Welsh. The first was that among the determined efforts of successive English kings, before and after the Norman Conquest, to dominate the Welsh, the primary example was Offa's Dyke, the building of which could be seen from a twelfth-century perspective to have marked a defining, in effect *originating*, moment in this attempted subjugation.

Secondly, Gerald's statement succinctly conveys the enduring sense of dispossession that Offa's Dyke cemented. The Mercian appropriations of British land were made to seem that much more permanent by the act of building the Dyke, and this must have had a devastating impact on those whose lands subsequently lay mostly to the west of the Dyke, but had once stretched uninterruptedly to the east of its line. The sense of injustice that such dislocation engendered was an enduring stain on Anglo-Welsh relations across many generations. The periodic violent eruption of Welsh military aggression throughout the Middle Ages could arguably be traced back to this defining episode of alienation.[8]

The politics of access and aggrandisement

> On (Offa's) western border, the dyke which bears his name is regarded as a more substantial structure than was once believed, and its interpretation as a work of compromise in a time of peace has given way to a perception of it as a work of almost studied contempt for the Welsh: no point in expanding further west, but necessary to prevent them from mounting smash-and-grab raids into English territory and then escaping back across the border with their cattle and crops.[9]

Whether or not the building of Offa's Dyke represented 'studied contempt' on that king's part, it was certainly an imperious response to the problems caused by the ongoing resentment that the British to the west no doubt felt about the loss of their lands in the lower Dee and middle Severn valleys and the more southerly lowlands.

One way to envisage Offa's Dyke is to consider it to have been of momentary importance only: Offa's campaigns to the west beyond Offa's Dyke could be held to have contradicted its purpose, while those of Coenwulf across Wales rendered it obsolete. However, it is possible to invert this particular lens to suggest that Offa's and Coenwulf's 'British wars' instead reveal its long-term strategic logic. It has long been noted that *despite* the existence of the Dyke there is considerable evidence for continued strife along the border.[10] Does this mean that the frontier work entirely failed to solve the problem of border warfare? The evidence of the Welsh annals, and the silence of the Anglo-Saxon sources concerning warfare in Shropshire, or Cheshire, or Gloucestershire, suggest rather the contrary. It is of interest in this context to note where the fighting concerned occurred, and when.

Broadly, the recorded engagements or campaigns appear to have been initiated either in the north or in the centre-south. Notwithstanding the 'testimony' of the now illegible inscription on the stone pillar at Valle Crucis near Llangollen, this conflict was recorded as having occurred only to the west of the projected line of Offa's Dyke and as having been initiated almost entirely by the Mercians. This could be taken to reflect the weakness of the Dyke in Flintshire and Herefordshire, but it could also be viewed in an entirely different way as, rather, an indication of the existence of Mercian 'unfinished business' in these territories, and therefore of a provisional approach to the definition of the frontier there. As such, it may be a reflection of the continuing *success* of Offa's Dyke in providing the spinal element of a scheme devised to define and stabilise the border in the areas north and south of the Severn at Welshpool that so little of the recorded warfare affected these areas.

What is clear from our discussion concerning the nature of the frontier and its people in Chapter 7 is that although there may have been an intention to 'check' British concerns to recapture extensive tracts of land colonised by the English and for the time being at least entirely lost to them, it is the extent of Mercian military penetration westwards that needs to be emphasised.[11] Offa's campaigns in the south to Brycheiniog and beyond, and Coenwulf's campaigns to the north against Gwynedd and towards Anglesey, represented deep incursions into British territory. In this context, Offa's Dyke could have been built, at least partly, in anticipation of the scale of possible British reaction to the further campaigns of conquest, or at least subjugation, westwards.

A tension can therefore be perceived to have existed between Mercian/English settlement consolidation, particularly in the middle Severn valley and areas southwards and northwards of it, and in the Forest of Dean area, and the expansion of Mercian power and influence in reducing the British kingdoms beyond the Dyke to dependencies, if not actually annexing them. The 'gaps' in Offa's Dyke could in this light be seen as positive points of departure for the sustenance of hegemony not only through the statement of building the great earthwork, but also by providing an at least two-point springboard for ongoing displays of military might at the expense of the Mercians' western neighbours.

It has recently been pointed out, however, that the political context of the creation of the Dyke can plausibly be cast also in reference to the history of dynastic struggle within Mercia itself, as with the case of St Guthlac in exile in Wales.[12] Such examples 'indicate that the borderlands of a kingdom were where rivals could best exploit the weaknesses in a regime. Control of a frontier, not just against the Welsh but also against such rivals, would thus have enhanced the stability of royal power.'[13]

It was, however, a wider Anglo-Saxon audience, as well as the British of whom he was a representative, who would have shared Asser's view of the overbearing character of Offa's kingship and policies, and of the place of the Dyke in furtherance of them. The Mercian dominance that the actions and attitudes of Offa exemplified were nowhere more effectively displayed than through the commissioning and conduct of the great linear earthwork as a 'public works' undertaking that was manifestly conducted on a scale that had not been seen in Britain, nor indeed across northern Europe, since the time of the Roman emperors.

The power-politics of display: Roman imperial echoes

> The frontier-line which Offa drew....can now be seen for what it is – a work of the Dark Ages which in the strength of its conception and the intelligence of its planning is comparable with Hadrian's Wall itself.
>
> Frank Stenton, *Foreword*, in Fox, 1955.[14]

The sophistication in the construction of Offa's Dyke that can now begin to be fully appreciated stands in contrast to the dykes so often regarded as somehow equivalent to it not only in the borderlands of Wales and England, but elsewhere in England itself.[15] It bears closer comparison with the Roman frontier works in northern Britain. Besides their equivalent 'sea-to-sea' concept and compass, these latter works were also highly engineered; and they were also designed, at least in part, to impress. It can hardly be a surprise, given the ambitious nature of Offa's kingship and its emulations of the Carolingian model, to find that Offa's Dyke, like Hadrian's Wall, features dramatic cross-cuts of the grain of the country, especially performative sections, and a refined choreography of form and placement in key locations. As was explained in Chapter 6, some features of Offa's Dyke (such as the angled turns) were perhaps directly imitative of Roman military works (Figure 9.4).

We have observed how Offa's Dyke was frequently positioned in such a way that it could be seen extending across tracts of landscape, especially when viewed along its course. The earthwork could be overseen from several vantage points along its course rising (especially when viewed northwards) around the flanks of hills and making dramatic descents around or down spurs. In this respect it mirrored the way that, in particular, the central section of Hadrian's Wall could also be observed from different points along its course snaking up the outer flanks of hill slopes and hugging the edges of prominent crags. Apart from these locational similarities, the quality of the engineering involved in the construction of the Dyke could sometimes approach Roman standards, as has been observed by more than one commentator.[16]

That this was a conscious replication of the northern frontier works of the Roman emperors cannot be proven, and it is perhaps unlikely that Offa himself ever viewed those works. It is, however, almost certain that he did have available to him Bede's description of Hadrian's Wall as 'a great ditch' and a bank which together stretched 'from sea to sea' (although Bede mistakenly thought that this edifice had been

FIGURE 9.4 Hadrian's Wall at Steel Rigg, west of Housesteads

The prospect eastwards along the stone-built lengths as they wind their way along the Whin Sill crags provides one of the most memorable images of the Roman wall. The maximisation of visibility and surveillance capacity making optimum use of broken terrain was effected highly skilfully both here and along Offa's Dyke.

FIGURE 9.5 The Great Bath with Bath Abbey church above it to the east

Both Offa and his son, Ecgfrith, are recorded as witnessing charters at Bath. It has been suggested that their interest in the place had as much to do with an intended emulation of the Frankish court at Aachen as with its frontier position in respect to the West Saxons.

built by the Emperor Severus).[17] Given that Bede's description included reference to the manner of construction of the Roman frontier work as 'a rampart…made of sods cut from the earth and… raised high above the ground like a wall', it does not seem impossible that the idea for the Dyke, in Offa's mind at least, stemmed from the Roman imperial example as portrayed by the celebrated Northumbrian monk.

If it did involve a referencing of Roman military works, therefore, Offa's Dyke can be seen as a further example of explicitly 'Roman' imperial dimensions to Offa's supremacist pretensions. As such, it could be regarded as parallel to the formulas used on official documents, the portraiture on coins that explicitly mirrored Roman imperial conventions, and the re-use of Roman materials in early 'Romanesque' buildings whose form represented among other things a decided break with the practices of the pagan past.[18] The difference between these various devices is one of scale: the work of building the Dyke, and its imprint on the geography of Britain, dwarfed the other enterprises. Such a 'Romanisation' of reference by Offa seemingly involved also a privileging of places that had particular Roman connections, whether for instance London, or Bath, or Leicester. Other such places evocative of *Romanitas* had an explicit further connection with the origins of Christianity, whether the locus of the martyr Alban at St Albans where Offa allegedly founded a monastery, or Canterbury itself, where St Augustine's mission had first focused its attention.

Bath has a particular resonance here, in reference to the way in which the Frankish court was developing a permanent place of residence close to the hot springs at Aachen in the early 790s, with Roman-style buildings recreated close to the vestiges of Roman Imperial structures.[19] Little is known of the pre-ninth-century Anglo-Saxon settlement at Bath, the spa town of *Aquae Sulis* famed across the Roman Empire for its thermal springs. That it occupied a strategic position on the Wiltshire river Avon in respect to both Mercia and Wessex had been clear for some time, parts of the course of that river having for some time formed part of the frontier between the two kingdoms.

Given its importance on the border between the two principal southern English kingdoms, Offa had expended considerable effort to secure control of Bath: and by the end of his life he had apparently established a royal residence there. Its planned importance to the Mercian regime is indicated by the fact that one of the few charters issued in Ecgfrith's name in 796 was described as having been formulated at the place called '*at the baths*'.[20] 'If the Mercian rulers wished to emulate their Frankish contemporaries and Ecgfrith's own consecration in 787 was inspired directly by that of Charlemagne's sons in 781 then Bath, with its antique architecture and hot springs, was the only candidate for an English Aachen.'[21]

Power in the frontier: the concept of a Mercian 'March'

If Offa's Dyke was never conceived as a frontier 'line' or as a stand-alone work, and was instead designed to be the key element in the creation of a frontier zone that with the benefit of hindsight set the framework for the Anglo-Welsh borderland for the next 700 years, the 'March' was as important as the Dyke itself. The Dyke is the main point of historical attention because Asser mentioned it, because it is such an impressive construction, and because it made the longest and deepest impression on medieval and later writers, especially in the role it came to have historically, of defining 'Wales'. However, it was the frontier itself that was arguably the focus of Mercian activity, and for which the Dyke was the principal, but not necessarily the only, manifestation.

The workings of a Mercian 'March'

The organisation of the frontier with the Dyke at its core may also have reflected the existence of the 'political places' where the earthwork stood in opposition to established, or former, centres of British power to the immediate west of the Dyke. The relation of the Dyke to a wider frontier landscape, that included British settlements to its east and English settlements to its west, indicates, however, the development of a 'march', a hybrid border region that rather than simply delimiting a frontier, created instead a buffer zone that was permeable when needed, and 'fixed' when needed.[22]

In respect to both the broader political scene that in the case of Offa extended to Rome (and even, in some commercial, cultural and diplomatic contexts probably also to Byzantium and the Islamic Caliphate), the Dyke in this way fully embodied the concept of 'the political' (Gladys Mary Coles' phrase 'a concept made material' finds particular resonance here). While on the ground along the frontier, there were places that were already 'political' inasmuch as they had been centres of power, in some cases long before the Dyke was built, the building of the Dyke nonetheless would have transformed their political nature. This is because it introduced a new tension by challenging both their dominance of the local landscape and their presence in a controlled frontier zone at all.

The idea was introduced in Chapter 7 that it may be possible to trace the breadth of that part of the eighth-century frontier zone from arrangements that are hinted at in eleventh century and later sources, supported by place-name clues. Moreover, it was just this zone that, in a somewhat different guise in the early Norman period, became a key part of the 'March of Wales'.[23] The breadth of this zone in the late eighth/early ninth century would have been variable according to changing circumstances. It may, for instance, have been relatively 'narrow' where the Dyke was located close to powerful and potentially aggressive neighbours. In key places the Dyke itself announced the power of Mercia through the scale, location and nature of the work. This was the case in several places: north of the Dee by Ruabon, close to the Vyrnwy-Tanat confluence at Llanymynech, opposite Montgomery and Frydd Faldwyn, and on the Wye above Tintern. Elsewhere, the existence of English settlements, and possibly also fortified places, created a broad zone extending some distance to the west and to the east of the Dyke. Here, the Dyke was frequently impressive in location and build, and often overlooked wide swathes of country, as was the case north of Oswestry, and in the stretch of country to the west of Shrewsbury and north of Montgomery. It was also the case in the Teme and Lugg valleys, in the Walton basin west of Presteigne, and in the Wye valley to the north-west and west of Hereford.

Among the practical consequences of the concept of frontier *depth,* where it existed, was that both English and Welsh communities could have contributed to its composition and character, as they were certainly to do in later centuries.[24] While some evidence was adduced for this in respect of the Presteigne area in Chapter 7, medieval documentary sources for other parts of the March of Wales may provide other indicators of relative span of the frontier east and west. One example of the way that the breadth of the frontier zone in the eighth and ninth centuries could have been reflected in arrangements documented for the twelfth century is through the charting of the extent of the Welsh and English dependencies of the lordship of Clun in the twelfth century.[25] Another example is the broad east–west span of the dependent chapelries of the deanery

FIGURE 9.6 Herrock Hill in the 'Marchia Walliae' of 1086, west of Presteigne

Offa's Dyke emphatically, if in earthwork terms, minimally, curves around the upper flank of Herrock Hill, seen in the near-distance here. Radnor Forest dominates the left skyline, and beneath it, at centre-left, is the Radnor Badin with its putatively early (?seventh-century) English settlements.

of 'Marchia' following a major ecclesiastical reorganisation in the Oswestry area in the twelfth century.[26]

In respect to the 'Domesday March' near Presteigne, it was noted how the medieval lordships extended further to the east and to the west than the spread of individual settlements said to lie 'in the March of Wales' in 1086, so it is clearly necessary to exercise caution in simply equating the two. It does, however, at least seem possible that the kernel of the idea of a 'lateral' March was put in place as part of the late eighth- and early ninth-century organisation of the frontier.

The medieval March was based upon essentially military lordships and was predicated upon a much 'wider' world of mixed tenures extending to France, Ireland and south-west Wales as well as to central, eastern and southern England.[27] It was also a frontier that was organised according to the interests of magnates who were attempting to operate independently of the medieval kings of England, in contrast to the apparent close inter-dependency of the elite in the Mercian realm under Offa and Coenwulf. Nonetheless, the idea of a coherent, if diverse, zone may perhaps have been well-understood in the high medieval period *precisely because* it was a concept that had lasted so long, and was an inheritance from the kings of Mercia.[28]

A European context for the March

It is surely no coincidence that the Mercian hegemony under Offa and Coenwulf saw an 'imperial statement' such as the Dyke conceived and executed on a grand scale. The Dyke may have been designed to reflect Offa's putative status as the (Mercian) inheritor of the mantle of the Emperors of Rome in Britain. However it was also an expression of a Mercian hegemony among whose aims was to emulate, and potentially in some ways to surpass, the achievements of the most substantial power in the world of eighth-century Western Europe, that of Francia, and its leader Charlemagne, whom Pope Leo III was soon to crown 'Emperor of the Romans'.[29] Such emulation and competition was nonetheless conducted in a late eighth- and early ninth-century western European world that was entirely dominated by the Frankish state and in which any Anglo-Saxon kingdom, however assertive, was inevitably a minor player. Carolingian influence upon Mercia was in this context reflected in very many ways, of which the anointing of a king's successor, the creation of a court circle, an interest in religious reform especially in terms of diocesan boundary changes, and the adoption of classicising material forms, perhaps especially architecturally, are but a few examples that have already been noted.

In this context it may be worth considering what light might be thrown on the Mercian western frontier and its hypothesised controlled region from an examination of the better-documented frontiers of the Carolingian polity. Both the Old English word *mearc* and the Old French *marche* could mean a 'boundary', but the concept of a 'border district' is documented only for the continental *marche*.[30] It has been claimed that 'the evidence of Offa's Dyke' itself shows that for the Mercians in the eighth century, their border with the British was conceived in contrast as a line.'[31] 'Yet perhaps it would be wise not to draw too strict a distinction between *mearc*, *marche* and their Latin derivations. After all, it seems clear from Domesday Book's usage that *marcha* could also mean border district.'[32] Among the Franks, the word *marca* was apparently used in documents interchangeably with the classical terms *limites*, *confinia*, *termini*, and *fines*. From this, it has been deduced that the *marca* was not understood by the Carolingian Franks necessarily in the way that modern geographers and anthropologists distinguish categorically between a linear boundary and a zonal frontier. Rather, the interchangeable terms noted above 'could refer to either a particular line or a swathe of land at the margin of the empire….Behind the words lies the fact that most Carolingian frontiers were *both* linear and zonal.'[33]

Moreover, the idea of a 'march' as at least a quasi-militarised buffer zone was emerging in mainland Europe at exactly the same time that Offa's Dyke was being built in Britain: 'the crucial shift in meaning occurred in the late eighth century, when the term (*marchia*) began to be used in a new way, particularly in Charlemagne's capitularies. It was then that it came to denote a border zone of the Carolingian empire for which particular legal and military arrangements had been made.'[34] Two important implications stem from a realisation that Offa's Dyke was contemporary with border regions becoming much more closely defined by the Franks, for instance in Italy and (in a direct parallel with the situation in western Mercia) against the Bretons. The first is that, regardless of disparities in the relative sizes of the polities, and who was emulating whom, common problems of defining areas within and outside the emerging state were finding parallel solutions in Francia and Mercia.[35]

The second implication is that, therefore, it may be reasonable to deduce that the better-documented Carolingian situation may offer some insights into how the western frontier of Mercia was perceived by the Mercians themselves, and how the 'controlled zone' was supposed to operate. So, for instance, such march-lands were seen not so much as militarised zones, but rather as regions where the danger of dwelling was greater than elsewhere: they were zones of 'ill-defined or un-defined domination'.[36] Importantly, the character of the military presence in such regions related strongly to campaigning out beyond them, so that for example 'Carolingian armies were expected to refrain from plundering until they reached the frontier'.[37] Some Frankish frontiers were yet more tightly controlled, at least economically. The capitulary of Thionville, of 805, for instance, records the existence of nine trading checkpoints on the eastern periphery of the empire.[38]

There is, however, a contrast to be drawn here between the way that Carolingian frontiers were defined, and the presence of Offa's Dyke amid the western Mercian frontier, since we have no record of either Charlemagne or his successors creating a similarly extensive linear work to match Offa's great earthwork. This may simply be a question of scale, in that the distances on

FIGURE 9.7 'Both linear and zonal': the frontier east from the Clun
Offa's Dyke conspicuously traverses the slope in the foreground, on Spoad Hill, with topography providing part of the framework for the visual definition of the frontier zone: here bordered by hills in the Bishop's Castle area.
PHOTOGRAPH: ADAM STANFORD/AERIAL-CAM, COPYRIGHT RESERVED.

FIGURE 9.8 'Areas of ill-defined domination': the Dyke in the Ceiriog uplands
West of Chirk, the Dyke encloses some areas with broad westerly, northerly and easterly prospects. These take in lands to the north and west that remained, probably firmly, under British/Welsh control: as here, with the distant north-westerly prospect of Ruabon/ Eglwyseg and Lantysilio Mountains above Llangollen, from Mount Wood above Nanteris. The back of the massive bank of the Dyke is visible beyond the field gate.
PHOTOGRAPH: ADAM STANFORD/AERIAL-CAM, COPYRIGHT RESERVED.

FIGURE 9.9 The Dyke at Orseddwen, looking south-eastwards

It is possible to gain the impression from reading Fox's accounts that the counter-scarp bank of the Dyke was a minimal and relatively rare feature. This aerial photograph overlooking Selattyn Hill (with the western suburbs of Oswestry in the background) shows that this is not the case, and our observations elsewhere indicate that the counterscarp was a normal, and not an exceptional build element that was often very prominent and substantial in size, as here. This photograph also serves to emphasise the extent of the Dyke in the landscape, and its contrast with shorter dykes both in Britain and on the Continent. Its great length and often massive build stands in marked contrast to Charlemagne's ultimately abortive 6.5 km long 'Karlsgraben' earthwork, for example.

REPRODUCED COURTESY OF A. WIGLEY: COPYRIGHT, SHROPSHIRE COUNCIL.

the Continent were so much larger, and the process of conquest was in many cases much swifter. However, it seems that Charlemagne did attempt to create his own symbolic 'frontier ditch', the 'Karlsgraben', across a four-mile (6.5 km) watershed between two tributaries of the Danube and Main rivers south of Nuremberg in northern Bavaria in the autumn of 793 at the height of his wars against the Avars. This was an abortive project, and Carolingian annalists writing in the early ninth century, after Charlemagne's death, expressed surprise and disappointment over this fiasco. It had involved the Frankish king and his entourage being present on site for several weeks, and the diversion of troops and levies to undertake the task, which both military incursions and possibly also weather and ground conditions put an end to before it was completed.[39]

It is difficult not to see an element of rivalry rather than simply emulation here. Offa successfully created a 'wall' that reflected those that the Roman emperors had built in Britain. He may well have actively promoted the concept of its vast extent in propaganda terms: like the Roman works, it extended 'from sea to sea'. Charlemagne could well have been aware of the existence of former Roman frontier works along the Rhine-Danube frontier, and the strange 'Karlsgraben' episode could have reflected a concern on his part not to be outdone by the presumptuous Mercian king.

Offa's Dyke and eighth-century frontiers

Given the lack of any contemporary eighth-century reference to Offa's Dyke, it may be tempting to dismiss the significance of Asser's statement, and to suggest that we somehow need to adjust our thinking about Offa's Dyke towards a more purely material and archaeological appreciation of it as simply another mid to late Saxon long-distance boundary. As suggested in Chapter 1, there are several reasons why such a temptation should be resisted, such as its naming and its lack of reliance on pre-existing boundaries.

So while it is possible to regard Offa's Dyke in generic terms as a long-distance boundary in a world in which such boundaries existed more widely, it merits an understanding in its own terms as a distinctive construction created at a particular juncture historically. However, in reviewing the place of the Dyke in the wider course of British and European history, it may be instructive to consider here how the Dyke has been viewed in these generic terms, in a little more detail. Was the Dyke just one manifestation of a longer-standing concern with major boundaries? Or was it an example of a particular point in time, for instance, when 'great men' strove to mark their presence by digging (massive) ditches?

Offa's Dyke as a boundary among others

In recent years, perhaps in part due to frustration with the manifest intractability of the questions of fact and interpretation surrounding Offa's Dyke, there has been a focus not on the uniqueness of the great earthwork, but rather upon its place among many other linear dykes or boundaries. One version of such a view is that the Dyke should be considered first and foremost, and generically, as a linear earthwork, and should therefore be compared closely with other linear earthworks likely to have been dug by the Anglo-Saxons, to seek to understand both its form and its purpose.[40] Study of Offa's Dyke in these terms should include comparison with obviously (though perhaps only superficially) similar linear dykes, but should extend to include frontiers created in the ninth and tenth centuries.[41] Moreover, it can be argued that such frontier works span a broader period of history than has hitherto been appreciated: from such structures as Bokerley Dyke in Hampshire/Dorset dating to the fifth century AD to less overtly dyke-like frontier-lines such as the ninth-century Danelaw boundary that ran extensively along Watling Street and the thirteenth-century boundary between the diocese of Rochester and of Canterbury.[42] In such perspective, the 'discontinuous' nature of Offa's Dyke needs no explanation, since most boundaries were of this character in the later first millennium and beyond.[43] As such, it used rivers, the coastline, or pre-existing roads, wherever this was more convenient and involved less need for laborious construction. Such a categorising view sets Offa's Dyke into a broader temporal and spatial frame, and indeed supports a questioning even of the very attribution of 'Offa's Dyke' as a work inspired or built by Offa himself, except perhaps as a mythological attribution that Offa's name itself might represent.[44]

This is a challenging perspective, and at first reading it might seem to represent a more strictly archaeological (rather than historical) one. However, it is in our view flawed in a number of respects. So, for example, it ignores the fact that the construction of Offa's Dyke could have involved much greater use of rivers than it did. While it could plausibly be argued that the Dyke used the Wye to the west and south of Hereford in this way, it did not use the Wye south of Monmouth in the same way. Although it used the middle Severn in the immediate area east of Welshpool in this way, it did not continue such a strategy southwards along the banks of the Severn, although it could have done. Although it could have used the Dee to 'produce' a frontier-line down to Chester, it did not do so.

Secondly, such a view suggests that all boundaries are ultimately the same, regardless of the political or historical circumstances obtaining at the time of their construction. We take the opposite view, that all boundaries are historically contingent: they have a purpose in a given time and at a particular place or region, and changing circumstances usually soon transcend that specific juncture. Thirdly, the generic view of dykes ignores the unique characteristics of the design and construction of Offa's Dyke. Moreover, removing the Dyke's naming into the realm of mythology involves discounting centuries of tradition and a clear historical attribution to King Offa, from Asser onwards. If it is only by recourse to a suggestion that, because other dykes are 'mythologically-attributed', so must Offa's be, that we can de-link this Dyke from the eighth-century Mercian king, then there seems no reason to abandon the various historical references (including that of Gerald of Wales in the eleventh century noted above). It is rather more logical, following Stenton, to see a considerable and particular significance in the fact that, of all the dykes that have existed in Britain and overseas, the only dyke to be named specifically for an individual appears to be Offa's Dyke. This particularity of reference correlates especially well with the observation that the Dyke is structurally unique.

A cross-continental perspective

More profound in its historical resonance is the suggestion that there was a particular pan-European, or even world-wide, 'moment' when to be a great leader and the commissioner of digging to create enormous but functionally irrelevant frontier works was briefly fashionable, and this took in the construction not only of Offa's linear work, but those of greater magnates including Charlemagne himself. 'Construction of great fosses happened at roughly the same time, in that 'long' eighth century during which central control, the assertion of rulers' authority, or state formation, all found new means of expression'.[45] What mattered was the capacity to bring subordinates together to exercise acts of construction, and this provides an explanation for a new exercise of royal or imperial authority through labour requirements: in Mercia, for instance, for landholders to contribute to bridge-work and fortress-work.

Moreover, 'digging ditches…was far too important to be overlooked by rulers whose capacity to coerce and to build support and consensus was always fragile, and open to question. Ditches were a project the ruler defined and whose execution he organised.'[46] And furthermore, 'it was not the finished product – the ditch as artefact which scholars contemplate today – that concerned the powerful in the early Middle Ages. Rather, it was the event of construction that mattered.'[47] This latter statement provides an important insight concerning the impetus for construction and the impact of the completion of such 'projects', but in the case of Offa's Dyke it tells only part of the story. The care with which it was built indicates that it was not only the event of the building, but also the visual impact and the excluding character of the Dyke that was designed to endure in the memory.

We have suggested that, at least for Offa, but probably also for those Mercian 'comitates' who saw their political fortunes wholly or largely bound up with his, the Dyke was at

FIGURE 9.10 Offa's Dyke on either side of the Teme valley, from Ffrydd Hill

'Digging ditches' marked, according to Paolo Squatriti, a key moment in the process of state-building in post-Roman Europe. It is true that Offa's Dyke represents an example of the aggrandisement involved, but its extent is without parallel in Europe. The view here is from the 'slight' build length north of Jenkins Allis, towards the Teme valley and the course of the Dyke along the hills on the horizon (Panpunton and Cwmsanahan).

one and the same time an instrument of control, a demonstration of the power and potential reach of the Mercian state, and a compromise in the progress of unfinished business to the west. This may moreover have involved a role for the Dyke in 'fixing' yet further the identity of the Mercians as a people surrounded on all sides by other kingdoms and peoples: by permanently making reference to a particular frontier at a particular time. Fundamental to an understanding of the development both of Mercian identity and to the creation of Offa's Dyke, therefore, is the concept and reality of the frontier, and beyond this the existence of a borderland in which there stood a boundary work that served as the 'spine' of that frontier.

In reference to the east-central European 'Limes', the Roman imperial frontier between the Rhine and the Danube, it has recently been stated that 'Frontiers originated in centrifugal forces and at least they are an integrating factor, because they are open to both directions, to the centre and to the margins. The Frontier is outward-oriented, and the main attention of the centre is concentrated on treasured space gained under calculated danger'.[48] This is said to contrast with the idea of the border, which is defined in an inwards-looking way as a consolidation of territory, a limitation to the expansion of colonisation, and as a definition of those beyond as well as within the polity.[49] Arguably, a more comprehensive strategy was involved in the creation of a 'March'. This was a strategy that involved both a linear work *and* a linear territory within which it existed. As such, the creation of the Mercian western boundary zone would, at one and the same time, have brought together the benefits of both an outwards-looking frontier and an inwards-focused border.

Offa's Dyke: a point in time, a frontier in transition

Not only did the Dyke reflect Offa's reasonable desire to create a more 'managed' western border: it was also an integral part of his wider strategies of political manipulation and controlled violence, of reference to kingly powers with an imperial cast, and of competition in a European dimension. The Dyke can be seen as having crystallised a number of aspects of Offa's hegemonic strategy. As such, regardless of what it has come to signify as a defining cultural boundary, as a construction located precisely in time and space it represents a particular historical *juncture* and circumstance. It involved a reaching back into an inherited past, evoking an imperial era and an inherited tradition of dyke-building at one and the same time. Equally, it managed to be innovatory in that it gave both the concept and the expression of the 'wall' and the 'frontier' a new twist, suited to the emerging politics of its day.

It is unlikely that any modern scholar will emulate Sir Frank Stenton in confidently assigning the building of the Dyke to the years immediately around 785, on the basis that this was the only period in which relative peace between Mercia and its British neighbours westwards was demonstrable. This peace is perhaps definable not only in the absence of reference to warfare, but also in the

FIGURE 9.11 Complexity and a possible 'gateway' at Carreg-y-big near Oswestry

The care with which the Dyke was located in the landscape west of Oswestry, and between the Afon Morda valley in the south and the Ceiriog valley near Chirk Castle in the north, is evident from many of the photographs, at ground level and from the air, used to illustrate this book. The build complexity was also remarkable, with multiple subtle adjustments nowhere more clear than here at Carreg-y-big, as discussed at length in Chapters 5 and 6.

REPRODUCED COURTESY OF A. WIGLEY: COPYRIGHT, SHROPSHIRE COUNCIL.

FIGURE 9.12 The Dyke crossing the southern flank of Graig Hill above the Clun

Both from the valley-bottom and as here seen from across the valley, the Dyke makes a striking ascent/decent of the lower slopes of Graig Hill, south from Hergan. The disposition of the earthwork across the south-facing slopes bordering the Clun valley is less dramatic, but no less sophisticated, than the descent/ascent on the north-facing side above Lower Spoad (Figure 5.27).

PHOTOGRAPH: ADAM STANFORD/ AERIAL-CAM, COPYRIGHT RESERVED.

possibility of travel for foreign 'diplomats' in the frontier zone. In this light it is revealing to note that following the general legatine Council in 786 presided over by Offa and by Ecgberht of Wessex, when part of the deputation went to Northumbria, the rest 'went into Offa's other dominions and into Wales'.[50]

It does seem reasonable to suppose that Offa was only able to countenance such a massive undertaking by the third or fourth decade of his reign. It might be supposed also, that it would have been just as plausibly a corollary of a period of warfare, wherever directed, as of one of 'peace'. It is perhaps more likely, therefore, that Offa's Dyke was built in the period between 785 and 795. That decade relates closely to what was identified in both Chapters 3 and 8, above, as a critical time in Offa's reign. In this light, the Dyke was a culminating work, not only in terms of it being the ultimate expression of physical frontier definition, but also as the crowning act of a process of more and more radical exercise of Mercian political control and statehood, and of Offa's personal and imperial ambitions.

If there was any particular subtlety to the reason for the construction of Offa's Dyke in a given year or years, it is entirely lost to us without the survival of any contemporary documentation from which to deduce a singular political strategy. Yet if there were differences in the political approach of Offa and of Coenwulf to both Dyke and frontier, it would be helpful to know how these 'played out' in reference to the different histories of their personal involvement. It would for instance appear that while Offa appears to have pursued an agenda focused upon the Wye valley and Hereford, Coenwulf's focus was more obviously upon the northern part of the frontier.

Offa and the Wye valley interruption

A mid-eighth-century pause in the 'moving frontier' in the area to the west of the Wye to the south of Hereford was probably due to the success of a strategy of containment of Mercian ambitions by Ergyng, with support of Gwent or Brycheiniog, or both, after the Mercian depredations during Aethelbald's reign. Offa contained a backlash to this early advance through his victory over a British force, from wherever drawn, in the vicinity of Hereford in 760. Peace could have been achieved by the subsequent establishment of treaty relations that involved a parallel ecclesiastical oversight of the two populations, as well as legal arrangements for the regulation of relations between the English and the Welsh in this area that was perhaps formalised much later on, in the 'Ordinance concerning the *Dunsaete*.'

Mercian awareness of the potential openness to Gwent-inspired attacks that such treaties involved may nonetheless have led to the development not only of formal defences for Hereford itself, but also to the construction of linear earthworks marking the frontier zone along at least parts of the eastern side of the Wye valley south of Hereford. The lack of a heavily-built length of the Dyke either north or south of the Wye in Herefordshire could, as was suggested in

Chapter 7, have represented a deliberate Mercian preparedness to annexe further British lands and to extend the frontier westwards in these areas as opportunities arose.[51]

Why, however, did Offa not apparently campaign in the north? One answer is that we do not know that he did not. Indeed, what evidence there is suggests that either he or Ecgfrith (or both) did campaign there in the last decade of the eighth century. Fox believed that Offa had died at Rhuddlan, and this was surely significant in respect to plans for the northern part of the frontier.[52] Moreover, at the very beginning of Coenwulf's reign, in 797 or 798, that king was required to respond to an attack upon a Mercian force located at Rhuddlan.[53] Such dispositions might well reflect the unfolding of a new phase of a wider strategy of expansion along alternate parts of the frontier where the scale and organisation of the opposing Welsh polities was judged to be weaker.

Coenwulf and the northern limits

As with Offa, a pattern to Coenwulf's involvement with the frontier can be reconstructed that both advances new perspectives and raises further questions to be addressed. The focus of Coenwulf's activity appears to have been upon the northern part of the frontier, although this no doubt reflects the biases and concerns of the Welsh sources that have survived into the present-day. It has important implications for both dykes. For example, if the new dating of Wat's Dyke to the early ninth century, based upon the work at Gobowen, is upheld through further evidence obtained in the coming years, it is clear that there is a need to try even harder to understand its relationship to Offa's Dyke.

FIGURE 9.13 The massive 'terminal' length of Offa's Dyke at Ffordd Llanfynydd

The most northerly known length of Offa's Dyke as a continuous earthwork is a massive embanked linear feature almost entirely obscured in the belt of trees at left (viewed from the north-west). It is also unusual in supporting a road along its crest. Hope Mountain is visible in the background of this view.

Offa's Dyke could have been built as an attempt to define the frontier once-and-for-all, and if so it could be envisaged as simply uncompleted beyond Treuddyn. This could have been due either to the death of Offa, or uncertainty as to whether the Vale of Clwyd might be incorporated within its compass, or both. Alternatively, Offa's Dyke may once have continued on a line towards Basingwerk, perhaps with an interruption in the Caergwrle area similar to the one that may have deliberately existed west of Hereford, in order to facilitate campaigning. In this way, the confusion between the dykes (and the naming of parts of the northern section of Wat's Dyke historically and locally as 'Offa's Dyke') would immediately become explicable, since the northern part of what later 'became' Wat's Dyke would initially have been built originally as part of the Offa's Dyke scheme.

This would imply not only that the northern part of Wat's Dyke followed an original earlier line, but also that the Gobowen dating itself relates to a re-use, or even the rebuilding on a slightly different routing, of an earlier monument. As such, it may have served as the first demarcation line of a western frontier, possibly dating to the period of earliest Anglo-Saxon settlement of the Cheshire plain in the seventh century rather than, as confidently asserted by Fox and Stenton, to Aethelbald's reign in the early eighth century. Originally it could simply have delimited that part of the Cheshire plain that extended southwards to the Dee as being Mercian territory, or it could have comprised a series of single straight lengths, as with the Rowe Ditch in north Herefordshire. In support of this thesis is the fact of the 'adjusted' northern course of both dykes. Why, for example, did Offa's Dyke turn north-westwards at Mount Sion, and not go straight on to the Dee estuary? This must surely have had to do with 'unfinished business' at the northern end of the frontier. But why, then, did Wat's Dyke turn in this same direction to take in the territory up to Basingwerk? Surely, this would reflect the prior existence of a line of Dyke that extended in a line parallel to the coast, northwards towards Basingwerk.

Whether or not this was the case, Coenwulf may subsequently have ordered 'Wat's Dyke' to be created, with a new course southwards to the Vyrnwy and an explicit linkage to pre-existing fortified places, in the most northerly of which (at Basingwerk), he died. This would have provided a more secure base for Coenwulf's campaigns into north Wales, the stability of these arrangements being registered by the fact that the Mercian 'high command' continued to use this route into Wales through the rest of the ninth century. Moreover, an extensive southwards 'extension' of a putative former 'most northerly' part of 'Offa's Dyke', built under Coenwulf entirely as 'Wat's Dyke', alongside the remaining 'Treuddyn' Offa's Dyke course northwards could have had the aim of changing a simple break into an extended open 'corridor'. This tallies well not only with the new dates for Gobowen, but at least one recent discovery of a coin of Coenwulf in an area close to the Dykes, north-east of Wrexham.[54] Does this latter in particular mean that Churchyard's idea of commercial exchanges between the Welsh and the English in just this area were based in a ninth-century reality?[55]

This question of the role of the Dyke and frontier in commerce is an aspect that has recently been the subject for some, albeit limited, discussion. In particular, it has been noted that the Dyke may have served as much as a customs barrier to regulate trade between Wales and Mercia, as to have served any specifically military purpose.[56] Gateways and route-ways have been seen as vital to this purpose, and one is put in mind immediately again of the capitulary of Thionville, of 805, and the nine trading checkpoints on the eastern periphery of the Carolingian empire that it records.[57] The mineral wealth of copper in the Llandudno area to the north-west and of lead to the north-east around Halkyn Mountain, as well as the brine springs of Cheshire to the east, provided ample reason for continuous commerce east and west across the frontier to the north. Meanwhile the 'salt-ways' of the *Hwicce* extending in all directions from Droitwich echo such economic activities further south.[58]

FIGURE 9.14 Coin of Coenwulf, from a location to the north-east of Wrexham

PHOTOGRAPH REPRODUCED COURTESY OF THE PORTABLE ANTIQUITIES SCHEME/BRITISH MUSEUM. COPYRIGHT RESERVED.

This perspective receives additional support when the focus is transferred from the extreme northern to the extreme southern end of the frontier. Fox's inferences about the importance of commerce along the Roman road from Gwent to Gloucester, and Noble's suggestion that Chepstow emerged as a frontier market are of immediate relevance here. Equally important, perhaps, is the role of the *Cantref Coch*, the 'Red District', located between the Wye and the Severn, that included much of the Forest of Dean and that was absorbed within the Diocese of Hereford at an early date. Recent investigations to the north of St Briavels, at Clearwell Quarry, involved the excavation of a series of three major clusters of ironworking furnaces and hearths that have been dated by radiocarbon to the late eighth or early ninth century.[59] They quite probably represent brief episodes in what was nonetheless a highly productive industry, but what is of most interest is that they are located in the area of the Mork Brook valley where the Dyke is associated with a 'Wyegate' recorded on a tenth-century charter. Moreover, this 'gate' is itself located close to an 'outwork', a loop of bank and ditch of closely similar character to the Dyke that extends down to the river-bank on the south side of the Brook. Could this encompass the site of a river-side wharf through which (perhaps along with other such places) the trade in iron and timber could be conducted?

One corollary to the 're-centring' of Wat's Dyke within the narrative of the Mercian hegemony of the late eighth and early ninth centuries involves looking again, if speculatively, at its naming. One way in which Wat's Dyke has always been regarded as standing in contrast to Offa's Dyke is that while the latter uniquely bears the name of the king who commanded its construction, the former was named after a mythical 'Wade' or 'Gado' (Old English, *Wada*).[60] It has in contrast been suggested, as noted above, that the 'Offa' that the longer

FIGURE 9.15 Wat's Dyke viewed from Mount Sion on Offa's Dyke

North-west of Wrexham, the two dykes are occasionally inter-visible, by the valley of the Cedigog. Wat's Dyke follows a course above, and immediately to the east of, the river Alyn which flows through the ravine beyond the houses in the middle-distance here.

of the two dykes was named after was in fact the mythical hero of that name that occurred in literature, rather than the most famous of the Mercian kings. It has not until now been proposed, however, that the latter idea could itself be stood upon its head: could not Wat's Dyke actually have been named also, after an *historical* figure?

Such an idea may not be as far-fetched as it at first sounds, if the 'new' Optically Stimulated Luminescence (OSL) dates at Gobowen correctly identify either its initial construction or its rebuilding in the third or fourth decade of the ninth century.[61] This is because it so happens that there was a senior Northumbrian leader called Wada whose existence is documented at just this time. He was a 'dux' who had led an army in rebellion against Eardwulf of Northumbria in 798, but was defeated at Billington Moor.[62] In 808, both Coenwulf of Mercia and Eanbald, Archbishop of York, were accused of having harboured Eardwulf's enemies, and it seems plausible that this Wada was among them. He was certainly still present in Mercia at that time, and could have remained a military commander.[63]

Is it feasible, then, to suggest that Coenwulf might have placed such a commander in charge of the northern frontier with Wales, with the specific responsibility of reinforcing the barrier that Offa's Dyke, either uncompleted or interrupted, had for at least a time comprised? Could it therefore also be the case that 'Wat's Dyke' was named after this Northumbrian warlord, 'Wada', just as Offa's Dyke was named after the man who ordered the creation of the longer linear earthwork?[64]

Offa's Dyke: a *contested* frontier-work?

Another interpretive possibility is that rather than being built as a single construction, the Dyke comprised a project that linked together a number of disparate sections of pre-existing cross-valley and cross-ridge dykes. In this light, could the north Herefordshire evidence as currently documented be read in a different way, as the opening elements of construction of what was designed to be just as massive an undertaking as further north? What the intermittent lengths of Dyke surviving in the Arrow valley and the major stretch across the valley west of Lyonshall would therefore signify is evidence for how the Dyke elsewhere gradually evolved in the course of the campaign of construction in each area.

This would certainly explain why seemingly detached sections of Dyke such as those in north Herefordshire remain as they are: according to such a view, they would simply have been awaiting incorporation into the 'Offa's Dyke scheme', even though it never did so incorporate them. Although this reasoning could result in the inference being drawn that Offa's Dyke was, as it currently exists, a multi-phase construction, created over a considerable period of time, there is little evidence at present to support such a view. This is because, as was noted earlier, the various design and build practices observed appear to have been applied in a continuous and methodical manner: it cannot convincingly be argued that they simply reflect an accumulated 'layering' of build and re-build. We do not have an indication of the build date of the Dyke at all, and this means also that we cannot distinguish between decades in its commissioning and construction. Moreover, we are unlikely to do so unless there is a remarkable discovery of a previously unknown late eighth or early ninth century manuscript, or the recovery and successful dendro-chronological dating of wooden piles underpinning its construction in several river-crossings. We therefore cannot know exactly the circumstances of its completion as a building project.

There is, however, a possibility that some adjustments were made to the location of the Dyke *as the process of its building occurred*. Here, we might start with the curious statements in the *Brut y Tywysogion* chronicle to the effect that in 776 the people of Gwent and Morganwyg rose up and attacked Mercia, and that they 'broke in Offa's Dyke even with the ground'; and that, in 784, after the Welsh/Britons had 'laid waste' Mercia, 'Offa made a dyke a second time nearer to him, further to the south-east, and leaving room for the territory between the Wye and the Severn, of Elystan Glodrydd, one of the five royal tribes of

Wales'.⁶⁵ The dates concerned are highly suspect, and the sources may reflect only the vestiges of an early folk tradition that was nonetheless recorded in the period after AD 1200. However, such events might account for the apparent 'displacement' of the primary 'key line' noted in Chapter 4, eastwards from the south Shropshire uplands towards the Wye west of Hereford. It might also provide a reason for the south-eastwards trending line of the Dyke in Herefordshire north of the Wye (and even, perhaps, its 'incomplete' nature here).

Hartshorne thought that the uprising concerned could account for the existence of Wat's Dyke,⁶⁶ but otherwise there is no substance to the idea, at least in physical terms, that Offa's Dyke was 'moved back' from a line once further forward into British territory. Or is there? The interesting configuration of Offa's Dyke at Llanymynech on the river Vyrnwy north of Welshpool was noted in Chapter 4, above, in reference to the eminence at Asterley Rocks on Llanymynech Hill, and the curiously-named Carreghofa parish at its foot, extending the short distance down to the Tanat/Vyrnwy confluence. In Chapter 7 this was explored further in reference to the 'political place' that the Dyke faced here, with the possible existence of an important centre at Meifod to the west. What was not discussed then, but may be of interest here, is an intriguing place-name, *Clawdd Coch*, the 'Red Dyke', belonging to a farm located on a very slight north–south ridge that crosses the flood-plain of the Vyrnwy immediately east of its confluence with the Tanat. Although this might have been the site of the medieval Carreghofa castle, the question arises as to whether this ridge was ever occupied by a dyke that might once have bisected Carreghofa parish. Excavations undertaken around 20 years ago of linear crop-marks north and south of that farm failed to demonstrate that these were Roman military structures, as had been supposed (there were no associated Roman artefacts), and a ditch in the northern area contained a burnt deposit dated to between the eighth and twelfth centuries.⁶⁷ The results of the investigations are too imprecise to confirm the alternative idea that this was a Mercian work (or works). However, given that it was a *Welsh* naming of 'Offa's Rock' that gave the place its name, it is perhaps worth raising the possibility that this was one location where the Dyke was pushed back, in this case from a former more forward line that had extended precisely to the Tanat/Vyrnwy confluence.

This idea cannot at present be substantiated further, and even the former existence of a dyke next to the confluence is somewhat speculative. However, the idea introduces an important further potential dimension to the 'Offa's Dyke story', that it could be worth exploring in the years to come. This dimension comprises not only again the proposition that there could, throughout much of the course of Offa's Dyke, have been time-depth to the process of construction. It also raises the possibility that, rather than the course of the Dyke having been, as in Fox's terms, 'negotiated', it may instead have been actively *contested* during the time of its imposition. Such resistance, perhaps preserved in the memories captured in the *Brut y Tywysogion*, may also have been echoed, in propaganda terms at least, in the 'text' recorded on the 'Pillar of Eliseg' that was raised by Concenn at Llangollen and that refers to the efforts of Elise to overturn the English incursions.

Some concluding thoughts: Offa's Dyke, landscape *and* hegemony

It was proposed in the introduction to this book that Offa's Dyke needs to be understood in reference not only to a local topographic and political setting, but also to a much wider, and in effect to a geo-political, landscape. The unfolding of the narrative has included setting out how such a task of new understanding might be approached. The scale of the undertaking of construction of the Dyke arguably reveals how radical the physical consequences of King Offa's quasi-imperial ambition for himself and for the Mercians could be. While it is a monument therefore to the intended expanding boundaries of the landscape of Offa's political ambition, arguably it did also represent something vital to Mercian interests, at least as perceived by the ruling elite. This may, in part at least, have reflected the intensity of colonisation of the areas to the east of the Dyke, particularly perhaps of those areas that had witnessed most resistance to the westwards expansion of Mercia in the seventh century. In this light, the

FIGURE 9.16 A 'frozen' strategy? The view northwards over the Clun valley

location of the Dyke where it is 'should probably be interpreted as the act of a strong, centralising kingship asserting its power in a newly integrated region.'[68]

The degree to which the Dyke may have represented a strategy for the westwards expansion of Mercia that became 'frozen' in time as Offa's successor carried through his execution of that strategy in subtly different ways has also been briefly explored here. In such perspective, the particular role of 'ambiguous places', such as Herefordshire and Flintshire may have been, is crucial rather than marginal, therefore, to an understanding of the place of Offa's Dyke in history, and in reflecting the tension between consolidation and aggrandisement in the expanding political horizons of the Mercian world.

One important thing to acknowledge about Offa's Dyke is that we should be wary of lighting upon a single purpose or a single significance for its construction. It could have been, and very probably was, *at one and the same time* a vainglorious enterprise designed to impress Offa's contemporaries, a response to a particular crisis or perceived threat, an act of permanent appropriation of the fertile or otherwise appealing parts of the borderlands, a device within an emerging long-term strategy for Mercian domination of Wales, and the central element in the creation of a distinctive frontier landscape integral to the emergence of a clear identity to the Welsh Marches that has endured until today.

Since his is the nearest contemporary observation about the Dyke that has come down to us, it is fitting to leave the last word on its hegemonic role to the closest thing that late ninth-century England had to a court historian. Asser, bishop of the West Saxon diocese of Sherborne, in Dorset, was clearly concerned in the relevant passage of his *Life* of King Alfred of Wessex not with Offa's Dyke as a phenomenon in its own right so much as with the reputation of King Offa himself: for which, arguably, the Dyke stood (and stands) as metaphor. It is important to remember that Asser was a Welsh cleric at the West Saxon court who celebrated among other things in his *Life* his patron's achievement as the saviour of all the peoples of southern Britain – English and Welsh alike – from the scourge of the Danes. He therefore mentions the Dyke simply as the perfect illustration of the nature, and ultimately the futility, of the famous Mercian king's achievement: as Keynes has put it (in effect recapitulating Asser's late ninth-century view), Offa bequeathed to Anglo-Saxon posterity only a reputation, not a legacy.[69]

We may take issue with such a view, not least given the sophistication of placement and construction of the great earthwork and the apparent complexity of the strategy of control and state-craft that it represents. Yet for Asser and his West Saxon audience, the Dyke was an object lesson in the wrong kind of kingship, one that in his eyes involved a preference for might over right. The Dyke was, in this light, no more and no less than a monument to hubris. The earthwork needed no other explanation, from Asser's perspective, than to say it was built by an ambitious and powerful king, as the crowning expression of his overbearing dominion over the kingdoms and provinces bordering Mercia. It is conceivable that Asser and his contemporaries may actually have believed that Offa's Dyke extended literally 'from sea to sea', even though it never precisely did. Such a misapprehension presents us with a culminating irony, that the very success of Offa's scheme was marked not so much by the continuity of the use of the earthwork, as of its advertisement. Only a relatively short while after its construction, and Offa's demise, 'his' Dyke had already grown in shared perception to be more than, at least physically, it ever really was.

EPILOGUE

Reconnecting Offa's Dyke in the twenty-first century

> Offa's Dyke…was probably built in the eighth century by order of King Offa of Mercia as an agreed boundary between his territory and that of the Welsh. Although the dyke no longer coincides with the border between Wales and England, the term is often used with this meaning.
>
> Meic Stephens, *Oxford Companion to the Literature of Wales*, 1986[1]

There are, as we have seen, some highly divergent views on the nature of Offa's Dyke, and there are few questions that are wholly resolved. Would it therefore perhaps be possible to suggest that we have not moved very far forward from Cyril Fox's conclusions of between fifty-five and eighty years ago paraphrased in the above quotation? In terms of definitive results from excavation, we must reluctantly conclude that this is the case. Nonetheless, the attribution to Offa does appear to be secure, and the scheme overall does seem to have been envisaged as a sea-to-sea effort facing all the British kingdoms of what became (in part through the impact of this monumental construction) Wales. While it was a unitary project it was not necessarily a completed one, nor even one that was designed in simple geographical terms ever to be 'complete' through spanning without interruption the whole extent of the territory between the Dee and the Severn estuaries. Such a provisional existence is reflected in the lack of evidence for maintenance of the structure, or any lasting infrastructure, and this no doubt also reflected the political dynamics of the later eighth century.

The legacy of the Mercian hegemony: sources and reputations

> The student of Offa, confronted with a massive 'public work' and an elaborate coinage, but without any documentation as to how either was managed, is not so differently placed from the student of Cunobelinus.[2]

We have not in this book laboured the difficulties of developing a history either of Mercia or of its western frontier in regard to the dearth of historical source-material, but the impact of this documentary near-void is nevertheless considerable. Offa's Dyke has been described by one historian recently as 'a monument without a history',[3] although if it is indeed such, it is part of a landscape and a kingdom which, for much of the crucial eighth and ninth centuries, are also beyond the reach of history, at least as can be written from its own sources. If not for the survival of the Worcester charters, for instance, there would be a manifestly huge gap in the existing record. We do not need to cite the activities of the Danish armies to explain this dearth of documentation, although their impact should not be underestimated; nor do we, as Simon Keynes has recently done, need to suggest that Mercia under Aethelbald, Offa and Coenwulf was a 'different sort of polity' that did not produce documents or histories.[4]

The reverse may in fact be the case. H. P. R. Finberg summarised the situation for the west of Mercia succinctly as long ago as 1961, when he pointed out that the repositories of many of the places where we would expect archival material for the Mercian polity to have survived were destroyed in the high medieval period even as there was arising a fully articulated interest in how England had come into existence. So, Pershore Abbey was destroyed by fire in 1002, and again in 1223. Hereford cathedral was burnt down by Gruffydd ap Llywelyn and his English allies in 1055. A conflagration at Gloucester in 1122 destroyed St Peter's Abbey together with all its treasures apart from 'a few books' and three garments for preaching. Most seriously of all, on 28th September 1151, close to the end of the civil warfare in the anarchy of King Stephen's reign, St Peter's Abbey at Winchcombe was also razed to the ground, 'cum scriniis, vestimentis, libris et cartis, ac edificiis omnibus', that is, with its parchments, vestments, books and charters, and all of its buildings.[5] As Finberg noted, 'These ancient minsters must have housed large numbers of pre-Norman documents, particularly Winchcombe, which in the ninth century appears to have been the recognised place of custody for the archives of the Mercian royal house'.[6] Moreover, if Mercia was a state in which literacy was so little valued or sustained, why did King Alfred himself make reference to a legal inheritance that included the laws and customs of King Offa? And, more especially, why did he make the efforts he unquestionably did to attract key individual Mercian clerics, 'certain luminaries', renowned for their scholarship, to the late ninth-century West Saxon court?[7]

In Chapters 1 and 8 we alluded to the 'revisionist' view of Offa's reign and the Mercian hegemony, formed by Simon Keynes, Janet Nelson and others. Keynes in particular has developed a 'realistic' assessment of Offa in respect to, and in comparison with, other great rulers of his day and the immediate century afterwards. This has of course to be understood in part at least in the context of the long-term focus of Keynes' research and writing on King Alfred of Wessex, and the relative wealth of documentation for the latter's reign. We have no portrait of Offa such as Asser and other contemporaries have left for Alfred, but Keynes has suggested that we do not necessarily need this in order to understand Offa in his own times, his own kingdom, and his own (uncompromising) terms:

> ...even to suggest the comparison (with Alfred the Great or Charlemagne) is to set (Offa) up as something which would misrepresent the kind of ruler that he was, and the kind of ruler that he claimed to be. Offa was driven by a lust for power, not

A visionary image? 'King Offa' tree on the Afon Clywedog

This carving by Simon O'Rourke was commissioned by The Woodland Trust within its Plas Power Woods reserve at Coedpoeth west of Wrexham.

PHOTOGRAPH:
© CHARMAINE HARRISON
http://charmingphotography.deviantart.com

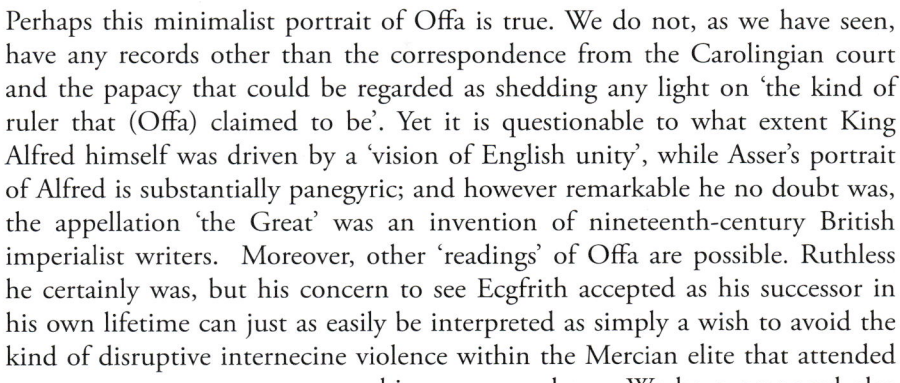

by a vision of English unity; and what he left was a reputation, not a legacy. Alfred made a point in his law-code of remembering Offa's legislation for his people; the chronicler Aethelweard described him as 'an extraordinary man' (*vir mirabilis*); and Aethelstan, son of King Aethelraed the Unready, bequeathed to his brother Edmund Ironside 'the sword which belonged to King Offa'.[8]

Perhaps this minimalist portrait of Offa is true. We do not, as we have seen, have any records other than the correspondence from the Carolingian court and the papacy that could be regarded as shedding any light on 'the kind of ruler that (Offa) claimed to be'. Yet it is questionable to what extent King Alfred himself was driven by a 'vision of English unity', while Asser's portrait of Alfred is substantially panegyric; and however remarkable he no doubt was, the appellation 'the Great' was an invention of nineteenth-century British imperialist writers. Moreover, other 'readings' of Offa are possible. Ruthless he certainly was, but his concern to see Ecgfrith accepted as his successor in his own lifetime can just as easily be interpreted as simply a wish to avoid the kind of disruptive internecine violence within the Mercian elite that attended his own ascendancy. We have proposed also that Offa's Mercian regime in effect secured continuity in what can be interpreted as its pragmatic promotion of Coenwulf during the crisis year of 896.

The views of modern historians concerning Offa have perhaps however been made to appear starker in their contrasts than is really the case. For example, Keynes suggested also that Stenton's opinion of Offa was simply that he was a 'visionary statesman'.[9] Keynes portrays Offa instead as a 'creature very different' from this, who 'achieved his purposes by an irresistible combination of intrigue, ruthlessness, and brute force.' More expansively, he has invited us to see Offa as 'a species of Mercian octopus: his tentacles reaching out over different peoples, smothering some and poised more threateningly over others, but united only in the head which remained firmly in the north-west midlands.' This view (no doubt unintentionally) misrepresents Stenton, who expressed on at least one occasion a more balanced and nuanced view of Offa: 'Alcuin, who admired (Offa's) strength, saw in his son's death a judgement on his ruthlessness. Nevertheless, as the history of his reign is traced from one fragment to the next, it gradually becomes clear that this formidable and unsympathetic king was a statesman.... No other Anglo-Saxon king ever regarded the world at large with so secular a mind or so acute a political sense'.[10]

Keynes' judgement on Offa also appears to have embodied a misunderstanding of the geography of Mercian power: it failed to take account, for example, of the fact that the 'head' of the 'octopus' was as often in Chelsea as in Tamworth, and that, especially towards the end of his reign, Offa was actively promoting places such as Bedford, Bath and Winchcombe, perhaps consciously, as new centres from which the ideology of Mercian hegemony could be promulgated. The conclusion that perhaps we should rather draw from this difference of interpretive emphasis from Stenton to Keynes is that the concept of what, among historians of Anglo-Saxon England at least, constitutes a 'statesman' changed significantly between, say, 1930 and 2000 AD.

Keynes was, however, surely right to suggest that Coenwulf's reputation has been overshadowed by Offa's.[11] We have therefore also been concerned to emphasise the degree to which Coenwulf sustained both Offa's policy and the regime itself. However, there were important contrasts not only in the terms of that policy but also in style of leadership between the two kings. The characters of Offa and Coenwulf may, for example, be revealed in the contrasting ways they dealt with their kin. Possibly significant here is that there is nowhere any mention of Offa's male kin other than his son, Ecgfrith. It is likely that they were seen as rivals, and instead the ubiquitous Brorda, a powerful but probably unrelated magnate, appears to have been the closest thing Offa had to a lieutenant. In contrast, two of Coenwulf's brothers, Cuthred and Ceolred, were not only named but were also promoted under his patronage.

The Offa's Dyke inheritance

It has been one of the key propositions of this book that while Offa's Dyke stands as a physical record of Offa and the power of the Mercian state, it also represents a less tangible inheritance. This relates among other things to the cultural heritage of Wales and England, but there may be yet wider dimensions to it. For example, the Dyke can be seen to stand as an enduring physical trace of a pan-European perspective lost to England under the deluge of the ninth century and later Viking incursions and the emergence of a more circumscribed view of the English international project. Taking the long view of history, we can perceive the building of Offa's Dyke as marking not a forging of nationhood as much as a parting of the ways in terms of the (then) future character of England: thanks to the depredations of the Danish armies later Anglo-Saxon history necessarily adopted a distinctly Scandinavian focus from the later ninth century onwards.

Offa's Dyke stands, as Patrick Wormald once observed, at the end of a tradition of earthworks created through massive mobilisation without (at least, surviving) written record.[12] However, the Dyke is important also because with the benefit of hindsight it anticipates as well, the Normans and the way they exercised power through the imposition of a will to dominate expressed, and largely achieved, through great works such as the mighty stone castles and their dependent boroughs. As we have seen, it arguably also represents in effect the origin of the 'March of Wales' that had so much influence on the course of English (and Welsh) medieval history.

In an English context, the 'inheritance' of Offa's Dyke may seem in comparison with Wales somewhat limited. For the Welsh people, the impact of the construction of the Dyke, especially in the period either side of the Norman Conquest, was considerable in serving as a perpetual reminder of the finality of the loss of so much land to its east. However, the border remained contested, from the attack on Hereford in 1055 to the revolt of Owain Glyndwr in the years around 1400. The confusion of identity this caused in noble families with connections among the Welsh, English and Norman nobility was nowhere more keenly expressed than in the person of Gerald de Barri: ostensibly a Norman who, as 'Giraldus Cambrensis', regarded himself as first a Welshman, Gerald 'of Wales', proud of the female line of inheritance through his mother, Angharad, daughter of the Welsh princess, Nest.[13]

The 'fossilisation' of boundaries that followed upon the Act of Union in 1536 left small areas of Wales administratively under English control, but the areas east of Offa's Dyke that were 'returned' to Welsh control, especially around Wrexham and in east Montgomeryshire, were often substantial. It was probably therefore not until the rise of a more acute national consciousness in Wales in the nineteenth century (whether ascribed to Romanticism or to a re-awakening of appreciation for Welsh literature) that bitterness over what the Dyke represented re-emerged strongly. Since that time, it has been seen by many in Wales as an instrument of English oppression and a mark of Anglo-Saxon (in the broadest sense) avarice.

Ideas about the Dyke's cultural legacy have usually been seen in terms of a simple opposition between the Welsh on one side and the English on the other. Yet in some respects later first millennium commentary, whether concerning the reported customs of the Godwins towards the Welsh found east of the Dyke in Cheshire, or the border strife of the eleventh century encapsulated in the sack of Hereford in 1055, has served more than the Dyke itself to reinforce this contrast. However, what also emerged more subtly was a hybrid 'Marches' culture, in which the interleaving of Welsh and English tenure and customs, as reflected in the 'Ordinance concerning the *Dunsaete*', or in the creation of composite jurisdictions such as the Lordship of Clun and the Deanery of Oswestry, reveal a different picture of co-operation and synergy rather than antagonism and strife.[14] The creation of the frontier zone that Offa's Dyke was the central part of was an important contributor to this process.

There are several dimensions to such a revised appreciation of legacy. For example, the *Maelor Saesneg*, the territory around modern day Wrexham, reflects a 'conceded' Welsh political resurgence. The very area that saw the 'tightest'

Offa's Dyke immediately south of Knighton, with Panpunton top left

The destruction of the length of Dyke just before the woodland here 'for agricultural improvement' (now reinstated as a hedgerow) was railed against by Professor John Earle following his visit here in 1856. Coincidentally, Frank Noble came to teach in Knighton secondary school in the 1950s and was instrumental in the founding of the Offa's Dyke Association, which now manages the Offa's Dyke Centre in the town.

AERIAL PHOTOGRAPH REPRODUCED COURTESY OF CLWYD-POWYS ARCHAEOLOGICAL TRUST.

drawing of the frontier in Offa's time (see above, Chapter 7) was in this way reabsorbed into Wales through an at least symbolic 'breaching' of both dykes. Although this has been discussed in the past mostly in reference to the particular history of Cheshire and Flintshire, the political resonances are wider. The point of reference here must surely have to do with the special historical significance of, and enduring Welsh attachment to, Bangor-is-y-coed (Bangor-on-Dee). This was the monastery whose monks had streamed out to join their warrior compatriots in meeting Aethelfrith, King of Northumbria in battle at Chester in around 616, to be slaughtered in their 'hundreds': British-Welsh memories are long. Nine hundred years later, Chester was too strategically significant to be conceded to the Welsh by the English kings and the lords of the March, but Bangor was clearly a compromise.

It is, moreover, not an accident that the Welsh/English cultural ambiguity is strongest in areas such as south and west Herefordshire, Wrexham, Flintshire and to a certain extent also Denbighshire. This has persisted even to the present day, and can be 'read off' in the north in the clear Merseyside as well as Welsh influences in local accents, and in Herefordshire in particular intonations of speech and in many local folk-tales and customs with a strong Welsh flavour, as recorded by Ella Mary Leather in her magnificent *The Folklore of Herefordshire*, published in Hereford in 1912.

A new era for Offa's Dyke and its archaeology?

Sir Cyril Fox noted as long ago as 1928 that:

> It would be absurd to suppose that all the problems presented by the Dyke in this (South Shropshire and East Radnorshire) sector have been solved, when one considers the variety of conditions and forces – political, military, physiographic, economic, financial, social, personal – operating to produce by their interaction the observed effects, and how few, if any, of these forces can be adequately assessed today.[15]

Addressing questions like 'what is the date of Offa's Dyke, and are all parts of it the same date?', 'what was the original extent of Offa's Dyke?' and 'to what extent was it really continuous from sea to sea?' remains fundamental to making progress in our understanding. Crucially, as we hope to have made clear through the pages of this book, it is not helpful to seek to foreclose further archaeological research on Offa's Dyke on the basis of a presumption that the 'Offa's Dyke Project' of the late twentieth century produced unassailable and definitive conclusions. In particular, in a situation where the form of the lengths of north–south oriented earthwork in Herefordshire down to the Wye (other than Rowe Ditch) and in west Gloucestershire exhibit such close similarity in location, design and build to those of the Dyke north of Rushock Hill, and where there are no other adequate explanations for their existence in such places and in such configuration, it is entirely unsupportable to dismiss them as having had nothing to do with 'Offa's Dyke'. Moreover, the arguments adduced to suggest that there is no *historical* reason, from early documentary sources, to indicate that these lengths were ever considered to be part of Offa's Dyke, have been found on closer scrutiny to lack substance.

The availability of modern radiocarbon or Optically Stimulated Luminescence (OSL) methods of dating, and of new characterisation and survey techniques (including radar and satellite based remote-sensing methods) means that there has never been a better time to initiate new closely-targeted fieldwork. This should include research excavations carried out on an appropriate scale, and of sufficiently sophisticated design, to select with careful consideration their location to answer clearly articulated questions.[16] In particular there have for example been no excavations undertaken so far to expose any length of the Dyke to examine the lateral build of the earthwork, as was achieved in the Wat's Dyke excavation at Gobowen near Oswestry. And as noted in Chapter 5, such exposure needs to be undertaken where the potential for results is greatest. So to move the debate onwards in a number of directions, there needs to be some examination of the Dyke in areas where it is better-preserved, as well as in areas

New housing on a former works site at Tatham, Ruabon, in 2010
Both the fabric and the setting of both Offa's Dyke and Wat's Dyke have come under increasing pressure in recent years, especially in the 'metropolitan' areas west of Wrexham.

where it has almost been obliterated as a surface feature. Losses and erosion continue in many places, but there are still very many miles of earthwork where a short length could be examined and carefully reinstated that could well provide significant new evidence about structure and (crucially) dating of at least key sections of the monument.[17]

Despite all this, one needs to be mindful that the complexities of the Dyke as a structure are such that there can be no 'magic bullet' that will solve the riddles overnight. Closer surface and analytical characterisation of the Dyke will, we hope to have demonstrated, yield new insights: and it will be the most thoughtful and meticulously conducted excavations (as ever has been the case) that will provide the most tangible advances in documentation and understanding. This must include information on the environmental context that will be gained by sensitive and targeted sampling of appropriate deposits, both in direct association with the Dyke, and nearby.

Offa's Dyke is nonetheless fascinating archaeologically in large measure for the very reason that in practical terms it is so hard to grapple with. This is not just a matter of scale, because in those terms the Hadrianic and Antonine northern Roman frontiers are a not dissimilar case. It is also, for instance, factors such as the dearth of artefacts associated with the Dyke and its contemporary military or civil landscape that render it so inaccessible. And yet Offa's Dyke exerted such a fascination for Cyril Fox that through his own 'great work' he elevated it to an iconic status for archaeologists. Far from denigrating that legacy, it is incumbent upon us today both to celebrate and to build upon it. We need to seek to understand the Dyke, too, in its own unique time and place for the discipline of archaeology: namely, the emergent field of landscape archaeology in the early decades of the twentieth century.

What we can understand about Offa's Dyke primarily from historical sources has, as noted above, recently been reviewed under the banner of its status as 'a monument without a history', and this echoes also a different way of describing the Dyke as 'the last great prehistoric achievement of the inhabitants of Britain.'[18] We should see the Dyke rather as a monument for which no conventional history exists, or is recoverable. That it has a history, however, is undeniable. Re-working and re-study of the available documentary evidence is therefore a valid potential contribution to set alongside the historiographical reviews that have characterised much of the recent literature. An example of the potential of careful source-criticism to throw new light upon key 'artefacts' is demonstrated by the recent discussion and debate over the exact form and meaning of the inscription upon the 'Pillar of Eliseg' at Llangollen.[19]

Offa's Dyke, then, should and does continue to inspire our curiosity and to engage our efforts to understand its character and achievement. In these terms we view this book not in any sense as the 'last word' on the subject, but rather as a point of departure. While we have tried to illustrate the extent of what is known, it needs also to be emphasised how much there is still to learn about the Dyke. If such extended focus as provided in this volume serves to engender new enthusiasm to explore the rich heritage that it embodies, it has succeeded in its purpose. In sum, what is now needed is a revisiting of the Dyke's subtleties and wider political setting in the light of twenty-first century technologies, thought and scholarship.

Re-connecting Offa's Dyke: localism, inheritance and diversity

As Britain's (and probably Europe's) longest earthwork monument, as the legacy of one of the most vigorous of England's early kingdoms, as the harbinger of more than a millennium of particular forms of Anglo-Welsh cultural interaction and interrelatedness, and as the key linking feature of one of Britain's most distinctive landscapes, Offa's Dyke has tangible international importance. It stands at the beginnings of modern Europe, and strongly exemplifies the complex processes by which new national and cultural identities were forged in the Early Medieval period. As such, the Dyke is a monument whose very existence in the form that we have outlined uniquely informs an understanding of the roots of the profound subsequent influence of European societies on world history. On the one hand it bridged landscape and culture at its widest scale, and on the other it evoked substantially a sense of destiny embedded in and characterised by the exercise of a culturally as well as politically cast hegemony that in some respects (including what could be termed its 'Anglo-centricity') has continued to the present day.

Yet, interestingly, this significance is by no means universally acknowledged or recognised within modern cultural-political narratives. Offa's Dyke was recently proposed for admission to the 'UK Tentative List of World Heritage Sites'. The application was not successful, and a primary reason given was that the historical value of the Dyke was held to compare unfavourably with other linear monuments defining politico-cultural boundaries (including the existing 'Frontiers of the Roman Empire' and 'Great Wall of China' World Heritage Sites).

It was therefore concluded that Offa's Dyke does not in that sense have the 'Outstanding Universal Value' which is the core quality which World Heritage Sites must demonstrate. Regardless of the validity of that assessment (and 'OUV' is meant to be an exacting standard), it is intriguing that a monument whose original political and cultural context is unequivocally expressed in the Asser reference (and which, in some degree, has had a related meaning ever since, as is most obvious in the fact that the Dyke still lies close to or on the present border between England and Wales) is nevertheless seen from a modern perspective as *less* clearly representative of political and cultural division between peoples than, for example, the Roman imperial frontier works which arguably have had no active meaning or relevance beyond their own time.

Perhaps part of this reluctance to acknowledge the outstanding significance of Offa's Dyke culturally and historically is explicable simply by the fact that manifestations of the past which are firmly in the past are sometimes easier to handle than those which more directly implicate the present-day, and which touch on cultural sensibilities which are still very much alive (such as ideas of English and Welsh identity and belonging). Perhaps there is something to learn here also about how we still regard the Early Medieval period (not for nothing formerly known as 'the Dark Ages'), and how modern perceptions continue to reflect a post-renaissance tendency to find Western origins and values more

Offa's Dyke at Discoed: prospective World Heritage Site, or not? *The Dyke occupies a notch cut into the hillside at lower left and it ascends the wooded hill to the north at centre right, across the Lugg valley. World Heritage Site status could provide a much-needed boost to the local economy, but more importantly would provide the monument, and the landscape in which it is located, with a conservation framework that it currently lacks. A recent planning proposal to construct a wind-farm with massive turbines on a prominent hilltop within this landscape has heightened awareness of the need to define an 'Offa's Dyke landscape setting' and to provide adequate safeguards for what remains a stunningly beautiful, but fragile, context in which one can appreciate the monument in something approaching its original 'visual envelope'.*

clearly defined in classical (and imperial) traditions than in the complex political and social processes which played out in the post-Roman period and beyond.

Perhaps there is here also even a long historical echo of the political appropriation of Anglo-Saxon history by the later West Saxon kings which explicitly involved excluding the achievements of the rival kingdom of Mercia from both the historical record and popular memory. The heartland of Mercia is forever partitioned and divided by the later Anglo-Saxon county boundaries which bisect the Tamworth area, to the extent that the centrality of that locality to midlands history is, on a daily basis, obscured. In much the same way, Offa's Dyke remains widely regarded as fragmented, incomplete, and no different to other much shorter linear boundaries of broadly the same period. Even its historical relationship to the genesis of the cultural and national identities, which, on the face of it, it so clearly seems to relate to, is sometimes forgotten.

Emerging political agendas may nonetheless also help to shape future perceptions of Offa's Dyke, and may provide a context for responding to the complex conservation challenge which, spread across two countries, six local authority areas, multiple ownerships, multiple environmental and land-use contexts and the interests of multiple stakeholders, Offa's Dyke also presents.[20] A key theme here is the shift towards a fuller appreciation of the value of the local, perhaps creating the possibility of 'connecting up' new ideas of shared community heritage with the complexities of a wider cultural inheritance.

One way forward for Offa's Dyke in this context is therefore to provide a context in which to encourage contacts, to foster improved awareness, and to promote access to the monument that involves more than just a casual (or even a continuous walking) encounter along paths and across lanes. Rather, it may be one that is grounded in personal or shared explorations that are informed by thinking about the complexities and the connections that are manifest on the one hand by the physical form and landscape placement of the Dyke, and on the other by its associations in the landscapes of the eighth century and today. In short, those local communities that have inherited the Dyke and its cultural and historical 'baggage' might begin investigating it at all levels, including the spheres of folklore and reminiscences, exploring the resonances of the monument both socially and culturally, and from north to south as well as east to west, working back from 'living memory'. The future of the Dyke in these terms lies not only with the promptings of historians and archaeologists (many of whom have lost interest in the particular in favour of the generic in cultural 'explanation'), and still less so of 'heritage professionals' (whose judgements in closed session determine even whether a complex case for the

'Mid-way' Path post at the crossing of the Clun valley in Shropshire

Dyke can be made in the forums of world heritage designation), as within a digitally mediated world, experienced and mapped by new generations through the recording and exploration of heritage in a variety of media.[21]

The last word in verse

The poem by Thomas Churchyard with which we opened Chapter 2 of this book illustrates a spirit of inquiry concerning the Dyke that remains strong today. The more contemporary piece by Gladys Mary Coles at the beginning of the book reflected a subtler understanding of Mercian history, of the landscape of the borderlands, and of the place of the Dyke within both. Moreover it is a perspective that is both philosophical and intelligently reflective. For Coles, the Dyke was representative of the continuing urge to delimit and demarcate humanity, and stands even today as a metaphor for the futility of conflict. It was a concept made material, and has long since returned to dust and the realm of concept.

But for other poets, as for Asser, the Dyke illuminates a key aspect of the personality of Offa himself. The remarkable poet with whose work we have chosen to close this book, Geoffrey Hill, was concerned to recover Offa and Mercia from the oblivion to which each were consigned by history, and by the 'loss' of the heartland of this midland kingdom to industry, roads, and shopping malls. Offa was, for this poet, among other things, 'overlord of the M5' (itself a significant image of the vaunting ambition of 'progress'). But whether or not the Mercian king was, as Simon Keynes has suggested, more the master of the 'A5' from London to Wales than the north–south motorway slicing through the Severn valley past Worcester,[22] Geoffrey Hill exhibited a fine grasp of the subtleties of Offa's mind and motivations:

King of the perennial holly-groves, the riven sandstone: overlord of the M5:

architect of the historic rampart and ditch, the citadel of Tamworth, the summer hermitage in Holy Cross: guardian of the Welsh Bridge and Iron Bridge: contractor to the desirable new estates: saltmaster: moneychanger: commissioner for oaths: martyrologist: the friend of Charlemagne.

'I liked that,' said Offa, 'sing it again.'

Geoffrey Hill[23]

APPENDIX

Selected Offa's Dyke profiles

These outline versions of drawn profiles are redrawn from the published surveys carried out by Sir Cyril Fox between 1927 and 1931, latterly assisted by C.W. Phillips. They were first published in successive numbers of *Archaeologia Cambrensis*, the journal of the Cambrian Archaeological Association; and then together in *Offa's Dyke: A Field Survey of the Western Frontier-Works of Mercia in the Seventh and Eighth Centuries AD* (Oxford University Press for the British Academy, 1955).

19 profiles have been selected from among the 44 profiles published in Fox's 1955 British Academy *Offa's Dyke* volume. The 19 profiles have been chosen as a representative sample of the total, to illustrate aspects of character and build discussed in detail in Chapter 5 of this book. Nearly every one of the 19 profiles is accompanied here by a bullet-point summary drawing attention to key features of the profile concerned.

The 19 profiles are presented here in (Fox's) numerical order, and proceed from north to south, on two consecutive pages.

The profiles reproduced here include an excavated section across the ditch at Chirk Park, and an excavated section through the bank at Forden, between Welshpool and Montgomery. 2 of the profiles are for lengths of the Dyke that face uphill, but, as in the field, the majority of profiles that can be drawn face down a slope westwards.

There are 14 examples here, where a steep west-facing slope has been enhanced, with 9 cases where there is clear evidence for a linear quarry at the rear (usually to the east) of the bank. Enhanced scarps on precipitous slopes are sometimes extended over a considerable area, as at Hergan Hill (Fox, XLV) and Caswell Wood, Tidenham (Fox, LIII).

Appendix: Selected Offa's Dyke profiles

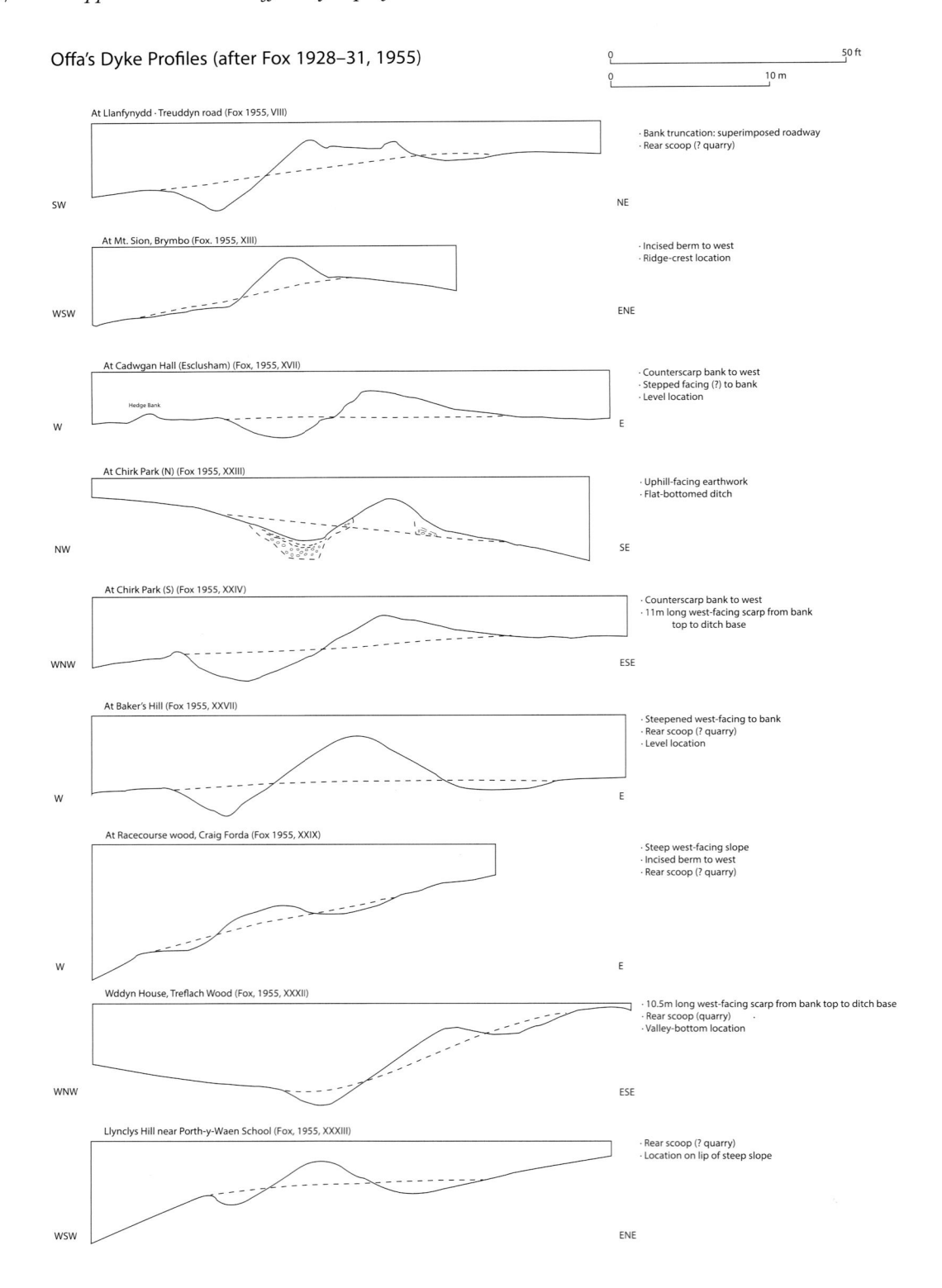

Offa's Dyke Profiles (after Fox 1928–31, 1955)

At Llanfynydd - Treuddyn road (Fox 1955, VIII)
SW — NE
- Bank truncation: superimposed roadway
- Rear scoop (? quarry)

At Mt. Sion, Brymbo (Fox. 1955, XIII)
WSW — ENE
- Incised berm to west
- Ridge-crest location

At Cadwgan Hall (Esclusham) (Fox, 1955, XVII)
Hedge Bank
W — E
- Counterscarp bank to west
- Stepped facing (?) to bank
- Level location

At Chirk Park (N) (Fox 1955, XXIII)
NW — SE
- Uphill-facing earthwork
- Flat-bottomed ditch

At Chirk Park (S) (Fox 1955, XXIV)
WNW — ESE
- Counterscarp bank to west
- 11m long west-facing scarp from bank top to ditch base

At Baker's Hill (Fox 1955, XXVII)
W — E
- Steepened west-facing to bank
- Rear scoop (? quarry)
- Level location

At Racecourse wood, Craig Forda (Fox 1955, XXIX)
W — E
- Steep west-facing slope
- Incised berm to west
- Rear scoop (? quarry)

Wddyn House, Treflach Wood (Fox, 1955, XXXII)
WNW — ESE
- 10.5m long west-facing scarp from bank top to ditch base
- Rear scoop (quarry)
- Valley-bottom location

Llynclys Hill near Porth-y-Waen School (Fox, 1955, XXXIII)
WSW — ENE
- Rear scoop (? quarry)
- Location on lip of steep slope

Appendix: Selected Offa's Dyke profiles   379

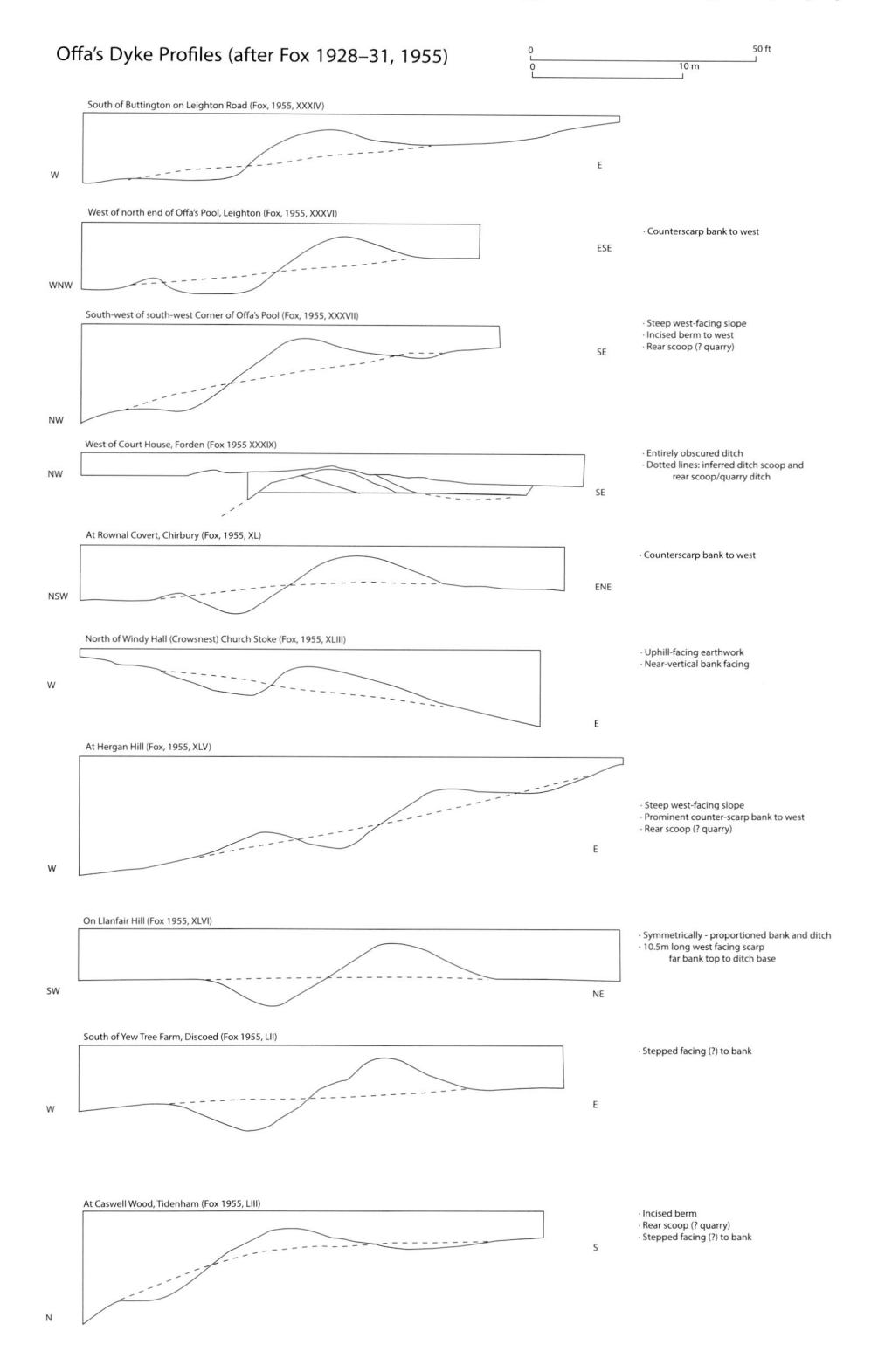

Offa's Dyke Profiles (after Fox 1928–31, 1955)

South of Buttington on Leighton Road (Fox, 1955, XXXIV)

W — E

West of north end of Offa's Pool, Leighton (Fox, 1955, XXXVI)

WNW — ESE

- Counterscarp bank to west

South-west of south-west Corner of Offa's Pool (Fox, 1955, XXXVII)

NW — SE

- Steep west-facing slope
- Incised berm to west
- Rear scoop (? quarry)

West of Court House, Forden (Fox 1955 XXXIX)

NW — SE

- Entirely obscured ditch
- Dotted lines: inferred ditch scoop and rear scoop/quarry ditch

At Rownal Covert, Chirbury (Fox, 1955, XL)

NSW — ENE

- Counterscarp bank to west

North of Windy Hall (Crowsnest) Church Stoke (Fox, 1955, XLIII)

W — E

- Uphill-facing earthwork
- Near-vertical bank facing

At Hergan Hill (Fox, 1955, XLV)

W — E

- Steep west-facing slope
- Prominent counter-scarp bank to west
- Rear scoop (? quarry)

On Llanfair Hill (Fox 1955, XLVI)

SW — NE

- Symmetrically - proportioned bank and ditch
- 10.5m long west facing scarp far bank top to ditch base

South of Yew Tree Farm, Discoed (Fox 1955, LII)

W — E

- Stepped facing (?) to bank

At Caswell Wood, Tidenham (Fox 1955, LIII)

N — S

- Incised berm
- Rear scoop (? quarry)
- Stepped facing (?) to bank

Notes

Introduction

1. Alternatively, the largely parallel Wat's Dyke may have in effect 'completed' its course northwards from the Treuddyn – Caergwrle area; or the northern part of Wat's Dyke may have originated as a separate but related 'Offa's Dyke' work.
2. See Chapter 2 for a discussion of this viewpoint expressed by David Hill and Margaret Worthington.
3. For discussion of the perspective, see Chapter 2 and for scrutiny of the evidence base, see especially Chapter 5, below. The orthodoxy has been developed not only through repetition by the authors of the thesis themselves (e.g., Worthington, 1999), but also by the settled view of historians who have made definitive statements to the effect in public broadcasts and publications (see Charles-Edwards, 2013a, 2013b).

Chapter 1

1. William Caxton (c.1420–1491), from the *Description of Britain* (1480), Chapter 5: The Principal Divisions of Britain', from the version rendered by Marie Collins (1988, 49–50). Caxton's principal source was Ranulf Higden's (c.1350) *Polychronicon*. By 'past Bristol' he was not making a topographical error, but was simply expressing a London-centred view: the Dyke begins at the other side of the Bristol Channel beyond Bristol. This is reasonably clear evidence that, from at least as far back as the Medieval period, the linear earthwork that follows the edge of the scarp slope high above the left bank of the Wye, was regarded as an integral part of Offa's Dyke.
2. Most of the course of the Dyke as it survived down to the late eighteenth century was described accurately for the first time by Thomas Pennant in 1783/4 (Pennant, 1991). In the northern part of its course it has nonetheless, at times, been confused with Wat's Dyke, the major linear earthwork that runs parallel with Offa's Dyke, but eastwards from it and extending further north to reach the sea at Holywell (Trefynnon) on the Dee estuary.
3. See Fox, 1955; Fox's view was actively promulgated also by Sir Frank Stenton, for instance in his Anglo-Saxon England (2nd edition, 1947). See Noble, 1983, and Hill, 2000, for summaries of the subsequent debates.
4. The 'ditch' is sometimes rendered as a notch cut in the west-facing scarp west of the bank, or as a level berm. A 'counter-scarp bank' is a small continuous earthwork bank running along the outer lip of the ditch, and standing therefore opposite (counter to) the main scarp (front) of the bank. This feature has been mostly eroded away in many places. As a result it has been under-recorded even though it occurs throughout the course of the Dyke.
5. The distances given here are deliberately approximate, and refer to what we might term 'map miles', in that if minor variations in the course of the 'frontier' are taken account of, the actual span is probably at least 20% longer than the figures given here. By adding these factors in, for example, Fox deduced a frontier spanning 149 miles. The question of the distinction between the Dyke itself and the frontier it formed a part of is central to the interpretation of Offa's Dyke, and will be touched upon several times in the book. See especially, Chapters 2, 7 and 9, below.
6. On measurements used throughout the book, see the prefatory notes, xii.
7. See Chapter 2, below.
8. Wood (1908), for example, identified a series of separate lengths of earthwork in the vicinity of, and southwards from, Hereford, as potentially part of Offa's Dyke and speculated about the place-name 'Clouds' at Checkley possibly referring to the Welsh 'Clawdd', or dyke.
9. See Hoyle and Vallender, 1997, 37. In the Gloucestershire study, lengths in the Collins Grove and Tumpshill areas were assessed as being similar in location and form to the Dyke south of Redbrook, but of more hybrid build. Hoyle and Vallender also noted four areas in the Bishopswood area east of the Wye on the border with Herefordshire where earthwork lengths similar to some of the Gloucestershire could be recorded. The case for the continuation east and south of Hereford was put at greatest length by J. G. Wood (1908), but was dismissed

10. The 1995 survey found evidence that in one of the large gaps, to the north and south of the Lancaut Peninsula, 'the monument is likely to have been destroyed by quarrying during the nineteenth century' (Hoyle and Vallender, 1997, 5).
11. With a surviving built length of this span comprising 81 miles of earthwork.
12. These characteristics are discussed in the context of its detailed course below; and at length in terms of repeated occurrences of different devices in Chapter 4.
13. These characteristics, and the locations of their observed occurrence, are described at length in Chapter 5.
14. For maps of these particular areas see Figure 1.16, 1.12 and again 1.16, respectively. The existence of the Dyke in a farmed landscape has also taken its toll, and Fox noted in 1928 that lengths of ditch in some fields had been filled in at locations not far from industrial activity that had caused greater damage (as at Ruabon, north of Wynnstay Colliery, the works from which had obliterated some lengths of the Dyke; Fox, 1955, 52). It is nonetheless salutary to observe also how much erosion, as well as the compromising of the setting of the earthwork, has occurred particularly in areas such as east Denbighshire since Fox carried out his survey over 80 years ago.
15. Fox attributed differential survival in the farmed landscape largely to the material that the Dyke was composed of. So where, for instance, as between the Vyrnwy and the Severn (see below), its bank was built from the alluvial silts, gravels, and clays of the floodplain, it tends to have been eroded into a broad profile; while, where dug for example from the Ordovician shales of the Long Mountain east of Welshpool, it has retained a sharp profile. Fox cited in support of this thesis a point where there was a sudden transition from one subsoil to another near the crossing of the Lack Brook on the southern margins of the Vale of Montgomery: 'On the northern flank of the small valley formed by this streamlet, Ordovician shales form the subsoil, but on the floor these are overlaid by stony clays probably of glacial origin. The result is that an exceptionally fine and clear-cut stretch of the Dyke gives way to a series of sprawling shapeless hummocks...' (Fox, 1955, 108).
16. On the relationship between Offa's Dyke and Wat's Dyke, see below and Chapter 9.
17. Fox, 1955, 5–28.
18. Field investigations in the late twentieth century led to the conclusion that the so-called 'Whitford Dyke' comprised two distinct linear features, complete in their own right, extending north and south from the Ysceifiog Bronze Age barrow and the Brynbella Mound respectively, and that some lengths of apparently linear earthwork nearby were in fact little more than hedge-banks (Hill and Worthington, 2003, 154–61). Recent field study has supported this interpretation, and has led to the conclusion that it was in origin a prehistoric feature, that may have been re-used as a later boundary (W. Britnell, pers comm., 2010).
19. Hill and Worthington, 2003, 181–4. Since the authors list excavations on the continuous earthwork section from Treuddyn to Herrock Hill only, as being 'on Offa's Dyke' it is difficult to use their Appendix 3 'Gazetteer of sites' as a reliable guide to the total for 'Fox's', or perhaps 'maximal', Offa's Dyke. Nonetheless, using this source, there have been 62 interventions on the 'minimal' Dyke (including a Shropshire County Council Highways cutting recorded on Polaroid film by the site engineer), 44 of which were 'project' led. Gloucestershire interventions total 12 (all at or nearby Buttington Tump), and Herefordshire 10 (mostly on Rowe Ditch), while the Flintshire total north of Treuddyn is also 12.
20. Ibid, 99–100. On p.102 this is given as 52 excavations, with another 30 mentioned as undertaken by 'other organizations' (our reading of the Appendix 3 figures for the latter, excluding those in northern Flintshire, gives a total of 27).
21. Fox, 1955, 40–4
22. At Sunnybank: Jones, 1992; and at Frith Farm: Turner-Flynn et al., 1995.
23. In September 2013, Ian Grant and a team from Clwyd-Powys Archaeological Trust carried out an archaeological salvage operation (involving cleaning and recording of sections and excavation of four sample excavation trenches of different sizes) at Plas Offa, Chirk. This followed the landowner's abrupt casual bulldozing of a 40m upstanding length of the bank of the Dyke immediately south of the A5 trunk road. One organic sample, from turf close to the base of 'Section C', produced a radiocarbon date calibrated to AD 541–651 (SUERC 51225). Another sample, from 'Section B', only 20m to the south, produced a date of AD 887–1019 (SUERC 51224). These contradictory results do not 'date' the Dyke: rather, they exemplify the difficulties inherent in spot-dating such an earthwork. For recording details of the investigation, see Grant, 2014.
24. By 'chronometric' here is meant any independent scientific dating technique derived from samples that are rigorously obtained from reliable contexts. Such contexts could include old land surfaces that might yield OSL (Optically Stimulated Luminescence) dates indicating approximately when that surface was last exposed to sunlight, radiocarbon dates on articulated bone or short-lived plant remains derived from primary

structural deposits sealed beneath the bulk of the bank, or basal layers of the ditch, and of dendro-chronological dates from timber posts or piles associated with the construction that might be preserved in waterlogged deposits in the flood-plain river-crossings. The latter could in principle place the construction to within a particular decade.

25 Hill and Worthington, 2003, 47ff. Many of the excavations were undertaken at too small a scale to bear the weight of the conclusions drawn from them. Others were carried out in less than optimal locations, mostly due to an otherwise laudable concern to minimise damage to the upstanding sections of the monument (ibid, 48). Some were in effect watching briefs carried out in unfavourable circumstances when machine cuts had been made through places where the Dyke was no longer visible; several for non-archaeological reasons, as at Tatham Road, Ruabon, where excavation carried out by the project team in advance of development was one of several that produced a 'negative' result (ibid, 80). As many as 14 among the at least 27 excavations on or near the 'continuous upstanding' sections of the Dyke seem to have been limited to the objective of testing for the presence/absence of the ditch. In some cases the circumstance of training excavations and sometimes adverse weather conditions hampered the results. In this light, the nature of the overall enterprise is more clearly apparent and the absence of dating conclusions becomes more explicable. The lack of provision for the sampling or analysis of radiocarbon dates is another possible explanation (ibid, 55, 61). Moreover, since the reporting of the excavations has only ever been in summary form, the published conclusions should be approached with caution (see also, Chapters 2 and 5, below).

26 Hannaford, 1998.

27 Hannaford (ibid) interpreted the date as indicating that Wat's Dyke was a probable frontier-work for a sub-Roman kingdom based upon Wroxeter, on the river Severn east of Shrewsbury.

28 Hayes and Malim, 2008. See Chapters 5 and 6, below, for discussion of these structural implications; for the dating implications, see Chapter 9.

29 Ibid. OSL dates do not have the same level of accuracy as high-precision carbon-14 dates, but the series of dates from the ditch for successive silting episodes are very largely consistent (the sample dates from lower ditch fills are earlier, those from higher up, later), and they correlate well with the single date from a buried soil under the bank (Hayes and Malim, 2008, 164–6; 173–5; Figures 26 and 27).

30 Ibid, 154–63. This agrees well with the conclusions of David Hill (at least as reported in Davies, 1990, from public lectures by Hill in the 1980s) that Wat's Dyke was a mid-ninth-century construction.

31 The new (2014) dates for the Plas Offa length notwithstanding (see n.23, above).

32 The Latin is from W.H. Stevenson, 1904. This differs in details of transliteration from that of W. H. Stevenson as given in Whitelock, 1979. We would like to thank Professor John Blair of The Queen's College, University of Oxford, for advice concerning the translation. We have tried to capture each word used in Asser's original carefully, and not to gloss that original. An example of such glossing in past versions is the repeated rendering of 'recent' as 'fairly recent' (for example, Keynes and Lapidge, 1983, 71). Such past treatment implicitly interpolates an opinion that Asser could not have regarded the events of a century before he wrote as 'recent'. Such a presumption pays too little heed, in our view, to the difference between the historical views of a Welsh bishop living in Anglo-Saxon Wessex and those of our own age. The exact meaning of 'formidolosus' is debatable: Keynes and Lapidge render it 'vigorous', but 'overbearing' could also convey its sense, as does the more neutral 'energetic' used here.

33 Keynes and Lapidge, 1983, 71; Asser, *Life*, 13–14. For the historical context of the marriage arranged between Beorhtric and Eadburh, see Chapters 3 and 8, below.

34 Some of the readings of Asser's statement published in recent years have not placed it fully enough in the context of the work concerned, the *Life* of Alfred, nor of the West Saxon court at the end of the ninth century. See our discussion of this point in Chapter 9, for a fuller treatment of this important subject.

35 So, for example, while not suggesting that there is positive evidence that the Dyke was *not* built in Offa's reign, Gareth Williams has suggested that recent research on the Danevirke, a linear dyke dug across the Jutland peninsula to delimit the southern boundary of Denmark, serves as a potential cautionary tale. This dyke has traditionally been attributed (from a reference in the Frankish Annals) to the Danish king, Godred, in AD808; however, archaeologically at least one part of the earthwork has now been dated to *c.*700, and 'no phase corresponding to Godred's reign has yet been identified' (G. Williams, 2001b, 302).

36 'Wansdyke' was 'Woden's dyke', named after the Anglo-Saxon/Germanic foundational god who presided over war, among other things (See Chapter 3 for discussion of the place of Woden in Mercian royal genealogy). Grimsdyke was named after 'Grimr, the 'hooded man', another name for Woden' (A. Williams 2009, 41). The Offa of legend was believed by the Anglo-Saxons to have ruled towards the end of the fourth century AD in

Angeln (Anglia), today the area north-east of Schleswig in Germany, immediately south of the border with Denmark near Flensburg, facing the Baltic Sea on the eastern side of what becomes (northwards) the Jutland peninsula. This was where the Angles (of East Anglia, Mercia and so on) were thought to have migrated from: see Chapter 3, below.

37 The crucial problem shared by all 'cautionary' approaches to the attribution (including a controversy, now largely dismissed, that arose over whether Asser was indeed the author of Asser's *Life* of Alfred; see Keynes, 2005) is that it involves regarding the famous comment as somehow invalid. An annalistic (for instance) attribution is, however, very much more likely to represent legend than one made in a court context where the presence is attested of several Mercian clerics presumably well able to contradict inaccuracy or hyperbole.

38 Given that the wealth of historical documentation for the period after 1100 would have made some mention of the enterprise as a contemporary or near-contemporary phenomenon; and given that the work would have bisected the tenanted holdings of the expansionary lordships of the medieval March.

39 As David Hill did in his review of border warfare (Hill, 2001).

40 See the review of the contributions of the medieval writers in Chapter 2, below. A useful succinct treatment of the relevant references has also recently been published (A. Williams, 2009).

41 It might also be taken to imply that there were in the medieval period many more surviving Anglo-Saxon documents available to commentators than have survived into the present day.

42 Fox, 1955, 1.

43 Worthington, 2005, 93.

44 A. Williams, 2009, 43, quoting Levison, 1946.

45 As will be noted variously below, the last of these ideas is now considered highly unlikely, the first is only partly the case, and the second is more applicable to some areas than to others. See Fox, 1955, 283, for commentary upon the wooded areas the frontier was presumed to have traversed.

46 This 'filling in' of the gaps is due in large measure to the (mostly unpublished) work of David Hill, Margaret Worthington and associates (referred to in Hill and Worthington, 2003, 163). As many as 62 excavations, undertaken mostly to trace the course between what Fox had recorded as gaps, were carried out at various points on Wat's Dyke by the project concerned between 1971 and 2002. Another 17 excavations were carried out by Clwyd-Powys Archaeological Trust and various archaeological contractors in the period 1984 to 1998. None of these 79 interventions apparently produced secure dating evidence, and it is only the work at Mile Oak and at Gobowen near Oswestry that has at last produced a full series of chronometric dates from determinate contexts.

47 See especially Chapter 4 for a discussion of these practices in reference to Offa's Dyke.

48 Interestingly, Hayes and Malim (2008, 177) assert the opposite. However, this is based upon the summary of their findings given by Hill and Worthington (2003, 101) and not upon their own, and other, published sections (for example, ibid, 65, Figure 23, which shows the section recorded at Redwood Lodge, Buttington), or upon the profiles recorded by Fox (1955).

49 Hayes and Malim, 2008, 177.

50 Ibid.

51 This similarity to some of the East Anglian dykes (see below) is among the reasons why Wat's Dyke has often been thought to be earlier in date than Offa's Dyke.

52 Hayes and Malim, 2008, 177. The results of the nine investigations summarised by Hayes and Malim (Ibid, Table 5) indicate consistencies in form and build of the bank within, but not necessarily between, different geographic sub-regions traversed by Wat's Dyke.

53 See Chapter 2, below.

54 Fox, 1955, 284–8. Fox saw 'the political and archaeological setting for the construction of Wat's Dyke' as most comfortably fitting into the reign of Aethelbald (716–757) at the culmination of a period of Mercian territorial expansion under Penda and Wulfhere during the mid- to late seventh century (see Chapter 3, below).

55 RCHM(E), 1975, 55–6; Bowen, 1990. It is beyond the scope of this book to provide an exhaustive comparative analysis of Offa's and Wat's Dykes with comparable dykes in the Welsh Marches of shorter length, nor of the scope of the Cambridgeshire dykes, none of which are longer than seven miles in length, or even as long as a 'maximal' Wansdyke stretching for more than 30 miles.

56 Instead, it links up at its western end with the major Roman road from Mildenhall to Bath. Fox and Fox (1958: 45) did indeed propose that East Wansdyke was a migration-period Saxon work. More recently, however, Fowler (2001) has suggested that the weight of contemporary evidence suggests that East Wansdyke was an uncompleted Romano-British work; while Reynolds and Langlands (2006) reject this in favour of the idea that a 'maximal Wansdyke' (including West Wansdyke and the Mildenhall to Bath Roman road) was a much later West Saxon frontier work. Meanwhile, Eagles and Allen (2011) see both East and West Wansdyke as essentially multi-period works.

57 For reviews of recent work on the Cambridgeshire dykes

58 Nor are these the only linear works in the area. The 'High Ditch' west of Wilbraham is generally considered to have functioned as a continuation of the Fleam Dyke westwards to the banks of the river Cam; the short and intermittent Mile Ditch extends north–south, to the west of Royston. In each case, they may be earlier (Iron Age or Romano-British) works.
59 See Malim *et al.*, 1997.
60 Malim, ibid; Malim, 2003.
61 Erskine, 2007.
62 White, 2003. A square farmstead-scale enclosure cut across obliquely by the Dyke, and excavated in 2003, was shown to date from the Iron Age and to have remained in use into the third century AD.
63 Detailed discussion of the Rowe Ditch is provided in White, 2003 and Ray, 2015, 209–10. The date of construction of Rowe Ditch and the Devil's Dyke may also be closely parallel.
64 Hankinson, 2002.
65 Hankinson, 2002; Hankinson and Caseldine, 2006.
66 Dyke at Birtley Cross: Herefordshire HER record reference (Primary Record Number): HSM 1679. For the significance of this part of the frontier, see the relevant section of Chapter 7, below (290–3).
67 See Chapters 4 and 5, below.
68 See Fox, 1955, 5–223; Noble, 1983, 1–31; 40–91. Hill and Worthington's (2003) description is interwoven with their commentaries upon excavations, but was also carried northwards from Rushock Hill to Treuddyn (descriptions of the course: 50–3, 58–9, 63–5, 69–74, 77, 79–80).
69 'Derwas' is itself an interesting place-name, since it combines the Welsh word *Derw* for 'oak' with the English word *waese* for a sometimes inundated area close to a major river.
70 Fox at this point amended his 1929 text in 1953 (1955, 87) to indicate that he thought that the nature of the floodplain here, perhaps in the eighth century occupied by a loop of the river Vyrnwy between Llandysilio and Llanymynech churches, may have obviated the need for the Dyke north of Llandysilio church. Our view, in contrast, is that the Dyke was deliberately sited here to follow the eastern side of a subtle floodplain ridge of Pleistocene origin that even now is respected by the course of the river on its western side.
71 See in particular, the discussion of 'political places' in Chapter 7, and the passages addressing the significance of 'Carreghofa' both as a place-name and a significant location, in Chapter 9.
72 See Chapter 3 for a discussion of how Pennant and his contemporaries portrayed the Dyke.
73 Noted here in the past tense because two-thirds of this length has been lost to quarrying, much of it caused by the linking up of several smaller quarries to form Llynclys Quarry since Fox's 1928 field season.
74 Fox noted in particular how along the top of the Craig Forda scarp the Dyke was cut as a notch maintained at a constant height of 1000 feet for over half a kilometre, with the river 400 feet below: "The choice of so dominating an alignment for the great earthwork is noticeable, influencing conclusions as to its purpose and significance" (1955, 61). These conclusions are supplied later in the same chapter (ibid, 79), and refer to the requirement simply that 'every effort is made to site it on dominant westward-facing slopes'.
75 It is not in fact the crest of Selattyn Hill that the Dyke gains, but a saddle just to its west. This was clearly a key sighting point, and Fox pointed out that between here and the Vyrnwy the direct line southwards deviates at most by only by around 800 metres (Fox, 1955, 80). More remarkably still, the alignment running northeastwards from here, crossing both the Ceiriog and Dee valleys to a point just to the north-west of Ruabon, and covering a distance of five miles deviates only by around 260 metres.
76 Pennant adduced some interesting reasons for the termination of the Dyke here in 1794 that even today are worth considering closely: see Chapters 3 and 7 for further discussion of this key point.
77 An earthen dyke known as the Tirymynach Embankment follows the Severn along its left (north) bank from a point immediately across the river at Buttington Bridge, which the Dyke approaches from the south. From four miles north of the bridge at Rhyd-esgyn the Embankment is mirrored by another dyke on the right (south) bank, but for most of the route the Embankment follows the course of the river alone. While it is clear that the central and northern sections of this earthwork are a post-Medieval flood prevention measure, the half-mile long stretch to the north of Buttington Bridge comprises two straight sections on different alignments, both of which have been eroded away by the Severn. Noble was convinced that, due to the presence of fords here, and from inferences from medieval and later documentary evidence, the Dyke once existed here close to the right (south) bank of the river. Despite careful searching and some test excavations of some of the local earthworks, no trace of any linear earthwork has been found here (Hill and Worthington, 2003, 67–70).
78 Much discussion of this idea from Fox onwards has failed to resolve the issue of whether the tradition of a road that preceded the Dyke here is based in anything more than surmise.

79 It has been suggested that this saddle marks the point where the ridgeway concerned is narrowest (Hill and Worthington, 2003, 120). This superficially plausible observation is in fact incorrect, since there is an alternative, narrower, point only half a mile to the east, at present-day 'Dog and Duck Cottage'.
80 Fox, 1955, 124–71.
81 This is discussed further in Chapter 7, below. In crossing the floodplain obliquely, the Dyke here departs from the usual practice of crossing river-valleys at the perpendicular (cf, the discussion of design and landscape placement in Chapter 4, below). Meanwhile, however, the Dyke mirrors the way in which it crossed the Teme valley further north, by linking across ridges that divide the floodplain.
82 See Whitehead, 1980.
83 This sighting is significant, because the Dyke does not extend to the summit, but rather it achieves it highest elevation at mid-slope on the southwards-facing flank of the hill. Noble (1983, 30), noted that the alignment of this stretch of the Dyke appears to have been 'set' from as far north as Rushock Hill.
84 Substantial sections of bank border the eastern side of the road in at least two locations, and there is a suspiciously steep drop from the road south-westwards around a bend just to the west of Little Batch Farm. This possible course is discussed further in Chapter 7.
85 The 'reading' of the route of the Dyke provided in the foregoing accords well with the testimony of Aubrey's correspondent Henry Milbourn, Recorder of Monmouth, in the 1680s. In responding to Aubrey's request for information about the Dyke, it is not surprising that Milbourn's closest knowledge was of the then well-preserved section across open country north of the Wye in Herefordshire (in probable contrast to the part 'buried' in dense woodland overlooking the Wye in west Gloucestershire). It is also of interest in this context to note that Thomas Pennant, writing in the late eighteenth century, describes the Dyke as extending northwards 'from the river *Wye*, along the counties of *Hereford* and *Radnor*…' (1784, I, 273).
86 See the discussion below, in Chapter 7, concerning the possibility that the area south of the Wye precisely here was the scene of a series of military encounters between the Mercians and the British throughout the eighth century.
87 Note that this is discussed further in Chapter 5, where the build evidence for 'primary' form is reviewed.
88 For example, the Dyke earthworks have been levelled across parts of St Briavels Common, where a pattern of piecemeal informal enclosure into a maze of pasture closes took place probably in the earlier post-medieval period. See again, Hoyle and Vallender, 1997.
89 *Contra*, for example, Hill and Worthington, 2003, 145. This may seem to some readers too sweeping a statement to be made without further corroboration. However, the detail of the evidence upon which this assertion is made are set out fully below, in Chapters 2, 4, 5 and 7.
90 Cf. Hoyle and Vallender, 1997, 5: 'to the north and south of the Lancaut Peninsula, the monument is likely to have been destroyed by quarrying during the nineteenth century'.

Chapter 2

1 Thomas Churchyard, *The Worthines of Wales* (Evans, 1776, 104; 'reprinted from the Edition of 1587'). Churchyard (or 'Churchyarde'), was a sometime military adventurer, poet and early antiquary whose rambling work on the 'Worthiness' of Wales, published in 1587, comprised a narrative in verse interspersed with prose commentaries, tracing a journey around Wales, in which Shropshire is included integrally, celebrating its historic, natural and familial wonders. Offa's Dyke is here 'within two miles' of Ruabon, and the Mercians are become 'Danes'. The 'free ground', in Churchyard's imagining at least, appears to be a trading zone between the two dykes, operating according to strictly enforced rules. Just why Offa's Dyke should also be 'called the Britons' strength' is opaque, unless this is recording another belief about the Dyke recorded along its course, that it was built by the Welsh at Offa's command (see, for instance, Hartshorne, 1841, 184).
2 See especially the discussion of Coenwulf and the northern end of the frontier in Chapter 9, 356–7.
3 Whitelock, 1969, 203–4. See Chapter 6, below, for further discussion of the potential significances of this event.
4 The version of Byrhtferth's record of these lost Northumbrian annals covering the years 732 to 802 was located in sections 58–68 of *Symeonis Monachi Opera Omnia* (See Hart, 2006; Lapidge, 1982). The Anglo-Saxon, Carolingian and papal dimensions of the entries are discussed at length by Story (2003, 93–133).
5 Seemingly, Reginald was the first to make this identification of the battle site with Oswestry. Such an identification has been widely followed to this day.
6 Quoted in A. Williams, 2009, 34–5.
7 For the *Brut*, see Hughes, 1980, 67 and Jones, 1971. The relevant entry is found only in one copy of one the fifteenth-century 'Brehinned y Saesson' ('Kings of the Saxons') version of the 'Brut'. The translation of the passage concerning Offa's Dyke is quoted from A. Williams, 2009, 35.

8   Williams, 2009, 35.
9   Gerald of Wales (*Giraldus Cambrensis*, or Gerald de Barri) was born of mixed Welsh and Norman ancestry at Manorbier in Pembrokeshire, in 1145/6, and wrote his *Description of Wales* probably between 1188 and 1198 (Thorpe, 1978, 16–17).
10 Thorpe, ibid, 266.
11 Ranulf Higden was born *c*.1280 and, as a monk at the Benedictine Priory of St Werburgh's, Chester, from 1299, wrote his *Polychronichon* (a discursive account of world history; in Book 2 of which he mentioned both Offa's Dyke and Wat's Dyke) in the years before 1342 (the *Polychronicon* itself was continued by others to 1377).
12 Collins, 1988, 49–50.
13 The question of the historically possibly complex inter-relationship between the Offa's and Wat's dykes in the development of the western Mercian frontier is discussed more fully in Chapter 9, below.
14 Lucy Toulmin Smith, 1907, 40.
15 Lit. the practice of being 'many-learned' (OED). Such men had usually been educated within the classical and clerical traditions at Oxford or Cambridge, or one of the ancient Scottish universities. Such scholars absorbed and integrated diverse information, in often idiosyncratic, sometimes ingenious, and at other times perverse, ways, and from a variety of sources including correspondents whose testimony they were rarely in a position to corroborate.
16 It was in fact first published in 1982, edited by the novelist John Fowles (Fowles, 1982).
17 Fowles, 1982, 884–5; Aubrey folio 87/59.
18 Pennant (below), 1783/4 (2nd edn 1810), p. 275, ascribes this edict to King Harold, citing Leland's (1535–43) *Collectanea*, iii, 230, and John of Salisbury (*Polycraticus*, c. 1159, vi, 6) quoted by William Camden, in his *Britannia* (1588), p.698.
19 This reference is significant enough that, and has been neglected to the extent that, it warrants further discussion in Chapter 7, below (p. 286).
20 By 'Wensditch' here, Aubrey was referring to the linear earthwork known as 'Wansdyke' that runs along the southern edge of the Marlborough Downs in Wiltshire, for much of its course overlooking the Vale of Pewsey.
21 Aubrey added here 'This paragraph is by the information of Henry Milbourn Esq. Recorder of Monmouth; and a good Antiquarie'. Milbourn's knowledge of the Dyke northwards from the section near the Wye in Herefordshire was evidently slight, and based presumably on not very accurate reports. The north Herefordshire Rowe Ditch near Leominster (and not *Lanterden* = Leintwardine) was clearly routinely being mistaken by some at this time for Offa's Dyke, as was Wat's Dyke to judge from the Basingwerk reference.
22 Alternatively, the name 'Bachy-hill' is an early toponym for Garnons Hill, upon which it is likely that Aubrey could have seen the Dyke. Possibly because of Aubrey's limited familiarity with local place-names, but possibly also connected with some genuine belief about the existence of fortifications in the Brilley area, there is confusion here between the hills on which the Dyke ran. See Chapter 7, below, for the potential significance of the name 'Merbach' (= 'boundary stream') for the early frontier locally.
23 MS copy in a private collection (inf. R. Silvester, Clwyd-Powys Archaeological Trust).
24 Lhuyd, 1696 ed. Morris, 1909–11. Unfortunately, the parochial enquiry returns were somewhat patchy (returns were gained for 137 of the civil parishes of Wales as defined in the mid-twentieth century) and there were none for parishes in Montgomeryshire and Radnorshire through which the Dyke runs, although there was one for 'Oswaldstrey' (Oswestry) in Shropshire (Emery, 1958). The compilation for Whitford parish (Flintshire) included a letter from John Aubrey in 1703 mentioning an earthwork forming part of the parish boundary near Newmarket that had, at least by 1832, long been known as 'Offa's Dyke' thereabouts (Fox, 1955, 5).
25 For instance, Hill and Worthington, 2003, 108–10; Edwards, 2009. Lhuyd was not the first to make a transcription, however, and he appears likely to have interpolated some of the partly-obliterated lettering. See below, this chapter, for mention of what reference Fox, and Hill and Worthington, have made to this stone; and Chapters 7 and 9, below, for further discussion of its implications.
26 '*Offa's Dike*, an entrenchment cast up by Offa, a Saxon king, to defend England against the incursions of the Welch, in 777. This dyke or ditch is yet visible on Brachy-hill, and and [*sic*] near Rhydor, Helig and Lanterden in Herefordshire, and is continued northwards from Knighton, over a part of Shropshire, and goes over the long mountain Kevn-Digoth to Harden-Castle, across the Severn and Landrinio-Common; from thence it passes the Vyrnwy again into Shropshire, not far from Ofswestry; in Denbighshire it is visible along the road between Rhyabon and Wrexham, and being continued through Flintshire, ends a little below Holywell.' (Luckombe, 1790).
27 Thomas Pennant, *A Tour in Wales* (1784), 272–5. (Bridge Books reprint, 1991).
28 The debt to the Ordnance Survey was for example explicitly acknowledged by H. L. Jones (1856a, 2).
29 Fosbroke 1833, 1835; Lane Fox and Boyd Dawkins, 1876.

30 Colt Hoare, 1812, 7. For a general account of the development of antiquarian thought, investigation and writing in Britain, see Nurse, Gaimster, and McCarthy, 2007.
31 Williams, 1850.
32 Jones, 1856a, 5.
33 Ibid. It is remarkable testimony to Jones' perspicacity that, with the exception of Llanymynech, it was at just these locations (at Ffrith near Caergwrle, at Forden, at Garnons near Kenchester, and at Buttington near Chepstow – although at the latter not on the projected line of the Roman road) that Cyril Fox chose to make his field investigations involving excavation in the following century, some 75 years later.
34 M'Kenny Hughes, 1893.
35 See, for example, the discussion in Hartshorne (1841, 181–209).
36 The detailed accounts of Jones (1856a) and Hartshorne (op. cit.) are particularly informative on this point.
37 Pennant, 1784, 273.
38 Fosbroke, 1833.
39 Fosbroke, 1835.
40 Ormerod, 1842 See also Ormerod 1856, and 1859.
41 Ormerod, 1856, 18. For 'Buttinton' read Buttington (in both cases), for 'Tiddenham', Tidenham.
42 Meyrick, 1834.
43 See, for example, Hartshorne, 1841.
44 Hartshorne, 1841; Jones, 1856a and 1856b.
45 This significant observation about the Dyke and the road north of Sarnesfield, which prefigures our own observations here, is to be found in Hartshorne, 1841, 187. See Chapter 7, pp. 285–8 for identification of the places noted here.
46 Jones, 1856a, 14.
47 Pennant, 1784, 274.
48 Hartshorne, 1841. See also, Fox, 1955, 5–28 for extended discussion of this vexed question; and Hill and Worthington, 2003, 154–61 for a summary account of late twentieth-century investigations that have thrown doubt on Fox's conclusions.
49 Jones, 1854.
50 Jones, 1856a, 9.
51 Guest, 1858, 338.
52 Fox also noted a lost deed mentioned in a letter of 1832 which apparently recorded the use of the Offa's Dyke name in Whitford Parish in the time of Edward VI in the mid-sixteenth century, and a 1703 letter from William Aubrey also mentions this section of the Dyke (Fox 1955, 5).
53 See, for example, the similar summary discussions of the historical background in Hartshorne (1841), Jones (1856a), Earle (1857), and Elias Owen (1896).

54 Earle, 1857, 203. Jones quoted an earlier travel writer who expressed the same problem in a more whimsical way: 'Near this town (Kington) we crossed Offa's Dyke, a great mud wall, said to be built formerly by Offa, King of Mercia: but how came the King of Mercia to build this wall cross all the island? There must have been other kings to join him; and it seems the Welsh were plaguy troublesome, when there must be a wall to separate them. But I cannot be of the common opinion that this was a defence against the Welsh; for how soon would they demolish such a mud wall if they were such terrible creatures? If they were such a parcel of poltroons, as some modern wits will infer from this silly fortification, what occasion was there for a wall at all against such worthless animals? Doth it not seem more likely, that upon a peace between the English and British princes, this ditch was cut as an everlasting boundary line between the two nations, and that they all joined in it.' (As quoted in Jones 1856a, 4–5: Jones did not identify the author of this presumably eighteenth-century statement, and neither was the exact date of the quotation given).
55 Hartshorne, 1841, 208.
56 Lane Fox and Boyd Dawkins, 1876.
57 Owen, 1896. Although the exact location of this feature is not clear from the plan, it may be the same right-angled turn in the earthwork that we note as existing on Llanymynech Hill within the hillfort, in Chapter 6, below.
58 Earle, 1857, 205–6.
59 For example, Ormerod, 1859.
60 M'Kenny Hughes, 1893.
61 Mortimer Wheeler, annual report of the Director of the National Museum of Wales, Bulletin of the Board Celtic Studies, 1923. Quoted in Hill and Worthington, 2003, 75.
62 Fox had been appointed to a joint post as Keeper at the National Museum and as Lecturer in Archaeology at University College, Cardiff, in 1924 (Fox, 1955, xxiii–xxiv; Scott-Fox, 2002, 55–62).
63 Fox, 1955, xxiii–xxiv. Quite possibly, Northcote Thomas' initiative had bolstered – or perhaps had even inspired – Wheeler's decision to recruit Fox and to institute the Offa's Dyke Survey in the first place.
64 Ibid, xxv.
65 On Offa's Dyke, Fox, 1926, 1927, 1928, Fox and Phillips, 1929, 1930, and Fox, 1931, respectively. On Wat's Dyke, Fox, 1934a. A brief general note on dykes was published in *Antiquity*, the archaeological magazine founded and edited by O.G.S. Crawford (Fox, 1929). The third volume of the *Inventory Survey of the Royal Commission on Ancient Monuments, Herefordshire* included an essay on Offa's Dyke and other linear works

66 in that county (Fox, 1934b). A fuller interim synthesis of the results of the survey was prepared, and published in *Yorkshire Celtic Studies* (Fox, 1938). The Sir John Rhys Memorial Lecture was published under the different title, 'The Boundary Line of Cymru' in the *Proceedings of the British Academy* (Fox, 1941).

66 As explained in general terms in Fox, 1955, xxiii–xxvii. See also Scott-Fox, 2002, 70–82; 114–29.

67 This was first published as 'The Boundary Line of Cymru' in the Academy's Transactions. In his 'Author's Preface' to the combined publication (1953) Fox noted how the British Academy funded the 'definitive edition' published on their behalf by Oxford University Press (1955, xxiii).

68 Stenton, 1955, xxi.

69 See Fox, 1955, 116–23. This idea seems to have occurred to Fox when he was analysing the rationale for the formation of the different kinds of alignment he had encountered along the Dyke south to the river Vyrnwy. For discussion of the evidential basis concerning alignments, and how his deductions about land-use relate to a current appreciation of the nature of that landscape, see Chapter 7 below.

70 There was possibly also a feeling that the field study needed to be drawn to a close, having lasted so many seasons.

71 Fox, 1955: Part II: 'VIII. Wat's Dyke: From the Dee Estuary at Holywell, Flintshire, to Maesbury, Shropshire, in the basin of the Middle Severn (1934)', 225–75.

72 Fox, 1955, Part I: 'IV. Offa's Dyke in East Denbighshire and North-West Shropshire (1928)', 47–83.

73 Op. cit., 73–4.

74 For example, the photograph looking east-south-east at Tintern in the Wye valley with the Dyke as a sky-line feature shows a stark winter scene (Fox, 1955, Plate XXXVI). Reproduced here as Figure 2.11.

75 As, for instance, on the 'Highbury plateau' south of Redbrook. Here 'the undergrowth…was too dense for the usual method of progression, and the survey was perforce made by incursion at selected points' (Fox, 1955, 187).

76 Fox, 1926. Fox, 1955: Part I: 'II. Offa's Dyke in north Flintshire (1926 and 1953)', 5–28.

77 Fox, 1927. Fox, 1955: Part I: 'III. Offa's Dyke in south Flintshire and east Denbighshire (1927)', 29–45.

78 Fox, 1955, Part I: 'IV. Offa's Dyke in East Denbighshire and North-West Shropshire (1928)', 47–83 (from Fox, 1928). This report/chapter also set the pattern for those that followed. The 'formula' comprised a prefatory introduction, then a detailed account of the course of the Dyke, then a commentary on the profile of the Dyke throughout this part of its course. These sections were in each case followed by further ones on gaps in the Dyke, earthworks on or near its course, and an overview of its form of construction. Finally, each account was concluded with a commentary section drawing out general points of comparison and interpretation. Each account was accompanied by the annotated map extracts, by a table of measurements, and by drawn profiles, as well as wider interpretive maps and by photographs. The 'three great stretches' (Fox, 1955, 82) were divided by the major changes in orientation at Ruabon and at Sellatyn Hill, described in Chapter 1.

79 For the latter, Fox, 1955, 82–3. The whole commentary section spanned seven pages of the 1955 volume (77–83).

80 Ibid, 81–2.

81 Fox, 1929. Fox, 1955: Part I: 'V. Offa's Dyke in East Montgomeryshire (1929)', 85–123.

82 And this was set out in a hand-drawn map (Fox, 1955, Figure 52, p. 122) of 'Offa's Dyke in Montgomeryshire' that showed the 'suggested distribution of arable and low-level woodland in the eighth century. (The upper levels were probably moorland pasture varied with patches of wood and scrub).'

83 Fox, 1955: Part I: 'V. Offa's Dyke in the Mountain Zone (South Shropshire and East Radnorshire) (1930)', 125–71. Original report: Fox, 1930.

84 Fox, 1955, 154. Fox later referred to this form of construction as being 'of 'boundary-bank' type' (1955, 218). He appeared unaware here (p. 154) that he had previously noted the existence of just such an eastern (albeit intermittent) quarry-ditch in various places such as Treflach (1955, 73–4) and Baker's Hill (ibid, 60–1), even if it does not in those northerly stretches accompany a slighter bank.

85 The incidence and significance of the different forms is discussed in some detail in Chapter 5, below, but is worth noting here that the slighter form *does* occur north of the Severn, as at Llanymynech Hill and at Craig Forda.

86 Fox, 1955, 160.

87 Fox, ibid (italics in the original). 'Reinforced' lengths were, according to Fox, those with a counterscarp bank present.

88 Ibid, 169. That is, already firmly established.

89 Ibid, 170.

90 Fox, 1955: Part I: 'VI. Offa's Dyke in the Wye Valley – Herefordshire and West Gloucestershire (1931)', 173–223. Original report: Fox, 1931.

91 See Chapter 7 for detailed and specific discussion of more recent ideas on this subject.

92 Fox. 1955, 216. This also was important due to the presence of the Roman road between Caerwent and Gloucester, that crossed the Wye just to the north of Chepstow and represented a major trade-route from Mercia into south Wales (ibid, 221–2).

93 Ibid, 216. See also, Faith (1994) regarding the wider significance of this charter for the estate at Tidenham in terms of the origins of medieval manorial practice; and further discussion regarding the local implications for the Dyke in Gloucestershire, in Chapter 7, below.

94 Fox had tangible evidence to support none of the inferences he made regarding Tidenham (see also Faith, 1994). He was undoubtedly right to stress the political and economic aspects of the frontier here, however. These aspects will be discussed further in Chapters 7 and 9, below.

95 Fox, 1955, 217. Fox adduced this inferred situation as yet further evidence that, in his wisdom, Offa had 'negotiated' the exact line of the frontier (ibid, 218).

96 This chapter of Fox, 1955, Part II: 'VIII. Wat's Dyke: From the Dee Estuary at Holywell, Flintshire, to Maesbury, Shropshire, in the basin of the Middle Severn (1934)', 225–75. The report: Fox, 1934.

97 Fox stated: 'Wat's Dyke is constructionally uniform, very much more so than Offa's Dyke' (1955, 258).

98 Ibid, 259. From his measured profiles, Fox compared 18 examples of the height of Wat's Dyke (producing an average of 1.3 m) with 42 examples of the 'normal' scale of Offa's Dyke which accounts for the whole distance covered by the latter north of the Severn (producing an average of 1.9 m). While the greatest recorded height of the bank of Wat's Dyke was 1.9 m, the greatest recorded height of the bank of Offa's Dyke was over 3m. It should be noted that this view has recently been contested in light of the excavated evidence particularly for Wat's Dyke ditch profiles, which has been taken to suggest that the latter was consistently the larger work (Malim and Hayes, 2008; Malim, 2009).

99 Fox, 1955, 277.

100 The 'agreed frontier' idea was clearly central to Fox's whole conception of the work, and his arguments in support of the thesis of a negotiated route were elaborate, but were not incontestable (1955, 279–81). That the small enclosure of Pen-y-Gardden fort overlooks the Dyke at Ruabon was deemed most important in reference to the proximity of the Pillar of Eliseg up the Dee valley just to the west, although the fact that Pen Offa fort stands immediately to the west of the Dyke overlooking the Walton Basin in Radnorshire, for example, but could not be defensible in the same terms owing to its isolation on the end of a ridge, was not given similar prominence. The fact that the Dyke rises up over the southern slopes of the Long Mountain south of Welshpool was seen as explicable not in terms of the dominant prospect therefore obtained over this part of the Severn valley (as adduced by Noble and others, and evident today), but because the lower slopes of the hill above the Severn were seen as prime cultivable land which the Kingdom of Powys did not wish to be ceded to the Mercians. The reason why the continuous Dyke only extended northwards from Sedbury to Redbrook in Gloucestershire was, according to Fox, because otherwise the frontier along the river itself would have complicated the payment of tolls to the Kings of Gwent for landings within the tidal limits of the Wye (Fox, 1955, 217).

101 Ibid, 282, 283. See Chapter 6, below, for a detailed reconsideration of how the Dyke-building project may have been organised.

102 Ibid, 284–5.

103 Ibid, 286: 'The 34 miles from the Severn at Buttington, Montgomeryshire, to Rushock Hill, Herefordshire, will have been built first, because it covered the vulnerable Mountain Zone …The 25 miles from the Severn at Llanymynech, Shropshire, to Pencoyd, Flintshire, set out in three magnificent major alignments, will have been constructed next … The remaining dyke-work is in areas less vital to Mercian security, being further from the heart of the kingdom, Tamworth.'

104 Ibid, 290.

105 Ibid, 290–2.

106 Although it should be conceded that at the time of his writing, there was a general acceptance that the post-Roman landscape involved extensive regeneration of woodland. This is a view substantially modified today but not entirely discounted from more recent evidence (see Chapter 7, below).

107 In particular, Hill and Worthington, 2003, 143–9. 'Why then is the section (of Fox, 1955) on west Gloucestershire in need of serious revision? Primarily because Fox was the 'inventor' of the section' (ibid, 145). As noted above, on the contrary the matter had been the subject of serious debate for more than a century before Fox's monograph was published.

108 The excavations and their results, set alongside other explorations of the structure of the Dyke, are discussed in Chapter 5, below.

109 Frank Noble is best remembered today (having died at the age of only 53 in 1980) for his indefatigable efforts to ensure that the Offa's Dyke Path, one of the very first group of long-distance walking trails to be designated in the early 1950s, actually became a reality. To this end, he negotiated access paths, encouraged local tourism, organised scrub clearance working parties, lectured widely, and laid the foundations for what would become the Offa's Dyke Centre at Knighton, from the late 1950s until 1971 (when the Path was officially opened), ultimately receiving the award of an MBE in recognition of his efforts in 1979. See Noble, 1969, 1975.

110 Noble, 1983, 1–12.

111 Ibid, 9.
112 The document and its implications have since been discussed by various authors (see for instance, Gelling, 1992, 113–18). It has only recently, however, been subject to close scholarly re-examination, which has suggested a slightly later date for its creation, in the late tenth or eleventh century (Molyneaux, 2011). We are grateful to John Blair for drawing KR's attention to the study and to George Molyneaux for sight of a copy of the article.
113 Noble, 1978.
114 Noble, 1983.
115 Cf. Shoesmith, 1980.
116 Noble, 1983, 9.
117 Ibid, 9.
118 Ibid, 2–3.
119 This has significant implications for an understanding of the economic context for the Dyke, that will be discussed in Chapter 9, below.
120 Fox, 1955, 187.
121 Noble, 1983, 8.
122 Ibid, 9.
123 In particular this derived from Wendy Davies' careful sifting of original material from medieval glosses and embellishments in the *Liber Landeniensis*. See Davies, 1978, 1979.
124 Noble, 1983, 27. Contrary to the view expressed by Hill (e.g., 2000), Noble did not originate the idea that 'cleared rides' might have existed where the Dyke was not built. In uncleared areas, Fox suggested, 'What *might* be necessary is unhampered *lateral* movement along the frontier; this could be attained by the clearance and maintenance of a broad ride through the woodlands' (1955, 210; emphases in original).
125 This is in the valley between Garbett Hall and Cwmsanahan Hill: see Figure 22.
126 Ibid, 42.
127 The Bwlch and Yew Tree Farm, Discoed, openings are discussed at some length in Chapter 6, below.
128 As with the Devil's Mouth cross-ridge dyke: Watson, 2002, 5.
129 Noble (1983, 89–90) followed an equation of the unusually large Domesday manor of Alretune with Trewern, and noted that it was the westernmost manor of Ruesset Hundred. The latter he recognised as a '-saete' settlement area, linked to a 'Rhiw' element presumably denoting the mountain known as The Breiddin. See Chapter 6 for an extended treatment of the questions both of deliberate settlement along the line of the Dyke and the provision of an 'infrastructure of defence' in these zones.
130 Ibid, 6. See the discussion of this length of Dyke in relation to Tintern in Chapter 4, and its built form in respect to the political landscape in Chapter 7.
131 Gelling, 1992, 101–124.
132 For the latter: Gelling, 1992, 119–22. Her ideas will be discussed further below, especially in the relevant sections of Chapters 6 and 7.
133 Hill 1974a, 1974b; Hill and Wilson, 1974; Hill, 1981, 1984, 1986, 1997b.
134 Hill, 1977a.
135 Ibid, 21. The italicised word was in the original. The statement suggests that Fox regarded the Offa's Dyke/Wat's Dyke 'problem' as solved by his work. It is possible to get this impression from Stenton's 'Introduction' to the 1955 volume, but not from Fox's own more considered assessment. Although the edited sections of Noble's M. Phil. dissertation were not to be published until 1983, Noble had submitted the thesis by 1977, and it seems highly unlikely that his (critical) views about Fox's work were unknown to Hill. Noble could hardly be regarded as a 'lulled student'. The suggestion that Fox's work had dealt 'only with aspects of the problem' is not explained further and is odd given that his survey was at the same time dismissed as being so monumental as to have discouraged further work by others.
136 These were identified on a plan prepared by Dominic Powlesland in 1976, although the more southerly of the Old Oswestry sites was specified in the 2003 volume gazetteer as having been excavated in 1977. Only seven of the 23 sites were discussed in this 1977 paper.
137 1977a, 23.
138 This aspect is dealt with at greater length when considering the totality of excavation results of this (and other) projects, in Chapter 5, below.
139 Hill, 1977a, 25–31.
140 For instance, Hill 1985; 1991. David Hill had intended to write up the results of his investigations more fully in retirement, but was prevented from doing so by ill health and other problems (David Hinton, pers. comm., 2011).
141 Hill, 2000a.
142 'Claim' because, despite the study concerned being (in the opinion of its co-ordinators) 'a spectacular achievement of fieldwork and excavation' (Hill and Worthington, 2003, 163), involving extending its known length from 20.75 miles to 38.6 miles, the evidence has not been documented more fully than in the 14-page summary of work on both dykes published by Hill more than twenty years ago (Hill, 1991).
143 Hill, 2000a, 200.
144 Ibid.
145 Ibid, 202, quoting Nash-Williams, 1950 (no page reference given).
146 Even if it is left unstated that the Dyke is not, in fact,

147 continuous given the six-mile interruption at the Severn near Welshpool.
147 V. E. Nash-Williams delineated this merely as a reference-point for noting the distribution of inscribed stones (Nash-Williams, 1950, 42–3).
148 Hill, 2000a, 203: 'If we construct a map which shows only the proven portions of Offa's Dyke … the relationship between the central Offa's Dyke and the possible Kingdom of Powys becomes apparent … if we superimpose the boundaries delineated in a recent work, notional though they are, onto a map of the same central area portion of Offa's Dyke, the potential correlation is demonstrated.' The 'recent work' cited was 'Keynes and Lapidge 1983', which was used to illustrate the situation in Alfred's reign (Keynes and Lapidge, 1983, Map 4, p. 95, 'Wales in the late ninth century') using modern political boundaries. Hill's 'superimposed' mapping (2000a, 204: Figure 4) simply involved replacing the modern eastern boundary of Wales with the line of the 'proven' Offa's Dyke. Hill deliberately mentioned Wendy Davies' strictures: she 'warns us against the facile naming and delimitation of early medieval kingdoms in Wales. The evidence does not exist for the accurate definition of the frontiers of the early Welsh Kingdoms' (ibid, 203), but he did not mention Davies' doubts expressed in the same chapter in which her warnings were expressed, that not only is Powys not documented as existing before AD 808, but that the lands between Brycheiniog east of Brecon and 'Powys' north of the Severn bordering Shropshire may have contained several early kingdoms (1982, 94–6).
149 Hill, 2000a, 203
150 Ibid, 198. Hill cited Hoyle, 1996, a summary account of the work, to suggest that there were 'five discrete lengths' of Dyke in Gloucestershire.
151 Hill, 2000a, 198.
152 Currie and Herbert, 1996, 249. The document concerned was from the Dunraven MSS (No. 271), at the National Library of Wales.
153 Hoyle and Vallender, 1997. See the relevant sections of Chapters 4, 5, 6 and 7, below, for details.
154 Hill, 2000a, 204. This substantially mis-represents Asser's account and its context (see Chapter 1, above, and the discussions in Chapter 9 and the Epilogue, below). Reference to the account of the 'Danevirke' in the Frankish annals (ibid, 205) is not helpful, because that work was much shorter, and crossed very different terrain (see Dobat, 2008, and Lund, 2009, for contemporary assessments).
155 Some have proposed alternative readings, and have queried whether the warfare concerned saw Powys instead supported by the Mercians against Gwynedd (Fitzpatrick-Matthews, 2001). The cairn upon which the Pillar stands has been the subject of recent intensive study by Howard Williams and associates from the University of Chester, and the pillar itself and its inscription have been the subject of in-depth scrutiny as part of the same project (Edwards, 2009). Most recently, David Stephenson (2012), while agreeing with Nancy Edwards that an earlier transcription by Robert Vaughan of Hengwrt in 1648 may be more reliable than the Lhuyd transcription of 1696, because 'no gaps have been inserted between the words of the inscription, and one would not expect word divisions on early medieval inscriptions in Wales in this period; therefore, in this respect, it may reflect the original more closely' (Edwards, 2009, 157), also points out that the degree of interpolation by Lhuyd materially affects the meaning of the original. A careful *re-reading* of the Vaughan version, in Stephenson's view, provides a key context for the Powysian resurgence. These aspects are discussed further in Chapter 7, below.
156 Worthington, 1999.
157 Ibid, 342.
158 Hill and Worthington, 2003, 40–1.
159 Ibid, 42. Not only does this indicate a lack of awareness of the medieval St Briavels reference, but also the several medieval references to 'Offa's Dyke' (however erroneously made, given that some refer to the earthwork we now understand as Wat's Dyke) in Flintshire.
160 The evidence for the form of the ditch and the bank especially, is reviewed in Chapter 5, below, while the evidence for build sequences and gateways (for example) is reviewed in Chapter 6.
161 Ibid, main account, 47–87; discussions, 87–102.
162 Ibid, 102.
163 Ibid, 101. The impressionistic nature of these conclusions is nonetheless evident when the published ditch profiles are examined carefully and the characteristics of the different build modes are examined in detail. For example, the generalised dimensions given for the breadth and depth of the ditch, presumably adduced from the very few fully-recorded excavated profiles, differ from those illustrated even in the same volume. Nor can the generalisations be sustained from examination of Fox's many drawn surface profiles, which demonstrate no 'consistent relationship' between ditch centre and bank crest, although some regularities do exist between different *kinds* of build in different categories of location. These aspects are documented further in Chapter 5, below.
164 Ibid.
165 Ibid.
166 Ibid, 105.
167 Ibid, 107–12.

168 Ibid, Figures 30 and 31. See Chapter 6, below, for an extended treatment of the same topics.
169 Hill and Worthington, 2003, 129–39. We do not regard the Rowe Ditch across the Arrow Valley as part of the 'Offa's Dyke' works, and are in agreement with Hill and Worthington that they represent the earthworks of a cross-valley dyke; but the characteristics of Rowe Ditch are quite unlike the length of dyke that crosses the Curl Brook valley to the west of Lyonshall, that has at least three key characteristics in common with Offa's Dyke elsewhere (see the detailed discussion in Chapter 7, below).
170 Ibid, 148. The certainty with which this is stated is surprising given that one of us (ILB) gained the impression from an interview with Margaret Worthington in 2000/1 that the direct on the ground knowledge of members of the 'Offa's Dyke Project' team, of the Gloucestershire part of the Dyke, especially northwards from East Vaga/Tidenham Chase, was slight.
171 Ibid.
172 Hill, 2000. In other words, neither the Ordnance Survey surveyors (who on some editions of their maps chose to be cautious and not to follow local tradition in naming the lengths concerned 'Offa's Dyke') nor Fox 'invented' the connection with Offa: this was, as noted above, a matter of either (medieval and later) documentary record, or local practice as recorded in the field.
173 Hill and Worthington, 2003, 146.
174 The Hill/Worthington account (2003, 145–7) conflates the southern portion of the 'Type A' earthwork of the Hoyle/Vallender survey, which traces a course *partly* 'on the crest of the river cliffs' (as at Plumweir) with the northerly length from St Briavels north to Redbrook, which is built along steep slopes and ridge-tops, but nowhere occupies land above 'cliffs'. The length of Dyke that crosses St Briavels Common and continues either side of it is of apparently slighter build, but it traces a course that links directly with the more prominent lengths to north and south, and its recorded form on the Common itself has been much compromised from field to field by later smallholding activity.
175 To take one of these aspects, Tim Malim has recently pointed out that the ditches found in very small-scale trenches at locations such as Bwlch/Newcastle Hill, Discoed, on a ridge to the south of the river Lugg crossing were not necessarily associated with the Dyke because they were: 'not on the same scale as the normal ditch dimensions and no evidence is cited to show that these ditches were contemporary with the original monument; they could be later field ditches that follow the line of the earlier boundary.' (2007, 27). Moreover, 'the presence of the ditch does not preclude an entrance through Offa's Dyke (at these locations); to the contrary it suggests a policy of controlled access, perhaps using planks to form a section of retractable bridge in the fashion used in later medieval castles to cross towers from one parapet walk to another' (ibid).
176 Hill, 2000a, 195.
177 Tyler (2011) has noted that David Hill concluded that there was no Dyke built along either side of the river Severn downstream from Buttington, but that Margaret Worthington still believed that there could be. We agree with Hill: it is evident from the way that the earthwork approaches the river in each direction, that the intention was to meet the river-bank and terminate there (See Chapter 4, below).
178 See Charles-Edwards, 2013a. The broadcast concerned included statements such as 'it is *not* true that (Offa's) Dyke stretches from sea to sea' and 'archaeological survey and excavation have shown that…its southern end was on Rushock Hill'.
179 The results of a preliminary exercise in such comparison are set out in Chapter 4, below. Meanwhile, the idea of a 'zonal' landscape in which the Dyke was located at the frontier will be discussed further in Chapter 7, below.
180 Feryock, 2001. Feryock's essay again reviewed most of the key questions, and much of the past commentary noted above, and especially the views of Fox, Noble and Hill and Worthington.
181 Observations on the lower Wye valley lengths: ibid, 170–2; 189–90. We concur with most of Feryock's views on this sector in these pages (if not her overall conclusions about it: ibid, 192), but do not accept the dismissal of the north Herefordshire lengths as entirely unrelated earthworks. See Chapter 7, below, for detailed commentary on these zones of the frontier and on the Dyke in north Herefordshire. See also Chapter 9, below, for discussion of the economic factors relevant to the lower Wye. The 'prediction' concerned the presence of extensive contemporary ironworking on the heights of the hills above the east bank of the river (ibid, 189–90).
182 Gloucestershire: Hoyle and Vallender, 1997. Short-dykes: Hankinson, 2002; Hankinson and Caseldine, 2006.
183 See Bapty, 2000; and online (2003), 'The Final Word on Offa's Dyke' (review of Hill and Worthington, 2003), at http://www.cpat.org.uk/offa/offrev.htm. The very recent (2013) Clwyd-Powys Archaeological Trust investigation of a damaged length of Offa's Dyke at Plas Offa, Chirk, just to the south of the crossing of the Dee, is pertinent here. Dates obtained (early in 2014) from deposits close to the base of the bank are apparently contradictory, but raise the possibility of earlier and later phases in the history of at least this stretch of Dyke.
184 Besides those commentaries noted below, produced by

Squatriti, A. Williams, and Tyler, see for example Nurse (2001), reproduced online at http://www.wansdyke21.org.uk/wansdyke/wanart/nurse1.htm, (accessed 15.12.2010). See also Keith J. Matthews, (2001) 'Wat's Dyke: a North Welsh linear boundary' at http://www.wansdyke21.org.uk/wansdyke/wanart/matthews1.htm, accessed 5.1.2011.
185 Squatriti, 2004.
186 Squatriti, 2002.
187 Discussed in particular in Chapter 9, below.
188 A. Williams, 2009.
189 Tyler, 2011.
190 Ibid. This aspect concerns the Roman imperial connotations of building such a vast frontier edifice: 'The balance of probability is that there were individuals in eighth-century elite circles who were aware of the imperial significance of frontier defences' (ibid, 159).
191 Hayes and Malim, 2008.
192 Malim, 2007. This important new work, and the conclusions that have and can be drawn from it, are considered at greater length in Chapters 5 and 9, below. One of the authors (KR) is particularly grateful to Tim Malim for information about the Gobowen site and (albeit brief) discussion of the implications.

Chapter 3

1 Camden, *Britannia*, Chapter 18, Shropshire. (1588).
2 The history of Mercia is obscure for reasons that will be touched upon at various points in this book, but since the renowned Anglo-Saxon historian Sir Frank Stenton first set out in some detail a Mercian historical narrative, interest in their story has been constant. Stenton set out at some length the course of Mercian history up to the late ninth century in his book contributory to the fourteen-volume *Oxford History of England* (Stenton, 1947, 35–57 and 200–33). For other historical overviews of the Kingdom of the Mercians, see Whitelock, 1979, 16–31; Brooks, 1989; Yorke, 1990, 100–27; Kirby, 1991, 77–141 and 163–209; Gelling, 1989a, 1992.
3 'Mercia' was rarely referred to as such by the Mercian kings. The charters of Offa, for instance, term him 'Rex Merciorum', king *of the Mercians*. This reflects a more general Anglo-Saxon tendency to think in terms of 'the folk', rather than of a bounded territory, and was also true of the West Saxons for example.
4 'Mercii' is the Latin word used without variance by the Northumbrian monk Bede and others to describe the Mercians, and in sources in the vernacular they are referred to as 'Mierce', the borderers. See below for discussion of how the use of this term has been and can be used to locate them geographically, and how its resonances probably changed in the period from 600 to 800 AD.
5 See Chapter 8, below, for discussion of this and parallel terms expressive of Mercian dominance of the Anglo-Saxon world in the eighth and early ninth centuries.
6 The career of Offa has inevitably been a primary focus for such re-appraisal as has so far occurred. See especially, Kirby, 1991, 163–79; Keynes, 2005. Our response to this re-appraisal permeates the arguments developed in Chapter 8, below, and is set out most directly in the Epilogue that follows Chapter 9.
7 This interpretation, based upon the idea that succession in a number of Anglo-Saxon kingdoms was indicated by the alliteration of the first letters of proper names, was first proposed by David Dumville (1977, 98) and has been promoted by Wormald (1982, 128, 138), Yorke (1990, 118–20), and Kirby (1991, 194), among others.
8 See Yorke, 1990, 118–23; Keynes, 2001a. Keynes in particular has questioned the existence of such a 'dynastic' pattern of succession, plausibly preferring instead the idea of an elite of leading Mercian families, from whose membership successive kings were severally drawn (ibid, 314–23).
9 This also has implications for how Offa's Dyke should be viewed historically. Such campaigning certainly demonstrates continuing military capacity and vigour, although the reasons for the campaigns, as we shall note especially in Chapter 9, below, appears to have had more to do with suppressing Welsh raiding and the public demonstration of martial capacity, than territorial acquisition.
10 Aethelflaed, the 'Lady of the Mercians', the daughter of Alfred of Wessex, became the wife of Aethelred, who ruled Mercia in succession to Ceolwulf II from 879 to his death in 911. Aethelred accepted the overlordship of Alfred from *c*.882 and jointly he and Aethelflaed accepted the over-rule of Edward the Elder after Alfred's death in 899. Aethelred campaigned independently against the kings of south Wales, was entrusted with control of London by Alfred in 886, and with Aethelflaed recovered much of Mercia hitherto lost to the Danes (see Keynes, 2001a).
11 For the zenith of Mercian power under Aethelbald, Offa and Coenwulf see Wormald, 1982; Kirby op. cit, 129–36 and 163–95; and Keynes, 2005.
12 See 'Uoden de cuius stripe: the role of Woden in royal genealogy', 111–32 in North, 1997, for an account of how by time of the late eighth century Anglian regnal lists, Woden had been assimilated into a scriptural view of kingly ancestry. On the politics of 'Woden descent', see John, 1996, 55–7.

13 On the location of 'Anglia', see Chapter 1, note 36. See also, Kirby, 1991, 12–14.

14 The reasons for this lack of documentation have long been debated. Recent consensus (John, 1996, 14; Keynes, 2005, 19) has it that the documents that we might expect to have survived in fact never existed. In the following passages we have drawn extensively upon Nicholas Brooks' carefully marshalled and closely argued introduction to the uncertainties and conundrums of early Mercian history (Brooks, 1989). This latter account acknowledges the debt owed to Sir Frank Stenton (1947, 38–42) for first defining the lineaments of the problem of Mercian origins. Brooks also noted the potential contribution to such studies of Wendy Davies' (1977) analysis of early Welsh annals for the light they may shed on aspects of the 'earliest' Mercian history. Some useful insights have also been provided by Barbara Yorke (2001), especially concerning the earliest Mercian kings.

15 The exception proves the rule here: for only a brief period from 903 to 924, there is a version of the *Anglo-Saxon Chronicle* known as the 'Mercian Register' that adds some details to the main Chronicle (Whitelock, EHD, 1979, 208–18).

16 The *Tribal Hidage* and its historical context have also been much debated. Its significance to the borderlands is explored in Chapter 6, below. 'Inner' Mercia here refers to what the Tribal Hidage describes as 'the first Mercia', an area that excluded for instance the Middle Angles to the south-east, or the western peoples including the Hwicce focused upon Gloucestershire and Worcestershire.

17 As noted below, the most obvious juncture for this would have been when the Northumbrians under their king Oswiu defeated Penda in the period immediately after 656. See Brooks, 1989, 167–8.

18 Stenton, 1947, 40. See also, Pelteret (2010, 35–6) on the location of Tamworth in relation to the Tame and Trent.

19 Bede, HE, III, 24 (McClure and Collins, 1994, 152). Despite its inevitable biases, Northumbrian and Christian, and its long apocryphal asides, Bede's *The Ecclesiastical History of the English People* written in 731 remains the only narrative source not only for Northumbrian events and the actions and motivations of its individual leaders and churchmen, but also for the impact of their neighbours, including the Mercians, on Northumbrian affairs in the hundred years before its compilation in 731.

20 There is a well-established series of early Anglo-Saxon cemeteries along the Trent valley, and these include those at Catholme in the Trent valley, and at Elford Hall to the south-east of its confluence with the Tame. Moreover, very recently beneath Lichfield itself, late Roman or sub-Roman period houses have been found that were cut through by the construction of sunken-floored buildings of likely late fifth-century or early sixth-century date (S. Dean, pers. comm.). See also, Welch, 2001.

21 Stenton, ibid; Brooks, 1989, 160. The reference is from the *Historia* II, 12, rendered in modern translation as 'Not giving him (i.e. Aethelfrith) time to summon and assemble his whole army, Raedwald met him with a much greater force and slew him on the Mercian border on the east bank of the river Idle' (McClure and Collins, 1994, 94; they identify the site of the battle as in the vicinity of Bawtry).

22 Although if this was the case, it was a name that the Mercians were soon using to refer to themselves.

23 Mann, 1998. These new provinces were: *Britannia Prima* (known to have been based upon Cirencester), *Britannia Secunda*, *Flavia Caesariensis*, and *Maxima Caesariensis* (known to have been based upon London).

24 Ekwall, 1960, 297; Greenslade, 1990, 4, proposed that a Welsh *luitcoit* ('grey wood') element derived from *Letocetum* was added to form a compound word with the Old English element *–feld*, ('common pasture'), 'Lichfield'. The suggestion was made that both names refer to a wooded district, and 'it may well be that in the seventh century the name Lichfield was used for an extensive area and only later came to be restricted to the cathedral and its environs.'

25 Greenslade (op. cit.); Round, 1992; Webster, 1994; White, 2007, 68, 72, 87.

26 White, 2007, 197–201.

27 This may be reflected also in the Welsh reference to the Mercians as 'Lloegrwys' or people of the border, although this may also have been used generically of the English at an early date: see Dumville, 1993, 8.

28 Gareth Williams (2010) has come to a precisely similar conclusion, noting that the walls of Wall remained visible through to the eighteenth century, and expressing surprise that it has taken the discovery of the Staffordshire Hoard for historians and archaeologists to realise this likelihood.

29 The idea that he was simply using a different calculus seems unlikely given that Bede was writing in the early to mid-eighth century, and was consciously referring to an era a hundred years earlier. Bede's perspective need not have been entirely 'political', however. Rather, it may reflect genuine uncertainty. So, for instance, he may himself have been skeptical of the total hidage given in the documents available to him because he says of the kingdom of 'Southern Mercia' that 'it was said to consist of 5,000 hides', in contrast to his comment on Northern Mercia, 'which is 7,000 hides in extent' (Bede, HE, III, 24: McClure and Collins, 1994, 152).

30 The relevance of the discussion of the name of the Mercians to the subject-matter of this book should be

obvious, and is a matter that we shall return to more than once: including at the end of this chapter.

31 The 'shiring' of these areas was a later development, a product of the developing English realm forged through an alliance between Wessex and Mercia under the leadership of the kings of Wessex in the late ninth and early tenth centuries. The northern part of Elmet is thought to have been annexed by the Deirans under Edwin at around the same time as the Mercians took control of the south, between c.620 and 650 (Kirby, 1991, 72, 77).

32 Succinct and useful summaries of the likely origins of the *Hwicce* and the *Gewisse* are provided in Sims-Williams, 1990, 29–39, and in Blair, 1994, 35–41, respectively.

33 Such an account skates over considerable swathes of territory and history, better documented elsewhere. See in particular, Gelling, 1989a and 1992, Dumville, 1989, and Sims-Williams, 1990. The 'indeterminate folk' include the 'western Hecani', the 'Westerna', and the 'Magonsaetan'. These peoples will be discussed at greater length in Chapter 7, below.

34 The particular Mercian concern with Kent and East Anglia, and the extraordinary strife involved as a result of their attempt to control and then subsume these kingdoms had much to do with international trade and their close proximity to the continent. However, it also reflected Mercian awareness of the historical situation of these kingdoms at the forefront of Anglo-Saxon settlement, leadership and Christianity. See Chapter 8 for further discussion of this dimension of the politics of hegemony in the late eighth and early ninth centuries.

35 Kirby, 1991, 82.

36 "At first sight Bede seems a simple monk who never held important office. But his *History* was commissioned by the Northumbrian king and he was freely given information from all over England as well as from the papal archives. He shows intimate familiarity with the world of high politics – especially as regards what it was expedient to ignore." (John, 1996, 51). John perhaps had in mind here, especially, the way in which Bede downplayed the contribution of the Mercian kings to the moulding the history of the Anglo-Saxons in the hundred years preceding the time of writing.

37 Brooks suggests (1989, 163–4) that the co-distribution of these possibly Penda-linked names may configure with those in the same areas with possible Creoda- and Pybba-linked names, indicating the likelihood that the earlier documented Mercian kingly lineage derived from this area also. See also, G. Jones, 1998.

38 Brooks, 1989, 167.

39 The northern part of Northumbria, the kingdom of Bernicia, never entered into an alliance with the Mercians.

40 Or, it could have been to emulate his illustrious predecessor Aethelfrith, whose own motivations for an attack on Chester c.616 may have included a wish to protect Anglians who were then settling in Lancashire, or even 'to bring an emerging independent Anglian principality beyond the Pennines under (his) authority' (Kirby, 1991, 72). See also, Higham, 1993a.

41 Despite alternative more northerly locations having been proposed, recent research has confirmed the likelihood that the site was near Oswestry. See Stancliffe, 1995; cited in Charles-Edwards, 2001, 93.

42 Bede, HE, III, 9 dates *Maserfelth* to 5th August in the 38th year of Oswald's reign (McClure and Collins, 1994, 119, 124). If Eowa and Penda fought in that battle on opposite sides, it would have seen 'Christian' Mercians fighting 'pagan' Mercians, with the latter prevailing. Gelling, 1992, 72–9, strongly questioned the traditional location of *Maserfelth* that far south, basing her arguments on doubts regarding the relevant place-name. However, the similarity between *Maserfelth* and names such as Maesbury and Maesbrook in the area to the east of Oswestry has more complex resonances in relation to both the later western frontier and Offa himself, and these will be explored in Chapters 7 and 9, below.

43 This is particularly significant because Oswald had previously married Cenwalh's sister. This inter-relation also serves to highlight how Wessex was perceived to be a key player in Anglo-Saxon inter-kingdom politics as early as the mid-seventh century.

44 Brooks, 1989, 167. Bede, HE, III, 6, and III, 16, terms Bamburgh 'the royal city' of the Bernicians, and suggests in the latter chapter that although Penda attacked Bamburgh, he did not destroy it (McClure and Collins, 1994, 119, 135). The battle in which Penda defeated the East Anglians has – on account of the date and likely place of manufacture of key datable items and the apparent stripping of military fittings – been one of the contexts suggested for the gathering together of the items in the 'Staffordshire Hoard' discovered near Lichfield in July 2009 (although in Penda's reign an equally plausible event was his attack on East Anglia in 654). This is discussed further in Chapter 8, below, with an alternative interpretive scheme for the composition of the 'hoard' as a group.

45 Kirby, 1991, 51.

46 For more on this question, see Tyler, 2005, and the discussion of the meaning of hegemony in reference to the 'Mercian supremacy' at the beginning of Chapter 8, below.

47 Bede at various points described 'the heathen Penda' in disparaging terms, but in the chapter he devoted to

48 Finberg, 1964, 68.
49 See especially, Davies, 1992, 99–102, for discussion of the relevant issues. This notion of mid-seventh-century settlement of the Shropshire plain is borne out by the discovery (in 2015) of a 'sunken-floored building' south-east of Shrewsbury (A. Wigley, pers comm.).
50 Higham, 1993, 142–4. Feryock, 2001, 181, 183.
51 As was briefly discussed in Chapter 1, above.
52 The earliest name of this people is uncertain, but later appears to have been the Magonsaetan. See Chapter 7, below, for a discussion of the peoples of the frontier.
53 Ray, 2015, 207–12, provides a review of the evidence.
54 See Sims-Williams, 1990, 47–51 for a discussion of Merewalh (also, Pretty, 1982 and Gelling, 1992, 81–3). See Chapter 7, below, for discussion of the relevance of Merewalh and the Magonsaetan to the eighth-century frontier in Herefordshire. The complexities of Magonsaetan and Hwiccian origins are also discussed at length in Sims-Williams, op. cit.
55 Oswiu thereby in effect appropriated the northern part of the Mercian kingdom, temporarily bringing the boundary between Northumbrian and Mercian spheres of control southwards to the Trent in its middle reaches.
56 This was certainly the impression that Bede (HE II.xxi) wanted to give.
57 Bede, HE, IV, 3 (McClure and Collins, 1994, 174).
58 We are grateful to Professor John Hines for this insight, and for pointing out that the question of when and how 'Middlesex' came be to identified as such remains an open one.
59 It seems likely that Wulfhere led a campaign through Berkshire as far south as the Solent and the Isle of Wight in the period around 670 (see Kirby, 1991, 115–16, in which he attempts to reconcile the relevant *Anglo-Saxon Chronicle* entry with Bede's account).
60 Bede, HE, IV, 21 (McClure and Collins, 1994, 207).
61 Stenton wrote "The reign of Aethelred…is more important in ecclesiastical than in political history" (1947, 201–2), a view seemingly coloured by Aethelred's abdication in 704 to retreat to the monastery of Bardney in Lindsey.
62 See Kirby, 1991, 126–7.
63 ASC A and E; This status of Somerton, located in south Somerset, is uncertain. It is said to have been the most important centre of the western part of the West Saxon kingdom beyond Selwood, as opposed to an eastern centre at Winchester.
64 Stenton, 1947, 203. The early history of Abingdon is complex, and still somewhat uncertain: see for example Blair, 1994, 64–5.
65 This has inevitably attracted a considerable amount of comment: see for instance, Brooks, 1971; Williams, 2005, 300–1. It is a matter we return to in Chapter 6, below.
66 Fox, 1955, 272–5.
67 For design and build of Offa's Dyke see especially Chapter 5 below.
68 Kirby, 1991, 135.
69 The events of this short period of chaos in the governance of Mercia were described in an unusually full entry preserved in a 'continued' version of Bede's *Ecclesiastical History*, of probable ninth-century origin, thus: '757. Aethelbald, king of the Mercians, was treacherously killed at night by his bodyguard in shocking fashion; Beornred came to the throne…in the same year Offa put Beornred to flight and attempted to conquer the Mercian kingdom with sword and bloodshed' (McClure and Collins, 1994, 297).
70 Stenton, 1947, 205. Kirby's chapter on Offa (1991, 163–79), remains the most balanced assessment of his reign yet written, anticipating as it does more recent reviews that suggest that Stenton's judgement of Offa's power and influence was overblown, especially in respect to Charlemagne.
71 Simeon of Durham, writing in 1104–1108 recorded this event from a version of the ASC now lost (Whitelock, EHD, 1979, 268).
72 Whitelock, EHD, 1979, 179: ASC 779. The significance of this is that Benson was a royal vill that was the centre of the largest royal estate in the middle Thames valley; as such it had probably been the principal Hwiccian royal centre, a likelihood underlined by its proximity to Dorchester-on-Thames, the site of the first bishopric in the region (cf. Blair, 1994, 39).
73 See below, this chapter; but for more detail on these other means of achieving and maintaining Mercian dominance, see especially Chapter 8.
74 Story, 2003, 169.
75 For the bald record of the event, ASC 794: Whitelock, EHD, 1979, 181. The sources concerned are the hagiographical works connected with the cult of St Aethelbert: see for example, Keynes, 2000.
76 This late eighth-century Mercian strategy of dynastic alliance is discussed further in Chapter 8, below
77 This aspect also is dealt with at greater length in Chapter 8.
78 This could be seen as a cynical move intended simply to ensure that Ecgfrith was anointed by a metropolitan authority, but there is some reason to believe that it also represented both an attempt at reform to better integrate the existing Mercian bishoprics, and to provide a more

substantial platform for sustaining Mercian dominance. In practice, it served to achieve all of these things, and may also have been envisaged as a means to bring all the Anglian peoples south of the Humber, including those of Lindsey and East Anglia, more firmly within the Mercian fold (Cf. Kirby, 1991, 173–4).
79 Kirby, 1991, 170.
80 This view has been contested in recent years. Catherine Cubitt (1995, 153ff) has for instance made a strong case that the visit was more concerned with securing a return to order in the Northumbrian court and church than with Mercia. Joanna Story (2003) has moreover emphasised the degree of Carolingian involvement and control involved through Bishop George of Ostia, who was at the Frankish court before travelling to England.
81 G. Williams, 2001a.
82 See Chapter 8, below, for further articulation of aspects of the role of coinage in both the economic and political strategy of Offa and Coenwulf.
83 Or, perhaps more accurately, 'should be beyond dispute': there is a revisionism regarding Offa and the Mercian kingdom at its apogee, that suggests that it was practically devoid of the literary apparatus of statehood (see for instance, Keynes, 2005). The cultural dimension in terms of sculpture, architecture and so on is dealt with in Chapter 8, below; the question of the character of the Mercian state, and of Offa himself, historically, is addressed in the Epilogue.
84 Story, 2003, 184–8. 'If Offa thought that he could attempt 'to deal on equal terms' with Charlemagne, therefore, he was mistaken, and the likelihood is that the Frankish court had come to see his ascendancy in southern England with misgivings, destroying as it had done the traditional shape of political power in the south-east' (Kirby, 1991, 176). For further discussion of the circumstances of the marriage negotiations, if such they were, see Chapter 8.
85 We follow Kirby in referring to Ecgfrith's successor and Offa's inheritor as 'Coenwulf', rather than 'Cenwulf' (cf both Stenton, 1947 and Keynes, 2005a) for the simple reason that this is how his name appears on his coins.
86 Letter of Alcuin to the Mercian ealdorman 'Osbert' (Whitelock, EHD, 1979, 855: No. 202). The full text goes on to say: 'For you know how much blood his father shed to secure the kingdom upon his son. This was not the strengthening of the kingdom, but its ruin.'
87 In other words that the 'vengeance' concerned could have been a divine one. There is some circumstantial evidence for the possibility that this death was not also due to an act of regicide, albeit that it derives from a corrupt medieval source: '(Offa's) son Egbert (Ecgfrith) succeeded to the glories of his rule; but, after having reigned one hundred and forty-one days, he was seized with a malady and departed this life' (*Chronicle of Crowland Abbey*, edited by Henry T. Riley, 1854, 12).
88 S151, granted at Chelsea, regarding land transferred to St Albans Abbey at 'Pinnelesfeld' (near Rickmansworth, Hertfordshire); a charter widely thought to be spurious in its present form, but containing some accurate information. See Cubitt, 1995, 275–6.
89 Fox (1955, 287) appeared to believe that this meant that Offa had died at or near Rhuddlan.
90 We know of this overture through the text of a letter of reply from Pope Leo in 798 (Whitelock, EHD, 1979, 861–2, N. 205). Leo also reprimanded Aethelweard for his dereliction of his post, and requested that Coenwulf should sustain the annual gift of 365 gold *mancus* (heavy coin) to the papacy from the Mercian kingdom for the benefit of the poor, that he claimed Offa had announced publicly at one of the Councils of 786.
91 ASC 798: Whitelock, EHD, 1979, 182: No. 1. The wording given here is that of the 'A' version of the Chronicle, thought to have been compiled at the Old Minster, Winchester. The 'F' version, a late composite assembled at Canterbury in the late eleventh or early twelfth century from various earlier versions and other sources available locally, added more detail: including that the Mercians had Praen's eyes put out and his hands cut off (Whitelock, EHD, 1979, 109–16, 182). Other sources indicate that he was then imprisoned at Winchcombe, in the lands of the Hwicce (see below).
92 ASC 802 (Whitelock, EHD, 1979, 1, 183). Kempsford is on the Thames, and this entry provides a clear idea where the northernmost point of the border of Wessex with Mercia lay at that time.
93 Quotations are again from ASC 802 (Whitelock, EHD, 1979, 183: No. 1). The significance of ealdormen leading 'regional' forces in campaigns is returned to in Chapter 6, below.
94 On Winchcombe, see Bassett, 1985, and Blair, 2005, 277–8. Recently, Bassett (2008, 213–26) has argued that the 'Period 1' defences at Winchcombe were secular in nature, rather than forming part of an ecclesiastical precinct, and that the balance of probabilities indicates that 'the first-stage defences found at Hereford, Tamworth and Winchcombe belong to the Mercian kings' overlordship in England' (ibid, 232), even though as yet there is no firm archaeological dating evidence for the earliest phases of development from any of these places. The reign of Coenwulf would be an appropriate juncture for such a move, since it is likely that it was in the ninth century, rather than earlier, that more permanent centres for the Mercian court were developing.
95 Once again, see Chapter 8 for further details.

96 See further discussion in reference to Coenwulf and the northern sector of the frontier in Chapter 9.
97 Finberg, 1964.

Chapter 4

1. C. H. Hartshorne, 1841, 184.
2. Ibid, 183.
3. Ibid, 184–5; 187–92.
4. As we observed in Chapter 2, the conclusion of the 'North-West Shropshire' report (Fox, 1928; Fox, 1955, Chapter IV), for example, comprises a number of text sections that summarise his evolving view of the relationship of the location and form of the Dyke to the challenges presented by topography, and that express his growing conviction that there was a design unity that was a deliberate product of 'one mind'.
5. This was no doubt due to his decision, presumably in the early 1950s, to create the unifying monograph by, in essence, reproducing the original reports in series, with minimal editing.
6. Fox and Phillips, 1929; Fox, 1955, 120. See the discussion of alignments, this chapter, below. Arguably, it was Fox's 'revelation' that alignments and the nature of the courses that the Dyke followed could be analysed to 'reconstruct' the eighth-century landscape it traversed, and his conviction that the line was negotiated, that prevented him from placing at centre-stage instead, the full implications of its placement in the landscape in terms of Mercian strategic advantage.
7. Noble, 1983; Hill and Worthington, 2003.
8. Fox, 1932. Scott-Fox, 2002, 122–5. This essay built upon Fox's earlier work with distribution maps to suggest the impact on cultural developments in prehistory of the existence of a broadly Upland and a generalised Lowland Zone within the British Isles.
9. As with his views on the productive capacity of the land and the existence of heavily forested areas on the frontier, the only 'evidence' Fox adduced for the reality of this 'natural divide' was the climatic maps and artefact distributions cited in his 'Personality of Britain' publication (Fox, 1932).
10. Fox, 1995, 286–7.
11. Ibid, 292.
12. As noted in Chapter 2, this is asserted, variously, in Hill, 2000; Hill, 2001; Worthington, 2005; Hill and Worthington, 2003.
13. The question of the character and identity of late eighth- and early ninth-century communities on either side of the frontier is discussed at greater length in Chapter 7, below; as is the idea that the frontier peoples both east and west of the Dyke were an amalgam of British and Mercian communities.
14. Fox regarded this consistency of line as an aspect of alignment, 'the plan and general layout in respect to the main features of the landscape' (1955, 278), and he noted stretches where deviation was notably slight, for instance 'in the Wrexham-Oswestry district, where the major alignments are 8, 7½, and 12 miles long, with maximal deviations from a dead-straight line of only 280, 300, and 750 yards respectively' (ibid). What this indicates about the way that the Dyke was built is discussed further in Chapter 6, below.
15. Fox, 1955, 80.
16. This introduces a distinction between Offa's Dyke, which existed as a particular *structure*, or linked series thereof, and more broadly the *boundary* of the Mercian kingdom, followed by either Dyke or river, or, for some, 'woodland' (in Fox's terms, 'dense woodland', in Noble's, a 'cleared ride'). This distinction was clearly made by some of the earlier writers such as Hartshorne (1841, 187: 'Offa's boundary commenced with the mouth of the Wye …'). We think that the more important distinction to be made, however, is between the frontier as a zone, and the Dyke as a spinal feature thereof: see Chapters 7 and 9 for a fuller exposition.
17. A projection of the '3 degrees 5 minutes' line southwards would easily have produced an alignment onto Hay Bluff, a course along the crest of the eastern scarp of the Black Mountains (following the course of the present-day Offa's Dyke Path), and a descent to the Usk Valley and the Bristol Channel. However, this would have involved the impracticalities of a Dyke reaching 2300′ above sea-level across upland mires (as opposed to a maximum of 1400′ on Llanfair Hill), and the political 'mountain' of achieving annexation of the Kingdom of Gwent. A 'displacement' eastwards was, nonetheless, according to the Welsh chronicle first recorded in the thirteenth century and known as the *Brut y Twysogion*, achieved by the incursions into Mercia of the armed forces of Gwent and Morgannwg (Glamorgan) in 784. This, it was claimed, prompted a rebuilding of the Dyke eastwards from an original course, involving leveling of an earthwork marking an earlier course of 'Offa's Dyke', and leaving a British territory ruled over by 'Elystan Glodrydd' and his descendants, 'between the Wye and the Severn' in the area of later Maleinydd (See Chapter 7).
18. The Dyke changed its orientation only once in this stretch down to the Wye at Bridge Sollers, to take up again a strictly north–south routing for just under a mile and a half (2.4 km) at Moorhampton in the valley of the Maddle Brook west of Hereford. The siting onto Ladylift Clump was noted above in Chapter 1, but also by Fox:

19. 'the straight stretch of Dyke across the Curl Brook, 800 yards long, is aligned on the crest of the southern spur of Burton Hill (Ladylift Clump), 933 ft. above O.D., which is immediately above Claypits, where the Dyke begins again' (1955, 209).
20. The Ordnance Survey revision of 1906–8 marked a 'course of' Offa's Dyke along a mile-long stretch continuing the line of 'Main Ditch' north of Buttington towards Trewern Hall, but Fox (1955, 89) rejected earthworks in this area as flood-banks or hedge-banks. Noble challenged such a view (1983, 89–91) citing medieval boundary disputes that he nonetheless conceded made no mention of the existence of Offa's Dyke in the Trewern area. Since then, Hill and Worthington (2003, 65–8) have undertaken three excavations close to the riverbank at Buttington without locating the Dyke positively. As a result 'We can now be reasonably sure that the Dyke did not cross the Severn at Buttington but continued on the east bank', although they were unable to trace it in the one trench they dug within the area, at Old Mills moat north of Trewern (ibid, 68–9). As noted below, however, the trend of alignments of the Dyke from well to the south indicates that the intention must have been to bring the Dyke to the south bank of the Severn at Buttington, or to have commenced its southwards course there.
21. Described in detail by Fox as a series running from north to south from Llanymynech village to the Severn (1955, 86–9).
22. A more direct line southwards from the chosen point of crossing of the river Vyrnwy would have brought the Dyke even closer to the strict north–south orientation. However, this would have necessitated crossing a longer stretch of unstable floodplain ground, and would have failed to close the topographic gap noted here, directly across the river from The Breiddin mountain. The slight displacement eastwards from an exact north–south line was, however, in effect 'made good' by the trend of the river itself, and that line was picked up at precisely the 'right' point of the southern bank of the Severn, at Buttington.
23. Literally, 'Offa's Rock'. The tiny parish of the same name occupies all the ground between the eminence of Llanymynech Hill/Asterley Rocks and the Tanat/Vyrnwy confluence. It was in this area (perhaps at Carreghofa Hall) that the medieval Carreghofa castle once stood, and there are clues from other place-names locally, that another boundary work may once traversed the lower ground here (see Chapter 9).
24. See below (pp. 133–5) for closer discussion of the Vale of Montgomery alignments and Chapter 5 for detail concerning build practices deployed in this location. See also, views towards the Dyke at Gwarthlow (Figure 4.21 below).
24. Although it should be noted that Fox (1955, 120) did not recognize this as an individual alignment at all. It ought to have been classed as his 'Type II' (below), but he presumably regarded its ends as not inter-visible.
25. And as such are discussed in terms of their identifiable presence in many places along the Dyke, in Chapter 5.
26. Fox, 1955, 118–23. Types I, IA, II, and III.
27. Fox's assumption appearing to be that the Dyke was laid out from one direction only, and not both, which seems somewhat odd.
28. Fox, 1955, 119.
29. Ibid.
30. Fox discussed only his first type of alignment, and its variant, in the subsequent report (and chapter) on South Shropshire and East Radnorshire, where nonetheless, in the hilly terrain, the 'demonstrably straight' sections are fewer in number and shorter in span. Ibid, 151–3.
31. Ibid, 121.
32. Fox, 1955, Figure 52.
33. The detail of alignment as reflected in the build of the Dyke in the Vale of Montgomery is discussed further in Chapter 5, below (pp. 194–8).
34. It is important to note that the achievement of the perpendicular crossing of the Camlad was a contributory factor in the choice of the particular location for the turn at Hem, but not necessarily the determining one. The importance of the site for its prominence and surveillance capacity is discussed in Chapter 7, below (pp. 278–9).
35. Fox, 1955, 141–6; 169; 218ff. See Chapter 5 for a detailed discussion of contrasting build forms.
36. The Welsh annals indicated the fighting of a battle 'at Hereford' in (or around) AD 760. This is discussed further in Chapter 7, below (pp. 273–4).
37. Again, see Chapter 7 (p. 277), below, for a discussion of the particular dominance involved (and Chapter 6 for the discussion of the angled turn on Llanymynech Hill here: p. 237, below).
38. As noted previously, while the Dyke does not cross the Wye after descending from Garnons Hill to the west of Hereford, the approach that the earthwork makes to the river is also on a tangent to it such that it overlooks the river and its flood-plain from the north-east over a two-mile course.
39. See Chapter 6 (p. 248, below) for further discussion of the likely surveillance role of such placement, and its relation to other features at Yew Tree Farm and at Bwlch, Discoed.
40. And here, the cleft was too narrow and deep to have ever permitted serious passage along its course.
41. This reflects some particular circumstances relating to the Presteigne area discussed further in Chapter 7.
42. See Malim, 2007, 27–8. The potential 'economic'

43. See, for instance, Fox 1955, 81–3; 279–81.
44. Hill and Worthington, 2003, 119.
45. Fox, 1955, 118.
46. Ibid.
47. Ibid, 94.
48. This aspect is considered in particular in Chapter 6, below.
49. See Fox, 1955, Plate VIIa, for his dramatic 1927 panoramic photographs of this length of Dyke before it became entirely obscured by mature oak trees, already in evidence in Plate VIIIb.
50. These occurrences are in the bottom of the valley descending westwards from Hewelsfield, and on the north-facing slopes rising towards Madgett Hill. See for example, profile 16370/1/10, Hoyle and Vallender, 1997, Fig 6iv.
51. Interestingly, both the stretch of the Dyke south from Buttington, and the stretch overlooking the Walton Basin, involve the making of subtle adjustments using short connecting straight lengths placed between longer straight stretches. This is a manoeuvre that enables an overall direct alignment to be maintained, adjusted for topography. It also just happens to maximise the visual impact of the monument within the landscape (see Chapter 5 discussion of alignments, for more detail).
52. For the 'angled turns', see Chapter 6, below
53. View-shed analysis involves the factoring in of elevation and topography to establish what can be seen from given vantage-points, usually after the virtual removal of obscuring vegetation. Light detection and ranging (LiDAR) is a method of airborne scanning that maps differences in elevation minutely. The manipulation of artificial shadow then enables the highlighting of subtle ground-surface variation, and, from an archaeological perspective, the pinpointing of characteristics of earthworks.
54. It is for this reason that, despite the occasional use of aerial photographs in this volume, most images used in illustration of points made here are views of the Dyke at or near ground-level. Comprehensive use of view-shed and LiDAR mapping would greatly enhance our record and understanding of the earthwork, but at present are beyond the resources of any study such as our own. Any future study such as that undertaken by the Gloucestershire County Council archaeologists in 1995 would need to integrate such mapping with field-based investigation.
55. The composite Welsh–English name is intriguing. The –low element suggests that an early burial (?prehistoric) mound may have surmounted the knoll, and this could have been a useful beacon or look-out location both during and after the Dyke construction works locally.
56. Hill and Worthington, 2003, 120.
57. Although this is not as simple an exercise as might at first be thought, as we discovered when attempting to apply viewshed analysis to the length of Dyke that traverses Herrock Hill and Rushock Hill in Herefordshire. The main problem encountered was the degree to which the viewers' perspective changes depending upon whether standing in front, behind, or on top of, the earthwork.
58. For a discussion of gates and associated possible look-out points and other 'surveillance' features, see Chapter 6.
59. With these observations we enter the field of politics, and the theme of the frontier that is explored in greater depth in Chapters 7 and 9, below.

Chapter 5

1. Hartsthorne, 1841, 184.
2. There is as yet no definitive published record of the number of excavations carried out on different parts of Offa's Dyke. The interventions recorded on the English Heritage on-line register, *Pastscape*, for example, amount to only 25. The closest approximation to a full list is in the 'gazetteer of sites' published as an appendix within the 'History and Guide' volume (Hill and Worthington, 2003, 181–7). This specifies 56 interventions on or by what the authors refer to as 'Offa's Dyke', from 'Newcastle Hill' (Bwlch, Discoed) in the south to Treuddyn in the north (although some 'sites' feature more than one excavation, as at Nutwood, Edenhope, where 'Site 128' had two interventions: 2003, 57; and at Mainstone nearby where 'Site 98' also comprised two cuts partially across the line of the earthwork: ibid, 56). Adding the interventions they list in Herefordshire and Gloucestershire on the earthworks that Fox included, but that they discounted, as part of the Dyke (but not on the 'Whitford Dyke' in Flintshire) this total increases to 84. The results of 40 of the above interventions between Discoed and Treuddyn were described in the chapter of the 'History and Guide' volume that outlined 'the evidence' for the Dyke. Curiously, although 7 excavations were detailed in north Herefordshire, none of these were located across (or even close to) earthworks that have in the past been claimed to be part of Offa's Dyke, except across the Rowe Ditch and at Garnons Hill. Equally, 12 excavations are listed as having been carried out in Gloucestershire, 8 of which were at Sedbury, but no details were provided about what was found at the other 4.
3. Fox, 1955, 81. See Chapter 6, below, for a detailed evaluation of methods of construction.

4   Ibid, 218.
5   Fox took the unusual step of illustrating the differences here not only by two drawn profiles less than 50 metres apart, but also by first including a sketch plan showing both the location of the two profiles relative to one another and then also the plan form of the two kinds of Dyke build (Ibid, 156: Figure 66).
6   Fox, 1955, 160. The reasoning for the interpretive linkages that Fox made between the form of the Dyke and the nature of the landscape in the eighth century is discussed further at the beginning of Chapter 7.
7   Although Fox himself chose not to see the contrasts as arising from substantial differences in date of construction, but rather to contrasts in the importance of different routes and the presence of vulnerable Mercian farming communities: Fox, 1955, 160.
8   Ibid, 200.
9   The question of how design and build may have been organised is discussed in Chapter 6, below.
10 This approximates most closely what Fox termed the 'normal' form.
11 Now, unfortunately, partly bulldozed and spread, or largely obscured by a hedge-bank.
12 Fox, 1955, 218–21. Close inspection of the latter two locations indicates considerable variability in the proportions of the build at different points, however, and that the course across Rushock Hill is much eroded, in part due to stone-robbing for nearby field-walls.
13 The interleaving of *substantial* and *scarp* modes is evident, for example, at Lord's Grove, Welsh Bicknor, at Wyegate Wood, and at Lower Meend. Moreover, the *slighter* mode is very evident across St Briavels Common and, where it is observable, along the cliffs from Wintour's Leap to Tutshill opposite Chepstow. See below for more detailed discussion of the build of the Dyke in Gloucestershire as recorded in the recent major survey project by the County Council's archaeology service.
14 This is the only study so far completed that has carefully documented the spatial incidence of different build forms (Hoyle and Vallender, 1997, Figs 4 A–D). The 'reduced' form of the earthwork across St Briavels Common no doubt reflects both geology and subsequent land-use, but may always have conformed to the *slight* mode of construction (Ibid, 38; Form 2 and Type B in the Hoyle/Vallender classification). Meanwhile, the Beachley peninsula length was confirmed as built in the *substantial*, and in the eastern half in the *monumental*, mode (Ibid, 37: also profiles, Fig. 6i). The stretch of Dyke located on the edge of the limestone scarp overlooking Tintern between Madgett Hill in the north and East Vaga/Dennell Hill in the south is either of *scarp* mode or *substantial* mode, or (as at the Devil's Pulpit and Lippetts Grove) a hybrid of the two (Ibid, 36; mostly Form 1 and Type A in the Hoyle/Vallender classification: see below, note 88). Indeed, at these locations the linear earthwork approximates closely the *monumental* mode. From Wyegate north to Highbury near Redbrook, the *substantial* mode predominates, with the *scarp* mode evident on some of the steeper slopes (again, mostly Form 1 and Type A in the Hoyle/Vallender classification). The hybrid character of the Dyke in Gloucestershire, and the nature of this mixing, was explicitly recognised in sections of the report, specifying 'Variability within and between the forms' and 'Change in form between contiguous portions of the monument' (Hoyle and Vallender, 1995, 24–5).
15 Indeed, this form Fox also termed, when he was summing up the Teme-Lugg stretch of the Dyke, the 'Cwmsanahan type with E. ditch, and mostly subnormal in size.' (1955: 144).
16 Fox, 1955, 156. However, he also noted how there was a small eastwards ditch behind the massive bank at Jenkins Allis. Moreover, further south at Jenkins Allis, the substantial west-facing bank has clearly been filled in at several points, indicating that the lack of a western ditch in the 'boundary bank' section to the north may be an artefact of more recent land use.
17 At Cwmsanahan Hill this artificially steeped scarp appears also to feature a ditch at its base (Figure 6.12).
18 See below for details of the build at Esclusham as revealed by this excavation (p. 181; Figure 5.13).
19 Fox, 1955, 103; Fig. 43, Fig. 45 ii; Plate XXI.
20 See the discussion of entrance-ways/gates in Chapter 6, below (pp. 228–34).
21 For the prehistoric dimension, recent work by Clwyd-Powys Archaeological Trust at Ysceifiog: W. Britnell, pers comm., November 2010. For the medieval interpretation, see Worthington, 2005, 91.
22 As in the case of two separate recording events at Chirk Castle, one of which involved the machine digging of a narrow oblique slot (see below).
23 Although these were recorded for the majority of substantial lengths, some were located quite close together, while other lengths featured no examples. A remarkable omission, for instance, was the Vyrnwy-Severn interfluve, where it was possible to record bank if not always ditch profiles. Also, no profiles were recorded for any of the Herefordshire lengths.
24 Fox, 1955, 39, 68, 108.
25 Hill and Worthington, 2003, 145.
26 Although there are, as suggested in Chapter 4, several locations where the Dyke is placed in this overtly unfavourable position topographically, it may be that Fox recorded so many profiles both to emphasise that this

27 situation does occur more often than might previously have been realised, but also to support the developing thesis derived from his study of the position of the Iron Age fort at Gardden near Ruabon, that the placement of the Dyke was 'negotiated' (see Appendix 1, below).

27 Hill and Worthington (2003, 123) make the general point that 'the surface evidence for changes in scale of construction can be misleading as the entire earthwork has been subject to different rates of erosion over the centuries'. It is not, however, 'rates' of erosion, but the incidence, cause and impact of erosion that have served to modify the 'as built' form in different ways and places. The degree and impact of erosion needs therefore to be assessed at each location, and where possible 'tested' by closer study, survey and intrusive investigation, rather than summarised through 'blanket' statements made about what can and cannot be deduced throughout the course of the earthwork from surface traces.

28 Fox, 1955, 109: Profile XXXIX.

29 This judgement is inevitably somewhat subjective. It is however made possible not only by the skill and attention to detail of Fox and his colleagues in the measured recording, but also by the foresight to have recorded the trend of the 'pre-Dyke' landscape on the profile itself.

30 It must be acknowledged that the distinctions can be over-emphasised, however, given the variability that is often evident along individual bank lengths. A good example is the two bank sections that were recorded only six metres apart at Ffrith Road, Knighton, one of which might be regarded to have a more symmetrical profile than the other (see below; Allen, 1988).

31 Only three profiles were recorded here, at Caswell Wood, Lippetts Grove, and the Devil's Pulpit (Fox, 1955, Figure 88).

32 In the report the earthwork forms were recorded as comprising a series of different numbered types (Hoyle and Vallender, 1997, 21–24). The figures given here represent, rather, our provisional interpretation of ditch character from the published profiles (Figs 6i to 6viii in Hoyle and Vallender). In our analysis, the remaining 4 profiles could not be assigned.

33 This has important implications for the course of the Dyke through the Old Red Sandstone area that is prevalent throughout much of Herefordshire, north and south of the Wye: even where the bank is present, if now slight, as at Yazor and north of the Wye at Garnons, the ditch is invisible at surface.

34 Such co-existence is evident at the Yew Tree Farm lengths at Discoed. One possibility is that, at least where there is a significant slope along the course of the Dyke (as also with the Yew Tree Farm lengths at Discoed), bank construction in some locations was designed specifically to avoid slippage and slumping, and to stabilise the build as it was made. The idea that construction in bays may have been a common practice will need more careful investigation during any excavations in the future which are carried out on well-preserved parts of the bank. Such excavations will need to involve more than simple cross-sectional excavation trenches. Whether the bays defined by edge-set stones extend right across the bank, or whether there was a central 'spinal' definition of any such bays will also have to await future explorations designed specifically to examine this possible build method. How extensive the deployment of this method may have been it is not yet possible to say: it may for instance have been reserved for steeper lengths of the Dyke, or for those at which, for whatever reason, a more elaborate treatment was deemed appropriate.

35 The only 'linear' excavation of the Dyke appears to have been the curious exercise carried out by Northcote Thomas and his associates near Selattyn Hill, noted in Chapter 2 (Hill and Worthington, 2003, 75).

36 Hill and Worthington, 2003, 101.

37 Fox, 1955, 70: Profile XXIII (Figure 31).

38 These three latter sites are the only ones for which full drawn sections were published in the Hill and Worthington volume (2003: 56, 65, 76). The fact that the ditch at Redwood Lodge is described as being 'the full 2m-deep ditch' in the text (Ibid, 64), when the accompanying drawing clearly shows it to have been close to 3m deep, does not inspire confidence in the reported dimensions for other sections where a drawn section is not reproduced as a figure. Doubts could be raised at Orseddwen as to whether the ditch was fully bottomed in the excavation, or whether the excavated trench extended far enough to have encountered the original ditch. However, since the excavation has not been published even to the extent of showing the exact location of the trench, or any details of the excavated contexts, it is at present impossible to judge the significance of the published, presumed summary, section drawing.

39 Allen, 1988, Site 9.

40 Ibid, 9–10. This relates strongly to a change in slope, and to Fox's record that the earthwork changed character as it rose up towards (or descended from) the north-facing flank of Ffrydd Hill here (1955, 141, and Figure 59).

41 Jones and Brassil, 1990.

42 Hill and Worthington, 2003, 69.

43 Ibid, 73. It is an unfortunate and uncomfortable situation whereby, of the 125 or so excavations listed in Hill and Worthington, 2003, as having been undertaken by those authors and their associates on (or looking for) linear earthworks along or near the postulated line of Offa's Dyke, or establishing the line of Wat's Dyke, not

a single one has, as far as we are aware, been published in any detail and to modern standards. The authors have described their work in particular on Wat's Dyke, proving they say that it is a continuous work almost 18 miles longer than previously thought, as 'a spectacular achievement of fieldwork and excavation'. Sadly, the results of this work have not been made available in such a way as to enable their contemporaries or successors to evaluate (and therefore to appreciate) the achievement.

44 Jones and Owen, 1988.
45 Turner-Flynn *et al.*, 1995.
46 Hill and Worthington, 2003, 85.
47 Lewis, 1963.
48 Ibid, 90, for example, wherein Figure 28 shows part-sections at eight locations where at least the upper deposits of presumed ditch lengths were intercepted.
49 Hill and Worthington, 2003, 122.
50 Rhodes, 1965.
51 For Redwood Lodge, Ibid, 65; figure 23. The primary sequence as shown in Figure 23 appears to comprise context 12 (initial silting), and then 11, 10 and 9. Next, it seems that 11 and 10 were truncated to both east and west sides of the ditch by a cut and thin lenses of (presumed) silt in a narrow band with U-shaped profile (contexts 5 to 8), before a normal pattern of silting resumed (4, 3, 2). At Ffrydd Road (Allen, 1988, 9, and accompanying figure), the first fill appears to be from initial weathering of stones from the face of the bank, and the more gradual silting following stabilisation is represented by at least one turf line. A major collapse of more facing stone occurred halfway through the silting sequence.
52 Hill, 1980, Site 22, p. 40 (bis).
53 Lewis, 1963.
54 Malim and Hayes, 2008, 166–72; 176–7. It should be noted also that the comparison is based upon the Hill and Worthington (2003) generalisations, which we have shown may be misleading.
55 Fox, 1955, 259. It should however be accepted that the deep slot found in the base of a number of sections of the Wat's Dyke ditch is what makes the profile consistent, and consistently deeper, on present evidence.
56 Fox, 1955, 40–4. The comment (Hill and Worthington, 2003, 78) that 'It is interesting that Fox should have chosen a site (to excavate) where the bank and ditch face uphill, an unusual situation along the course of the entire Dyke' is contradicted by the observation that Fox recorded ten locations where the Dyke faces uphill in this way (see pp. 148–9, above).
57 Fox, 1955, 40–4. 'The top of this hole, which was 1 ft. 8 in. deep, was blocked by three waterworn boulders; there was *no filling*, and no trace of decayed wood. A post must have been placed in it shortly before the bank was thrown up and wedged in position with stones. *When the bank was under construction the post was withdrawn*; the boulders remained in, blocking the hole and preventing its being filled with soil.' (Ibid, 41; emphasis in the original). The void was alternatively the result of decay of a post *in situ*, and the stone infilling the void derived from the mound of such stones found mostly westwards of this post-hole (Fox, 1955, Figure 17). For the question of whether 'marker features' existed for the planned course of the Dyke, see Chapter 6.
58 Fox's 'partial section' was reproduced within his Figure 17 (1955, 42). A series of 'sandy patches' shown on the section through the bank could either represent sandy subsoil or the basal traces of turves. The 'interval' is a line of such patches in the upper part of the section could simply represent a pause in the mounding of the bank.
59 Fox, 1955, 77; 70: Profile XXIII, Figure 31.
60 Caeau-Gwynion section: Fox, 1955, Fig. 31, p.70. Court House, Forden, section: Fox, 1955, Fig. 48, p. 109.
61 Fox, 1955, 77. This section through the Dyke was 'perched' at the top of the vertical quarry-face, so Fox was unable to make a measured drawing of it.
62 Ibid.
63 Ibid: Fox was still able to observe this section, albeit by then covered in vegetation, in 1928. He did make another cutting through the bank of the Dyke at Garnons, but published no observations about its form or composition (1955, 203–4).
64 Allen, 1988. Even then, although clear and succinct, at three pages in length David Allen's report could hardly be described as very detailed. It is helped enormously by still providing the most informative drawn sections so far published (see Figure 5.12).
65 Ibid, 8.
66 Ibid.
67 Ibid.
68 The excavation was directed by Ken Brassil for Clwyd-Powys Archaeological Trust (Jones and Brassil, 1992). See also Turner-Flynn et al, 1995, for the (limited) results of a subsequent archaeological field evaluation at Ffrith Farm.
69 Hill and Worthington, 2003, 81–2. The published part-section (Ibid, 88: Figure 27), 7 metres wide and seeming to be wholly within the bank, is difficult to understand. It appears to show a dump of stones beneath the highest part of the surviving bank, filling but also over-spilling a shallow metre-wide slot (see 'marking-out features', Chapter 6, pp. 217–18, below).
70 Jones, 1990.
71 Lewis, 1963.
72 Hill and Worthington, 2003, 57. This comment was made in reference to the section across a 'badly eroded

area of bank'. No information was given about the other section where the bank 'still stood a metre high' but was said to have been masked at surface by the build-up of erosion silts on its eastern side.
73. Ibid, 56: 'The section did not add to our knowledge as it was entirely consistent with upcast from the ditch and no new evidence for the structure of the bank was observed'.
74. Ibid, 69.
75. Blockley, 1997. The slope of deposits from west to east within this surviving bank was such that it was interpreted that the crest of the bank lay to the west of the exposed section, and that the line of the A483 road followed the course of the ditch locally (ibid, 5).
76. Hill and Worthington, 2003, 64. The western edge of this deposit is shown on the published section (65; Figure 23) as being fully half a metre thick and retained by a hollow on the lip of the ditch.
77. Ibid, 77.
78. Ibid, 60–1.
79. Ibid, 80–1.
80. Jones and Owen, 1988.
81. Hayes and Malim, 2008, 156; Figure 10.
82. Such features were for instance noted by Fox (1955, 129). Hill and Worthington (2003, 123) state that the Dyke 'would appear to have been constructed mainly of turf from a wider than normal area, or of earth taken from the scoops to the east of the bank that have been observed in some places, particularly on aerial photographs', although evidence for the former is not adduced to support the idea, and the only published mention of the location of such scoops is made in reference to the Clwyd-Powys Archaeological Trust's excavations at Ffrith Road, Knighton (ibid, 54).
83. As Noble noted at several points in his own account (1983), this probably reflected Fox's concern to complete the more southerly parts of his survey in less time than it had taken to complete the more northerly parts.
84. For instance in the Edenhope Hill area, 'on the steepest slopes material is derived from spoil holes on the E. side' (Fox, 1955, 129), but the pits concerned were only very rarely mapped, except where the quarry-pits approximate an east ditch. Fox did in effect record the presence of quarried areas in some of his profiles, however. Of 10 profiles recorded between Selattyn Hill and Treflach in the course of the Dyke between the Ceiriog and Vyrnwy rivers, fully 7 indicated areas of quarrying to the rear of the bank (Ibid, Figures 32 to 34).
85. 'Extensive quarries on the inner side of the monument ... (are) a more or less ubiquitous feature of the monument in Gloucestershire' (Hoyle and Vallender, 1997, 4).
86. Allen, 1988.
87. Hoyle and Vallender, 1997, 21.
88. Ibid. That these quarries were dug at the time that the bank was built is shown by the fact that 'The inner side of the bank always appears to slope down into the hollow of the quarries without an intervening berm of any kind' (Ibid).
89. This is not simply a matter of randomly digging a couple of locations to see what can be found. What is required, rather, is a systematic approach to examining a given length of Dyke (or two or three such in contrasting locations), in which the suite of features is mapped, and selected areas then sampled through excavation.
90. Fox, 1955, 143.
91. As deduced from Hill and Worthington (2003) and from the map drawn by Dominic Powlesland to accompany an article summarising the early progress of the project (Hill, 1977). A short article entitled 'Land-systems mapping and the new Offa's Dyke survey' (Robinson, 1985) also refers to work at Ruabon, where Fox's explanation of the route is challenged in reference not to the form of the Dyke, but the course chosen to take advantage of a side-valley leading southwards down to the river Dee.
92. Hill and Worthington, 2003, 171; Figure 56. Margaret Worthington provided a detailed account (as part of 'Appendix 1: Research Strategies of Offa's Dyke Project') of the survey method used during the project to record the earthworks of Offa's Dyke (ibid, 167–72). She noted that "This system of recording is given in detail below because, *although the result will not be found in this book*, it has contributed greatly to our understanding of the monument and this understanding is discussed in the preceding chapters" (ibid, 167: emphasis added). It is not exactly clear why such an archive as is illustrated (ibid, Figures 55 – two profiles across the bank and ditch – and 56 – a schematic longitudinal section) was not used to provide a more detailed characterisation of the Dyke in the book. Nor is it indicated where or when the results of such a more detailed survey might appear. The statements that "our detailed survey of *a number of lengths of the monument* has also shown…" (ibid, 101; emphasis added), and that "the survey is far from complete" (ibid, 172) do not indicate the likely appearance of a full account anytime soon. Where the survey took place, the cross-monument profiles were recorded at fixed intervals of 100 m, "regardless of its state of preservation at that point", and were designed "to give a representative sample of the present state of the earthwork" (ibid, 169). Meanwhile, the 'longitudinal section' was a continuous record in those areas surveyed, measuring in parallel the top of the bank, the bottom of the ditch and 'ground level' to the west of the earthwork. Readings were taken "on the perceived line of the crest of the bank" (ibid, 170), and this ought therefore to

be an important source of information on its form in the late twentieth century (although as noted above, modern methods of recording will no doubt produce a more three-dimensional characterisation). This was an interesting and pragmatic solution to the problem of making a 'running' record of the earthwork using simple technology. However, the use of LiDAR combined with modern analytical field survey based upon use of differential GPS equipment is likely to produce a more complete record.

93 Hill and Worthington, 2003, 123.
94 Hoyle and Vallender, 1997. The sophistication of the Gloucestershire County Archaeological Service survey, although undertaken primarily for conservation purposes, is at present unmatched anywhere along the Dyke. It involved the definition of a series of build forms and their variants (Ibid, 21–4; and Figure 4, A–D). Broadly, their Form 1 corresponds to the *scarp* mode of construction but is defined mostly in reference to the bank profile, and especially to the steepened front that Fox recorded in profile at numerous locations in Gloucestershire and elsewhere. Form 1 often features the scale of bank associated with the *substantial* mode elsewhere, whereas Form 1a was noted as having a bank of lesser proportions. Form 2 corresponds closely to the *slight* (Fox's 'boundary bank') mode, occasionally featuring a quarry ditch to the rear and a shallow ditch to the front, while Form 3 also corresponds to the *scarp* mode but is mostly defined in reference to the existence of a terrace or notch forwards from the front of the bank.
95 It is important to note that statements that suggest that the 1995 survey established, for instance, that 'there are three separate monuments, none dated and only one short length bearing any resemblance to Offa's Dyke' (Worthington, 2005, 93) have served substantially to misrepresent its findings. As we have noted, the 'one short length that bears any resemblance to Offa's Dyke' is, rather, one of the most monumental lengths that exist anywhere along the course of the Dyke: fittingly so, given that it marks the southern terminus of the monument in a dramatic location. Nor is it the only part of the Dyke in Gloucestershire built to such a scale, as the length either side of the Devil's Pulpit demonstrates. The comment about the 'three separate monuments' appears to gloss the complexity of the situation: the survey identified at least eleven spatially distinct lengths. The comment about the lack of dating evidence signifies nothing given that so far there are no scientific dates for the monument anywhere along its entire course.
96 On the hybrid character of some stretches, it was noted, for example, that: 'It is commonplace for variants of Form 1 to be contiguous with, and merge into variants of Form 4' (Hoyle and Vallender, 1997, 24). The existence of the different forms also appears to correlate not only with geology, but also with historic land-use: Type 1 is prevalent in areas unsuitable for cultivation (due no doubt largely to the rocky nature of the terrain), while Type 2 is prevalent where, as on the Old Red Sandstone, the soil is suitable for cultivation: the latter again, just as in Herefordshire (Ibid, 29–32).
97 Fox, 1955, Figures 41 to 43; table showing alignments defined and classified, p. 120; map of Offa's Dyke in Montgomeryshire, p. 122.
98 Everson, 1991.
99 The idea that the location of the field boundaries and tracks built up to or across the Dyke might instead have been determined by the prior existence of a 'groove' at such points has apparently never occurred to any commentators on the build of the Dyke.
100 Fox, 1955, 145; Figure 62. These approximate respectively to our *substantial* and *slighter* build modes, as described above.
101 In Welsh, 'bwlch' means 'gap, pass, or notch' (Evans and Thomas, 1987, 62), corresponding closely therefore to the English 'yat' (OE 'geat': gate or pass), cf Symond's Yat, on the Wye on the border between Herefordshire and Gloucestershire. The significance of this name is discussed further in Chapter 6.
102 It continued at this scale, if somewhat reduced by erosion, to a ridge-top by Pen Offa farm immediately to the east of the spur on which stands the circular embanked enclosure known as Castle Ring, on what is labelled 'Newcastle Hill' on the 1:12500 map that Fox annotated for his survey.
103 For the sake of clarity both the alignments and other features noted are marked on the plan shown here. The counterscarp bank along the ditch edge here may have been spread from its original east–west profile by the creation of a vehicular track on top of it, but its dimensions are nonetheless considerable even to this day, standing a metre above the ground to the west, and being over 6 metres in breadth from east to west.
104 This is just 2 miles south from the Spoad length described above, and 10 miles north of the Discoed length.
105 Fox, 1955, 135.
106 The co-occurrence of placement of the Dyke around a prominent west-facing scarp, just below the crest; the use of the scarp mode of construction; the deployment of the adjusted-segmented bank construction form; and the creation of a right-angled turn overlooking a strategic location are all fundamental features of the design and built form of the Dyke throughout its course.
107 There is no indication, however, that this observation has been made previously.

108 Fox, 1955, 74. These were illustrated in his published profiles 'no. xviii, Fig 30; no. xxiv, Fig 31, and no xxvi, Fig 33'.
109 This also had a hedge-bank on top of it, but like the other two examples was sited exactly upon the outer lip of the ditch (1955, 71: Profile XXX, Figure 32).
110 Ibid, 128, 129.
111 Ibid, 131–2; Figure 54. (see p. 154).
112 Ibid, 156: 'sketch plan: profile LI'.
113 Or indeed, the occasionally massive counter-scarp bank observable at Lippetts Grove and elsewhere along the stretch of Dyke between Madget Hill and Plumwier Cliff in Gloucestershire.
114 Hill and Worthington, 2003, 76, where the possible presence of such a feature was noted. However, the implausible section drawing (90, Figure 28) does not clarify either its form or indeed its stratigraphic relationship with the ditch fill.
115 Rhodes, 1965.
116 Fox, 1955, 154, 160, 163: Figure 69.
117 Hill and Worthington, 2003, 75–6.
118 Hoyle and Vallender, 1997, 48.
119 Ibid, 49.
120 For further discussion of this point, see Chapter 7 below.

Chapter 6

1 Fox, 1955, 282–3.
2 'Dux' was a term that in middle Saxon parlance often referred to local leadership of a 'people'. Use of the term in the early eighth century seemingly referred to a local kingship, but by the end of the century, in Mercia at least, the equivalent term that was used more frequently was 'ealdorman'. Kirby (1991, 11–12) has discussed the likely significance of this change in nomenclature in detail, for instance charting the variable references to 'rex', 'subregulus' (under-king), 'princeps' ('prince' – perhaps in a similar way to which Welsh kings in the thirteenth century became, in deliberate subordination to the English king, 'princes'), 'dux' ('leader, duke'), 'praefectus' ('prefect', 'junior leader'), 'comes' or ('companion', 'count'). He carefully traced this 'descent' among the Hwicce, in respect to Offa's charters.
3 The hide was a unit of land of variable extent, in Bede's time defined as the area in any one region or locality capable of supporting a family working the land. Subsequently, the hide became the basic unit in an artificial system for the assessment of land for purposes of taxation (see Keynes and Lapidge, 1983, 237, n.36). David Hill, and others, have suggested the way in which Offa's Dyke could have been built, by extrapolation from the provisions of the later 'Burghal Hidage', a ninth- or early tenth-century document specifying how the walls of fortified centres or *burhs* of the West Saxon kingdom were to be maintained (Hill, 1977; 1987; 2000; Hill and Worthington, 2003, 116–18).
4 This does not however mean that individual stretches of the earthwork could not have been built by different teams of people: only that we cannot simply assume that contrasts in build and contrasts evident at the junctions of lengths with contrasting forms were derived from this cause.
5 That this has long been appreciated is illustrated by the quoted passages, both from the same page of C. H. Hartsthorne's article of 1841, with which we opened Chapters 4 and 5.
6 Wood, 1987, 77.
7 The date that Fox and Stenton seized upon was AD 785. The 'cattle-rustling' idea stems from the provisions of such documents as the *Ordinance concerning the Dunsaete* (q.v.) where detailed provisions are made for compensation arising from such nefarious activities.
8 See Chapter 7 for discussion of the evidence for communities on both sides of the line of the Dyke.
9 Work for the Herefordshire historic landscape characterisation project in 1999–2002 and for the Arrow Valley landscape change project in 2003 defined these relationships closely from a combination of map-work, field (and aerial) survey, and excavation. Rowe Ditch clearly cut across the grain of all earlier land boundaries (White, 2003, 39–42).
10 Again, see especially Chapter 7, below.
11 Hill and Worthington, 2003, 123–124.
12 This is described at length in Bede's *History*. A young princely retainer of Ecgfrith of Northumbria, having been knocked unconscious and wounded in the battle with Aethelred's Mercian army on the Trent, revived after the battle was over, and, upon capture, passed himself off as a peasant and, to avoid discovery of his rank, 'declared that he had come to the army in company with other peasants to bring food to the soldiers' (Bede, HE, iv, 22; McClure and Collins, 1994, 208–9). The significance of this event was noted in Abels, 1988.
13 For example, Fox, 1955, 41; Hill and Worthington, 2003, 84, and 87–9.
14 Moreover, although Fox assumed that this post had been placed along, or close to, the centre-line of the bank of the Dyke, it could have formed part of a revetment to the rear of the 'core' of the bank. This possibility is enhanced in reference to the section-drawing (Fox, 1955, 42, Figure 17, Profile X) which shows a concentration of large stones to the west of this post-hole, towards the (modern) road that apparently follows the line of the ditch. These could

15. Hill and Worthington, 2003, 87
16. Ibid, Figure 27.
17. Ibid, 89.
18. Allen, 1988, 8.
19. The presence of a 'marker bank' was claimed also at the recent excavation at Gobowen, Oswestry, on Wat's Dyke (Malim and Hayes, 2008). However, this was a 'spread bank', and could just have easily simply been the primary dump. A similar phenomenon, albeit in the construction of Iron Age hill-fort defences, was observed in excavations in 2008 at Credenhill near Hereford (see Ray, forthcoming, 2015, Chapter 4 for a discussion of the build practices recorded at this site).
20. Although not a panacea, the approaching wider availability of detailed LiDAR (Light Detection and Radar) data will enable the likely presence and possible form of such features to be identified, preparatory to the conduct of the necessary field-based ground-truthing (including occasionally excavation). The resource of time necessary even to the preliminary identification task should not, however, be underestimated.
21. Bosworth and Toller, 1898, 203 (Charter, Kemble iii, 438).
22. Ibid, 204 (Charter, Kemble iii, 48).
23. Ibid, 203 (Charter, Kemble iii, 169).
24. Fox, 1955, 283, Note 1.
25. See especially, Abels, 1988, 43–57. See also, Brooks, 1971 and G. Williams, 2001b, 2005.
26. This was opposed to folk-land, the inalienable holding of land by a kin-group. It is generally understood by Anglo-Saxon historians that book-land was developed in the seventh century to enable the church to hold land outside the sphere of the folk-group. This, like many of the subjects touched upon in this chapter, is a complex one that has fascinated historians from F. W. Maitland (1897; 1987) onwards. It is one of the defining questions the discussions of which have contributed to an understanding of the origins of feudalism. Although it cannot be discussed in any detail here, readers are referred to more recent, if controversial, treatments such as those by Eric John (1960) who suggested that it was kings rather than the clergy who promoted book-land in their own interests, to the brief but useful discussion by Patrick Wormald (1982a, 95–9), and to contemporary revisiting of the issues by Stephen Baxter (2007, 125–51) and by Ann Williams (2003).
27. The relation of military and other requirements to hidage has been examined at greatest length in recent years by Richard Abels (1988). The specifically eighth-century and Mercian context of military organisation and service has been discussed more recently by Gareth Williams in two essays in particular (G. Williams, 2001b; 2005).
28. It is perhaps necessary to point out (cf. Wormald, 1982a, 97) that such formulas of immunity from military duties and works do not feature in the earlier charters and such formal grants were not therefore developed specifically to give such immunity. Charters from the eighth century onwards increasingly feature three elements: the inscription in Latin detailing the donor and recipient and the terms of the grant, the bounds in Old English specifying the extent of the holding, and the witness-list beginning with the most senior witness (usually the king, although this is sometimes added later as an endorsement), and extending to magnates, churchmen, and other officials.
29. Cf. Baxter and Blair, 2006; Blair, 2005b.
30. Birch 124 is a Worcestershire charter attributed to Coenred and dated 709, granting land at Oldberrow (now in Warwickshire) to Bishop Ecgwine of Worcester. It refers to the 'common burdens' of bridge-work, fortress-work and service in the army, but the attached bounds were said by Finberg to indicate that it derived instead from Berhtwulf's reign, 840–852 (Finberg, 1961, 88).
31. Sawyer, 1968, S92. For discussion of the significance and context, see also Brooks, 1971, 76; Sims-Williams, 1990, 136; and G. Williams, 2005, 103–4.
32. The key section of the Gumley grant reads '*Huius rei gratia hanc donationem meam me vivente concede, ut omnia monasteria et ecclesiae regni mei a publicis vectigalibus, operibus, oneribus absolvantor, nisi in instructione archium vel pontium quae nunquam ulli possunt laxari.*' A range of 'public undertakings, works and burdens' is significantly noted here, that include the building or maintenance of bridges and the creation of fortresses but are not limited to these specific responsibilities. A supplement to the letter from Boniface to Aethelbald in 746 was to Archbishop Cuthbert of Canterbury, wherein he complains that churchmen were themselves being forced by the king to labour on royal projects (Whitelock, 1979, included with Item 177; Williams, 2005, 103).
33. Issued at the Council of Clofesho, 742: Sawyer, 1968, S134; H. PRO E 164/27; transcription at http://www.aschart.kcl.ac.uk/content/charters/text/s0134.html: accessed 12/08/2010. The quoted section reads: '*nisi expeditione intra Cantiam contra paganos marinos cum classis migrantibus......ac pontis constructionem et arcis minitionem*'. See also Abels, 1988, 54, for further discussion.
34. The Dorset occurrence is noted in the *Anglo-Saxon Chronicle* ('A' version) under the year 787. See below on

the significance of this event and the record of it.
35 Fox, 1955, 283, Note 1. He quoted W. H. Stevenson in suggesting that the repeated substitution in Worcester charters of terms indicative of *weall-geworc* rather than *burh-bot* represented a deliberate distinction between work towards the building of different kinds of structure.
36 By 'the army' is meant here the *fyrd* or 'host', the armed body of men assembled for a particular purpose or campaign. See Williams, 2005.
37 A well-documented contemporary example of this practice was when Aethelmund, the *dux* of the Hwicce, led a military force into Wessex on the same day as the accession of Ecgfrith to the Mercian throne in the late summer of 796 (Kirby, 1991, 187).
38 See the sections on architecture in Chapter 8, below, for example (pp. 323–5).
39 See Chapter 2.
40 Hill and Worthington, 2003, 126.
41 Earle, 1857, 205–6. The most recent discussion of this question (A. Williams, 2009, 47–8) has noted that the term 'wealhgefera' was later amended to read 'wealhgerefa', perhaps in the belief that the earlier reference had transposed the letters in the word, and that 'reeve' made more sense of the term for King Alfred's official.
42 The men concerned were those who '*quos* sa*xonice nominauimus Wahlfaereld*'. Sawyer, 1968, S207. This referred to an estate in Worcestershire and is therefore pertinent to the management of the frontier (A. Williams, op. cit, 48).
43 ASC A 787. EHD.
44 Gelling, 1992, 101–24: 'The Eighth Century: The Building of the Dyke'.
45 Gelling, 1989. The problems with accepting the generality of this thesis are several. Not only does the word have a more general applicability denoting simply a 'fortified manor' (Ekwall, 1960, 77), but other more specialised cases include the association of settlements with monastic enclosures also sometimes denoted 'burh' (Blair, 1995, 251, note 21). An element of the distribution may also reflect the provision of fortified places around the perimeters of sub-kingdoms, as argued for the Hwicce (Sims-Williams, 1990, 366–8). See Draper, 2008, for further discussion.
46 These were 'ac-tun' and 'eik-tun' names, which were concentrated in western Shropshire: Gelling, 1992, 123–4. Gelling suggested that these were places to which oaks may have been brought for use in such works. If this is the case, the occurrence of the place-name Ackhill, in the Lugg valley to the north-east of Discoed, at the base of slopes on which the Dyke was built only a kilometre to the west, could be of considerable potential significance.

47 Although it should be noted that is likely that only the defences of the residences of higher ranking individuals could be so designated: see Draper, 2008, 248.
48 See discussions below, for instance in Chapter 8, regarding the relation of 'wics' to the political economy of Offa and Coenwulf.
49 Gelling, 1989, 146; 1992, 121–2. The implications for the frontier are discussed further in Chapter 7. Gelling was not, apparently, aware of the speculations of Earle (1857) in this direction.
50 Fox, 1955, 113, 158.
51 Noble, 1983, 82. Noble also reasoned that if pre-existing English farmlands were divided by the Dyke but continued to be farmed by the communities concerned, they would have to be accessible.
52 Fox, 1955, 36, 75; Plate XVII. Unwarranted, because the 'gap' is very narrow and appears to be a location from which material has been removed rather than there being a former gap that has partly been infilled by slippage.
53 Hill and Worthington, 2003, 76; Figure 28.
54 Ibid, 89.
55 Ibid, 97. They further wrote that 'it clearly cannot be proven that Offa's Dyke was built without any entrances through it…(but) it does seem a distinct possibility' (ibid, 95) and, less cautiously, that 'there appear to be no gateways through the original monument' (ibid, 101).
56 Ibid, 91.
57 Malim, 2007, 27.
58 Finberg, 1972, 141–2. See below for the discussion of roads in the frontier regions.
59 Fox, 1955, 169. The route is important, not so much in reference to the mountain eminence of Radnor Forest itself, as to the route-ways around it to north and south. It is worth noting, in this light, that a route-way from Bleddfa to the north and another from New Radnor and Kinnerton to the south of the main massif, converge on the col at Beggar's Bush, immediately to the west of Bwlch.
60 Cf. Fox, 1955, 158, described this course and its 'opening' at what he termed 'Newcastle Hill', after the adjacent plantation.
61 Fox's representation of this feature on his Figure 62 (1955, 145) shows very clearly the character of this twin 'in-turn' and illustrates how the 'ridge-way' appears to curve southwards and then eastwards to pass through the gap concerned. His observation concerning the build-size of the earthwork as it approaches the gap is also important here, as noted below (1955, 169).
62 Fox, 1955, 158.
63 Hill and Worthington, 2003, 53.
64 Unfortunately, the published section drawing is, in common with the other nine such sections deployed to illustrate the presence of the ditch at potential 'gateways',

65 Evans and Thomas, 1987, 62.
66 Ekwall, 1960, 543.
67 We have noted that the metalling recorded here, associated in the Hill/Worthington intervention with post-medieval pottery, could have been associated with a medieval or later re-cutting of the route-way before the construction of the present road; it does not necessarily preclude an original entrance here. Houghton also found metalling on the route-way that approaches the Dyke along the Kerry Ridgeway from the west, but this too seems more likely to represent a late fore-runner to the present lane rather than the Roman road that the excavator supposed it to be (Hill and Worthington discussion, 2003, 91–2; see also Malim, 2009, 27).
68 Fox, 1955, 105: Figure 45, i–iii.
69 Tim Malim (2007, 26–8) has recently reviewed Hill and Worthington's assertion that there were 'no or few' gateways, and has pointed out that 'the presence of the ditch does not preclude an entrance through Offa's Dyke; to the contrary it suggests a policy of controlled access, perhaps utilising planks to form a section of retractable bridge in the fashion used later in medieval castles to cross towers from one parapet walk to another' (ibid, 27). For Tamworth defences, see Bassett, 2008. For Anglo-Saxon bridges, see Blair, 2001.
70 Malim, 2007, 27.
71 Ibid, 32.
72 At Pole Plantation, Leighton, Fox found the course of the Dyke difficult to trace across the south-facing slopes, perhaps due in part to the presence of a deeply down-cutting stream that may have eroded the slope locally. South of the stream, it is clear that the Dyke approached (or left) the south bank of the stream at the perpendicular to its course.
73 Noble, 1983, 46, gives an account of this feature derived from study of the site following clearance of vegetation to create the Offa's Dyke Park (next to the existing Centre) in 1970, and an (unpublished) excavation by David Hill and associates in 1973 which interpreted wall tumble in the ditch sealing medieval pottery as the remains of Knighton's medieval town wall (see also the paragraph-long description in Hill and Worthington, 2003, 54–5).
74 One of which, at Ruchock Hill, is along that part of the Dyke that Hill and Worthington accepted as the 'real' Dyke, and the other of which, at Lyonshall, is along a 'rejected' length.
75 Fox, 1955, 153.
76 Ibid, 178, Figure 73. The north-eastwards trending arm of the turn appears only as a thin line broken line on the annotated map extract, indicating the bank as a much slighter feature than it in fact comprises. Until recently, the eastwards-trending bank and ditch of this right-angled turn was not only of much more massive proportions than the stretch immediately southwards from the turn, but was much better preserved. Failure to act upon the recommendation of English Heritage 'monument protection' advisers to Schedule this eastwards-trending part of the earthwork here has enabled arable conversion of former pasture and consequent heavy plough, planting and harvesting damage to the bank to occur.
77 Fox, 1955, 153.
78 Noble, for instance, saw this angled turn as having to do with setting up an alignment down into the Wye valley, owing to the fact that the eastern attached length aligns onto Ladylift Clump southwards (1983, 30).
79 The existence of a possible Mercian centre here may indeed explain why the Dyke takes the otherwise eccentric course that it does in a wide loop around just this area. See Chapter 7, below.
80 Fox, 1955, 153.
81 Ibid. The idea that 'the builder of the northern portion was forced to diverge from what he naturally regarded as the ideal line, in order to link up', though a neat conceit on Fox's part, does however contradict the idea that the meeting-place was pre-arranged.
82 Fox, 1955, 153; Hill and Worthington, 2003, 52–3.
83 Ibid, 138.
84 The complexities of the Anglo-Saxon 'relationship' to their inheritance of roads and how they perceived their different meanings is complex. See Pelteret, 1984, for a discussion of the West Saxon and wider context.
85 Della Hooke has made some interesting observations (1985, 122–6) about the network of saltways in Worcestershire and neighbouring counties, emanating from Droitwich. She has also mapped, and named from charter evidence, route-ways major and minor, in the lands of the Hwicce (ibid, 202–22).
86 See the opening discussion in Chapter 7 for further commentary on this point.
87 Whitelock, 1979, EHD: No. 109 (557–9); Finberg, 1961, No. 418 (141–2).
88 Fox, 1955, 285–286.
89 Hankinson, 2002.
90 Ibid, 7–8.
91 Watson, 2002, 16.
92 Nigel Baker, pers comm, October 2010.

93 Hankinson, 2002, 9.
94 Fox, 1955, 114.
95 Ibid.
96 Perhaps surprisingly, Fox's statements about the site have aroused little subsequent comment. Clwyd-Powys Archaeological Trust staff (Chris Martin, Jeff Spencer, pers comm., November 2010) are of the opinion that Caer Din conforms to the sub-oval plan of several other later prehistoric hill-top sites in the region. The Soldier's Ring at Llansatffraid-ym-Mechain near Llanymynech, for instance, is in plan an irregular elongated oval, but parts of its perimeter are straight. Beacon Ring fort also at 400 metres (although much larger than Caer Din) crowning the hill above Leighton also features similar straight lengths. This is itself only half a mile east of Offa's Dyke: so it could – in the absence here also of definitive dating evidence – be argued that this site also experienced 'Mercian modification'! The 'non-rectilinear form' argument can also be over-played, moreover, given that the probable late ninth/early tenth-century 'Burghal Hidage' fortress at Chisbury occupied the Iron Age hillfort there, and that other such sites in Wessex occupied likely prehistoric promontory forts, as at Lydford and Malmesbury (see Haslam, 1984a, 1984b, for a review of such sites; see also Hill, 2000b).
97 Musson and Spurgeon, 1988. It should be noted, however, that the date was obtained from a sample of wood very close to the old land surface, and the actual date of construction could therefore be substantially later (cf. Arnold and Huggett, 1995, 171).
98 Musson and Spurgeon, 1988, 102–7.
99 Arnold and Huggett, 1995.
100 Musson and Spurgeon, 1988, 104–7.
101 See below for its proximity to sites immediately beyond the Dyke to the west. Its form, as well as its location in terms of proximity to the rear of Offa's Dyke, is interestingly mirrored by the circular enclosure site at Rhos near Four Crosses between the Severn and Vyrnwy south of Llandysilio.
102 Gelling, 1982, 116–17.
103 Ibid, 106. The excavation (Hill and Worthington, 2003, 67–68) was undertaken to see if Offa's Dyke was represented by the earthworks, but produced no clear indications of anything.
104 Jeremy Haslam (1987) has proposed that a series of fortresses was created in Mercia under Offa towards the end of the eighth century. Basing his arguments upon the suggestion by Brooks (1971, 72) that the reservation of bridge-work and fortress-work implied a connection between the two, Haslam identified as many as 16 possible Mercian defended bridge-head *burhs*, primarily from topographical inference. While among those listed, Bedford, Nottingham and Northampton have produced Ipswich ware that might imply a contemporary royal or commercial settlement, none of the 16 sites concerned have produced clear dating evidence for defences before the late ninth century. See also, Bassett, 2008; Draper, 2008.
105 Fox, 1955, 138.
106 Discussed in detail in Chapter 7, below.
107 It may be no more than coincidence, but at exactly this point (SO 27006375) the parish boundary between Discoed and Evenjobb, which has risen through Cwmadee from the north-east to join the Dyke at Bwlch, then abruptly leaves it to continue westwards towards Beggar's Bush.
108 Lewis, 1963, cited in Hoyle and Vallender, 1997.
109 Professor John Blair has independently observed the interesting location of this enclosure, although only in respect to locations forward of the Dyke, looking down into the Teme valley. He has noted (pers comm., KR, 15.10.2012) that it is inter-visible with the castle hill at Knucklas (see Chapter 7, p. 279; Figure 7.9), via an intermediate earthwork at Upper Trebert, and suggests that this may have been part of a deliberate scheme of Mercian oversight of the vicinity of the Dyke.
110 See, for instance, Squatriti, 2002 (and Chapter 9, below).
111 These points about the political context and scope of the development of the western frontier are the subject of particular focus in Chapter 9, below.

Chapter 7

1 Howe, 2008, 10.
2 Moreland, 2000, 82–7, points out the increasing evidence in East Anglia and the East Midlands for a shift from the cultivation of lighter soils and the location of settlements in such areas, to the more challenging but also more productive claylands. Rippon, 2007, 114–120, reviews the increasing amount of archaeological and palaeo-environmental evidence. See also Burghart and Wareham, 2008, for discussion of alternative ways in which the evidence can be interpreted.
3 Rippon, 2007, 117.
4 Blair, 2005; Keynes and Lapidge, 1983.
5 Only three sites, in areas in reasonable proximity to the northern sections of the Dyke, and to the landscape through which Wat's Dyke runs, have produced pollen sequences with radiocarbon dates that enable some linkage to the eighth-century environment. See Dark, 2000, 130–69.
6 1610 ± 75 BP (Q-1231): Beales, 1980. The long sequence obtained from the silt beneath the open water mere is

7. Lindow Moss sequence: Branch and Scaife, 1995. The dated sequence from Wellington Quarry just to the north of Hereford might also be cited in support of this trend: see Jackson and Miller, 2011.
8. The terminal date was 1055±72 BP: Beales, 1980; Dark, 2000, 144.
9. Fox, 1955, 145.
10. By 'alluviated' we mean here valleys whose lower profiles have become filled up with silts washed downstream from higher in their catchments. This reason for the lack of visibility of the Dyke as a surface feature at these locations was not apparently fully appreciated at either end of the twentieth century. A potentially important corollary is that, given the low velocity of sediment transport, particularly on the Camlad, organic remains of piles to secure the Dyke foundations may survive in these places and may present us with the opportunity to use dendro-chronology to date the creation of the works here.
11. Fox, 1955, Fig 69, p. 163.
12. Ibid, 115–16.
13. Quotation from: Hill and Worthington, 2003, 77–8. For the original report, see Jones and Owen, 1988.
14. Jones, 1992, 71.
15. Malim and Hayes, 2008, 155–6.
16. Everson, 1991.
17. 'These differences in the form of the Dyke as it is presently encountered, both between substantial sections and in specific details, are therefore intelligible as the effects of precisely the land-use changes that can be invoked ... to explain the cultivation remains that abut the Dyke' (Everson, 1991, 59).
18. Everson, 1991, 60–1. This is a subtle argument, and Barker pointed out that the case was only solvable in reference to excavation beneath the bank of the Dyke itself, in the immediately adjacent locality: '... the Dyke, a massive earthwork and a major disruption of the landscape, may have distorted pre-existing features... Clearly the only way to find out is to excavate the Dyke here, and I believe that there are powerful arguments for doing this, and in the near future' (ibid, 61). The urgency Barker advocated was due to the nature and scale of contemporary erosion.
19. Fox, 1955, 122 (Figure 52).
20. See for example, Hooke, 2010, 118–30.
21. Ibid, 193–217.
22. See Rumble, 1996a for a modern translation of the provisions of the Tribal Hidage; and Rumble 1996b, for a listing of 66 different interpretations of the date and/or purpose of the document from Kemble in 1849 to Higham in 1995.
23. Keynes, 2005, 11.
24. An alternative and perhaps more plausible reason for the inclusion of Wessex is that the document was 'inherited' by the West Saxon kingdom after the decline of Mercia (see P. Featherstone, 2001). Keynes (1995, 21–5; 2005, 11) nonetheless noted how the Tribal Hidage makes most sense as a Mercian production and that the reigns of either Aethelbald or Offa provide an equally plausible context for its compilation as the reign of Wulfhere in the previous century; Storey (2003, 174) suggested that it 'most probably belongs to the period of Mercian hegemony'.
25. For example, Hart, 1977.
26. For instance, Pretty, 1989.
27. Both Sims-Williams (1990, 18) and Gelling (1992, 83–4) have adopted this view.
28. Sims-Williams, op. cit, 41–3.
29. While it is possible that the 'Magonsaetan' were the 'Westerna' of the Tribal Hidage, there are plausible arguments against this identification. There is also some suggestion that they were known as the 'Hecani' or 'Western Hecani'. Although this involves 'going further than the present evidence allows' (Sims-Williams, 1990, 43) it is tempting to see the people who became known as the 'Magonsaete' as the 'western' branch of the 'Hecani', the latter equating with the Hwicce. If the cognate element in the name 'Gewisse' locates an eastern branch of the same people in the Thames valley their combined territory would approximate the Dobunnic sphere in the Romano-British period and this might account for the strong British element that appears to have survived into Anglo-Saxon times in all three areas.
30. Sims-Williams, 1990, 17–18
31. Higham, 1993, 71; fig. 3.2. See also Bassett, 2000, which appears to regard all such peoples of the west as necessarily hybrid, due to the fact that there are no known early pagan cemeteries west of the Severn.
32. See the discussion in Chapter 6, above, concerning the meaning and value of hidages.
33. Ibid, 31.
34. Ibid, 47.
35. Liebermann, 2010, 23ff; 192–3.
36. Ibid, and VCH Shropshire; see also information on Maesbury.
37. Liebermann, 2010.
38. For Hahlsaete, see Gelling, 1992, 119; For Staple, see Thorn and Thorn, 1983.
39. See Molyneaux, 2012, for a re-appraisal of the *Ordinance* document which favours a re-dating of the document to the tenth or early eleventh century.

40 See Coplestone-Crow, 2009, 11–15; Sims-Williams, 1990, 45–7; Gelling, 1992, 114–19.
41 Molyneaux also questions (2012, 249) the usual reading of the preamble of the *Ordinance* as: 'This is the ordinance that the English *witan* and the counsellors of the Welsh people have established among the Dunsaete', suggesting instead that it might be read as having been 'the Welsh counsellors among the Dunsaete' who established the ordinance. His view is that, comparing the document with other such agreements elsewhere, including between Anglo-Saxon groups, it is more likely that it was drawn up by a local *witan*, and not the '*witan* of the English people'. The latter would, according to Molyneux, imply, incorrectly, that it was a major treaty between the English and British peoples (which is what some former interpretations, from Fox and Noble onwards, have seen it as). This idea that the Ordinance represented a local arrangement is more plausible, but it might rather therefore be read as meaning: 'This is the ordinance that has been established among the *Dunsaete* by the English witan and the counsellors of the Welsh people, both drawn from the people who live there'? This would suggest that, among the *Dunsaete* (a group who established ordinances in the regular Anglo-Saxon manner, and therefore presumably under Mercian authority), an ordinance for the regulation of interactions between the 'signatories' was drawn up by the counsellors of both English and Welsh inhabitants.
42 See Higham, 1993b.
43 Gelling, 1992, 119.
44 Ibid, 105.
45 Ibid.
46 Gelling, 1992, 106ff.
47 Ibid, 108–9: Figures 43b and 43c
48 Stenton, 1947, 212–13, concerning Burlingjobb; but see Gelling, 1992, 110–11, on the significance of the –ing and –hope elements in both this and Evenjobb.
49 As in the case of Bulllinghope south of Hereford: see below.
50 See this chapter, below: sections on Presteigne and on the wider borderlands.
51 For example, Wood, 1987, 77, cited at the beginning of Chapter 6, above. Interestingly, Fox was more equivocal about the connection, stating that: 'Whether the Dyke was intended to prevent or make more difficult cattle raids is an arguable point' (1955, 170).
52 Keynes, 2005b, 10. The inference that earlier writers, including Fox, thought that the Dyke was not a considerable work is somewhat misleading. However, it is regarded now as more positively 'martial', and Keynes' gloss that it represented no wish for the Mercian state to expand further west may be correct, but only if annexation, rather than domination, was its aim.
53 Cf. Noble, 1983, 104–7, reproducing and quoting directly from Corpus Christi, Cambridge, MS 383; for example: 'if anyone follow the track of stolen cattle from one river bank to the other, then he must hand over the tracking to the men of that land, or show my some mark that the track is rightfully pursued' (ibid, 105, first provision); and 'Neither is a Welshman to cross over into English land, nor an Englishman to Welsh, without the appointed man from that land, who shall meet him at the bank and bring him back there again without any offence' (ibid, 107, sixth provision).
54 Davies, 1990, 67. The particular events outlined in this section are not referenced here in detail. The relevant material is discussed in Davies, 1982; 1990; Sims-Williams, 1990; and Charles-Edwards, 2005.
55 Davies, 1982, 94.
56 Ibid, 82–3.
57 The transcriptions concerned were by Robert Vaughan in 1648 and by Edward Lhuyd in 1696 (see Chapter 2, above).
58 See Fox, 1955, 80–1, n.2.
59 See, for example, Edwards, 2009, 163.
60 Ibid, 168–9. She also suggests that its location, on top of a probable prehistoric round cairn, and in a highly visible location ringed by hills, may have provided an appropriate setting for the public recitation of Powysian royal genealogy and accounts of the exploits of its earlier rulers.
61 Stephenson, 2012, 43.
62 Stephenson (ibid, 44), notes that 'the landscape on the Mercian side became much more anglicised, with British place-names rarer in Shropshire, particularly western Shropshire, than in Herefordshire…And perhaps it may reveal a programme of deliberate re-population after losses caused by pestilence and war'.
63 Ibid, 41.
64 Noble developed this idea furthest, in reference to the 'Ordinance concerning the Dunsaete', which successive commentators have suggested sought to regulate relations between English and Welsh occupants of a single political entity.
65 Although this may have been the case by the time, in the later ninth century, that there was a common enemy to oppose, in the form of the Danish armies and Viking war-bands.
66 Davies, 1982, 93.
67 Davies, 1982, 102. See also, Sims-Williams, 1990, 46.
68 Noble, 1983, 10; Sims-Williams, 1990, 46–7: the dynasty ends with Gwrgan ap Cynfyn, the grandson of Peibio ab Erb, who was the contemporary of Iddon, the king of Gwent who was a contemporary of Cadwallon of Gwynedd, who as we saw in Chapter 1 was killed fighting

the Northumbrians in 634. Iddon is the earliest king noted as granting land in Gwent in the Llandaff charters.
69 Coplestone-Crow (2009, 13–14) has attempted to reconstruct the bounds of the kingdom using a multiplicity of clues, suggesting for instance that an association recorded in 1330 and traceable back to Domesday between the church at Lugwardine to the east of Hereford and three churches in Archenfield indicates that they all formerly formed part of Ergyng. He linked this to similar references concerning Ledbury and Yarkhill, noting that the northern boundaries of Greytree, Winslow and Winstree hundreds link these places in a line that could mark a former northern boundary of Ergyng.
70 Mann and Vaughan, 2008.
71 Sims-Williams, 1990, 46, n.149.
72 Ibid, 45–6. The term 'anergyng' apparently denoted, deliberately, that the area concerned was once a part of Ergyng, but by 1086 was not. The hybrid nature of the
73 The gift to Gloucester Abbey by Nothheard, ealdorman of the Magonsaete, of four *manentes* (hides) of land in an unspecified location in Archenfield in 823 or 825 indicates the likely reality of mixed occupation of the lands of Ergyng by that time (Coplestone-Crow 2009, 76). Such an equation of 'Webtree' with the 'Dunsaete' would add weight to the idea that the name of the latter grouping referenced what today is the hilltop at Dinedor Hill, the prominent western end of which is crowned by an Iron Age hillfort.
74 Thorn and Thorn, 1983, 179b. The similarity between the terms of the Ordinance and the customs recorded in 1086 do perhaps indicate the likelihood that they referred to the same geographic area, and that the Dunsaete reference is to a population of wholly intermixed British and English origin.
75 Davies, 1982, 94.
76 ASC 'Mercian Register', 916. Whitelock, 1979, 214.
77 These latter 'built' facings are complemented along several parts of this dramatic stretch of the Dyke in Gloucestershire by the kind of 'sculpting' of the living rock exploiting the natural bedding planes to produce a wall-like effect that we have also observed at Cwmsanahan and that are discussed in Chapter 5, above (Hoyle, pers comm.).
78 Noble, 1983, 6. Noble mis-quotes Ekwall in suggesting that the name Dindyrn (Liber Landav, c.1150), with alternative contemporary MS versions 'Dindirn', 'Tindirn' and 'Tindryn', translates as 'the prince's stronghold'. Rather, Ekwall has 'the king's fort' (1960, 475).
79 See R. Faith (1994) regarding the complexities of the Tidenham estate and the existence (or otherwise) of a major British centre at Tintern.
80 Although it is difficult to fully appreciate the impact today, since the view over the valleys to the west is obscured by tree-cover.
81 Noble, 1983, 84. There may be a hint of something yet more complex going on here. Carreghofa parish is bisected by a routeway that extends from the north bank of the river Vyrnwy northwards to Carreghofa Hall on the east bank of the river Tanat. North of the Hall, there is a fragment of linear earthwork sited north–south along the crest of the bank directly overlooking the Tanat. A farm placed towards the southern end of the routeway is called 'Clawdd Coch', the 'Red Dyke'. Could the routeway and its continuation northwards as an earthwork overlooking the Tanat represent the former line of the Dyke here? And if so, could the placing of the Dyke on Llanymynech Hill be a response to the British over-running of an earlier line, as mentioned in the *Brut y Twysogion* record for 784? This may seem a far-fetched idea, but it represents an example of the potential intricacies of the formation of the frontier, and of the Dyke itself, that are in need of further exploration in the years to come. See Chapter 9, 360–2, below.
82 The site known as The Soldier's Mount, less than two miles to the west, is a good candidate. This covers the summit of Foel Hill above Afon Cain and overlooks also Llansantffraid-ym-Mechain on the Vyrnwy close to the Tanat confluence. It has a clear view eastwards towards the southern end of Llanymynech Hill by Asterley Rocks (that is, precisely where the elaboration we discuss here is prominent).
83 Noble, 1983, 86.
84 Fox, 1955, 92; Figure 38.
85 Ibid, 94.
86 This close siting of the two dykes together in the Dee valley here makes the point about reinforcing a blocking of access to and from Bangor regardless of which was the earlier of the two linear earthworks.
87 Although this could also be a factor of preservation.
88 It may in fact be mirrored by a West Saxon re-working of the multi-phase West Wansdyke as a contemporary and complementary Mercian-facing frontier work. See Erskine, 2007.
89 As recorded in the Welsh annals. See below for a discussion of the place of Hereford at the frontier and in relation to Offa's Dyke.
90 The sources are medieval and hagiographical, but they relate to the foundation of the cathedral. See Blair, 2005, op. cit. See also, Blair, 2001, 8–11; Sims-Williams, 1990, 90–1; Keynes, 2000, 9–10, for an evaluation.
91 One piece of material testimony to the location of the legend is the discovery, during the dredging of a pond close to the church in the nineteenth century, of a large

92 For Freen's Court see Ray, 2015, 219–21. For Wellington Saxon mills, ibid, 221.
93 For Bullinghope and the enclosure at Rotherwas, ibid, 205–6; 212.
94 This is a point made by both Margaret Gelling (1992, 103–5) and Della Hooke (1986).
95 Recent work immediately to the south of Hereford, for instance, has shown that the landscape was opened up by cultivation in the Middle Bronze Age and continued to be open farmland into the medieval period, when cultivation was intensified still further. See Ray, 2015, 105, 273.
96 Ray, 2015, 209.
97 Fowles, 1982, 884–5; Aubrey folio 87/59. In a Memorandum he added: 'the range of Hills lyeing north and south (of the Wye?) are the first that terminate the fair level/plain of Herefordshire towards Wales'. This again appears to reference his first-hand observation of the Dyke there.
98 Hill and Worthington, 2003, 135–7. Fox's comments about 'forest so dense' here have, as we noted in Chapter 3, proved not only too easy a target, but also too tempting a distraction, for late twentieth-century investigators here: as did the presence of the north Herefordshire Rowe Ditch nearby.
99 However, since the seventeenth century, the hills concerned have been subject to both landscaping (for landscape parks associated with great houses) and industrial exploitation. A case in point is Garnon's Hill, where not only quarrying for Old Red Sandstone gritstone and calcreted limestones but also the digging of 'hundreds of small' marl-pits for agricultural lime has peppered the ridge across which the line of the Dyke appears to have run (Brandon, 1989, 45–46). This may in large measure explain the lack of success that Hill and Worthington (2003) had in locating any remains of the Dyke here.
100 See Copleston-Crow, 2009, 23–6 for further discussion of the limits of 'Straddle' in 1086 and thereafter.
101 Ibid, 21–3.
102 Sims-Williams, 1990, 52.
103 'Garth', in Welsh: Evans and Thomas, 1987, 232.
104 Fox, 1955, 215
105 Again, see the discussion of this stretch of the frontier in Chapter 7, below.
106 Hill and Worthington, 2003, 158–61.
107 A charter for Hope dated May 1378 and cited in the 1912 RCAHMW Inventory of Flintshire, Volume I, mentions 'Offediche' three times along the course of the bounds of the town.
108 And, interestingly, this is an idea promoted at least since Thomas Pennant was writing, in the late eighteenth century.
109 This may also make sense of the traditional, allegedly simply confused, local naming of the northern part of Wat's Dyke as instead 'Offa's Dyke': 'It is a singular circumstance, that from the village of Hope to Basingwerk Abbey, the Dyke is called Clawdd Offa, or Offa's Dyke' (Hartshorne, 1841, 196).
110 Copleston-Crow, 2009, 18–19.
111 Ibid, 18.
112 Copleston-Crow, 2008, 131.
113 Ibid.
114 Ibid.
115 Ekwall, 1960, 497.
116 Liebermann, 2010.
117 This was a Mortimer stronghold, conventionally dated to c.1180–1200, and was thought to have been built to 'oppose' the de Say castle at Stapleton. More recently, the dating has been revised to the end of the eleventh century. The form of the castle is intriguing, since it would appear that an earthen ring-work has been inserted into one end of an earlier, and longer, rectangular fortification aligned east–west along the ridge (information from Clwyd-Powys Archaeological Trust and (KR) site inspection).
118 Lieberman, 2008, 2010.
119 Blair, 2005, 287–8.
120 Gelling (1989, 199–200) saw the appearance of the 'string' of -saete names along the frontier explicitly as potential evidence for just such a reorganisation.
121 See Rodd, 1958, 118, for a mapping of Hezetree and Elsedune Hundreds. In light of the discussion of the Presteigne area above, and the question of the depth of the frontier zone, this breadth of the hundred, taking in both the Lugg and the Hindwell Brook crossings, is clearly significant. The eastern termination of Lentuerden Hundred at the Leintwardine (former Romano-British) enclosed settlement, Hezetree Hundred at Burrington, and Elsedune at Eardisland/Burton, and the association of all of these settlements with the north–south Roman road, 'Watling Street West', may hint at a quasi-military organisation of the frontier here and elsewhere.
122 We are grateful to Paul Selfe and the members of the Eardisland History Group for drawing our attention to these field names from the Eardisland Tithe Award map.
123 To the north-west of Forden Gaer fort, 'an aisled hall … was initially identified from crop-marks and later confirmed through trial excavation in 1987. The form of construction and and size of the hall are comparable with later Saxon royal palace sites of the 9th to 11th centuries' (Jones, 2010, 245). This site has recently (2010) been further excavated by Kevin Blockley, and

124 Although Gelling (1992, 122) thinks that the version of this name recorded in 1284, 'Treboreward' may represent a Welsh version of Burwarton, indicating another 'burhweard' name.
125 Not only does this place still retain its rectilinear Romano-British bank and ditch defences from the time when it operated as a staging-post on Watling Street West (the Roman road that connected Caerleon-on-Usk with Chester on the Dee), but it also has a medieval church carefully sited just within and partly over the mid-point of the eastern side of the enclosing bank. The identification from a site within the north-western quadrant of the enclosure of a sherd of Stafford ware of tenth–eleventh century date indicates a possible continuing administrative or high-status role for the place.
126 This is a location coincidental with the western boundary of Staple hundred immediately across the Wye at Brobury.
127 Gelling, 1989, 146.
128 Gelling, 1992, 122.
129 Wrockwardine, described as 'an important multiple estate in the Wrekin area' features a hill-top site that has been thought likely to be a royal 'caput' or vill (Hooke, 1986, 33). It is perhaps also of some interest that some other places well to the rear of the Dyke were certainly fortified with palisades, as apparently was Newport, Shropshire, which in 963 was referred to as Plesc, 'a fortified or palisaded place' (The Victoria County History, Shropshire).
130 Noble, 1983, 47.
131 For Kingsland, see Coplestone-Crow, 2009, 126.
132 Fox, 1955, 216–17. Fox was interested in the idea of the rental arrangement with the 'shipmen' because he sought an historical or cultural link between the known extent of the Dyke northwards.
133 See, for instance, Lieberman, 2008.
134 See Berry, 2010.

Chapter 8

1 John, 1996, 54.
2 Kirby, 1991, 186; Story, 2003, 144–5. Story also notes research that suggests that Ecgberht's father Ealhmund was the king of that name who ruled Kent as an 'indigenous' king in the early 780s before the kingdom was in effect annexed by Offa, and suggests that this situation represents a policy of Charlemagne to try to ensure at least a degree of Kentish independence from Mercia, in pursuit of Carolingian trade and political interests. See also, Keynes and Lapidge, 1983, 236, n.30.
3 It is pertinent to point out that, towards the end of one of the most extended reviews of the eighth-century Mercian regime, and of Offa's reign in particular, Simon Keynes wrote (2005, 18): 'We still lack an extended study of the 'Mercian Supremacy' in which distinctions might be made between the successive phases of its history, establishing how its nature changed from one period to the next.' This lack is nowhere more keenly evident in the need for re-appraisal of the reign and person of Coenwulf.
4 Such a view of a Mercian 'path to statehood' is contested by a number of authorities (see, for instance, Keynes, 2005). While it lacked developed institutions, it is nonetheless evident for example from the documentation of bridge-work and fortress-work that it must have had at least the rudiments of a bureaucracy.
5 For the former, see for instance Martin, 2005.
6 See Keynes 2005, 14–18.
7 A view most famously championed by Sir Frank Stenton (1947), but upheld into more recent times by Eric John (1996) and to some extent by Patrick Wormald (1982). The reference to 'hegemony' was Damian Tyler's (2005a; see also Tyler, 2005b). Tyler has thrown much useful light on the nature of Penda's dominance over his contemporaries, particularly in the period from 642 to 655. He has noted the use of hegemonic devices such as we have noted here, but also focuses upon how difficult the exercise of dominance was for Penda as a pagan king in an era of kingly conversion to Christianity.
8 Keynes, 2005.
9 Ibid.
10 See especially, Featherstone, 2005.
11 Kirby, 1991, 165. The joint kingship of Kent with an east Kent and west Kent sub-kingdom, with Rochester the separate bishopric for the latter, is seen to be reflected in the witnessing of grants east and west of the upper Medway. Rochester's 'capital' status in contradistinction to Canterbury was perhaps underlined by its becoming the site of a mint in Coenwulf's reign.
12 See Kirby, 1991, 167. Offa's statement came to light when Coenwulf in turn revoked the same grants in 799 (Whitelock, EHD, 1979, 510–511: No. 80). Ecgberht was apparently in close friendship with Archbishop Jaenberht, who was such a fierce opponent of Offa's policies towards Kent and the metropolitan authority of the church at Canterbury.
13 We find Simon Keynes' published commentaries on Offa somewhat paradoxical in this regard. When writing with Michael Lapidge on Asser's *Life* of Alfred and associated

texts, he appears to have accepted the sophistication of the Mercian court (see for example Keynes and Lapidge, 1983, 26, 259–60 in respect to the role of four 'learned men' whom Alfred had deliberately recruited from among the Mercian clergy because of the lack of such intellectuals in Wessex; and ibid, 305 n. 5 and 309, n. 24, regarding Offa's law code). However, in more recent writing (see especially Keynes, 2005) he has emphasised the qualitatively less developed character of the Mercian court under Offa especially.

14 The deacon, scribe, teacher and scholar Alcuin of York (c.735–804) was one of Charles the Great's leading advisers during the period c.782 to 794, at which point he was appointed as Abbot of the royal monastery at Tours in the Loire valley in France. Alcuin was influential in several ways at Charlemagne's court, introducing new standards of grammar, calligraphy and Latin pronunciation, revising church liturgy, drafting key statements of royal policy, and teaching not only the royal family but also a cohort of young churchmen.

15 For instance, Abbot Gervold of St Wandrille: see section on 'trade', below.

16 Quoted in Wormald, 1982, 101.

17 This was part of the 'Avar treasure' gained as a spoil of war.

18 Wormald, ibid.

19 For a detailed account of the politics behind the papal legates' visit and its context within the sphere of Carolingian diplomacy, see Story, 2003, 55–92. For the role of Alcuin's 'political theory' of kingship in the formulation of the canons promulgated at and through the Councils of 786, see Cubitt, 1995, 153–90, and especially 168–85. For the context of Cynewulf's participation, Keynes, 2005, 11.

20 See especially, Nelson, 2005 and Keynes 2005b. The contradiction was of the judgements of Stenton, Evison, and Wormald. Nelson (2005, 128–31) pointed out that although 'greater Mercia' (including East Anglia and Kent) might have extended to as much as 100,000 square kilometres, the Carolingian empire was at least 12 times this size; and the nature of Charlemagne's political control was both more direct and more intensive.

21 Storey, 2003.

22 Nelson (2005, 139–43) largely dismissed the terms with which Charlemagne addressed Offa as either flattery or mere convention, but the case can be carried too far. The fact remains that the only other contemporary ruler that Charlemagne addressed in these terms was the Byzantine emperor, and that, if Charlemagne did indeed regard Offa as so puny, what possible advantage could he have seen in trying to arrange the marriage of his eldest son to Offa's daughter in the first place? (cf. Story, 2003, 185–186).

23 'There are also some grounds for the suspicion that Offa was afraid of Frankish overlordship being asserted in England' (Dumville, 1997, 359).

24 This is perhaps preferable to Wallace-Hadrill's somewhat more convoluted explanation for Charlemagne's reaction, that he was concerned that Offa would use Bertha as a hostage: see Story, 2003, 185. The episode and its significance for Frankish-Mercian relations in general and the status of the relationship between Offa and Charlemagne in particular, have been discussed at length in recent years. For instance, Joanna Story (2003, 184–8) has highlighted the role of Abbot Gervold of St Wandrille, a monastery on the coast of Flanders, in mediating economic relations and resolving the dispute, while pointing out that Charlemagne was loathe to see any of his daughters married abroad. Janet Nelson (2001, 132–4) has expressed the view that Charlemagne was bound to have been dismissive of the idea of marrying his second daughter, Bertha, to Ecgfrith, given that serious negotiations had already taken place concerning the idea that his eldest daughter might marry the son of the Byzantine Emperor. Also, she suggested that Charlemagne saw Offa's request as an opportunity to take serious affront, that was politically expedient to him at the time. Rosamond McKitterick, meanwhile (2008, 282–4), has questioned whether there ever was a marriage proposal, and has suggested that the dispute may have concerned neither Offa nor Mercia, but instead arose between Charlemagne and Pope Hadrian, concerning Northumbria.

25 Stenton's pronouncement that 'the chief interest of (Coenwulf's) reign lies with his relations with the two southern archbishops of his time' (1947, 223) is clearly in need of substantial revision. For Keynes, 'if Offa is cut down to size, King Coenwulf emerges as a worthy successor to his eighth-century predecessors' (2005, 18).

26 Kirby, 1991, 179; 185–7.

27 See, for example, Kirby, ibid.

28 Ibid. On Cuthred's death in 807, he consolidated the Mercian regime's control further by taking the Kentish throne directly into his own hands.

29 Kirby, 1991, 179.

30 S153. The overblown form used in the Latin text of the charter for lands in Kent was 'Ego . . . . . ente rector et imperator Merciorum regni. anno secundo imperii nostri'. (http://ascharters.net/charters/153?q=&page=, accessed 23.11.2010. cf. Wormald, 1982, 101). The charter was witnessed by both archbishops Aethelheard and Hygebehrt, and, perhaps significantly by Brorda ahead of (and in isolation from) the other secular witnesses and styled 'chief minister' in the formula: 'Signum manus Brordan principis'.

31. Kirby, 1991, 169–70. Kirby perceptively observed, however, that both Coenwulf and Leo had their own reasons to denigrate the reasons that Offa had for trying to create a Mercian archdiocese at Canterbury's expense, and that Offa himself appeared to hold Canterbury in high regard, despite the ferocity of Jaenberht's opposition to his plans (ibid, 172).
32. See Story, 2003, 202–3.
33. See above.
34. Although without any immediate connection with a previous Mercian 'royal' family, Coenwulf was a prince who 'would seem to have been a member of a very powerful kindred, some of whose landed estates were centred on the region of Winchcombe' (Kirby, 1991, 177).
35. Although again, this apparent situation may simply be a reflection of gaps and biases in the available documentation.
36. This important observation was made by Eric John in his perceptive essay 'Thought and action under the Mercian hegemony' which we quoted from at the beginning of the chapter (John, 1995, 50).
37. Tyler, 2005b, 28.
38. Ibid.
39. 'Imperium' was a term that Bede used, to distinguish between ordinary kingly authority, and the control exercised in over-lordship over other kingdoms: see Nelson, 2005, 127.
40. This was vividly expressed by Stenton: 'The great Mercian kings of this age created a political system which included every kingdom in southern England. This system permitted every variety of relationship which could then exist between men of dependent kingdoms and an overlord….but overlordship soon passed into political authority when the overlord was an autocrat like Aethelbald or Offa and, as time went on, more than one insignificant local king exchanged his ancestral rank, and the claim to independence which it implied, for the security of a provincial ealdorman under Mercian patronage.' (1947, 234).
41. Story, 2003, 178–80. As with several other aspects of Offa's political strategy, this was a Carolingian innovation and was being promoted elsewhere – as in Northumbria – under direct Carolingian patronage.
42. S 164, initially issued at Croydon. The phrase used was 'rex Merciorum atque provincie Cancie'.
43. Kirby, 1991, 167–8.
44. The terms used are interesting, if not entirely revealing: Offa and Cynewulf 'convenerunt in unum concilium' (met together in a council) at the time of the envoys' visit in 786 (cf. Keynes, 2005, 11). This could have represented a reconciliation between the kings, but was more likely to have been at the insistence of both Charlemagne and Pope Hadrian.
45. See discussion of Gervold of St Wandrille, below.
46. Story, 2003, 209–10. Charlemagne died in 814. Story notes the rash of diplomatic missions that Coenwulf dispatched to Rome early in his reign to secure the suppression of the Lichfield archdiocese and the removal of Eadberht Praen (with four formal Mercian missions, at least one of which was headed by Archbishop Aethelheard himself). She moreover cited the embassies to Rome and to Louis the Pious' Frankish court in the later years, c.818–821, of the Mercian king's dispute with Arcbishop Wulfred over the Kentish royal monasteries, as evidence that contradicts Kirby's suggestion (1991, 187) that Coenwulf was 'increasingly estranged from the political community of Frankish Europe'.
47. Story, 2003, 211. This also not only illustrates the role of key monastic communities in the political machinery Mercian regime, but suggests too that some degree of control was exercised over the 'direction of approach' of diplomatic missions to the Mercian heartlands.
48. Whitelock, EHD, 1979, 527–8: No. 91).
49. James, 1917. For commentary, see for instance Keynes 2000, and Blair, 2001.
50. MEC = *Medieval European Coinage* reference number (P. Grierson and M. Blackburn, 1986). After Gannon, 2003, 32, Fig. 2.10. Drawn by Tim Hoverd.
51. BMC = *British Museum Catalogue* (Kearey, 1887) After Gannon, 2003, 33, Fig. 2.12, (a). Drawn by Tim Hoverd.
52. Gannon, 2003, 31–3.
53. Kirby, 1991, 174–5.
54. Ibid, 174.
55. Brorda is referred to by this term when he witnessed a charter in favour of the bishop of Worcester late in Offa's reign (Whitelock, EHD, 1979, 507–8: No. 78).
56. Story, 2003, 188, citing the York Annals and ASC, D and E versions, for 792.
57. Stafford, 2005, 41.
58. Keynes, 2005, 11.
59. Cubitt, 1995, 54: Charter S1430, the relevant text reading: 'factum est pontificale conciliabulum in loco famosa qui dicitur Celchyð præsidentibus duobus archiepiscopis Iamberhto scilcet et Hygeberhto mediante quoque Offan rege cum universis principibus suis' (http://ascharters.net/charters/1430?q=&page=, accessed 12/9/2010).
60. Whitelock, EHD, 1979, 861: No. 205.
61. Kirby (1991, 169) for instance pointed out that there may have been a genuinely pastoral concern that Canterbury could not effectively influence or regularize the subordinate bishoprics effectively, when these numbered as many as twelve, and in the context of

62 These are the only English examples of the striking of a coin in the name of a queen consort. 'The coins may indicate that Cynethryth had real political power alongside her husband, or they may have been struck specially for gifts to the Church from Cynethryth. The most likely explanation is that Offa knew that some Roman emperors had issued coins in the names of their wives, and was trying to act like an emperor himself.' (The British Museum website, 'Silver coin of Cynethryth, wife of Offa of Mercia', http://www.britishmuseum.iorg.explore/highlights/highlight_objects/cm/s/silver_coin, accessed 11/01/11). See also Webster and Backhouse, 1991. At one point it was suggested that the coins of Cynethryth were deliberately modelled upon those of the Empress Irene of Constantinople, also minted in the late eighth century. However, no issues of the latter monarch have been found that antedate those of the Mercian queen.

63 Story, 2003, 182.

64 Gannon, 2003, 41.

65 Kirby, 1991, 187; Yorke, 2003, 53–7. The symbolism of Mercian control over these two monasteries was bound up, among other things, with the tradition that the first landing of the Augustinian mission from Rome that led to the (re)conversion of Kent, was on the Isle of Thanet (and the related Kentish tradition that the church at Minster was first built in commemoration of that event); and the construction of the first church at Reculver on the site of the principium, or headquarters building at the centre of the late Roman 'Saxon Shore' fort.

66 Stafford, 2001, 41. The charter concerned, S 165 of 811 concerning lands in Kent, where she witnessed as 'filia regis' alongside her male kin Coenwald and Cyneberht.

67 Ibid, 42.

68 Kirby, 1991, 31. This has been explored further elsewhere: 'To carry the Carolingian analogy of Ecgfrith's consecration at Chelsea in 787 to its logical conclusion, Offa would have required a sub-kingdom for his son. Where more obvious than the kingdom of Kent which, by 785 Offa had secured for Mercia, having removed its native dynasty? And what could be more appropriate, for a Kentish king, than a Frankish bride named Bertha? There was a powerful resonance here for an Anglo-Saxon audience of the successful union between the Merovingian princess, also named Bertha, and the Kentish 'Bretwalda' Aethelberht, which had presaged the arrival of St Augustine's mission to convert the English. Offa's dynastic aspirations cannot have been more explicit; in marrying his son to a Frankish princess named Bertha he was laying claim to the memory and inheritance of Aethelberht, the first Christian king of the English and (the first) *Bretwalda* ' (Story, 2003, 185–6).

69 For Offa and Bardney, see Kirby, 1991, 180, n.7, sourcing the information from Alcuin's 'Bishops, Kings and Saints of York'. For Coenwulf and Gloucester, Finberg, 1972, 153–66.

70 On the cult of St Oswald, see papers in Stancliffe and Cambridge, 1995.

71 What we term 'capitulary' here is more accurately a 'report' back to the Northumbrian and English Councils, but it was close in character to the formal capitularies issued as summaries of the proceedings of church councils in Carolingian Europe. 'The format of the legates' document was, therefore, innovatory and sophisticated in that it seems to combine something of the ritual of Anglo-Saxon charter diplomatic with the new type of legislative document emerging in Francia – the capitulary' (Story, 2003, 83).

72 The lineaments of the debate can be found in Wormald, 1991. The treatment of the issue in Keynes and Lapidge is particularly useful: the reason why Alfred was in such a good position to know about Offa's law-encoding efforts was on the one hand that his wife Eahlswith's brother was a Mercian ealdorman and her mother had been abbess of a Mercian royal monastery, and on the other, he had purposely recruited four leading Mercian clerics to his court specifically because of their learning (Keynes and Lapidge, 1983, 241, n. 58, and 92–3, 259–60, n. 162–7, respectively).

73 Wormald, 1991, 32.

74 Vince, 2005, 183. Vince points for example to the fact that much of the north and west Midlands appears to have managed without the use of pottery in this period, and how, in this huge zone, 'archaeological sites are almost barren of artefacts'.

75 The very recent appreciation of the likely status of Bidford-on-Avon in Warwickshire as a 'Productive Site' where trade was regulated at a nodal point of the inland communications network in Mercia, is a case in point (Naylor and Richards, 2010). It is of interest, in view of the potential role of such places as points of taxation, that 26.3% of the total coin count from the site belongs to the two decades from 790 to 810 (ibid, Figure 5b).

76 See especially, Metcalf, 1960.

77 The whole subject of the Mercian coinage under Offa and Coenwulf has been extensively re-appraised in Rory Naismith's *Money and Power in Anglo-Saxon England: The Southern English Kingdoms, 757–865* (2012). This not only includes an overview of the development of the coinage in the Mercian regime between 757 and c.825 (ibid, 100–6), but provides an extremely important

78 For overviews of the role of coinage, particularly in Offa's reign, see Blackburn, 1995; Chick, 1997 and 2005; Williams, 2005; Naismith, 2012.
79 The location of the East Anglian mint during Offa's reign is uncertain. While Ipswich is the most obvious candidate, Dommoc/Dunwich has also been considered likely, and if the new patterns of distribution are a reliable guide (see Chick, 2005), a location between Great Yarmouth and Lowestoft appears probable.
80 The most extensive exposition of *wics* as kingly emporia remains Hodges, 1989, 69–114.
81 The reaction to the Hodges thesis has been varied, with critical comments in Moreland, 2000, and Vince, 2005. Another view is that set out in Hamerow (2007).
82 See Bassett (2008) for a recent review of the evidence for dating of the earliest defences at the four latter places.
83 Moreland, 2000, in particular discusses the significance of styli and 'productive sites' at length, and notes the diversity of possible functions for such sites; Vince, 2005, stresses the range of sites. Blair, 2005, notes the likelihood of an ecclesiastical link at many such sites.
84 Maddicott, 2005; Hurst, 1997.
85 At Wellington (by Marden), the discovery of a broken quern-stone inserted as a repair to the base timbers of a mill whose principal timbers date to the first half of the eighth century is strongly suggestive of royal control over such facilities in Offa's reign (Ray, 2015, 221) and potentially provides a link to the industrial-scale corn-drying ovens discovered in the earliest levels at nearby Hereford (Shoesmith, 1980).
86 Story, 2003, 186.
87 Whitelock, EHD, 1979, 341: No. 20. Gervold's role is discussed at length by Story (2003, 186).
88 See Gannon, 2003; Naismith, 2012, 47–69; 80–6.
89 A view that Gannon, 2003, 16–17, in a useful summary of the debate over the significance of Anglo-Saxon coinage, attributes in general terms referring more to earlier coins, to the Oxford numismatist D. M. Metcalf.
90 Gannon, 2003, 33
91 Ibid, 2003, 32–3.
92 Ibid, 59–61.
93 Ibid, 142.
94 *After* Gannon, 2003, Figures 2.52 and 2.53; drawn by Tim Hoverd.
95 Webster and Backhouse, 1991; Cramp, 2005; the quotation is from Thurley, 2010.
96 Parsons and Sutherland, 2013.
97 Eaton, 2000, 129–43; Eaton, 2001.
98 Story, 2003, 175: although noting Fernie's opinion (1983, 116–21) that the columns could have been inserted in the tenth or eleventh century.
99 See Peacock, 1997, for discussion of the re-use of these columns. Designed by Odo of Metz and built between 792 and 805 (Conant, 1959, 46–51), the palace at Aachen included a bath within the Emperor's apartments (which according to his biographer, Einhard, Charlemagne used daily), an audience chamber, an assembly hall and throne room, quarters for court officials, and courtyard that could accommodate up to 7000 people. Its architecture self-consciously echoed both the buildings of the Vatican and the late Roman imperial complexes in Ravenna.
100 John Blair, for one, appears to think so (2005, 275): 'For an English Aachen the only possible choice was Bath, where hot water still welled up from its holy spring through the stupendous ruins of the great bath, flanked northwards by the churches of the minster overlying the temple of Sulis Minerva. Ecgfrith may not necessarily have shared Charlemagne's taste for holding court in the bath, but he must have been alive to the current resonances of assemblies at hot springs, as well as to the generally Roman and imperial connotations of recycling monumental ruins.'
101 Cramp, 1977; Jewell, 2001.
102 Hawkes, 2001.
103 Ibid.
104 Rodwell, Hawkes, Howe and Cramp, 2008.
105 HE IV.3: 'Chad's place of burial is a wooden coffin in the shape of a little house, having an aperture in its side, through which those who visit it out of devotion can insert their hands and take out a little of the dust' (McClure and Collins, 1994, 178).
106 The term mancus was used for a gold coin, or its equivalent weight in gold (4.25g), or as a unit of account equivalent to 30 silver shillings. It was modelled on the Arabic dinar, its name derived from the Arabic 'manqush', meaning 'something struck'. The earliest issues in England as on the Continent appear to have been modelled upon the 157 AH (AD 773–774) issue of the Caliph al-Mansur which may have circulated widely in Europe in the years following this. Its creation and use, especially in Italy, appears to have been a deliberate attempt to provide an alternative to the Byzantine 'solidus'. See Blackburn, 2007, 56–9, for discussion of the literary sources and the mancus.
107 A coin minted by Paendraed in the 780s for instance featured a design copied directly from a gold aureus of Augustus from the mint at Lyon (Blackburn, 2007, 62).
108 Blackburn, 2007, 56–64. See moreover, Williams, 2001a,

109 See Naismith, 2012, 112–14.
110 Naismith (ibid, 115) has introduced a note of caution here, however, by noting the highly variable meaning of the term *vicus*, which instead , 'in the context of eighth- and ninth-century London might also have been used of an estate near or within the (walled) city, specifically one held by the king'.
111 Blackburn, 2007, 64.
112 That this also reflects a trading connection and rivalry with Francia should be noted here also. In its use of the term 'vico' the London *mancus* is most closely paralleled by coins being issued from Dorestad which was at its zenith at just this period. This suggests that the rivalry with Charlemagne exhibited by Offa continued into Coenwulf's reign, with London being promoted by the latter as a rival to Dorestad (Williams, 2006).
113 Leahy and Bland, 2009. The 4,000 fragments and items of 'the hoard' (at May 2014) include 69 elaborate sword pommels wrought in gold and 10 in silver, 8 sword pyramids in gold and 1 in silver, and more than 207 sword hilt plates (178 gold, 29 silver), while the fragments of decorative wrought gold or silver edgings number at least 80, and there are also over 350 fragments of decorative plates and panels from helmets or shields, mostly in silver (Leahy and Bland, 2009, 44).
114 Even such an apparently straightforward reconstruction of the physical context of deposition is not without controversy. Tim Tatton-Brown, for instance, has written to a leading archaeological magazine to suggest that the finds context is implausible, and the 'hoard' may have been dumped near a main road having been found in another context altogether, perhaps in nearby Lichfield (Tatton-Brown, 2011). More recent close examination of the context, including a detailed appraisal of the aerial photographic record by Alison Deegan, has come to the conclusion that there probably existed a prominent natural hillock close to Watling Street, which was the attraction of the location as a place to bury the group, and that its survival until recently was due to the location of this latter place under what was later a hedge-bank, removed only in recent years (Cool, 2012, 11–16).
115 More precise quantification is emerging as a result of further laboratory analysis of the finds (Cool, 2012). More items were recovered from the surface of the field following ploughing early in 2012.
116 There is a danger that an historical understanding of the 'hoard' as derived from principles of archaeological analysis is entirely submerged under the weight of scholarly opinion regarding the 'predominant' styles (and likely manufacture dates) of the objects concerned. For instance, it is stated without qualification in a recently published authoritative survey of Anglo-Saxon art that 'The hoard was buried towards the end of that (seventh) century' (Webster, 2012, 122) when in fact no such certainty exists concerning the *date of deposition*.
117 We offer the following alternative interpretation for the context of assembly (and explicitly not for the date(s) of manufacture) of the assemblage of items not as a way of trying to suggest that the manufacture of the vast majority of the pieces was later than expert opinion currently assesses them (the later seventh-century date of which is undoubtedly closely accurate), but rather as a means of introducing a specific *contextual* rigour to the attempt to understand each of these three circumstances.
118 Webster, op cit, 122–6. See Okasha, 2009, for an assertion that the later dates are the only acceptable ones for the inscription. The contrary view has been taken by Chris Fern, whose assessment is written into the project design for the current intensive study of the hoard (Cool, 2012). He has suggested that since this is the only item that *might* be later in date, it is more methodologically sound to deduce that it is the script of the inscription that might be anomalous, and it is earlier in date.
119 Webster, ibid, 124. It is, we would submit, dangerous to take at face value the idea that the hoard items represent a hitherto unsuspected tradition of such elaborate metalworking based in Staffordshire itself, in the absence of any such finds contexts such as a burial that can firmly be placed in a local context of use and deposition. So far, there are less than a handful of similar finds from 'central Mercia', and these have all been un-contextualised discoveries of individual pieces.
120 Brooks, 2009.
121 This includes the 'missing' belt-fittings which, according to Chris Fern (Cool, op. cit), would be expected to have been present along with the sword/seax fittings and helmets. See also, Fern and Speake, 2014.
122 Okasha, op. cit.
123 Felix's *Life* of St Guthlac: see Roberts, 2001. The significance of the Guthlac connection was picked up directly by Elisabeth Okasha (2011): 'Felix quoted both versions of the text in the Vita. The version from Numbers occurs when Guthlac meets Aethelbald, who subsequently became king of the Mercians, ruling from 716 to 757. Guthlac foretells the future to Aethelbald and in the process says *et fugient a facie tua qui te oderunt*, 'those who hate you shall flee from your face'. This may

be of no significance whatever, but if this expression had a particular resonance for the Mercian regime as a prophetic indication of 'manifest destiny' in their overlordship of their neighbours, its appearance as an embellishment either to a Mercian weapon (or, for that matter, to a book of psalms in the personal ownership of royalty) would be readily explicable.

124 See Chapter 3, above, for an outline of the martial events affecting the Mercian kingship in the seventh and eighth centuries. Given the apparent date of most of the items, the fact that the number of pommels closely approximates an anticipated number of members of an elite 'war-band' of the seventh century, and the presence of portable crosses with martial gear, a view of mainstream specialists is that the hoard was buried as a consequence of a Mercian victory sometime in the 670s or 680s (Williams, 2010). Given the presence of putative Northumbrian items, Gareth Williams (2010) has noted that the battle at the Trent in 679, documented by Bede, and in which Aethelred defeated Ecgfrith of Northumbria so decisively that the latter kingdom never again threatened the independence of Mercia, was a battle 'in the right area at the right time'. Yet while this might explain the presence of several items with possible Northumbrian resonances and parallels, it would not so easily accommodate the East Anglian or broadly south-eastern/Kentish style pieces.

125 Offa was depicted wearing both diadems and individual brooches and pendants on his coinage. The images are in no sense 'portraits', and are clearly modelled on Roman imperial prototypes, but they do convey a sense in which it was a known characteristic of Offa to display such items, and Offa, like Einhard suggests that Charlemagne did, was probably known for the wearing of his sword in public. This may not only explain why Charlemagne selected the fine Avar example (as a gift from one connoisseur or 'gladophile' to another), but also why the 'sword of king Offa' had been handed down the generations of West Saxon and English kings to become part of the bequest of the aetheling Aethelstan, the son of king Aethelred, to his brother Eadmund, as mentioned in his will of c.1015 (Whitelock, 1930, 171).

126 That display was a significant aspect of Mercian elite dress and that the items concerned could be standardised, is perhaps illustrated by the six closely similar yet extravagantly decorated silver disc brooches found buried together at Pentney, Norfolk in 1977, and dated to the early ninth century (Webster, 2005, 275–7).

127 The fact that there are as many as six individual gold snake representations (and that are sinuous and not coiled or interlaced) among the hoard items, and that some of these have such attachment strips, is not without potential relevance here. Given what we have noted above, about snakes and Offa's coinage, and although it is an observation no doubt more comfortably cast in the court of the late fourteenth-century English king Richard II than of Offa (and therefore very much an interpretive leap in the context of Middle Saxon Mercia), could these items in some way have been 'emblematic' of the kingship of Offa himself?

128 Story, 2003, 182.
129 See note 121, above.

Chapter 9

1 D. Whitelock, 1979, 22–3.
2 See Story, 2003, for an extended discussion of the implications of this correspondence and that of the Northumbrian cleric Alcuin, discussed in Chapter 8.
3 It is this aspect of Offa's Dyke build, featuring carefully designed treatments of individual traverses (especially of hillsides and valleys) that above all distinguishes Offa's Dyke from other contemporary or near-contemporary linear works. So the notion that 'a simple bank and ditch, while demanding a great deal of labour, required no particular engineering skills: ditch digging and earth moving were commonplace activities for early medieval peasants' (Tyler, 2011, 159) may have been true for the peasants, but is need of some qualification in respect to those responsible for designing and orchestrating the work.
4 Such turns are also a feature of other dykes such as Wansdyke East and Bokerley Dyke, but are not deployed to the same visual effect. Fox noted the presence of some of them, but as noted in Chapter 6, chose to explain their presence in terms of treaty agreements.
5 Fox, 1955, 214–15. Fox's immediate point of reference was the difficulties of being sure that the traces of potential Dyke in Herefordshire were genuinely so. His focus was directed towards the 'uncharacteristic' lengths of Dyke that approximated the scale of hedge-banks (the *slighter* mode of construction). He suggested that 'detached' lengths must be 'in direct extension of characteristic portions, on an alignment such as the Dyke might be expected to take'. Moreover they 'must, to be acceptable, throughout their length follow the alignments which are usual in the case of the Dyke and be continuous' (ibid, 215).
6 Such deliberate permeability, if such it was, may have applied to the area north and east of Treuddyn in Flintshire, to the apparently Dyke-less stretch along the middle Severn near Welshpool, to south Herefordshire,

7. Gerald of Wales, c.1190, *Description of Wales*, Book II, Chapter 7 (Thorpe, 1978, 266).
8. In recent decades Welsh perspectives on this have oscillated between nostalgic negativity and optimism. Some Welsh historians have, for example, viewed the impact of the building of the Dyke as largely positive for the emergence of a distinctive Welsh identity: 'But this earth embankment, the largest man-made boundary in western Europe, was also an acknowledgement of the otherness of Wales….its very presence helped to shape the extent of Wales and, in the long term, to exercise a profound effect on its people's sense of identity' (Jenkins, 2007, 37).
9. Keynes, 2005b, 10. The inference that earlier writers, including Fox, thought that the Dyke was not a considerable work is somewhat misleading. However, it is regarded now as more positively 'martial', and Keynes' gloss that it represented no wish for the Mercian state to expand further west is made in hindsight, and need not have any bearing upon contemporary actions, as witnessed by the northern campaigns of Coenwulf. We have not addressed directly the persistent idea that the Dyke was built to deter cattle-raiding, which is upheld in passing commentary in both popular and scholarly works, and for which there is no evidence apart from the *Ordinance concerning the Dunsaete* which makes it clear that this could occur in both directions, and on the part of both Welsh and English 'rustlers'. Examples of such commentary are the quotation from Michael Wood in Chapter 7, and the recent work on the medieval March by Liebermann (2010, 104–5).
10. Summarised, for example, in Hill, 2001.
11. 'For the meantime' being the period between the construction of the Dyke and the reclamation by the Welsh of parts of the lands to its east, for instance in the area around Wrexham, and in Montgomeryshire.
12. Charles-Edwards, 2013, 423.
13. Ibid.
14. F. M. Stenton, 1955, xxi.
15. Where, as noted Chapter 1, there was nonetheless a long tradition of such works stretching back not only into the sub-Roman period, but beyond at least as far back as the Iron Age.
16. For example, Fox (1955, 94), speaking of the stretch of the earthwork near Leighton, opposite Welshpool: 'There is a Roman quality about engineering work of this class that compels admiration. The directness of the approach to the plateau up a slope which, for 70 yards, has a gradient of 1 in 2 is especially striking; the Dyke is aligned exactly on to the margin of the plateau.'
17. McClure and Collins, 1994, 15 (HE I, 5). Alcuin wrote a letter to Offa in late 792 or early 793 in answer to an enquiry from the Mercian king about the procedures for the succession to the See of Canterbury, in which he made direct reference to Bede's *Ecclesiastical History*, in the clear expectation that Offa would have access to its text (Levison, 1946, 242–7).
18. So, also, Tyler (2011, 159): 'Though greater in physical scope, the dyke parallels other manifestations of Offa's concern to augment his position and image by any and all possible means. These included the use of grandiose royal styles in charters, the minting of pennies bearing his name and image, the promotion of Lichfield, the Mercian bishopric, to the status of an archdiocese, his presidency of pan-English church councils, the anointing of his son Ecgfrith as (future) king, and his correspondence with Charlemagne.'
19. Williams, 2009, 42.
20. Ibid.
21. Ibid. See also note 100, Chapter 8 (above), and Blair, 2005, 275, quoted therein.
22. Squatriti, 2002; Smith, 1995, op. cit. As Maund, 2006, 40, put it: Offa's Dyke was 'unlikely to have been a simple defence, but it may have marked a frontier, or buffer zone, or a barrier to raiding parties, or a line to which Anglo-Saxon settlers within the Welsh border (zone) might retreat'. All of these are characteristics of a march-land (see below, in reference to the contemporary Carolingian situation).
23. The 'March of Wales' is of course a mercurial term, that could mean different things at different times in the medieval period, at different localities within the borderland: for the terms themselves, see Mann, 1996.
24. Liebermann, 2010, 42–51; Map 8.
25. Suppe, 1994
26. Liebermann, 2010, 8–12.
27. The 'middle March', taking in Shropshire, Herefordshire and (at least) Brycheiniog and Montgomery in Wales, for example, was a zone that was made, and remade, at various points in the high medieval period. See Brock Holden, 2000, 2008.
28. It is worth noting here that Frank Noble also recognised the possibility of an early origin for the 'march': 'the use of the term ('in marca de Walis', in his rendering of the Domesday reference), in relation to manors that had lain waste from long before the arrival of the Normans, seems evidence enough that the 'Marcher' status of this area was not a Norman innovation' (1983, 59).
29. On Christmas Day, AD 800, thus symbolically re-creating the Empire in the west, deemed lost in the first decades of the fifth century, 400 years earlier.
30. Liebermann, 2010, 8.
31. Ibid.

32. Ibid.
33. Smith, 1995, 176–7.
34. Liebermann, 2010, 11.
35. Frank Noble had early on noted the coincidence between the building of Offa's Dyke and the Carolingian situation: 'Such arrangements (as that for the exchange of cattle across the frontier zone, as indicated in the Ordinance concerning the Dunsaete) have been common enough on borders in many parts of the world…(such as) the more extensive creation of marches, or marks, by Charlemagne in the period when Offa's Dyke was being constructed.' (Noble, 1983, 59).
36. Smith, 1995, 179.
37. Ibid, 177.
38. Ibid, 179.
39. Squatriti, 2002, 11–15. Allegedly, Charlemagne allowed himself to be persuaded to this presumably largely emblematic task by 'certain people who claimed to know such things' (ibid, 11). One might be tempted to speculate that these 'certain people' were a party of Mercian officials seconded from work on Offa's Dyke, were it not for the timing of this event during the period when Franco-Mercian relations are thought to have been at a low ebb!
40. Malim, 2007.
41. Wileman, 2003.
42. Reynolds and Langlands, 2006.
43. Ibid. The argument made concerning Wansdyke was that in the seventh to eighth centuries at least, the two distinct lengths (East and West) may have been linked together as a frontier work by a demarcation line that followed part of the Roman road between Mildenhall (*Cunetio*) east of Marlborough and Bath, along the line of the later A4 Great West Road.
44. Wileman, 2003; Yorke, 2005; Reynolds and Langlands, 2006.
45. Squatriti, 2002, 40.
46. Ibid.
47. Ibid.
48. Moschek, 2009, 15.
49. Ibid.
50. Kirby, 1991; Cubitt, 1995; Keynes, 2001b. Curiously, it has been suggested very recently that the dynastic references of the 'Pillar of Eliseg' are so closely computable that the building of Offa's Dyke, in assumed response to the alleged mid-eighth-century 'resurgence' of Powys, can be dated precisely to the decade 750 to 760 (Charles-Edwards, 2013a). The manifold problems of interpretation of that inscription have, in contrast, been reviewed closely by Stephenson (2012).
51. Such 'opportunistic' extension of Mercian control chimes well with what the Welsh Annals attest, namely periodic expeditionary activity by Mercian forces entering Wales from Cheshire and Herefordshire. It corresponds also, with 'the desire to protect those lands in Shropshire that had been systematically anglisised under royal authority' (Charles-Edwards, 2013b, 427), although we might add 'and the economically-important Forest of Dean in Gloucestershire'.
52. Fox, 1955, 287. Fox suggested that the slight nature of the earthwork here reflected 'the exhaustion of both King and people' or difficulties that had arisen due to 'either a breakdown of the peace with Powys, or a failure to come to terms with Powys' (ibid).
53. Equally, it could be asked 'why did Coenwulf not campaign westwards through Herefordshire?' The simplest answer would be that Offa may have already achieved what the Mercians had set out to do, in the Wye valley region west of Hereford.
54. Portable Antiquities Scheme reference CPAT-4AAF81, from near Wrexham.
55. Again, Fox believed that the incomplete 'Flintshire' part of the Dyke was begun from the coast at Prestatyn at least in part 'because of the value to (the) Mercian economy of the lead (silver) mines of the Halkyn – Llanasa ridge' (1955, 287).
56. Malim, 2007. These aspects were discussed briefly above, also (Chapter 6, pp. 232–3) in the context of the presence and working of possible gateways through the Dyke.
57. Smith, 1995, 179.
58. Malim, 2007; Malim and Hayes, 2008 for the north; Hooke, 1985, 1986 for the *Hwicce*.
59. Pine et al, 2010. Prefiguring this discovery, Feryock wrote of the lower Wye sector in 2001: 'Though wide, the river Wye is fordable in many places, even at its deepest southern end. Perhaps the dykes (*sic*) were built to prevent people coming across the river and taking the resources of Forest of Dean, known to be an important industrial source of iron and wood since Roman times. The dyke on the cliff could more effectively prevent entry into the forest from the river than any obstacle along the water's edge. *The dyke could also have been built here to control access to the exposed hilltops where the wind would help to fire the many iron smelters which may once have been worked in this area.*' (Feryock, 2001, 189–90; emphasis added).
60. Fox, 1955, 288.
61. Hayes and Malim, 2008.
62. Story, 2003, 202.
63. Ibid.
64. This idea will no doubt be regarded as, at best, highly speculative. However, the aim is to try to draw out the potential implications of deploying evidence that has long been available for such scrutiny, but has so far

65 See Jones, 1955. Caution needs to be exercised in using these sources. For example, phrases found in some versions of the *Brut*, such as that Offa's Dyke extended from sea to sea, do not constitute independent Welsh sources at all: rather, they were interpolations derived from English medieval sources ultimately traceable back to Asser (see Thomas, 1975). Elystan Glodrydd subsumed the district of Elfael, with its chief centre at Painscastle. This does indeed lie between the Wye and the Severn, but in Radnorshire.

66 Hartshorne, 1841, 183.
67 Silvester, 2008.
68 Tyler, 2011, 160.
69 Keynes, 2005. See the Epilogue below, for further assessment of the validity of this claim.

Epilogue

1 Stephens, 1986, 436.
2 Wormald, 1991, 25. Wormald made the point here and elsewhere that the study of the history of the early Middle Ages is in many respects not so different from the study of prehistory.
3 Williams, 2009.
4 Keynes, 2005b.
5 Levison, 1946, 253.
6 Finberg, 1972, 11. Wulfred, Archbishop of Canterbury in Coenwulf's and Ceolwulf's reigns, outlived them both and in 825 at that year's Council at Clofesho he settled a dispute with Coenwulf's daughter Cwoenthryth, abbess of 'Southminster' (Minster-in-Thanet), making it an express condition of the reconciliation that the names of lands transferred to him should be erased 'de antiquis privilegiis quae sunt aet Wincelcumbe', that is, 'from the old (charters of) rights that are (lodged) at Winchcombe (Abbey)'. (Levison, 1946, 252).
7 On Alfred's attitude to Offa's 'law code' (whether or not formalised as such), see Keynes and Lapidge, 1983, 305–6, note 5). The clerics concerned were Werferth, Bishop of Worcester, Plegmund, Archbishop of Canterbury (who is noted explicitly as 'a Mercian by birth'), and the priests and chaplains Aethelstan and Werwulf ('Mercians by birth and learned men'), all of whom Alfred 'summoned…to him from Mercia'. In this way, 'The king's desire for knowledge increased steadily and was satisfied by the wisdom and learning of all four men' (Asser, *Life* of King Alfred, chapter 79. Keynes and Lapidge, 1983, 92–3, and note 167). The suggestion could be made that this was a 'late flowering' of Mercian scholarship, but such an idea seems unlikely given that the late ninth century was regarded by contemporaries as a time of intellectual diminution from past glories (Ibid, n. 167).
8 Keynes, 2001, 341; see also, Keynes, 2000; 2005; for Offa's relations with Charlemagne critically re-assessed see Nelson, 2001; for the 'remembered' Offa, see Martin, 2005.
9 Keynes, 2005a, 14.
10 Stenton, 1947, 222–3.
11 Keynes, 2005, 18.
12 Wormald, 1982, 121.
13 Thorpe, 1978. See also, Kightly, 1988, 6–9.
14 Suppe, 1994; Liebermann 2008, 2010
15 Fox, 1955, 171.
16 No better time, apart, however, from the present difficulties in securing funding for such investigations, which will necessarily have to be supported by adequate finance for specialist analyses. So, for example, attempts were made by the present authors on more than one occasion in the period 2010–12 to achieve funding for new recording and investigations of Offa's Dyke through a variety of proposed projects and partnerships. These applications for funding were unsuccessful due largely to the extent and quality of 'competition' from other projects, but also to some extent precisely because the view has seemingly become widespread that the 'problems' of Offa's Dyke have all been solved by the small-scale, part-time, and substantially unpublished, archaeological summer-school work of David Hill and associates.
17 This was a point that was forcefully made by Philip Barker as long ago as 1991 in reference to Dudston Fields near Montgomery and the active erosion of the Dyke earthworks in many places: 'It would of course be necessary to excavate one or more lengths of the Dyke in detail from the top downwards, on the model of the Hen Domen excavation, in order to recover the maximum possible information from all levels' (Barker in Everson, 1991, 61). He also noted that well-preserved lengths of the Dyke should in particular be examined, because it is only in these places that traces of any palisade structure might be traced, and in which extensive areas of pre-Dyke land surface would survive.
18 Williams, 2009; Wormald, 1982, 121.
19 See Edwards, 2009; Stephenson, 2012.
20 See Bapty, 2000.
21 This is very much what the Offa's Dyke Association,

formed by Frank Noble and others in the 1960s, has sought to do.

22 Keynes, 2005, 10. 'The hermitage in Holy Cross' is the church of St Michael in Lichfield; the Welsh Bridge is one of the two ancient bridging-points of the river Severn at Shrewsbury. Simon Keynes implied here that Hill did not adequately know either his geography or his Anglo-Saxon history since surely it was the A5 and not the M5 that Offa was overlord of. This misses entirely the subtlety of Hill's allusion. The point about the M5, apart from being a metaphor of modern power (and to some extent, futility), is that it serves for Hill in this poem as a modern echo of the line of Offa's Dyke, dividing an 'inner' Mercia from a western world.

23 Mercian Hymns, I, in *Geoffrey Hill: Selected Poems* (Penguin Books; 2006, 6). With copyright permission from author and publisher.

List of figures

1.1 Offa's Dyke and Wat's Dyke in west-central Britain (map)
1.2 Offa's Dyke at Mainstone, Shropshire, looking north
1.3 The northern course of Offa's Dyke south to the Clun valley, and Wat's Dyke (map)
1.4 The southern course of Offa's Dyke, south from the Clun valley to the Severn Estuary (map)
1.5 At Sedbury, Gloucestershire, by the Severn estuary
1.6 On the Clun uplands, south of Llanfair Hill
1.7 Excavations on Wat's Dyke at Gobowen in 2006
1.8 East Wansdyke at Baltic Farm, Bishop's Canning, Wiltshire
1.9 The Devil's Dyke in Cambridgeshire, near Newmarket (Suffolk)
1.10 The North Herefordshire Rowe Ditch
1.11 Offa's Dyke north of Carreg-y-big, viewed from the south-east
1.12 Offa's Dyke from Derwas on the Severn north to Trefonen (map)
1.13 Llanymynech Hill and Whitehaven Hill viewed from Bryn Mawr
1.14 Offa's Dyke from Treflach and Trefonen north to Chirk Park and Caeaugwynion (map)
1.15 Aerial view northwards from above Baker's Hill
1.16 Offa's Dyke from Caeaugwynion and Plas Offa north to Llanfynydd and Treuddyn (map)
1.17 The northern extremity of Offa's Dyke from near Brymbo
1.18 Offa's Dyke from Derwas along the Severn and south to Forden (map)
1.19 At The Stubb, looking west towards Kingswood
1.20 Offa's Dyke from Forden south to the Kerry Ridgeway (map)
1.21 At Dudston Fields, Chirbury, looking south
1.22 Offa's Dyke from the Kerry Ridgeway south towards Cwmsanahan Hill (map)
1.23 At the crossing of the Clun valley, north of Spoad
1.24 Offa's Dyke from Cwmsanahan Hill south towards Rushock Hill (map)
1.25 At Jenkins Allis south of Knighton, looking north
1.26 Offa's Dyke from Rushock Hill south to the river Wye (map)
1.27 At the Curl Brook valley, Lyonshall, Herefordshire, looking south
1.28 Offa's Dyke from Lydbrook south to Bigsweir (map)
1.29 At Madgett Hill, looking north
1.30 Offa's Dyke from Wyegate Hill to Sedbury Cliffs (map)
2.1 Sir Richard Corbett's 'Manor of Leighton' from Powis Castle
2.2 Offa's Dyke at Pen-rhos, south of Brymbo, looking south
2.3 Aerial view of Offa's Dyke at Ffrydd, south of Knighton
2.4 The site of the Oswestry Field Club's excavations at Carreg-y-big
2.5 Fox's annotated map extract of for Offa's Dyke south of Knighton
2.6 The site of Fox's 1927 excavation by Ffrith post office, Denbighshire
2.7 Offa's Dyke in Montgomeryshire (Fox, 1955, Fig. 52)
2.8 From Sarnesfield Cross south towards Burton Hill, Herefordshire
2.9 At Sedbury Park, Gloucestershire: view towards Chepstow
2.10 Offa's Dyke at Yew Tree Farm, Discoed, crossing the Lugg valley
2.11 The Devil's Pulpit length seen from Tintern (Fox, 1955, Plate XXXVI)
2.12 View north towards Orseddwen, north-west of Oswestry
2.13 Offa's Dyke at Garnons, near Kenchester, to the west of Hereford
2.14 At Knighton: the site of 'Offa's Dyke Project' excavations in 1973
2.15 The 'Pillar of Eliseg' to the north-west of Llangollen
2.16 The location of excavations at Plas Offa, Chirk, 2013
3.1 Mercia and major Anglo-Saxon kingdoms in southern Britain (map).
3.2 Wall, in Staffordshire: Romano-British buildings
3.3 The boundaries of late Roman provinces and distributions of early Anglo-Saxon brooch-types (map)
3.4 The hills south-west of Oswestry, viewed from near Watling Street
3.5 Cropthorne, Worcestershire: early eighth-century cross-head
3.6 Seckington, Warwickshire: view south towards Tamworth
3.7 Coin of Offa, moneyer Ebba (British Museum)
3.8 All Saints Church, Brixworth, Northamptonshire
3.9 Tamworth, Staffordshire: the Tame bridge and the castle
3.10 Winchcombe, Gloucestershire

List of figures

4.1 Orientation and seas: Offa's Dyke southern limit at Sedbury Cliffs.
4.2 Major 'stances' of the Dyke, facing the uplands (schematic map)
4.3 South-west facing orientation: the Teme valley from Panpunton Hill
4.4 Offa's Dyke on the south bank of the river Dee near Chirk
4.5 Offa's Dyke approaching the middle Severn valley from the north
4.6 The west-facing slopes of the Long Mountain, from Buttington Bridge
4.7 Along Offa's Dyke at Mainstone, looking southwards
4.8 Crossing the flood-plain of the river Lugg near Discoed
4.9 Approaching the crossing of the Teme, overlooking the valley
4.10 Offa's Dyke north of the Afon Morda valley, looking south
4.11 Offa's Dyke negotiating the crossing of the Ceiriog valley at Chirk
4.12 Blocking routeways and valleys: the Dyke north from Crowsnest
4.13 Offa's Dyke traversing the Kerry Ridgeway: from the north
4.14 A gently-curving course around a west-facing hill-top: Llanfair Hill
4.15 Craig Morda from the south, from just west of the Dyke
4.16 The Hindwell Brook and the valley below Burfa Camp
4.17 Offa's Dyke at Caeaugwynion, south of the river Dee
4.18 The long diagonal traverse of the southern slopes of Evenjobb Hill
4.19 The long diagonal traverse of the north-western flank of Selattyn Hill
4.20 Offa's Dyke crossing the Clun valley, viewed from the north-west
4.21 The Dyke at Gwarthlow, viewed from the west
4.22 The Dyke silhouetted on the skyline: Baker's Hill from the west
4.23 Eastwards towards Clun from the southern limit of Graig Hill
4.24 Looking westwards up the Clun valley over Newcastle village
4.25 View north along the Dyke, south of Gwarthlow
5.1 Offa's Dyke above Garbett Hall, continuing to Cwmsanahan Hill
5.2 Along the prominent ridge overlooking the Ceiriog valley above Bronygarth
5.3 The 'slighter' mode of construction: at Rhos-y-meirch
5.4 The 'scarp' mode of construction: at Hergan
5.5 A 'hybrid' length of Offa's Dyke at Lippetts Grove, Gloucestershire
5.6 Contrasting Dyke forms and build modes in Gloucestershire (map)
5.7 Contrasting profiles of Offa's Dyke on Long Mountain, after Fox
5.8 The *monumental* build mode well-preserved: above Garbett Hall
5.9 Bank length with possible slab-defined bays at Discoed on the Lugg
5.11 The excavated ditch at Ffrydd Road, Knighton: in section
5.12 The bank and ditch in the well-recorded Ffrydd Road investigation
5.13 A 20 metre long section through Offa's Dyke at Esclusham
5.14 The stony 'foundation deposit' beneath Wat's Dyke at Gobowen
5.15 Section through the bank exposed in the side of a track at Bronygarth
5.16 Possible roughly-coursed stone facework on the bank at Llanfair Hill
5.17 Surviving bank facework at Madgett Hill, Gloucestershire
5.18 Former quarry for Offa's Dyke stone on Madgett Hill, Gloucestershire
5.19 The bank and part-infilled rearward former quarries at Madgett Hill
5.20 The eastern quarry-ditch on Panpunton Hill, north of Knighton
5.21 Subtle scale and form adjustments: above Garbett Hall
5.22 Analytical field survey of Offa's Dyke at Dudston Fields
5.23 Dudston Fields: complexities of alignment
5.24 Dudston Fields bank/ditch lengths and segments
5.25 At Dudston Fields: the adjusted bank segments
5.26 The stance of adjacent Dyke lengths at Discoed (plan)
5.27 The continuously-adjusted bank lengths on the hill above Lower Spoad
5.28 Detail of the adjustment of bank lengths above Lower Spoad
5.29 Longitudinal bank and counterscarp bank profiles at Baker's Hill
5.30 Clearly co-adjusted bank lengths at Llanfair Hill, looking north
5.31 Fox's photograph of distinct bank segments at Fron Farm
5.32 'Adjusted-segmented' lengths on the western flank of Rushock Hill
5.33 'Adjusted-segmented' bank lengths at the Devil's Pulpit
5.34 Precision design: a 'compensating' build at Llanfair Hill
5.35 Dyke length adjustments around the crest of Llanfair Hill (1)
5.36 Dyke length adjustments around the crest of Llanfair Hill (2)
5.37 The counterscarp bank at Llanfair Hill, looking north

5.38 The Offa's Dyke 'wall': crossing the southern flank of Graig Hill
6.1 Landscape impact: Offa's Dyke traversing dramatic topographies
6.2 By the Devil's Pulpit, Gloucestershire: LiDAR plot
6.3 The process of establishing Offa's Dyke length by length
6.4 A 'frontier patrol' in the landscape?
6.5 Supposed 'gateway' at Jenkins Allis south of Knighton
6.6 Dyke configuration at a likely gateway at Bwlch, Discoed
6.7 The Dyke north of the Kinnerton-Presteigne ridge-way
6.8 Candidate gateways: the case of Carreg-y-big, Oswestry
6.9 The 'angled turn' on Rushock Hill, from the west
6.10 An angled turn and possible gateway at Hergan
6.11 The angled turn at Cwmsanahan Hill, overlooking the Teme valley
6.12 Indicative plan of the configuration of Offa's Dyke at Cwmsanahan Hill
6.13 The Rowe Ditch traversing the Arrow valley in Herefordshire
6.14 Burfa Camp and the course of Offa's Dyke from Herrock Hill
6.15 The Dyke north of Garbett Hall, with a small 'fort'/watchtower
6.16 An array of construction devices at Madgett Hill, Gloucestershire
7.1 Offa's Dyke north of Trefonen, from the east
7.2 The junction of slight and substantial mode builds at Jenkins Allis
7.3 Fox's 'reading' of contemporary land-use from the form of the Dyke
7.4 The middle Severn valley near Buttington, looking north
7.5 Offa's Dyke overlooking the Walton Basin at Herrock Hill and Burfa
7.6 From Offa's Dyke at Pont Adam, Ruabon, towards Llangollen
7.7 Tintern from the Pulpit Rock, Devil's Pulpit, Gloucestershire
7.8 Offa's Dyke, Montgomery and the Kerry Ridgeway, south from Hem
7.9 Knucklas viewed from the Dyke south of Cwmsanahan Hill
7.10 Offa's Dyke at Pont Adam, Ruabon, looking north
7.11 Old Radnor Hill as seen from Offa's Dyke on Evenjobb Hill
7.12 Towards the Severn Estuary, from Offa's Dyke near Sedbury Park
7.13 Offa's Dyke west of Lyonshall in north Herefordshire
7.14 Continuous lynchet formed from the bank of the ?Dyke near Weobley
7.15 Wood-bank or *slighter* mode Dyke length at Crump Oak, Broxwood
8.1 Tamworth: Market Street and the Town Hall from the west
8.2 'Offa Rex' pennies, promoting a particular view of Mercian kingship
8.3 Penny of 'Cynethryth Regina', promoting Mercian Queenship
8.4 The site of the monastery at Reculver, Kent, in the late Roman fort
8.5 Winchcombe, a key place in a western Mercian 'capital territory'
8.6 Gold's Clump, Watling Street, Hints, west of Tamworth
8.7 Pennies of Offa, with contrasting drapery styles
8.8 Brixworth Church: evoking Roman imperial structures
8.9 The 'Lichfield Angel' stone-carving, probably from St Chad's shrine
8.10 Gold *mancus* of Coenwulf, found at Biggleswade in Bedfordshire
8.11 Gold ornamental mount from the 'Staffordshire Hoard'
8.12 Inscribed gold strip from among the 'Staffordshire Hoard' items
9.1 Power in the landscape: Offa's Dyke crossing the Vale of Montgomery
9.2 At the Devil's Pulpit, Gloucestershire: Offa's Dyke distinctiveness
9.3 View south-east across the Shropshire Plain from Plascrogen
9.4 Hadrian's Wall at Steel Rigg, west of Housesteads
9.5 The Great Bath with Bath Abbey church above it to the east
9.6 Herrock Hill in the 'Marchia Walliae' of 1086, west of Presteigne
9.7 'Both linear and zonal': the frontier east from the Clun
9.8 'Areas of ill-defined domination': the Dyke in the Ceiriog uplands
9.9 The Dyke at Orseddwen, looking south-eastwards
9.10 Offa's Dyke on either side of the Teme valley, from Ffrydd Hill
9.11 Complexity and a possible 'gateway' at Carreg-y-big near Oswestry
9.12 The Dyke crossing the southern flank of Graig Hill above the Clun
9.13 The massive 'terminal' length of Offa's Dyke at Ffordd Llanfynydd
9.14 Coin of Coenwulf, from a location to the north-east of Wrexham
9.15 Wat's Dyke viewed from Mount Sion on Offa's Dyke

Bibliography

Abels, R. (1988) *Lordship and Military Obligation in Anglo-Saxon England*. London, British Museum Press.

Allen, D. (1988) Excavations on Offa's Dyke, Ffrydd Road, Knighton, Powys, 1976. *The Radnorshire Society Transactions*, 58, 7–10.

Allott, S. (1974) *Alcuin of York: His Life and Letters*. York, William Sessions.

Archibald, M. M. (2005) Beonna and Alberht: Coinage and Historical Context. In D. Hill and M. Worthington (eds.) *Aethelbald and Offa: Two Eighth-Century Kings of Mercia*, 123–32. Oxford, British Archaeological Reports (British Series, BAR 383).

Arnold, C. J. (1991) Excavation of Offa's Dyke, Chirk Castle. *Denbighshire Historical Society Transactions*, 40, 93–97.

Atherton, M. (2005) Mentions of Offa in the *Anglo-Saxon Chronicle*, *Beowulf* and *Widsith*. In D. Hill and M. Worthington (eds.) *Aethelbald and Offa: Two Eighth-Century Kings of Mercia*, 65–74. Oxford, British Archaeological Reports (British Series, BAR 383).

Audouy. M. (1984) Excavations at the Church of All Saints, Brixworth, Northamptonshire, 1981–2. *Journal of the British Archaeological Association*, 137, 1–44.

Bailey, K. (1989) The Middle Saxons. In S. Bassett (ed.) *The Origins of Anglo-Saxon Kingdoms*, 108–22; 265–9. Leicester University Press.

Bailey, R. N. (1980) *The Meaning of Mercian Sculpture*. Sixth Brixworth Lecture (1988): Vaughan Papers in Adult Education (Leicester University).

Balkwill, C. (1993) Old English *wic* and the origin of the hundred. *Landscape History*, 15, 5–12.

Bapty, I. (2000) Datganiad Cadwraeth Clawwd Offa/Offa's Dyke Conservation Statement, pp. 44. Welshpool, Clwyd-Powys Archaeological Trust. (available online at http://www.cpat.org.uk/offa/odcs.pdf).

Bapty, I. (2004) 'The Final Word on Offa's Dyke?' Clwyd-Powys Archaeological Trust website (available online at http://www.cpat.org.uk/offa/offrev.htm).

Bassett, S. (1985) A probable Mercian royal mausoleum at Winchcombe, Gloucestershire. *Antiquaries Journal*, 65, 82–100.

Bassett, S. (2000) How the west was won: the Anglo-Saxon take-over of the West Midlands. *Anglo-Saxon Studies in Archaeology and History*, 11, 107–18.

Bassett, S. (2006) Boundaries of Knowledge: Mapping the Land Units of Late Anglo-Saxon and Norman England. In W. Davies, G. Halsall, and A. Reynolds (eds.) *People and Space in the Middle Ages 300–1300*, 115–142. Turnhout (Belgium), Brepols. (Studies in the Early Middle Ages).

Bassett, S. (2008) The Middle and Late Anglo-Saxon Defences of Western Mercian Towns. In S. Crawford and H. Hamerow (eds) *Anglo-Saxon Studies in Archaeology and History* 15, 180–239. Oxford University School of Archaeology.

Baxter, S. (2007) *Earls of Mercia: Lordship and Power in Late Anglo-Saxon England*. Oxford University Press.

Baxter, S. and Blair, J. (2006) A Model of Land Tenure and Royal Patronage in Late Anglo-Saxon England. In C. P. Lewis (ed.) *Anglo-Norman Studies: Proceedings of the Battle Conference 2005*, 19–29. Boydell and Brewer, Woodbridge.

Beales, P. W. (1980) The Late Devensian and Flandrian vegetational history of Crose Mere, Shropshire. *New Phytologist* 85, 133–161.

Berry, J. (2010) Leintwardine. In B. C. Burnham and J. L. Davies (eds) *Roman Frontiers in Wales and the Marches*, 305–307. Aberystwyth, Royal Commission on the Ancient and Historical Monuments of Wales.

Blackburn, M. (1995) Money and Coinage. In R. McKitterick (ed.) *The New Cambridge Medieval History*, 2, c.700–c.900, 538–59. Cambridge University Press.

Blackburn, M. (2001) Coinage. In M. Lapidge, J. Blair, S. Keynes and D. Scragg (eds.) *The Blackwell Encyclopaedia of Anglo-Saxon England*, 113–116. Oxford, Blackwell.

Blackburn, M. (2007) Gold in England during the 'Age of Silver' (Eighth–Eleventh Centuries). In J. Graham-Campbell and G. Williams (eds) *Silver Economy in the Viking Age*, 55–98. Walnut Creek, California, Left Coast Press.

Blair, J. (1994) *Anglo-Saxon Oxfordshire*. Stroud, Sutton Publishing. (Oxfordshire Books).

Blair, J. (1996) Palaces or minsters? Northampton and Cheddar reconsidered. *Anglo-Saxon England*, 25, 97–121.

Blair, J. (2001) Bridges. In M. Lapidge, J. Blair, S. Keynes and D. Scragg (eds.) *The Blackwell Encyclopaedia of Anglo-Saxon England*, 74. Oxford, Blackwell.

Blair, J. (2005) *The Church in Anglo-Saxon Society*. Oxford University Press.

Bland, R. and Leahy, K. (2009) *The Staffordshire Hoard*. The British Museum Press.

Blinkhorn, P. (forthcoming) *The Ipswich Ware Survey*. Medieval Pottery Research Group.

Blockley, K. (1997) Veterinary Surgery, Four Crosses, Llanymynech: Archaeological Watching Brief. Cambrian Archaeological Projects, Report 67. (Copy on file at Clwyd-Powys Archaeological Trust Historic Environment Record, Welshpool).

Bosworth, J. and Toller, T. N. (1898) *An Anglo-Saxon Dictionary*. Oxford, The Clarendon Press. (online version: http://www.ling.upenn.edu/_kuristo/germanic/oe_bosworthtoller_about.html. (Accessed 15.10.2010)

Bowen, H. C., ed. B. Eagles (1990) *The Archaeology of Bokerley Dyke*. London, Her Majesty's Stationery Office.

Branch, N. P. and Scaife, R. G. (1995) The stratigraphy and pollen analysis of peat sequences associated with the Lindow III bog body. In R. C. Turner and R. G. Scaife (eds) *Bog Bodies: New Discoveries and New Perspectives*, 19–30. London, British Museum Press.

Brandon, A. (1989) *Geology of the country between Hereford and Leominster*, British Geological Survey Memoir for 1: 50 000 geological sheet 198 (England and Wales). London, Her Majesty's Stationery Office.

Brødersen, K. (2009) "The grand old lady still has plenty of surprises left": Hadrian's Wall. In N. Fryde and D. Reitz (eds.) *Walls, Ramparts and Lines of Demarcation: Selected Studies from Antiquity to Modern Times*, 5–11. Munster, Lit Verlag.

Brooks, N. P. (1971) The development of military obligations in eighth- and ninth-century England. In P. Clemoes and K. Hughes (eds.) *England Before the Conquest: Studies in Primary Sources Presented to Dorothy Whitelock*, 69–84. Cambridge University Press.

Brooks, N. P. (1989) The formation of the Mercian kingdom. In S. Bassett (ed.) *The Origins of Anglo-Saxon Kingdoms*, 159–70. Leicester University Press.

Brooks, N. (2009) Comment attached at http://www.staffordshirehoard.org.uk/commentary (Accessed, 25.02.2010).

Brown, M. P. and Farr, C. A. (eds.) *Mercia: An Anglo-Saxon kingdom in Europe*. London, Continuum.

Burghart, A. and Wareham, A. (2008) Was there an Agricultural Revolution in Anglo-Saxon England? In J. Barrow and A. Wareham (eds) *Myth, Rulership, Church and Charters: Essays in Honour of Nicholas Brooks*, 89–100. London, Ashgate.

Charles-Edwards, T. M. (2001) Wales and Mercia, 613–918. In M. P. Brown and C. Farr (eds) *Mercia: An Anglo-Saxon kingdom in Europe*, 89–105. Leicester University Press (2nd edn, London, Continuum, 2005).

Charles-Edwards, T. M. (2013a) Offa, King of the Mercians. *Anglo-Saxon Portraits*, 10. BBC Radio 3. First broadcast: 25th January 2013. http://www.bbc.co.uk/programmes/b01pz17l accessed 05/02/13.

Charles-Edwards, T. M. (2013b) *Wales and the Britons, 350–1064*. Oxford University Press.

Chick, D. (1997) Towards a Chronology for Offa's Coinage: An Interim Study. *The Yorkshire Numismatist*, 3, 47–64.

Chick, D. (2005) The Coinage of Offa in the light of Recent Discoveries. In D. Hill and M. Worthington (eds.) *Aethelbald and Offa: Two Eighth-Century Kings of Mercia*, 111–122. Oxford, British Archaeological Reports (British Series, BAR 383).

Churchyard, T. (1587) *The Worthines of Wales*. See Evans, T. (1776).

Clapham, A.W. (1927) The carved stones at Breedon-on-the-Hill, Leicestershire, and their position in the history of English art. *Archaeologia*, 77, 219–40.

Colt Hoare, Sir Richard (1812) *The Ancient History of Wiltshire*. EP publishing/Wiltshire County Library reprint, 1975.

Conant, K. J. (1966) *Carolingian and Romanesque Architecture 800 to 1200* (Second Edition). London, Penguin Books.

Cool, H. E. M. (2012) *Contextualising Metal-Detected Discoveries: Staffordshire Anglo-Saxon Hoard*. Barbican Design Associates Assessment and Project Design: Project 5892.

Coplestone-Crow, B. (2009) *Herefordshire Place-Names*. Hereford, Logaston Press.

Cowie, R. (2001) Mercian London. In M. P. Brown and C. A. Farr (eds.) *Mercia: An Anglo-Saxon kingdom in Europe*, 195–209. Leicester University Press (2nd edn, London, Continuum, 2005).

Cramp, R. J. (1977) Schools of Mercian sculpture. In A. Dornier (ed.) *Mercian Studies*, 191–233. Leicester University Press.

Cubitt, C. (1995) *Anglo-Saxon Church Councils c.650–c.850*. Leicester University Press.

Currie, C. R. J. and Herbert, N. M. (1996) *A History of the County of Gloucester, Volume 5: Bledisloe Hundred, St. Briavel's Hundred, the Forest of Dean*. (A. P. Baggs and A. R. J. Jurica eds., The Victoria County History of Gloucestershire). The University of London.

Darby, H. C. and Terrett, I. B. (1954) *The Domesday Geography of Midland England*. Cambridge University Press.

Dark, P. (2000) *The environment of Britain in the first millennium A.D.* London, Duckworth.

Davies, W. (1977) Annals and the origins of Mercia. In A. Dornier (ed.) *Mercian Studies*, 17–29. Leicester University Press.

Davies, W. (1978) *An Early Welsh Microcosm: the Llandaff Charters and South-East Wales in the Early Middle Ages*. London, Royal Historical Society.

Davies, W. (1979) *The Llandaff Charters*. Aberystwyth, The National Library of Wales.

Davies, W. (1982) *Wales in the Early Middle Ages*. Leicester University Press.

Davies, W. (1990) *Patterns of Power in Early Wales* (O'Donnell Lectures delivered in the University of Oxford 1983). Oxford, Clarendon Press.

Davies, W. and Vierck, H. (1974) The contexts of the Tribal Hidage: social aggregates and settlement patterns. *Fruhmittelalterliche Studien*, 8, 223–293.

Dobat, A. (2008) Danevirke Revisited: An Investigation into Military and Socio-Political Organisation in Southern Scandinavia (c. AD 700–1100). *Medieval Archaeology* 52, 27–67.

Dolley, R. H. M. (1958) Two stray finds from St. Albans of coins of Offa and of Charlemagne. *British Numismatic Journal*, 28, 459–466.

Dornier, A. The Anglo-Saxon monastery at Breedon-on-the-Hill, Leicestershire. In A. Dornier (ed.) *Mercian Studies*, 155–168. Leicester University Press.

Draper, S. (2008) The Significance of Old English *Burh* in Anglo-Saxon England. *Anglo-Saxon Studies in Archaeology and History*, 15, 240–253.

Dumville, D. N. (1976) The Anglian collection of royal genealogies and regnal lists. *Anglo-Saxon England*, 5, 23–50.

Dumville, D. N. (1977) Kingship, genealogies and regnal lists. In P. Sawyer and I. N. Woods (eds) *Early Medieval Kingship*, 72–104. Leeds University Press.

Dumville, D. N. (1989) The Tribal Hidage: an introduction to its texts and their history, in S. Bassett (ed.) *The Origins of Anglo-Saxon Kingdoms*, 225–230. Leicester University Press.

Dumville, D. N. (1993) Essex, Middle Anglia, and the expansion of Mercia in the South-East Midlands. In D. N. Dumville (ed.) *Britons and Anglo-Saxons in the Early Middle Ages*. Aldershot, Variorum/Ashgate.

Dumville, D. N. (1997) The Terminology of Overkingship in Early Anglo-Saxon England. In J. Hines (ed) *The Anglo-Saxons from the Migration Period to the eighth Century*, 345–365. Woodbridge, Boydell.

Eagles, B. and Allen, M. J. (2011) A reconsideration of East Wansdyke; its construction and date – a preliminary note, in S. Brooks, S. Harrington and A. Reynolds (eds) *Studies in Early Anglo-Saxon Art and Archaeology: Papers in Honour of Martin G. Welch*, 147–155. Oxford: British Archaeological Reports, BS 527.

Earle, J. (1857) Offa's Dyke, in the neighbourhood of Knighton. *Archaeologia Cambrensis* (Third Series) 10, 196–209.

Eaton, T. (2000) *Plundering the Past: Roman Stonework in Medieval Britain*. Stroud, Tempus

Eaton, T. (2001) Old ruins, new world. *British Archaeology* 60.

Edwards, N. (2009) Rethinking the Pillar of Eliseg. *The Antiquaries Journal* 89, 143–177.

Ekwall, E. (1960) *The Concise Oxford Dictionary of English Place-Names* (Fourth Edition). Oxford University Press.

Emery, V. E. (1958) A map of Edward Lhuyd's *Parochial Queries In Order to a Geographical Dictionary, &C, of Wales* (1696). *Transactions of the Honourable Society of Cymmrodorion*, 1958, 41–52.

Erskine, J. G. P. (2007) The West Wansdyke: an appraisal of the dating, dimensions and construction techniques in the light of excavated evidence. *The Archaeological Journal* 164, 80–108.

Evans, H. M. and Thomas, W. O. (1987) *Y Geiriadur Mawr: The Complete Welsh-English, English-Welsh Dictionary* (2nd edition, ed. Williams, S. J.). Llandyssul, Gomer Press.

Evans, T. (1776) *Thomas Churchyard: The Worthines of Wales: A Poem. Subtitled: A True Note of the auncient Castles, famous Monuments, goodly Rivers, faire Bridges, fine Townes and courteous People that I have seen in the noble Countrie of Wales*.

Everson, P. (1991) Three case studies of ridge and furrow: 1. Offa's Dyke at Dudston in Chirbury, Shropshire. A pre-Offan field system? *Landscape History* 13(1), 53–63.

Faith, R. (1994) Tidenham, Gloucestershire, and the history of the manor in England. *Landscape History* 16, 39–52.

Faith, R. (1999) *The English Peasantry and the Growth of Lordship*. Leicester University Press.

Featherstone, P. (2001) The Tribal Hidage and the Ealdormen of Mercia. In M. P. Brown and C. A. Farr (eds.) *Mercia: An Anglo-Saxon kingdom in Europe*, 23–34. Leicester University Press (2nd edn, London, Continuum, 2005).

Fern, C. and Speake, G. (2014) *Beasts, Birds and Gods: Interpreting the Staffordshire Hoard*. Alcester, West Midlands History.

Fernie, E. (1983) *The Architecture of the Anglo-Saxons*. London, Batsford.

Feryock, M. (2001) Offa's Dyke, Chapter 8 in S. Zaluckyj, *Mercia: The Anglo-Saxon Kingdom of Central England*, 163–192. Almeley, Logaston Press.

Finberg, H. P. R. (1964) Mercians and Welsh. *Lucerna*, X, 66–82.

Finberg, H. P. R. (1972) *The Early Charters of the West Midlands* (2nd edition). Leicester University Press.

Fisher, J. (ed.) (1917) *Tours in Wales (1804–1813) by Richard Fenton*. London, Cambrian Archaeological Association/Bedford Press.

Fitzpatrick-Matthews, K. J. Wat's Dyke: A North Welsh linear boundary. Wansdyke Project 21 (http://www.wansdyke21.org.uk/wansdyke/wanart/matthews1.htm. Accessed 05.02.2010)

Fosbroke, T. D. (1833) Investigation of Offa's Dyke. *Gentleman's Magazine*, 102 (2), 500–503.

Fosbroke, T. D. (1835) The Real and Pretended Offa's Dyke. *Gentleman's Magazine*, 104 (1), 490–491.

Fowler, P. (2001) Wansdyke in the Woods: an unfinished Roman military earthwork for a non-event. In P. Ellis (ed) *Roman Wiltshire and After: Papers in Honour of Ken Annable*, 179–198. Devizes: Wiltshire Archaeological and Natural History Society.

Fox, A. and Fox, C. (1958) Wansdyke Reconsidered. *Archaeological Journal*, 115, 1–48.

Fox, C. (1923) *The Archaeology of the Cambridge Region*. Cambridge University Press.

Fox, C. (1926) Offa's Dyke: A Field Survey. First report: Offa's Dyke in Northern Flintshire. *Archaeologia Cambrensis*, 81(1), 133–179.

Fox, C. (1927) Offa's Dyke: A Field Survey. Second Report: Offa's Dyke from Coed Talwrn (Treuddyn Parish), Flintshire, to Plas Power park (Bersham Parish) Denbighshire. *Archaeologia Cambrensis*, 82(2), 232–268.

Fox, C. (1928) Offa's Dyke: A Field Survey. Third Report: Offa's Dyke from Plas Power park, Bersham Parish, Denbighshire, to the river Vyrnwy on the boundary between Llanymynech (Shropshire) and Carreghofa (Montgomeryshire) parishes. *Archaeologia Cambrensis*, 83(1), 33–110.

Fox, C. (1929) Dykes. *Antiquity*, Vol. 3, No. 10 (June 1929), 135–154.

Fox, C. (1931) Offa's Dyke: A Field Survey (Sixth Report). Offa's Dyke in the Wye Valley. *Archaeologia Cambrensis*, 86, 1–74.

Fox, C. (1934a) Wat's Dyke; a field survey. *Archaeologia Cambrensis*, 89, 205–278.

Fox, C. (1934b) Offa's Dyke in Herefordshire. In, *An Inventory of the Historical Monuments of England, Herefordshire. Volume III: North-West Herefordshire*, xxx–xxxi. The Royal Commission on the Historical Monuments of England. London, Her Majesty's Stationery Office.

Fox, C. (1938) The Western Frontier of Mercia in the VIIIth Century. *Yorkshire Celtic Studies*, being the Transactions of the Yorkshire Society for Celtic Studies, Volume 1, (1937–8), 3–10.

Fox, C. (1941) The Boundary Line of Cymru: The Sir John Rhys Memorial Lecture, 1940. *Proceedings of the British Academy*, 26, 275–300.

Fox, C. (1955) *Offa's Dyke. A field survey of the western frontier works of Mercia in the seventh and eighth centuries AD.* London, The British Academy.

Fox, C. and Phillips, D. W. (1929) Offa's Dyke: A Field Survey (Fourth Report). Offa's Dyke in Montgomershire. *Archaeologia Cambrensis*, 84, 1–60.

Fox, C. and Phillips, D. W. (1930) Offa's Dyke: A Field Survey (Fifth Report). Offa's Dyke in the Mountain Zone. *Archaeologia Cambrensis*, 85, 1–73.

Fryde, N. and Reitz, D. (eds.) (2009) *Walls, Ramparts and Lines of Demarcation: Selected Studies from Antiquity to Modern Times.* Munster, Lit Verlag.

Gannon, A. (2003) *The Iconography of Early Anglo-Saxon Coinage.* Oxford University Press.

Ganz, D. (2010) 'The Text of the Inscription', Staffordshire Hoard Symposium:finds.org.uk/staffshoardsymposium; accessed 3/10/10.

Gelling, M. (1989a) The early history of western Mercia. In S. Bassett (ed.) *The Origins of Anglo-Saxon Kingdoms*, 184–201. Leicester University Press.

Gelling, M. (1989b) The place-name Burton and variants. In S. C. Hawkes (ed.) *Weapons and Warfare in Anglo-Saxon England*, 145–153. Oxford University Committee for Archaeology.

Gelling, M. (1992) *The West Midlands in the Early Middle Ages.* Leicester University Press.

Grant, I. (2014) *Offa's Dyke De138, Chirk, Wrexham: Survey, Excavation and Recording.* Clwyd-Powys Archaeological Trust Report 1224.

Greenslade, M. W. (ed.) (1990) Lichfield: History to c. 1500, in M. W. Greenslade (ed.) *A History of the County of Stafford: Volume 14: Lichfield*, 4–14. London, Victoria County History, University of London. (URL: http://www.british-history.ac.uk/report.aspx?compid=42336 (Accessed: 27.11.2009).

Greenslade. M. W. and Baugh, G. C. (eds) (1976) *The History and Antiquities of Staffordshire by Stebbing Shaw.* EP Publishing and Staffordshire County Library.

Guest, E. (1858) On the Northern Termination of Offa's Dyke. *Archaeologia Cambrensis* 4 (Third Series), 335–342.

Hamerow, H. (2007) Agrarian production and the emporia of mid Saxon England, c. AD 650–850. In J. Henning (ed) *Post-Roman Towns, Volume 1: The Heirs of the Roman West*, 219–232. Berlin, Walter de Gruyter.

Hankinson, R. (2002) *The Short Dykes of Mid- and North-East Wales: Project Report.* Welshpool, Clwyd-Powys Archaeological Trust (Report 495).

Hankinson, R. and Caseldine, A. (2006) Short Dykes in Powys and Their Origins. *Archaeological Journal*, 163, 264–269.

Hannaford, H. (1998) An Excavation on Wat's Dyke at Mile Oak, Oswestry, Shropshire. *Transactions of the Shropshire Archaeological and Historical Society*, 73.

Hart, C. (1977) The Kingdom of Mercia. In A. Dornier (ed.) *Mercian Studies*, 45–62. Leicester University Press.

Hart, C. R. (ed. and tr.) (2006) *Byrhtferth's Northumbrian Chronicle: An Edition and Translation of the Old English and Latin Annals.* The Early Chronicles of England 2. Edwin Mellen Press. (Edition and translation of the first five sections).

Hartshorne, C. H.(1841) *Salopia Antiqua, or an enquiry from personal survey into the 'Druidical', military and other early remains in Shropshire and the North Welsh borders.* London, John Parker.

Haslam, J. (1984a) The Towns of Wiltshire. In J. Haslam (ed.) *Anglo-Saxon Towns in Southern England*, 87–147. Chichester, Phillimore.

Haslam, J. (1984b) The Towns of Devon. In J. Haslam (ed.), 249–283.

Haslam, J. (1987) Market and fortress in England in the reign of Offa, *World Archaeology* 19, 76–93.

Hawkes, J. (2001) Constructing Iconographies: Questions of Identity in Mercian Sculpture. In M. P. Brown and C. A. Farr (eds) *Mercia: An Anglo-Saxon kingdom in Europe*, 230–245. Leicester University Press (2nd edn, London, Continuum, 2005).

Hayes, L. and Malim, T. (2008) The date and nature of Wat's Dyke. *Anglo-Saxon Studies in Archaeology and History*, 15, 147–179.

Higham, N. J. (1993a) *The Kingdom of Northumbria, AD350–1100.* Stroud, Alan Sutton.

Higham, N. J. (1993b) *The origins of Cheshire.* Manchester, Manchester University Press.

Higham, N. J. (2005) Guthlac's Vita, Mercia and East Anglia in the first half of the Eighth Century. In D. Hill and M. Worthington (eds.) *Aethelbald and Offa. Two Eighth-Century Kings of Mercia*, 85–90. Oxford, British Archaeological Reports (British Series, BAR 383).

Hill, D. (1974a) Offa's and Wat's Dykes: some exploratory work on the frontier between Celt and Saxon. In T. Rowley (ed.) *Anglo-Saxon Settlement and Landscape*, 102–107. Oxford, British Archaeological Reports (British Series, BAR 6).

Hill, D. (1974b) The interrelation of Offa's and Wat's Dyke. *Antiquity* 48, 309–312.

Hill, D. (1977a) Offa's and Wat's Dykes: some aspects of recent work, 1972–1976. *Transactions of the Lancashire and Cheshire Antiquarian Society* 79, 21–33.

Hill, D. (1977b) Notes, on Offa's Dyke and Wat's Dyke, in 'Medieval Britain in 1976' (ed, L. Webster and J. Cherry), *Medieval Archaeology* 21, 219–222.

Hill, D. (1981) Notes, on Offa's Dyke and Wat's Dyke, in 'Medieval Britain in 1980' (ed, S. M. Youngs and J. Clark), *Medieval Archaeology* 25, 184–185.

Hill, D. (1985) The Construction of Offa's Dyke, *Antiquaries Journal*, 65, 140–142.

Hill, D. (2000a) Offa's Dyke: pattern and purpose. *Antiquaries Journal* 80, 195–206.

Hill, D. (2000b) Athelstan's Urban Reforms. *Anglo-Saxon Studies in Archaeology and History*, 11, 173–185.

Hill, D. (2001) Mercians: The Dwellers on the Boundary. In M. P. Brown and C. A. Farr (eds) *Mercia: An Anglo-Saxon kingdom in Europe*, 173–182. Leicester University Press (2nd edn, London, Continuum, 2005).

Hill, D. (n.d.;1980) An Outline of Archaeological Approaches to the Offa's Dyke, with Particular Reference to the Work of the Univesity of Manchester. (Draft MS, pp.55, on file at

Clwyd-Powys Archaeological Trust Historic Environment Record, Welshpool).
Hill, D. and Matthews, S. (2004) *Cyril Fox on Tour 1927–1932*. Oxford, British Archaeological Reports (British Series, BAR 364).
Hill, D. and Rumble, A.R. (eds.) (1996) *The Defence of Wessex: The Burghal Hidage and Anglo-Saxon Fortifications*. Manchester University Press.
Hill, D. and Wilson, D. (1974) Frontier dykes in the Wrexham area, recent work, 1972, *Journal of the Chester Archaeological Society*, 58, 93–96.
Hill, D. and Worthington, M. (2003) *Offa's Dyke: History and Guide*. Stroud, Tempus
Hill, D. and Worthington, M. (eds.) (2005) *Aethelbald and Offa: Two Eighth-Century Kings of Mercia*. Oxford, British Archaeological Reports (British Series, BAR 383).
Hinton, D. A. (1990) *Archaeology, Economy and Society: England from the Fifth to the Fifteenth Century*. London, Seaby.
Hinton, D. A. (2004) Lost Hikers (review of Offa's Dyke: History and Guide). British Archaeology, 74.
Hodges, R. (1989) *The Anglo-Saxon Achievement: Archaeology and the beginnings of English society*. Ithaca, New York, Cornell University Press.
Holden, Brock W. (2000) 'The Making of the Middle March of Wales, 1066–1250', *Welsh History Review* 20, 207–226.
Holden, Brock W. (2008) *Lords of the Central Marches: English Aristocracy and Frontier Society, 1087–1265*. Oxford University Press.
Hooke, D. (1985) *The Anglo-Saxon landscape: the kingdom of the Hwicce*. Manchester University Press.
Hooke, D. (1986) *Anglo-Saxon Territorial Organisation: The Western Margins of Mercia*. University of Birmingham Department of Geography, Occasional Publication 22.
Hooke, D. (1999) Mercia: Landscape and Environment. In M. P. Brown and C. A. Farr (eds.) *Mercia: An Anglo-Saxon kingdom in Europe*, 160–172. Leicester University Press (2nd edn, London, Continuum, 2005).
Hooke, D. (2010) *Trees in Anglo-Saxon England*. Woodbridge, The Boydell Press.
Howe, N. (2008) *Writing the Map of Anglo-Saxon England: Essays in Cultural Geography*. New Haven, Yale University Press.
Hoyle, J. (1996) Offa's Dyke Management Survey, 1995–6, *Glevensis* 29, 29–33.
Hoyle, J. and Vallender, J. (1997) Offa's Dyke in Gloucestershire: Management Survey (3 volumes). Gloucestershire County Environment Department, Archaeology Service.
Hughes, K. (1980) The Welsh Latin chronicles: *Annales Cambriae* and related texts. In K. Hughes (ed. D. Dumville) *Celtic Britain in the Early Middle Ages: Studies in Scottish and Welsh sources*. Woodbridge: Boydell and Brewer.
Hurst, J. D. (ed) (1997) *A Multi-Period Salt Production Site at Droitwich: Excavations at Upwich* (CBA Research Report 107). York, Council for British Archaeology.
Jackson, R. and Miller, D. (2011) *Wellington Quarry, Herefordshire (1986–96): Investigations of a landscape in the Lower Lugg Valley*. Oxford, Oxbow Books.

James, M. R. (1917) Two Lives of St. Ethelbert, king and martyr. *English Historical Review* 32, 214–244.
Jenkins, G. H. (2007) *A Concise History of Wales*. Cambridge University Press.
Jewell, R. (2001) The Classicism of Southumbrian Sculpture. In M. P. Brown and C. A. Farr *Mercia: An Anglo-Saxon kingdom in Europe*, 244–262. Leicester University Press (2nd edn, London, Continuum, 2005).
John, E. (1960) *Land Tenure in Early England*. Leicester University Press.
John, E. (1996) *Re-assessing Anglo-Saxon England*. Manchester University Press.
Jones, G. (1998) Penda's footprint: Place-names containing personal names associated with those of early Mercian Kings. *Nomina*, 21, 29–62.
Jones, H. L. (1854) List of the Pre-Historic Remains of Wales. *Archaeologia Cambrensis* (New Series) 5, 83–84.
Jones, H. L. (1856a) Offa's Dyke and Wat's Dyke. *Archaeologia Cambrensis* (Third Series) 2, 1–23.
Jones, H. L. (1856b) Offa's Dyke. *Archaeologia Cambrensis* (Third Series) 2, 151–154.
Jones, N. (1992) Offa's Dyke, Sunnybank, Ffrith. *Archaeology in Wales* 32, 70–71.
Jones, N. (2010) Forden Gaer. In B. C. Burnham and J. L. Davies (eds) *Roman Frontiers in Wales and the Marches*, 243–245. Aberystwyth, Royal Commission on the Ancient and Historical Monuments of Wales.
Jones, N. and Brassil, K. (1990) Offa's Dyke, Esclusham, Wrexham. *Archaeology in Wales* 30, 65.
Jones, N. and Owen, W. (1988) Offa's Dyke, Home Farm, Chirk Castle. *Archaeology in Wales* 28, 70.
Jones, T. (1955) *Brut y Tywysogion or the Chronicle of the Princes, Red Book of Hergest Version*. Cardiff, University of Wales Press.
Keynes, S. (2000) Diocese and Cathedral before 1056. In G. Aylmer and J. Tiller (eds) *Hereford Cathedral: A History*. London and Rio Grande, Hambledon Press.
Keynes, S. (2001a) Mercia and Wessex in the Ninth Century. In M. P. Brown and C. A. Farr (eds.) *Mercia: An Anglo-Saxon kingdom in Europe*, 310–328. Leicester University Press (2nd edn, London, Continuum, 2005).
Keynes, S. (2001b) Offa. In M. Lapidge, J. Blair, S. Keynes and D. Scragg (eds.) *The Blackwell Encyclopaedia of Anglo-Saxon England*, 340–341. Oxford, Blackwell.
Keynes, S. (2001c) Coenwulf. In M. Lapidge, J. Blair, S. Keynes and D. Scragg (eds.) *The Blackwell Encyclopaedia of Anglo-Saxon England*, 111–113. Oxford, Blackwell.
Keynes, S. (2001d) Jaenberht. In M. Lapidge, J. Blair, S. Keynes and D. Scragg (eds.) *The Blackwell Encyclopaedia of Anglo-Saxon England*, 257–258. Oxford, Blackwell.
Keynes, S. (2005) The Kingdom of the Mercians in the Eighth Century. In D. Hill and M. Worthington (eds.) *Aethelbald and Offa. Two Eighth-Century Kings of Mercia*, 1–26. Oxford, British Archaeological Reports (British Series, BAR 383).
Keynes, S. and Lapidge, M. (1983) *Alfred the Great: Asser's Life of King Alfred and other contemporary sources*. London, Penguin Books.

Kightly, C. (1988) *A Mirror of Medieval Wales: Gerald of Wales and His Journey of 1188*. Cardiff, Cadw: Welsh Historic Monuments.

Kirby, D. P. (1991) *The Earliest English Kings*. London, Unwin Hyman.

Lane Fox, Col. A. and Boyd-Dawkins, W. (1876) Offa's Dyke: a short account of the examination of Offa's Dyke, made in the Autumn of 1870. *Montgomeryshire Collections* 9, 411–412.

Lapidge, M. (1982) Byrhtferth of Ramsey and the Early Sections of the *Historia Regum* attributed to Symeon of Durham. *Anglo-Saxon England* 10, 97–122.

Lapidge, M. (2001) Alcuin of York. In M. Lapidge, J. Blair, S. Keynes and D. Scragg (eds.) *The Blackwell Encyclopaedia of Anglo-Saxon England*, 24–25. Oxford, Blackwell.

Leah, M. D., Wells, C. E., Stamper, P., Huckenby, E. and Welch, C. (1998) *The Wetlands of Shropshire and Staffordshire*. University of Lancaster.

Leahy, K. (2009) The Staffordshire Hoard: Discovery and Initial Assessment (pdf. Attached at www.staffordshirehoard.org.uk. Accessed 29.11.2009).

Leahy, K. and Bland, R. (2009) *The Staffordshire Hoard*. London, The British Museum Press

Levison, W. (1946) *England and the Continent in the Eighth Century*. Oxford University Press.

Lewis, C. P. (2007) Welsh Territories and Welsh Identities in Late Anglo-Saxon England. In N. Higham (ed) *Britons in Anglo-Saxon England*, 130–143. Woodbridge, Boydell.

Lewis, J. M. (1963) A section of Offa's Dyke at Buttington Tump, Tidenham. *Transactions of the Bristol and Gloucester Archaeological Society* 82, 202–204.

Lieberman, M. (2008) *The March of Wales, 1067–1300: A Borderland of Medieval Britain*. Cardiff, University of Wales Press.

Lieberman, M. (2010) *The Medieval March of Wales: The Creation and Perception of a Frontier, 1066–1283*. Cambridge University Press.

Lluyd, E. (1696), ed. Morris, R. H. (1909–11). *Parochalia, being a summary of answers to parochial queries in order to a geographical dictionary, etc, of Wales. Archaeologia Cambrensis* supplements, 1909–1911.

Luckombe, P. (1790) *England's Gazetteer; or an accurate description of the Cities, Towns and Villages in the Kingdom, Volume 2*. London, Robinson and Baldwin.

Lund, N. (2009) Danewerke. In N. Fryde, and D. Reitz (eds.) *Walls, Ramparts and Lines of Demarcation: Selected Studies from Antiquity to Modern Times*, 57–65. Munster: Lit Verlag.

Maddicott, J. R. (2005) London and Droitwich, c.650–750: trade, industry and the rise of Mercia. *Anglo-Saxon England* 34, 7–58.

Maitland, F. W. (1897) Book-land and Folk-Land. In *Domesday Book and Beyond: Three Essays in the Early History of England*, 244–258. Cambridge University Press. (re-issued, 1987).

Malim, T. (2003) *The Anglo-Saxons in South Cambridgeshire*. Cambridgeshire County Council.

Malim, T. (2007) The origins and design of linear earthworks in the Welsh Marches. In *Landscape Enquiries* (Proceedings of the Clifton Antiquarian Society, Bristol, 8) 13–32.

Malim, T. (2009) Grim's Ditch, Wansdyke, and the Ancient Highways of England: Linear Monuments and Political Control. In *Early Medieval Enquiries*, (Proceedings of the Clifton Antiquarian Society, Bristol, 9) 148–179.

Malim, T., Penn, K. Robinson, B., Wait, G. and Welsh, K. (1997) New evidence on the Cambridgeshire Dykes and Worsted Street Roman Road, *Proceedings of the Cambridge Antiquarian Society* 85, 27–122.

Mann, A. and Vaughan, T. (2008) Archaeological Evaluation at Bullingham Lane, Bullinghope, Herefordshire. Worcestershire County Council Historic Environment and Archaeology Service, Report 1632. (On file at Herefordshire Council Historic Environment Record).

Mann, J. C. (1998) The Creation of Four Provinces in Britain by Diocletian. *Britannia* 29, 339–341.

Mann, K. (1996) 'The March of Wales: A Question of Terminology', *Welsh History Review* 18, 1–13.

Martin, R. (2005) The Lives of the Offas: the Posthumous Reputation of Offa, King of the Mercians. In D. Hill, and M. Worthington (eds.) *Aethelbald and Offa: Two Eighth-Century Kings of Mercia*, 49–54. Oxford, British Archaeological Reports (British Series, BAR 383).

Matthews, S. (2005) Legends of Offa: the Journey to Rome. In D. Hill and M. Worthington (eds.) *Aethelbald and Offa: Two Eighth-Century Kings of Mercia*, 55–58. Oxford, British Archaeological Reports (British Series, BAR 383).

Maund, K. (2006) *The Welsh Kings: Warriors, Warlords and Princes*. Stroud, Tempus.

McClure, J. and Collins, R. (eds) (1994) *Bede: The Ecclesiastical History of the English People, The Greater Chronicle, Bede's Letter to Egbert*. Oxford University Press (Oxford World Classics; original edn, Oxford 1969)

McKitterick, R. (ed) (1995) *The New Cambridge Medieval History, Volume 2*. Cambridge University Press.

McKitterick, R. (2008) *Charlemagne: The Formation of a European Identity*. Cambridge University Press.

Meaney, A. (2005) Felix's *Life of Guthlac*: History or Hagiography. In D. Hill and M. Worthington (eds.) *Aethelbald and Offa: Two Eighth-Century Kings of Mercia*, 75–84. Oxford, British Archaeological Reports (British Series, BAR 383).

Meyrick, S. R. (1834) On the course of Offa's Dyke, *Gentleman's Magazine*, Vol 103 Part 1, 504.

M'Kenny-Hughes, T. (1893) On Offa's Dyke. *Archaeologia* (Second Series) 3, 466–484.

Molyneaux, G. (2011) The *Ordinance concerning the Dunsaete* and the Anglo-Welsh frontier in the late tenth and eleventh centuries. *Anglo-Saxon England* 40, 249–272.

Moreland, J. (2000) The significance of production in eighth-century England. In I. L. Hansen and C. Wickham (eds) *The Long Eighth Century*, 69–104. Leiden, Brill.

Moschek, W. (2009) The Limes: Between open Frontier and Borderline. In N. Fryde and D. Reitz (eds.) *Walls, Ramparts and Lines of Demarcation: Selected Studies from Antiquity to Modern Times*, 13–29. Munster: Lit Verlag.

Musson, C. and Spurgeon, C. J. (1998) Cwrt Llechrhyd, Llanelwedd: An Unusual Moated Site in Central Powys. *Medieval Archaeology* 32, 97–109.

Naismith, R. (2012) *Money and Power in Anglo-Saxon England: The Southern English Kingdoms, 757–865*. Cambridge University Press.

Nash-Williams, V. E. (1950) *The Early Christian Monuments of Wales*. Cardiff, The University of Wales.

Naylor, J. and Richards, J.D. (2010) A 'Productive Site' at Bidford-on-Avon Warwickshire: salt, communication and trade in Anglo-Saxon England. In S. Worrall, G. Egan, N. Naylor, K. Leahy and M. Lewis (eds.) *A Decade of Discovery: Proceedings of the Portable Antiquities Scheme Conference, 2007*, 193–200. British Museum, London/Oxford, British Archaeological Reports (British Series) 520.

Nelson, J. (2001) Carolingian Contacts. In M. P. Brown and C. A. Farr (eds.) *Mercia: An Anglo-Saxon kingdom in Europe*, 126–143. Leicester University Press (2nd edn, London, Continuum, 2005).

Noble, F. (1969). *The Shell Guide to Offa's Dyke Path*. London, Shell Corporation.

Noble, F. (1975) *The ODA Book of Offa's Dyke Path*. Knighton, Offa's Dyke Association, Offa's Dyke Services. (Foreword by Lord Hunt).

Noble, F. (1978) *Offa's Dyke Reviewed*. (M.Phil, Open University). Microfilm version, Offa's Dyke Association, Knighton, Powys.

Noble, F. (1983) *Offa's Dyke Reviewed* (ed. M. Gelling). Oxford, British Archaeological Reports (British Series) 114).

North, R. (1997) *Heathen Gods in Old English Literature*. Cambridge University Press.

Nurse, B., Gaimster, D. and McCarthy, S. (eds) (2007) *Making History: Antiquaries in Britain, 1707–2007*. London, Royal Academy of Arts.

Nurse, K. (2001) 'A famous thing…that reaches farre in length' *New Welsh Review* 52, 21–27.

Okasha, E. (2009) 'The Staffordshire Hoard inscription', Staffordshire Hoard Symposium:finds.org.uk/staffshoard symposium; accessed 3/10/10.

Ormerod, G. (1842) An Account of Some Ancient Remains in the District adjacent to the Wye and the Severn, in the counties of Gloucester and Monmouth, *Archaeologia* 29, 13–19.

Ormerod, G. (1856) Letter concerning the southern termination of Offa's Dyke, in H. L. Jones, Offa's Dyke and Wat's Dyke. *Archaeologia Cambrensis* (Third Series) 2, 18–20.

Ormerod, G. (1859) *Remarks on a line of earthworks in the parish of Tidenham, Gloucestershire known as Offa's Dyke*. Printed Privately.

Owen, A. transl. (1864) *Brut y Tywysogion*: the Chronicle of the Princes *Archaeologia Cambrensis*, 3rd Series, Volume X, supplement, 401–453 (numbered in text, 1–143).

Owen, A. E. (1896) Offa's Dyke. *Montgomeryshire Collections* 29, 93–111.

Parry, C. (1990) A survey of St. James's church, Lancaut, Gloucestershire *Trans Bristol Gloucesetershire Archaeol. Soc.*, 108, 53–103.

Parsons, D. (2001) The Mercian Church: Archaeology and Topography. In M. P. Brown and C. A. Farr, (eds.) *Mercia: An Anglo-Saxon kingdom in Europe.*, 50–68. Leicester University Press (2nd edn, London, Continuum, 2005).

Parsons, D. and Sutherland, D.S. (2013) *The Anglo-Saxon Church of All Saints, Brixworth, Northamptonshire: Survey, Excavation and Analysis, 1972–2010*. Oxford, Oxbow Books.

Peacock, D.P.S. (1997) Charlemagne's Black Stones: The re-use of Roman Columns in Early Medieval Europe. *Antiquity* 71, 709–715.

Pelteret, D. A. E. (1984) The roads of Anglo-Saxon England. *Wiltshire Archaeological and Natural History Magazine* 79, 155–163.

Pelteret, D. A. E. (2010) The role of rivers and coastlines in shaping Early English history. In W. North (ed) *Haskins Society Journal* 21, 21–46. Woodbridge, The Boydell Press.

Pennant, T. (1781) *Tours in Wales Vol II*. (Rhys, J., ed. 1883). Caernarvon, Humphreys.

Pine, J., Allen, J., and Challinor, D. (2010) Saxon iron smelting at Clearwell Quarry, St. Briavels, Lydney, Gloucestershire. *Archaeology of the Severn Estuary*, Volume 20 (for 2009), 9–40.

Pretty, K. (1982) Defining the Magonsaete. In S. Bassett (ed.) *The Origins of Anglo-Saxon Kingdoms*, 171–183. Leicester University Press.

Ray, K. (2015) *The Archaeology of Herefordshire: An Exploration*. Hereford, Logaston Press.

Reynolds, A. and Langlands, A. (2006) Social Identities on the Macro Scale: A Maximum View of Wansdyke. In W. Davies, G. Halsall, and A. Reynolds (eds.) *People and Space in the Middle Ages 300–1300*, 13–42. Turnhout (Belgium), Brepols. (Studies in the Early Middle Ages).

Rhodes, J. (1965) Offa's Dyke in Lippet's Grove, Tidenham. Unpublished MS at Gloucestershire HER (Primary Record Number 6817).

Richards, M. (1969) *Welsh Administrative and Territorial Units*. Cardiff, University of Wales Press.

Riley, H. T. (1854) *Ingold's Chronicle of the Abbey of Croyland*. London, H. Bohn

Rippon, S. (2007) Emerging Regional Variation in Historic Landscape Character: The Possible Significance of the 'Long Eighth Century'. In M. Gardiner and S. Rippon (eds) *Medieval Landscapes*. Macclesfield, Windgather.

Roberts, J. (2001) Hagiography and Literature: The Case of Guthlac of Crowland. In M. P. Brown and C. A. Farr (eds) *Mercia: An Anglo-Saxon kingdom in Europe*, 69–86. Leicester University Press (2nd edn, London, Continuum, 2005).

Robinson, P. (1985) Land-systems mapping and the new Offa's Dyke survey. *Archaeology in Clwyd*, 7, 18–19.

Rodd, F. (Lord Rennell of Rodd) (1958) *Valley on the March: a history of a group of manors on the Herefordshire March of Wales*. Oxford University Press.

Rodwell, W. (1995) Lichfield Cathedral. *Medieval Archaeology* 39, 241–242.

Rodwell, W., Hawkes, J., Howe, E. and Cramp, R. (2008)

The Lichfield Angel: A spectacular Anglo-Saxon painted sculpture. *The Antiquaries Journal* 88, 48–108.

Rollason, D. (2009) 'St. Aethelberht of Hereford and the Cults of European Royal Saints'. Hereford Cathedral.

Round, A. (1992) Excavations on the Mansio Site at Wall (*Letocetum*), Staffordshire, 1972–78. *Transactions of the South Staffordshire Archaeological and Historical Asociation* 32, 1–78.

Royal Commission on the Historical Monuments of England (1975) *An inventory of the historical monuments in the county of Dorset, Volume 5, East Dorset*.

Rumble, A. R. (1996a) An edition and translation of the Burghal Hidage, together with Recension C of the Tribal Hidage. In D. Hill and A. R. Rumble (eds) *The Burghal Hidage and Anglo-Saxon Fortifications*, 14–35. Manchester University Press.

Rumble, A. R. (1996b) The Tribal Hidage: An Annotated Bibliography. In D. Hill and A. R. Rumble (eds), 182–188.

Sawyer, P. (1968) *Anglo-Saxon Charters: An Annotated List and Bibliography*. London, Royal Historical Society.

Scott-Fox, C. (2002) *Cyril Fox. Archaeologist Extraordinary*. Oxford, Oxbow Books.

Sharp, S. (2005) Aethelbert, King and Martyr: the Development of a Legend. D. Hill and M. Worthington (eds.) *Aethelbald and Offa: Two Eighth-Century Kings of Mercia*, 59–64. Oxford, British Archaeological Reports (British Series, BAR 383).

Shaw, Stebbing (1798) *The History and Antiquities of Staffordshire*. London, J. Nichols and Son. (see Greenslade and Baugh, 1976).

Silvester, R. (2008) Abertanat, Llantsantffraid and Clawdd Coch: Barri Jones's Excavations in Montgomeryshire. *Studia Celtica* 42, 27–53.

Sims-Williams, P. (1990) *Religion and Literature in Western England, 600–800*. Cambridge University Press.

Smith, J. M. H. (1995) *Fines Imperii*: the Marches. In McKitterick (ed), 169–189.

Squatriti, P. (2002) Digging Ditches in Early Medieval Europe. *Past and Present* 176 (1), 11–65.

Squatriti, P. (2004) Offa's Dyke between nature and culture. *Environmental History*, 9 (1), 9–36.

Stafford, P. (2001) Political Women in Mercia, Eighth to Early Tenth Centuries. In M. P. Brown and C. A. Farr (eds.) *Mercia: An Anglo-Saxon kingdom in Europe*, 35–49. Leicester University Press (2nd edn, London, Continuum, 2005).

Stancliffe, C. (1995) Where was Oswald killed? In C. Stancliffe and E. Cambridge (eds) *Oswald: From Northumbrian King to European Saint*, 84–96. Stamford, Paul Watkins

Stancliffe, C. and Cambridge, E. (eds) (1995) *Oswald: From Northumbrian King to European Saint*, 84–96. Stamford, Paul Watkins

Stenton, F. M. (1947) *Anglo-Saxon England* (2nd Edition). Oxford University Press.

Stenton, F. M. (1955) 'Foreword' In Fox, C. *Offa's Dyke. A field survey of the western frontier works of Mercia in the seventh and eighth centuries AD*, xvii–xxi. London, The British Academy.

Stenton, F. M. (1970) Medehamstede and its colonies. In D. M. Stenton (ed) *Preparatory to Anglo-Saxon England, being the collected papers of Frank Merry Stenton*, 179–192. Oxford University Press.

Stephenson, D. (2012) Offa: the View from the West. In H. Hidden (ed.) *'Ruling and Dividing': Offa's legacy in the Northern Marches*, 39–47. Report of the 6th seminar of the Old Oswestry Landscape and Archaeology Project: Oswestry, Shropshire.

Stevenson, W. H. (1904) *Asser's Life of King Alfred, together with the Annals of St Neots erroneously ascribed to Asser*. Oxford, The Clarendon Press.

Story, J. (2003) *Carolingian Connections: Anglo-Saxon England and Carolingian Francia, c.750–870*. Aldershot, Ashgate.

Suppe, F. (1994) *Military Institutions on the Welsh Marches: Shropshire AD 1066–1300*. Woodbridge, Boydell and Brewer.

Tatton-Brown, T. (2011) The Emperor's New Gold? *Current Archaeology* 250, January 2011, 4.

Thomas, W. Gwyn (1975) Offa's dyke and the *Brut*. *Antiquity* 44, No. 194, 131–2.

Thorn, F. and Thorn, C. (1983) *Domesday Book, Herefordshire*. Chichester, Phillimore.

Thorpe, L. (1978) *Gerald of Wales: The Journey Through Wales and The Description of Wales*. London: Penguin Books (Reissued, 2004).

Thurley, S. (2010) Making England: The Shadow of Rome 410–1130. *Gresham College Lectures, 2010*, 3/11/2010, http://www.gresham.ac.uk/printtranscript.asp?EventId=1083.

Toulmin Smith, L. (ed.) (1907) *The Itinerary of John Leland In or About the Years 1535–1543, Parts I to III*. London, George Bell and Sons.

Turner-Flynn, B., Garner, D. J., Sproat, D. and Walker, W. S. (1995) Ffrith Farm, Ffrith, near Wrexham: An Archaeological Evaluation. Earthworks Archaeology, report E140. (On file at Clwyd-Powys Archaeological Trust Historic Environment Record, Welshpool).

Tyler, D. (2005a) Orchestrated Violence and the 'Supremacy of the Mercian Kings'. In D. Hill and M. Worthington (eds.) *Aethelbald and Offa: Two Eighth-Century Kings of Mercia*, 27–34. Oxford, British Archaeological Reports (British Series, BAR 383).

Tyler, D. (2005b) An Early Mercian Hegemony: Penda and Overkingship in the Seventh Century. *Midland History* 30, 1–42.

Tyler, D. (2011) Offa's Dyke: a historiographical appraisal. *Journal of Medieval History*, 37:2, 145–161.

Vince, A. (2001) The Growth of Market Centres and Towns in the Area of the Mercian Hegemony. In M. P. Brown and C. A. Farr (eds.) *Mercia: An Anglo-Saxon kingdom in Europe*, 183–193. Leicester University Press (2nd edn, London, Continuum, 2005).

Watkins, A. W. (1904) Offa's Dyke and the Gap in the Weobley District. *Transactions of the Woolhope Naturalists' Field Club*, 1904, 246–250.

Watson, M. (2002) *Shropshire: An Archaeological Guide*. Shrewsbury, Shropshire Books.

Watts, M. (2002) *The Archaeology of Mills and Milling*, Stroud, Tempus.

Webster, G. (1994) *Wall Roman Site, Staffordshire*. English Heritage.

Webster, L. (2001) Metalwork of the Mercian Supremacy. In M. P. Brown and C. A. Farr (eds.) *Mercia: An Anglo-Saxon kingdom in Europe*, 263–277. Leicester University Press (2nd edn, London, Continuum, 2005).

Webster, L. (2012) *Anglo-Saxon Art*, London, The British Museum Press.

Webster, L. and Backhouse, J. (eds.) (1991) *The Making of England: Anglo-Saxon Art and Culture, A.D. 600–900.* London, British Museum Press.

Welch, M. (2001) 'The Archaeology of Mercia' In M. P. Brown and C. A. Farr (eds.) *Mercia: An Anglo-Saxon kingdom in Europe*, 147–159. Leicester University Press (2nd edn, London, Continuum, 2005).

White, P. (2003) *The Arrow Valley, Herefordshire: Archaeology, Landscape Change and Conservation.* Herefordshire Studies in Archaeology, 2.

White, R. (2007) *Britannia Prima: Britain's Last Roman Province.* Stroud, Tempus.

Whitehead, D. (1980) Historical introduction, 1–6. In R. Shoesmith, *Hereford City Excavations, Volume 1, Excavations at Castle Green.* Council for British Archaeology, Research Report 36.

Whitelock, D. (1930) *Anglo-Saxon Wills.* Cambridge University Press.

Whitelock, D. (1979) *English Historical Documents, 1, c.500–1042.* 2nd edn. London, Eyre and Spottiswoode.

Wileman, J. (2003) The Purpose of the Dykes: Understanding the Linear Earthworks of Early Medieval Britain. *Landscapes* 2, 59–66.

Williams, A. (2003) How Land was Held before and after the Norman conquest. In R. W. H. Erskine and A. Williams (eds.) *The Story of Domesday Book.* Chichester: Phillimore.

Williams, A. (2009) Offa's Dyke: a monument without a history? In N. Fryde, and D. Reitz (eds.) *Walls, Ramparts and Lines of Demarcation: Selected Studies from Antiquity to Modern Times.*, 31–56. Munster: Lit Verlag.

Williams, Archdeacon (1850) Offa's Dyke. *Archaeologia Cambrensis* (New Series) 1, 72–73.

Williams, G. (2001a) Mercian Coinage and Authority. In M. P. Brown and C. A. Farr (eds) *Mercia: An Anglo-Saxon kingdom in Europe*, 210–228. Leicester University Press (2nd edn, London, Continuum, 2005).

Williams, G. (2001b) 'Military Institutions and Royal Power' In M. P. Brown and C. A. Farr (eds.) *Mercia: An Anglo-Saxon kingdom in Europe*, 295–309. Leicester University Press (2nd edn, London, Continuum, 2005).

Williams, G. (2005) Military Obligations and Mercian Supremacy in the Eighth Century. In D. Hill and M. Worthington (eds.) *Aethelbald and Offa: Two Eighth-Century Kings of Mercia*, 103–110. Oxford, British Archaeological Reports (British Series, BAR 383).

Williams, G. (2006) Striking Gold. *British Museum Magazine*, Summer 2006, 36–38.

Williams, G. (2010) Wealth and Warfare: interpreting the contents of the Staffordshire Hoard. Talk at the Society of Antiquaries of Scotland. (http://screencast.com/users/simongilmour/folders/Society%20Lecturers/media/67e95639–5806–4f60; accessed 27/08/14).

Williams, G. and Cowell, M. (2009) A gold mancus of Coenwulf of Mercia and other comparable coins. *The British Museum Technical Research Bulletin* 3, 31–36.

Wood, J. G. (1908) Saxon dykes. *Victoria County History of Hereford*, Volume 1.

Wood, M. (1987) Offa. In M. Wood, *In Search of the Dark Ages*, 77–103. New York and Oxford, Facts on File Publications.

Wormald, P. (1982a) The Age of Bede and Aethelbald. In J. Campbell (ed.) *The Anglo-Saxons*, 70–100. London, Phaidon Press.

Wormald, P. (1982b) The Age of Offa and Alcuin. In J. Campbell, (ed.) *The Anglo-Saxons*, 101–128. London, Phaidon Press.

Wormald, P. (1991) In search of King Offa's 'Law-Code'. In I. Wood and N. Lund (eds.) *People and Places in Northern Europe 500–1600: Essays in Honour of Peter Hayes Sawyer*, 25–45. Woodbridge, The Boydell Press.

Worthington, M. (1999) Offa's Dyke. In M. Lapidge, J. Blair, S. Keynes and D. Scragg (eds.) *The Blackwell Encyclopaedia of Anglo-Saxon England*, 341–342. Oxford, Blackwell.

Worthington, M. (2005) Offa's Dyke. In D. Hill and M. Worthington (eds.) *Aethelbald and Offa: Two Eighth-Century Kings of Mercia*, 91–96. Oxford, British Archaeological Reports (British Series, BAR 383).

Yorke, B. (1990) *Kings and Kingdoms of Early Anglo-Saxon England*. London, Seaby.

Yorke, B. (2001) The Origins of Mercia. In M. P. Brown and C. A. Farr (eds) *Mercia: An Anglo-Saxon kingdom in Europe*, 13–22. Leicester University Press (2nd edn, London, Continuum, 2005).

Yorke, B. (2003) *Nunneries and the Anglo-Saxon Royal Houses.* London, Continuum.

Yorke, B. (2005) Aethelbald, Offa and the Patronage of Nunneries. In D. Hill and M. Worthington (eds.) *Aethelbald and Offa: Two Eighth-Century Kings of Mercia*, 43–48. Oxford, British Archaeological Reports (British Series, BAR 383).

Index

Italics indicate inclusion in Figures on the page concerned

TOPOGRAPHICAL INDEX

Aachen (Germany) 325
Abermule (Montgomery) 39
Abingdon Abbey (Berks/Oxford) 108
Ackhill (Discoed) 409 (n.46)
Acton Beauchamp (Herefs) 256, 325
Alberbury (Shropshire) 266
Alyn, river/valley 39, 289
Anglesey, see Ynys Môn
Aran Mountains 151
Arrow river/valley 104, 168, 216, 229, 291, 358
Asterley Rocks, see Llanymynech
Avon (Wilts/Somerset) river/valley 343

Bagillt (Flints) 24
Baker's Hill (west of Oswestry) 33, 35, 66, *139*, 144, 161, 190, *204*
Bala Lake, see Llyn Tegid
Bamburgh (Northumberland) 103
Bangor-on-Dee (Bangor-is-y-coed) 281, 290, 370
Bardney Abbey (Lincs) 106, 315
Basingwerk (Holywell, Flints) 17, 24, 58, 84, 118, 357
Bath 283, 316, 325, 343–4, *343*, 368
Beachley (peninsula, Gloucs) 16, *53*, 75
Bedford 316, 319, 368
Benson, (Bensington, Oxford) 110, 310
Berwyn Mountains 126–7, *128*
Biggleswade (Beds) 327,
Billington Moor (Lancs) 358
Bishop's Castle (Shropshire) 57
Bishopswood (Gloucs/Herefs) 18, 177
Black Mountains (Brecknock) 128, *128*, 138
Blackwardine (east of Leominster, Herefs) 295
Blockley (Worcs) 311
Blodwel Rock (west of Oswestry) 33, 145, 277
Bollingham (Herefs) 295
Bradwell-on-Sea (Essex) 324
Brecon 275
Bredwardine (Herefs) 293, 295
Breedon-on-the-Hill (Leicestershire) 311, 315, 325
Breiddin, The, mountain (north-east of Welshpool) 29, 31–2, 104, *130*, 131, *132*, 247, 266
Brentford (Middx) 316

Bridge Sollers (Herefs) 13, 18, 50, 138, 274, 289
Brixworth (Northants) 323, 324, *324*
Brockweir (Gloucs) 149
Stream 136–7
Brompton Bridge (Montgomery) 155, 142
Bronygarth (Chirk) 162, 140, 167, 201, 203
Brymbo (Denbigh) 16, 38, *61*, 63, 126–7, 137, 144, 169, 290
Brymbo Hill 144
Brynbella Mound (Flints) 70
Bryn Melin (Flints/west of Wrexham) 38
Bucknell (Shropshire) 250
Builth Wells (Rads) 245
Bullinghope (Hereford) 104, 273, 285
Burfa Bank/Camp (Rads) 146, 147, *148*, 168, 171, 246, *247*, 258
Burton Court (Eardisland, Herefs) 294
Burton Hill (Weobley, Herefs) 50, *74*, 128
Buscot, Oxfordshire 228
Buttington (Montgomery Welshpool) 16, 31, 39–41, 59, 63, 80, 131, 180, 294, 268, 277, 294
Redwood Lodge 180, 182
Buttington Tump (Gloucs) *53*, 177, 182, 186, 213, 249

Caebitra, brook 43, 136, 142, 155, 172, 259
Caeaugwynion (Chirk) 34, 149, *149*, 161, 180, 182
Caer Caradoc 250
Caer Din (fort, Springhill, Shropshire) 245, 249, 411 (n. 96)
Caergwrle (west of Wrexham) 36, 39, 357
Caerwent (Monmouth) 74
Camlad, river 41, 43, 136, 142, 194, 259, 294
Cannock (Staffs) 328
Cannock Chase (Staffs) 95
Canon Bridge (west of Hereford) 50
Canterbury 112, 115, 298, 302, 304, 306–7, 313, 318
Christ Church 309
St. Augustine's monastery 324
Carreghofa, see Llanymynech
Carreg-y-big (west of Oswestry) 35, 67, *139*, 217, *233*, *354*
Cascob/Cascob Brook (Rads) 152, 199

Castell Dinas Brân (Llangollen) 162
Caswell Wood (Gloucs) 276
Castor (Hunts/Cambs) 325
Cedigog, river/valley 36, 38, 127
Cefn (Llangollen) 140
Cefn (Montgomery) 131
Cefn Bychan (east of Llangollen) 36
Ceiriog, river/valley 13, 127, 136, 140, 167, *168*, 169, 190, 192, 201, 203, 209, *348*
Chelsea (Middx) 117, 307, 313, 315, 316, 368
Cheltenham (Gloucs) 151
Chepstow 16, 17, 57, 79, 129, 282, *282*, 358
Cherry Hill (Fownhope, Herefs) 289
Chertsey Abbey (Surrey) 105
Cheshire/Shropshire Plain 38, 123
Chester 158, 351, 370
Chichester (Sussex) 25
Chirbury (Shropshire) 169, 197 (see also, Dudston Fields (Chirbury/Montgomery)
Chirk (Denbigh/Clwyd) 129, 140, *141*
Chirk Castle Park 16, *34*, 36, 167, 209, 180, 185, 281
Church Stoke (Montgomery) 266
Cirencester (Gloucs) 102, 316, 323
Clearwell Quarry (Gloucs) 358
Cleeve Hill (Gloucs) 151
Clun (Shropshire) 13, 17, *18*, 159
Clun Forest 126, 128, 338, *348*,
Clun, river/valley 13, 43, 45, 136, 142, 151, 154, *159*, 168, 169, 190, 201, 203, 201–2, 239, 266, *375*
Clwyd, Vale of 115, 290, 357
Clwydian Mountains 39
Clywedog, river/valley 24, 36, 136, 138, 140, 186
Coedpoeth (west of Wrexham) 36, 83, 161, 217
Colchester (Essex) 25
Conwy (Caerns) 270
Cookham (Berks) 108, 309, 316
Corndon Hill (Shropshire/Montgomery) 126, 298
Cotswold scarp (Gloucs) 151
Coxbury (Gloucs) 54, 146, 150
Craig Forda (west of Oswestry) 33, 145, 158
Craignant (Selattyn, Oswestry) 36, 126, 130, 162, 234

Topographical Index

Crediton (Devon) 256
Criggion (east of Welshpool) 131
Croft (Leicestershire) 307, 315
Croft Ambrey (Herefs) 151
Cropthorne (Worcs) *108*, 325
Crosmere (Kenwick, Shropshire) 256, *257*
Crowland Abbey (Lincs) 107
Crowsnest (Kerry Ridgeway/Montgomery) 43–4, *141*, 160, 245
Curl Brook (Herefs) 50, 136–7, 168, 288
Cwm (Montgomery) 43, 149
Cwm Ffrydd (Clun Forest, Shropshire) 44, 138
Cwmsanahan Hill (Clun Forest, Shropshire) 44, 46, 121, *137*, 138, 146, 161, *168*, 171, 204, 213, 234, 237–40, *238*, *239*, *241*, 279
Cwm Whitton Hill (Presteigne, Rads) 47, 248
Cymau Hall (Flints/west of Wrexham) 38

Danube, river/valley 350, 353
Dean, Forest of (Gloucs) 233
Dee, river/valley 13, 24, 36, 57, 126–7, 129–30, *129*, 162, 169, 185, 338–40, 345, 351, 357
  Dee estuary 68, 124, 365
Deganwy (Caerns) 118, 270
Derwas (north of Welshpool) 31, *31*, 33, 40, 131
Devil's Dyke (Newmarket, Cambs/Suffolk) 68
Devil's Pulpit (Tidenham, Gloucs) 81, *82*, 89, 172, *173*, 190, 206, *207*, 212, 220, 237, 276, *276*, 279, 337
Discoed (Presteigne, Rads) 81, 125–7, *136*, 138–9, 142, 152–3, 154, 160, 178–9, 199, 203, 212, 228–9, 230–2, *230*, 248, 257, 291–2, *374*
  Bwlch 152, 153, 199, 228–9, 230–2, *230*, *248*, 257, 292, 336
  Yew Tree Farm 81, 152, 153, *178*, 179, 192, 198–201, 210, 213, 248, 335
Dorset 223, 227
Droitwich (Worcs) 283, 240, 316, 320
Dudston Fields (Chirbury, Shropshire/Montgomery) 43, 169, 195–8, *195*, *196*, *197*, *198*, 203, 223, 232, 261, 279, 412 (n. 17, 18)
Dunwich (?'Dommoc', Suffolk) 316

East Vaga (Tidenham, Gloucs) 17, 146, 168, 234, 276
Edenhope (Clun Forest, Shropshire) 43, 138, 146, 153
Edenhope Hill (Shropshire) 44, 179, 210, 212, 250
Eglwyseg (Llangollen) 290
  Eglwyseg Mountain 126
Eglwyseg river 162
Eign Brook, valley (Herefs) 243
English Bicknor (Gloucs) 13, 18, 171
  Collins Grove 168
Erddig (Wrexham) 24
Eryri (Snowdon, Caerns/Gwynedd) 118

Esclusham (west of Wrexham) 167, 171, *181*, 181
Evenjobb (Rads) 245
Evenjobb Hill (Rads) 47, 146, 150, 171, *230*, 281, *281*
Evesham (Worcs) 325
Eywood Park (Herefs) 49

Fflos, the (Montgomery) 42
Ffrith (Flints/west of Wrexham) 19, 38, *38*, 39, 70, 146, 217
Ffrith Hall (Flints) 38, 70
Ffrydd (Knighton) 47, 144, 166, *352*
Ffrydd Road (Knighton) 218
Fladbury (Worcs) 325
Fleam Dyke (Cambs) 68
Flint 290
Flixborough 319
Forden (Montgomery) 41, *42*, 76, 132, 167, 217, 246, 294
  Court House, 175, 185
  Forden Gaer (Roman fort) 294, 415 (n.123)
Four Crosses (north-west of Welshpool) 130
Fownhope (Herefs) 244
Fron Farm (Denbigh) 205, *205*
Furrow Hill (Rads) 47, 138, 248

Gaer, The, (Thornbury, Montgomery) 42
Garbett Hall (Clun Forest, Shropshire) 121, *121*, 151, 168, *178*, 192, *193*, 207, 240, *249*, 250
Garnons Hill (Herefs) 50, 76, 88, 138, 148, 168, 242
Glasbury (Rads) 270
Gloucester 316, 366
  St Peter's Abbey 366
Glymorlas (Wrexham) 281
Gobowen (north of Oswestry, Shropshire) 92, 183, *183*, 356–7, 359, 371
Goodrich (Herefs) 50
Graig Hill (Clun Forest, Shropshire) 45, 212, *354*
Gwarthlow (Montgomery) 155
Gwenfro river/valley 136–7, 205, *205*
Gwent uplands *128*, 129

Halkyn Mountain (Flints/north-west of Wrexham) 39, 358
Hammerwich (Staffs) 316
Harleys Mountain (Herefs) 126
Hawthorn Hill (Presteigne, Rads) 47, 79, 144, 152, 192, 239, 248, 249
Hem (Montgomery) 41, 132, 136–7, *141*, 194, *278*, 279
Hengwn Hill (Rads) 248
Hentland (Herefs) 63
Hereford 1, 6, 13, 18, 22, 50, 109, 110, 240, 243, 264, 270, 273–5, 283–4, 289, 338, 345, 351, 355, 357, 366, 369–71
  Cathedral 366

Hergan/ 'Hergan Corner' (Clun Forest, Shropshire) 45, 151, 170, 172, 211, 234–7, *238*
Herrock Hill (Herefs) 49, 84, 136, 148, *148*, 171, 206, 234, *234*, 250, 282, 291, 293, *345*
Hexham (Northumberland) 324
Highbury/Highbury Plains (Lower Redbrook, Gloucs) 52, 146, 148, 154, 168
Hindwell, brook (Rads/Herefs) 47, 136, 147, 169, 171, 268, 282, 291, 293
Hints (near Wall, Staffs/Warks) 320
Holmes Marsh (Lyonshall, Herefs) 50, 79, 287
  Crump Oak Wood (south of Holmes Marsh) 287, *288*
Holywell (Flints) 18, 24
Hope Mountain (Flints/west of Wrexham) 38
Hopyard Wood (east of Llangollen/south of Ruabon) 36
Humber river/estuary 97, 118, 303

Ipswich (Suffolk) 312, 319

Jenkins Allis (Knighton) 47, *47*, 191, 210, 229, 258, *258*

Kempsford (Wilts) 116
Kenchester (Roman town, west of Hereford) 242
Kerry Ridgeway 12, 17, 42, 43–4, *44*, 72, 108, *133*, 138, *141*, 143, 144, 145, 149, 160–1, 232, 242, 266, 278
Kidderminster (Worcs) 307
Kington 22
Kingswood (Montgomery) 41, 50, 277
Kinnerton-Presteigne ridgeway 229–32, *230*, *231*, 248
Kinsham (Herefs) 291, 292
Knighton 13, 39, 47, 69, 72, 83, 88, 127–8, *137*, 138, 144, 146, 161, 166, *168*, 171, 191, 206, 218, 219, 234, 248, 258, *370*
Knill (Herefs) 169, 245
Knuck Bank (Clun Forest, Shropshire) 44
  Middle Knuck 149, 236
Knucklas (Rads) 237, *241*
Knucklas Castle 279, *280*

Lack Brook (Montgomery) 155
Ladylift/Ladylift Clump (Weobley, Herefs) 49, 50, 79, 128, 286, 288
Lancaut (Gloucs) 169
Leicester 99, 324, 343
Leighton (Montgomery) 41, 132, 147, 167, 171, 234, 277
  Hope Farm (Leighton) 232
Leighton Park (Montgomery) 41
Leintwardine (Herefs) 295, 416 (n.125)
Leominster (Herefs) 229, 286, 295
Lichfield (Staffs) 99, 105–6, 304, 306, 307, 310, 312, 313, 315, 317, 325, 328

Topographical Index 441

Lindisfarne Abbey (Northumberland) 223
Lindow Moss (Cheshire) 256
Lippetts Grove (Gloucs) 146, 147, 171, *172*, *173*, 210, 219, 234, 276–7
Llandrinio (north-east of Welshpool) 31
Llandysilio (north-east of Welshpool) 32
Llandudno (Caerns) 358
Llanelwedd, Court Farm 246
Llan-faes (Ynys Môn, Anglesey) 118
Llanfair Hill (Clun Forest, Shropshire) *44*, 47, 121, 169, 176, *186*, 203, 204, *205*, 207–8, *208*, *209*, 210, *210*, 211, 212, *217*, 219, 224, *227*, 240
Llanfair Waterdine (Shropshire) 295
Llanfynydd (Flints) 13, 38, 147, 169, 184, 356
Llangollen 71, 89, 112, 130, 272, 280, 338, 373
Llangorse (Lake, east of Brecon) 275
Llanyblodwel (west of Oswestry) 33
Llanymynech (Shropshire/north-east of Welshpool) 31, 345, 361
  Llanymynech Hill 31–3, 131–2, 138, 145, 158, 169, 206, 237, 244, 277, 279
  Asterley Rocks 132, 237, 277, 361
  Carreghofa 132, 277, 361, 400 (n.22)
Llynclys (Shropshire) 171
Llynclys Hill (Shropshire) 16, 32–3, 145
Llynclys Quarry (Shropshire) 16, *32*
Llyn Tegid (Bala Lake) 151
London 107, 115, 117, 302, 307, 312, 315, 316, 318–19, 327, 343, 376
  Aldwych 318, 327
  'Lundenwic' 319
Long Mountain (Montgomery) 41, 126, *139*, 145, 158, *176*, 278
Long Mynd (Shropshire) 126, 142
  dykes on, 243
Lugg, river/valley 47, 127, 136, *136*, 140, 144, 152–5, 163, *178*, 190, 199, 236, 240, 248, 257, 268, 284–5, 291–2, 345, *374*
Lugwardine (east of Hereford) 295
Lydbrook/ Lower Lydbrook (Gloucs) 13
Lyonshall (Herefs) 49, 50, 128, 137, 146, 168, 234, 235, *285*, 286–7, 358
  Lyonshall Park (Wood) 49, 235

Maddle Brook (Herefs) 50
Madgett Hill (Gloucs) *52*, 54, 74, *173*, 187, *190*, *191*, 234, *251*
Madley (west of Hereford) 50
Maesbury (Shropshire) 18, 24, 84, 162
Main, river/valley (Germany) 350
Mainstone (Clun Forest, Shropshire) *44*, *133*, 149, 180, 182, 187
Mansell Gamage (Herefs) 148
Marden (north of Hereford) 284, 295
Mardu Brook (Rads) 45, 235
Mathrafal (site, west of Welshpool) 246
Mechain (dyke) 243,
Meifod (settlement, west of Welshpool) 246, 277, 361

Mellington Hall/Park (Shropshire) 42, 132, 232
Merbach Hill (west of Hereford) 58
Middlewich (Cheshire) 296, 320
Minera (west of Wrexham) 148
Minster-in-Thanet (Kent) 117, 314, *315*
Moel-y-Mab (Montgomery) 41
Mold (Flints) 1, 13, 39, 290
Monmouth 1, 13, 125–8, 274, 286, 289
Monnow, river/valley 273
Montgomery 13, 17, 185, 194, 197, 259, 278, *278*, 345
  Castle 155, *196*, 198, 278–9
  Vale of, 57, *74*, 80, 127, 132, 142, 163, 167, 169, 188, 193, 194, 216, *223*, 229, 242, 245, 259, 262, *337*, 338
Morda, river/valley 33, 136, 139, 140, 161, 162
Mordiford (east of Hereford) 292
Morfe/Kinver 95
Morlas, brook 36, 136, 139
Mork Brook (Gloucs) 136–7, 358
Monmouth 351
Mount Sion (Brymbo, Denbigh) *38*, 357

Nantcribba Gaer (fort, Forden, Montgomery) 58, 246, 294
Neath, brook 32
Nercwys Mountain (Denbigh) 39
Newcastle Hill/Pen Offa (Rads) 47, 168, 171, 230, *230*, 248, 257
Newcastle-upon-Clun *159*, 201, 234
Northampton 99, 319–20
Nottingham 319
Norton Canon (Herefs) 287
Nuremberg (Germany) 350

Old Oswestry (Shropshire) 24, 83
Orseddwen (Sellatyn, Oswestry) 83, *84*, 228, 232, *349*
Oswestry (Shropshire) 13, 16, 56, 66–7, 83, 102, 140, 144, 145, 152, 161, 167, 219, 237, 256, 266, 290, 338, 339, 345–6
Otford (Kent) 110, 310

Panpunton Hill (north of Knighton) 80, *129*, 144, 146, 171, *191*, 239, *370*
Pedwardine (Brampton Bryan, Herefs/Shropshire) 295
Penkridge (Staffs) 265
Pen Offa (Rads) 47
Pentre (Montgomery) 131, 133, 145, 147
Pentre Bychan (south-west of Wrexham) 36, 144
Pentre-shannel (west of Wrexham) 149, 167
Pen-y-coed (Flints/west of Wrexham) 38
Pen-y-Gardden, fort (Ruabon) 71, 140, 280, *281*
Perrystone (Herefs) 289
Pershore (Worcs, monastery at) 366
Peterborough 99, 324

Pewsey, Vale of (Wilts) 25–6
Pilleth (Rads) 152, 153
Pinner's Hole (Knighton) 234, 240
Plas-crogen (Shropshire) *339*
Plas Offa (Chirk) 92, 185
Plumweir Cliff (Gloucs) 146, *173*, 190, 276–7
Polesworth (Warks) 316
Porth-y-Waen (Shropshire) 190, 213
Powis Castle (Welshpool) 150
Prestatyn (Denbigh) 18, 68, 289
Presteigne (Rads) 138, 139, 147, 163, 169, 179, 199, 230–1, *231*, 236, 248, 282, 290–3, 338, 345

Quentovic (coastal port near Étaples, northern France) 321

Radnor Forest 126, *128*, *133*, 152, 230
  Llan Fawr 152
Radnor, Old 291, *281*
Ravenna (Italy) 325
Reculver (Roman fort, Kent) *315*, 324
Redbrook/Lower Redbrook (Gloucs) 16, 52, 146, 148, 168, 177
Redlake valley 250
Repton (Derbyshire) 311, 315, 324
Rhine, river/valley 353
Rhos (north-east of Welshpool) 32, *130*, 167
Rhosllanerchrugog (Denbigh/Wrexham) 16
Rhos-y-meirch (south of Knighton) 144, 169
Rhuddlan (Denbigh/Clwyd) 115, 290, 356
Richard's Castle (Herefs/Shropshire) 292
Ripon (Yorks) 324
Rochester (Kent) 106, 302, 328, 316
Rome 304, 307, 313, 323–4
  St Peter's Church (Vatican) 324, 327
Ross-on-Wye 13, 50, 125, 273
Rotherwas (south of Hereford) 285
Rownall Covert /Coppice 41–2, 136, 155, 194
Ruabon (Wrexham) 16, 19, 36, 126, 130, 144, 193, 345
  Pont Adam 272, *281*
  Ruabon Mountain 36, 126–7, *128*, 148, 162
  Ruabon School 169, 185, 280
Rushock Hill (Herefs) 1, 13, 16, 22, *48*, 49, 88, 128, 171, 206, *206*, 234, 235, 259, 283, 288, 371

St Albans (Herts) 25, 316, 343
St Briavels (Gloucs) 209, 358
St Briavels Common (Gloucs) 17, 52, 62–3, 89, 144, *173*, 177
Sandbach (Cheshire) 325
Sarnesfield (Herefs) 49, 50, 79, 242, 287
Seckington (Warks) 109, *109*, 315
Sedbury (Gloucs) 17, *17*, 68, *78*, 125, 154, 169, 177, 186, 210, 249, 282, *282*
Selattyn Hill (west of Oswestry) 33, *35*, 36, 83, *84*, 126, 139, 150, *151*, 162, 169, 209, 217, 219, 228

442 Topographical Index

Selley (Shropshire) 39, 79, 72, 166, 172, 174, 207
Severn, river/valley 13, 16, 29, 31–3, *40*, 40–1, 57, 80, 123–4, 126, 130, 171, 182, 187–8, 268, 271, 338–40, 351, 358, 376
  Middle Severn 29, *40*, 193
  Severn Estuary *53*, 16, 17, *17*, 31, 169, 282–3, *282*, 365
Shrewsbury 130, 158, 266, 272, 280, 345
Silchester (Hants) 25
Snowdon, mountain, *see* Eryri
Somerset (Somerset) 107
Soughton (Flints) 290
Southampton 319
  'Hamwih' (at Southampton) 319
Spital Meend (fort, Gloucs) 169, *173*
Spoad/Lower Spoad (Clun valley, Shropshire) 45, *45*, 154, 201, *201*, 202, *202*, 234, 239
Spoad Hill 161, 202–3
Springhill Farm (Clun Forest, Shropshire) 202
Stapleton (Herefs) 291, 292, 295
Staunton-on-Arrow (Herefs) 242, 265, 291
Steel Rigg (Housesteads, Northumberland) *342*
Strata Florida Abbey (Cards) 56
Stretford (Herefs) 240
Stubb, The, (Kingswood, Montgomery) 41, *41*, 50, 132
Sutton St Michael (Marden, near Hereford) 284, 319–20
  Freen's Court 284
Sutton Walls (hillfort, north of Hereford) 285

Tame, river/valley 214, 265
Tamworth (Staffs) 232, *305*, 307, 315, 319, 325, 332, 368, 375
Tanat, river/valley 32–3, 36, 127, 130, 138, 140, 158, 162, 237, 277, 345, 361

Tatham (Ruabon) 36, 280–1, *372*
Teme, river/valley 13, 46–7, 80, 128, *129*, 136, 138, 140, 146, *168*, 170, 204, 206, 237, 239, *241*, 266, 268, 291, 345, *352*
Thames, river/valley 101, 107, 307, 310, 315
  Thames estuary 101
  Middle Thames valley 107
Thionville (Metz, NE France) 347
Thornbury (Montgomery) 42
Tidenham (Gloucs) 16, 146, 161, *173*, 210
Tidenham Chase (Gloucs) 17, 62, 89, 219
Tintern (Monmouth) 81, *82*, 146, *173*, 206, 219, 276, *276*, 345
Tirymynach (Welshpool) 130
Titley Mill (Herefs) 49, *49*, 168
Treflach (Shropshire) *34*, 146, 171, 175, 185
Trefonen (Shropshire) 13, *31*, 33, *34*, 149, 167, 210, *257*
Trelystan Hill (Montgomery) 41
Trent river/valley 118, 214
Trewern (Welshpool) 130, 246
Treuddyn (Clwyd) 1, 13, 18, 23, 31, 38, 60, 125, 127, 147, 169, 261, 289–90, 357
Tutshill (Gloucs) 16, 54, 146
Tyn-y-coed (Denbigh) 148

Unk, river/valley 43–4, 136, 138, 142
Usk, river/valley 273, 275

Valle Crucis Abbey (Llangollen) 280, 340
Vyrnwy, river/valley 17, 22–3, 32–3, 36, 123, 127, 130–1, 138, 140, 158, 169, 171, 182, 187, 206, 237, 345, 361

Wall (*Letocetum*, Staffs) 98–9, *100*
Walton Basin (Rads) 47, 125, 146, *148*, 149, 171, 282, 345

Welshpool 12–13, 16, 29, 32, 40–1, 125, 127, 130, 131, 167, 171, 246, 351, 361
Weobley (Herefs) 287, *287*, 294
Wergan's Wood (Gloucs) 213
Whitehaven Hill (Oswestry, Shropshire) *32*, 33
Whitton Hill (west of Presteigne) 144
Wigmore (Herefs) 240, 292
Winchcombe (Gloucs) 117, *117*, 307, 315, 316, *316*, 319, 332, 366, 368
  St Peter's Abbey 366
Wing (Bucks) 323
Woonton (Lyonshall, Herefs) 50
Worcester 117, 264,
Worgan's Wood (Gloucs) 234
Worthen (Shropshire) 294
Wrekin, The (hill, Shropshire) 104, 263, 266
Wrexham 16, 19, 22, 24, 167, 171, 217, *358*, 369
Wroxeter (Roman town, east of Shrewsbury, Shropshire) 41, 298, 308, 316, 319, 325
Wye, river/valley 13, 16, *48*, 50, 54, 58, 63, 74–5, 78–9, 125–6, 128, 138, 146, 152, 169, 177, 206, 219, 233, 244, 270, 273–4, 282–3, 286, 289, 338, 345, 351, 355, 358, 371
Wye cliffs 209
Wyegate (Gloucs) 146, 358
Wynnstay Colliery (Ruabon, Wrexham) 16, 280

Yarkhill (Herefs) 265
Yazor/Moorhampton (west of Hereford) 50, 137, 146, 168, 286
Yeavering (Northumberland) 103
Ynys Môn (Anglesey) 118, 341
York 307, 319
  'Eoforwic' 319
Ysceifiog Circle (Flints) 70, 289

SUBJECT INDEX

Aachen (Germany) 325
Aelfflaed, daughter of Offa of Mercia, m. Aethelred I, king of Northumbria 111, 113, 305, 312
Aelfthryth, youngest daughter of Offa of Mercia 111
Aethelbald, king of Mercia 94, 101, 107–9, 117, 223, 244, 256, 263, 271, 273, 300, 308, 309, 331, 366
Aethelberht, king of East Anglia 111–12, 114, 284, 309, 312, 332
  execution of 114, 284
Aethelberht, king of Kent 302, 317
Aethelburh, daughter of Offa of Mercia 314
Aethelflaed, 'lady of the Mercians', daughter of Alfred of Wessex 94, 274–5
Aethelfrith, king of Northumbria 370

Aethelheard, archbishop of Canterbury 115, 117, 307, 313
Aethelheard, king of Wessex 256
Aethelmund, Ealdorman of Mercia 116
Aethelred, king of Mercia 106
Aethelred I, king of Northumbria 111, 114, 303, 312
Act of Union between Wales and England, 1536 AD 369
Ahlmund, moneyer to Offa 312
Alban, martyr, saint 343
Alcuin (Northumbrian cleric, at the court of Charlemagne) 23, 115, 300, 303–4, 314, 367–8, 417 (n.19)
Alfred, king of Wessex 94, 273, 317, 366 (*see also*, Asser, Aethelflaed)
  Mercian clerics at court of 366

angel carvings, Mercian (Breedon, Lichfield, q.v.) 300, 325–6
Anglo-Saxon Chronicle 56, 226
Anna, king of East Anglia 331
Annales Cambriae 270, 288, 340
Archenfield (in south Herefordshire; *see also* 'Ergyng') 79, 80, 267, 274
Arosaete (people, Warks) 265
Ashwell Street (Roman Road, Cambs) 27
Asser (Bishop of Sherborne) 20–3, 88, 334, 341, 351, 363–4, 366–7, 374, 376
  Life of King Alfred 20–3, 56, 62, 86, 88, 383 (n.32)
Aubrey, John *Monumenta Britannica* (c.1690 AD) 58, 286
Avars ('Huns'; people) 303, 350
  swords and silks of 333

Subject Index 443

Avon (river, Wilts/Somerset) as boundary between Mercia and Wessex 283

Barker, Philip 262
Bede (monk, Northumberland) 23, 97, 101, 342–3
   HE (*Ecclesiastical History*) 23, 395 (n.19, 29), 396 (n.36)
Beonna, king of East Anglia 109, 112,
Beorhtric, king of Wessex 21, 111, 116, 227, 314
Beornred, king of Mercia in 757 AD 109
Beornwulf, king of Mercia 94, 118, 332
Berhtwulf, king of Mercia 94
Bertha, daughter of Charlemagne 113, 305, 317
Bertha, daughter of King Pippin, m. Aethelberht, king of Kent 317
Berthwyn, 'bishop of Ergyng' 273–4
Biblical images of kingship (eg on coins) 308
'black stones' (?porphyry columns, imported to Aachen) mentioned by Charlemagne 325
Blair, John 293, 383 (n.32)
Boniface, monk, missionary (St.) 108
'book-land vs 'folk-land' explained 222, 408 (n.26)
Boyd Dawkins 65
Breedon-on-the-Hill (Leics), Archangel Gabriel carving 325
Britannia, province of Roman Empire 98
bridge-work and fortress-work 222–4, 320
brooches, Anglo-Saxon types 98, *100*
Brooks, Nicholas 330–1
Brorda, Mercian nobleman, late eighth-/early ninth century, 'patricius' 115, 312, 368
Brown, Michelle 331
Brut y Tywysogyon ('Chronicle of the Princes') 56–7, 360–1
Brycheiniog, kingdom of 274–5, 341, 355
Brynbella Mound, Flintshire (Fox excavations at) 289
Buca, *comes* (q.v.) of Aethelbald of Mercia 256
'Burghal Hidage' (West Saxon document concerning fortified places) 81, 214
Burgred, king of Mercia 94, 226, 275
burh (places) 227, 294
burhweard (OE, 'fort-guardian') 227–8, 294
'Burton' (place-name) 227, 293–4
Buttington (battle at, in 894 AD) 56
Byrhtferth, monk of Ramsey Abbey (Peterborough) 56
Byzantium 326, 344

Cadwallon, king of Gwynedd 102
'Caer Din', fort on Kerry Ridgeway (q.v.) 245, 248
Camden, William *Britannia* (1588) 93, 118
Cannabacae (hemp) pollen 256
cantref boundaries 243
'Cantref coch' (Forest of Dean) 358
Capitulary of Thionville, 805 AD 347

Caradog ap Meirion, king of Gwynedd 115, 118
Carolingian
   court 114
   diplomacy 112
   relations with Mercia 301–4, 307, 346–7
   'Renaissance' 113
Caxton, William 10, 381 (n.1)
   Description of Britain (1588 AD) 57
Ceolwulf I, king of Mercia 94, 223
Ceolwulf II, king of Mercia 94
Chad, missionary to Mercians, Saint 317
   shrine of (in Lichfield cathedral) 325–6, 326
Charlemagne, king of the Franks, Holy Roman Emperor 110, 113, 116, 298–300, 302–5, 307, 309, 310, 321, 324–5, 334, 344, 346–50, 352, 366
   'Karlsgraben' earthwork, Bavaria, built by 350
Charles, eldest son of Charlemagne 111, 113, 305
charter, granted at 'Ismere' (=?Kidderminster) 307
charters (land diplomas) 95, 215, 219–20, 222, 243, 274
charters, Kentish 214, 223
charters, Mercian
   style of 301, 308, 312, 408 (n.28)
   witness lists for 301
   Worcester 223, 366–7
Chertsey Abbey, charter 105
chronometric dating 382–3 (n.24)
Churchyard, Thomas (poet, scholar) 55, 58, 75, 376, 386 (n.1)
   Worthines of Wales (1587 AD) 55
clergy 95
cloaks, trade in 303
'Clofesho', Council at 307, 315
Clwyd-Powys Archaeological Trust 18
Coelred, king of Mercia 106–7, 368
Coenred, king of Mercia 106
Coenwulf, king of Mercia 93–4, 114–19, 223, 244, 290, 298–9, 303, 306–8, 312–13, 315, 323, 328, 332, 340, 345, 355–7, 366, 367–8
   as scion of Mercian regime 114–15
   coinage of 118, 323, 327–8, 358
   gold *mancus* (coin) of 327–8, *327*, 420 (n.106)
   and London 421 (n.112)
   'emperor' 117–18, 306–7
   political use of history 316–17
   relations with Charlemagne 418 (n.46)
   strategy of assertion 115–17
   succession to Ecgfrith in 796AD 398 (n.87)
coinage in Mercian economy/political economy 318, 321–3
Coles, Gladys Mary (poet) vi, 344, 376
Colt Hoare, Richard 61

comes (companion of king or leader) 222
Concenn, king of Powys 89, 271
copper, as a resource 233
Councils (Church) 304
Cramp, Rosemary *108*,
Cropthorne (Worcs), cross-head at *108*,
Cuthred, Mercian king of Kent, brother of Coenwulf 116–17, 306, *327*, 332, 368
Cuthred, king of Wessex 107–8, 268
Cwoenthryth, daughter of Coenwulf 117, 314–15, *315*
Cyfeilog, bishop of Archenfield 274
Cynan ap Rhodri, king of Gwynedd 118
Cynehelm (Kenelm), son of Coenwulf of Mercia 312,
Cynethryth, Queen of Mercia, wife of Offa of Mercia 113–15, 314, *314*, 315, *315*, 419 (n.62)
Cynewulf, king of Wessex 304, 309

'damp oak woodlands' (Fox) 23
Danevirke, dating of 383 (n.35)
Danish armies 366, 368
David, (biblical) king, archetype 322
Davies, Wendy 269
Deanery of Oswestry 369
Deira, kingdom of 101–3
Diocletian, Emperor of Rome 98
Dunsaete (people) 244, 266–7
   identity of 267
   Ordinance concerning (q.v.)
'dyke', Anglo-Saxon terms for 220–1, 227
dykes, early
   Bokerley Dyke (Dorset) 27, 351
   Bran Ditch/Heydon Ditch (Cambs) 26
   Brent Ditch (Cambs) 26
   Cambridgeshire (all) 225
   'Clawdd Coch' (nr Llanymynech) 361
   cross-valley and cross-ridge 360
   Devil's Dyke (Cambs/Suffolk) 26, 65
   Fleam Dyke (Cambs) 26, 65
   Grim's Ditch (north Oxfordshire) 21
   on Long Mynd (Shropshire) 80
   Late Iron Age 25, 27
   Middle Bronze Age 25, 27
dux term explained 407 (n.2)

Eadberht Praen, of Kent 115–16, 306, 312, 332
Eadburh, daughter of Offa of Mercia, m. Beorhtric, king of Wessex 21, 111, 116
Eadhun, moneyer at Canterbury 322
Eadwald, king of East Anglia 306
Eahlflaed, wife of Peada (q.v.), sister of Osthryth (q.v.) 106
Eahlmund, king of Kent 302
Ealdhun, reeve of Kent 302
Ealdred, 'dux' of *Hwicce* 309
Eanbald, archbishop of York 359
Eardwulf, king of Northumbria 116, 307, 312, 359
Earl Harold (Godwin) 56

Earle, John, Professor 65, 87, *370*
East Anglia, kingdom of 93, 94, *96*, 101, 111, 305, 309, 312, 316, 318, 324, 330–1
East Saxons 101
Ebba, moneyer to Offa *112*
Ecgberht, king of Kent 302
Ecgberht, king of Wessex 298, 306, 332,
Ecgfrith, king of Mercia 110–11, 113–14, 283, 300, 305, 312, 344, 356, 368
 anointing of 110–12
 circumstances of death of, in 796AD 398 (n.87)
 death of 113–14
Ecgfrith, king of Northumbria 106,
economy and environment, eighth-century 255–7
Edgar, king of West Saxons, king of the English 242
Edward, king of England, 'The Confessor' 56
Edward the Elder, king of England 274
Edwards, Nancy 271–2
Edwin, king of Northumbria 102
Elise, king of Powys 86, 271–2, 280
Elmet, kingdom of 99
 enclosures, defended 227
Elystan Glodrydd, district of 360
English communities, on both sides of Offa's Dyke 216
Eowa, brother of Penda of Mercia (q.v.) 309, 317
Ergyng, kingdom of 50, 81, 267, 273, 293, 355
 extent of 414 (n.69, 73)
Evans, John (of Llwyn-y-Groes) 60
Everson, Paul 261

Felix, monk (author of *Life of St Guthlac*) 107, 331
Feryock, Marge 91
Finberg, H. P. R. 119, 366
Fodbroke, T.D. 61–2
Forthere, Bishop of Sherborne 256
Fowler, William 58–9
 'The Mannor of Leighton' (map, 1663 AD) 58–9, 59
Fox, Cyril (Sir) xiii, 3, 10, 18, 19, 23, 27, 33, 47, 60, 61, 67–77, 122–4, 126, 133–5, 143–4, 147, 162, 164, 165–7, 173–7, 179–80, 184–5, 192, 193–4, 199–200, 214, 216, 221, 223–5, 227, 229, *229*,230, 234,–5, 237, 244–5, 247, 255, 257–62, 275, 280, 286, 289, 336, 365, 371–2 (see also, below, Offa's Dyke, various: for example, 'mountain zone', alignments; and 'Offa's Dyke: A Field Survey', monograph)
 as 'inventor' of Gloucestershire lengths of Offa's Dyke 390 (n.107)
 dykes profiles study (Offa's Dyke and Wat's Dyke) 17
 excavation methods of 70, 76
 excavations on Offa's Dyke (see also 'Offa's Dyke' and 'Offa's Dyke excavations' entries, below) 402 (n.55–8), 404 (n.55, 56, 57, 58)
 experience of Cambridgeshire dykes study 68
 'Mercian school of field-engineering' 173, 214
 methods and conclusions questioned 76–7, 83, 86–7, 90
 Personality of Britain (1932) 123
 routeways and gates, Offa's Dyke (see 'Offa's Dyke' entries, below) 409 (n.59–61)
 study of borderland 'short dykes' 73
 survey and recording methods of 68–71, 69, 122
 survey of Wat's Dyke 75
 use of Ordnance Survey maps 192–4
Franks, kingdom of/Francia 110, 303, 346–7
 influence upon Mercia 346
frontier, Mercia with Wales/Britons 6, 19, 93, 119
 as a patrolled line 78
 in Herefordshire 283–9
'frontier patrol' 226–8
frontier zone, of which Offa's Dyke a part 336, 344–7
frontiers as 'treasured space, gained under calculated danger' (Moschek, 2009) 353

'Gart Mailauc' (battle site, c.722 AD, located ?east of Hereford) 288–9
Gelling, Margaret 77–8, 82, 227–8, 247, 268–9,
Gentleman's Magazine 62
George, bishop of Ostia 317
Gerald of Wales (*Giraldus Cambrensis*) 56, 339, 352, 369
 Descriptio Kambriae ('Description of Wales', c.1190 AD) 56, 339
Gervold, Abbot of St. Wandrille (overseer of port of Quentovic) 320–1
Gewisse, early Anglo-Saxon kingdom of (also, people) 100, 102, 104
Glyndwr, Owain 369
Godwin family, West Saxon magnates 369
'great dykes', as special category of linear earthwork 221
Greenwich Meridian, Offa's Dyke in relation to 125
Gregory I, Pope 307
Gruffydd ap Llywelyn, king of Gwynedd, overlord of Wales 366
Guest, Edwin 64
Gumley (Leics), synod of 108, 223, 408 (n.32)
Guthlac, warrior, monk, of Crowland (St.) 107, 317, 331, 341
Gwent, kingdom of 81, 267, 273, 276, 355, 360
Gwynedd, kingdom of 93, 103, 118, 270, 290, 341

Hadrian, Pope 310, 313
Hadrian's Wall *96*, 157, 213, 247, 250, 342–3
Haestingas (Sussex, people) 110
Hahlsaete (people) 266
Hartshorne, Revd Charles. H. 63, 65, 122, 164, 165, 361
 Salopia Antiqua 122
Heahberht, king of Kent 302
herepath (=army-road) 240
heriot, practice of 330
Higden, Ranulf *Polychronichon* (1299AD) 57
Highland Zone/Lowland Zone of Britain (Fox) 123
Hill, David 82–91, 193, 261
 and Gloucestershire lengths of Offa's Dyke 84–6
 and Worthington, Margaret 84–91, *229*, 231, 237
 critique of conclusions of 89–91
 'Hill-Worthington orthodoxy' 91
 Offa's Dyke History and Guide (2003) 87–9
Hill, Geoffrey 376
Historia Regum (York) 56
Howe, Nicholas 254
Hoyle, Jon *173*, 189, 190, 193, 381–2 (n.9, 10)
Hwicce, kingdom of (people) 100, 102, 106, 111, 117, 224, 298, 307, 309, 315
Hygeberht, archbishop of Canterbury 313
Hywel ap Caradog, king of Gwynedd 118

Ibba, moneyer to Offa 323
Icknield Way 27
Ine, king of Wessex 107, 317
iron, as a resource 233
Iron Age forts 75
Islamic Caliphate 344

Jaenberht, archbishop of Canterbury 112, 307, 310, 313
John, Eric 298
John of Salisbury *Polycraticus* (1159 AD) 56
Jones, H.L. (fl. 1856 AD) 61

Kent, kingdom of 101, 111, 115–7, 223, 301–2, 304, 309–10, 318, 324, 330–2
Keynes, Simon 263, 269, 363, 366, 376
'Kington'-type names 296–7
Kirby, David xiii, 306

landscape
 eighth-century 255–7, 262
 political 1, 6
lead, as resource 233
'-leah' element place-names 216, 268
Leather, Ella Mary 371
Leland, John *Itinerary in Wales* (1539–45) 57
'Lene', community of 242
Leo III, Pope 115, 313, 346

Lhuyd, Edward (1659–1709), antiquary 59, 86, 413 (n.57)
  Parochalia 59
'Lichfield Angel' (carving) 300, 325–6
Lichfield, archdiocese of 113, 115, 117
LiDAR imaging 151
Limes (Roman, a frontier zone) 57–8, 353
Lindsey, kingdom of/province of Mercia 93, 100, 106, 309
Llandaff charters 79, 274, 288
llys, court 275
Lordship of Clun 345, 369
Luckombe, Philip England's Gazetteer (1790 AD) 59–60
'Lugharness' district (north Herefordshire) 291, 338

'Maelor Saesneg' (in Wrexham area) 369
Magonsaete (people) 80, 264–5, 267, 309, 412 (n.29)
Malim, Tim 92, 232–4, 410 (n.69)
mancus (gold coin, *see under* 'Coenwulf', above)
Mang, moneyer at London and Canterbury 318
'March of Wales' 345–6, 369
Maserfelth, battle of (near ?Oswestry) 56, 102, 104, 162, 266
mearc (OE, boundary) 292
merchants, English, on Continent 303–4
Mercia, kingdom of 50, 96, 222, 224, 234, 255, 268–9, 272, 278, 283, 298, 305, 319, 323, 330, 336, 341, 343, 346–7, 352, 353–4, 365–8, 375
  alliance with Gwynedd 102
  alliances with Wessex and Northumbria 111, 298
  'Anglian empire' of Mercia 312
  army, nature of 216, 221, 269
  border with Powys 392 (n.148)
  bureaucracy of (emergent) 234, 308
  'capital territories' of 315–16
  coins of 112
  'command economy' in 318
  core area/'heartlands' of 97–9, 101, 124, 216, 263, 318, 375–6
  correspondence with Papacy and Charlemagne's court 334
  'court culture' of 314, 332–3
  diplomacy of 311–2
  female royal kin 313–15
  'Greater Mercia' 107
  hegemony of 93, 308–9
    defined 299–300
    legacy 365–8
    'material of Mercian hegemony' defined 299–300
    political mechanisms supporting 308–17
  kings of 234, 267–8
  law codes of 317
  'Mercian March' as a hybrid buffer-zone 344
  patterns of alliances of 103
  power, geography of 368
  royal archives of, (probably) at Winchcombe 366
  'Supremacy' of 94, 250
  warfare as policy of 309–10
  western (region) 227
  western frontier of 118–19, 123, 130, 216
Mercian Hymns (verse cycle, Geoffrey Hill) 376
Mercians 55, 142, 162
  as border people ix, 93, 95, 98, 394 (n.3, 4)
  bridge-building of 229
  cadre of specialised officers for public works 225
  campaigns against Britons/Welsh 93
  campaigns against Kent 111
  campaigns against West Saxons 116
  clerics at court of King Alfred of Wessex 366
  colonisation of borderlands 72
  early history 395 (n.14)
  early settlement of frontier zone 124, 397 (n.49)
  fortress-building 215–16, 223, 245, 247
  history 376
  Mierce (people) 93, 95, 97
  military service, terms of/exemptions from 222
  moneyers for 112
  origins 95–101
  origins, dual settlement thesis 99
  workforce of 216, 221
Meresaete (people) 266
Meurig ap Tewdrig, king of Gwent 273
Middle Angles 103, 105
Middle Saxons/Middlesex 101, 105
Milbourn, Henry (Recorder of Monmouth) 286, 386 (n.85), 387 (n.21)
minsters 227
mint at Rochester 328
mints, increased production of 318–19
M'Kenny Hughes 61–2
Mitchell, Bruce xiv
monasteries, as property of elite 106
Morganwydd, kingdom/region of 360
Mortimer, Ralph de 292
Musson, Chris 261–2

Naismith, Rory 419 (n.77)
Nelson, Janet 366
Nico Ditch (Manchester) 104
Noble, Frank 77–82, 226, 228–9, 229, 251, 254, 258, 268, 277, 284, 289, 293, 358, 370, 390 (n.109)
  critique of conclusions of 81–2
  study of 'central border' area 79–80
Northumbria, kingdom of 96, 101–3, 105–6, 107, 111, 114, 118–19, 303–5, 309, 316–17, 313, 318

Oelf and Oelfwine, aethelings of Northumbria 312
Offa, king of the East Saxons 106
Offa, king of Mercia 21–3, 71, 87, 93–4, 101, 109–14, 115, 117, 119, 126, 222, 223, 244, 284, 293, 298–308, 310, 313, 315, 318, 323–4, 326–7, 334, 334, 339–43, 345–7, 351–6, 362–4, 366–8, 370, 376
  as 'presiding genius over' creation of Offa's Dyke 214, 225
  assertion of power 110
  campaigns in Wales 275
  close associates of 214
  coinage of 112–13, 301, 311, 314, 317–18
    'Offa Rex' pennies 311, 318, 323
  death of 114
  emulating Charlemagne's model of kingship 342
  gift exchange with Charlemagne 303
  in Hereford 56
  interest in Bath 283
  marriage dispute with Charlemagne 303–4
  'minimalist' view of 367–8
  'new politics' of 111–12
  'overlord of the M5' 376
  political symbolism of coinage of 322
  portraits 322
    drapery 322, 323
    snake symbols 322
  political use of history 316–17
  regicide as instrument of policy of 312
  relations with Charlemagne 417 (n. 22–4)
  relations with church 112–13, 313
  reputation of 301
  'statesmanship'/hegemonic leadership of 300–5
  zenith of power of 112–14
Offa's Dyke
  abrupt changes in scale and build of 147, 181, 199, 258–9
  alignments of 122, 131–5, 257, 259
    at Dudston Fields (Chirbury/Montgomery) 196, *196*
    in Vale of Montgomery 132–5
    north of Welshpool 130–1
    'straight alignments' 193–4, 199–200
    types of (Fox) 133–5
  along the middle Severn valley 400 (n.19)
  apparent absence of 385 (n.77), 393, (n.177)
  and eighth-century landscape 76, 84
  and the frontier in Herefordshire 283–9
  and the frontier in north-east Wales 289–90

and Wales/England national border 76
and Welsh identity 7
'angled turns' along course of 234–41
as a barrier 219–21
as a *contested* frontier-work 360–1
as a frontier-marker 119
as an index of eighth-century land-use 72, 76, 80
as a line within frontier zone 78, 57–8
as a memorial (?intended) to Offa (Whitelock) 334
as military work 221, 226
as 'a monument without a history' 365, 373
as the only dyke named after a real-life person 352
as a negotiated frontier work 10, 143, 162, 216, 390 (n.100)
as part of strategy of political control 135, 138
as a potential World Heritage Site 373–4, 374
as a 'register' of eighth-century land-use (Fox) 257–9, *260*
as representing:
　a long-distance boundary among other such lines 350–1
　a particular historical juncture 353
　'a strategy frozen in time' 363
　'studied contempt' for the Welsh (Keynes) 340
　'unfinished business' in respect to Wales 341
as structurally-unique 352
as a wholly-designed structure 135, 161–3
at Llanymynech 385 (n.70)
at Long Mountain (profile across) 176
attribution to Offa 10, 75, 93
　'cautionary approaches' to 384 (n.37)
bank of
　boulders at rear of 184–5, 188
　facings *178*, 181, 186, 188, 212, 218–19
　foundations 165, 188
　profiles 176–7
　levelled upwards, to maintain bank height 207
　segments, overlapping terminals of 196–8, 199, 209
　short component lengths, standardised 198
'bastions' on (Revd Elias Owen) 65
berms along, questioned 212
British/Welsh kingdoms and districts west of 269–75
Bronygarth, track cutting through Dyke at 184, 192
build characteristics of 12, 16, 52, 68, 164–213, 217–19, 228–40
　shared throughout 164
　variation in scale 165

built under direct control of Offa 75–6
careful siting of 122–3, 135–54
characteristic features of (according to Fox) 336
compared with other dykes 11, 65, 67,
compared with Wat's Dyke 11, 22–5, 183–4
condition of 16–17, 32
conservation of 65
consistency of line of 125–6
construction of 215–19, 222–6 (see also 'bank', above; 'ditch', below; pits and quarries, below)
　'adjusted-segmented' build 203–8, 209, 279
　as an act of appropriation 250
　by local levies or conscripted force 224
　camps for builders 216
　cellular build, in 'bays' (possible) 218–19, 403 (n.34)
　contrasting modes 165–74
　details 164
　devices 335
　dumps of material for 218–19, 221
　'formula' 173
　'fully engineered' 336
　'hybrid' construction modes/scales 171
　impact on contemporary observers 215–16
　in segments 219, 335
　'interleaved' construction modes/scales 171
　junctions between segments 219
　leaders responsible for particular lengths 215
　length of time to complete 224
　'marker bank' for indicating intended course 188
　methods as understood from surface traces 175–9, 219
　overseen by professional cadre of officers 225
　physical scar caused by 152
　primary builds 218–19
　processes 219
　timber bank components (potential) 164
　variation in scale 165
'continuous' or 'basic' Dyke (after Hill/Worthington) 84–5, 88
contrasting build types of 72–3
controlling or regulating movement 142
control points along 80, 228
correlations: built form, alignment, location (Fox) 166
counterscarp bank of 12, 16, 209–11, 213
course of 1, 13, 23, 29–54
　across hills and vales 154–6
　from the middle Severn valley north to Treuddyn 29–39
　from the middle Severn valley south to Sedbury 39–54

crossing of Kerry Ridgeway (Fox) 143
date of 4, 10, 19–21, 56, 61–2, 184–5, 353 (Stenton), 355
design of 69, 72, 87–8, 335
'designers' of 140
design practices for 5, 24, 52, 225
ditch of 87
　as understood from excavations 179–84
　profiles 165, 175–6
ditch, linear, to east of 218, 402 (n.16)
early antiquarian comment on 57–9
economic, regulatory, and revenue-raising role of 234, 358
elaborated lengths of 275–83
Elm Villa 'bank' (Gloucs, opp Chepstow) 78–9
English settlement west of 268–9
erosion/destruction of lengths of 65, 146, 164, 196
excavations of (see 'Offa's Dyke excavations', below)
extent of 2, 13, 16–17, 83
　'sea to sea' 56, 65, 75, 86
'façade' along 279
　creation of 208–13
　revetment/facings 219
　'stepped' 212
fields, pre-existing building of 216
gaps in 72, 84–5, 341
gateway(s) through 72, 81, 86–7, 172, 228–34
　at 'Hergan Corner' 172
geology of underlying rocks 164–5, 218, 382 (n.15)
　variations affecting form of Dyke 164–5, 174, 177, 184, 187
glacis-like slope to front of bank of 212
Gloucestershire lengths integral to 62–3, 86, 88–9, 393 (n.170, 172, 174, 181)
Gloucestershire lengths questioned 85, 86, 88–9
hegemonic role of 6–7
in European history 373
in Herefordshire 63, 170, 285–9
in Montgomeryshire (map, Fox, 1955) 72
in the 'mountain zone' 227
landscape placement 334
　along contours, facing west 145–6
　approaching river-valleys 137–9
　ascents/descents of steep slopes 147
　ascents/descents of spine of ridge 147–8
　as mid-slope feature 154
　as sky-line feature 154, 156,
　crossing flood-plains 135–7
　curving over west-facing summits of hills 143–5
　expedience in siting of 143

facing uphill, to the west/on east-facing slopes 148–9, 175
for optimal surveillance use 162
impact 217, 226
in respect to hills 142–51
occurring as work progressed (Fox) 162
reasoning for (Fox) 144
legacy/inheritance of 368–71, 373
locational practices for 5, 13, 32, 35–6, 41
maintenance, lack of 365
'marking out' features of 83, 87, 188, 217–18
medieval commentary upon 56–7
Mellington Park 'outwork' of 72, 172
military patrols along (possible) 65, 77
'mirrored' oversight of valleys 139–40
monumental construction mode of 169, 176, 177, *178*, 257
'mountain zone' of (cf. Fox) 43, 72–3
multiple phases of construction of 62
naming of 22
natural environment as principal influence upon siting of 124
'normal', reinforced', 'weak' and 'boundary-bank modes of construction (Fox) 166–7
north–south orientation of 125–6
northern terminus of 63–4
not an impermeable barrier 142
Offa as 'presiding genius' over (Fox) 214, 225
operation of, when in use 226–8, 234
oversight of valleys 139–40
'outstanding example of its type and period in north-western Europe' (Stenton) 69
'outworks'
 at Mellington Park (Vale of Montgomery) 232
performative character/lengths of 160, 275–283
physical/geographical relation to Wat's Dyke 39
politics as principal influence upon siting of 124
profiles across (*see also*, 'bank' and 'ditch', above) 174–7
at Long Mountain 176
protective role of 160
provisional nature of 365
purpose of 10, 56, 65–6, 71, 77–8, 81
 barrier 56, 65–6, 77–8, 81
 connective 338
 economic, regulatory, and revenue-raising 234, 358
 multiple 363
 strategic 2
 treaty fulfilment 66, 71, 162,
quarry-pits, scoops, quarries and terracing for 12, *52*, 188–92, 200, 218–19

rivers integral to route of 126, 130
Roman imperial resonances of 342–3
'Roman' quality of engineering of (Fox, at Leighton) 278
route-ways across/intercepted by 227, 242, 230–4, 261
scarp construction mode of 170–1, 177, 181
Severn (river) as proxy for 40
shift in major alignment of (reasons for) 127
sighting-points along 194
slighter construction mode of 169–70, 171, 200, 236, 257–8
stances of, facing west 33–4, 41, 127, 140, 162
strategic location of 33, 36, 43
substantial construction mode of 167–9, 171–2, 176, 177, 181, 199, 236, 257–8
'surveillance infrastructure' for 336
surveillance, sophistication of 234, 249
'tangible international importance' of 373
terminus, southern, at Sedbury ('terminal flourish') 282–3
timber bridge(s) across 232
traditions concerning 57, 64,
uniformity of design and build of 215, 226
unitary construction of 4, 5, 16,
valleys 'stopped up' by 140–3
views of and from
 along the Dyke 160–1
 from the Dyke 157–9
 from the east 161
 from valleys 154
 from the west 152, 155–6, 156, 157,
visual dominance of 162
wall-like appearance/ character of 181, 212–13, *212*, 213, 219, 240
woodland cleared for 216
workforce for building 214, 221, 224
'work gangs' (and difference in competence of) 165
Wye cliffs, loss along 146
Offa's Dyke: A Field Survey (Fox), monograph (1955) 3, 10, 68, 75, 90,
 annotated extracts from Ordnance Survey maps (1955) *69*
 annotated photographs from *82, 153*
 chapter formula 389 (n.78)
 measured profiles 390 (n.98)
Offa's Dyke excavations 70, 76, 83–92, *92*, 164, 174, 182–88, 190, 217–18
 at Brompton Hall, Vale of Montgomery 188
 at Bronwylfa Road, Esclusham Farm 186
 at Bryn Hafod, Forden 217
 at Buttington Tump, Sedbury 182, 183, 186
 at Caeaugwynion, Chirk 180, 182, 185

at Carreg-y-big, Selattyn 217
at Coedpoeth 186, 217
at Court House, Forden 175, 185, 261
at Esclusham 171–2, 180, *181*, 183, 186, 213
at Ffrith Farm, Llanyfynydd 182
at Ffrith Hall 184
at Ffrith village 184, 404 (n.57)
at Ffrydd Road, Knighton 179, 180–1, 180, 182–3, 185, 190, 217, 404 (n.51)
at Four Crosses, Llandysilio 182, 187
at Home Farm, Chirk Castle 182, 188
at Johnstown, Ruabon 188
at Lippetts Grove, Tidenham 182
at Mainstone, Shropshire 180, 182–3, 187
at Nutwood, Edenhope 186–7
at Old School House, Llynclys 182
at Orseddwen, Selattyn 180, 228–9
at Plas Offa, Chirk 382 (n.23)
at Porth-y-Waen, Shropshire 183
at Redwood Lodge, Buttington 180, 182–3, 188 , 404 (n.51)
at Schoolfield, Llanyfynydd 182
at Sunnybank, Ffrith 186, 261
at Woodside, Selattyn 188
by Cyril Fox 404 (n.55, 56, 57, 58)
totals of 401 (n.2)
Offa's Dyke Conservation Project (Gloucestershire County Council/English Heritage/J. P. Hoyle, J. Vallender) 173, 189, 190, 193, 381–2 (n.9, 10), 402 (n.13, 14), 406 (n. 94, 95, 96)
Offa's Dyke Path (national walking trail) 7, 13, 375
Offa's Dyke Management Project (Cadw/ English Heritage) 91
'Offa's Dyke Project' (University of Manchester) 19, 84, 87, 261, 371, 382 (n.18–20), 383 (n.25)
 critique of results of 89–91
 investigations (details concerning) 403 (n.38, 43), 405 (n.92)
 'research strategies' of 405 (n.92)
Okasha, Elizabeth 331
'Ordinance concerning the Dunsaete' 77, 81, 266–7, 272, 355, 369, 413 (n. 41, 53), 414 (n.74)
Ordnance Survey 60, 62
Osbern, fitz Richard 292
OSL (Optically Stimulated Luminescence) dating 20, 358, 371
Osred, king of Northumbria 312
Osthryth, queen of Aethelred, king of Mercia 106
Oswald, king of Northumbria 56, 317,
Oswiu, king of Northumbria 263
Owen, Revd Elias 65

palisade, timber (Sutton, north of Hereford) 284

Papal legates/legatine Council (786 AD) 304, 355
Pascal I, Pope 117
Peada, son of Penda 105
Pecansaete (people) 99,
Pencasaete (people) 99, 265
Penda, king of Mercia 101–4, 105, 118, 162, 266, 301, 309, 317, 331, 338
Pennant, Thomas, topographer Tour (1773/1784 AD) 60–2, 64, 75, 381 (n.2)
'Perfeddwlad' (Dyffryn Clwyd, Rhos, Rhufoniog, Tegeingl) 290
'Pillar of Eliseg' (Llangollen) 71, 89, 162, 271–2, 280, 373
  inscription (note on) 392 (n.155)
plague, c.759 AD 272
'political places' 255, 275
'political sense of place' 254
pottery
  Continental imports 319
  'Ipswich ware' 319
Powys, kingdom of 50, 71, 85, 90, 93, 124, 162, 255, 270–2, 277, 279, 338
'productive sites' 319–20
provinces, late Roman (Britain) 98, *100*,

quernstones, Mayen lava (from Germany) 320, 325

'Reconnecting Offa's Dyke: localism, inheritance, diversity' 373–6
reeves (officials) 226
Reginald of Durham *Life of King Oswald* (c.1165 AD) 56
Relations between Welsh and English, at the frontier 77
Rhiwsaete (people) 266
ridgeway routes 228, 230–2
Roman Ridge Dykes (Sheffield) 104
Roman
  Empire 346
  imperial frontier works 226, 353, 372, 374
  military officers and engineers 221
  models of kingship 308
  'spolia' (re-used building materials – stone, tile) 323–4
routeways, inherited and used by Anglo-Saxons 240–2, 320
Row Ditch, Hereford 243
Rowe Ditch (Pembridge, Herefs) 28, 28, 58, 104, 242–3, 243, 296, 357, 371
  gateway through 229
Royal Commission on the Ancient and Historical Monuments of Wales (RCAHMW) 289

royal 'vills' 227, 319
Ruabon Mountain 'dykes' (discounted) 244

salt, as resource 233
  at Droitwich (Worcs) 320
'saltways' 240, 320
Scandinavian raiders 223
scriptoria, monastic scribing workshops 321
'short-dykes' (eastern Wales) 72, 80, 243
  Lower Short Ditch 72
Sigered, king of Kent 302
Sigered, ruler in Essex 309
Squatriti, Paolo 220–1, 352
  'digging ditches' as a 'moment' in time 220–1, 223, 352
'Staffordshire Hoard' 300, 328–33, *330, 331*, 421–2 (n.113–129)
  archaeological contexts pertaining to 328–9
  assembly of (possible) 329–30
  burial of (possible) 329
  sword pommels 328
Stenton, Frank (Sir) 68, 216, 222, 303, 342, 352, 368, 381 (n.3)
Stepelsaete (people) 266
Stephens, Meic 365
Stephenson, David 272
strongholds in frontier zone (possible) 244–7
Symeon of Durham, c.1129 56

Tatton-Brown, Tim 421 (n.114)
Temesaete (people) 266
'theatre of landscape' concept 160
Theodore, Archbishop of Canterbury 106
Thomas, Northcote 66
Tidenham charter 74–5
Tiw, god 95
Tomsaete (people) 95, 105, 265,
trade tolls (Francia/Mercia), 303, 321
Trent, battle on river 106
'Tribal Hidage', document (?tribute list) 95, 99, 103, 263–5, 412 (n.24)
Tyler, Damian 92, 308

Vale of Pewsey, battle at 106
Vallender, J. *173*, 189, 190, 193, 381–2 (n.9, 10)
Vaughan, Robert 413 (n.57)
Viking incursions 368
visual modelling devices 151
view-shed analysis 151, 158

Wada, Northumbrian general 359–60
wahlfaereld 226
Wansdyke (Wilts/Somerset) 21, 25–7, 58, 104

  Dating of 384 (n.56)
  East Wansdyke (Wilts) 26, 27, 225,
  West Wansdyke (Somerset) 27
'-wardine' place-names 292, 295–6
watch-towers, fortified 249–50
  as look-out posts 247–9
Watling Street 94, 96, 98, 266, 351
Wat's Dyke 108, 114, 118, 122–3, 163, 173, 183–4, 188, 224–5, 244, 261, 266, 281, 290, 356–9, *359*, 371
  compared with Offa's Dyke 22–5, 55, 60, 63–4, 69–70, 75–6, 83, 183–4
  course of 16–17, 19–20, 22–5, 27, 39
  dating and comparisons 384 (n.46, 48, 52, 54, 55)
  excavation, Gobowen (Shropshire) 20, 21, 29, 183, *183*, 188, 261, *359*, 371
  excavation, Mile Oak (Shropshire) 20
  physical/geographical relation to Offa's Dyke 39
  Welsh and English communities alongside one another 57
Wensaete (people) 267
Weogoran (people) 265
Weohstan, Ealdorman of Wessex 116
Wessex, kingdom of 96, 106–8, 125, 256, 263, 304, 343
West Saxons 94, 113, 223, 256, 263
'Westerna' 264–5, 412 (n.29)
Wheeler, Mortimer (Sir) 3, 66
Whitelock, Dorothy 334
'Whitford Dyke' (Flints) 17–18, 174, 289,
wics (trading places) 227, 319, 327
Williams, Ann 91
Williams, William *Flintshire and Denbighshire* (map, 1754) 60
Winwaed, battle of 103, 105, 263,
Woden, god 95
Wood, J. G. 289, 381 (n.8, 9)
Wood, Michael 215–16
Woodland in 'pre-Dyke' borderland 74
World Heritage Sites 373–4
Wormald, Patrick 317, 368
Worthington, Margaret 85–6, 89, 193
writing styli (metal scribing tools) 319
Wrocansaete (people) 100, 106, 263–7
Wulfhere, king of Mercia 101, 105–7,
Wulfred, archbishop of Canterbury 116–17, 307, 314
Wulfric, King Alfred's 'Welsh reeve' 226

yat (OE, 'gate') 232
'Ysfeiliog Circle', Flintshire (Fox excavations at) 70